12,167

Kitchen and Cooking Secrets

12,167

Kitchen and Cooking Secrets

everyday tips, hints, techniques and more

Susan Sampson

For complete cataloguing information, see page 684.

Disclaimer
The recipes in this book have been carefully tested by our kitchen and our
tasters. To the best of our knowledge, they are safe and nutritious for ordinary
use and users. For those people with food or other allergies, or who have special
food requirements or health issues, please read the suggested contents of each
recipe carefully and determine whether or not they may create a problem for
you. All recipes are used at the risk of the consumer.

We cannot be responsible for any hazards, loss or damage that may occur as
a result of any recipe or tip use.

For those with special needs, allergies, requirements or health problems, in
the event of any doubt, please contact your medical adviser before using any
recipe or following any tip.

Design and Production: Kevin Cockburn/PageWave Graphics Inc.
Editor: Sue Sumeraj
Copy Editors: Jo Calvert, Jennifer MacKenzie, Teresa Makarewicz
    and Emily Richards
Proofreader: Sheila Wawanash
Indexer: Gillian Watts

We acknowledge the financial support of the Government of Canada through
the Book Publishing Industry Development Program (BPIDP) for our
publishing activities.

Published by Robert Rose Inc.
120 Eglinton Avenue East, Suite 800, Toronto, Ontario, Canada M4P 1E2
Tel: (416) 322-6552 Fax: (416) 322-6936

Printed and bound in Canada

1 2 3 4 5 6 7 8 9 WC 17 16 15 14 13 12 11 10 09

Contents

Introduction

Many a conversation starts out like this: "Mmmm, what's your secret?"

The secret never remains a secret. Cooks are generous. They like to nourish and share. Cooking secrets are passed down from mothers to daughters, writers to readers. Friends exchange them. Chefs proclaim them. They wind up online, on-air in cooking shows, in print in newspapers, magazines and cookbooks. Cooks discover them by experience or by accident (sometimes gory). They are hidden in the nooks and crannies of recipes.

Okay, so they're not really secrets. Just undiscovered territory. What's obvious to one cook is a revelation to another.

As a food columnist for the *Toronto Star*, I cooked constantly but never experimented systematically. Once I stepped off the treadmill of newspaper deadlines to write this book, I took a breath and asked: How can I make it easier, faster, cheaper, prettier, better?

Collecting "secrets" is addictive. Once I started, I couldn't stop. I'm still at it.

The result is this compendium of kitchen wisdom. There are thousands of tips, hints, observations and techniques on these pages. I tested as many as I could. I confess that I couldn't test them all — I'd be puttering in the kitchen into retirement age if I did. When experience whispered in my ear and I was reasonably sure a tip would work, I let it through.

Along the way, I learned two things: Many routes lead to the same destination. Nothing is sacred.

Perfection is a matter a taste, especially with comfort foods such as roast chicken or apple pie. A technique that one cook swears by, another shrugs off. Just because a famous chef says something, just because you read it in a magazine, doesn't mean it is written in stone. Cooking is full of controversy and debate. Answers lie in the murky depths of food science, sometimes waiting to be discovered.

Still circulating is a large group of vintage "secrets" dating back to the days of housewifery, when the lady of the home was a proud and frugal household engineer. Our standards have understandably slipped, but we're looking back at the old ways as we worry more about the environment and the economy.

For better or worse, cooks have thought of it all. There's no such thing as too bothersome, too frugal or too silly. Are you really going to pick out grape seeds with the tip of a hairpin or wrap your cheese in a cabbage leaf? Do you want to tie a big batch of lettuce in a clean pillowcase and tumble it in the dryer on the air setting?

Please don't think of cooking tips as rules. In the kitchen, as in the world at large, most rules are just guidelines. Browse. After all, there's more than one way to skin a peach.

Cooking is an art and a science. If the experiments in chemistry and physics classes in high school had involved cooking, I wouldn't have been so bored. A recipe is, after all, a chemical formula. But if everything you need to know were written there in black and white, lugging a cookbook would double as a weight-training session. There's a dash of magic in the mix. It happens when experience combusts with instinct. Don't have that — yet? Keep stirring. Keep experimenting. That's the joy of cooking.

Feeding Tipoholics

Eight places to find kitchen tips:

- Newspapers. Check out my "Fare Lady" column and recipes in the *Toronto Star*.
- Culinary, home and women's magazines.
- Cookbooks.
- Meat, fish, egg and produce marketing boards.
- Product packages.
- Websites for food lovers.
- Vintage housewifery books.
- In your own head. Heed the light bulb that comes on over your head as you cook. You know more than you think you do.

Five handy websites:

- **The Cook's Thesaurus:** An encyclopedia of ingredients, synonyms and substitutions. With clear pictures! Log on to foodsubs.com.
- **Recipesource.com:** A recipe-sharing free-for-all that started way back in 1993. Includes 70,000 recipes, no frills. Be careful: These are untested.
- **Epicurious.com:** Multi-media how-tos and recipes.
- **Baking911.com:** A riotously laid out guide to baking and making sweets.
- **Chow.com:** A smorgasbord, nicely served up. Sharing, recipes, videos.

Acknowledgments

I owe many thanks:

- To my favorite testers, my picky daughters, Eva and Emma, and omnivorous husband, Robert.
- To my mother, Margit Horvath, and mother-in-law, Christel Sampson, who wash dishes as fast as I can dirty them. Their steady help and support makes my life so much easier.
- To food writing colleague Jennifer Bain, who inspired me with her passion for getting it right and learning more.
- To Mary McGrath, former *Toronto Star* home economist, whose recipes helped me grow up as a cook.
- To *Toronto Star* editor Lesley Ciarula Taylor, who kicked my butt to start collecting "secrets." I foolishly asked: "What secrets? Doesn't everybody know all this?"
- To Robert Rose publisher Bob Dees, for believing in me, and marketing manager Marian Jarkovich and editor Sue Sumeraj for their hard work and kind help.
- To the designers at PageWave Graphics, Kevin Cockburn, Andrew Smith and Joseph Gisini, who had their hands full with this one.

Tools

Recipes

Kitchen Tools Hall of Fame

The Number One Kitchen Tool: Your Hands

- Tough or gentle, endlessly versatile, your hands are the best tools. Wash them well, then don't be afraid to get messy. If you were the kind of kid who liked finger-painting, you'll enjoy separating eggs in your palm, rubbing butter into flour for

Top 7 Kitchen Tools Beginning with the Letter S

1. **Scissors:** Are two blades better than one? For a lot of chores, scissors are faster and easier than knives. More, much more, on this later.

2. **Scraper:** So much can be done with this flat, flexible metal rectangle with a handle: scrape dough from a work surface; transfer food from the cutting board to a measuring cup or skillet; sweep peelings off the counter into a compost bin; smash garlic cloves; level flour in a measuring cup; cut bars, brownies or butter; divide or score dough; create chocolate curls; press the last bit of icing out of a piping bag; sweep leftover food off plates on their way to the dishwasher; scrape burnt pans. Metal scrapers with a ruler printed on the blade are handy. Avoid the plastic ones.

3. **Serrated peeler:** The serrated peeler removes the fine skins of tomatoes, peaches, kiwis — even bell peppers. So say goodbye to blanching. And is the wee store label stuck to the fruit? Use a serrated peeler to get it off.

4. **Skimmer:** Never mind the slotted spoon — use a skimmer. It has a long handle and a wire basket or metal net. It comes in small, medium and giant. The traditional Asian ones with bamboo handles are called spiders. Skimmers strain, lift and transfer. Extract a pile of fries from oil or dumplings from stock. Blanch a series of vegetables in the same pot. Strain (without draining) pasta. Get a fine-mesh skimmer to clean the scum off stock.

5. **Offset spatula:** This spatula has a long, narrow, thin metal blade with a dogleg at the handle. It's also called a baker's spatula, and comes big and small. Sure, it's great for spreading icing, but you'll find many other uses for it: loosen around the edges of a casserole, baking dish, cake or loaf pan and extract the first piece; flip a crêpe; smear spread on a wrap or sauce on a pizza; gently tilt a roll in the oven to check how browned the bottom is.

6. **Sprayer:** You can't have too much spraying action. Get the retractable-hose sink sprayer and the spraying faucet attachment, too. Clean. Rinse. Cool.

7. **Stools:** A cheap plastic stool will get a good workout every day. Kick it across the floor to the spot below the cupboard you want to explore. Alleviate backache by resting one foot on it as you work at the counter. If you're short and holding the electric hand mixer at a tedious angle, step up on the stool and look down into the bowl instead of fighting arm cramps. For serious climbing and stability, you'll also need a folding step stool.

pie pastry, squashing canned tomatoes between your fingers or prodding a barbecued steak to check if it's done.

More Top Kitchen Tools
Disher
- More than a mere scoop, a disher has a spring-loaded attachment that sweeps the inside of the cup. For even scooping, the round ones are better than the oval ones. You can scoop and measure at the same time. Use a large disher to fill muffin cups or to scoop mashed potatoes into cafeteria-style balls, a medium disher for meatballs, a small one for cookie dough, a tiny one for truffles.
- Though it's no good for ice cream, the disher is often mistaken for an ice cream scoop.

Gripper
- I call this "The Hand." It's a pole with a trigger at one end and suction-cupped pincers at the other so you can squeeze and retrieve items from on high. It'll make you feel like you're working at Ye Olde General Store. Strong enough to hold a can, "The Hand" lets you extend food storage space to the farthest reaches of a cupboard.

Microwave
- Melt, reheat, steam. The microwave can't be beat if you think of it mainly as a food prep tool rather than a cooking/defrosting appliance.

Pizza Wheel
- Dip a pizza wheel in flour or oil to prevent sticking and you're ready to put it to work with no pizza in sight. When rolling pie dough, clean up the ragged edges and refine the circle. Cut strips for a lattice pie crust. Slice puff pastry or phyllo. Trim fondant. Cut designs in tortillas, flatbreads or large pancakes. Slice quesadillas into wedges. Use a pizza wheel along with a metal ruler to cut straight lines or squares.

Rasp Grater
- When you want something finely grated, this is what you should pick up, not that clunky old box grater. This super-sharp, flat, hand-held tool evolved from the carpenter's rasp. The best-known brand is Microplane. Expect the finest citrus zest and the fluffiest flakes of Parmesan. Purée ginger and garlic.
- When zesting, don't hold the lemon in one hand and run the rasp over it. Bolster the rasp at an angle against the cutting board and run the lemon up and down its length.

Tape Measure
- Forget sizing by eye. Steal a retractable tape measure from your toolbox and make it standard equipment in your kitchen drawer. A ruler is good too. Measure thickness, length and diameter. They're never quite right when you guess. Meatballs and cookie dough rounds, for example, are always bigger than you think, and they tend to increase in size as you daydream.

Weigh Scale
- It's amazing how many cooks fumble along without one. Recommended: measuring by weight rather than volume, and dividing by weight. When arithmetic is involved, flicking the switch from ounces to grams will make calculations easier.
- To check the accuracy of your scales, weigh several consumer products, such as butter or chocolate bars. (Don't forget that package weights refer to contents only; that tin can doesn't count.)

Hall of Shame: 20 Silly Kitchen Tools to Avoid

1. Electric pot stirrer
2. Battery-powered salad spinner
3. Tuna can drainer
4. S'mores maker
5. Steak toaster
6. Pop-up hot dog and bun toaster
7. Toaster sandwich bags (cram a whole sandwich in your toaster)
8. Peanut butter lid equipped with a crank
9. Peanut butter and jam spreader (double-ended and color-coded for the confused)
10. Hard-cooked egg caddy (just spin the eggs to tell them apart, for heaven's sake)
11. Egg cuber (to prepare square hard-cooked eggs)
12. Ball-shaped ice cream maker that you roll around the yard
13. Green bean guillotine and slicer (done one by one, yawn)
14. Crunchy cereal bowl (with a built-in platform so the cereal doesn't soak in the milk)
15. Banana slicer
16. Hard plastic banana suitcase
17. Silly Feet cake stands and cupcake holders (they add clown feet to your serving ware)
18. Automatic potato peeler (spuds clunk around alarmingly in the water and look like they were shaved by a blind barber)
19. Toast stamper (bite into Mickey Mouse's head, a "hangover cure" message or other images)
20. A clip that holds your wooden spoon to the edge of the pot

Zip-lock Bags

- The potential uses for these sturdy plastic bags go far beyond storage and freezing (see page 44 for examples). I always stock the tiny snack size, medium and large freezer bags, and the large perforated vegetable bags.

A Silly Kitchen Tool That Makes Sense

Onion mask (you'll look like a scuba diver when you chop onions)

Two Silly but Fab Kitchen Tools

- Voodoo doll toothpick holder
- Corn zipper (to strip kernels from the cob)

A Kitchen Tool That Seems Silly at First but Becomes More Attractive as the Cook Ages

Electric flour sifter

The Scoop on Kitchen Supplies

Cookware

Cookware Categories

✧ Choosing cookware is a balancing act. Factors to juggle: How well and evenly does it conduct heat? How durable is it? How much does it cost? The wild card: good looks.

- **Stainless steel:** Sturdy. Expensive but not over the top. Looks good. Poor conductor, so the base should include aluminum or copper. Quality is reflected in the alloy, such as 18/0, 18/8, 18/10. The 18 is the percentage of chromium. The second number is the percentage of nickel — the higher the better. These numbers are being phased out, though.
- **Aluminum:** Lightweight. Cheap. Heats up fast. Conducts well. Soft. Reacts with acidic foods.
- **Anodized aluminum:** Quality cookware, coated with a hard gray finish. Resists scratches and sticking. Good alternative to nonstick cookware. Looks ugly.
- **Copper:** Best conductor. No hot spots. Heats and cools super-fast. Beautiful but high-maintenance; needs polishing. Reacts with acidic foods.
- **Clad:** Hybrid of aluminum or copper with stainless steel, with good qualities of both.
- **Cast iron:** Heavy. Lasts forever. Cheap. Has power of nostalgia on its side. Heats up slowly but conducts heat evenly. Food can be seared at very high heat. Comfortable on the stove, in the oven, on a barbecue grate or over a campfire. Grandma's original nonstick cookware. Must be seasoned; consumers mistakenly believe that means arduous maintenance. Most likely to set off the smoke alarm or send you to the burn unit. Reacts with acidic foods.
- **Enameled cast iron:** Expensive. Comes in alluring, happy colors. Requires no seasoning, but doesn't have the nonstick qualities or searing ability of bare cast iron.
- **Nonstick:** Coated aluminum. Easy to clean. Not good over high heat. Foods don't sear properly. Prone to scratching when used with metal utensils. Flakes as it degrades; health scares have made it controversial. Must be replaced every few years.
- **Non-metal cookware:** Mainly for baking. Poor heat conductors. Can chip and crack. Ceramic cookware includes glazed or unglazed terracotta, which conducts heat poorly but contains it well. There's clear heatproof glass (Pyrex) or glass ceramic (Corningware). The latter can be used on the stovetop. Silicone is light, flexible and famous for its ability to withstand high temperatures.

✧ Stainless-steel cookware manufacturers warn consumers never to use high heat, even to boil water.

ⓝ is for Non-reactive

Recipes often warn us to use non-reactive pans. Aluminum, copper and cast-iron pans, bowls and other equipment react with acidic foods, egg yolks and vegetables such as asparagus and artichokes. These chemical reactions can create bitter flavors and strange colors.

◆ Check the base of a pan. It should be as thick as the sides. Too thin, and poor heat distribution leads to hot spots. Burnt food will be the reward for your frugality.

L is for Leaching

When we cook, some of the metal from the pan leaches into the food and we ingest it.

• Acidic foods and leafy vegetables absorb aluminum from pans. Anodized aluminum has a coating that reduces leaching.
• Large amounts of copper are toxic. Copper pans are clad with metal such as stainless steel so the copper doesn't come in contact with food. Scouring can scrape away this protective layer.
• Cooking in cast iron provides a source of iron.
• Small amounts of iron are ingested from food cooked in stainless-steel cookware.
• Never store food in aluminum, copper or cast iron. Don't store acidic foods such as tomatoes or stewed rhubarb in stainless steel.

◆ Use a pan the same size as the element. You'll save energy and get better results.

4 Nonstick Rules

1. Do not cut food in a nonstick skillet.
2. Don't try to sear meat or fish, or caramelize onions, in a nonstick pan.
3. When storing nonstick cookware, line it with paper towels or another buffer so it doesn't scratch from contact with other metals.
4. Throw out a nonstick pan if the coating is deeply scratched, peeling or flaking.

◆ On a gas burner, keep the flame within $\frac{1}{2}$ inch (1 cm) of the base of the pan. It should not flare up the sides. This wastes energy and discolors the pan.

S is for Sauté Pan

A sauté pan is wide like a skillet but slightly deeper, with straight sides and a lid. So now you know.

◆ Choose a round Dutch oven. The oval shape is not as good for the usual first step of browning meat on the stovetop.

Mythstake

Plastic handles won't necessarily melt in the oven. Most quality stovetop cookware has sturdy, welded plastic handles that are rated to withstand moderate oven temperatures. As insurance, wrap handles in foil before putting a pan in the oven for, say, a frittata. If something will bake for a long time, use a proper roasting pan or Dutch oven.

◆ To tighten a lid, cover the pot with foil, then put the lid on.

T is for Thermal Shock

Don't put a cold pan on a very hot burner or a hot pan in cold water. Thermal shock can cause warping and buckling.

◆ To keep cookware in good condition, fill it with hot water and soap immediately after using it. Let it stand until lukewarm. Exception: cast iron.

Cast-Iron Pans

◆ Always preheat a cast-iron pan before cooking in it.

◆ For the first few weeks of a cast-iron pan's life, cook mainly fatty foods, such as bacon. Avoid watery dishes and acidic dishes, such as stews that include tomatoes. Acids eat away at the protective coating.

Tarte Tatin

The key to tarte Tatin is evaporating the juices from the apples. This allows the syrup to thicken into a dark, rich, apple-flavored caramel, and the apples themselves to scorch attractively. And the key to evaporating the juices is to start on the stovetop. Cast iron is perfect for this method. In fact, no other pan will work properly. **Makes 10 to 12 servings**

- **10-inch (25 cm) cast-iron skillet**

Tips

I like to use Granny Smith apples because they are tart and the sauce is so sweet, but you can use any firm, not too sweet pie apple, such as Northern Spy.

Use a rich, tart-style pâte brisée rather than a flaky pie pastry.

This makes a good master recipe for caramelized apples. After turning the apples, continue to cook them in the pan until tender.

Variations

Cut corners and use packaged puff pastry.

If desired, omit the final sprinkling of sugar at the end.

6 tbsp	unsalted butter	90 mL
1 cup	granulated sugar	250 mL
7	Granny Smith apples (about 2¾ lbs/1.375 kg)	7
8 oz	cold pastry for a single-crust pie	250 g
1 to 2 tbsp	granulated sugar	15 to 25 mL

1. In the skillet, melt butter over medium heat. Sprinkle 1 cup (250 mL) sugar over the bottom of the pan. Heat, without stirring, for 2 to 3 minutes or until all the sugar is moistened, bubbles start to pop over the surface and small areas turn golden. Continue cooking, stirring occasionally, for 2 minutes or until the mixture is an even caramel color and butter separates out at the edges. Let cool for 30 minutes. The mixture will firm up.

2. Meanwhile, peel, core and quarter the apples from top to bottom. Arrange apples on their cut sides in a tight overlapping circle on the caramel around the edges of the pan. Fill in center. The apples should be snug, but you will probably have some pieces left over.

3. Cook over medium heat until juices evaporate and the bottoms of the apples are a golden caramel color and are starting to scorch at the ridges, about 15 minutes. Remove pan from the heat and flip each apple with a carving fork or tongs. Return to the heat and cook for 5 minutes, occasionally pressing apples gently down into the caramel to scorch the ridges. Let cool for 15 minutes. Meanwhile, preheat oven to 400°F (200°C).

4. On a lightly floured work surface, roll out pastry to an 11-inch (28 cm) circle. Working quickly, place it over the apples and push in the edges with a blunt knife.

5. Bake until pastry looks firm and golden, apples are tender but not mushy, and caramel is dark brown but not blackened, about 15 minutes. Let cool for 5 minutes. Place a heatproof serving dish over skillet, grip tightly using oven mitts and invert. Drizzle juices from the pan over the apples.

6. Sprinkle apples with 1 to 2 tbsp (15 to 25 mL) granulated sugar. Use a kitchen torch to caramelize the sugar.

✦ Too many folks toss out cast-iron pans because they are dismayed by rust patches, burnt-on crud and discolored food. These sad pans have to be cleaned and seasoned, but the job is not onerous and the payoff is wonderful. Clean and season a cast-iron pan while it is still warm, but not hot.

3 Ways to Clean a Cast-Iron Pan

1. Scrub a lightly soiled pan with a stiff brush or plastic pot scrubber in warm water.
2. A paste of oil and coarse salt works great. It scrubs off rust spots and crusty patches left after cooking. Afterwards, wipe out the paste, polish the pan with an old kitchen towel and rinse in lukewarm water.
3. If you have a wood fireplace and a hopelessly crusty pan, stick it in the fire for a few minutes to combust the crud into ash.

⚡ Lightning Won't Strike If ...

- You wash a cast-iron pan with soap. In most cases, you won't need it. But simply wiping the dry pan is ridiculous advice. In most cases, it will be smelly and sticky. What about that blackened catfish? The first time you use it, and periodically as needed, wash your cast-iron pan with hot, soapy water, rinse it well and dry it with a kitchen towel. If there's a heavy buildup, scour it with steel wool.
- You don't heat a seasoned pan in the oven. Always season a cast-iron pan after using it. But for a lightly soiled pan, that might mean applying a thin coat of oil while it is still warm, then storing it. If the pan has been scrubbed with soap, put it in the oven for sure.

Ⓢ is for Seasoning

To season a cast-iron pan, you apply oil to create a black, shiny, smooth, slick coating. This takes time. The pores must absorb the oil. After its first seasoning, the pan is ready to use but not mature. Seasoning is ongoing. Don't do it just once a year. Seasoning keeps the pan nonstick and prevents rusting. Food sticking stubbornly is a sign that the pan is not seasoned properly. As they season, cooks develop a relationship with their cast-iron pans.

6 Steps to Seasoning a Cast-Iron Pan

1. Start with a clean pan. If the pan is new, wash it with hot, soapy water and a stiff brush. Dry the pan well.
2. Apply a thin coat of oil or shortening all over the pan — inside and out, top and bottom, handle and lid. Use your fingers, a clean cloth or a pastry brush to rub it in. Avoid paper towels; they leave flecks. Don't use butter, margarine or flavored shortening.
3. Line the lower rack of the oven with foil to catch drippings.
4. Put the pan on the middle rack, upside down so the oil doesn't build up inside. Bake at 350°F (180°C) until very hot, up to 1 hour for a newer pan. You can reduce the time by cranking up the heat to 400°F (200°C).
5. Wipe off any excess oil. Otherwise, fat buildup will make the pan smoke. (The pan should smoke, however, when other fats are added during cooking.)
6. Store the pan in a cool, dry place. It needs air, so take the lid off to prevent moisture from collecting and causing rust. Place a paper towel in the pan to absorb stray oil and moisture.

✖ No-Nos

- Never soak the pan.
- Never scour the pan with abrasive cleansers.
- Never put the pan in a dishwasher. It removes the coating and opens the door to rust.
- Never air-dry. Dry the pan right after cleaning it. Cast iron will stain the towel, so use an old towel or paper towels.
- Don't boil water in a cast-iron pan.

Ways to Recondition a Rusty, Crusty Old Pan

- Pour in a solution of 2 parts vinegar and 1 part water. Leave it until the rust lifts. Rub stubborn spots with crumpled foil. Rinse.
- Scour it with steel wool. Wipe out the loose dirt. Place it over medium-low heat and add oil to coat the bottom. Heat for 5 minutes, then turn off the burner. Add salt to form a paste. Scrub the pan with paper towels. Rinse it in hot water.

❖ It's better to hand-wash pricey enameled cast-iron cookware. The dishwasher is safe, but will eventually dull the finish. Do not use harsh abrasive cleaners.

Ovenware

Tips for Even Baking

- Cheap, thin metal pans are no bargain. They warp at high temperatures and have hot spots that cause uneven baking.
- Food browns more evenly in round pans. Food browns more in the corners when you use a square pan.
- Keep pans clean. Blackened spots on metal pans can cause uneven baking.

❖ A filled silicone baking dish can be wobbly. Put it on a pizza peel or a rimless baking sheet to transfer it to the oven.

❖ You can label sizes on the bottoms of baking dishes with a permanent marker.

🌼 *Being Green*

Dark pans and glass ovenware save energy.

Dark **VS.** Shiny?

Shiny baking dishes reflect heat. They create thin, more evenly browned crusts, especially in baked goods. So do disposable aluminum pans. Dark pans absorb heat. Baked goods cook faster in dark pans and the crusts are browner and heavier. Glass pans are not good conductors, so they need time to warm up.

For some recipes, you may be able to compensate for dark and glass pans. Reduce the oven temperature by 25°F (14°C) and perhaps increase the baking time by 5 minutes for every 30 minutes specified in the recipe.

Clay and Ceramic

- Soak unglazed clay bakers in water for about 20 minutes and pat them dry before using.
- Don't start a clay baker in a cold oven; it may crack.
- Sudden temperature changes can damage earthenware (clay) glazes.
- You can use a mesh pad to scrub a clay baker, but never soap.
- Be suspicious of glazed ceramic cookware you bring home from abroad. It may not be made to high standards. The cookware may crack in the oven. The lead content may be unacceptable. Use it decoratively only.

❖ Add a cup of water to the bottom of a broiling pan before using it to cut down on burnt grease and smoke. Line the bottom of the pan with parchment to make cleanup easier.

- ✧ When lining a baking sheet to catch drips from anything from pie to ribs, avoid foil. It bakes onto the pan. Parchment is better.

Making Do

- If you don't have a small roasting pan, use a cast-iron or ovenproof skillet with a rack in it.
- If you don't have a tube pan, put an empty tin can in the center of a round baking dish. Grease the can if the recipe calls for it. Pour in pie weights to make sure the can stays put.

Baking Sheet **VS.** Jelly Roll Pan?

A baking sheet (also called a cookie sheet) is flat. Jelly roll pans have short rims. Many of us use jelly roll pans as baking sheets. So few people make jelly rolls now that these pans have to be called rimmed baking sheets. Otherwise, people would just scratch their heads.

Knives

Signs of a Good Knife

- It balances on the index finger between the blade and handle.
- The end of the blade, or tang, extends right to the end of the handle.

Steel **VS.** Ceramic?

- Carbon steel is an iron and carbon alloy. Carbon steel knives are very sharp, but get stained and rusty.
- Stainless steel is not quite as sharp but is worth the compromise. High-carbon stainless steel is forged with a greater amount of carbon to give it an edge.
- Ceramic knives are lightweight but close to diamond hard. They won't rust. They stay sharp a long time, but require special sharpening equipment.
- There are also titanium blades (lighter and more flexible than steel, but not as hard or sharp) and laminates (forged with two types of metal).

How to Hold a Chef's Knife

- Curl your middle, ring and pinkie fingers under the bottom of handle. Rest your index finger on the flat side of the blade, near the handle. Place your thumb on the opposite side, past the bolster (where the blade and handle meet). That should maintain a 90-degree angle.

German **VS.** Japanese?

- German-style knives are stainless steel. They are better for tackling heavy jobs, such as splitting a squash or chopping through bones. In comparison to Japanese-style knives, they have thicker blades and a thickened bolster (guard) where the blade and handle meet.
- Japanese-style knives are made with carbon steel, stainless steel or a laminate of the two that exposes only the sharp carbon edge. They are better for fine slicing and carving. The edges can chip more easily. People with small hands may prefer them.

✗ No-No

Don't put good knives in the dishwasher. The edges can get damaged and blunted, and the heat can harm the handles. Though fine knives are advertised as dishwasher-safe, manufacturers still advise cleaning by hand.

Slicing and Dicing

- ✧ Chefs cut so neatly and evenly because they are taught to always create at least one flat surface first. It's safer that way, too. Examples: Take a slice off the end of a cantaloupe. Halve a carrot lengthwise. Turn a potato into a rectangle.

Four Dice Sizes

- **Fine dice:** $1/8$ inch (3 mm)
- **Small dice:** $1/4$ inch (0.5 cm)
- **Medium dice:** $1/2$ inch (1 cm)
- **Large dice:** $3/4$ inch (2 cm)

✥ To prevent staining from acids, rinse a knife immediately after cutting, say, a lime.

ⓙ is for Julienne

Trim a vegetable (or other food) into a rectangular shape. Slice it thinly. Stack the slices. Cut them into matchsticks. Voila — you've just julienned them!

8 Tricks for Slicing and Dicing

Here's how to cut, chop, slice and dice without it turning into a horror movie:

1. Use a chef's knife (with a triangular blade) in a rocking motion, pivoting the handle end up and down without lifting the point of the knife from the board.
2. Use a slight sawing motion when you slice. Your knife will feel sharper.
3. Serrated knives should be long, so you can get a good sawing motion without crushing.
4. Whenever possible, cut away from you, not toward you.
5. Always curl in the fingertips of the hand holding the food, like claws. This not only protects your fingertips, but lets you use your knuckles as a cutting guide.
6. For precision, use the index finger sitting on the food to align the knife. Keep the side of the blade lightly in contact with the front edge of your index finger as you make each cut.
7. If you are cutting on the diagonal, move your fingers on the diagonal too.
8. When chopping with a cleaver, move your arm, not your wrist. You'll have more force.

Cutting Tricks

- For faster cooking, expose more surface area. Think diced carrot vs. coins vs. whole carrot.
- To get even slices from a soft fruit or vegetable, such as a tomato, prick one side lightly with the tines of a fork. Use the dots as cutting guides. Use a small serrated knife.
- Wedges will be more even if you cut them from the wide side up.

ⓒ is for Chiffonade

Shred vegetables or greens into thin strips. Voila — it's a chiffonade! The name is derived from a French term for rags.

Keeping Knives Sharp

✥ Does your knife need sharpening? Slash the edge of a sheet of paper. A dull knife will tear the paper. A sharp one will cut cleanly.

5 Ways to Stay Sharp

1. A knife fanatic will insert knives into the block with the blades facing up. The knives rest on their spines instead of their cutting edges.
2. Steel knives can be stored on a wall-mounted magnetic strip.
3. Never toss a working knife naked into a drawer, where it will jostle. At the very least, protect the blade in a plastic sleeve.
4. Don't cut on stone, glass or metal. Wood and plastic cutting boards are easier on the cutting edge.
5. Flip the knife over and use the spine, rather than the business end, to scrape food off a cutting board.

Sharpener VS. Steel?

A sharpener sharpens. A steel maintains the edge. Don't confuse the two. The steel is a thick rod or skewer with an abrasive surface, like a giant nail file. Choose a steel that is longer than the knife. Before using the knife, run it over the steel. This refreshes and realigns the edge, but the knife has to be sharp to begin with. A sharpener grinds the edge of the knife to a fine point.

Factoid A blunt knife is more dangerous than a sharp one. A dull knife requires more force, and catches and drags. There's a greater chance the knife will slip and cut you.

Mythstake

The steel should not be held in the air like a sword as you gleefully rub the knife over it. Well, maybe the gleeful part is okay. As for the steel, hold it steady against the counter at a slight angle, as if you were stabbing the counter. Bring the knife down one side of the steel in an arc from the base to the tip. Then do the same on the opposite side of the steel.

Steel Tips

- Test your steel by running a fingernail around the circumference. You should feel grooves. If you don't, replace it.
- You may use a steel sporadically or each time you wield a knife. Wipe it after each use, as it picks up microscopic metal filings that clog the grooves.
- If honing the knife doesn't make much difference, sharpen the knife.

Gadgets and Gizmos

Baking Stone

✧ A baking stone absorb moistures and distributes heat evenly. Normally used for pizza, a stone is also useful when you're baking bread, rolls, pies, pastries, biscuits and cookies.

Ways to Clean a Stone

- Scrape it while it's hot.
- Scrub it with a brush and water.
- Rub it with a salt water paste.

But no matter what you do, the black splotches are there to stay.

✧ Keep a pizza (or another dish) piping hot by serving it on a stone. Do not set the stone directly on a table or counter.

✗ No-Nos

- Never use a stone over a direct flame.
- The barbecue is no place for a stone.
- Don't put a cold stone in a hot oven.
- Don't put a hot stone in cold water.
- Stones are absorbent. Don't put them in soapy water. Don't rub a stone with vinegar.

Brushes

✧ Two ways to squeeze grease, marinade or glaze from a pastry brush:
- Run a scraper over it.
- Press it against the side of a bowl and run a spatula over it.

Keep It Clean

To clean a kitchen brush, squirt dish soap onto the bristles. Massage them. Rinse the bristles under running water.

Can Opener

✦ A can opener should glide better if it's first dipped in very hot water.

Keep It Clean

To clean a grotty can opener, feed a thin kitchen towel through the jaws.

Chopper

Lightning Won't Strike If ...

You use a chopper instead of a knife. Chefs will mock you for this one. But you don't need fine knife skills, or even a fine knife, when wielding a chopper. It saves hauling out the food processor. And smacking the chopper gets rid of frustration. Just don't use it when finesse is required.

Chopsticks

✦ You can buy plastic training chopsticks with the tops joined. Or, to improvise your own, put a roll of cardboard or a section of a paper towel roll between two chopsticks at the top end, then secure it with an elastic band in a figure eight. (A toilet paper roll would also work, if you don't find it unappetizing.) You'll need 1 or 2 inches (2.5 or 5 cm) of clearance between the chopsticks, depending on the size of your hand.

Cutting Board

✦ Plastic and wood cutting boards have the most give and are best for knives, with the latter being kinder on serrated knives. It's normal for a knife to score the wood or plastic. Glass and stone cutting surfaces are terrible for knives. Don't use them. All work and no give makes my knife a dull boy.

Plastic VS. Wood?

This is an ongoing debate, thanks to contradictory studies. Plastic cutting boards apparently harbor less bacteria, but germs may not live as long on wood cutting boards. Plastic is easier to clean. Wood looks nicer.

✦ A subset of the wood category is the so-called commercial-grade cutting surface, made of pressed paper coated with resin. It won't harbor bacteria, doesn't need oiling, won't warp and can be put in the dishwasher. This type of board is supposed to be knife-friendly, but it's hard to get past the awful scraping sound it makes.

---

5 Keys to Wielding Chopsticks

1. Don't hold chopsticks too close together or try to scissor them. Move only the top chopstick.
2. Hold the bottom chopstick stationary in the valley between your thumb and index finger. Stabilize it by pressing your ring finger against the chopstick.
3. Hold the top chopstick against the side of your middle finger, with your index finger on top and your thumb on the opposite side. Move it up and down against the bottom one.
4. Don't hold chopsticks too close to the top. They should have about 4 inches (10 cm) of clearance at the eating end. If you are using them to stir-fry or sauté, hold them halfway down, with about 6 inches (15 cm) of clearance.
5. Keep the tips evenly aligned.

4 Ways to Preserve a Wood Cutting Board

1. Dry it upright to prevent moisture from seeping in.
2. Prevent cracks by oiling it when it starts to look dry.
3. To revive an old board, scrub it clean with sandpaper, then rinse, dry and oil.
4. Season it with mineral oil, not vegetable oil. The latter can go rancid and taint food.

How to Oil a Wood Cutting Board

1. Warm a bowl of mineral oil in the microwave.
2. Apply it with a soft cloth, following the grain. Don't forget to oil the sides.
3. Let the oil soak in just until it is absorbed. Wipe off any excess.

For the first seasoning of a new board, apply three coats of oil before using it. Let the oil soak in for 4 to 6 hours each time. Thereafter, oil the board once a month.

✧ Use a cutting board as a trivet under a slow cooker or bread machine so it doesn't overheat the counter.

Safety Tips

- Throw out cracked, worn cutting boards. Bacteria lurk in those crevices, nicks, scratches and grooves.
- To avoid cross-contamination, reserve separate cutting boards for meat and vegetables. It also makes sense to keep one for fruit, sweets and desserts only. You don't want garlicky mango mousse.

Ways to Sort Cutting Boards

- Use color-coded boards, say red for meat and green for vegetables.
- Mark boards with a permanent marker or scratch a notch or symbol into the surface.
- Simply buy different designs.

✧ Anchor a cutting board so it doesn't slide around. Two anchors:
- Put a damp towel underneath it. The towel also absorbs stray juices.
- Put a rubber mat under it.

✧ For camping or a picnic, roll up a thin, flexible plastic cutting board.

Keep It Clean

First, rub the cutting board with a scraper. Rinse it with cold water, not hot. You don't want to cook or glue any food particles to the board. If the board was used to cut chicken or other germy raw foods, spray it with a bleach solution, then rinse. If the board still smells of onion, fish or other unpleasant odors, rub it with a used lemon rind or a wedge of lemon, a paper towel dipped in vinegar, a sprinkling of baking soda or a spoonful of mustard powder. Rinse. Wash the board with hot, soapy water. Rinse and dry well.

✧ Two ways to create a temporary work surface in a small kitchen:
- Lay a firm cutting board across the top of the sink.
- Pull out a drawer and cover it with a large cutting board. (A baking sheet will also work.) You can pull out the drawer underneath for security. Don't put anything too heavy on the board.

Ice Cube Tray

✦ An ice cube tray is less likely to cement to the floor of the freezer if you stick a sheet of waxed paper under it.

Mandolin

✦ Cooks are using the mandolin in the wrong direction. It's counterintuitive, but you should work with gravity, not against it. Two keys to working with gravity:

• Think of the mandolin as a ski ramp. You want to ski smoothly down with your vegetable victim — elbow raised, pushing the victim toward the counter.

• Keep the high end of the mandolin on the same side as your working hand — the right if you are right-handed. If the high end is at your left, you are awkwardly pushing down toward the counter with your elbow lowered. That's not a smooth run for your vegetable victim — or you.

♛ A Golden Rule

Always use a pusher/guard. Setting it aside because it's awkward is not worth the pain and horror of a mandolin slash.

✦ Two ways flesh meets blade on the scary mandolin:

• You are most likely to be injured when you get down to a nub of food, pull it off the guard and doggedly try to slice it freestyle.

• You are second most likely to be injured when slicing a hard, sticky vegetable such as a sweet potato. It catches or drags, then suddenly gives way.

Meat Pounder/Mallet

Pounder VS. Mallet?

A mallet is like a double-headed hammer, with smooth and grooved ends. A pounder has a flat head and a handle. It can be wielded in a stamping motion.

Keep It Clean

To clean a mallet, especially after pounding meat, spray the hottest tap water over the grooves. It will cook the meat fibers stuck in the crevices, and the force of the spray will flush them out. Then wash the tool in soapy water.

Mortar and Pestle

> **Factoid** The mortar is the bowl. The pestle is the pounder.

✦ When using a mortar and pestle, sprinkle in coarse salt or sugar, depending on the recipe, for better grip.

Making Do

Improvise with a small, deep bowl, preferably metal, and a sturdy glass spice bottle. Press the spices in a smooth motion; don't whack at them.

✦ When pulverizing spices and mixing pastes, grind the pestle in circles around the bottom of the mortar. It's easier, more effective and less frustrating than pounding up and down against the sides of the bowl like a Neanderthal.

Reamer

✦ Use a citrus reamer over a sieve set in a bowl. You catch the seeds that way.

Ring Mold

✦ To transfer English muffin dough in a ring mold, slip a thin, wide metal spatula underneath.

- Ring molds are sometimes called tart rings because professional bakers use them. But they are not just for baking. Standard 4-inch (10 cm) molds are particularly handy. Three ideas for a ring mold:
  - Fry a round egg. Break it into a ring in the skillet.
  - Make round pancakes. Pour the batter into rings on the griddle.
  - Sculpt a layered lunch like a chef. Gently pat, say, a circle of toast, a tomato slice, tuna salad and salad greens into the ring. Slowly pull the ring off.

- Always oil a ring mold to prevent sticking.

Rolling Pin

- Store a rolling pin away from sharp objects so it doesn't get dinged or nicked.

Keep It Clean
Wipe a wooden rolling pin with a damp cloth. Don't soak it — water will make it warp.

Salad Spinner

- Dry a salad spinner basket by spinning it empty. Drain and wipe.

Scissors

3 Ways to Hone Kitchen Scissors and Poultry Shears

1. Cut strips off sandpaper, rough side up.
2. Cut foil.
3. Cut steel wool.

Note that if the scissors are dull, not much will help.

- Always keep sturdy, sharp scissors in your knife block. If you are cutting something sticky, flour or oil the blades, or dip your scissors in a tall glass of cold water as you work.

Sifter

- Don't fill a sifter more than halfway. The light mechanism will strain. Sift in batches.

Making Do
Don't have a sifter? Use a fine-mesh sieve. Hurry it up by stirring the contents with a spoon.

- Hit the sifter with the base of your palm, like hitting a tambourine, to speed it up. You can also rap it with a spoon if you don't mind dents.

✗ No-No
Don't wash a sifter. Little lumps of flour will solidify, get trapped in the mechanism and rattle endlessly. Just sift, shake vigorously, then wipe with a clean cloth.

Silicone Mat

- Use a silicone mat with the smooth side up.

Keep It Clean
Clean the mat with a damp cloth or warm, soapy water, then pat dry.

- Although people keep these rolled up, a silicone mat is supposed to be stored flat to prevent fiberglass filaments from breaking and crackling. If you don't care to store it flat, roll it around an empty paper towel tube and secure it with an elastic band.

Spray Bottle

Keep It Clean

To clean or unclog the spritzer of a spray bottle without emptying the bottle, remove the top with the tube, place it in a glass of warm, soapy water, then spray repeatedly. To rinse, switch to cold water and spritz.

Being Green

Vegetable washes come in effective spray bottles — better than the ones you pick up at the dollar store or drugstore. So reuse them.

Strainer

Strainer **VS.** Sieve **VS.** Colander?

A strainer can be any type of filter. A sieve is a strainer made of wire mesh or perforated metal. It is used to strain, sift and purée. Though it doesn't have to be, we generally think of a sieve as shallow, with fine mesh and a long handle. A colander is a bowl-shaped sieve and can be made of perforated metal or plastic.

✧ If a strainer is lying too low in a bowl, perhaps sitting in strained liquid, place it on top of a small inverted bowl or cup.

⒟ is for Drum Sieve

A round sieve with mesh stretched straight across it is called a drum sieve, although it looks more like a tambourine to me. Five uses for a drum sieve:

1. It's great for rinsing and draining vegetables or other food in a single layer.
2. When you're puréeing and straining out seeds, it gives you a large, stable surface to push food through.
3. It's an efficient sifter that sits nicely over a large bowl.
4. It makes a good drying screen for herbs or mushrooms.
5. It can double as a splatter screen.

✧ Use a sieve to toss blueberries or nuts in flour for baking. The excess falls through.

✧ Pushing food through a sieve to extract seeds and to purée fruit or vegetables seems like the dullest, most irritating chore in the kitchen. Three ways to press food through a sieve more efficiently:
  - Push and stir with a heavy whisk.
  - Press on the pulp with a small metal bowl.
  - Use the back of a ladle in a circular motion.

⒞ is for Chinois

A chinois is a cone-shaped sieve. It's easier to press food through a chinois. The chinois is also commonly used to strain soup stock and for sifting.

✧ Fine-mesh strainers that are bowl-shaped are less awkward to use than those with long handles.

Keep It Clean

Clean the fine mesh of a sieve using the sprayer attachment on your sink. Turn the sieve upside down and press the sprayer systematically over the surface.

✧ One of my handiest gadgets is an over-the-sink strainer. Handles hook over the edges of the sink and pull out to fit sinks of different widths.

Thermometer

✧ If you are using an electric stove, temperatures will not register evenly. They will bounce around as the element alternately heats and cools.

◇ Thermometers get damaged easily and the readings go screwy. Don't jostle them in a drawer. Two ways to protect the tips of thermometers:
● Store them upright in a cup or container padded with paper towels.
● Place them in a padded plastic storage tub.

4 Ways to Test Accuracy

1. Set a candy thermometer in boiling water for 10 minutes. Make sure it doesn't touch the bottom of the pot. It should register 212°F (100°C) at sea level.
2. Stick an instant-read thermometer in boiling water and hold it briefly until the temperature rises to the maximum reading, which will hopefully be the boiling point.
3. Take the temperature of ice water. Stick the tip of the thermometer in the corner of one compartment in an ice cube tray. The compartment should contain a melting ice cube sitting in a bit of water. The thermometer should read just above freezing, 33°F to 34°F (0.5°C to 1°C).
4. Fill a plastic cup with crushed ice and just enough water to float it. Stir while taking a reading with the thermometer. It should read close to the freezing point, 32°F (0°C).

Making Do

If you lose the clip off your candy thermometer, twist some foil into a rope. Secure one end around the head of the thermometer and the other around the handle of the pan.

Tongs

◇ Do yourself a favor and buy spring-loaded tongs with a locking mechanism that keeps them compact in the dishwasher or drawer.

Torch

◇ A kitchen torch will give you more control, browning the top of a dish more evenly than the broiler. It is not just for crème brûlée, either. You can use a kitchen torch to:
● Brown the top of a cheesy casserole.
● Create a crunchy sugar topping on rice pudding, or simply brown the pudding.
● Set a glaze on meat and fish.
● Blister the skins of tomatoes and peppers.
● Lightly brown cheese sauce on eggs, pasta or a sandwich.

Making Do

If you don't have a kitchen torch, grab a welding torch from the tool room in the basement.

Wooden Spoons

◇ Wooden spoons absorb and transfer flavors and odors. We shouldn't really use them, but we love them anyway. It helps to use separate spoons for sweets and savories. You can tell them apart by making notches or burn marks on the handle.

◇ Soak new wooden spoons in mineral oil. They'll be less absorbent and easier to clean. You can also soak a new spoon in vinegar, but it will stink for weeks.

◇ Instead of fussing with a pot holder, lift the hot metal handle on a lid using the handle of a wooden spoon.

Containers and Wraps

Bags

❖ To seal a plastic storage bag, cover the ends with foil and press with a hot iron to melt them.

❖ Store garbage bags at the bottom of the garbage can, under the current bag.

❖ Keep a net bag hanging on the kitchen door for dirty towels.

 **KID STUFF**

Turn brown paper lunch bags into masks for kids' crafts.

Cheesecloth

❖ When you're straining food through a sieve lined with cheesecloth, the final step is to push on the solids. Instead of pushing with a spatula, twist the top of the cheesecloth, lift and squeeze. You'll get the most liquid out of it.

❖ Two reasons to dampen cheesecloth before lining a strainer:
- The cloth will stay put better.
- It won't absorb or steal juices.

❖ Here's a clever way to drain food in cheesecloth, particularly homemade cheese or yogurt cheese: Pick up the edges of the cloth and tie it into a bundle. Tie the ends to a wooden spoon. Balance the bundle over a deep bowl or pot.

Foil

❖ Spray foil with oil when covering a dish in the oven to prevent it from sticking and pulling at the top layer.

Mythstake

Common wisdom is that the shiny side of aluminum foil deflects heat. So foil is put matte side up to cover a casserole, shiny side up to wrap pot handles in the oven. You can do that if it makes you feel efficient. But scientists have found that the difference is barely perceptible, a matter of mere seconds in cooking time.

✗ No-No

Don't use foil to wrap food with acidic ingredients, such as tomato sauce. Acid can attack the foil, and it may react with the food.

How to Line a Baking Dish with Foil

1. Turn the dish over and press heavy foil over it.
2. Remove the foil, turn the dish and drop in the shaped foil.
3. Crimp the foil over the edges of the dish.

The result is tidy and there's less chance of the foil ripping.

🌺 *Being Green*

Foil can be washed, dried, folded and reused.

❖ Insulate picnic food by wrapping it in two layers of foil and putting it in the cooler.

Jars

How to Prevent Sticky Lids on Jam, Honey and Condiment Jars

- Before putting away the jar, wipe the rim and threads.
- Put waxed paper on top of the jar before screwing on the lid.

- Stretch plastic wrap on top of the jar before covering it.
- Rub petroleum jelly on the threads.
- Rub mineral or vegetable oil on the threads.

8 Ways to Loosen a Tight, Sticky Lid

1. Get a good grip on stubborn lids with rubber gloves.
2. Tap around the perimeter with a wooden spoon or the handle of a knife.
3. Rap the jar upside down on the counter.
4. Run hot tap water over the lid.
5. Wrap a towel soaked in hot water around the jar.
6. Put the jar upside down in a bowl and pour in hot water to cover the lid.
7. Use a nutcracker to grip and loosen tight tops on small bottles.
8. When all else fails, break the suction by prying under the lid with the pointy tip of a church key can opener.

Parchment Paper

Ways to Deal with Parchment (or Foil) That Curls or Shifts

- Pull it along the square edge of a counter to uncurl it.
- Clip it to a baking sheet with clothespins.
- Secure the corners with dabs of dough.
- Stir together a flour paste to glue the edges.
- Weigh it down at the corners with metal spoons.

Parchment Liner Techniques

- Cut the right size of parchment liner for a baking pan: Place the bottom of the pan on top of the parchment. Trace around it with a pencil. Cut slightly inside the line. Place the side you drew on face down in the pan (just in case).
- If you want to work faster, use the sharp tip of a scissors blade to score an outline around the pan, then pull on the paper.
- To make a parchment circle for the bottom of a tube pan, cut the circle, fold it in half, then cut out a semicircle. The hole should just accommodate the funnel.

P is for Poaching Paper

If you need to cover your food without bringing it to a boil, a lid is too heavy-handed. Use poaching paper. This parchment "lid" rests directly on top of the food and its liquid. It is also known as a self-baster. Poaching paper protects food from drying, but lets steam escape.

How to Form (Sort-of) Round Poaching Paper

1. Cut out a parchment paper square a bit larger than the diameter of the pan you are using.
2. Fold the square into quarters.
3. Beginning at the closed tip, fold it diagonally into a cone shape, leaving the top about 2 inches (5 cm) wide. (Or you can roll it like a cone.)
4. Hold the paper in the center of the pan to assess the distance to the rim.
5. Cut off the part that projects more than 1 inch (2.5 cm) past the edge of the pan.
6. Cut off a tiny piece no more than $\frac{1}{8}$ inch (3 mm) at the small tip to form a vent for the center.
7. Unfold the paper. It ends up a bit oval. Trim the edges if you wish.

Plastic Wrap

❖ For a tighter seal, place some plastic wrap directly on the food, then stretch another piece over the dish.

❖ Plastic wrap won't stick? Moisture will help, but won't necessarily cure the problem. Three ways to moisten wrap:
- Wipe the surface with a damp cloth.
- Moisten the edge of the dish you are covering.
- Moisten your hands and press the wrap down over the dish.

Ways to Find the Edge of Plastic Wrap

- Rub along the roll with a toothbrush.
- Rub flour around the roll.
- Tuck a square of paper into the roll so you can always find the edge.

Twine

4 Kitchen Twine Holders

1. Put a ball of twine in a plastic tub. Fish it out through a hole poked in the top. Pull and cut as needed.
2. Store it in a funnel. Pull the string through the funnel's tube so it doesn't get tangled.
3. Put loose twine in an old piggy bank.
4. Dispense twine via an inverted flowerpot on a saucer or base.

Zip-lock Bags

❖ To make it easier to ladle food into a storage bag, put the bag in a bowl or a narrow pan, such as an asparagus pot, and fold down the edges.

Ways to Seal a Zip-lock Bag Tighter

- Stick a straw in one corner. Close the zipper. Suck, pinch and finish closing the zipper all the way.
- Close the zipper almost all the way. Stick the bag in water up to the edge. Squeeze out air and quickly finish closing the bag.

❖ Freeze small portions in snack-size zip-locks. Since they're not made thick for the freezer, stack them in a freezer bag or a plastic tub.

🌱 *Being Green*

You can clean and reuse zip-locks. Turn them inside out. Squeeze and swish them vigorously in a sink of hot, soapy water. Rinse them. Stand them up on a rack to dry.

Linens and Decor

Aprons

Lightning Won't Strike If ...

You don't wear an apron. An apron doesn't give enough coverage and can be uncomfortable. But you should cover up with something. Slip that something over good clothes if you're dressed for guests.

Alternatives to Aprons

- Wear a clean old T-shirt.
- A roomy T-back exercise tunic gives good coverage without being too warm.
- If you have a sense of humor, wear a lab coat. In a weird way, it's appropriate.
- Cover up with a man's big, old cotton shirt.

Candles

Cures for Candles

- Fix a warped taper. Let it soften in hot water, then roll it on a tabletop.
- If you care enough, renew a candle by rubbing paste wax or furniture polish over it.

Chairs

- ✧ Dining chairs and upholstered kitchen stools get stained quickly. Have them upholstered with two layers of cloth. When the time comes, pull off the top layer. It will still match the other chairs, so you won't have to reupholster the set.

- ✧ You can turn a tall kitchen stool into a regular chair by cutting off the legs.

Table Linens

- ✧ To reduce creases in table linens, you can hang them or roll them instead of folding.

Waste Not

A worn tablecloth can be recycled into napkins. Hem the edges or add decorative trim.

- ✧ If you're short on storage space, hang placemats on pant hangers in a kitchen closet.

- ✧ To keep cloth placemats and napkins flat, hang them on a clipboard.

Towels

- ✧ Always reaching for that towel, but it's never in the right place? Three ways to keep a towel close at hand:
- Use a large pin to secure it to the waistband of your pants.
- Tuck it beneath your apron strings.
- Wear a belt while cooking and tuck the towel into it.

✗ No-No

Don't use polyester kitchen cloths or towels. They aren't absorbent like cotton.

Thinking Outside the Box

Multitasking Kitchen Items

✤ Kitchen equipment is marketed for specific purposes, but we need not be so single-minded. If a handy tool seems more at home in the bathroom or the tool shed, so what? Shoppers don't have to stick to fancy kitchen stores, either. There are many utilitarian, unusual and inexpensive tools to be found at restaurant supply outlets. Hardware stores have their charms too.

Aluminum Pan

✤ A thawing tray works on the principle that aluminum conducts heat from the air into the food. You don't need one. Just fill an aluminum pan with boiling water and let it sit for 2 minutes. Drain it and put the frozen food in it. Repeat when the pan cools, turning the food.

✤ To clean silverware, sprinkle a spoonful of baking soda and/or salt into an aluminum pan filled with water. Bring it to a boil, then remove it from heat. Dip in the silverware and wipe it clean.

Making Do
If you don't have an aluminum pan, use a heavy metal bowl or skillet lined with aluminum foil.

Asparagus Pot

✤ Deep and narrow, with an inset basket, the asparagus pot is the right shape for a number of jobs:
- Boil corn on the cob.
- Steam whole stalks of broccoli.
- Deep-fry a small batch.
- Press the pot into service as a wine cooler.

Baking Sheet

✤ Keep unused burners on the stove clean by covering them with inverted rimmed baking sheets (or aluminum pie plates).

WAY OUTSIDE THE BOX

Having a party? An old rimmed baking sheet lined with a cooling rack will hold wet boots.

Bamboo Steamer

✤ Use large stacking bamboo steamers for storage. When you need one for steaming, empty it into a bag temporarily.

Baskets

✤ Separate the lids from cookware and stack them sideways in a plastic basket. You'll save space and they won't scatter all over the cupboard.

✤ Stack your plastic containers and stash all the lids in a basket alongside.

✤ If you don't have net domes to protect food from bugs in the backyard, invert a woven basket over your dish.

✤ Woven plastic berry baskets work well as small strainers.

Baster

✧ Use a baster when you need to:
- Drizzle carefully or add drops of liquid or oil.
- Vacuum scum from simmering beans or stock.
- Suck up fat from a greasy pan.

Keep It Clean

To clean a baster or medicine dropper, suck up soapy water and press it out a few times. Remove the squeeze bulb. Place the tube against the tap and run water through it.

Bottles

✧ Cut off the top section of a plastic bottle to use as a funnel.

✧ For a small job, a large wine bottle will double as a rolling pin. Fill it with ice water.

✧ Recycle a small squeezable mustard bottle as a drizzler. The pop top keeps the contents fresher.

✧ A squeeze bottle may be awkward to balance upside down when you're trying to get the last remaining contents, such as honey, ketchup or barbecue sauce, to ooze to the top. Steady it by planting it in a bowl of unshelled nuts or fruit.

Brushes

✧ Use a vegetable or potato brush to clean a wire rack with crumbs or bits of icing clinging to it.

WAY OUTSIDE THE BOX

A pastry brush is great for applying hair dye evenly to your roots.

6 Uses for a Pastry Brush

1. Treat it like a mini broom and sweep crumbs off the counter or stovetop.
2. Brush flour off the base of your stand mixer or food processor.
3. Sweep zest or chopped herbs to the side of the cutting board or into a small bowl.
4. Poke a grater to free it of zest or dry cheese particles.
5. Brush out a coffee/spice grinder.
6. Sweep debris off the gills of mushrooms.

Cans

✧ Remove the top and bottom of a tuna can and use it as a ring mold or cookie cutter.

✧ Turn a coffee can into an ice pack for a cooler. Fill it with ice cubes and put the lid on.

Cast-Iron Pan

✧ Use a cast-iron pan as a stand-in for a pizza stone. Turn it upside down.

✧ Substitute a cast-iron pan for a plancha (a heated iron grill) to lightly char vegetables such as asparagus and mushrooms. The veggies can be oiled and salted beforehand.

✧ Enameled cast iron holds the cold. Fill it with ice water, cover it and let sit for 5 minutes. Drain and dry it. Now you can fill it with chilled food, such as macaroni salad.

Cheese Slicer

✧ Cut a thin ribbon from firm butter, to melt on toast or for baking.

Chopsticks

✧ Use a chopstick (or the handle of a wooden spoon) to gently separate the skin from the flesh of a turkey in want of stuffing or seasoning.

✧ Run a chopstick around the edge of a mason jar to release air bubbles in preserves. It's nimbler than a spatula.

✧ Wield chopsticks to tuck garlic cloves or slices, whole dried chile peppers or dill sprigs decoratively against the side of the jar when canning pickles.

✧ Instead of tongs or a fork, use chopsticks to turn delicate meat or vegetable chunks in a skillet — if you're nimble with them.

✧ Hold a chopstick across the lip of a pan of potatoes you are draining. They are less likely to tumble out.

Cocktail Shaker

✧ Blend a flour or cornstarch slurry for gravy in a cocktail shaker. Pour it out through the strainer.

✧ Grab the cocktail strainer if you need to quickly strain a small amount of liquid for a sauce.

Colander

✧ If you don't have a steamer basket or insert, improvise with a steel colander and a large lid.

Cutlery

✧ To hold a recipe card, stick it between the tines of a fork. Stand the fork in a glass.

✧ Toss a small spoon in the bottom of a double boiler. It will rattle a warning when the water runs too low. (You can also use the lid of a jar.)

✧ Use two spoons nestled together to crush candies or pills.

♛ A Golden Rule

Elaborate place settings can be confusing. All you need to remember about the cutlery is to work your way from the outside in, toward your plate.

Coffee Filter

✧ Borrow the permanent mesh coffee filter from your machine and put it to work as a small strainer. Don't try this with paper coffee filters — you'll die waiting.

✧ A paper coffee filter works as an impromptu cover for a measuring cup in the microwave.

Coffee/Spice Grinder

✧ You can use a coffee or spice grinder as a mini food processor, though it is harder to clean. Two other uses:
  • Make a small amount of bread crumbs by tossing chunks of bread into the grinder.
  • Pulverize candy to sprinkle on cake or cookies, or to stir into coffee or tea.

Cookie Cutter

✧ Use a cookie cutter to:
  • Cut fruit, vegetables and cheese into cute shapes.

- Punch out the makings of crustless tea sandwiches from single slices.
- Cut dainty rounds from a single-layer rectangular cake. Glaze and serve.

Corncob Holder

✦ A corncob holder is good for piercing potatoes or squash before cooking.

Dishwasher

✦ Cook fish in the dishwasher. Hold the detergent.

Egg Carton

✦ If you don't have enough ice cube trays, put a thoroughly washed plastic egg carton to work. An added benefit: It closes to prevent spills.

✦ Use an egg carton to transport hard-cooked eggs.

WAY OUTSIDE THE BOX

Recycle an egg carton in the tool room to separate and hold screws, nuts, bolts and washers.

Dishwasher Salmon

You can cook exceptionally moist fish in the dishwasher. Do not, of course, do dishes at the same time. **Makes 4 servings**

Tips
The cooking time will vary with individual dishwashers and water temperatures.

This technique works with other kinds of fish, whole or filleted.

1¼ lb	skinless salmon fillet (about 1¼ inches/3 cm thick)	600 g
2 tsp	melted unsalted butter	10 mL
¼ tsp	ground lemon pepper	1 mL
	Sea salt	
4	lemon wedges	4

1. Halve salmon lengthwise along the seam. Put each piece on a large buttered sheet of foil, tucking under the thin ends of the fish. Drizzle 1 tsp (5 mL) butter over each piece. Sprinkle with lemon pepper and salt.

2. Make watertight packets by holding up and aligning the edges of the foil, then crimping them several times until the foil lies flat against the fish. Press the foil to mold it around the salmon. Wrap each packet in another large sheet of foil.

3. Place the packets on the top rack of the dishwasher. Run the normal wash cycle for about 45 minutes or until salmon is opaque and flakes easily with a fork. (Do not use the whole wash cycle or the dry cycle.) Cut each piece in half before serving.

☺ KID STUFF

Save plastic egg cartons as containers for paints.

Egg Slicer

✧ An egg slicer is perfect for more than just eggs. Try it for slicing:
- Mushrooms
- Truffles (how ignoble, especially if you're using a plastic slicer)
- Soft fruit, such as kiwis, strawberries and bananas
- Cooked halved small beets (larger whole beets can be cut evenly with an apple wedger — although you end up with a "core")

Escargot Plate

✧ Use an escargot or devilled egg plate as a palette for food dyes if you're painting with several colors.

Foil

✧ For a makeshift trivet, scrunch foil into a roll, then shape it into a ring.

✧ If you don't have a cookie sheet, cover an oven rack with a double layer of heavy foil. (The lines are liable to show through if you press it on too tight.)

✧ In an emergency, foil can double as gift wrap (as can a dismantled brown paper bag). Dress it up with a colorful ribbon.

Fondue Fork

✧ Though the prongs are a bit too far apart, a fondue fork will do as a seafood pick.

✧ Use a fondue fork to prick the skin of a duck or goose during cooking to release fat.

Frozen Vegetables

✧ A bag of frozen vegetables makes a flexible ice pack.

Glass Bowl

✧ Replace the top of a double boiler with a heatproof, see-through glass bowl. (Just make sure there are no cracks or chips in the glass.) You can push the food aside to check how much water you have and how bubbly it is.

Glasses

✧ Use a glass (or cup) as a spoon rest next to the stove. It takes up less space and catches drips better than a flat plate.

✧ If you don't have a round cookie cutter, use a wine or juice glass, depending on the size you want, to cut pastry or cookie dough.

✧ Measure tablespoons (15 mL) in shot glasses.

✧ Use a shot glass to press flat small balls of cookie dough.

✧ If a couple of glasses (or bowls) are stuck together, spray the top one with cold water. If that doesn't work, fill it with ice.

Grapefruit Spoon/Knife

✧ A grapefruit knife is small and curved, with serrated edges. Use it to:
- Easily separate the flesh from the shell of a tomato half.
- Coax mini cupcakes, muffins and tarts out of their tins. (Careful: This may scratch a nonstick pan.)

- The grapefruit spoon, shaped like a shovel with a pointed end and serrated edges, is versatile:
  - It works on papaya, kiwi, mango and prickly pear, too. Scoop and eat.
  - Seed a cucumber that has been cut in half lengthwise.
  - Carve and scoop the flesh from baked potatoes en route to becoming potato skins.
  - Scrape seeds from a squash.
  - Excise eyes and rub dirty patches off potatoes.

- You can seed halved chile peppers and tomatoes with a grapefruit spoon or knife.

Grater

- Use a rasp grater to sand scorched bits off burnt pastries, rolls and toast.

- Shred peeled garlic in the small teardrop holes of a rotary cheese grater. To chop it, use the small grater holes.

- "Chop" chocolate into shavings with a rotary cheese grater. Chill the chocolate first.

- Use a rotary grater to grind small quantities of nuts.

Ice Bucket

- Keep cookies fresh in an insulated ice bucket.

Ice Cream Scoop

- Use an ice cream scoop to scrape seeds from squash or pumpkin.

Ice Cube Tray

- Beware: Some liquids and foods, particularly tomato-based ones, leave permanent stains on white plastic ice cube trays.

Jars

- Store odds and ends by hanging them from a shelf. Screw the lid of a small jar onto the "ceiling" of a cupboard. Fill the jar and screw it onto the lid. The jar hangs, and can be removed with a quick twist of the wrist. Marinated artichoke jars are a good size.

Lids

- When freezing burger patties, separate them with lids from yogurt tubs and the like. Don't use waxed paper or foil; they stick.

- They do actually make a tool for this, but if you don't have one, use the lid of a mason jar to make uniform patties for mini burgers and fish cakes. Pat your mixture into the lid. Push off the screwband.

- Use the flat lid of a mason jar to strip scales from a fish. Be careful: It's easy to scrape or tear the skin.

☺ KID STUFF

Drip-proof a kid. Make a slit in the center of a plastic lid from a yogurt, sour cream or cottage cheese container. Jab the stick from a Popsicle or ice cream treat though it to form a little plate that catches drips.

17 Uses for an Ice Cube Tray

1. Freeze tomato paste or sauce by the tablespoon (15 mL).
2. Do the same with stock for small jobs or, better, concentrated stock.
3. Freeze tamarind paste.
4. Be prepared for your morning smoothie. Dice fruit and spoon yogurt into ice cube trays. When they're frozen, place the right amounts for one smoothie into individual zip-lock bags.
5. Make mini frozen pops. Freeze juice. When it's almost firm, stick in a toothpick or half a Popsicle stick.
6. Once a lemon or lime is zested, it dehydrates and rots. Squeeze it and store the juice in cube form. You can throw in the leftover zest, too.
7. Purée leftover cooked vegetables and freeze them in cubes. Add a bit of butter or oil to a cube to create a sauce for fish or poultry.
8. Chipotle chile peppers in adobo sauce are sold in small cans, but a little goes a long way. Mash the goods with a fork and freeze by the teaspoon (5 mL).
9. Make pesto cubes to season soups, stews or sauces.
10. Meat likes a little demi-glace. It's expensive. Save it in cubes.
11. Freeze single egg whites and prepped yolks. Then you can just count out whites for that angel cake or meringue. Or take one of each if you need a whole egg.
12. Purée ripe fruit and freeze it in cubes for shakes, lemonades or blender cocktails.
13. Make juice cubes to use in fruity party drinks so they won't dilute. Or go low-cal with flavored water. How about club soda served with apple juice ice cubes?
14. Pour leftover brewed coffee or tea into an ice cube tray. Use the cubes to chill iced coffee or tea, or when baking to replace some of the water in your recipe.
15. If you don't drink much wine, freeze the leftovers for cooking. A little bit will lift a dish.
16. Baby likes small portions. Make homemade baby food and freeze it in cubes.
17. Add vermouth to your martini in the form of an ice cube.

Lobster Pick

✧ A lobster pick will help you get to the delicious marrow in osso buco or beef bone soup.

Marshmallows

✧ No holders? Catch drips on a birthday cake by pushing candles into colored mini marshmallows.

Mats

✧ Woven rubber matting made for crispers and scatter rugs can prevent sliding in other locations too. Put a mat under a mixing bowl to prevent bouncing and slipping while you're whisking and whipping.

✧ Line a drawer with a rubber mat to prevent utensils from jostling.

- Use a mat as a soft liner between nonstick pans so they don't scratch.

- Scrape chopped vegetables onto a plastic placemat, or sift flour onto it. Fold up the sides for easy transfer to a pan or mixing bowl. (A flexible plastic cutting board does the same job.)

- Use an old plastic placemat as a drawer liner.

Meat Grinder

- You can use a meat grinder to crush fruit and vegetables.

Meat Pounder/Mallet

- Use the grooved head of a mallet to gently stamp cookie dough with an interesting diamond pattern.

- Crack peppercorns.

- Crush ice in a paper bag.

- Shell nuts.

Muffin Tin and Liners

- Use an old muffin tin to hold separate colors of icing, dye for eggs or even paints for kids.

- For well-rounded cookies, bake the dough in a muffin tin. Make sure you put enough dough in each cup to spread to the edges.

- Put recipe ingredients in paper muffin/ cupcake liners instead of little bowls. If they get dirty, toss them out. You'll have less cleanup. (Candy cups come in handy, too, for seasonings.)

Melon Baller

- Use a 1-inch (2.5 cm) melon baller to core apples and pears without cutting them into quadrants. Cut the fruit in half from top to bottom. Scoop out a ball at the core. Scrape the remaining core up to the top.

Netting

- Save the plastic netting used to package onions. Bundle it and tie the ends. You now have a dish scrubber.

Oil Mister

- Spraying is fun, so why limit yourself to just oil?
  - Spray on thin barbecue glaze instead of brushing it on.
  - Spray soy sauce onto vegetables, stir-fries and steamed fish.
  - Spray balsamic vinegar or thin vinaigrette onto salad.

Oyster Knife

- You can cut chocolate with an oyster knife. Use a stabbing killer grip.

Paper Towels

- Use a paper towel when you run out of coffee filters.

Pastry Blender

- Break up partially thawed ground meat, or fresh ground meat that clumps, before or after cooking.

- Press a grid pattern onto cookie dough (you can also use a potato masher). Flour your tool first.

✧ Mash eggs handily for egg salad.

Peeler

✧ Remove scales from a fish, from tail to head. Work under running water.

✧ Create carrot "noodles," or ribbons. Steam the ribbons with a spoonful of water in the microwave for 30 seconds. Rinse with cold water and drain. Limp ribbons are easy to curl or drape.

✧ Make butter curls.

✧ Scrape the hard casing off salami or dry smoked sausage.

WAY OUTSIDE THE BOX

A peeler can be pressed into service as an emergency pencil sharpener, though it doesn't do a great job.

Pie Plate

✧ If you need a see-through lid for a pan, use a glass (Pyrex) pie plate. As with all glass cookware, remember not to set the hot plate down on a cold surface or pour cold water into it.

Pizza Stool

✧ Keep the little plastic stool that pizza chains sit in the middle of their pies to prevent the box from sticking to the cheese.
• Put a stool or two on top of a cake to keep plastic wrap from sticking to the icing.
• Put stools on top of a stored casserole to prevent plastic wrap from disturbing a cheese or crumb topping.

Pizza Wheel

WAY OUTSIDE THE BOX

Use a pizza wheel to unstick a window frame that has been painted shut.

Plastic Wrap

✧ If water is slowly leaking out of the kitchen sink, line the drain with plastic wrap before putting in the stopper. Note: This doesn't work with a regular plastic plug; it floats.

Plastic Containers

✧ Turn a large ice cream tub into a container for plastic bags. Cut a hole in the bottom big enough to pull out the bags. Fill it from the top.

😊 KID STUFF

Make a drinking box for a kid. Punch a hole in a yogurt tub or other small plastic container and stick a straw through it.

Plates

✧ Use paper plates as buffers. Place them between stacked china plates or line nonstick cookware to prevent scratches. (You can also use old towels or facecloths.)

✧ If pots and pans are leaving scuff marks on your shelves, put paper plates underneath them.

✧ Peel vegetables over a plain, cheap, unwaxed paper plate. Throw in the trimmings from the cutting board. Fold the lot and toss it in the compost bin.

- Grind pepper or sift flour onto flexible paper plates, then fold to pour.

- No need to flip food in the air like a chef. Use two dinner plates to turn rösti potatoes, for instance. Slide them onto the first plate. Cover them with the second plate. Invert. Slide them back into the pan.

4 Ways to Warm Dinner Plates

1. Heat them in a pile for 5 to 10 minutes in an oven set no higher than 200°F (100°C).
2. Wipe each plate with a damp cloth and microwave briefly.
3. Put them in a sink of hot water. Drain and dry when you are ready to use them.
4. Use the heat cycle of the dishwasher.

Popsicle Sticks

 KID STUFF

Give kids Popsicle sticks, instead of potentially dangerous knives, to smear butter or peanut butter on bread.

Potato Chip Tube

- Transport homemade cookies in a potato chip tube.

- Store homemade croutons.

Potato Masher

- Crush soft fruit and tomatoes with a potato masher when you don't want to attack them with a chopper or food processor.

- Use a masher to dip truffles, pretzels or cookies into molten chocolate.

- Here's a quick way to drain a can of tomatoes: Hold a masher over the mouth of the can while pouring out the juices.

Potato Ricer

- Use a ricer to squeeze water out of cooked spinach.

Racks

- Prop a long flat rack over the sink for rinsing and draining food.

- Need a large cooling rack? Put an oven rack to work.

- Stack cookware lids in an old dish rack.

- Use the V-rack from the roasting pan as a cookbook holder.

Ways to Save Space

- Space is at a premium in a busy working kitchen. You can hang utensils and tools, as well as pans, from an overhead pot rack.
- Attach one of those high-tech wire racks to the wall, put in metal S-hooks and hang anything from ladles to pots. The racks come in sections, so you can cover as much surface as you need. (I used this method way back when my age wasn't as close to the square footage of my kitchen.)

Rice Cooker

- You can use a rice cooker for Israeli couscous, oatmeal and a plethora of grains.

28 Uses for Kitchen Scissors

1. Shred fresh herbs. Roll leaves into a cigar, then snip thin slices off the end.
2. For an instant garnish, snip and slice herbs or green onions directly onto a dish.
3. To chop parsley, cilantro or other herbs, put them in a jar or measuring glass and snip away.
4. Snip, don't chop, chives. Hold a bunch tightly in one hand and snip with the other. You can also do this with other herbs. Hold them in a tight bouquet.
5. Chop tomatoes in the can or in a measuring cup. Holding one side of the scissors handle in each hand, snip until you feel very little resistance. For a finer result, pour out the juice first.
6. Snip sun-dried tomatoes into slivers.
7. Quickly trim the stem ends of green beans. Hold a handful at a time.
8. Trim the leaves from the base of a cauliflower.
9. Instead of cutting, shave black spots off cauliflower with one blade of your scissors. It looks neater. (You can also use a small, sharp knife for this job.)
10. Cut dried chile peppers in half. (Then brush off the seeds.)
11. Sliver dates and other dried fruit.
12. Halve or quarter marshmallows.
13. Evenly trim the edges of pie pastry after laying it in the baking dish.
14. Divide yeast dough — cutting it with scissors is easier than using a knife.
15. Cut stale bread into cubes for croutons.
16. Snip hunks off bread straight into the food processor for fresh bread crumbs.
17. Neatly trim the ragged whites on poached eggs.
18. Remove sausage casings. Run cold water over the sausages for a minute to make them easier to slit.
19. Trim the fat from meat.
20. Cut pork crackling.
21. Snip raw bacon right into the skillet.
22. Cut boneless chicken.
23. Cut the tips off chicken wings.
24. Trim the sharp fins of a whole fish before cooking it.
25. Cut fresh or cooked lasagna noodles to fit your pan. (By the way, remember to slightly overlap the noodles.)
26. Cut yourself a slice of pizza.
27. Slice unruly spaghetti strands on your plate — if no one's looking.
28. Serve French onion soup with scissors alongside to snip the stringy cheese.

Rolling Pin

✧ Roll soft crackers and cookies into crumbs.

✧ Crush spices.

✧ Make like an old European lady and pound your butter to soften it for pastry.

Rubber Bands

✧ Save the colorful wide rubber bands from vegetables.

• Wind bands around the ends of tongs for better grip. Use them to pick up hot ramekins and extract mason jars from boiling water.

- When opening a jar, get a better grip by placing a rubber band around the lid.
- If tongs or poultry shears keep popping open in the drawer, secure the ends with rubber bands.
- Hold the lids on pots and casserole dishes when transporting them. To secure a casserole dish, run a rubber band from one handle to the knob on the lid. Repeat on the other side.

Shakers

- Fill large salt or spice shakers with flour, confectioner's (icing) sugar or vanilla sugar for sprinkling, or with baking soda for cleaning jobs.

Skewer

- Keep a short, thin, round metal skewer beside the stove to test for doneness. It's more subtle than a paring knife or fork for potatoes, longer than a toothpick for baked goods and perfect for poking a roast chicken to see if the juices run clear without making a large cut.

- Potatoes, stuffing and other foods cook faster if you push steel skewers or nails into them. The metal conducts heat to the interior.

- Clean solids out of a metal latte straw by pushing a skewer into it.

- Use a long skewer to root around in the drain and poke at any obstructions.

- Use a skewer (or a large knitting needle) to swirl the batter for a marble cake.

Slow Cooker

- Use the Low setting to keep food warm for a party, buffet or big dinner. To ensure that germs don't proliferate, heat the food before putting it in the slow cooker.

- Serve hot cider, chai, spiced tea or punch in a slow cooker set on Low, so guests can help themselves.

WAY OUTSIDE THE BOX

Heat stones in a slow cooker for a hot stone massage.

Spaghetti

- A length of raw spaghetti can be used as a long match for flambéing or lighting a barbecue. Just light the end.

- Use spaghetti as a cake tester.

Sponge/Scrubber

- Put a dry sponge in the vegetable crisper to soak up excess moisture or, vice versa, store a damp sponge in the crisper to add humidity.

- Duct-tape a sponge or dishcloth to a yardstick to help you clean under appliances and in tight spaces.

- Use a large scrubber/sponge to hold food being sliced in a mandolin. The thick scrubber side works as a food guard, and it's easier to hold because it molds to the food. Beware: This is not a license to come close to the blades.

- Scrub vegetables with a clean dish scouring pad.

Sugar Disc

✦ Moistened clay discs are buried in brown sugar to prevent drying and clumping. You can also use a disc to keep moisture in a cake tin or cookie box, a bag of desiccated coconut or dried fruit, or a tub of popping corn.

Tea Bag

✦ Can't find the plug? A used tea bag will hold the water in a sink for a while.

Tea Ball

✦ Fill a tea ball with confectioner's (icing) sugar (or paprika or ground cinnamon) and sprinkle it instead of dusting through a small sieve. If you use the type with fine mesh and tong handles, you can scoop the icing sugar directly.

✦ When making chutney or a curry, put the whole spices in a tea ball. They will be easier to remove.

Toaster Oven

✦ The top of a toaster oven gets warm. It's a good place to warm up your breakfast or lunch plate and mug.

Toothpick

✦ Scrape out the gunk between the cabinetry and the edge of the stove with a toothpick (or a thin knife).

Tostoñera

✦ A tostoñera is used as a plantain press. But you can use it to press uniform circles of dough for mini tart shells or to flatten cookie dough evenly.

Trays

✦ Indented plastic trays from manicotti boxes and cookie packages are good for transporting fragile éclairs or cannoli. A baguette pan would work too.

Tubes

✦ Save sturdy cardboard tubes from rolls of parchment paper, foil, paper towels, toilet paper and twine.
• Stuff small plastic produce bags into an empty tube and toss the tube in a drawer.
• Protect knives in a drawer with sheaths made from tubes.
• Tongs don't or won't lock? Shove the ends in a tube cut to fit. This works for poultry shears too.

WAY OUTSIDE THE BOX

Slit the tube from a roll of paper towels and pad a hanger with it.

Waxed Paper

✦ To help them slide, rub warm oven racks with waxed paper (or an old candle or paste wax). Do the same with a sticky drawer.

✦ Make a pan less sticky. Heat it and rub it with a large sheet of waxed paper.

✦ You can use waxed paper as shelf paper. Dampen it lightly to make it adhere.

✦ Save the waxed paper inserts from cereal boxes for freezer packaging.

✦ Put a large sheet of waxed paper under the bowl of a stand mixer to catch spills. (Or use a kitchen towel.)

25 Uses for Zip-lock Bags

1. Seal burger, meatloaf or meatball mixture in a zip-lock and knead to blend. It's almost like using your hands, but less icky.

2. Pound meat in a zip-lock. The bag is thicker than plastic wrap, which tears under the duress. The meat pounder will stay clean, as juices and bits of meat will be contained.

3. You can not only marinate in a zip-lock, but also mix the marinade in it. Shake or squeeze to blend the ingredients.

4. Toss a brick in a zip-lock or fill it with water. Seal it and use to submerge meat floating in brine.

5. Oil meat and vegetables for roasting or grilling. Doing this in a zip-lock is less messy than smearing it with your hands or brushing, and less oil is required.

6. If you are salting and draining sliced or shredded eggplant, cucumber, zucchini or potato in a colander or sieve, fill a large zip-lock with water and place it over the vegetables to provide even pressure.

7. Put a roasted pepper in a zip-lock. Cool it briefly. Massage the skin through the plastic to tease it off.

8. Chop nuts quickly in a zip-lock. Whack the bag with the side of a mallet a couple of times.

9. Chill a work surface for pastry or truffles by leaving ice-filled zip-locks on it for half an hour. (You can also put a baking sheet over the surface and place ice on top.)

10. One step is better than two. Grate cheese or carrots directly into a large bag. Seal and store.

11. Use a perforated vegetable zip-lock as a salad spinner. Do this outside.

12. Store party foods such as salads in zip-locks instead of bowls. The fridge won't get so overcrowded.

13. Control your portions. Separate a big batch of leftovers into individual zip-locks and freeze them for instant TV dinners.

14. Brown bagging? Make a salad. Divide it into individual-serving bags. When the time comes, add dressing and shake. Lazy teenagers like this too. You can use the same idea when transporting a salad to a party or picnic. When you get there, squirt in the dressing and turn the bag gently from side to side.

15. Make sorbet. Stick a bag full of sorbet mixture into the freezer. Forgo the stirring. Instead, massage the bag every once in a while.

16. Slit the sides, slide in cookie dough or pie pastry, and roll without sticking.

17. Convert a zip-lock into an impromptu piping bag. Snip off a corner and insert the coupler and tip. The tip should stick about $\frac{1}{2}$ inch (1 cm) through the opening. Fill the bag with frosting. Use the snack-size bags for tiny amounts of trim or rosettes.

18. When handling crumbly cookie dough, such as for shortbread, toss the crumbs into a zip-lock and press the contents into a block or disc. This also works for pie pastry that doesn't come together easily.

19. To add filling to cookies, turnovers or blueberry buns, cut a small hole in one corner of a bag and squeeze.

20. Turn a zip-lock into an ice pack. Fill it with water, place it in a serving bowl and freeze it. The bag will keep its shape. Cover it with a clean towel. Serve salad, condiments or the like in a bowl over top. You can also put food directly on ice. Just put a piece of foil over the zip-lock.

21. If the phone rings while you're handling dough or messy meatloaf mix, slide your hand into a bag before you pick up.

22. Keep a kitchen scale clean, yet still see the readout. Store it in a perforated bag that breathes. You can weigh items right on the plastic. Then give it a wipe or change the bag.

23. Slide a recipe sheet or card into a plastic bag while you're cooking. No stains or splatters.

24. Cover a small cookbook with a zip-lock.

25. Turn a perforated zip-lock into an herb terrarium. Put a small pot in it. Seal the top.

Wok

✦ Use the domed lid of a wok to cover a hunk of something on the grill without closing the lid.

Zester

✦ Use a lemon zester to shred a bit of Parmesan.

Versatile Household Supplies

Bandana

✦ Don't want hair to fall in the food, but feel silly in a chef's hat? Use a motorcycle bandana. It's shaped like a cap, with a flap and ties in the back. You can get one lined with netting and a sweatband. Harley designs even come with flames — perfect for the kitchen.

Blow-Dryer

✦ Aim a blow-dryer inside a bottle or jar to dry it quickly.

✦ For a silky, lustrous finish on a frosted cake, run a blow-dryer on low heat — briefly — over the frosting.

✦ Dry fruit fast. Wipe it with a towel, then blow-dry on the cool setting.

Box Cutter

3 Uses for a Box Cutter

1. Slash bread before baking.
2. Cut fondant or pastry cleanly.
3. Slice fresh homemade pasta.

(If you have a scalpel or a plain razor blade hanging around, that works too.)

Bricks

✦ Use a brick covered in foil to press grilled cheese or panini, push halved chicken against the barbecue grate or submerge brined meat.

Brushes

3 Uses for a Paintbrush

Add new paintbrushes — whether marketed for walls or for art, tiny and delicate or big and wide — to the kitchen arsenal.

1. Paint barbecue sauce on meat with a wide brush.
2. Apply shimmer to a cake with a small brush.
3. Grease pans quickly by applying oil with a big brush.

10 Uses for a Toothbrush

Keep an old toothbrush beside the sink with your scrubbing tools. You can dip it in an abrasive cleanser, vinegar or dish soap for cleaning jobs.

1. Brush the clogged holes in a garlic press or grater.
2. Scrub between the buttons and in the vents on a mixer, blender, pasta machine or other appliance.
3. Scrub the moving parts of a can opener.
4. Clear the food holder of a mandolin and brush the nooks near the sharp business end of the blade. You don't want to be anywhere near those with your bare fingers.
5. Clean the crevices on the top of a filtered water jug.
6. Brighten scratched plastic plates with toothpaste on the brush.
7. Scrub the crevices in a stained colander.
8. Scrub the dirty crevices and hinges of bivalves.
9. Clean a stalk of celery.
10. After cooking, scrub away debris under your fingernails if they are long.

❖ Use a baby bottle brush to clean deep, narrow glasses.

❖ A shaving brush can stand in as a pastry brush.

Clamps

❖ Sometimes known as locking forceps, this surgical tool looks like serrated scissors that clamp shut. You can use it to get a grip on slippery jobs, such as pulling pin bones from fish or pin feathers from poultry.

Clips

❖ Hang a recipe sheet or card on a magnetic binder clip on the fridge door. Or use a big binder clip and hang it from a knob.

❖ Use binder clips to close potato chip bags and other open packages.

Clothespins

❖ Close potato chip and snack bags.

❖ Secure cheesecloth to the rim of a sieve. (Large paperclips work too.)

Comb

❖ Make designs in frosting with a comb.

❖ Clean a kitchen broom by stroking it with a comb.

Crayon

❖ Rub chipped wood with a crayon to disguise the scar.

Dumbbell

❖ You can pound meat thin with a dumbbell.

Eraser

✦ Rub and clean the metal contact points on an appliance.

✦ Rub small burnt spots on wood. An eraser will get rid of some of the discoloration.

Floss

✦ Unflavored dental floss comes in handy. (Fishing line does similar jobs.)
● Cut soft cheese, such as goat cheese.
● If dough is sticking to a pizza peel, slide floss under it before putting it in the oven.
● If you run out of kitchen string, substitute floss. Use it to truss poultry, for example.

Envelope

✦ Make a disposable funnel using an envelope with the bottom corner snipped off. Use a small one to fill salt and pepper shakers. Use a large brown one for bigger jobs.

Gloves

✦ Wear thin latex or other disposable gloves while cutting jalapeños or working with food dye or vegetables that stain, such as beets. They're more comfortable and maneuverable than dishwashing rubber gloves. You can buy gloves cheap in bulk at a medical supply store or in small packets at the drugstore.

✦ If latex or rubber gloves are hard to pull on, sprinkle baby powder inside.

✦ Dry gloves by fitting them over a bottle.

Grease Pencil

✦ Use a grease pencil to jot dates on butcher's paper, zip-lock bags and the lids of mason jars and plastic storage tubs.

Hairpin

✦ You can pit cherries with a large hairpin, although the fruit will end up ragged at the top. Insert the looped end into the stem end of the cherry, press down to the bottom of the pit, flip and twist out.

✦ If you are a masochist, you can scrape seeds from a grape with the end of a hairpin.

Hand Vacuum

✦ Move a hand vac into the kitchen. It makes short work of crumby cleanup jobs.
● Suck debris off the dinner table or kitchen island after the kids eat.
● Vacuum crumbs out of the cutlery drawer.
● Quickly suck burnt bits of bread out of the toaster. Pull out the crumb tray and vacuum it clean.
● Before washing cupboard shelves, vacuum them.

Hanger

✦ A wire hanger cut in the center makes a portable paper towel holder.

Ice Pack

✦ Gel ice packs are handier and tidier than loose ice. They mold to the shape of different dishes and foods.

• Cool a baking sheet or platter by putting a frozen flexible gel ice pack under or in it. If you need a cold bowl, leave an ice pack sitting in it for 5 minutes.

• For a quick ice bath for blanched vegetables, toss an ice pack in the water. The miniature ice packs work nicely.

Jug

✦ Those large commercial wide-mouth plastic jugs (like the ones containing Epsom salts) are great for salt and sugar in the pantry. Clean them out well.

Kitty Litter

✦ Sprinkle litter in the bottom of a garbage can to catch leaks and absorb odors.

Knobs

✦ If the handle falls off a pot lid, replace it with a metal knob or cabinet pull from the hardware or home decor store. You can also do this if you want the lid to withstand higher temperatures.

Magnifying Glass

✦ Whipping reading glasses on and off while following a recipe is so tedious. Boomers with fading eyesight can rest a magnifying glass over the ingredient list to see those little fractions.

Makeup Sponge

✦ You can grease pans with a fresh makeup sponge.

Medicine Dropper

✦ Keep a clean medicine dropper in the kitchen. Here are some uses for it:

• Dispense drips or dashes of dye and extracts.

• Decorate a plate, say with polka dots of chocolate syrup surrounding a tart.

• Drizzle reduced balsamic vinegar onto grilled fish or chicken.

• Test how much liquid the full dropper dispenses and use it in place of a measuring spoon for small amounts.

Mouse Pad

✦ Slip an old mouse pad under a mixing bowl to keep it steady.

✦ Use it as a cushion between nonstick pans.

Music Stand

✦ Hold an open cookbook or recipe sheet on a music stand.

Newspaper

✦ To store glass, wrap it in a couple of layers of wet newspaper. It clings and dries into a protective coating.

Pantyhose

✦ Use pantyhose instead of cheesecloth as a filter. Stretch it over a sieve. Use new hose, and launder it without soap. I prefer the knee-highs.

✦ Air and hang onions and garlic bulbs in pantyhose, with knots between each one. They keep better when separated.

✦ Pull pantyhose over food in the freezer to secure wrappings, such as foil.

* Save the waistbands from pantyhose to clamp garbage and compost bags more securely to their bins.

Petroleum Jelly

* Rub the base of a candleholder with petroleum jelly to keep dripping wax from sticking.

Picture Frame

* Having a school bake sale? Use those clear plastic picture frames that stand up by themselves to hold descriptions and prices. The frames also come in handy at buffets or dessert stands.

Pillowcase

* Making salad for a crowd? Put the lettuce in a pillowcase and spin it dry outside.

Pipe Cleaner

* Weave a pipe cleaner between the tines of a fork when you are polishing tarnished silver.

Plastic Report Cover

* Cut a plastic report cover to use as a knife sleeve.

Pliers

* Reduce your chance of burns by pulling out a hot oven rack with pliers or a vise grip (locking pliers). This is less clumsy than oven mitts. (Tongs work too, but the grip isn't as firm.)

* Use pliers to pull a baking sheet from the oven.

* Pull off chicken skin or bits of gristle, silverskin or hard fat from meat with pliers. Pliers are especially good for stripping those slippery drumsticks.

* A vise grip can be used to crack nuts without a lot of pressure.

* Use pliers to crack hard claw shells on crustaceans.

Powder Puff

* Dust the cutting board and counter lightly with flour using a fresh cosmetic powder puff.

Sand

* After gluing together broken glass or another item, bury it in sand to apply even pressure and hold the edges together.

Scraper

* Scrape dried-on food from baking sheets, pans and dishes.

* If you have no bench scraper, try a paint scraper. If you need a big one, try a drywall taper. A car ice scraper is also useful.

Shoe Organizer

* Is kitchen space tight? Hang a shoe bag on the door. The compartments will hold anything from utensils to spices in small zip-locks.

Shower Cap

✧ A shower cap works as a recyclable bowl cover.

Soap Pump Dispenser

✧ Fill a dispenser with oil and pump it out. This works great. It dispenses little squirts neatly into a pan, so you don't use too much oil. There's no dripping spout. So who needs an oil can?

✧ Other neat potential oil dispensers: an old Worcestershire or soy sauce bottle, a water bottle with a pop top, a squeezable ketchup bottle or a sippy cup.

Stones

✧ Frozen stones can replace ice cubes on a buffet table to keep food cold.

Thimble

✧ Slip a thimble over your thumb as protection while you're grating cheese or vegetables.

Toque

✧ A toque makes a fine tea cozy.

Tweezers

✧ Be your own food stylist. Use tweezers to manipulate small garnishes.

✧ Pick capers and green peppercorns out of brine with tweezers.

✧ Look for long-handled tweezers in kitchen supply stores.

Wallpaper

✧ Use leftover scraps of wallpaper to line shelves and drawers.

✤ Before shopping for a small appliance — especially a newfangled type like, say, a coffee pod system, or something pricey, such as an espresso maker — ask a friend if you can test-drive hers first.

✤ You won't use it if you have to lug it. And if you won't use it, some recipes will seem too intimidating. Appliances that should live on the counter: bread machine, food processor, stand mixer, blender. The attachments can live in a drawer.

✤ Grind ice cubes in your blender, food processor, coffee/spice grinder or garbage disposal to hone the blades. Four to six cubes should do the job.

Blender

✤ For the most velvety purées for soups and desserts, choose a blender over a food processor.

How Good Is Your Blender?

• A simple test is how well it pulverizes ice. Good: slushie consistency. Bad: watery chunks.

✤ For the best blending, put liquids in first, then solids in small chunks. You need adequate liquid.

✤ For smoothness, drop frozen fruit or ice cubes one at a time into the blender while it's running.

✤ Don't wiggle the jar while the blender is running. You'll break it.

Keep It Clean

Right after using the blender, fill it with hot water, squirt in dish soap, cover and pulse. Fill it almost to the top to reach the lid too. Rinse with warm water. Now pulse without the lid to dry it a bit.

Coffee/Spice Grinder

✤ When using a spice grinder, turn it upside down and pulse briefly to clear the blades and coax the debris into the lid. This makes the spices easier to remove and measure. You can do the same with coffee.

Keep It Clean

To clean a coffee or spice grinder, pulverize raw rice or process a piece of bread torn into chunks. They'll scrape it clean and absorb oils. You can also run coarse salt through it.

Deep-Fryer

✤ When buying a deep-fryer, look for one with sections that separate easily for draining and cleaning, and with minimal small parts and nooks for the oil to gum up in.

OUTSIDE THE BOX

You can blanch or boil vegetables in a clean deep-fryer. Fill it partway with water, heat to boiling, then lower in the basket with the vegetables.

Electric Skillet/ Griddle

✦ When using an electric skillet or griddle, insert the detachable temperature control cord into the pan before plugging it into the socket. Do the opposite when disconnecting. This lessens the chance of a shock.

Food Processor

♔ A Golden Rule

Do not overload the bowl of the food processor.

✦ Make friends with the pulse button. You'll be less likely to purée when you want to chop.

✦ Two reasons to spray or smear the discs and blades of a food processor with oil before use:
  ● They will be easier to clean.
  ● It will be easier to chop something sticky, such as dried fruit.

✦ If you don't need to use the feed tube, keep the lid clean by covering the bowl with plastic wrap before twisting on the lid.

✦ The blade won't fall out of the food processor when you pour if you stick your finger in the slot at the bottom.

A Food Processor Is Not Always the Answer

✦ A kitchen without a food processor is like a farm without a tractor. This mechanized workhorse quickly chops, shreds, slices and mixes. It is a jack of all trades, but not a master of all.
  ● Don't rely on a food processor for puréeing. A blender does that best.

Buy a separate blender and a separate electric mixer, rather than food processor attachments for these functions.

● Don't purée onions until they weep bitter tears. If you must, cut an onion into large chunks and pulse carefully until it is chopped medium, not minced. Add a bit of cold water and use the water in cooking. Still, onions chopped by hand are superior and onions puréed using a grater don't taste as angry.

● Don't try to mash potatoes in a food processor. You'll get a paste fit for kindergarten arts and crafts hour.

● Don't process potatoes for latkes. The fine grating disc yields hard, mealy little worms that seem to take forever to cook. Chopping creates chunks that cook unevenly. Both methods fail to produce the crisp lace you want at the edges.

● Mashing banana in a food processor is overkill. Your baked goods will be leaden.

● Don't chop candy or nuts. The result is a blend of powder and coarse bits.

● Don't chop candied ginger. It turns into paste.

● Don't chop chocolate unless you want it powdery. Also, the chocolate may overheat and melt in the machine. If you want ground chocolate, prevent overheating by adding 2 tbsp (25 mL) granulated sugar per 4 oz (125 g) chocolate. Normally, you don't want chocolate to be cold when you are chopping it, but it should be cold or frozen if you're using a food processor. Pulse to chop.

⊟ Fast Fix

After making pesto or another oily mess in the food processor, toss in hunks of stale bread and pulse them into crumbs. This mops up the machine. Then use the crumbs as a topping for a casserole.

- Is food sticking to the blades? Scrape the bowl. Pulse to harness centrifugal force to clear the blade. Scrape the bowl again.

Grill/Panini Press

- You can cook vegetables such as bell pepper, zucchini, eggplant and mushrooms in a contact grill/panini press. Slice them no thicker than 1 inch (2.5 cm).

Keep It Clean

To clean a contact grill/panini press, immediately unplug it and put a soaking wet dishcloth between the plates. Leave it for 5 minutes, then wipe. The towel must be very wet or it will cook. Don't use paper towels; they dry up and stick.

Microwave

A Bit of Science

Electromagnetic waves bounce off the surfaces in the microwave oven into the food, and are then absorbed. Microwaves penetrate food from $\frac{3}{4}$ to 1 inch (2 to 2.5 cm). This causes water molecules in the food to vibrate, producing friction and heat. Microwaved food cooks from the inside out. The oven itself remains cool.

- After water, fat absorbs microwaves the best.

- To test the power of a microwave, fill a 2-cup (500 mL) glass measure with 1 cup (250 mL) of water. Microwave it on High until the water boils.
  - If it boils in less than 2 minutes, the wattage is over 700.
  - If it boils in 3 minutes, the wattage is 600 to 700.
  - If it boils in 3 to 4 minutes, the wattage is 500 to 600.
  - If it takes more than 4 minutes, the wattage is less than 500.

9 Ways to Improve Microwave Cooking

1. Arrange food in a circle, like the spokes of a wheel, for even cooking.
2. Favor the edge of the rotary tray. More microwaves connect with food there than in the center.
3. Elevate food. Put it on an upside-down glass bowl.
4. Use round dishes. Square dishes overcook food in the corners.
5. The friction continues after the food is removed from the oven (up to 30 minutes for a large cut of meat), so it's best to undercook food and let it stand.
6. Cover food to cut down the cooking time. Always leave a vent for steam to escape. You can use a paper plate as a lid. Or use a damp paper towel to cover dry food such as rice or to wrap around stale bread.
7. When reheating, use High power for liquids, Medium (50%) for dense foods and Medium-High (70%) for other dishes. Defrost at Medium-Low (30%).
8. To cook a regular recipe in the microwave, decrease the liquid by 25%. You'll also need to brown meat beforehand.
9. Use clear glass so you can see the food cooking. Not all plastic is suitable for the microwave, and metal causes arcing.

- Salted food heats faster in the microwave.

- The microwave does better with fish than with meat, and does best with vegetables.

A is for Arcing

Arcing looks like a bolt of lightning, with an accompanying zap instead of a rumble of thunder. It is caused when the microwaves hit metal. Double-check that dishes and cups have no metal trim. You can use small amounts of foil to shield foods, but keep it 2 inches (5 cm) away from the sides of the oven.

Is It Microwave-Safe?

✧ Some heat from microwaved food will transfer to dishes. Not all glass or plastic is microwave-safe. It may overheat. Three tests:

● Fill a dish halfway with water and heat it on High power until the water is steaming but not boiling. If the dish can be held comfortably on top, it's okay. If it's too hot to hold, it's not safe. If it's uncomfortably warm, it can be used at 80% power.

● Fill a container three-quarters full with water. Heat it on High for 1 minute per cup (250 mL) of water. The water should be hot. It does transfer some warmth, but the container should not be unbearably hot.

● Put an empty dish in the oven. Set a ¼-cup (50 mL) glass of water at the opposite end of the turntable (so you don't run the oven empty). Zap for 30 seconds on High power. If the dish is hot, it is not microwave-safe.

✗ No-Nos

• Never use plastic unless it is clearly labeled microwave-safe. Chemicals from certain plastics can seep into food. The new steaming bags are okay.

• Never recycle margarine, yogurt, sour cream or cottage cheese tubs for the microwave.

• Never run the microwave empty. This damages it.

✧ To refresh stale chips, cereal or crackers, heat them for about 30 seconds on High power. The time depends on the amount.

✧ Your microwave can't tell the difference between food splatters and food you are heating to eat. Keep the oven clean. Splatters slow down cooking.

Ways to Prevent Microwave Explosions

• Pierce foods with a skin or membrane to let air escape. Pierce a whole potato or eggplant. Remove a 1-inch (2.5 cm) strip of skin from an apple.

• Stir thick liquids, such as soup, before and during heating; otherwise, they may erupt like a volcano.

Keep It Clean

• Heat 1 cup (250 mL) water on High power for 1 minute to loosen crud. Then wipe. You can add lemon juice, vinegar or baking soda to freshen the scent.

• Bring 1 cup (250 mL) water with 1 tbsp (15 mL) bleach to a boil. Let it sit for 5 minutes, then wipe. This loosens splatters and lessens odors.

• Freshen up the microwave by heating 1 cup (250 mL) water and the peel and juice of 1 lemon in a large bowl. Boil it on High power for 5 minutes. Wipe the oven.

• Fill a medium bowl with 2 cups (500 mL) water and 2 tbsp (25 mL) baking soda. Boil it on High power for 5 minutes. Let it sit for 30 minutes in the oven. Remove the bowl and use the liquid to wipe the oven clean.

• Cover a baked-on spill with a damp paper towel. Microwave on High power for 10 seconds. Wipe the spill while the oven is still warm.

• Scrub splatters with abrasive baking soda and a cloth dampened in hot water.

Mixer

Quick Tips
- Get a hand mixer with a built-in timer.
- Use a deep, narrow bowl for mixing.
- For small quantities, use one beater in an electric hand mixer and a small bowl.

✧ When adding flour or confectioner's (icing) sugar to a mixture, moisten it first with a spatula so you don't stir up a cloud when you start the beaters.

✗ No-No
Don't be tempted to stick a spoon in the bowl while using a mixer.

✧ To encourage sticky batter, dough, cream or meringue to leave the beaters of a hand mixer, turn it to high speed and carefully raise it up. Centrifugal force splatters the batter onto the sides of the bowl.

✧ After scraping the bowl, dislodge batter from the spatula by wiping it across the beaters.

Keep It Clean
- To clean an electric mixer, beat a bowlful of hot, soapy water.
- To dry the clean beaters of a hand mixer, hold the mixer downward in the air and turn it to high speed. The water flies off.

Pressure Cooker

Factoid A pressure cooker increases the pressure and raises the boiling point of water. Food cooks at a higher temperature and thus is done faster.

✧ A general rule for adapting recipes to a pressure cooker is to decrease the cooking time by two-thirds.

✧ Make stock fast with bones or a turkey carcass by using a pressure cooker.

Slow Cooker

♛ A Golden Rule
Avoid lifting the lid of a slow cooker. It loses heat quickly. Buy a slow cooker with a clear lid. Every time you take off the lid, you need to add 15 minutes of extra cooking time.

5 Adaptations When Switching to a Slow Cooker

1. Brown the meat and drain the fat before transferring it to the cooker.
2. Substitute evaporated milk for dairy products that will separate with long cooking.
3. Use reduced-sodium or salt-free stock. The saltiness intensifies as the stock reduces all day.
4. Add soft vegetables or fast-cooking vegetables close to the end of the cooking time or they will dissolve.
5. Reduce the liquid in the recipe. If you end up with too much liquid, strain the food, then reduce the liquid on the stove.

Major Appliances

Refrigerator and Freezer

Temperature Tips
- The fridge should be set at 33°F to 40°F (1°C to 4°C) to stop bacteria from multiplying.
- The freezer should be at 0°F (−18°C) or below to freeze food quickly and keep it in prime condition. Freezer compartments in refrigerators don't usually maintain that sort of deep freeze. Reserve them for short-term grab-and-go foods.
- Check fridge and freezer temperatures with a free-standing thermometer. Move it around the compartment to get a set of readings, likely different.

ⓖ is for Gasket
The gasket is like weather-stripping for the refrigerator and freezer, except it seals in the cold, rather than keeping it out. The gasket should be tight. A common test: Close a sheet of paper or a bill in the door. If you have to tug it out, the gasket is fine. If it glides out, the gasket should be replaced. I put several random fridges and freezers to the test. None passed. So is there a gasket crisis?

❖ Don't make a fridge or freezer work hard to keep its cool:
- Choose a cool, ventilated location. Bad ideas: beside the stove or water heater, or next to a sunny window. The basement is ideal for the freezer.
- Place the fridge or freezer at least 1 inch (2.5 cm) from the wall to let air circulate. If the coils are exposed, set the appliance 2 to 4 inches (5 to 10 cm) from the wall.

- Put the fridge or freezer on a level surface. Use a shim if necessary.
- Don't put warm food in the fridge. The temperature will rise and adjacent foods will be affected. Cool hot food down quickly before you refrigerate it. Transfer the food to a shallow container and set it in an ice water bath. Warm food is off limits in the freezer, too. It will ice up.

❖ An informal test: Press your finger into the butter. It if dents, the fridge is too warm.

Keep It Clean
- Don't use harsh detergents to clean a fridge or freezer, particularly the gaskets.
- To get rid of spills and nasty odors, first remove all the food. Wipe the interior surfaces of the appliance with a mild solution made of 4 cups (1 L) warm water and 1 tbsp (15 mL) baking soda or ⅓ cup (75 mL) vinegar. Dry well with a clean cloth.
- You can clean the exterior with warm, soapy water.
- Dusty coils at the back of a fridge or freezer can make the motor run hot. Vacuum them with a brush attachment or pass a hand vacuum lightly over them.

❖ How to combat musty odors in an empty fridge or freezer:
- Try activated charcoal from a drugstore or pet shop. Put it on a piece of paper at the bottom of the appliance for a few days. Repeat if necessary. Rinse and dry the appliance. Then turn it on.
- Sprinkle used coffee grounds on the bottom.
- Sit a large bowl of vinegar in the appliance.

Frost-free **VS.** Manual Defrost?

Frost-free sounds more convenient. Too bad the temperature has to fluctuate and the air circulate more to get rid of frost. This prompts ice crystals to form on food and promotes freezer burn. Not to mention that the ice cream won't stay firm enough. You have to clean out a frost-free freezer at least once a year, just like a manual freezer.

✧ Defrost a freezer once a year or when there's ice more than $\frac{1}{4}$ inch (0.5 cm) deep over a large area. If there's so much ice the job can't be done in 2 hours, you've waited too long.

Chest **VS.** Upright?

It's easier to find stuff in an upright freezer. An upright takes up less floor space and is easier to organize. However, a chest freezer may use less energy and thus cost less to operate.

Oven

✧ Oven temperatures are notoriously variable. Experts usually recommend using a freestanding thermometer to check, then adjusting to compensate — although it seems silly to accept the reading of a gadget you pick up for a few bucks over that of an expensive appliance. If in doubt, don't fool around. Ask a repairman to recalibrate the oven.

Oven Temperature Ranges

- **Very low:** 200°F to 275°F (100°C to 140°C)
- **Low:** 300°F to 325°F (150°C to 160°C)
- **Medium:** 325°F to 350°F (160°C to 180°C)
- **Hot:** 375°F to 400°F (190°C to 200°C)
- **Very hot:** 425°F to 500°F (220°C to 260°C)

---

10 Freezer Defrosting Tips

1. Don't just turn it off, unplug it.
2. Keep frozen food firm. Wrap packages and tubs in newspaper to insulate them. Stuff them into picnic coolers and insulated bags. When you run out of those, turn to cardboard boxes.
3. If the manual says it's okay, put pans of boiling water inside the freezer to hasten melting. Close the door for 15 minutes.
4. Stuff terrycloth towels around the base of the freezer to soak up water. Put buckets and large storage tubs on the floor of the appliance to catch drips.
5. Don't stab at the ice with knives or picks. Puncture wounds can damage the lining and equipment. You can use a blunt scraper, but carefully.
6. Use a dustpan to scoop up melting ice.
7. Did you know that your freezer probably has a plug inside at the back? Pull it. Water should flow through a tube at the back. Direct it into a pail.
8. Put a fan in front of the freezer with the door open to blow air into it as you work. The ice will melt faster.
9. When you're done, clean and wipe all the surfaces. Use a blow-dryer or fan to dry the interior completely.
10. Plug the freezer back in. Close the door. Chill for half an hour before putting the frozen food back inside. Mark the packages with an X as a reminder to use them promptly.

- If you use a freestanding thermometer, check the temperature next to the food you are cooking.

✗ No-No

Don't leave a thermometer in the oven during the self-cleaning cycle.

---

4 Ways to Prevent Uneven Heat

1. Rotate baking dishes. All ovens have hot spots, and the temperature varies from side to side and back to front.
2. Leave 2 inches (5 cm) of space between pans in the oven, and between pans and the oven walls. The hot air needs to circulate.
3. Avoid using two shelves. If you must, stagger the dishes for minimal overlap.
4. Keep the oven clean. It will heat more evenly and accurately than an encrusted one.

- Look inside the oven before turning it on. Check that the racks are in the right position and no bakeware or broiling pans have been left inside.

- Don't open the door too much. The temperature drops drastically each time you do so.

⚡ Lightning Won't Strike If ...

You don't preheat the oven at the beginning when the recipe tells you to. Odds are you won't be ready when the oven is. Save energy by preheating right before you're ready to put the food in the oven.

- You can cheat on preheating when you have a very large hunk of meat that's going to cook for hours anyway. But that's it. In all other cases, preheat — especially if you are baking.

♛ A Golden Rule

Never preheat to a higher temperature to speed things up. Not everything benefits from a blast of heat.

- If you don't have an actual middle rack, use the lower middle position rather than the upper middle. Food is raised up a bit anyway. You want to avoid too much browning on top.

✗ No-No

Don't open the oven door while broiling in an electric oven, unless your manual says otherwise. This releases smoke and prevents the food from cooking.

- When roasting at 450°F (230°C) or higher, always start with a clean oven. Otherwise, it will smoke.

Mythstake

The recipe — and oven temperature — is not written in stone. You can fiddle with the temperature knob if you need to adjust the cooking time for a dinner party, or if your dish is browning too quickly or slowly.

Ways to Cool the Oven Quickly

- Leave the door open.
- Put a large pot of cold water inside.

is for Convection

A convection oven uses a fan to move heat around. This makes the heat more effective, the equivalent of an extra 25°F to 50°F (14°C to 28°C). Food cooks faster and more evenly, even if it is spread out on several racks. The heat circulation encourages steam to evaporate faster from baked goods, so they become flakier. Fat is rendered more quickly from meat, so it browns better.

Coping with Convection

- Reduce the temperature by 25°F (14°C) if you are using a convection oven for a standard recipe.
- Read the manual. There are different settings for baking and roasting.
- You will probably be able to switch between convection and regular baking. You can use the standard setting for slow-cooking, then turn the convection on at the end for better browning.
- Use the convection setting to brown smaller cuts that roast too quickly to brown nicely, such as squab.
- The longer the cooking time, the more time you save with convection. Think turkey vs. cookies.
- Use baking pans with low sides to take advantage of the air circulation.

Ways to Make Spill Cleanups Easier

- Line the oven floor with heavy foil.
- Place a silicone mat on the bottom rack or the floor of the oven, depending on the design.
- Put pies and casserole dishes on a baking sheet.

Keep It Clean

- Toss salt on spills on the floor of the oven to prevent smoking while baking. Once the oven has cooled, scrape up the mess.
- Remove the racks during the self-cleaning cycle. It can strip the shiny coating and they won't slide as easily.

- To clean the oven, pour ½ cup (125 mL) ammonia into a small bowl. Place it in the oven, close the door and let it sit overnight. Wipe. Scrub stubborn spots with steel wool. Rinse with warm, soapy water. Or, the next morning, wipe the inside of the oven with the ammonia. Then rinse well.
- The bathtub is the easiest place to soak and clean oven racks (and barbecue grates). To dissolve crud, lay the racks on rags or old towels in the tub. Fill the tub with warm water and ½ cup (125 mL) ammonia. Let it sit for an hour. Drain and rinse. You need the window open for this one.

✘ No-No

Don't use oven cleaner or abrasive cleansers inside a self-cleaning oven.

Being Green

- Here's a green way to clean the oven: Make a paste with 6 tbsp (90 mL) baking soda, ¼ cup (50 mL) vinegar and 3 drops of dishwashing liquid. Scrub.
- Cut grease in the oven without chemicals. Make a paste of 1 cup (250 mL) each salt, baking soda and water. Spread it on the walls of the oven. Close the door. Heat to 500°F (260°C), then turn off the oven. Let cool, rinse and wipe.

Stove

Ways to Subdue the Heat

- Use a cast-iron pan to create gentle heat. Invert it over a burner, then put your working pan on top.
- To prevent burning, use a flame tamer between the burner and the bottom of a pot. These are sold in hardware stores and cookware shops.

- Temperatures don't change quickly enough on an electric stove. If you need fast action, use two burners and two different settings, and move the pan from one to the other.

- Put copper squares on your electric burners to distribute heat. Copper is a great conductor. These copper heat diffuser plates are sold online and in kitchenware shops.

Keep It Clean

Before cooking, dab a thin layer of dish soap on the stove. Spills and burnt spots will be easier to wipe off.

Dishwasher

Aluminum Warnings

- Don't put aluminum in the dishwasher. It gets gray and even pitted. For example, the aluminum beaters from a stand mixer will end up with a sooty black coating. Rub it off with a wet coarse cloth.
- Aluminum should not touch other metals in the dishwasher, either. The contact creates a reaction that corrodes and dulls.

- Put cutlery face up in the cutlery tray. It gets cleaner that way. Exception: sharp objects.

- To empty the cutlery tray faster, sort knives, spoons and forks into separate compartments as you load the dishwasher.

✖ No-No

Never use dish soap in the dishwasher. You'll get crazy sudsing action.

- To maximize the efficiency of your dishwasher:
  - Give it a head start. Turn the tap on and let it run until it's as hot as it gets. Then turn on the dishwasher.
  - Don't divert water from the dishwasher by running taps while it is filling. It takes plenty of water to get dishes their cleanest.

Keep It Clean

- To make the dishwasher sparkle and smell fine, fill the soap cups with vinegar and baking soda. Turn on the rinse cycle.
- To rid the dishwasher of soap scum and calcium deposits, add 1 cup (250 mL) vinegar and run it empty on the rinse cycle.

Shopping and Storing

Recipes

Shopping

♛ A Golden Rule

You'll be healthier and wealthier if you shop around the perimeter of the store for the freshest, least-processed foods. Whenever possible, avoid the processed, packaged products that live mainly in the aisles.

✪ Waste Not

Less food goes bad if you shop more often than once a week. Produce is not meant to hang around. Neither is fish. Neither is bread.

♡ Healthier Eater

• Don't shop hungry. Have a snack before you hit the aisles. This is healthy as well as economical. You'll buy less junk food. Heck, you'll simply buy less food.

• A high-profile brand with a health-endorsement logo isn't necessarily better for you than a similar, cheaper generic brand. Companies pay for their use of the logos by donating to the charitable programs of health foundations.

• Read labels. You'll be surprised and disgusted by what you discover. Example: Some packaged cereals and waffle/pancake mixes don't contain real berries, but colored bits of apple and artificial flavor instead.

• Let children prepare their own lists of (relatively healthy) items they can pick up and put in the shopping basket. It will keep them busy, so they'll spend less time whining for cookies and dyed cereals.

• Fat-free doesn't mean sugar-free or calorie-free. Don't be fooled.

13 Money-Saving Tips

1. In order to figure out a budget, you have to figure out what you're spending. Save all your grocery receipts for a month.

2. Always shop with a list. Veer from the list only for great specials.

3. Popular and pricey products are displayed at eye level at the supermarket. Look up and down for bargains.

4. Put on your glasses and check the unit pricing on the shelf.

5. Check prices in different departments. Examples: You can buy juice frozen, refrigerated or from the aisles. You can get cheese at the deli section or in the dairy case.

6. You've got to spend to save. Buy in bulk — but only if it makes sense.

7. If a special you want is sold out, ask for a rain check.

8. Buy store brands. They cost less. Some brand-name companies quietly make generic products for supermarket chains.

9. Assess meat by the cost per serving rather than the cost per pound.

10. Buy large cuts of meat and carve them up yourself.

11. Save deli counter cash by roasting your own turkey breast and beef.

12. Avoid cut fruit and vegetables, and bagged salads.

13. Don't buy shampoo and deodorant at the supermarket. Toiletries often cost more there.

❖ Keep a running grocery list on the fridge door. A magnetic, erasable whiteboard works well. The family can add to it, and so can you, when anything comes to mind.

How to Speed Up Your Shopping Trip

- Set up your list to correspond with supermarket aisles or sections.
- Shop on Wednesday, or maybe Tuesday, which are the least busy days in supermarkets.

❖ Wipe the handle of the shopping cart. It's covered with germs. Some supermarkets offer wipes.

Bulk-Purchasing Tips

- If you're cooking for one or two, find shopping companions. Divide the cost and the spoils.
- Join forces in an informal buying co-op with friends and neighbors, or join a real co-op.
- You may be able to buy by the case at the supermarket. Ask.
- If you see a great in-store special on a product you use a lot, and you have the freezer or cupboard space, buy multiples.
- Buy large packages and divide them up when you get home — right away.

Mythstake

Think the products at the ends of the aisles are on sale? Not necessarily. They just look like they are. Companies may pay for prime display space to feature their products. A product on sale should clearly note before and after prices.

Tips for Coupon Clippers

- Use a coupon only if you want that particular product or brand.
- Check the competitors' prices. They may be cheaper, even after you factor in the coupon.
- Write your grocery list on the back of an envelope and stuff it with the coupons you can use.
- Write an X beside an item on your list if you have a coupon for it.
- Get more bang out of your coupon by holding onto it until the product is on sale.
- If you have a lot of valuable coupons that are about to expire, go on a shopping expedition (if you have the storage space).

6 Places to Get Coupons

1. Clip them from flyers and ads.
2. Email companies to ask for them.
3. Check manufacturers' websites.
4. Go to online coupon-distribution sites.
5. Watch for them hanging in supermarket aisles and stuck to product wrappers.
6. Swap coupons with friends.

❖ Carry personalized sticky address labels so you can enter contests with minimal fuss.

Being Green

Look for local fruit and vegetables in season. Imported produce is often picked unripe and may travel for a week. Even organic produce, if grown far from where you live, can have a huge carbon footprint. Developing countries have less stringent rules about the use of pesticides and herbicides, and may fail to enforce any regulations they do have.

🌹 Being Green

- Buying or collecting reusable totes is not enough. You actually have to tote them into the supermarket.
- "Organic" is not one straightforward, clear, comprehensive and all-encompassing designation. Standards vary from place to place, from stringent to lenient, and organic means different things to different folks. It is more helpful to ask specific questions about a product. Ask the farmer, the butcher or fishmonger, the shop owner who sources her own products. Check labels. Do some research.

✧ Sustainably raised fish may be wild or farmed. For example, salmon can be farmed organically or conventionally.

✧ Categories to focus on if only part of your grocery budget is spent on organics:
- Thin-skinned produce you often eat without peeling, such as apples, grapes and tomatoes (as opposed to produce protected by thick skins you remove, such as avocados, citrus fruit or pineapples)
- Produce with the least pesticide residues. Some studies say onions retain the least, peaches and apples the most. Asparagus, broccoli, cabbage, corn, eggplant and peas are also cited as vegetables with lower pesticide residues. Bell peppers, carrots, celery, kale, lettuce, cherries, pears and strawberries generally have higher pesticide residues.
- Soy foods (soybeans are likely to be genetically modified)

- Meat from animals that were not fed hormones and antibiotics, and were put out to pasture or given organic feed
- Dairy products
- Eggs

✧ Meat may be specified as free-range, grass-fed or naturally raised, but not be strictly or completely organic.

---

11 Questions to Ponder

1. Are there any artificial ingredients?
2. Is this treated with preservatives?
3. Was this genetically modified?
4. Were pesticides or fungicides used?
5. Was this irradiated?
6. What did the animal eat? Examples: Was it grass-fed or grain-fed? Was it given flaxseed, rich in omega-3 fatty acids? Did the feed contain animal byproducts?
7. Was the animal fed hormones or antibiotics?
8. Was the animal confined or allowed to roam?
9. Was the animal treated humanely? Was it allowed to be true to its nature?
10. Is the farm or production facility inspected regularly?
11. Is the operation sustainable, or is it a monument to greed and shortsightedness?

Tips for Shopping at Farmers' Markets

- Don't make a list. Be spontaneous and flexible.
- For the best selection, shop in the morning, when stalls are fully stocked. For the best deals, arrive late in the day.
- When you first arrive, scout the market for the best stalls and freshest produce.
- Beware of resellers. Not all produce and products at farmers' markets come straight from farms. Some vendors unload rejected fruit and vegetables they have purchased from wholesalers. Different markets have different policies regarding resellers. Ask.
- Get to know the harvest seasons or look online to fine out what is ripe and ready in your area.
- Ask farmers when the food was picked. The answer should be "yesterday" or even "this morning."
- A farmer's products may be organic without being certified as such. Ask how each product was grown, raised or produced.
- Amuse yourself by trying unfamiliar or strange-looking produce. Ask the farmer how to store and prepare it.
- You'll get dirt on your hands. Bring some moist wipes.
- Don't expect to pay discount prices for everything. There are many exceptional products at exceptional prices. There are also bargains, especially if you buy produce by the basket.
- Buy in bulk, then act fast: Freeze or preserve the excess.
- Expect to pay cash. Bring small bills and change.
- Take a cart or bundle buggy. Bring your own bags, or use a roomy backpack to keep your hands free.

Storing

♛ A Golden Rule

This twist on a newspaper adage works in the kitchen, too: When in doubt, throw it out.

Old **VS.** Spoiled?

If it's old, it's stale and unpleasant, but can still be eaten. If it's spoiled, it's contaminated and can poison you. The two often, but not always, go together. Bacteria, mold, yeast, oxidation, and enzymes that cause browning and ripening all make food go bad.

Expiry Dates

✧ Expiry dates on cans, bottles and packages are not food-safety dates. They're food-quality dates determined by the manufacturer. They give you an idea when the food was packaged and help you guesstimate when it might spoil. But they are not carved in stone.

Types of Dates

- "Best before," "best if used by," "use by" and "packaged on" dates indicate when a product will pass its peak quality. If the package says "use by," deterioration after the specified date may affect the food's safety.
- "Sell by" dates cue a store how long to display a product. The consumer can safely eat it afterwards.

✧ Don't feel secure because an expiry date is far away. Don't feel alarmed if it has passed. Food can be wholesome after the expiry date or past its prime before the date. The more "irregularities" (as bureaucrats say) in your storage method, the less accurate the expiry date.

Factors That Affect Expiry Dates

When was it opened?

- If you break the seal not long after the "best before" date, the product will probably be fine — even sensitive food such as sour cream.
- Keep track by marking the date on a can, bottle or package you've just opened, especially jars of condiments and pickles that hang around endlessly.

How hardy is it?

- Some products, such as eggs or bread, can be consumed a couple of weeks beyond the "best before" date. Mind you, the eggs may be watery and the bread good only for crumbs.
- "Best before" dates are most important when dealing with dairy and meat products. You can be more lax with packaged processed goods (such as cookies), although flavor and nutritional value may be affected.

How was it stored?

- Was it promptly stashed in the fridge, or was it left languishing on the counter to dry up or breed bacteria? Was it hauled to a picnic? Improperly stored, it may be fit only for the trash can, even though the expiry date is far off.

Where was it stored?

- Products that can be kept in the pantry, such as ketchup, last longer in the fridge.
- Foods stored in the fridge's chilly interior stay fresher than foods stored on a shelf in the door.

✧ If you do use something after the expiry date, use it right away and cook it thoroughly.

- Packing, processing or manufacturing dates stamped on products may be open or coded.
- **Open dating:** The actual calendar date is given. This is mainly used on perishable foods such as meat, eggs and dairy products. Open dates help the store determine how long to display a product and help the consumer decide how long to keep it.
- **Coded dating:** Dates are coded in strings of letters and numbers. The codes vary from company to company. Parts of the code may refer to manufacturing information such as the plant or the lot number. Coded dates help companies rotate and keep track of inventory, especially in the case of recalls. The meaning of these codes is not meant to be obvious to the consumer.

- There's gold hidden in them there codes. Too bad they look like gibberish. You can, however, get help deciphering them:
- Go to a company's website and search "best before dates" or "code dates." Some sites have up-front explanations in the FAQ.

- Email a company and ask how to read its codes.

Storage Solutions

♛ A Golden Rule
Throw out dented or bulging cans.

- Heat and light leach out nutrients and color. The pantry cupboard is a better place to store food than the counter, and opaque containers keep food better than clear ones. Label each container. Otherwise, accept the trade-off and use clear tubs so you can see what and how much you've got at a glance.

Mythstake

Consumers think some products last forever. Not true. Once a package has been opened, flavors fade, and air, germs and mold play their tricks. Dried beans get tough. Pickles blacken. Condiments go off. Chocolate blooms. Vinegar becomes cloudy.

6 Coding Examples

1. The numbers 1 through 9 are used in place of the months January through September, then the letters O, N, D or A, B, C are used for October through December.
2. The months are indicated by the letters they begin with, except for duplicates, such as J.
3. The year is written as the last number only, such as 8 for 2008.
4. The date is written as the day of the year, with January 1 as 001 and December 31 as 365. Then one number is added to indicate the year, such as 3658 for December 31, 2008.
5. The first letter indicates the factory, followed by four numbers indicating the month and day the product was processed, followed by one number for the year.
6. The month (by letter) is followed by the year, the plant designation (by letter), then the date. Example: February 10, 2009 is coded as F9A10.

Maximum Storage Times

Time passes, even for condiments. Here are some maximum storage times for opened jars and bottles.

Item	Pantry	Fridge
Worcestershire sauce	1 year	
Mustard	1 month	1 year
Ketchup	1 month	6 months
Barbecue sauce	1 month	4 to 6 months
Prepared horseradish		3 to 4 months
Mayonnaise		6 to 8 weeks
Pickles		1 to 2 months
Salsa		2 weeks
Olives		2 weeks

7 Tips for Storing Home Preserves

1. You can keep high-acid foods, such as tomatoes, for 12 to 18 months, and low-acid foods, such as meat or vegetables, for 2 to 5 years, but the quality suffers. Try to use them up in 1 year.

2. Preserves and pickles are best stored between 50°F and 70°F (10°C and 21°C). Don't keep them near hot pipes, the water heater or furnace, or in a cold attic.

3. If your storage spot is cold, insulate preserves by wrapping the jars with newspapers, then put them in a box and cover the box with blankets.

4. If canned food accidentally freezes, it won't spoil unless the seal has broken. The food may soften, though.

5. Keep preserves out of direct sunlight. Light leaches out the color. Store jams and jellies in a dark place, wrap them in newspaper or place them in boxes.

6. To save space, store preserves in the cardboard boxes that mason jars are sold in. These boxes have dividers for individual jars. Here's a system: Set preserves right side up and empties bottoms up, so you can immediately see which is which. Storing empties upside down also protects the rims, maintaining their ability to form perfect seals.

7. Once opened, preserves can be kept in the fridge for a month, or for a shorter time at room temperature. Jams and jellies may weep in the fridge.

✦ Choose the right size of storage tub for the food. Too much air or headspace promotes staleness and freezer burn.

✦ How much wrapping do you need? Wrap until you can't smell the food. Odors mingle in the fridge and cupboard.

No-No

Never use the water in a can. Drain and rinse canned goods, except for fruit packed in juice or syrup.

Get Organized

- Arrange your pantry, fridge and freezer using a system that food-service pros call FIFO: First In, First Out. Write the date of purchase on each can or package to help you out.
- Keep inventory-control lists taped inside your cupboard doors. The lists don't have to be fancy. Just write on lined sheets, creating different categories. Add and cross off items. Mark with an X to indicate you're running low. That way, you'll know what you have and needn't go digging.

 Healthier Eater

Keep a snack shelf in the cupboard and a bin in the fridge with healthy, ready-to-eat foods divided into reasonable portions for your children. Discourage mindless eating in front of the TV.

Better Leftovers

Stop storing leftovers in covered serving bowls or pots in the fridge. These leftovers hog space, dry out, spill, and absorb odors or cause them. Transfer food to plastic tubs with airtight lids.

 **Waste Not**

Revive stale crackers and chips on a baking sheet in a 300°F (150°C) oven for 1 or 2 minutes.

Refrigerating and Freezing

Climate Zones in the Fridge

- The back is the coldest part of the fridge. Also cold zones: the meat keeper, the back section of the middle shelf and, in some models, the top shelf.
- At the front, from the middle to the bottom, the temperature is moderate.
- Shelves on the door can be up to 5°F (3°C) warmer than the interior.
- The crispers are more humid to prevent produce from shriveling.

5 Food Storage Tips

1. Stash meat and fish at the back of the fridge.
2. If you want soda pop super-cold, place it at the back of a shelf.
3. Store dairy products at the top, not in the door.
4. Alas, the butter compartment in the door is not best for butter, an egg keeper in the door not best for eggs. Keep them inside the fridge, with butter well wrapped and the eggs covered.
5. Condiments and vinegary sauces are fine on shelves in the door.

Crisper Tips

- Adjust the vents to let in more cold air and decrease the humidity.
- Line crispers with paper towels to absorb moisture. The produce will stay fresher longer, the drawer cleaner.
- If you don't have enough crisper space, store produce in a large plastic tub with an airtight lid in the moderately cold zone.

- The freezer works best when it's packed. The fridge works best when it's not packed. In the freezer, frozen packages keep each other ice-cold. In the fridge, cold air needs to circulate.

- Ways to maximize the efficiency of a loosely packed freezer:
  - Cram it with pop bottles or storage tubs filled with water.
  - Make enough ice cubes for an army at cocktail hour.

Get Organized

- Solidly frozen food is safe indefinitely, but it's not good indefinitely. It starts to look and taste bad if it's stored too long.
- Organize your freezer space into food groups: meat and fish, fruit and vegetables, cooking ingredients (from nuts to tomato paste), leftovers, desserts and ice cream, and prepared commercial foods.
- Put older packages at the front of the freezer so you use them first.
- Looking for stuff in a chest freezer can be like conducting an archeological dig. Keep similar items in stackable plastic boxes that are easily shifted.
- You don't need to root around with the door open, losing cold air and wasting energy. Use a steno pad with a pencil stuck in the spiral wire as an inventory-control tool. List a separate category of food (meat and fish, prepared foods, ingredients) on each page. Cross off or add to the lists whenever you visit the freezer. Don't know what to cook? Flip through the pages.

- Make big batches on weekends and freeze them in individual portions.
- Funny how frozen food becomes unrecognizable as time passes and your memory fades. What is it? What does it weigh? When was it frozen? Label all foods with item, month and, yes, year, just in case.

Making Do

You don't need to buy fancy labels. A roll of masking tape and a permanent marker make a cheap, effective "system." The tape is easy to peel off and the length can be customized. You can also save free labels or press file-folder labels into service.

✧ Avoid the wet, sticky hand problem. Write on the labels before slapping them onto bags and tubs. Label bags and tubs before filling them.

♛ 3 Golden Rules

1. Freeze sooner rather than later.
2. Freeze quickly, defrost slowly.
3. Seal it well, use it soon.

☼ A Bit of Science

- Freezing doesn't kill bacteria, molds or sometimes even parasites. It does put them in stasis, so they can't spoil the food and poison you. Once thawed, however, the critters are back in business. Bacteria hit their stride above 40°F (4°C), the average fridge temperature. That's why it's best to thaw food in the fridge.
- When food is frozen, the cells fill with ice crystals that puncture the cell walls. Thus, thawed food is soft and leaky. Slow freezing and fluctuating temperatures cause the formation of big crystals. The bigger the crystals, the worse the damage. The faster something is frozen, the smaller the crystals. That's why manufacturers flash-freeze.

✧ Always drain and dry food thoroughly before freezing. Moisture creates destructive ice crystals on the surface.

✧ Freeze fresh and fast. The fresher the food when it's frozen, the better the taste after thawing, and the better the color and texture. Don't use the freezer as a dumping ground for suspicious food. Freezing will arrest its decay, but, as it thaws, it will succumb quickly to any taint.

How to Freeze Food as Quickly as Possible

Cool it well beforehand.
- Chill cooked food in ice water and drain well before freezing.
- Whether it's meat you just brought home from the supermarket or a cooked casserole, put it in the fridge first, until it's cold inside and out.
- Use a quick-freeze shelf, if you have one.

Think small.
- Freeze small items, such as berries and meatballs, in a single layer on a baking sheet, then package them.
- Dole food into bags and tubs in small quantities sized for individual meals or recipes.

Put to-be-frozen food in the coldest parts of the freezer.
- The back and the walls are coldest. The bottom rack is colder than the top.
- Exception: Place delicate baked goods on top of other packages and away from the walls.
- The door on an upright freezer is the worst spot. Don't store hard-to-freeze items, such as ice cream or frozen juice concentrate, in the door.

Leave space between packages.
- Let cold air circulate around unfrozen food.
- Stack packages after they're frozen.

Don't overwork the freezer.

- Don't add too much food at once. This raises the temperature inside the freezer and slows down the freezing action.
- Add the amount of food that will freeze in 24 hours. One source calculates that at 2 to 3 pounds (1 to 1.5 kg) per 1 cubic foot (0.028 cubic meter) of freezer space.

♛ A Golden Rule

Food tastes best when it's fresh. Consider freezing the inferior alternative.

Wrapping and Packing

✧ Not sealing packages properly, then letting them languish in the deep freeze — we've all done it. We may as well throw the food away right now and toss our money out the door after the garbage truck.

Ⓑ is for Burn

The freezer is a dry place. Loss of moisture and exposure to cold air causes freezer burn. Leathery spots and a grayish-brown color are its bad signs.

Food with freezer burn is safe, but not worth eating. The texture is like cardboard, the flavor bland and the odor strange. You can cut away "burned" portions before cooking.

Proper packaging prevents freezer burn. Keep the packaging tight against the food, and press or suck out any air, if possible, before sealing.

Best Freezer Wrappings

- Vacuum-packing. Freeze vacuum-packed food unopened.
- Plastic freezer bags with zipper locks. These have a larger surface area and are more shallow than storage tubs, so the food inside freezes faster. They are perfect for soft or sloshy foods. When

frozen, they can be stacked like books. Portions are smaller in zip-lock bags, so they defrost faster.

---

4 Tips for Sealing a Freezer Bag

1. Lay the filled bag on its side.
2. If the filling is soft, press it flat, squeezing the air toward the top. Seal the bag quickly.
3. If the filling is liquid, let it flow almost to the top of the bag. Rub the air bubble at the top, to "burp" the bag. Fold over the top and squeeze out the air. Seal the top while it's folded.
4. To remove the air from a freezer bag containing a bumpy item, such as a chicken, put it in cold water, keeping the top just above the water line, then seal it quickly.

Alternatives to Freezer Bags

- Foil. Use only the heavy kind and only in combination with another wrap, as foil rips easily. Tightly cover the foil with plastic wrap, slip it into a zip-lock bag or secure it in clean pantyhose.
- Rigid containers with airtight lids. Plastic storage tubs pose problems, since getting the size right is difficult. Too much headspace will fill with frost, created by moisture drawn from the food. However, if the tub is filled right to the top, the food will expand and push up the lid.

✧ Leave about $1/2$ inch (1 cm) headspace (preferably no more) in filled containers. The less air, the better the food keeps, but you have to allow for expansion. The exceptions are loosely packed whole vegetables such as asparagus, bony meat and bread.

Making Do

- Waxy ice cream or milk cartons can be pressed into service as freezer containers. Fill them almost to the top. Seal spouts with duct tape. To use the food frozen, cut away the carton. Or thaw the food and pour it out through the spout.
- Empty sour cream, cottage cheese or yogurt tubs can be filled and sealed.
- When freezing a large quantity of liquid, you can guard against spills by pouring it into a zip-lock bag set inside an old coffee can.

6 Steps for Wrapping a Packet for the Freezer

1. Place the food in the center of butcher paper or foil.
2. Pull both ends up to meet, then fold them together twice to make an interlocking seam against the food.
3. Turn the packet seam down.
4. At one end, fold each corner over toward the center, forming a triangle, as though you're wrapping a present. Fold the triangle up over the packet and seal it with tape.
5. Run your hands over the packet toward the open end to push out any air.
6. Fold the open end into a triangle, smooth it down over the packet and seal.

Containers to Avoid

- Glass jars, which may crack (mason jars are sturdiest)
- Supermarket foam trays for meat (don't freeze meat in its flimsy packaging)
- Dishes
- Cookware

✧ Crumpled waxed paper can be crammed into the headspace on top of food packed into rigid containers, to reduce the frost.

✧ Before sealing a plastic storage tub or ice cream carton, cover the surface of the food with plastic wrap.

✧ Use duct tape to seal packets.

✧ Large, irregularly shaped foods, such as roasts or poultry, should be swathed tightly in lots of plastic wrap.

Wraps to Avoid

- Waxed paper (it gets soggy and sticks)
- Supermarket plastic tote bags
- Old plastic bread bags
- Thin supermarket produce bags

✧ Double- and triple-wrap to be safe rather than sorry. You can use various combinations. Examples: Top butcher paper with foil, then put the package in a plastic bag. Use plastic wrap in combination with a plastic tub.

Multi-Wrapping Ideas

- If you don't want to unwrap your supermarket meat, cover the packet with heavy foil, then slip it into a zip-lock bag or a tub.
- To prevent freezer burn and ice crystals on ice cream, wrap the container in foil.

Mythstake

Don't be fooled by what you see in the supermarket. Commercial giants have access to special freezing techniques and equipment, and packaged foods are pumped full of additives and chemicals to make them behave. Your frozen food won't look or taste the same.

- Layer individual steaks, chops, burger patties, pancakes and other foods between sheets of parchment. Waxed paper and foil are more apt to stick and tear.

Produce

- You can't simply toss fruit and vegetables into the freezer. Most have to be prepped to prevent browning and mushiness, and to keep them colorful. Three preparations:
  - Acidulation (treating with an acid)
  - Sugar packs
  - Blanching

No-No

Do not pack and freeze produce while it is still warm or even at room temperature. Wash fruit and immerse blanched vegetables in ice water first.

Fruits

- Fruits that tend to brown (including apples, peaches, apricots, pears, plums, nectarines, cherries and mangos) benefit from a meeting with citrus. Four ways to acidulate before freezing:
  - Toss with lemon juice.
  - Soak in water with lemon juice.
  - Pack together with citrus fruit.
  - Toss with ascorbic acid and sugar.

Types of Fruit Packs
- **Dry pack:** The fruit is frozen without sugar. This works well with berries, grapes, rhubarb, and fruit destined for jams and jellies.
- **Wet pack:** The fruit is crushed in its own juices. No sugar is added. This is a good choice for naturally sweet fruit, and fruit (such as mangos and melons) that keeps best when puréed.

- **Dry sugar pack:** The fruit is gently stirred with granulated sugar until the sugar dissolves. This works well with juicy fruit such as plums and peaches. Toss the fruit with sugar immediately before freezing. Sugar draws out the juices.
- **Syrup pack:** The fruit is frozen in a sugar-water solution. This is a good method for whole fruit, fruit that discolors and fruit intended for compotes.

---

5 Syrup Tips

1. Use light or medium syrup, made with 1 to 2 cups (250 to 500 mL) granulated sugar per 1 cup (250 mL) water.
2. The sugar can simply be dissolved in the water, but it's better to boil the solution for 5 minutes, then chill it before using.
3. You can replace some of the sugar with corn syrup or honey.
4. You can add anti-browning agents to the syrup.
5. The syrup should cover the fruit completely. To keep the fruit submerged, crinkle a piece of parchment and put it on top.

- Sliced strawberries are best frozen in a dry sugar pack, whole strawberries in a dry pack or syrup pack.

Other Preparations
- If you intend to use frozen fruit for preserves, measure and freeze it in portions required by the recipe, and label each clearly.
- Damaged fruit may be cut into chunks, then crushed or puréed before freezing.
- Remove cherry stems and pits before freezing.
- Hull strawberries before freezing.

✧ You can pack blueberries directly into freezer bags. They won't clump when frozen. Just make sure they're dry when packed.

Fruits That Don't Freeze Well
- Citrus fruit
- Sweet cherries (sour cherries are okay)
- Pears

7 Fruit Thawing Tips

1. Fruit packed with sugar thaws faster than fruit packed in syrup. Both types thaw faster than dry-packed fruit.
2. Fruit thawed in the fridge loses less liquid than fruit thawed at room temperature or in the microwave.
3. Thaw fruit for pie filling just until you can separate it into pieces. You'll lose fewer juices that way.
4. Frozen fruit is best served while it still contains ice crystals. When fully thawed, it tends to be soggy.
5. To quickly defrost frozen juice concentrate, pulse it in the food processor.
6. When cooking with fruit that is thawing, make allowances for any added sugar and for the increased juiciness. Drain the fruit, then use only part of the juice, reduce it or add more thickener.
7. If you have leftover thawed fruit, cook it so it keeps better.

✧ Purée frozen fruit to use in sauces or ices.

Vegetables

A Bit of Science
Enzymes lead to chemical reactions that cause ripening, deterioration and decay. Freezing slows enzyme activity but doesn't halt it. Cooking does. So most vegetables should be blanched, steamed, boiled or baked before being quick-frozen.

The Worst Vegetable for Freezing
- Eggplant

Other Vegetables That Don't Freeze Well
- Beets
- Cabbage
- Celery
- Cucumbers
- Endive
- Garlic
- Green beans
- Leafy greens (including lettuce and watercress)
- Mushrooms
- Onions
- Peppers
- Radishes
- Tomatoes
- Zucchini

✧ You know this, but just in case ...do not freeze any ingredients for green salad.

✧ For better results, sauté mushrooms in butter or oil until golden, before freezing.

✧ You don't need to blanch onions or peppers. Chop and freeze them on a tray, then pack them into bags. They will be limp when thawed, so use them only for cooking.

4 Reasons to Blanch

1. It brightens the color.
2. It removes surface bacteria and dirt.
3. It softens vegetables, making tight packing easier.
4. Blanched vegetables are firmer when thawed.

✧ Note recipe times. Under-blanching stimulates the enzymes you want to stop. Over-blanching makes the vegetables limp and robs them of nutrients.

Steam VS. Boiling Water?

Steam-blanching is gentler than blanching in boiling water, so it can be done longer. Choose boiling for vegetables or greens, such as spinach, that require quick heating. Steam-blanch watery vegetables, such as corn.

5 Corny Tips

1. Freeze shucked corn on the cob while it's fresh. Don't wait a couple of days. Blanch it first.
2. Corn on the cob should be partially thawed before boiling to allow the cob to heat through by the time the corn is cooked.
3. Freeze blanched ears of corn individually in foil. Unwrap and butter each frozen ear, then rewrap in the foil and bake at 400°F (200°C) for 45 minutes. The result is a bit chewy.
4. Raw corn kernels turn gummy when frozen. Blanch each ear of corn, then cut off the kernels for freezing.
5. Don't let corn sit after thawing. It's so soggy.

⚡ Lightning Won't Strike If ...

You stash overripe whole tomatoes in the freezer. Collect enough and you've got the makings of tomato soup or sauce, but that's all they're good for. When they thaw, the skins slip right off.

✧ To improve their texture, overripe tomatoes can be chopped and zapped in the microwave for 30 seconds before freezing.

✧ To freeze cabbage, coarsely cut or shred it, then blanch in boiling water for 2 minutes. Drain, cool it in ice water and drain again. Stuff it into airtight bags. Thawed cabbage is good only for cooking.

✧ Cook pumpkin, squash and sweet potatoes before freezing. Note: Vegetables that are fully cooked before freezing are not as good when thawed and reheated.

Potato Tips

• Mashed potatoes can be frozen in mounds or patties on a baking sheet, then put into freezer bags. They are not very good.
• Stuffed baked potatoes are okay after freezing.

✧ You can cook most frozen vegetables without thawing them first. Exceptions: Broccoli and leafy greens, such as turnip greens and spinach, will cook more evenly if partially thawed.

✧ To preserve nutrients, steam frozen vegetables instead of boiling them or cook them in as little water as possible. Use about $\frac{1}{4}$ cup (50 mL) water for every 1 cup (250 mL) of veggies.

❖ Use a fork to separate clumps of frozen vegetables so they cook more evenly.

❖ Add unthawed vegetables to soups and stews near the end of the cooking time.

Dairy

❖ Freeze dairy products in their unopened packages.

⚡ *Lightning Won't Strike If ...*

- You freeze milk, cream and buttermilk. Ice crystals ruin dairy products. These are prone to grittiness and curdling when frozen, but all is not lost. Once thawed, they are fine for baking and, in many cases, for cooking. Frozen skim and 2% milk are better than whole milk.
- You freeze cheese. It can become too gritty, chalky or spongy to eat outright, but you can use it for cooking or grate it as a topping. In a random test, thawed blue cheese, Parmesan and Brie all turned out okay to use. Freezing is disastrous for fresh cheeses.

❖ Milk can be frozen for 3 months. Thaw it in the fridge.

Cream Caveats

- Freeze heavy cream, but avoid freezing 18%, 10% or sour cream.
- Thawed cream works best in frozen desserts, in small amounts. It will whip, but not as well, and separates quickly afterwards. It's better to freeze cream whipped rather than unwhipped.
- Frozen coffee cream creates a greasy film on hot drinks.

❖ Before using thawed milk or cream, whisk or shake it.

❖ Unsalted butter freezes better than salted. The latter also becomes saltier.

❖ Moisture and salt levels determine how well cheese freezes.

4 Cheese Categories

1. Fresh cheeses — such as cottage cheese, cream cheese and fresh mozzarella — become watery, grainy or mealy when frozen.
2. In firm, moist, light cheeses, such as Havarti, ice crystals cause crumbling after thawing.
3. Hard cheeses, such as Parmesan, freeze the best.
4. Salty cheeses, such as feta, have to be colder to freeze well, so they are prone to developing more ice crystals.

❖ The texture of frozen, thawed cheeses makes them difficult to cut. Freeze semisoft, firm and hard cheeses in pieces of 1 lb (500 g) or less, or slice or shred cheeses before freezing them.

♻ Waste Not

Grate leftover nubs of cheese, then freeze them to use in sauces or casseroles.

❖ Thaw cheese in the fridge. It thaws unevenly at room temperature and may develop a slimy surface. Change the wrapping after thawing.

Eggs

❖ Freeze eggs in the amounts you need for specific recipes.

✗ No-Nos

- Never freeze eggs in their shells.
- Don't freeze cooked egg whites. They get rubbery or spongy.

◆ Thaw frozen eggs in the fridge. Let them come to room temperature before using.

---

4 Ways to Freeze Eggs

1. Lightly whisk whole eggs with granulated sugar or corn syrup. Use ¾ tsp (3 mL) sweetener per 1 cup (250 mL) eggs.
2. Blend in ¼ tsp (1 mL) salt per 1 cup (250 mL) whole eggs.
3. You can freeze egg whites, as is, for 4 months, no problem.
4. Egg yolks get gummy and thick when frozen. Stabilize them by adding ½ tsp (2 mL) salt per 1 cup (250 mL) yolks. As for sugar or corn syrup, 1 to 2 tbsp (15 to 25 mL) are recommended per 1 cup (250 mL) yolks, but the results are poor.

Meat and Fish

◆ Big cuts and roasts can be frozen longer than chops; they don't dry out as fast.

◆ Freeze ground beef pressed flat in a zip-lock freezer bag.

◆ Meat and poultry with more fat can't be frozen as long. Fat goes rancid. A turkey might last 1 year, a duck 3 months.

◆ Remove the giblets from poultry and freeze them separately. The bird will defrost faster.

◆ Do not stuff a turkey or chicken before freezing. Manufacturers have special equipment and methods to ensure food safety. Home kitchens don't.

◆ As archaeologists have discovered, you can freeze flesh in a block of ice. Just don't leave it frozen so long that it becomes an ancient artifact.

Icy Techniques

• Put individual fish fillets, steaks or chops in a loaf pan or baking dish that just accommodates them in a single layer. Line the pan first with a parchment sling for easier removal. Pour in enough water to thinly cover the fish or meat. Once it's frozen solid, remove it from the pan or dish and wrap it tightly.

• Freeze a whole, unwrapped fish until it is solid. Dip it into ice water and freeze again. Continue dipping and freezing until the ice coating the fish is ⅛ to ¼ inch (0.25 to 0.5 cm) thick. Package it in freezer wrapping.

◆ Thaw meat and fish completely before breading or stuffing it.

◆ Fish remains juicier and more delicate in texture if thawed slowly in the fridge before cooking.

◆ You don't need to thaw shrimp before cooking.

Prepared Foods

◆ Don't tie up baking dishes and pans in the freezer. Line them with foil or parchment before filling them. Once the food has frozen, remove it and seal it in plastic. Cook it from frozen.

◆ Freezing finger sandwiches and canapés seems drastic, but it can be done. Five tips for freezing sandwiches:
• Use fairly fatty fillings so the bread doesn't get soggy. Go for butter, however, and avoid mayonnaise.

- Sandwiches with eggs or crisp greens don't freeze well. Opt for ground meat, fish, hard cheese or peanut butter.
- Keep the sandwiches away from the cold walls of the freezer.
- Thaw finger sandwiches and canapés, still wrapped, in the fridge.
- It's better to cut sliced bread into cute shapes with cookie cutters, then freeze it unfilled. Thaw it only partially before spreading on the filling.

✧ Freeze meatloaf unbaked, then cook it from frozen. It will take $1\frac{1}{2}$ to 2 times longer to cook than it would normally. Hasten the process by using high heat at first. Cover it with foil and cook in a 400°F (200°C) oven for 20 minutes. Remove the foil. Reduce heat to 350°F (180°C) and cook until a thermometer inserted in the center registers at least 160°F (71°C), about 60 minutes.

✧ Undercook dishes that will be frozen, such as lasagna and casseroles. Specifically, undercook the vegetables.

✧ Once it has been frozen, cooked meat does best in stew, sauce or stock. To freeze a cooked roast or bird, slice it and cover it with stock.

✧ Leave potatoes out of soups and stews for the freezer. Add them when you're reheating the dish. If you must put them in before freezing, undercook them.

OUTSIDE THE BOX

To save freezer space and feel efficient, reduce stock to a concentrate first.

✧ If you're freezing what is destined to become a creamy soup, leave out the milk or cream. Add it when you're reheating the soup.

✧ Omit crumb or cheese toppings from casseroles going into the freezer. They get soggy. Sprinkle them on after thawing.

8 Types of Prepared Food to Avoid Freezing

1. Cooked pasta or rice. (It will be mushy and/or granular.)
2. Fried food. (The coating will no longer be crispy, and meat or fish will be tough and dry. If you have some, don't try to reheat it by frying. Thaw and bake it at 400°F/200°C.)
3. Breaded raw meat or fish. (If you have some, uncover it and thaw it on a rack to keep the coating drier. Bring it to room temperature before frying; otherwise, the coating will burn before the inside is done.)
4. Sauces and dressings thickened with egg, such as mayonnaise, hollandaise or custard.
5. Gravy or other fatty sauces thickened with flour. (They get gluey and separate. After thawing, try to repair the damage by adding stock or cream, then whisking.)
6. Sauces with a lot of milk or cheese. (They curdle. After thawing, whisk in some stock or cream.)
7. Leftover canned vegetables and legumes. (Water chestnuts, for example, become spongy and inedible, and baked beans turn to mush.)
8. Corn tortillas. (They puff, separate and crumble when thawed.)

Make-Ahead Retro Ham Loaf

I was naughty and desperate, so I shoved a bunch of leftover Easter ham in the freezer. Thawed ham is terrible, all spongy and tough. This was the only way I could save it. Of course, there's no need to start out with ham that has been frozen. This meatloaf tastes Spam-like, but is strangely appetizing. **Makes 8 servings**

- **9- by 5-inch (23 by 12.5 cm) loaf pan**

Tips

Don't trim all the fat off the ham.

Don't be tempted to add salt.

1 tbsp	unsalted butter	15 mL
4 oz	mushrooms, sliced	125 g
2	slices whole wheat sandwich bread, torn	2
1	onion, chopped	1
¼ cup	coarsely chopped green bell pepper	50 mL
2	cloves garlic, chopped	2
1¼ lbs	cooked ham, trimmed and cut into chunks	600 g
2	large eggs, lightly beaten	2
¼ tsp	freshly ground black pepper	1 mL
1 lb	ground pork	500 g
¼ cup	ketchup	50 mL
2 tbsp	packed brown sugar	25 mL
1 tbsp	cider vinegar	15 mL

1. In a small skillet, melt butter over medium heat. Sauté mushrooms until softened and turning golden brown at edges, about 5 minutes. Scrape into a sieve. Let drain and cool to room temperature.

2. In a food processor fitted with a metal blade, pulse bread into crumbs. You should have about 1¼ cups (300 mL). Scrape bread crumbs into a large bowl.

3. In the food processor, finely chop mushrooms, onion, green pepper and garlic. Scrape onto bread crumbs.

4. In the food processor, pulse ham until finely ground. Add to bread crumb mixture, along with eggs and pepper. Combine thoroughly. Add pork and combine, but do not overwork. Transfer to loaf pan and pat into a loaf. Cover with plastic wrap, then foil. Freeze for up to 3 months.

5. Preheat oven to 400°F (200°C). Remove wrappings from the loaf, then place the foil over the top. Bake 30 minutes. Reduce heat to 350°F (180°C) and bake for 1 hour. Remove the foil and bake for 45 minutes or until juices are bubbling and a thermometer inserted in the center registers 160°F (71°C). Drain, if necessary.

6. Stir together ketchup, sugar and vinegar. Smear mixture over the loaf. Increase heat to 400°F (200°C). Return loaf to the oven and bake for 30 minutes or until topping is sticky and browning at the edges.

- Prepared foods containing meat, eggs and dairy products should thaw in the fridge. Baked goods and breads can thaw on the counter.

♛ A Golden Rule

If you can stir it (soup), reheat it from the frozen state. If you can't stir it (a casserole), thaw it in the fridge first, so it cooks evenly.

Reheating Tips

- Always rinse ice crystals off frozen food. They taste bad.
- Speed the reheat in the top of a double boiler, if the dish would defrost haphazardly in the microwave, leaving some parts cooked and others still frozen.
- If a dish is saucy or creamy, reheat it in the microwave.
- You can reheat frozen food more evenly in a heatproof dish set inside a larger pan of hot water in a 350°F (180°C) oven.
- Don't put a cold glass dish in a preheated oven. Preheat the dish and the oven together. Freezer to oven–safe cookware is preferable.

Seasonings

- Freezing affects the seasoning of dishes. Season them lightly, then adjust when reheating. Some notes on frozen seasonings:
- Salt is less potent.
- Pepper, cloves and celery seeds get stronger and/or bitter.
- Curry tastes musty.
- Paprika changes flavor.

Baked Goods and Desserts

- Generally, it's best to freeze baked goods at the earliest stage you can manage. Cookie dough freezes better than baked cookies. Unfrosted cake holds up better than a frosted one. Yeast breads are best frozen as dough.

Baked Goods and Desserts to Avoid Freezing

- Thin cookies such as tuiles (they're too fragile)
- Boiled icings and glazes (they become frothy and weepy)
- Custards, creamy pies, some pumpkin pies (they get watery and lumpy, and the pastry gets soggy)
- Meringues (they turn spongy and rubbery; apply meringue after a dessert has thawed)
- Gelatin desserts
- Jelly preserves (they get weepy, but jams are okay)

✘ No-No

Never freeze baked goods while they are still warm. Moisture condenses on the outside. The interior dries out, but the surface turns gummy when the item is thawed.

- If it's easy, do a test-run. Freeze one cookie, say, and see how it turns out.

5 Cookie Dough Tips

1. Cookie dough freezes well. Wrap it in plastic, then put it in a freezer bag.
2. Freeze dough in logs that you can slice and bake from frozen.
3. Freeze it in a disc, then thaw just until you can roll it out. About 15 minutes should do it.
4. Freeze cookie dough in balls on a baking sheet until they are solid, then transfer them to a freezer bag.
5. Avoiding freezing thin cutouts. It's better to freeze the entire dough, then thaw, roll and cut out shapes.

Good Cookie Doughs for Freezing

- Shortbread
- Chocolate chip cookies
- Peanut butter cookies
- Refrigerator cookies
- Sugar cookies

---

4 Frosted Cake Tips

1. Freeze cake, frosting and filling separately.
2. Frost a cake after it's thawed and ready to serve.
3. For freezing, stick to uncooked frosting, such as mock buttercream made with butter and confectioner's (icing) sugar, which you can thaw and whip.
4. If you want to freeze a frosted cake (say someone brought it), freeze it solid on a baking sheet, then cover the frosted surfaces with waxed paper and wrap it tightly. Unwrap it before thawing at room temperature.

Baked Cookie Tips

- To freeze baked cookies, pile them in single layers between waxed paper or parchment. Wrap them well. Put them in a hard container so they don't break.
- Don't freeze iced or decorated cookies. Decorate them after they thaw.

Ways to Thaw Baked Cookies

- Heat them on a rack in a 300°F (150°C) oven until crisp.
- Let them sit at room temperature on a wire rack lined with paper towels to absorb any moisture.

✧ Freshen up thawed, baked cookies quickly in a 350°F (180°C) oven.

✧ Brownies and other squares freeze well. Freeze the whole block. Frost and cut them after thawing.

✧ Fatty pastries — such as pies, tarts and rich cookies — can be successfully frozen baked or unbaked.

✧ To avoid smooshing delicate pastries, freeze them on a baking sheet first, then wrap them tightly.

✧ Layer cakes, cupcakes, angel food cakes, chiffons and sponges, fruitcakes and steamed puddings are fine to freeze.

✧ Wrap cake tightly in plastic, then in foil. It should keep for 1 month.

✧ Bake cheesecake before freezing. Wrap it tightly.

♲ Waste Not
Cut rich cheesecake into individual slices before freezing.

---

2 Pie Pastry Tips

1. It's best to freeze pie pastry in discs. Thaw it until it is just pliable enough to roll out. It should still be cold.
2. Bake frozen pie shells without thawing.

✧ Tips for making your own frozen pie shells:
- Line a pie plate with rolled dough, then freeze and remove it.
- You can stack the shells. Use saved, store-bought aluminum pie plates as dividers to prevent breakage.
- You can freeze rolled dough in aluminum pie plates, stack them, then bake the pies in the same plates.

OUTSIDE THE BOX

You can freeze filling in a pie plate. When you're ready to bake, toss the frozen disc into a pie shell.

✧ If the filling is soft, freeze the pie before wrapping it.

✧ Pies filled with fruit, nuts or meat taste better if they are frozen unbaked, but they can be frozen after baking.

Tips for Freezing Unbaked Fruit Pies

- Brush the bottom crust with butter to prevent sogginess.
- Add a third to a half more thickener to the filling.
- Brush butter onto the top crust.
- Don't cut vents or prick the top until just before baking.
- Don't glaze the top with an egg wash or cream until just before baking.

✧ Muffins, quick breads, biscuits and waffles can be frozen after baking or cooking. Don't put on any toppings or glazes until are thawed and ready to serve.

✧ Thaw frozen muffins and quick breads in the microwave. Use Medium (50%) power.

✧ Baked goods are either dry or soggy when thawed, never in between. If they're soggy, wrap them in a paper towel. If they are dry, wrap them in a damp paper towel and zap them in the microwave.

How to Bake a Pie from Frozen

1. Prick or slice the top.
2. Brush melted butter onto the top.
3. Bake in center of a 400°F (200°C) oven for 20 minutes.
4. Reduce heat to 350°F (180°C). Bake until top is browned and filling is bubbling, 60 to 80 minutes.
5. Use a pie-crust protector or cover the edges with foil so they don't brown too much.

3 Baked Bread Tips

1. To freeze baked bread, cool it completely, wrap it in heavy foil, put it in a freezer bag and push out the air before sealing.
2. Slowly defrost the wrapped frozen bread in the fridge.
3. To crisp the crust, put the loaf, still in its foil, in a 400°F (200°C) oven.

Make-Ahead Peach Berry Pie

Make the filling with luscious seasonal fruit. Slip it into a pie shell, freeze it and whip it out when you need it. **Makes 10 servings**

• 9-inch (23 cm) pie plate

Tips

Choose peaches that are ripe but firm.

Use any type of cream.

If you want to bake this without freezing it, reduce the cornstarch to 2 tbsp (25 mL).

2 to 2½ cups	thinly sliced peaches (unpeeled)	500 to 625 mL
½ cup	granulated sugar, divided	125 mL
1 tbsp	freshly squeezed lemon juice	15 mL
	Pastry for one 9-inch (23 cm) double-crust pie	
2 cups	thinly sliced strawberries	500 mL
2 tbsp + 2 tsp	cornstarch	35 mL
2 tbsp	whole milk or cream	25 mL

1. In a large bowl, stir together peaches, $\frac{1}{3}$ cup (75 mL) of the sugar and lemon juice. Let stand for 30 minutes.

2. Meanwhile, on a lightly floured work surface, roll out half the pastry into a 12-inch (30 cm) circle. Transfer it to the pie plate. Refrigerate it for 15 minutes, along with the remaining dough.

3. Add strawberries to peaches.

4. In a small bowl, stir together cornstarch and 3 tbsp (45 mL) of the sugar. Stir into the fruit mixture. Scrape mixture into the pie shell.

5. Roll out the remaining dough into a 10-inch (25 cm) circle. Lightly moisten edges and place over filling, moistened side down. Press together top and bottom crusts. Trim edges and crimp. Cover tightly with plastic wrap, then foil. Freeze for up to 4 months.

6. Preheat oven to 400°F (200°C). Remove wrappings from the pie. Cut vents in the top crust. Brush top with milk, then sprinkle with the remaining sugar. Bake in center of oven for 20 minutes. Shield edges with a pie-crust protector or foil. Reduce heat to 350°F (180°C) and bake for 60 to 80 minutes or until top is browned and juices are bubbling through the vents.

Preserving

Equipment

Boiling Water **VS.** Pressure?

High-acid foods, such as fruit jams and jellies, are sterilized in a boiling-water canner. Low-acid foods, such as vegetables and meat, must be processed in a pressure canner so they won't cause botulism. Four exceptions:

- Tomatoes are borderline acidic. Process them in a pressure canner, or add 1 tbsp (15 mL) lemon juice per 2 cups (500 mL) tomatoes when using a boiling-water canner.
- Pickles, made with cucumbers and other vegetables, are protected by vinegar or brine.
- Sauerkraut is fermented. Lactic acid, produced by fermentation and brining, is protective and imparts tang.
- Chutneys and relishes are made with vinegar or citrus juice.

Making Do

Don't have a boiling-water canner?

- Use a soup pot. Put a round rack on the bottom. Or put the deep-fryer basket in the pot.
- For small batches, use an asparagus pot with a basket insert.
- Try a pasta pot with an insert.

❖ When storing a boiling-water or pressure canner, pack crumpled paper towels or newspapers in the bottom and around the rack to absorb moisture and odors. Put the lid on loosely, upside down.

❖ Beware: Jars can crack if they bounce around and hit the bottom of the pot as it boils. Use a rack or lay a towel in the bottom of the pot.

Keep It Clean

- To remove hard-water scale from a canner, fill it with a solution of 1 cup (250 mL) vinegar and 3 quarts (3 L) water. Bring to a boil, then remove from heat and let stand for several hours.
- Moisten a cloth with vinegar to wipe mineral and water-spot residues from canning pots and jars.

✖ No-Nos

- Ignore recipes that omit the boiling-water processing after the jars are filled. Bacteria can enter jars as they are filled, but the jam may have cooled down too much to kill them. Some recipes tell you to just turn the filled jars upside down. It's not enough. Also, the weight may break the seal and disturb the gelling.
- Discard any mason jars with chips or cracks.
- It seems like overkill, but jar manufacturers warn us not to use metal utensils. Metal can damage the rims, creating cracks that prevent a perfect seal.
- Never reuse the flat lids from mason jars. That red, rubbery coating on the perimeter is a sealing compound. It softens in boiling water and wears out. Used a second time, the lid may not form a perfect seal. The metal itself may get pitted from contact with acids. (You can reuse the screw bands unless they are rusty or dented.)
- Never use old-fashioned wax seals.
- Acidic ingredients react with aluminum, iron and copper cookware and utensils. Cook preserves in a stainless-steel pan.

Soft Spreads

A Bit of Science

When Grandma was in the kitchen making preserves, she should have been wearing a lab coat instead of an apron. Jams and jellies depend on the delicate dance between fruit pectin, acid and sugar. Getting the ratio right is tricky. We should always be open to experimentation in the kitchen, but, when preparing preserves, it's wise to stick to reliable recipes.

✧ Boiling fruit bubbles up a lot. Use a pan that holds three times the quantity of your fruit mixture.

What Kind?

- **Jelly:** Made with fruit juice and sugar. Translucent, firm and thin.
- **Jam:** Made with crushed or chopped fruit. Not as firm as jelly.
- **Conserve:** A jam that contains mixed fruit, citrus rind, raisins or nuts.
- **Preserve:** Made with small, whole fruit or chunks in slightly jelled syrup.
- **Marmalade:** Bittersweet jelly, usually citrus, with chopped peel suspended in it.
- **Chutney:** Somewhere between jam and pickles. Contains coarse fruit, vinegar or citrus juice and pungent spices.

✧ Speed up homemade preserves by cooking the fruit in a pressure cooker.

is for Pectin

Pectin is a substance in fruit and vegetables that binds cell walls. In combination with acid and sugar, it forms a gel. Pectin thickens preserves until they are set but still soft.

The amount of pectin varies with the fruit or vegetable. It also varies within specific fruit, depending on the type and ripeness. It varies by location; there's more pectin in the flesh closest to the skin.

Not all fruits have enough to make a jam or jelly gel. They need a pectin boost.

How to Boost Pectin

Add some apple.

- Apples are high-pectin fruit. You can add chopped apple, juice pressed from fresh apples or syrup made from the pectin-rich skin and cores. Unfortunately, this is not an exact science.

Add packaged pectin.

- It comes in powder and liquid, but, heck, they are not interchangeable. Otherwise, packaged pectin removes guesswork.
- The bad news is that you have to add a ghastly amount of sugar. It overwhelms the fruity flavor of your preserves. Add a bit of lemon juice to fight the sweetness. (Lemon blueberry is a successful combo.)
- Use commercial pectin at room temperature.
- Don't overdo it. After adding the pectin, boil hard for just 1 minute.

Use some underripe fruit.

- Fully ripened fruit has less pectin. Use three-quarters ripe fruit and one-quarter slightly underripe fruit in your preserves.
- If you use too much underripe fruit, the preserves will be cloudy.

Mash and grate fruit, rather than puréeing.

- The former releases pectin. The latter weakens its gelling power.
- Use a potato masher or fork to crush fruit, especially tender berries or peaches.
- Some cooks find a food processor okay for firmer fruit such as plums. Be careful: Pulse only and chop coarsely.

Boil hard.

- Long simmering and slow cooking destroy pectin. A darker color and caramel scent are signs of overcooked fruit.

✘ No-No

Don't try to turn jam into a dumping ground for overripe or bruised fruit. It has less pectin and less acidity.

Ways to Make Preserves Out of Season

- If you're busy getting the kids off to school in September or otherwise occupied in the summer, freeze fresh fruit and get back to it. Blueberries, cranberries, currants, rhubarb and strawberries are good candidates. Measure them into portions and label before freezing. Thaw just until they are still firm with some ice crystals. Add pectin.
- Use canned fruit. You'll need to add pectin.

Factoid Dream on, but fruit and vegetables are at their peak for preserves 6 to 24 hours after harvesting.

Fruits High in Pectin and Acid

- Apples (sour, depending on ripeness) and crabapples
- Blackberries (if sour)
- Cranberries
- Currants
- Gooseberries
- Grapes (depending on variety)
- Lemons
- Plums
- Quinces

Fruits Low in Pectin or Acid

- Ripe apples
- Ripe blackberries
- Sour cherries
- Grapefruit
- Oranges

2 Pectin Tests

1. To test whether a fruit has enough pectin to gel, boil a small amount of juice for 3 minutes. Cool it and pour 1 tsp (5 mL) into a small tub or jar, then add 1 tsp (5 mL) rubbing alcohol. Shake gently, then let stand for 5 to 10 minutes. The pectin should form a soft, transparent glob. Do not taste! This is poison.
2. Some jelly makers are more meticulous: If the gel is in a single mass, they advise using equal quantities of sugar and juice. If the gel is in two or three blobs, $\frac{2}{3}$ to $\frac{3}{4}$ cup (150 to 175 mL) sugar per 1 cup (250 mL) juice is recommended. If it's in particles, the recommended quantity is $\frac{1}{2}$ cup (125 mL) sugar per 1 cup (250 mL) juice.

Fruits That Need Added Pectin, Acid or Both

- Apricots
- Blueberries
- Cherries
- Figs
- Guavas
- Peaches
- Pears
- Pineapple
- Prune plums
- Raspberries
- Rhubarb
- Strawberries

No-No

Do not double jam or jelly recipes. The preserves may not set, even if you use store-bought pectin.

✧ If you're using commercial pectin, there's no need to worry. The acid is included.

---

3 Acid Test Steps

Fruit that's low in acid requires a citrus boost, usually in the form of lemon juice.

1. Combine 1 tsp (5 mL) lemon juice, 1 tbsp (15 mL) water and ½ tsp (2 mL) granulated sugar.
2. Compare it to the taste of the fruit juice you are using.
3. If the juice is sweeter, add 1 tbsp (15 mL) lemon juice per 1 cup (250 mL) fruit juice.

✧ Not enough acid? Jam or jelly won't set. Too much acid? Jam or jelly will weep.

Three Sweet Tips

- Don't cut the amount of sugar in any preserves recipe. If there isn't enough, the preserves won't gel.
- Don't add too much sugar. The preserves will end up syrupy, not gelled.
- Jam and jelly recipes usually call for granulated white sugar. Honey or corn syrup may be substituted for part, but not all of it. They change the chemical structure, so the preserves won't gel.

✧ When making jam, crush the lower layers of fruit to create some juices when you start cooking. This prevents scorching, and you won't have to add too much water.

Flavorful Additions

- Make jams, jellies or marmalades fruitier by using fruit juice instead of water.
- Add a cheesecloth bag or tea ball filled with spices when simmering the fruit.
- Once the fruit is skimmed and stirred, add a dash of complementary liqueur. Example: Add Apfelkorn to Granny Smith apple jelly.

Ways to Reduce Scum

- Skimming and stirring the preserves prevents floating fruit and foam.
- Add a spoon of butter to boiling jam.

Juicy Tips for Jelly Makers

- To maximize juiciness for jelly, fruit can be layered with sugar and left to macerate for 24 hours before cooking.
- Sometimes frozen fruit is better for jelly because it releases more juices.
- You can make jelly using commercial pectin and store-bought juice or frozen concentrate.

---

3 Reasons for Cloudy Jelly

1. The jelly bag was squeezed. Let cooked fruit drip through, overnight if necessary. Don't try to extract the last drop.
2. The fruit was cooked too long before straining. Cook the fruit until it is just tender. Or simply heat it enough to encourage it to release juices.
3. The fruit mixture was allowed to sit before being poured into the sterilized jars. Pour immediately.

✧ Make jelly in small batches or it may set too soft. Use no more than 4 cups (1 L) juice per batch. Larger quantities have to be boiled longer.

Triple-Berry Jelly

Beginners will appreciate this simple, tasty recipe that pairs berries with liqueur.
For the freshest flavor, don't cook the delicate berries, just heat to extract their juices.
Makes about 4 cups (1 L)

- **8 hot 4-oz (125 mL) mason jars with two-piece lids**

- **Jelly bag or sieve lined with cheesecloth**

3 pints	mixed raspberries and blackberries	1.5 L
3 cups	granulated sugar	750 mL
2 tbsp	lemon juice	25 mL
1	pouch (3 oz/85 mL) liquid pectin	1
¼ cup	strawberry-flavored liqueur	50 mL

1. In a large bowl, using a potato masher, crush berries one layer at a time, transferring them to a large saucepan as you work. Let stand for 1 to 2 hours, to let the juices release.

2. Heat the pan over low heat until berries start to steam. Simmer for no longer than 5 minutes.

3. Line a damp jelly bag or sieve with damp cheesecloth and set it over a medium bowl. Pour in berry mixture and wait until most of the juices appear to have finished dripping into the bowl. Do not squeeze.

4. Transfer juice to a medium saucepan. Add sugar and lemon juice. Bring to a boil over high heat. Stir in pectin. Boil hard for 1 minute, then remove from heat. Stir, skimming scum from surface, for 5 minutes. Stir in liqueur.

5. Quickly pour hot jelly into prepared jars, leaving ¼ inch (0.5 cm) headspace. Wipe rims. Center lids on top and screw on bands until fingertip-tight. Process jars for 10 minutes in a boiling-water canner.

6. Transfer jars to the counter and let cool, undisturbed, for 24 hours. Store in a cool, dry, dark location.

Jelly Bag Tips

- Wet the jelly bag first, so it doesn't suck up the precious fruit juice.
- Rinse the jelly bag in boiling water after using it.
- You can improvise a jelly strainer. Dampen cheesecloth. Lay three layers at overlapping angles in a large sieve. Place the strainer over a large bowl.

♻ Waste Not

When making apple jelly, recycle the strained leftover pulp into applesauce.

Marmalade Tips

- The pith and pips of citrus fruit have lots of pectin. Tie them up in cheesecloth and cook them along with the rind.
- If you don't cook citrus rinds until they are soft before adding them to the syrup, the marmalade will be too stiff.

Is It Done?

- ❖ It can be tricky figuring out when jams, jellies and marmalades made without pectin have reached the gel stage.

Three Tests for Doneness

The temperature test

- This is the most reliable. Let the preserves reach a temperature 8°F (4°C) above the boiling point of water. At sea level, this is 220°F (104°C). Use a candy thermometer.

The cold test

- Chill a small plate in the freezer. Spoon about 1 tbsp (15 mL) preserves onto the plate. Return it to the freezer for 2 minutes. Remove the pan of preserves from the heat while you await the verdict. If the test spoonful moves slowly when the plate is tilted, the preserves are ready.

- To test for specifics, run your finger through the cold blob of jam or jelly. If the two sides slowly move together, the preserves will be soft. If the sides don't move and the surface wrinkles when nudged, the preserves will be firm.
- If the preserves are not gelled enough, return the pan to the heat. Remember, they simply may not have enough natural pectin; don't boil them forever.

The sheet test

- This is for jellies. Dip a small, cold spoon into boiling jelly. Raise it about 1 foot (30 cm) above the pan away from the steam, then hold it horizontal to let the jelly run off the side, not the tip. The jelly should sheet — that is, fall in a sheet with a single drop at the bottom, rather than several drops.

Preserves Doctor

The chutney or relish is watery.

- Strain it. Boil the liquid until it has reduced. Return the liquid to the solids and process again.

The jam, jelly, chutney or relish didn't set, or you forgot an ingredient.

- Boil it in a pan over high heat for 1 minute. Add commercial pectin and boil hard for 30 seconds. Process again.

Bottling

⚛ A Bit of Science

Boiling-water processing kills germs and spores, and drives the air out of the jars, so that the food contracts and a vacuum is created as the jars cool. The lid is sucked down and sealed tight.

- ❖ Use the size of mason jar specified in the recipe. The size affects the processing time.

Master Plan
Bottling Jam or Jelly

1. Wash mason jars in hot, soapy water and rinse them well. There's no need to dry.
2. Start to cook the jam or jelly mixture. (Or, if the cooking time is unusually short, say less than 5 minutes, prepare the equipment first.)
3. Heat the jars on a rack in a boiling-water canner.
4. Bring a small pan of water to a boil, drop in the lids, turn off the heat and cover. There's no need to heat the screw bands. If you want to, toss them in with the lids to keep them clean and out of the way.
5. Transfer jars to the counter.
6. Remove the fruit mixture from the heat when it's done. Stir it for 5 minutes, skimming the scum with a spoon.
7. Working with one jar at a time, place a canning funnel in the mouth of the jar. Ladle in hot preserves, leaving 1/4 inch (0.5 cm) headspace.
8. Run a rubber spatula around the edges to release air bubbles. Add preserves to adjust the headspace.
9. Wipe the rim and threads of the jar.
10. Center the lid on top and screw on the band until fingertip-tight.
11. Return the jars to the rack in the canner. Make sure they are covered by 2 inches (5 cm) of water.
12. Process by boiling for the time specified in the recipe — 10 to 15 minutes is in the ballpark, though the time is less for some jellies. Start timing when the water returns to a boil.
13. Remove the jars and let them cool completely on a rack.
14. Check the seals.
15. Wipe the jars. Remove the screw bands or replace them lightly.
16. Label and store the jars.

Heating Mason Jars

- Place jars in the canner, leaving at least 1 inch (2.5 cm) between each jar, and fill the canner with hot water until the jars are submerged. Bring to a boil.
- If the jars filled with preserves will be boiled for more than 10 minutes or processed using a pressure canner, the empty jars needn't be boiled at length. Just bring the water to boil, turn off the heat and cover the pot.
- If the jars filled with preserves will be boiled for less than 10 minutes, sterilize the empty jars by boiling them in the canner for 10 minutes. Then turn off the heat and cover the pot.
- To prevent mineral deposits on the glass, add a bit of vinegar to the water in the canner.

4 Ways to Prevent Jars from Cracking

1. Don't put cold jars into boiling water.
2. Don't put jars, empty or full, into a hot oven. You may, however, heat the jars in a dishwasher on the heat drying cycle.
3. Don't put hot jars on a cold, hard surface. They may crack when you pour in the hot preserves. Put them on a cutting board, towel or rack. This also prevents damage to the counter. You can put the jars upside down on a rack to help them dry.
4. Don't pour hot food into cool jars.

✧ Use a clean facecloth or dishcloth moistened with hot water, or paper towels, to clean the jar rims and threads. Bits of preserves stuck to a rim can prevent a tight seal and make it difficult to screw on the band properly.

Two Lid Tips

- The flat lids don't have to be boiled, just heated. You just want to soften the sealing compound.
- Don't boil or simmer the screw bands. They'll burn your fingers if they're too hot.

ⓗ is for Headspace

Leave no more than a ¼- to ½-inch (0.5 to 1 cm) space at the top of the filled jars. The less air in the jar, the better. If too much air is left, it can't be sucked out during processing, and the surface of the preserves is more likely to discolor. If the jar is filled too full, the preserves are more likely to get trapped between the rim and the sealing compound. Either way, the jar may not seal properly.

Handy Tools

- Use a wide-based canning funnel when filling jars.
- Lift the lids out of hot water with a magnetic wand.
- Grip and transfer the jars (empty or filled) from hot water with a jar lifter — short, wide tongs with coated ends.

Making Do

If you don't have a jar lifter, use long silicone-coated tongs to pick up a hot empty jar. Insert one arm of the tongs into the jar.

ⓕ is for Fingertip-Tight

Center the lids on the jars, then screw on the bands just until you encounter resistance, no more. This is fingertip-tight. It allows steam to escape during the processing in boiling water. If the band is too tight, pressure builds in the jar and the lid may buckle, marring the seal. A jar can even break.

✧ When boiling the preserves, make sure the jars are at least 1 inch (2.5 cm) apart and covered by 2 inches (5 cm) of water.

> ### Ways to Make Jams and Jellies Firmer
>
> - Cool them slowly at room temperature, not in the fridge, for 24 hours.
> - After removing them from the canner, don't shake or tilt the filled jars as they cool. This disturbs the gelling. You don't have to pour the water off the tops.

✧ The screw band loosens as the jar cools. Don't tighten it. The sealing compound may get damaged, and you don't want to break the vacuum.

✧ To check the seal, remove the screw band after the preserves have cooled. Six signs of a good seal:

- Listen for a popping sound as each jar cools.
- Hold the jar at eye level and look across the top of the lid. It should be concave (curved down slightly) in the center.
- Press the lid with your finger. It shouldn't spring up.
- Tap the lid lightly with a spoon. It should ring, not sound dull.
- Check the preserves. They should not be pressed up against the lid.
- Pick up the jar by the edges of the lid. It should hold firmly. (Beware of nasty surprises.)

✧ Screw bands are usually removed before the preserves are labeled and stored. You don't need them, and rust may develop under them. If this offends your sense of order, screw them on lightly.

Ways to Deal with Improperly Sealed Preserves

- Refrigerate them. Eat them within 1 month.
- Reprocess them within 24 hours. Check each jar for defects; replace it, if necessary, and use a new lid.

❖ If your storage area is damp, wipe the outside of the jars with vinegar to combat mold.

❖ Want your preserves to wear little ruffled skirts when they are ready to make an appearance? Cut a circle of lightweight cloth (about 4 inches/10 cm larger than the lid diameter) with pinking shears. Center it over the lid, then screw the band on top.

Pickles

Keys to Crisper Pickles

- Cut a thin slice, about $\frac{1}{16}$ inch (2 mm) thick, from the blossom end of the cucumber. It contains enzymes that cause softening.
- Ice the sliced cucumbers. Toss them with pickling salt, then pack ice cubes on top. Refrigerate the lot for 3 hours. Rinse and drain. Let the pickling games begin.

Vinegar Tips

- Use 7% pickling vinegar for more astringency and crispness. You can also use regular vinegar if it has at least 5% acidity. Supermarket vinegars are usually in the 5% to 6% range. If a recipe specifies the acidity of the vinegar, follow it exactly.
- Wine vinegars are all over the place in acidity. They inject uncertainty into a recipe. Don't use wine vinegar unless the recipe calls for it.

✖ No-No

Don't try to pickle waxed cucumbers. The wax won't let the pickling liquid penetrate.

❖ Cucumbers and other vegetables must be submerged in pickling liquid. Weigh them down with a small can or a zip-lock bag filled with water.

❖ Excess pickling solution can be reused. Solution already used on pickles cannot.

❖ Homemade tomato juice tends to separate. Before canning, combat this with quick heating to destroy the enzymes that cause the juice to separate from the flesh. Bring a small amount of crushed tomatoes to a gentle boil. Continue adding and heating tomatoes in layers as you crush them.

3 Ways to Prevent Discoloration

1. Use distilled water to make pickles. Soft water is best. Minerals in hard water can react with tannins, sulfur compounds and acids in foods, making them turn black, brown or gray.
2. Avoid aluminum and iron cookware and utensils.
3. Use pickling salt. Table salt has iodine and anti-caking ingredients that can darken pickles and cloud their brine.

♛ A Golden Rule

Add vegetables to the mason jar, then add the hot pickling liquid — not awkwardly vice versa as in some recipes.

☼ A Bit of Science

Chemical reactions can turn garlic cloves in pickles green or blue. The pickles are still safe to eat. Garlic may discolor in reaction to vinegar, trace minerals in your water or certain metal cookware or utensils. Never use copper, iron or aluminum pans or tools when pickling. The iodine in table salt can also cause discoloration. Immature garlic is particularly prone to turning green or blue.

❖ Add pickling extras — such as garlic cloves or slices, whole dried chile peppers or dill sprigs — to the jar first. It's more convenient than trying to cram them in after you've put in the vegetables.

Pickled Asparagus Tips

- After trimming the asparagus, choose one stalk that fits your mason jar perfectly and use it as a template. That way, all the stalks can be trimmed to the same length quickly, in batches, with the template alongside.
- Cut tender 1-inch (2.5 cm) lengths from the discarded bottoms. Preserve them in a small jar with leftover pickling liquid.
- It's easier to pack asparagus stalks tightly into a jar that is lying on its side. Trying to shove asparagus into an upright jar is awkward and causes breakage. (Set a jar on its side to pack in long cucumber wedges, too.)

❖ Wait at least 3 weeks before eating homemade pickles, to allow them to mellow.

♻ Waste Not

You can put leftover pickle juice — homemade or commercial — to use. Drop in thinly sliced semicircles of raw zucchini or cucumber, or firm, cooked green beans or asparagus. Let them stand for at least a day. They won't be pickled per se, but it's an interesting way to eat them.

❖ For best flavor, chill homemade pickles before serving.

OUTSIDE THE BOX

- You can fry pickles. They taste good that way. Cut them in ¼-inch (0.5 cm) coins, dip them in a batter that includes a bit of pickle brine or juice, then fry until golden and crisp, about 2 minutes. You can use a tempura batter or a thicker, fish-style batter.
- You can bake pickles. They taste good that way. Cut them in little pieces, wrap them in dough and bake at 400°F (200°C) for 10 to 15 minutes or until golden brown. I recommend using sweet gherkins and cheesy dough.

Pantry Basics

Recipes

Flours

Hard VS. Soft?

Flours are described as being hard or soft, depending on the protein content. During milling, in the case of white flour, the germ and bran are removed. The endosperm is ground and separated into "streams," some high in protein, some high in starch. These streams are used to blend different flours.

Standard Types of White Flour

- Bread flour is high in protein.
- Cake and pastry flours are low in protein. Cake flour is a bit softer than pastry flour, but the two are often sold as one blend.
- All-purpose flour is made from hard and soft flours.

> **Factoid** Flours differ dramatically around the world. This can wreak havoc on far-flung cooks trying to follow the same recipes. For example, all-purpose flours are softer in the American South, harder in Canada.

Waterworks

- Flour can vary by 20% in its ability to absorb moisture.
- The gluten content of flour affects how it absorbs water. Hard flour absorbs more.
- Flour absorbs water from the air. On humid days, add less water.
- Flour can absorb water if improperly stored.
- Flour can dry out during the winter.

A Bit of Science

The wheat kernel, or wheat berry, has three parts: The bran is the husk. The germ is the seed. The endosperm is the inner part of the kernel; it has starch and protein.

Making Do

- To substitute all-purpose flour for bread flour, add 1 tbsp (15 mL) more all-purpose flour per 1 cup (250 mL) bread flour. Or vice versa.
- To substitute all-purpose flour for cake/pastry flour, subtract 1 tbsp (15 mL) all-purpose flour per 1 cup (250 mL) cake/pastry flour. Or vice versa.

G is for Gluten

When water is combined with flour, the glutenin and gliadin proteins form gluten. Sheets of elastic gluten trap and hold gases and bubbles created by yeast and other leaveners. In the oven, the proteins become firm but the air spaces remain.

- Sometimes you need lots of gluten; sometimes you don't. The type of flour you choose depends on what you're making. (Hard flour has more protein, and thus more gluten potential.) Gluten is good for strength, bad for tenderness. The vigor of your mixing is also a factor.
- Say "yes" to gluten for yeast breads, stretched strudel pastry, and pasta and pizza dough.
- Say "no" to gluten for cakes and pie pastry.
- Say "sort of" to gluten for muffins, quick breads, squares, puff pastry, choux pastry, popovers and Yorkshire puddings, and pancakes.

- To develop fully, gluten requires moisture and kneading. To prevent gluten development, handle dough gingerly and briefly.

- Gluten interferes with the action of baking soda and baking powder.

- Gluten loses strength as it ages.

Bleached VS. Unbleached?

White flour is bleached to remove its yellowish tinge and make it more uniformly absorbent. Bleaching also removes some chemicals that interfere with gluten development. Unbleached flour has more nutrients. It makes sense to use bleached flour for white cake, unbleached for golden pizza crust.

Lightning Won't Strike If ...

You use unbleached flour in a recipe that calls for bleached flour. Some cooks insist that bleached flour makes finer dough that rises higher. However, you won't notice any glaring difference. If you're a stickler, add slightly more water to unbleached flour.

- Instant flour is a granular type that's easier to mix into liquids without creating lumps. Use it in sauce or gravy.

S is for Self-Rising

Sometimes called self-raising, this white flour contains salt and leavening agents. Avoid it unless a recipe calls for it.

Making Do

Don't have self-rising flour? For each cup (250 mL) the recipe calls for, stir or sift together 1 cup (250 mL) all-purpose flour, 1½ tsp (7 mL) baking powder and ½ tsp (2 mL) salt.

- Whole wheat flour is made from the complete wheat kernel. Because it has fewer of the proteins that form gluten, it

can't rise as well. For lightness, combine with white flour.

- Advice is all over the place on mixing wheat flour with a flour that has low or no gluten. As a starting point, go half and half.

♡ Healthier Eater

You can add goodness by substituting whole wheat flour for some of the white flour in a recipe. Expect the result to be denser, heavier and coarser.

- Only wheat flour has enough gluten to make proper bread and baked goods. Without gluten, dough will not rise, no matter how much gas is produced by yeast or other leaveners.

- Soft wheat flours and non-wheat flours can by supplemented with starch-free pure gluten flour, or vital wheat gluten.

D is for Durum

Durum wheat has the highest amount of protein, and durum flour is the hardest. Do not confuse durum wheat semolina (a coarse flour) with soft wheat semolina (the farina, or Cream of Wheat, used in cereals and puddings).

- Choose durum wheat semolina for pasta that holds its shape yet remains soft.

Making Do

If you don't have any durum wheat semolina for pasta, use bread flour. If you substitute all-purpose flour for the durum, the pasta tends to get mushy unless it's eaten promptly after cooking.

- Rye flour has some gluten, but not enough to make a light bread. Blend it with wheat flour.

✧ Use buckwheat flour in small doses, in combination with other flours. It's slightly bitter.

6 Reasons to Sift Flour

1. Manufacturers sift flour to get rid of lumps. The package may be labeled "presifted," but the flour will still settle, so sift when the recipe calls for it.

2. Cake flour is lumpy, so you have to sift it. You don't need to sift all-purpose flour.

3. Sifting helps you blend flour evenly and effectively with dry ingredients such as baking powder, salt or cocoa powder. Sift them together. Ignore recipe instructions that tell you to sift the flour first.

4. Moisture in the air affects the volume of flour. It settles more if it's moister and heavier.

5. Different flours absorb liquid at different rates. If you are mixing flours, sift them together.

6. You can blend sifted flour more easily into a batter and thus avoid overmixing it. Baked goods will be lighter.

✧ Sift onto a sheet of waxed paper or a cheap paper plate, then roll up the sides to use it as a funnel.

⚡ *Lightning Won't Strike If ...*

You sift flour after measuring rather than before. It's annoying to sift, then measure. The difference is imperceptible in most recipes. Others you can adjust.

✧ Use a whisk to stir seasonings into flour for breading.

✧ Don't store flour in its paper bag. Transfer it to a clear container or tub with an airtight lid.

✧ White flour lasts for about 1 year in the cupboard, or indefinitely in the fridge or freezer.

♛ A Golden Rule

Always refrigerate or freeze whole wheat flour, and it will keep for 6 to 12 months. Because of the oils in the germ, it has a shelf life of just 2 to 3 months in the cupboard.

✧ You can use frozen flour. It doesn't clump.

✧ When baking, let frozen flour stand at room temperature for a couple of hours before using, so it doesn't alter baking times. An exception: It's good nice and cold for pie pastry.

☺ KID STUFF

Use flour and water as safe glue for toddlers' crafts.

Grains

◈ Presoak grains (from barley to bulgur to buckwheat) for 4 to 8 hours. They will cook faster and be more tender.

Better Leftovers

Toss cooked grains — such as wheat berries, bulgur, barley or wild rice — with chopped vegetables and salad dressing.

◈ Good news: Adding salt to grains and cereals during cooking helps them keep their shape and taste better. Bad news: The grains won't absorb as much liquid, so they may not be as tender.

◈ To prevent gumminess, add grains to rapidly boiling water and stir for a minute. That way, they quickly suck up hot liquid.

♻ Waste Not

Chop cereal crumbs left in the bottom of packages in a food processor. Use them for breading or crispy casserole toppings.

◈ Cover cooked cereal, such as Cream of Wheat or porridge, while it's hot. This keeps it softer and prevents a crust forming on top.

Ways to Reheat Cereal

- Scrape it into the top of a double boiler set over simmering water. Cover and heat.
- Add a bit of milk or water before microwaving it.

OUTSIDE THE BOX

Crunchy cereal, trail mix or granola is good at breakfast, lunch or dinner. Sprinkle it over yogurt, salad or ice cream.

◈ If you prefer crispy clumps in your homemade granola, don't stir it during baking.

Barley

Pot VS. Pearl?

Barley is "pearled," or polished and rounded, using abrasive discs. Pot barley (also called Scotch barley) is not as refined and takes longer to cook. Barley groats are even less refined; only part of the husk is removed.

≡ Fast Fixes

- Quick-cooking barley is pre-steamed.
- Barley may be cracked into faster-cooking grits.

Buckwheat

Buckwheat Groats VS. Kasha?

The groats are the hulled kernels of buckwheat. Roasting the groats turns them into kasha.

◈ Kasha comes in whole kernels, and fine, medium and coarse granules. The whole kernels and medium granules are the most frequently used. Whole kasha is more toothsome. The fine granules cook the quickest.

- Whole kasha is tastier if it's toasted. Stir it constantly in a dry pan over medium-high heat for 2 minutes before adding boiling water.

- For fluffier granulated kasha, stir it constantly with an egg white in a dry pan over medium-high heat for 2 to 3 minutes before adding boiling water. (Some cooks use a whole egg.) This coats the granules so they don't stick together. Whole kasha doesn't need to be stirred with egg because the bran coating keeps the kernels separate.

- You could toast granulated kasha for 1 minute before coating it with egg.

- Add at least 2 cups (500 mL) boiling water per 1 cup (250 mL) kasha, or $2\frac{1}{2}$ cups (625 mL) water if you have coated the grains with egg.

- Cover and simmer kasha for about 10 minutes or until it is tender and the water is absorbed.

- Buckwheat groats and kasha can be cooked in the microwave.

Master Plan
Microwaved Whole Kasha

1. Put kasha in a microwave-safe bowl. Microwave, uncovered, on High for 3 minutes, stirring halfway through, to toast it. Or toast it in a pan before microwaving.
2. Stir in boiling water. Cover the bowl with plastic wrap, leaving a small vent.
3. Microwave on High until kasha is tender and water is absorbed, about 10 minutes per $\frac{1}{2}$ cup (125 mL) whole kasha.

- Don't try to fluff together microwaved whole kasha and an egg. It gets clumpy.

Master Plan
Microwaved Kasha Granules

1. Put granulated kasha in a microwave-safe bowl. Stir in 1 slightly beaten egg per 1 cup (250 mL) kasha.
2. Microwave on High for 1 minute, breaking up clumps with a fork halfway through and at the end.
3. Stir in boiling water. Cover the bowl with plastic wrap, leaving a small vent.
4. Microwave on High until kasha is tender and water is absorbed, about 12 minutes per $\frac{1}{2}$ cup (125 mL) medium kasha granules.

- One cup (250 mL) whole kasha makes about $3\frac{1}{2}$ cups (875 mL) cooked. One cup (250 mL) granulated kasha makes about 4 cups (1 L) cooked.

Gussy It Up
- For deeper flavor, substitute stock for the water.
- Stir in chopped dried fruit after cooking.
- Stir sautéed mushrooms into cooked kasha.
- Stir finely chopped green onions or sautéed onions into cooked kasha.

Oats

Four Categories
- Oat groats are whole kernels that are roasted and hulled. They are chewy and take a long time to cook. The groats are also ground to make oat flour. Oat bran is the outer coating of the groats.
- Groats are steamed and flaked to make rolled oats, sometimes called old-fashioned oats. Rolled oats come in large-flake and quick-cooking versions. Cut into smaller pieces and rolled thinner, quick-cooking oats are a good choice for cookies.
- Instant oats are groats that have been cut, rolled thin, cooked, dried, salted and usually flavored. You just stir in boiling water for porridge.

- Steel-cut oats are groats that have been chopped into granules. The result is chewy and filling. They are also known as Irish or Scotch oats.

✧ Spray the porridge pan or microwave-safe bowl with oil or rub it with butter before using. This reduces sticking.

4 Ways to Improve Porridge

1. Use skim milk instead of water for a creamy texture.
2. Soak the oats overnight in the milk. This can also reduce a compound that inhibits the absorption of calcium in the body.
3. First, toast the oats in the pan or in a separate large skillet until golden.
4. Add salt near the end of cooking. The oats will be less chewy.

OUTSIDE THE BOX

- Cook oatmeal overnight in a slow cooker, so it's ready for breakfast. Steel-cut oats are best for this.
- You can cook oatmeal in a rice cooker.

Ⓢ is for Spurtle

Scots stir oats with a wooden spurtle, a.k.a. a theevil. They don't want to tear the oats and make the porridge mushy, so they use this tool. It is a thick dowel with a carved easy-grip end. You can make do by stirring with the handle of a wooden spoon.

✧ Before use in baking, you can tenderize oats. Boil or scald the liquid in the recipe, then pour it over the oats. Let cool completely before adding yeast or leavening.

Quinoa

> **Factoid** Quinoa is pronounced "keen-wa."

✧ Cook quinoa like rice, but not for as long.

 **Healthier Eater**

Quinoa contains more protein than any other grain. It also contains all eight essential amino acids.

✧ Before cooking, thoroughly rinse quinoa under running water to remove its bitter coating.

Creamy Steel-Cut Oats

Porridge purists swear by steel-cut oats. They are like the muscular version of rolled oats.
Makes 3 cups (750 mL), or 4 servings

Tip

Use a nonstick pan for easier cleanup.

1 tbsp	unsalted butter	15 mL
1 cup	steel-cut oats	250 mL
3 cups	skim milk	750 mL
¼ tsp	salt	1 mL

1. In a medium saucepan, melt butter over medium-high heat. Add oats and stir for about 2 minutes or until lightly toasted. Stir in milk. Bring to a simmer, stirring lightly and quickly to free any oats from the bottom of the pan.

2. Reduce heat to medium-low or low to maintain a gentle simmer. Cover and simmer, without stirring, for about 20 minutes or until thickened.

3. Uncover and sprinkle with salt, stirring once. Simmer for about 10 minutes or until most of the liquid is absorbed and oats are tender but chewy.

Pasta and Noodles

Pasta

✧ One lb (500 g) dry pasta makes about 8 cups (2 L) cooked pasta.

✧ You can substitute $1\frac{1}{2}$ lbs (750 g) fresh pasta per 1 lb (500 g) dry pasta.

4 Ways to Size Pasta Servings for a Main Dish

1. Allot 3 to 4 oz (90 to 125 g) dry pasta (whatever the shape) per person.
2. Cook 6 oz (175 g) fresh pasta per person.
3. Serve $1\frac{1}{2}$ cups (375 mL) cooked pasta (either dry or fresh) per person.
4. To guesstimate how much spaghetti or linguine you need to serve two, grasp the pasta in a circle formed by your thumb and middle finger (or index finger if you have large hands).

✧ Roll out fresh pasta a bit at a time. Keep the rest of the dough covered with a dampened towel or plastic wrap.

✧ Don't pull on the fresh dough rolling out of the pasta machine.

✧ Be patient. Start with the wide slot on the pasta machine and keep decreasing the setting.

✧ Store fresh sheets of pasta on a baking sheet, preferably nonstick. Slip waxed paper or parchment paper between each layer. Cover the baking sheet with plastic wrap.

OUTSIDE THE BOX

- Use a clothes drying rack to hang freshly cut pasta.
- Hang freshly cut pasta from the slats of your top oven rack inside the oven.

✧ In comparison to dry pasta, fresh pasta takes a third of the time to cook.

⚡ Lightning Won't Strike If ...

You boil different pasta shapes for one dish. You may have to use up whatever's on hand. Add the pasta to the boiling water at intervals, according to size.

✧ To whiten pasta, bleach it with a spoonful of white vinegar in the boiling water.

🌼 Being Green

Save energy by cooking pasta with the burner turned off. Scatter dry pasta into a pot of boiling salted water. Stir until the water returns to a rolling boil. Quickly slap on the lid. (If you are worried that the lid doesn't fit tightly enough, first cover the pot with a kitchen towel or foil.) Turn off the heat and leave the pot on the burner for 15 minutes.

A is for Al Dente

Al dente means "to the teeth," or toothsome. It can be described as tender but firm. Pasta should offer a slight resistance when bitten, but be easy to chew, without any dryness. Al dente can also be used to describe rice, grains and even vegetables.

Is It Done?

- Pasta is al dente.
- You see no white at the core when you cut it.

✧ Spaghetti and linguine are slippery customers. To test a strand, fish it out with a serrated knife.

Making Do

Don't have a pasta pot? Make an easy pasta lifter. Put a large mesh strainer or frying basket in the pot before adding the pasta to the boiling water.

To Rinse or Not to Rinse?

✧ Our jury of cooking peers votes against rinsing, but the decision is not unanimous. Here are the rinsing pros and cons:
- Rinsing removes the surface starch. This starch glues the sauce to the pasta. However, it also glues the pasta strands or shapes to each other. This can be remedied in other ways, but is a big problem with lasagna noodles.
- Rinsing stops pasta from continuing to cook in its residual heat and getting mushy.
- Rinsing makes pasta cold. So, if you're using it in a salad or want to hold it for later, rinsing is good.

✧ Make lasagna without a struggle: Rinse the noodles in cool water. Lay them side by side on a smooth kitchen towel. No sticking and less tearing are the rewards.

10 Ways to Prevent Clumping and Sticking

1. Rinse dry pasta before cooking it.
2. Cook pasta in lots of water. This allows the pasta to roll around and liberates the starches on its surface. Bonus: The pasta cooks more evenly. Per 1 lb (500 g) pasta, use 6 quarts (6 L) water and 2 tbsp (25 mL) salt.
3. Add a dash of oil to the cooking water. This is a must for lasagna, but optional for other pastas. Alternatively, you could oil the bottom of the pot before adding the water. This will make the cleanup easier, with fewer glued-on remnants of pasta. Bonus: Adding oil to the water reduces boilovers. The bad news: Oil discourages sauce from sticking to the pasta. Add too much oil and the sauce will slide right off.
4. Don't bring pasta and water to a boil together. Drop pasta into boiling water. It will be less likely to glue together.
5. Keep the water at a rolling boil. You want the starch on the surface to cook, so the strands don't stick to each other or the pot. Add pasta slowly so the water doesn't stop boiling.
6. After adding pasta, stir until the water returns to a full boil. Keep stirring for the first minute of cooking.
7. Spray your colander with oil before draining the pasta.
8. If bits of pasta cling stubbornly to the pot after you drain it, splash in cool water, swish and drain again. Do this while the pot is still warm.
9. Precook the pasta, then reheat it in boiling water, cafeteria-style.
10. Oil or butter the serving bowl.

♔ A Golden Rule

Always reserve some of the pasta cooking water. Use it to thicken or thin the sauce. Add a bit to boost the sauce with starch. Add a bit more if your dish is too dense or sludgy. You can also pour warm cooking water over pasta that is cooling down too quickly.

 Healthier Eater

You can make low-cal pasta sauce with pasta cooking water, fine vinegar and olive oil.

✧ Slightly undercook pasta destined for salad, as it will soften in the dressing.

Pasta with Mushrooms and Greens

You don't need a heavy, rich sauce to make pasta delicious. The cooking water is the base for this one. **Makes 4 to 6 servings**

Tip

Use fine vinegar and artisanal oil in the sauce.

Variations

I used beet greens because that's what was in the fridge. You can use any kind.

Use another vinegar, as long as it's subtle. Try champagne vinegar, but avoid balsamic and cider vinegars.

Try roasted nut oil in the sauce instead of olive oil.

1 lb	linguine	500 g
¼ cup	extra virgin olive oil, divided	50 mL
8 oz	cremini mushrooms, sliced	250 g
	Sea salt	
4 cups	loosely packed shredded beet greens	1 L
3 tbsp	sherry vinegar	45 mL
1½ tsp	sea salt	7 mL
	Freshly ground black pepper	
¼ cup	freshly grated Parmesan cheese	50 mL

1. In a large pot of boiling salted water, cook linguine for about 12 minutes or until tender but firm. Drain, reserving 1 cup (250 mL) of the cooking water.

2. Meanwhile, in a sauté pan, heat 1 tbsp (15 mL) of the oil over medium heat until shimmery. Add mushrooms. Sprinkle with salt to taste. Sauté for about 5 minutes or until softened and golden and any liquid has evaporated. Scrape into a bowl.

3. In the same pan, heat 1 tsp (5 mL) of the oil over medium heat. Stir in greens. Sauté for 1 to 2 minutes or until wilted. Drain in colander.

4. In a large measuring cup, whisk together pasta cooking water, vinegar, the remaining oil, salt and pepper to taste.

5. Transfer pasta to serving bowl. Pour in cooking water mixture. Let soak for 5 minutes.

6. Sprinkle Parmesan over pasta. Scatter mushrooms over the center. Scatter greens around the perimeter.

Ways to Cool Pasta Quickly for Salad

- Drain it in a colander. Place the colander in a large bowl half full of ice water. Let stand until the pasta is cold. Drain well.
- Toss pasta with a bit of oil and spread it on a baking sheet. Or spread pasta on an oiled baking sheet.

❖ Never let drained pasta languish in the colander. It molds into a dome as it cools.

4 Ways to Unglue Cooked Pasta

1. Pour hot pasta cooking water over it while pulling and plucking with tongs.
2. Spray it with hot water.
3. Fold in some oil.
4. Place the pasta in a heatproof bowl or pan. Add some sauce or oil. Heat it in a 325°F (160°C) oven or on the stove over medium heat. Stir occasionally. (This doesn't work in the microwave.)

❖ Remedies for the pasta cook in a holding pattern:
- If you have a pasta pot or a makeshift insert, pull it out and set it in the sink. Otherwise, use a skimmer to scoop the pasta into a colander. Do not drain the hot cooking water in the pot; cover it and leave it on the stove. When the sauce is ready, dip the pasta into the cooking water to reheat it.
- Toss the pasta with oil until coated. Put it in a heatproof bowl and cover with foil. Set it in a 200°F (100°C) oven. When you are ready to add the sauce, first toss the pasta with some leftover cooking water.

❖ Pasta cools quickly, so serve it in warmed bowls. Two ways to heat a serving bowl:
- Run hot tap water over it.
- Fill it with hot pasta cooking water.

Match Pasta to the Sauce

- Serve thin, delicate strands, such as angel hair pasta, only with light sauces.
- Toss thicker strands, such as fettuccine, with smooth, thick sauces.
- Pasta with tubes or ridges, such as rigatoni or radiatore, are best with chunkier sauces.
- Use macaroni or spirals in pasta salads.
- Shells go well with seafood sauce and tuna salad. They suit the theme and hold chunks of seafood in their little cups.

Ways to Help Sauce Cling to Pasta

- Choose a pasta shape with more exposed surface area, such as farfalle or linguine.
- Toss cooked pasta with grated Parmesan before adding the sauce.
- Avoid oiling or buttering the pasta before adding the sauce.

❖ To condition pasta and deepen the flavor, return the drained pasta to its pot. Add a ladleful of sauce and a small hunk of butter. Over medium heat, stir for 30 to 60 seconds. The pasta will suck up the sauce. Serve it with the rest of the sauce ladled over top, as usual. I saw a mobster on *The Sopranos* do this.

⩣ Fast Fix

You can divide cooked pasta into individual portions in medium zip-lock bags, then freeze. When you are ready to sup, drop the contents into boiling water.

Spaghetti Eva

I originally prepared this quick hit with cooked plain spaghetti that had been languishing in the fridge, along with whatever else I could find while rooting around. I was going to call it Spaghetti with a Greek Accent. My daughter Eva, however, insisted it be named after her because she enjoyed it so much. "But you don't even like zucchini," I protested. "I like zucchini now," she said. Music to a mother's ears! This works with 4 cups (1 L) leftover cooked spaghetti that has been warmed in boiling water. But here's the recipe if you want to make it from scratch. **Makes 4 servings**

• **Preheat oven to 400°F (200°C)**

8 oz	spaghetti	250 g
3	zucchini (about 1 lb/500 g), halved lengthwise	3
1	extra-large tomato (about 12 oz/375 g), halved at equator	1
4	slices bacon, chopped	4
1 tbsp	extra virgin olive oil	15 mL
1	onion, chopped	1
3	large cloves garlic, minced	3
½ tsp	sea salt	2 mL
	Freshly ground pepper	
8 oz	firm feta cheese, cut into ½-inch (1 cm) cubes	250 g

1. In large pot of boiling salted water, cook spaghetti for 10 to 15 minutes or until al dente. Drain.

2. Meanwhile, place zucchini and tomato on a baking sheet, cut sides down. Roast in preheated oven for 10 minutes. Transfer tomato to a cutting board. Return zucchini to the oven and roast for about 5 minutes or until just tender.

3. Pull off and discard skin from tomato. Discarding core, coarsely chop flesh.

4. Transfer zucchini to the cutting board. Cut each half lengthwise into 3 pieces, then crosswise into ½-inch (1 cm) pieces.

5. In a large skillet, sauté bacon over medium-high heat for about 3 minutes or until crispy. Add oil, then stir in onion and garlic. Reduce heat to medium and sauté for about 3 minutes or until softened and golden. Add tomato, zucchini and their juices. Add salt and pepper to taste. Cook, stirring gently, for 3 to 5 minutes or until most of the liquid evaporates.

6. Toss in spaghetti and feta until coated and warmed through. Remove from heat. Taste and adjust the salt.

✦ Take control of your spaghetti. Pick up a few strands with your fork and twirl them in a spoon. "Few" is the key. Diners complain that the fork-and-spoon technique doesn't work. That's because a hearty forkful twirls into a mouthful big enough for a hippo.

✦ You can refrigerate leftover cooked pasta for a day or two in a tub of cold water so it doesn't clump. It will get pasty if left too long, though.

Better Leftovers

Turn leftover spaghetti (or other shapes) into a pasta pie.

Spaghetti Pie

This "pie" is red, white and green like the Italian flag. You can use any leftover pasta, but small or thin types are preferable. **Makes 6 servings**

- **Preheat broiler**

- **12-inch (30 cm) ovenproof nonstick skillet**

Variation

If you want to make this from scratch, cook 8 oz (250 g) pasta, then drain and let cool to room temperature.

2 tbsp	extra virgin olive oil, divided	25 mL
1	onion, halved and thinly sliced	1
2	cloves garlic, minced	2
6	large eggs	6
1 tsp	dried Italian seasoning	5 mL
1 tsp	kosher salt	5 mL
	Freshly ground black pepper	
4 cups	leftover cooked spaghetti, at room temperature	1 L
1	tomato, cut into 1/4-inch (0.5 cm) dice	1
1/4 cup	dry grated Parmesan cheese	50 mL
2 tbsp	finely chopped fresh parsley	25 mL

1. In skillet, heat half the oil over medium heat until shimmery. Sauté onion and garlic for about 5 minutes or until softened. Remove from heat.

2. In a large bowl, whisk eggs, Italian seasoning, salt and pepper to taste. Add spaghetti and scrape in onion mixture. Toss with tongs until pasta is coated and there are no clumps.

3. In the skillet, heat the remaining oil over medium heat until shimmery. Add spaghetti mixture and sprinkle tomato on top. Cook, lifting the edges to let uncooked egg run underneath, for about 5 minutes or until the bottom is browned and slightly crusted. While the top is still wet, sprinkle with Parmesan.

4. Put the skillet in the oven and broil for 2 to 3 minutes or until the top is set and golden. Sprinkle with parsley. Cut into wedges.

- ◇ If you plan to freeze pasta, cook it until it's not quite done. Let it cool briefly. If desired, toss it with oil before freezing.

- ◇ To reheat pasta, drop it into boiling water, as they do in cafeteria pasta bars. It should take no more than 1 minute. To thaw frozen pasta, do the same, but let it boil longer.

- ◇ Keep small cans of vegetable cocktail in your pantry to pour into tomato pasta dishes when reheating.

Rice Noodles

⚡ Lightning Won't Strike If ...

You boil rice noodles (also called rice sticks). It's traditional to soften them in tepid water. A step up from that is pouring boiling water over them in a bowl and letting them soak. Some recipes even tell you to add raw rice noodles to a stir-fry on the stove, then toss them in to soften and suck up liquid — with dubious results. The best and easiest method: Simply cook rice noodles in boiling water until they're wilted, then drain and rinse. Just be quick or they'll get mushy.

Couscous

Mythstake

Couscous is not actually a type of grain. Made from durum wheat semolina, it is rubbed into granules and dried — more of a pasta than a grain.

- ◇ Traditional Middle Eastern couscous is steamed over stew for a long time. The packaged couscous in North American supermarkets is precooked. You simply rehydrate it.

Master Plan
Couscous

1. Put couscous in a bowl.
2. Pour in 2 cups (500 mL) boiling water per 1 cup (250 mL) couscous, stirring with a fork to separate the grains and allow them to absorb more water.
3. Cover and let stand for about 5 minutes or until water is absorbed.
4. Fluff couscous with a fork. Don't stir it with a spoon.

- ◇ Add butter to couscous via the boiling liquid, not afterwards. Drop 1 tbsp (15 mL) butter into 2 cups (500 mL) boiling water, then stir until melted before pouring it over the couscous.

- ◇ Another way to make couscous: Steam it.

Gussy It Up
- Play with the liquid. Use stock or cider.
- Add tomato paste to the boiling liquid.
- Stir herbs, nuts or dried fruit into the cooked couscous.

Israeli Couscous

Mythstake

Israeli couscous and regular couscous are not actually alike. Israeli couscous looks like pearls of pasta. It is made of large pellets of semolina. It is not precooked. *Ptitim* is the Hebrew name for it.

- ◇ For fluffier, nutty Israeli couscous, toast it before boiling. In a skillet, heat 1 tbsp (15 mL) olive oil over medium heat. Add couscous and toast for 1 to 2 minutes or until golden. Toasting seals the surface starch. The pearls will be less likely to turn mushy as they absorb moisture.

3 Ways to Cook Israeli Couscous

1. Cook it like pasta. Boil it in salted water for 10 to 12 minutes.
2. Cook it like rice. Use 1¼ cups (300 mL) water per 1 cup (250 mL) Israeli couscous. Cover and simmer it over low heat for 12 to 15 minutes or until the water is absorbed.
3. Cook it like risotto. Add ladlefuls of hot stock, stirring constantly, until it is tender and swollen.

OUTSIDE THE BOX

- Serve Israeli couscous with sauce, like pasta.
- Add Israeli couscous to finished soup.
- Make pasta salad with Israeli couscous.

Rice and Wild Rice

♕ Three Golden Rules

- The usual ratio of water to rice is 2:1, but err on the side of a bit less water — the rice will be nicer.
- Before cooking, always rinse rice. This makes it less sticky. It also swishes away debris and any dirt or foreign material clinging to the grains. Some foreign rice is coated with talc, which is considered a health hazard.
- The shorter the grain, the stickier the rice.

✧ One cup (250 mL) raw rice makes 3 to 4 cups (750 mL to 1 L) cooked rice, and serves four as a side dish.

✧ To guesstimate how much rice you need per person, place it on a sandwich plate in proportion to the amount of space it would occupy on a dinner plate. Then cook it. (This works for pasta, too.)

Rice Specs

✧ Rice is classified by the grain, the variety and the way it's been processed.

Long-Grain Specs

- The length is more than three times longer than the width.
- It swells lengthwise when it's cooked.
- It's lower in starch than medium- and short-grain rice.
- The cooked grains remain separate, light and fluffy, and tender-firm.
- Types include basmati, jasmine and Wehani.

✧ Use long-grain rice for main dishes, pilafs and salads, and as a bed for stews, curries and sauces.

Medium-Grain Specs

- The length is two to three times longer than the width.
- The cooked grains are moist and tender, and tend to cling together.
- It is starchier than long-grain rice, and creamy.
- It goes from fluffy to clumpy as it cools.
- Types include Arborio and carnaroli.

✧ Use medium-grain rice for dishes that are creamy, but not glutinous, such as risotto, desserts, paella, croquettes, meatloaf and rice balls (arancini).

Short-Grain Specs

- The length is less than two times longer than the width.
- The grains are oval or almost round, and are softer than those of medium-grain rice.
- It's the highest in starch, so the grains stick together and are easy to pick up with chopsticks.
- Types include sushi rice, glutinous rice and forbidden rice.

✧ Use short-grain rice for sushi, puddings and molds.

> **Factoid** Confusion over rice classifications arises because the United States slots them into three size categories, while other countries simply sort them into long- and short-grain types.

✧ Some rices — such as the super-absorbent Spanish paella rices, Bomba and Valencia — hover on the borderline between medium- and short-grain.

Ⓐ is for Aromatic

Rices with a popcorn or nutty scent are described as aromatic. Examples are jasmine, basmati and black rice.

Ⓖ is for Glutinous Rice

This rice is bred to be starchy. Glutinous rice may be called sticky rice, sweet rice or mochi rice. It can be white or black. It is usually, but not always, short-grain. Some Thai glutinous rices are long-grain.

Ways to Cook Glutinous Rice

- Want it chewy? Steam it wrapped in cheesecloth or a lotus or banana leaf, or steam it atop a lettuce leaf.
- Want it creamy? Boil it. Boiling makes it fall apart, but that may be exactly what the recipe requires.

❖ Choose glutinous rice for rice pudding.

OUTSIDE THE BOX

Give rice pudding a tropical touch. Substitute coconut milk for the milk or cream.

Brown **VS.** White?

Brown rice is the entire grain, including the bran and germ. White rice is stripped of these nutritious components when it is polished. Brown rice takes about 45 minutes to cook — more than twice as long as white rice. It remains chewy. Most varieties of rice come in brown and white versions.

❖ White rice keeps indefinitely in a sealed tub in the pantry. Refrigerate brown rice if you expect to keep it for more than 6 months. You can also freeze it.

Mythstake

Parboiled doesn't mean precooked. Parboiled rice, or converted rice, is boiled or steamed in the husk. This pushes the nutrients to the center of the grain. Converted rice is the darling of the food-service industry. Do not confuse this firm, beige rice with crumbly, precooked and dehydrated instant rice.

❖ Advantages of converted rice over standard white rice:
- It is more nutritious.
- It remains firmer after cooking.
- The grains stay separate and fluffy.
- It holds its shape and texture in long-simmered soups and stews.

❖ Rinse raw rice until the water runs clear. An exception: If you want the cooked rice sticky, just do a fast rinse. Two unusual ways to rinse rice:
- Put rice in a freestanding sieve, then place it inside the saucepan you will use. Spray and swish repeatedly. Lift out the sieve and shake it. Drain the pan.
- Set up a rice fountain. Place the rice in a medium bowl. Put this bowl in a small pan in the sink. Tilt the bowl so that the water from the tap runs in one end and flows out the other. Run the water very slowly. Swish the rice occasionally, then drain.

❖ You may want to soak rice, as well. Do this after rinsing it. Soaking is standard for short-grain rice, optional for long-grain rice. Three reasons to soak rice:
- It expands the grains. Soaking lengthens the grains of basmati, for instance.
- It promotes even cooking.
- It shortens the cooking time.

Rice with a Portuguese Accent

This rice should be firm and not too sticky, so I like to use converted (parboiled) rice. The recipe was inspired by the rice served at a Portuguese wedding. The hosts were my neighbors, the Do Coutos, who kindly and regularly deliver links of their home-smoked, spicy chouriço sausages to me. **Makes 4 to 6 servings**

Tips

The olives are usually served whole, but you can pit them if you wish.

Piri piri is Portuguese hot sauce.

Variation

Turn this into a meal by adding cooked clams or shrimp.

2 cups	water	500 mL
	Salt	
1 cup	converted (parboiled) rice, rinsed	250 mL
¼ cup	extra virgin olive oil	50 mL
½ cup	minced red bell pepper	125 mL
1	shallot, minced	1
¼ cup	finely chopped, skinned chouriço sausage (mild or spicy)	50 mL
1	clove garlic, minced	1
1 to 2 tbsp	tomato paste	15 to 25 mL
	Piri piri sauce	
15 to 20	black olives	15 to 20
	Chopped fresh parsley	

1. In a medium saucepan, bring salted water to a boil over high heat. Stir in rice. Reduce heat to low, cover and simmer for about 20 minutes or until rice is just tender and water is absorbed. Remove from heat and let stand, uncovered, for 5 minutes.

2. Meanwhile, in a small skillet, heat oil over medium-low heat until shimmery. Sauté red pepper and shallot for about 10 minutes or until very soft but not browned, reducing heat to low if necessary (the mixture should poach rather than fry). Stir in sausage and garlic; sauté for about 5 minutes or until softened. Stir in tomato paste to taste.

3. Fluff rice with a fork. Gently blend in red pepper mixture. Season to taste with piri piri sauce and salt.

4. Transfer rice mixture to a serving platter. Scatter olives on top and garnish with parsley.

Amounts and cooking times vary for different types of rice. Here are some guidelines for 1 cup (250 mL) rice.

Type	Amount of liquid	Cooking time
Long-grain white	1¾ to 2 cups (425 to 500 mL)	15 minutes
Medium- or short-grain white	1½ to 1¾ cups (375 to 425 mL)	15 minutes
Parboiled	2 to 2½ cups (500 to 625 mL)	20 minutes
Brown	2 to 2½ cups (500 to 625 mL)	45 minutes

✧ Compensate for soaking rice by reducing the amount of cooking water. Use up to ¼ cup (50 mL) less liquid per 1 cup (250 mL) soaked rice. The cooked rice will be drier and less sticky.

✧ Just to drive yourself crazy, note that the amount of water doesn't necessarily double when you double the amount of rice.

✧ Older, drier rice sucks up more water. So does rice cooked with acidic ingredients, such as tomatoes.

✧ Risotto rices (such as Arborio and carnaroli) and paella rices (such as Bomba and Valencia) are super-absorbent. One cup (250 mL) rice may suck up 3 to 6 cups (750 mL to 1.5 L) liquid, depending on the cooking method.

Measuring and Cooking Tricks

• Pour rice into a saucepan. It doesn't have to be measured. Shake the pan to help it settle. Rest the tip of your index finger on top of the rice (don't push it down to the bottom). Add just enough water to reach the crease on your first knuckle. That's about 1 inch (2.5 cm) water over the rice. Sprinkle with salt. Bring the water to a rolling boil over high heat. Stir the rice once. Reduce the heat to medium, then boil the rice, uncovered and undisturbed, until there's barely a thin layer of water on top and holes appear across the surface. Reduce the heat to the lowest setting, then cover and cook the rice, without peeking, for 15 to 20 minutes (the time depends on your stove).

• Pour rice into a saucepan. The amount doesn't matter. Shake the pan to help it settle. Place your hand flat on the rice. Pour in water until it reaches three-quarters of the way up the length of your hand. Add salt and cook the rice the classic way.

Master Plan
Classic White Rice

1. Rinse and drain the rice.
2. Put it in a medium saucepan. Add about twice as much water as rice, and some salt.
3. Bring to a boil over medium-high heat. Give it a big stir, then cover the pan and reduce the heat to low. Cook for 15 to 20 minutes or until the rice is tender and the water is absorbed.
4. Remove the pan from the heat. Uncover and let stand for 5 minutes.
5. Fluff the rice with a fork. Do not stir it with a spoon.

✧ When rice comes to a boil, give it a stir before putting on the lid. Less will stick to the bottom of the pan.

✗ No-No

Put a lid on your curiosity. Never peek at rice while it's cooking the classic way. The steam will escape.

❖ Cooked rice will be fluffier if you give any extra moisture time to evaporate. After you remove it from the heat, let the rice stand, uncovered and undisturbed, for 5 minutes.

P is for Parching

Add a nutty flavor and separate the grains by toasting rice in oil or butter before boiling it. This is called parching. The term "parched rice" also refers to a type of heat-treated Indian rice and to wild rice that is roasted after harvesting to evaporate moisture and loosen the husks.

OUTSIDE THE BOX

- Cook it like pasta. No need to rinse first. Just toss it into plenty of boiling salted water and cook until tender, about 12 minutes for white rice. (Start testing after 10 minutes.) Drain well.
- Steam it. White rice steamed over simmering water takes about 1 hour.
- Bake it. In a small casserole dish, stir together rice and boiling liquid. Cover and bake in a 400°F (200°C) oven until the liquid is absorbed, about 45 minutes for white rice.
- Microwave it. In a large, microwave-safe bowl, stir together 1½ cups (375 mL) water and 1 cup (250 mL) rice. Cover with plastic wrap and slit a vent at the center. Microwave on High for 12 to 15 minutes. Let stand, covered, for 5 minutes. Note: You can buy rice cooker bowls specifically for the microwave; they work well.

Factoid Electric rice cookers know when to turn themselves off because the temperature rises as soon as the water is absorbed.

Gussy It Up

- Use a liquid other than water. Try stock or consommé, or tomato or vegetable juice. Try fruit juices, such as apple or orange, diluted with water 1:1. Do the same with coconut milk. Splash in a bit of wine. Use up the cooking liquid left from boiling or steaming vegetables. Add soaking liquid from mushrooms.
- Flavor rice with onions and herbs. Sauté them in a skillet. Gently stir them in after the rice is cooked.
- Add pesto to hot cooked rice.
- Make it Rice-a-Roni style. Melt some butter and toast raw rice with broken bits of vermicelli, then add stock and boil as usual. Use about ⅔ cup (150 mL) white rice, ⅓ cup (75 mL) broken thin egg noodles (sold for soup) and 2 cups (500 mL) chicken stock.
- Stir some cooked wild rice into hot white rice. This is lovely along with chopped nuts, herbs and dried cranberries.

Master Plan
Soaked Basmati Rice

1. Rinse rice until the water runs clear. Soak in cold water for 30 minutes. Drain.
2. Put basmati in a saucepan. Per 1 cup (250 mL) rice, add 2 cups (500 mL) water and 1 tsp (15 mL) butter or oil.
3. Bring to a boil over medium heat and boil for 5 minutes. Reduce the heat to low, cover and simmer for about 5 minutes or until the water is absorbed.
4. Remove from the heat and let stand, covered, for 1 to 2 minutes.
5. Fluff the rice with a fork.

Rice Doctor

The rice has absorbed all the water, but isn't tender.
- Pour in ¼ cup (50 mL) water. Cover and cook for another 5 minutes.

The rice is almost tender, but it's slightly wet.
- Remove the pan from the heat. Cover and let stand for 5 minutes.

The rice is tender, but it's watery.

- Remove the lid. Turn off the heat, but leave the pan on the burner. Don't stir or the rice will get too sticky.
- Spread the rice on a baking sheet and dry it in a 200°F (100°C) oven.

The rice is scorched.

- You can reduce (not repair) the damage. Without disturbing the burned bottom, scoop the rice into a fresh pan. Place a slice of bread on top to absorb the burnt odor. Cover and let stand for 10 minutes. (If the burned rice is not yet tender, add a bit of water before topping with the bread.)

The grains are sticky rather than separate and fluffy.

- Switch to long-grain rice.
- Never stir rice while it cooks. This crushes the grains and releases starch.
- Add butter or oil to the cooking water. Use 1 tsp (5 mL) butter or oil per 2 cups (500 mL) water.
- Add 1 tsp (5 mL) lemon juice per 2 cups (500 mL) water. (This also bleaches the rice.)
- Fluff rice with a fork, not a spoon.

Ways to Hold Cooked Rice

- Keep it warm and even out the texture. Once the liquid is absorbed, but the rice is still slightly firm, remove the pan from the heat. Cover and let stand for up to 30 minutes.
- Help it stay warm and fluffy. Cover the rice with a dry pita round, then replace the lid. You could also use a slice of bread or a crumpled paper towel. Let it stand for up to 30 minutes.
- Keep it hot. Cover the dish and put it in a 350°F (180°C) oven for up to 30 minutes.

✧ Rice can be molded. Pack hot rice into a greased ramekin or custard cup. Let it stand for 3 to 4 minutes. Turn it out onto the serving plate. This works for long- and short-grain rices, but the sticky rices mold best.

OUTSIDE THE BOX

- Paella is tricky. It can turn out sludgy or gluey. Cheat by making a mock, deconstructed paella. Prepare the rice, then stir in the other ingredients.
- If a wide paella pan doesn't fit on your stove burners, use a gas barbecue.

Risotto Rules

- Use warmed stock.
- Go slowly. Add a ladleful of stock (½ to 1 cup/125 to 250 mL) at a time.
- Cook over medium-low heat. The stock evaporates too quickly if it boils.
- Add seasonings lightly, then adjust them at the end. The stock reduces and concentrates.
- Risotto should be creamy, but not soupy.
- Sauté fast-cooking ingredients, such as shrimp, then stir them in at the end.

⚡ *Lightning Won't Strike If ...*

- You don't stir the risotto every second. While multitasking, stir it frequently and be vigilant.
- You serve the risotto in a bowl. Purists worry that the sides will retain heat and the rice will continue to cook. However, a wide pasta bowl is fine and lovely.

Master Plan
Classic Risotto

1. Bring a saucepan of stock to a simmer on the burner alongside your risotto pan, then keep it warm over low heat.
2. In your risotto pan, over medium heat, sauté onion in oil until softened. Stir in garlic and any vegetables, such as chopped peppers.
3. Increase heat to medium-high, then add rice, stirring for about 1 minute until

thoroughly coated. It should turn shiny and translucent, but not brown.

4. If you're using wine, now's the time to add it. Stir and scrape the bottom of the pan as you do.

5. Reduce heat to medium-low or low. Pour a ladleful of stock onto rice, then stir until only a small puddle is left at the bottom of the pan. Continue adding stock by the ladleful and stirring until rice is tender but still firm. Do not rush. The risotto should be creamy and slightly wet. How fast it's done and how much stock you need depends on the shape of the pan and the heat. Think 20 to 30 minutes.

6. About 5 minutes before risotto is done, you can add fast-cooking items such as peas or chunks of fish.

7. Remove the risotto pan from the heat. Now's the time to stir in Parmesan, butter cubes, greens (such as arugula), or pieces of cooked meat or fish.

8. Transfer to a serving dish. Garnish with anything from chopped parsley to olives.

✧ To make risotto in advance, you can cook it halfway, then finish it just before serving. However, it will harden if it cools too much.

Rice with a Spanish Accent

Use absorbent Spanish paella rice, such as Valencia or Bomba. The final dish should be moist, but not gloppy. **Makes 4 to 6 servings**

4	slices bacon, chopped	4
1	onion, halved and thinly sliced	1
2	cloves garlic, minced	2
1 cup	paella rice, rinsed	250 mL
2 cups	canned diced tomatoes with juices	500 mL
1 cup	water	250 mL
1	green bell pepper, finely chopped	1
1½ tsp	sweet smoked Spanish paprika	7 mL
1 tsp	sea salt	5 mL
	Chopped fresh cilantro	

1. In a medium saucepan, sauté bacon over medium heat for about 5 minutes or until crisp. Using a slotted spoon, transfer it to a plate lined with paper towels.

2. Add onion and garlic to the pan drippings and sauté for about 2 minutes or until softened. Add rice, stirring to coat for 1 minute. Add tomatoes and their juices, water, green pepper, paprika and salt. Reduce heat to low, cover and simmer for about 15 minutes or until rice is tender and liquid is absorbed. Uncover and let stand for 1 minute. Taste and adjust salt, if desired. Fluff with a fork.

3. Transfer to a serving dish. Sprinkle with bacon and cilantro.

Microwave Shiitake, Carrot and Cilantro Risotto

Making risotto in the microwave cuts down on all the stirring. **Makes 6 servings as a side dish**

Tip

This is a fine vegetarian meal. Make it vegan by using oil instead of butter and avoiding the cheese.

Variations

Use sliced cremini mushrooms instead of the shiitakes.

Use dried mushrooms; soak them and add the strained soaking liquid to the rice in place of some of the stock.

Use other fresh herbs instead of cilantro.

¼ cup	unsalted butter	50 mL
1	small onion, chopped	1
1	clove garlic, chopped	1
1 cup	Arborio rice	250 mL
3 cups	vegetable stock	750 mL
6 oz	shiitake mushrooms, stemmed, caps sliced (about 2 cups/500 mL)	175 g
1	small carrot, finely shredded (about ½ cup/125 mL)	1
½ cup	chopped fresh cilantro	125 mL
½ tsp	kosher salt	2 mL
	Freshly ground black pepper	
	Grated Parmesan cheese (optional)	

1. In a large, microwave-safe dish, microwave butter on High for 1 minute or until melted. Stir in onion and garlic. Microwave on High, uncovered, for 2 minutes. Stir in rice until coated. Microwave on High, uncovered, for 2 minutes. Stir in stock and mushrooms. Microwave on High, uncovered, for 20 minutes or until creamy and tender. Remove from microwave. Stir in carrot and cilantro. Let stand for 5 minutes. Stir in salt, pepper to taste and Parmesan to taste (if using).

Gussy It Up

- If you are adding seafood, pour the juices or cooking liquid into the stock for risotto.
- If you are adding rehydrated dried porcini mushrooms, strain and add the soaking liquid to the stock for risotto.

Better Leftovers

Recycle cold leftover risotto into arancini. Roll risotto into dense 2-inch (5 cm) balls, tucking a surprise (such as a tiny cube of mozzarella) into the center of each. Roll each ball in dry bread crumbs. In a skillet, heat 1 to 2 inches (2.5 to 5 cm) of olive oil over medium-high heat. Fry arancini, turning occasionally, just until warm inside and golden brown outside, about 5 minutes. Serve hot or at room temperature.

Three Mock Risottos

- In a saucepan, over medium heat, sauté chopped onion and any other vegetables in oil until softened. Stir in rice until coated. Add the standard amount of liquid needed for classic boiled rice. Cover, reduce heat to low and simmer gently for 12 minutes. Remove the lid.

Quickly place any greens and bits of meat you desire on top. Cover and cook for 8 minutes. Remove from heat. Stir in butter and cheese.

- Use the microwave. Always microwave risotto uncovered. For 1 cup (250 mL) rice, microwave ¼ cup (50 mL) butter and/or oil on High for about 1 minute. Add onion and garlic and microwave on High for 2 minutes or until softened. Stir in rice until coated. Microwave on high for 2 minutes. Stir in 3 cups (750 mL) stock and microwave on High for 20 minutes or until creamy and tender. You can add vegetables at the same time as the stock or halfway through the cooking time, depending on how firm they are. Herbs or finely shredded vegetables such as carrots can be stirred in at the end of the cooking time. Let stand for 5 minutes. Stir in salt, pepper and cheese.
- Brown rice doesn't lend itself to risotto, but you can take a stab at an imitation. Using equal amounts of rice and water, soak short-grain brown rice overnight. Drain, reserving the soaking liquid. Add soaking liquid to stock and/or wine to make about 3½ cups (875 mL) liquid per 1 cup (250 mL) rice. In a saucepan, over medium heat, sauté rice in oil, stirring to coat. Stir in liquid and bring to a simmer. Reduce heat to low, cover and simmer for 30 minutes. Uncover and simmer for about 20 minutes or until creamy and tender and the liquid is absorbed. Stir in salt, pepper and cheese.

✧ To cool rice faster, rinse it quickly with cold water, then drain well.

✧ To dry cooked rice faster for salad or fried rice, spread it on a baking sheet. Pat it dry with paper towels, but do not press or you will release the starch. Keep the rice aired until it is dry. (This works for cooked grains, such as bulgur or quinoa, too.)

Keys to Rice Salad
- Rinse the cooked rice to wash off the starch.
- Add the dressing while the rice is still warm, so the rice can suck it up.
- Do not refrigerate the rice. It will get cold and hard.

Better Leftovers

Make fried rice. This dish was actually created as a way to salvage old, cold rice.

Keys to Better Fried Rice
- Dry the rice at room temperature.
- Scrape the rice into a storage tub with an airtight lid, and refrigerate it overnight.
- Separate the clumps with moistened hands.
- Start cooking with cold rice.
- Don't skimp on the oil. There's a reason it's called fried rice.
- Stir-fry over medium-high heat.
- Do not stir constantly. Let the rice start to stick to the pan.
- Don't use a nonstick pan.
- It's traditional to add eggs, but you want chunks, not curdles. Scramble the eggs in a separate skillet, then fold them into the finished fried rice. If you want to use the same pan, push the finished rice aside, pour the eggs into the pan, then let them set before stirring them together.

✧ You can cook extra rice and refrigerate it up for up to 3 days for fast fried rice or pudding.

✧ To cook rice you intend to freeze, use less water and remove it from the heat while it's still firm.

5 Ways to Reheat Rice

Add 2 tbsp (25 mL) liquid per 1 cup (250 mL) rice.

1. Cover and heat the rice in a pan over medium heat on the stove or in a 350°F (180°C) oven for about 5 minutes.
2. Warm rice in the top of a double boiler set over simmering water.
3. Put rice in a steamer insert over simmering water.
4. Cover and microwave rice on High for about 1 minute per 1 cup (250 mL) rice. For frozen rice, make that 2 minutes.
5. If the rice is frozen, drop it into boiling water, then drain it.

Wild Rice

✧ Before cooking, rinse wild rice in cold water several times to wash away debris.

✧ Some people soak wild rice before cooking, but it's not worth the bother. It only shaves about 15 minutes off the cooking time. The texture remains the same.

Mythstake

Wild rice is not a type of rice. It's the seed of a water plant. The long, slender, dark brown grains have a nutty flavor. They remain chewy, so don't keep cooking in the hopes of attaining tenderness.

✧ Cook wild rice in plenty of salted water. Use 4 parts water to 1 part wild rice.

Is It Done?

- Wild rice takes about 45 minutes to cook.
- Simmer until the kernels start to split, exposing the cream-colored centers.

✧ For fluffier wild rice, take the pan off the heat at the end of cooking time. Let it stand, covered, for about 30 minutes before draining.

OUTSIDE THE BOX

- Stir cooked wild rice into soup.
- Make stuffing with a combination of wild and regular rice.

Corn Products

A Bit of Science

Corn may be the world's most versatile crop. Everything from the husk to the kernel is utilized, in livestock feed, laundry starch, solvents, cosmetics, even folk art. The cook encounters corn in many guises, from powdery starch to swollen hominy, oil to alcohol.

Corn Flour

Cornstarch VS. Corn Flour?

Cornstarch is a powder ground from the endosperm, or starchy heart, of the corn kernel. Corn flour is finely milled corn. The term "corn flour" is sometimes used interchangeably with "cornstarch," particularly in British recipes. This can cause confusion.

Making Do

If you don't have corn flour, pulverize cornmeal in a blender or food processor.

M is for Masa Harina

For tortillas, choose this Central American take on corn flour. It is made from corn kernels cooked with limewater, soaked and pulverized into a dough called masa, then dried and powdered. Masa harina is not a substitute for corn flour or cornmeal (or vice versa).

Cornmeal

❖ Cornmeal can be yellow, white or blue. White corn kernels are smaller. Blue ones have more protein.

Stone-Ground VS. Standard Milling?

Cornmeal is made of dried, ground corn kernels. Standard cornmeal is milled using steel rollers.

Stone-ground cornmeal retains some of the hull and germ (seed), and is more nutritious.

Characteristics of Stone-Ground Cornmeal

- It is coarser.
- It has yellow and black speckles.
- It goes bad faster.
- It takes longer to cook.
- It is more nutritious.

A Good Sign

Fresher cornmeal tastes "cornier."

❖ Regular cornmeal keeps indefinitely in a cool, dry, dark place. Stone-ground cornmeal should be stored in the fridge.

❖ Before you cook with cornmeal, decide what grind you need: fine, medium or coarse.

> **Factoid** Cornmeal mush is made around the world, in forms such as grits, polenta and mealie pap.

P is for Polenta

Polenta is an Italian cornmeal mush. You can eat it as porridge or play polenta geometry with firm squares, triangles, sticks, balls or other shapes.

Polenta Formula

- One cup (250 mL) cornmeal, 4 cups (1 L) water, 1 tsp (5 mL) salt. For smoothness, stir 1 tbsp (15 mL) butter or oil into the warm cooked polenta.

❖ One cup (250 mL) cornmeal yields 3½ to 4 cups (875 mL to 1 L) polenta.

❖ Stir polenta once every minute while it's simmering in a saucepan over medium-low heat. It could take 20 to 30 minutes to cook, depending on the grind.

Avoid Going Stir-Crazy
- Cook polenta in a double boiler.
- Bake the polenta.
- Use a rice cooker.

Master Plan
Polenta in a Rice Cooker
1. Pour in the blended ingredients, then cover and flip the switch.
2. Once the mixture is boiling, stir it every 10 minutes. The rice cooker may snap from the "On" position to "Warm," but the polenta will still bubble.
3. Keep cooking until it is tender, at least 30 minutes.

⨸ Fast Fix
True polenta is made with medium or coarse cornmeal. You can cheat for speed with fine cornmeal, also sold as quick-cooking polenta. It should cook in no more than 10 minutes.

4 Ways to Prevent Lumps

1. Whisk cornmeal into boiling salted water slowly and gradually.
2. Blend the cornmeal with a third of the cold water from the recipe. Stir that into the rest of the water, which should be boiling.
3. Start by whisking together all the cold ingredients.
4. Choose coarser cornmeal. The finer it is, the more prone to lumping.

Smooth and Easy Polenta

For the creamiest polenta, simmer it in a double boiler. **Makes about 3¾ cups (925 mL), or 4 servings**

- **Double boiler**

Tip

If you don't have a double boiler, bring the cornmeal mixture to a boil in a medium saucepan, then scrape it into a heatproof bowl set over simmering water. Don't forget to cover the bowl.

4 cups	cold water	1 L
1 cup	medium-grind cornmeal	250 mL
1 tsp	kosher salt	5 mL
1 tbsp	extra virgin olive oil	15 mL

1. Bring water in bottom of double boiler to a simmer on medium-high heat. Turn heat to low.
2. In the top of the double boiler, whisk together 4 cups (1 L) cold water, cornmeal and salt. Place it directly on a burner over medium-high heat and bring to a boil. Place it over the simmering water. Cover and cook, stirring occasionally, for 45 to 60 minutes or until tender and creamy. Stir in oil.

Baked Polenta

Here's another way to reduce the work when making polenta. It is not quite as smooth as the type made in a double boiler. **Makes about 3$\frac{1}{2}$ cups (875 mL), or 4 servings**

- **Preheat oven to 350°F (180°C)**

- **9-inch (23 cm) square baking dish**

Variation

You can start polenta on the stove and finish it in the oven. Bring salted water to a simmer over medium-high heat. Slowly whisk in the cornmeal, then bring to a boil. Scrape it into the baking dish. Shorten the baking time by 5 to 10 minutes.

4 cups	cold water	1 L
1 cup	medium-grind cornmeal	250 mL
1 tsp	kosher salt	5 mL
1 tbsp	extra virgin olive oil	15 mL

1. In baking dish, stir together water, cornmeal and salt. Bake in preheated oven, uncovered, for 45 minutes or until thickened and creamy.

2. Stir in oil. Return to oven and bake for 10 minutes.

Gussy It Up

- Substitute cream for some of the water.
- Use stock instead of water.
- Stir in freshly grated Parmesan.
- Fold in chopped fresh herbs or arugula.
- Sandwich sauce and/or fillings between polenta layers.

✧ Polenta sets as it cools, so you can slice it into shapes. Five ways to make polenta shapes:

- Line a baking pan with a long sheet of oiled foil (the ends should extend beyond the pan). Spread $\frac{1}{2}$ to 1 inch (1 to 2.5 cm) layer of hot polenta in the pan. Refrigerate until set. Use the foil ends to lift out the polenta. Cut it into squares or triangles, or use cookie cutters to create circles or other shapes.

- Make a polenta "pie" in a round cake pan lined with parchment. Once it sets, cut wedges.
- Spread warm polenta in a decorative mold, and let cool.
- Spoon warm polenta into a tube pan with a removable bottom. Let cool, then serve the polenta ring with sauce or meat in the center.
- With moistened hands, pat cooled polenta into balls or roll it.

Better Leftovers

You can turn firm, cold polenta into mushy, warm polenta. Add a bit of boiling water to thin it, whisk vigorously, then place it over the bottom of a double boiler with simmering water. Or purée it in a food processor with a bit of water, then reheat it in the microwave or on the stove. It will thicken as it warms, but won't harden again. This is the best way to deal with thawed frozen polenta squares, which are squishy and rubbery.

> ## Ways to Finish Polenta
>
> - Make it crispy. Fry shapes in butter or oil in a skillet. Or brush them with butter or oil, then grill or broil them, turning once, until they're golden.
> - Make it softer. Warm polenta on a buttered baking sheet in a 375°F (190°C) oven.

✧ To keep polenta from drying out in the fridge, brush the top with soft butter or oil, then cover with plastic wrap.

Cornstarch

> ## Ways to Avoid Lumps
>
> - Make a paste with cornstarch and some of the cold liquid from the recipe. Introduce it by whisk to a hot — not boiling — liquid.
> - Mix cornstarch with some of the sugar and/or salt from the recipe before slowly stirring it into a cold liquid.

Grits

Quick VS. Instant?

There are three types of grits: traditional, quick and instant. Quick grits are ground finer to cook faster. Instant grits are partly cooked, then dried, so you can just add boiling water. Quick and instant grits are bland and relatively smooth.

✧ Grits are dried corn granules. When made from hominy, they're called hominy grits. During grinding, dried,

hulled corn kernels shatter into grits and a lighter cornmeal. The latter is sieved out. Grits may be standard milled or stone-ground.

✧ You can keep grits fresher in the freezer.

Ⓗ is for Hominy

Hominy refers to big, starchy corn kernels, soaked in lye or limewater to loosen and remove the hulls and germs. Hominy grits are sold dried or canned.

✧ Before cooking stone-ground grits, swish them in a bowl of cold water, then skim the chaff (seed casings and other bits of plant debris) that floats to the surface. You can skim with a small sieve or pour it off with some of the water.

✧ Some cooks soak grits before cooking, for tenderness, but this is not common.

✧ Simmer standard grits for at least 30 minutes. Stone-ground grits take 3 to 4 times as long; add liquid as needed.

✧ Stir grits constantly to prevent sticking and stop a skin from forming.

✧ Grits get creamier the longer they cook.

✧ You can prepare grits in a slow cooker.

✧ Grits can be started on the stove and turned into a casserole. Simmer them for about 30 minutes. Stir in some cheese and eggs. Cover and bake at a low temperature, no higher than 325°F (160°C).

Better Leftovers

Grits firm up in the fridge. Cut them into squares or fingers, coat with seasoned flour and deep-fry until a crispy crust forms.

Popcorn

✧ Keep popcorn fresher and more poppable by storing it in the freezer. Bring it to room temperature before popping.

⚛ A Bit of Science

Popcorn may be dried, but it still has to be moist. The water inside the kernel causes it to explode in the heat. Older popcorn is drier, so it doesn't pop as well. One cup (250 mL) popcorn should quadruple in volume.

✧ Popcorn with added moisture works best in a hot-air popper. It may become chewy when popped in oil.

3 Ways to Add Moisture for Fluffier Popcorn

1. Soak kernels in water for 5 to 10 minutes. Drain just before popping.
2. Sprinkle warm water on the kernels 1 hour before popping. Use 2 tbsp (25 mL) water per 1 cup (250 mL) kernels.
3. Put 1 cup (250 mL) popcorn in an airtight plastic storage tub, stir in 1 tbsp (15 mL) water, cover and refrigerate it overnight before popping.

♡ Healthier Eater

• A hot-air popper yields the most healthful snack. But even popping corn in oil in a large pot on the stove is better than using those microwavable bags with nasty trans fats. Check the labels.
• To pep up air-popped corn without adding too many calories, spread it on a baking sheet, spray it with olive oil, then sprinkle on salt and spices.

✧ Strange, but generic popcorn often pops better than a premium brand.

✧ For kettle popcorn, use 4 parts kernels to 1 part oil, rather than the standard 3:1. The popcorn will be drier, lower in calories and fluffier.

Master Plan
Kettle Popcorn

1. In a large pot, heat the oil over medium heat until it is shimmery. Add the kernels and cover.
2. Slip on oven mitts to prevent burns. When you hear the first kernel pop, start shaking the pan. Vent the lid slightly to allow steam to escape, and shake the pan constantly for about 2 minutes or until you hear a 2-second gap between pops.
3. Averting your face from the steam, carefully remove the lid. Immediately pour the popcorn into a large bowl.

✧ To test if the oil is hot enough for popcorn, toss in a kernel. It should immediately dance around and become surrounded by tiny bubbles.

✧ You don't have to measure the oil. Pour enough popcorn kernels into a large pot to loosely cover the bottom in a single layer. Pour in enough oil to barely cover the bottom of the pot. Heat them together. This method takes 3 to $3\frac{1}{2}$ minutes.

Ways to Get Rid of Unpopped Kernels

• Pour popped corn into a deep-fryer basket and shake it. The unpopped kernels will fall out instead of breaking your teeth.
• Using a large skimmer with a loosely woven wire basket, scoop popped corn, shake it to liberate the hard kernels and transfer the popcorn to a large bowl.

✧ For buttery flavor, add about a tablespoon (15 mL) of butter or margarine to the oil when popping corn. Don't use too much; these burn at high temperatures. Don't use light butter or margarine with a high moisture content; it spatters.

✧ Add salt after the kernels have popped; it can toughen the popcorn otherwise.

✧ Put melted butter on popcorn first, then the salt and other dry seasonings. This gives them something to stick to instead of falling to the bottom of the bowl.

Gussy It Up

- Shake in smoked or gourmet sea salt.
- No need for pricey sprinkles. Simply shake in supermarket spice blends. Tex-Mex and Cajun seasonings are good.
- Sprinkle on grated dry Parmesan or powdered Cheddar. The latter is sold in bulk food stores.
- Toss in broken pretzels.

- Combine popcorn with small dried fruits and roasted nuts.
- Mexicans top popcorn with honey, caramel sauce or salsa, as a special treat.
- Caramel corn and similar flavored popcorns are set in the oven. Toss the popped kernels quickly and evenly with caramel until coated. Spread them on a rimmed baking sheet. Heat in a low oven, 250°F to 300°F (120°C to 150°C), stirring often, until crunchy. Store caramel corn in an airtight container at room temperature.

Better Leftovers

To reheat popcorn, put it in large microwave-safe bowl, cover it with a damp paper towel and microwave on High for 1 minute.

Factoid Cooks who ship homemade cookies and breads to loved ones have found that air-popped corn makes great packing material.

Legumes

Bean Math

- One cup (250 mL) dried beans swells to about 3 cups (750 mL) cooked beans.
- About 2½ cups (625 mL) dried beans weigh 1 lb (500 g).
- There are about 1½ cups (375 mL) beans in a 14-oz (398 mL) can and about 2 cups (500 mL) in a 19-oz (540 mL) can.

✧ You can rinse beans in the can. Punch two holes at opposite ends on the top with a church-key opener. Direct running water into one hole. Continue until the water runs almost clear, shaking and draining the can a couple of times.

✧ Place dried beans, lentils and split peas in a sieve set in a bowl. Rinse under running water until the water is no longer foamy.

✧ Soaking lentils and split peas is optional. If you want them to suck up water (and flavor) from the dish, don't soak them. If you do soak them, don't leave them in water for more than a couple of hours; they start to taste sour.

♛ A Golden Rule

For soaking, use 3 cups (750 mL) water per 1 cup (250 mL) dried beans.

✧ Discard any dried beans that float. They may be moldy.

Reasons to Soak Dried Beans Overnight

- It softens them.
- They will hold their shape better when cooked.

Quicker Soaks

- Cover dried beans with cold water, bring to a boil, simmer for 2 minutes, remove them from the heat, cover tightly and let soak for 1 hour. Drain.
- Cover dried beans with the hottest tap water. Cover and let soak for 4 hours. Drain.

⚡ Lightning Won't Strike If ...

You fail to soak dried beans before cooking them. They will, however, take a lot longer to cook.

✧ To the soaking water, add 1 tbsp (15 mL) oil per 1 cup (250 mL) dried beans. The beans will be more tender and the skins less likely to split during long simmering.

✧ Two techniques to help you prepare dried beans more spontaneously:
- Soak, drain and freeze the beans. Cook them as you normally would.
- As an alternative to canned beans, soak and cook an entire package of dried beans. Drain and freeze in can-sized portions.

✧ Cook dried beans over low heat. If they boil too vigorously, the surface will get mushy while the interior remains hard.

✖ No-No

If the cooking water boils off the beans, don't pour in cold water. The skins may burst off. Add boiling water from the kettle.

✧ To test whether beans are done, blow on the skins. They should split.

Bean Doctor

Overcooked beans? Turn them into a dip. Drain them well and purée in the food processor.

❖ Beans cooked with sweet ingredients hold their shape better.

Mythstake

No, salt does not toughen beans. You can add it to the cooking water. Just be moderate.

❖ Even for beans, there comes a time when you should throw them out. The older and drier the beans, the longer they take to cook — never mind the soaking. If they're really old and hard, they can cook all day and stay tough.

❖ To loosen a can-shaped blob of refried beans, mash it with a fork.

3 Ways to Tenderize Legumes

1. Cook them in bottled spring water.
2. Cook until they're softened before adding tomato, wine or other acidic ingredients. These extend the cooking time, prevent softening and toughen the skins.
3. Add baking soda.

Tenderizing Legumes with Baking Soda

- Add baking soda to the soaking water for beans or dried chickpeas (especially those destined to become falafels).
- Add baking soda to the cooking water for beans. Use about 1 tsp (5 mL) baking soda per 2 to 3 cups (500 to 750 mL)

soaked beans. This softens the skins dramatically.

- Bring canned legumes to a boil in their liquid with baking soda. Use 1 tsp (5 mL) baking soda per 19-oz (540 mL) can. Immediately drain and rinse. Proceed with your recipe. This is a great way to make fluffier hummus.

❖ You can make bean flour by pulverizing dried beans in a coffee grinder, then straining. Use it to thicken or fortify dishes.

☼ Healthier Eater

Moisten a sandwich sans mayo or butter. Mash cannellini beans (white kidney beans) with a little olive oil and use this as a sandwich spread.

❖ Before using Chinese fermented black beans, rinse and chop them.

6 Ways to Reduce Gas

1. The longer beans soak, the less flatulence they cause.
2. Blanch beans in boiling water, drain right away and rinse in cold water. (This will also reduce the amount of scum.)
3. Discard the soaking water. Always cook beans in fresh water.
4. If using canned beans, drain and rinse them. Never use the liquid in the can.
5. Add a pinch of baking soda to beans while they cook.
6. Chew a supplement called Beano just before eating. It contains an enzyme that breaks down complex sugars to make them more digestible. (The Beano solution applies to any food with lots of fiber.)

- To peel cooked or canned chickpeas, put them in a bowl of cold water and rub the skins with your fingers. They should float to the top. Pour off the water with the skins.

- If hummus is too thick, stir in some warm water or lemon juice.

- The cooking time for lentils varies according to their freshness, so be prepared to wait. Fresher lentils will be ready faster.

L is for Lentils du Puy

These are premium lentils that hold their shape better when cooked. Small and dark green, they are also known as French lentils.

- For brighter lentils, blanch them in boiling water and rinse them before cooking.

My Best Hummus

This beloved recipe has evolved over the years. **Makes 2¼ cups (550 mL)**

Tip

Tahini is sesame seed paste. It is sold in many supermarkets.

1	can (19 oz/540 mL) chickpeas	1
1 tsp	baking soda	5 mL
4	cloves garlic	4
¼ cup	tahini	50 mL
2 tbsp	extra virgin olive oil, divided	25 mL
3 to 4 tbsp	freshly squeezed lemon juice (1 lemon)	45 to 60 mL
3 to 4 tbsp	hot water	45 to 60 mL
Pinch	cayenne pepper	Pinch
¼ tsp	kosher or sea salt	1 mL
⅛ tsp	freshly ground black pepper	0.5 mL
	Chopped fresh cilantro	
	Whole black olives	

1. Pour chickpeas and their liquid into a small pan. Stir in baking soda. Bring to a boil over high heat. As soon as the foam rises and large bubbles begin to form, remove from heat. Drain and rinse immediately under cold water. Drain well.

2. In a blender, pulse garlic until minced. Add chickpeas, tahini and 1 tbsp (15 mL) of the oil; purée until a coarse paste forms. Add 3 tbsp (45 mL) each lemon juice and hot water, cayenne, salt and black pepper. Blend on high until smooth and fluffy and the color has turned from tan to lighter café au lait. Add the remaining lemon juice, if desired. Adjust thickness by adding the remaining water, if desired.

3. Scrape into a shallow bowl. Drizzle with the remaining oil. Sprinkle with cilantro to taste. Scatter olives over top.

Nuts and Seeds

✧ The best storage containers for nuts are their own shells.

✧ The oils in nuts and seeds make them go rancid quickly in the cupboard. Store them in the fridge or freezer. You can freeze nuts right in their shells.

A Bad Sign

If nuts rattle in their shells, they are old and dry.

✧ Frozen nuts and seeds needn't be thawed before using, unless you are adding them to a batter.

4 Ways to Brown Nuts and Seeds

1. For the most even color, roast them on a rimmed baking sheet in a 300°F (150°C) oven until barely golden. Shake the sheet and/or turn the nuts a few times with a spatula. You can preheat the baking sheet for speedier results.
2. Toast them in a roomy skillet over medium heat until they start to become brown and fragrant. Shake the skillet frequently.
3. Brown them in a toaster oven.
4. Use the microwave. Spread the nuts or seeds on a glass plate. Microwave on High, stirring once every minute, until they are golden. Hazelnuts and cashews brown in about 5 minutes, sunflower seeds in about 3 minutes.

✧ Tough nut to crack? Pour boiling water over hard cases, such as Brazil nuts, then let them soak for 10 minutes.

✧ To get rid of shell fragments, swish cracked nuts in a bowl of cold water. Skim the bits of shell that float.

✧ To skin hazelnuts and peanuts, first roast them in a 350°F (180°C) oven for 10 to 20 minutes. Wrap the warm nuts in a kitchen towel and rub vigorously.

✧ Watch carefully. The color of nuts and seeds continues to deepen after they are removed from the heat. They can go from browned to burned in a blink, so transfer them from the baking sheet or skillet right away.

✧ No matter what the recipe says, toast nuts before chopping them, not after. Chopped nuts toast unevenly and the finer particles burn.

OUTSIDE THE BOX

You can roast nuts in their shells. In a 375°F (190°C) oven, walnuts are ready in 15 to 20 minutes. Hazelnuts, almonds and smaller nuts will take less time. To test, crack open one roasted nut. If it's still pale, return the nuts to the oven. Let them cool before serving.

Reasons to Roast Nuts in Their Shells

• They smell and taste better.
• They are easier to crack.

- For extra flavor, you can toast nuts before baking with them. But think twice. They'll be fine in muffins, but will scorch in a pecan pie.

- Get rid of the fine crumbs in a batch of chopped nuts by shaking them in a sieve. Your cake will be tidier, your curry less gritty.

Better Spiced Cocktail Nuts

- To help the seasonings stick, first stir nuts with egg white or simple syrup until coated.
- If you're using egg white, drain the nuts well before dumping them into the spice mixture.
- Embellish by using maple syrup or honey instead of simple syrup.
- Toss the coated nuts with the spice mixture in a large plastic bag.
- Roast the nuts in a single layer, well spread out.
- Cool the nuts completely before storing, or they will be chewy.

Master Plan
Candied Nuts

1. In a pan, stir together 1 cup (250 mL) each water and sugar. Bring to a boil over high heat.
2. Add nuts. Reduce heat to medium-high and simmer until golden and crispy, but not brown (about 15 minutes for walnuts). Watch closely after 10 minutes; they can burn suddenly. Drain.
3. Fill a small pan halfway with vegetable oil. Over medium-high heat, bring to about 350°F (180°C). In batches if necessary, add nuts and fry, stirring constantly, until brown (2 to 3 minutes for walnuts).
4. Using a skimmer, transfer nuts to a rimmed baking sheet lined with parchment. Sprinkle with salt and/or spices. Let cool.

- For spicy candied nuts, add 1 tsp (5 mL) cayenne pepper to the syrup.

Making Do

Need unsalted nuts, but have only salted ones? Rinse them under cold water and pat dry.

- Grind nuts with some of the sugar from the recipe so they don't get oily or clumpy.

Almonds

How to Blanch Almonds

1. Put whole almonds into a bowl. Cover with boiling water, then soak for 2 to 3 minutes. Drain. Rinse under cold water. Drain well.
2. Dump them onto a kitchen towel and rub vigorously to loosen the skins. For a good grip, use a square of paper towel or the corner of the kitchen towel. Dip your fingers occasionally into cold water, as the skins are sticky.

- To soften almond paste or marzipan, zap it in the microwave for a couple of seconds.

Almond Paste VS. Marzipan?

Almond paste is an ingredient. Marzipan is a confection. Almond paste is blended from blanched almonds and sugar, and maybe glycerin to keep it supple, maybe almond extract to boost the flavor. Almond paste is used in confections, such as rum balls. It is also used to make marzipan. In that case, more sugar, as well as dye, is blended in. Egg whites are added to bind the marzipan and keep it pliable. Marzipan's finer texture allows it to be molded or rolled into cake decorations and fanciful shapes. It's cute when it mimics fruit.

- ❖ Wrap almond paste and marzipan in plastic, then seal it in a zip-lock bag.

Chestnuts

Chestnut **VS.** Horse Chestnut?

Chestnuts are housed in shiny brown shells covered by bristly pods, or burrs. The meat looks like a tiny brain. Consumers are most familiar with the fine marron, which has one nut in each burr. The cheaper châtaigne has two or three. Don't bother trying to eat the chestnuts that fall off that tree down the street. They are horse chestnuts — hard and bitter.

- ❖ Two lbs (1 kg) chestnuts in the shell yield 1 lb (500 g) shelled chestnuts.

Three Good Signs

- Look for smooth, glossy shells.
- Squeeze the shell to make sure it is firm and full.
- Choose large, heavy chestnuts.

Two Bad Signs

- Holes are signs of insect activity.
- Watch out for spots of mold.

- ❖ Store chestnuts in an airtight container in the fridge, not in a bowl or plastic bag on the counter.

Reasons to Slit the Shells Before Roasting

- It vents steam and prevents explosions.
- The chestnuts will cook faster.
- They will be easier to peel.

- ❖ Use a small serrated knife to slit the shell. Slash. Don't cut deeply. Two ways to slit the shell:
  - Slash an X across the top of the flat side.
  - Cut a slit all the way around the equator.

- ❖ Roast chestnuts, slit side up, until the cuts gape.

4 Ways to Cook Chestnuts

1. Roast them on a rimmed baking sheet in a 400°F (200°C) oven for 15 to 20 minutes.
2. Microwave them on a plate, 6 at a time, on High for 30 to 60 seconds.
3. Boil them in lightly salted water for 10 to 20 minutes or until tender.
4. Roast them in a cast-iron pan over the proverbial open fire, preferably while singing carols.

is for Tan

The tan is the brown, furry skin clinging to the meat of the chestnut. The shell must be removed and the stubborn tan peeled off while the chestnut is hot.

Ways to Make Chestnuts Easier to Peel

- Condition them with oil before roasting. Place the chestnuts in an ovenproof skillet over high heat. Drizzle with oil (1 tsp/5 mL oil per 1 lb/500 g chestnuts) and shake until coated. Transfer to a hot oven. Roast, then peel one at a time.
- Boil chestnuts, a few at a time. Remove them, one at a time, to peel.
- Wrap roasted chestnuts in a kitchen towel and let stand for 5 minutes to soften the skins.
- If the tan seems hopelessly stuck, dunk shelled chestnuts into boiling water for 1 minute.

Is It Done?

* Insert a metal skewer into one chestnut via the slit. The flesh should be soft and golden.

* You can boil peeled chestnuts in water or milk. Then mash, if desired. This is also a remedy for leathery chestnuts or a prelude to puréeing.

Substitutes for Fresh Chestnuts

* Vacuum-packed chestnuts. They are the best substitutes.
* Canned or bottled chestnuts. These are sometimes bathed in syrup.
* Dried chestnuts. Soak these overnight, then simmer before using.

How to Make Chestnut Purée

1. Soften the chestnuts, if necessary. Work on them while they are warm.
2. Chop them in a food processor.
3. Push them through a sturdy strainer, food mill or potato ricer.

⫶Fast Fix

Save yourself the work and buy plain, canned chestnut purée. Beware: Some brands are sweetened and flavored with vanilla.

ⓒ is for Chestnut Flour

Chestnut flour may be made from raw or dried chestnuts. Use it as a thickener, an unusual ingredient in pancakes or quick breads, or in gluten-free recipes. In baking, you can replace up to one-quarter of the white flour with chestnut flour, but experimentation is required. Freeze chestnut flour; it goes rancid quickly.

Pistachios

* You can buy shelled pistachios in bulk food stores.

Red VS. Beige?

Once upon a time, pistachio shells were dyed red to hide stains and to stand out in vending machines. Modern harvesting methods eliminated the stains. As for consumers, most of us prefer to eat pistachios without being caught red-handed.

Factoid Don't crack a tooth for nothing. Closed pistachios are immature. As a pistachio kernel grows, it expands until its shell splits.

Nut Butters

* Once natural peanut butter, another nut butter or sesame seed paste (tahini) has separated, stirring the oil back into the solids requires strength, patience and a tolerance for messy jobs. It's easiest to prevent it from happening in the first place.

Remedies for Separation Anxiety

* Turn the jar upside down overnight. Stir the nut butter. Flip and stir regularly.
* Store nut butters in the fridge. The oil will become more viscous and less likely to separate and seep to the top.
* Scrape separated nut butter into the food processor and pulse.

* Mice seem to like peanut butter better than cheese. Smear it on a trap.

KID STUFF

Serve a peanut butter and banana sandwich like a hotdog. Put a whole banana in a toasted hot dog bun smeared with peanut butter.

Flaxseeds

 Healthier Eater

To obtain the benefits of flaxseeds, grind them before using. Otherwise, they go in one end and out the other. You can pulverize flaxseeds in a coffee/spice grinder. Or buy ground flaxseed.

Poppy Seeds

3 Ways to Tenderize Poppy Seeds

1. Cover them with warm milk from the recipe and soak for at least 1 hour.
2. Some European ladies swear by grinding them.
3. They can be steamed, then crushed.

✧ Tenderize poppy seeds before baking cakes or muffins.

✧ The best poppy seeds have a bluish tinge.

✧ You can boost the flavor by toasting poppy seeds in a dry skillet over medium heat until fragrant.

Sesame Seeds

✧ Sesame seeds are usually beige, but don't be alarmed if you see brown, red or black ones.

Ways to Intensify the Flavor of Sesame Seeds

• Spread them on a rimmed baking sheet. Toast in a 350°F (180°C) oven, stirring often, for 5 to 7 minutes.
• Toast them in a small skillet over medium heat until they turn golden and become fragrant, 2 to 5 minutes.
• Crush them between your fingers to release the fragrant oils. This is easiest with toasted or frozen sesame seeds.

 is for Tahini

Sesame seed paste originating in the Middle East is called tahini.

✧ Tahini separates, so stir it well before measuring.

✧ Tahini solids can turn into cement when the oil separates out. Put chunks into the blender with some oil or hot water, then pulse until smooth. (You can do the same with natural peanut butter.)

✧ When mixing tahini sauce, use a blender or a food processor. A whisk won't get it smooth enough. The blender makes it smoothest, but is harder to scrape clean.

Fats

Animal VS. Plant?

Unsaturated oils from plant sources are considered healthier to eat than saturated fats from animals. Unsaturated fats are divided into polyunsaturated, such as safflower oil, or monounsaturated, such as olive oil.

❤ Healthier Eater

There are "good fats" and "bad fats." The baddies include shortening and lard. "Good fats" include fish oil, olive oil, avocado oil and canola oil. Just don't go hog wild with these, or you'll fatten up like one. All fats have the same amount of calories.

Solid VS. Liquid?

Saturated fats, such as butter and lard, are solid at room temperature. They mainly come from animal sources, but the group includes tropical oils such as coconut and palm kernel oils. Unsaturated fats, or oils, are liquid at room temperature. In the fridge, they become sluggish, but not solid.

Ⓗ is for Hydrogenation

Hydrogenation creates a hybrid. Hydrogen molecules are pumped into liquid fat to turn it into solid fat such as margarine and shortening. Hydrogenation produces the most evil fats, the trans fats. So why do it? Trans fats are cheaper than butter, extend the shelf life of processed foods and make products creamier or crisper. Consumer disgust has spurred the development of margarines without trans fats. Check labels. Note that trans fats do occur naturally, but in trace amounts.

Ⓕ is for Fractionated

Fractionated oils may be separated into their fatty-acid components to produce thinner and thicker oils. Thicker fractionated oil may be a substitute for hydrogenated oil full of trans fat. Thinner fractionated oil has the advantage of remaining soft and flowing in the cold, not sluggish.

Butter

✧ The butter keeper in the fridge door is actually a bad place to store butter. Butter should be kept colder and tightly wrapped.

A Bad Sign

Stale butter looks darker on the surface.

✧ Store butter in an airtight tub or wrap it in foil. It tends to absorb odors or flavors from the fridge.

Ways to Freeze Butter

- Wrap sticks in foil. After freezing, break or cut off chunks.
- Cut it into pats. Freeze the pats on a tray. Transfer them into a plastic tub, separating layers with parchment.

Ⓑ is for Butter Bell

Butter keeps better when sealed with water. That's the principle behind the butter bell, or crock. Butter at room temperature is pressed into the domed lid. The dome holds about ½ cup (125 mL). It sits in a base filled with cool water. The butter remains spreadable, but doesn't go bad as quickly.

- Change the water in a butter bell every second day.
- To flavor the butter, you can add garlic or herbs to the water.

Making Do

You can improvise a butter bell. Push softened butter into a rounded ramekin or teacup and invert that into a small bowl of water.

Ways to Cut Butter

- To get a couple of tablespoons (25 mL), cut right through the foil wrapper of a stick of butter. Return the rest of the wrapped stick to the fridge.
- Use a sharp knife to score each tablespoon (15 mL) mark printed on the wrapper. Unwrap and cut as needed.
- To cut a package of butter into even cubes, start by cutting it lengthwise into 4 same-size sticks. Slice each stick lengthwise into thirds. Turn the stick so the slices are stacked. Cut the stack lengthwise into thirds. Cut the thirds crosswise into cubes. Repeat with the remaining sticks.
- If you need tiny cubes to dot a casserole or pie, it's faster to shred very cold butter with a box grater, then sprinkle it on.

✧ To cut a block of butter straight from the fridge, run the knife under hot tap water for a few seconds. The cuts will be tidier.

Salted VS. Unsalted?

Butter is about 80% fat. The rest is water and milk solids. Salt is added to butter to preserve it and make it tastier. Salted butter is best as a spread. Unsalted is best for cooking.

✧ Unsalted butter doesn't last as long as salted butter. You can freeze it.

Reasons to Cook with Unsalted Butter

- The flavor is more pure.
- It has less moisture.
- It scorches less readily.

- You have more control over the amount of salt in your food.
- In baking, salt toughens glutens and frightens yeast.
- Salt masks rancidity.

✧ Different brands have different levels of salt, from 1% to 3%. Generally, if you substitute salted butter for unsalted, cut the salt in the recipe by $\frac{1}{2}$ to 1 tsp (2 to 5 mL) per 1 cup (250 mL) butter.

C is for Cultured

Plain butter is made with pasteurized cream. Cultured butter is ripened, or matured, by adding bacteria that produces lactic acid, which adds a bit of tang.

6 Ways to Soften Butter Quickly

1. Chop it into bits, arrange in a single layer and let stand at room temperature for about 10 minutes.
2. Shred refrigerated or frozen butter with a box grater and let stand at room temperature.
3. Microwave it. Zap an unwrapped 4-oz (125 g) stick on Medium-Low (30%) for 1 minute. If you cut the stick into 4 chunks, it'll take about 45 seconds. Err on the side of hardness. The butter may hold its shape, but be molten inside. If you see puddling, you've zapped it too long.
4. Put wrapped butter in a zip-lock bag and immerse it in hot tap water.
5. Cut it into chunks. Warm a fork by dipping it into boiling water, then press it onto the chunks.
6. Is the butter too cold to spread on your toast? Shave it with a cheese slicer.

◆ Store butter curls, balls and molded shapes in an airtight tub of cold water in the fridge.

◆ When making curls, the butter should be firm, but not too cold. Otherwise, the curls will crack. You can dip the curler into warm water before using it. If your curls aren't perfect, finish twisting each ribbon quickly by hand.

◆ Serve curls, balls or shapes on crushed ice or, better, on a rack over ice.

© is for Compound

Compound butter is the fancy name for flavored butter. You can add almost anything to softened butter. Roasted garlic and herbs are favorites. A more unusual combo is honey and sea salt.

Master Plan
Compound Butter

1. Soften butter to room temperature.
2. Blend in herbs and seasonings with a fork.
3. Center the butter blend on a square of parchment or plastic wrap. If it is too soft to be rolled, refrigerate it briefly. Otherwise, roll it into a cylinder. Twist the ends or seal them with elastic bands.
4. Refrigerate until firm. Roll the cylinder occasionally to maintain the shape.
5. To use the butter, slice off coins.

◆ A better way to make herb butter: Coarsely chop the herbs. Add the butter and continue chopping. This prevents the herbs from darkening and there's less mixing work.

♻ Waste Not

Save butter wrappers for greasing cake pans, baking sheets and griddles. Fold the wrappers and stash them in a zip-lock snack bag in the fridge. Before using, rub a wrapper between your palms to soften the butter.

◆ Instead of brushing a pan or griddle with butter, you can hold a stick by the wrapper and rub it over the cooking surface.

© is for Clarified

When butter is clarified, the oily part is extracted and the milk solids and moisture are discarded. Clarified butter will endure higher heat without burning.

Easy Ways to Clarify Butter

• In a small saucepan, melt butter over low heat, then remove it from the heat and let stand for 30 minutes. Skim any foam. Carefully pour off the oily top layer. Discard the milk solids at the bottom.

• In a small saucepan, melt butter over medium-low heat until it starts to bubble. The foam will turn white, then start to brown. When you start to see brown bits clinging to the bottom of the pan, remove the pan from the heat. Strain the butter through a fine sieve lined with cheesecloth.

• In a small saucepan, melt butter over medium-low heat. Gently simmer for 2 minutes. Remove from heat and let cool. Cover and refrigerate overnight. Poke a hole near the edge and drain off the milky liquid.

• Melt butter in a bowl in the microwave on High until foamy and hot, about 1 minute for ½ cup (125 mL). Remove it from the microwave and let stand until firm. Poke a hole in the top and drain off the milky liquid.

• Use the Defrost setting to melt the butter in a bowl. Remove it from the microwave and let stand for about 5 minutes or until separated. Skim any foam. Pour out the clear oil. Discard the milk solids at the bottom.

- Use unsalted butter to make clarified butter.

- Instead of brushing butter onto dough and the like, you can spray on clarified butter with an oil mister. Prevent it from going sluggish by setting the mister in a bowl of hot water.

Ⓖ is for Ghee

Indian clarified butter is called ghee. It is simmered to evaporate all the moisture and to brown the milk solids. This gives it a nutty flavor. In some cities, ghee is easier to find in supermarkets than standard clarified butter.

- Half a cup (125 mL) unsalted butter yields about $\frac{1}{3}$ cup (75 mL) browned or clarified butter.

- Butter burns easily. When frying with it, keep the heat low and add some oil to stop it from browning too much.

Master Plan
Browned Butter

1. In a small skillet, warm butter over medium heat until it starts to bubble. Beware of eruptions; the water in the butter may spurt up from the bottom of the pan.

2. Once the foam subsides, the milk solids coagulate into specks that change from white to deep brown in 8 to 10 minutes. When the butter is fully brown, but not black, remove it from the heat and strain immediately. Browned butter can burn in the blink of an eye.

- Use a shiny pan for browning butter so you can assess the color of the milk solids.

- You can make homemade butter on purpose or discover how by accident after overbeating cream. It tastes clean, clear and light. It goes rancid quickly, so keep it refrigerated.

Homemade Blender Butter

Homemade butter tastes so fresh and is easy to make — no churner required. **Makes about $\frac{1}{2}$ cup (125 mL)**

Tip
This works well with any heavy cream. I tested it with whipping (35%) cream.

1 cup	heavy or whipping (35%) cream	250 mL
$\frac{1}{2}$ cup	ice water	125 mL
	Salt (optional)	

1. In a blender, blend cream on high for about 15 seconds. Add ice water and blend on high until butter globules rise to the top.

2. Line a sieve with cheesecloth and place over a medium bowl. Scrape blender contents into the sieve. Let drain for 30 to 45 minutes. Press out any extra moisture.

3. Transfer butter to a small airtight plastic tub. Stir in salt to taste (if using). Keep refrigerated up to a week.

Homemade Beaten Butter

Don't cry over curdled, excessively whipped cream. Keep going and make butter.
Makes about $1/2$ cup (125 mL)

Tip
I used whipping (35%) cream. Any kind of heavy cream will work.

1 cup	heavy or whipping (35%) cream	250 mL
	Salt (optional)	

1. Pour cream into a large bowl. Using an electric mixer, beat on high speed, beyond stiff peaks, until yellow, clumpy and watery. Keep beating until clumps cling to the bowl and milky liquid collects in the center, about 10 minutes using a heavy-duty stand mixer, longer using a regular or hand mixer.

2. Line a sieve with cheesecloth and place it over a medium bowl. Scrape the beaten cream into the sieve and let drain for 30 to 45 minutes.

3. Gather the cheesecloth into a bundle. Squeeze it to extract the last bit of liquid and compact the butter.

4. Transfer to a small airtight plastic tub. Stir in salt to taste (if using). Keep refrigerated up to a week.

✿ Waste Not

• Keep the milky residue drained from homemade butter to use in coffee or for cooking.

❖ If you want to replace regular butter with whipped butter in baking or cooking, measure by weight rather than volume.

♡ Healthier Eater

• Whipped butter is aerated to stretch it out, so a little goes a long way, which dieters may appreciate.
• You can stretch butter even more (and cut calories) by whipping it with milk and gelatin.

Margarine

❖ Margarine is an emulsion of refined oil and water, with milk products, salt, colorants and vitamins. For baking, it has little to recommend it.

Mythstake

Margarine is reviled, but there's no truth in the tale that it was originally created to fatten turkeys — which all died. It was actually invented by French chemist Hippolyte Mège-Mouriés. In 1869, he won the French emperor's competition for the best butter substitute.

Block VS. Tub?

The softer the margarine, the less trans fat. Whenever possible, go for the spreadable margarine in tubs rather than the hard blocks like butter.

❖ Margarine must be refrigerated.

❖ To keep soft tub margarine firmer, you can freeze it.

Stretched Butter

Frugal homemakers and calorie-watchers may prefer to "stretch" their butter supplies.
Makes about 2 cups (500 mL)

Tip

Serve this at room temperature. If it's too firm for your liking, reduce the amount of gelatin.

1 cup	unsalted butter	250 mL
2 tbsp	unflavored gelatin powder	25 mL
1 cup	whole milk	250 mL
	Salt (optional)	

1. Place butter in a large bowl and let stand at room temperature until softened but still cool to the touch.

2. Pour milk into a measuring cup, sprinkle with gelatin and let soften for 5 to 10 minutes. Transfer to the top of a double boiler, over simmering water. Heat, stirring to dissolve gelatin, until barely warm. Remove from heat and let cool to room temperature.

3. Using an electric mixer on medium speed, gradually add the milk mixture to the butter, mixing until blended. Increase speed to high and whip until fluffy and smooth, with no visible globules. Stir in salt to taste (if using).

4. Pour into molds, cover and refrigerate up to a week.

 Healthier Eater

Look for the newer non-hydrogenated brands of margarine.

Rendered Fat

 is for Cracklings

Cracklings are the connective tissues and other solids left after fat is rendered. The term is most often used in connection with pork or duck.

❖ Rendering involves heating solid chunks of saturated fat or fatty meat to extract liquid fat, also known as drippings. Rendering is out of fashion, but remains popular among some Europeans. They do it to make tasty spreads and cooking fat. Rendering also occurs naturally during roasting.

Master Plan
Rendered Fat

1. Dice fat or fatty meat and place in a small skillet.

2. Add a small amount of water, say ½ cup (125 mL). Heat slowly over medium-low heat, pressing the fat occasionally with the back of a spoon or, better still, a potato masher. Do not let the drippings smoke or burn.

3. When the cracklings are browned and firm and the water has evaporated, remove from heat.

4. While the rendered fat is still warm, strain it through a sieve lined with cheesecloth and placed over a bowl. You can eat the cracklings.

5. Keep the rendered fat refrigerated or frozen.

L is for Lard

Lard is the best-known rendered fat. Soft and silky, it is rendered from pork. Some cooks still swear by it for frying. It's supposed to make flakier pie crusts and biscuits, too, but is not suitable for cakes.

✧ Lard has its advocates because it contains less saturated fat than butter. Some supermarket lards were hydrogenated, but manufacturers seem to have ceased and desisted. Check the package; you don't want a double whammy of saturated and trans fats.

S is for Suet

Suet is the solid white fat from an animal. The term is used most often in connection with beef. Beef suet is chopped and used in steamed English puddings. Drippings are also rendered from suet.

✧ The best types of suet and lard come from around the kidneys.

S is for Schmaltz

The drippings rendered from chicken fat are called schmaltz. (The term is sometimes applied to goose or duck fat, too.) Schmaltz is sold in butcher and specialty shops, but you can easily make it at home from fat pulled out of a chicken.

Ways to Save Rendered Duck Fat

- If you're searing the breast or leg, pour off the drippings halfway through the cooking time, or the fat will start to burn. It goes from clear white to golden. The less color, the better.
- If you are roasting a whole duck, suck out drippings frequently with a baster, or tilt the pan and ladle them out.

OUTSIDE THE BOX

Make a play on beurre manié, a sauce thickener usually made with butter, by mixing schmaltz and flour into a paste. Roll it into balls and freeze them.

Shortening

✧ Shortening is a soft fat made with refined oil. It is usually hydrogenated and aerated — great for baking, bad for your health. However, a type without trans fat has been developed.

✧ Shortening can be stored at room temperature.

Oils

Answers to Pressing Questions

- Oils are pressed from nuts, seeds, vegetables and fruit. For some, particularly nut or sesame oils, the nuts and seeds are roasted before pressing.
- "Expeller-pressed" is the term for oil obtained simply by squeezing and straining in a mechanical press. The friction can heat the machinery and start to cook the oil. When oil is pressed without excessive heat, it is called "cold-pressed." Water may be used to cool the machinery.
- "First cold-pressed" is put on olive oil labels to impress. It dates back to a time when presses could extract less than half the oil from a batch of olives. So hot water was added to the pulp and the producer took a second whack at it. Modern presses extract the majority of the oil the first time around.
- "Expeller-pressed" and "cold-pressed" are usually used in reference to higher-quality nut and seed oils, and olive oil.

- Simple pressing doesn't efficiently remove all the oil and doesn't work on every type of grain or seed. Manufacturers turn to heat and solvents to extract every drop.

✧ Do you need cooking oil or flavoring oil? It's ideal to keep one generic cooking oil (refined) and several flavoring oils (unrefined) in your pantry.

Refined **VS.** Unrefined?

Oils are either filtered in their crude state or refined. Unrefined oils taste and smell like their source. Refined oils are stripped, neutralized and deodorized. The payoff: They stand up to higher temperatures and have a longer shelf life. Many oils, such as peanut and olive oils, come in refined and unrefined versions.

✧ Unrefined oils taste distinctive. Drizzle them on dishes as a finishing touch. They generally don't stand up well to the heat of cooking. Extra virgin olive oil is an exception, but you must still lower the temperature.

10 Uses for Unrefined Oils

(Particularly delicate nut and seed oils)
1. In salad dressings
2. In sauces
3. Drizzled over steamed vegetables
4. In or over mashed potatoes
5. Drizzled over polenta
6. Stirred into rice (especially with herbs)
7. Swirled in a pleasing pattern over soup
8. As a dip for crusty bread
9. Over yogurt for breakfast
10. Drizzled over ice cream

✧ To pep up a boring refined oil, such as canola, add a few olives (preferably oil-cured). Store it in the refrigerator.

✧ Two reasons refined oils are perfect for frying and long cooking:
- They have undergone flavor lobotomies.
- They have higher smoke points.

✧ Oil can combust on its own. If it starts to smoke, immediately remove it from the heat.

S is for Smoke Point

Smoking is a bad habit when it comes to cooking, too. The smoke point is the temperature at which a fat starts to break down. It emits nasty chemicals and bad smells, and threatens to catch on fire. So ignore recipes that tell you to heat oil until it smokes.

✧ The smoke point of a fat depends on the type and how it was processed. Smoke points range from about 225°F to 520°F (107°C to 270°C).

F is for Flash Point

This is the temperature at which a fat will ignite when the vapor meets a flame. The smoke point warns you that the flash point is approaching.

✧ Avocado oil is usually noted as the oil with the highest smoke point, but grapeseed oil is vying for the title. Corn, peanut, safflower and soybean oils also have high smoke points.

C is for Canola

There is no such plant. Healthful canola oil is extracted from a type of rapeseed. The name is a blend of the words "Canada" and "oil."

✧ Safflower oil is touted for salad dressing because it doesn't turn to sludge in the fridge.

✧ Coconut oil is waxy and solid at room temperature. It is extracted from dried coconut flesh. Though saturated, it is sometimes dubbed a "good fat" because of the source.

Palm Fruit **VS.** Palm Kernel?

Red palm fruit oil is not to be confused with its cousin, palm kernel oil. The latter is extracted from palm nuts. Palm oils are high in saturated fat. Palm fruit oil, however, has far less saturated fat and is filled with healthy carotenoids (antioxidants).

✧ You can buy a blend of palm fruit oil and canola to give dishes a golden glow. Use it on an egg white omelet or brush it onto poultry.

🌸 *Being Green*

If you see a generic label that says "vegetable oil," the product likely includes soybean oil. Soybeans are one of the world's most genetically manipulated crops.

Going Nuts

✧ Unrefined nut oils are as wildly delicious as they are wildly expensive. Add them to cooked food at the last minute. Buy unrefined nut oils — such as walnut, almond, hazelnut, peanut and pistachio — in tiny quantities. Three reasons to buy these oils in small bottles:
- They are pricey.
- They taste and smell so distinctive and intense that a little goes a long way.
- They go rancid quickly.

✧ Oils pressed from roasted nuts (as opposed to simple dried nuts) keep longer and taste stronger. However, you should still store them in the fridge.

✧ You can dilute precious roasted nut oil with canola oil, half and half, without ruining its effect — particularly for salad dressings.

Making Do

To mimic roasted nut oil, blend toasted nuts with a neutral oil.

1. Put toasted nuts (such as walnuts, pecans, hazelnuts or cashews) and a mild oil (such as canola) in a small saucepan. Use equal quantities of nuts and oil; 1 cup (250 mL) of each will yield $\frac{1}{2}$ cup (125 mL) of nut oil.
2. Gently simmer over medium heat for 5 minutes.
3. Purée the mixture in a food processor.
4. Pour it into a sieve lined with cheesecloth set over a bowl. Let it drip through, stirring occasionally with a small spoon or spatula to loosen the solids. This can take all day.
5. The resulting oil will be cloudy. If you want it less sludgy, purée the mixture more coarsely.
6. Save the aromatic solids. You can add them to curry or baked goods.

Sesame **VS.** Toasted Sesame Oil?

Dark Asian sesame oil is made from toasted sesame seeds. It comes in small bottles for a reason. This oil is not meant for frying. Use it sparingly as a seasoning in stir-fries, marinades, sauces and dips. If you do apply heat, be brief. It burns easily. Regular, clear, light sesame oil is fine for cooking and salads. It can be found mainly in health food shops.

✧ Grapeseed oil is the darling of chefs. It is extracted from grape seeds, particularly those left over from winemaking. This type of oil offers a pleasing whiff of grape.

Healthier Eater

Flaxseed oil is the richest plant source of omega-3 fatty acids. Linseed oil is another name for it. Be judicious with flaxseed oil. It is strong-tasting, plus you should consume no more than 1 to 3 tbsp (15 to 45 mL) a day. In higher doses, it can cause diarrhea or other health effects. Treat flaxseed oil as a dietary supplement. It is not suitable for cooking.

✧ Hempseed oil is made from the seeds of the cannabis plant, but doesn't contain the compound that makes marijuana smokers high. Hempseed oil is fine for dressings and sauces, but not for frying.

Grades of Olive Oil

✧ Olive oils are graded according to their acidity. The better the oil, the lower the percentage of oleic acid (a type of fatty acid). How the oil tastes, how it was pressed and whether it was subjected to heat and chemicals also play a part in the grading. Six grades of olive oil, in descending order:
- Extra virgin
- Virgin
- Fino (a blend of extra virgin and virgin oils)
- Olive oil (a blend of refined and virgin oils)
- Pomace
- Lampante

✧ Premium extra virgin oils are called estate or artisanal oils.

P is for Pizzicante

This Italian term describes a peppery tingling at the back of your throat. It is a sign of a fine olive oil.

Two Bad Signs

- Fine olive oil will have green highlights, but turns more golden over time. It should not be a vibrant green after a year.
- Cucumber or banana odors are signs of rancidity.

Mythstakes

- Olive oil does not have to be olive green. The color can range from champagne to deep green. It depends on the color of the olives when they were harvested. Olives change color as they ripen. Sometimes leaves are tossed in with the olives to give the oil a vibrant hue.
- No, the best olive oil is not necessarily from Italy. It may come from top producers such as Spain and Greece, or places as far-flung as Tunisia or New Zealand. In North America, California makes the best olive oils. It's better to judge an olive oil by the grade, brand and production methods than its source.

9 Potential Qualities of Artisanal Olive Oils

1. They're made from olives from a single grove.
2. They're made using a single variety of olive.
3. The olives are not harvested all at once, but only picked when ready.
4. The olives are picked green, just on the verge of ripening.
5. They are kept cool, below room temperature, while waiting at the mill.
6. They are pressed right after picking or, if held for a short time, kept cool at about 60°F (16°C).
7. Stems and leaves are removed before the olives are pressed.
8. The olives are pitted before pressing. Pits yield a lot of oil, but can impart bitterness.
9. The trip from the mill to the bottle takes only a few hours.

✤ If the label says "virgin," the oil is pressed and unrefined.

Ⓟ is for Pomace

Pomace is the pulp left after oil is extracted from the olives. Solvents are used to extract more oil from the pomace, then a bit of virgin oil is mixed in. Pomace oil is rarely seen in stores, but is used commercially.

Ⓛ is for Lampante

Lampante is made by refining defective or rancid olive oil, so is not suitable for consumption. In ancient times, it was used as lamp oil.

✤ Olive oil with defects (such as high acidity or overpowering bitterness) is refined. The result is tasteless, so it is boosted with some virgin or extra virgin olive oil. Such blends may be misleadingly labeled "pure" or "lite."

Mythstake

"Lite" does not mean fewer calories. Lite olive oil simply has a milder taste and odor. There are no "lite" standards. This product may be carefully filtered, or a blend of inferior refined and virgin oil, or a combination.

Reasons Not to Buy Refined or Lite

- Refined oil is better for frying than virgin oil, and has a higher smoke point, but other vegetable oils do the job better.
- If you want olive oil flavor (and quality), you want extra virgin.

A Reason to Buy Lite

- If you're baking with olive oil, you may prefer the subtler flavor of lite.

OUTSIDE THE BOX

You can bake a cake with olive oil. Choose a mild or fruity one. Fans rave that cakes made with olive oil stay fresher longer because of the antioxidants.

♡ Healthier Eater

The sooner the olives are harvested, the more antioxidants they offer.

✤ Oil made from under-ripe olives is pungent and somewhat bitter. Oil made from ripe olives is nuttier or fruitier.

✤ Match delicate olive oil with mild food, robust oil with pungent food. Four matches:
- Delicate oil with tender greens and mild cheeses.
- Fruity oil for pasta, chicken breasts and salads.
- Grassy oil with beans, greens and bare pasta.
- Oil that tastes peppery or strongly of olives with hearty bread for dipping.

✤ Exposure to air, light, heat and moisture makes oil rancid.

✤ Smells that are signs of rancidity:
- Fishy
- Soapy
- Cheesy
- Musty

✤ Flavors that are signs of inferior or defective olive oil:
- Almond
- Brininess
- Burnt taste
- Cucumber
- Metallic
- Wine or vinegar

✦ Wipe an oilcan, bottle, sprayer or pump after using it. Greasy spots attract dust.

7 Ways to Keep Oil Fresher

1. Buy oil in small quantities. Check expiry dates.
2. Buy oil in a tinted bottle or transfer it to an opaque container.
3. Don't keep oil near the stove. (This is also a fire hazard.)
4. Don't keep oil on a windowsill.
5. Tightly screw on the cap.
6. Store oil in a cool, dark place.
7. Decant small amounts for use into an oilcan.

⚡ Lightning Won't Strike If ...

You refrigerate oil. Sure, avoid it if you can. Oil gets cloudy and viscous in the fridge, and picks up moisture. However, some sensitive, precious oils (such as gourmet nut oil) will go rancid in a heartbeat otherwise. In the case of unrefined nut oils, as well as hempseed and flaxseed oils, refrigeration is the lesser of two evils. You can also store them in the freezer.

✦ Bring oil to room temperature before using it.

✦ Frozen oil deteriorates quickly when thawed. Use it promptly.

Cooking with Fat

⚛ A Bit of Science

The saying that "fat equals flavor" is scientifically accurate. Fat is the repository of odors in meat, and the odors determine the flavors.

✦ You can substitute one refined oil for another.

✦ Don't directly substitute a liquid fat for a solid fat. To make the recipe work, you have to play with the amounts of fat, plus make other adjustments. Example: When mixing cake batter, the butter is creamed and aerated. If you substitute oil, you must beat the egg whites to greater stiffness for more lift. Substituting one solid fat for another can be problematic, too. Lard, for example, is all fat, while butter is four-fifths fat.

✦ Conversions are tricky. It's better to get a different recipe that calls for the fat you want to use than to try to doctor the recipe you have. This is especially true when baking.

5 Substitutions

1. In a recipe that calls for melted butter or margarine, substitute oil but reduce the amount by 20%.
2. To switch oil for butter, reduce the amount by 15% to 20%. However, other adjustments will be necessary.
3. In place of butter, use 20% less lard or rendered fat.
4. To substitute shortening for butter, use equal amounts by volume. The air in the shortening compensates for the moisture in the butter. If measuring by weight, however, use 20% less shortening.
5. Substitute an equal amount of block margarine for butter, or vice versa. They have similar moisture levels. Spreadable tub margarine, however, doesn't work with this equation. The results will be moister, softer and crumblier.

D is for Displacement

It's easier to measure solid fat by displacement than to cram it into a cup. If you want, say, $\frac{1}{2}$ cup (125 mL) solid fat, fill a 1-cup (250 mL) measure halfway with water, then add enough fat to push the level to the 1-cup (250 mL) mark.

✧ To drizzle oil more judiciously, use the cap.

♡ Healthier Eater

Commercial oil sprays have additives and propellants. Fill a pump bottle or mister and use it instead.

✧ To condition fresh oil for frying, some cooks add 1 tbsp (15 mL) old, used oil per 1 cup (250 mL) fresh.

✪ Waste Not

To better preserve a paste, liquid or minced vegetable in the fridge, pour a thin layer of oil over top. Pour off the oil before using or tilt the container to move the oil aside before scooping. Try this with pesto, curry paste and flavor essences.

✧ To grease your hands quickly and lightly, spray them with vegetable oil.

✗ No-No

Homemade herb and garlic oils are not recommended because they are good growth mediums for the bacteria that cause botulism. If you do make these, pay particular attention to ensuring that the garlic and herbs have no moisture clinging to them. Keep these flavored oils in the fridge and use them within 2 or 3 days.

Recycling Fat

✧ Recycling grease after deep-frying is economical but unwise. With each use, it degrades and the smoke point gets lower.

♛ A Golden Rule

You can't recycle oil endlessly. Two or three times is a sane maximum.

✧ To increase the number of times you can recycle oil, lard or shortening, add a bit of fresh fat each time you fry.

✗ No-Nos

• Never leave grease sitting in a deep fryer.
• Never reuse unfiltered frying oil. Strain it through a sieve lined with cheesecloth, or pour it through a metal mesh coffee filter. Store it in an airtight bottle or tub in the refrigerator.
• Don't reuse oil for different foods. Frying doughnuts in the same oil you used for fish is an extreme example. If you are storing two kinds of frying oil, label the containers.

✧ Keep recycled grease in the fridge.

---

3 Ways to Deodorize Used Oil

1. Fry parsley sprigs.
2. Fry celery.
3. Fry a knob of peeled ginger.

✧ It's better to use recycled oil in small amounts for sautéing.

Signs That Recycled Grease Is Exhausted

• It's dark.
• It's thick and sluggish.
• It gives food a bad taste.
• It starts to smoke over medium heat.

Condiments and Flavorings

♻ Waste Not

- To use every last bit from a bottle of ketchup, mustard, barbecue sauce or other thick condiment, add some vinegar to the container and shake it. Use rice vinegar; it's mild.
- Add a bit of water to the remnants in a barbecue sauce bottle and shake it. Use as a marinade.
- Mix vinaigrette in a jar with mustard dregs. You'd add a dollop of mustard to the dressing anyway.
- Add vinegar and oil to an almost empty salsa bottle and make tomato salad dressing.

✧ How to get ketchup, barbecue sauce or oyster sauce flowing from a glass bottle:
- Introduce air by inserting a straw to the bottom. Remove the straw and pour.
- Shake the bottle from side to side, rather than smacking the bottom.

Making Do

- If you run out of prepared mustard, stir together 1 tsp (5 mL) mustard powder, 1½ tsp (7 mL) wine, white wine vinegar or flat beer, and a pinch of sugar to make a paste. You can also add a drop of oil. Let it mellow for 1 hour. It'll still be hot enough to clear your sinuses but not so bitter.
- Out of tomato paste? Substitute the same amount of ketchup. Reduce the sugar in the recipe or add freshly squeezed lemon juice. This works only when you need a small amount.
- Make your own ketchup. In a medium saucepan, combine a 14-oz (398 mL) can of tomato sauce, 3 tbsp (45 mL) white vinegar and ¾ cup (175 mL) granulated sugar. Simmer over medium-low heat for about 1 hour or until thickened, dark and reduced to 1 cup (250 mL).

Salsa

OUTSIDE THE BOX

- You can boost burger, meatball or meatloaf mixtures with a bit of salsa.
- You can add salsa to soup. Stir it in, or put a dollop on creamy soup as a finishing touch.

Soy Sauce

Light VS. Dark Soy?

Light soy sauce is clear brown and has a beany aroma. It is saltier than dark soy. Use it either as a seasoning or as an ingredient in delicate or lightly cooked dishes. Don't confuse it with the lower-sodium soy sauces, also described as light. Dark soy sauce is closer to dark brown, slightly thicker, and has a bit of shine. It adds deeper color and flavor, and is used mainly for cooking. Try it in stews and other long-simmering dishes.

Vinegar

✧ If a vinegar is too sharp, dilute it with red or white wine.

Buyer Beware

- Caramel coloring or sugar listed on the ingredient label is a sign of lower-quality balsamic vinegar or malt vinegar.

✧ When you don't want balsamic vinegar to discolor a dish, use white balsamic. This milder version is made from white wine vinegar.

❖ Add a splash of vinegar to cut the fat in a rich sauce or oily dish.

Master Plan
Balsamic Syrup

1. Pour balsamic vinegar into a small saucepan. Bring it to a boil over medium-high heat.
2. Reduce heat to low and simmer, uncovered, until vinegar is syrupy and reduced by half.
3. Transfer the syrup to a squeeze bottle and refrigerate it.
4. Decorate plates with splashes of balsamic syrup.

❖ Homemade flavored vinegar poses a botulism risk. In addition, once the solids are exposed to air, they can get moldy.

Safety Tips for Homemade Flavored Vinegar

- Steep crushed garlic in the vinegar for no more than 24 hours.
- Strain out the solids after steeping, or discard them after the bottle is opened.
- Store vinegar in a glass bottle, with a cork or top that won't corrode.
- Don't keep the vinegar for longer than 1 or 2 months.

Master Plan
Flavored Vinegar

1. Clean, sterilize and dry a bottle.
2. Put in flavorings such as citrus zest, raspberry or sprigs of tarragon, but don't overcrowd the bottle. For a pretty effect, thread fresh fruit onto a bamboo skewer.
3. Pour in vinegar right to the top, immersing all the solids.
4. Cover tightly and steep for 2 to 3 weeks.

OUTSIDE THE BOX

Raspberry vinegar mixed with club soda or fizzy mineral water makes a refreshing summer drink.

Wasabi

❖ To turn wasabi powder into paste, stir together equal parts of powder and water in a small bowl. Let it stand for 15 minutes.

Mythstake

No, wasabi is not a type of horseradish. The two are not related. Chances are you've never eaten real wasabi. Here's the scam: Real wasabi is hard to grow. Supplies are limited and expensive. The generic stuff we get with sushi here is dried horseradish and mustard, dyed green.

Spices and Seasonings

✦ Spices lose their power within months. Buy small quantities.

Two Good Signs

• Sniff. The spice should still prickle the nose.
• Check the color of red and green spices and herbs. It should be bold. Faded means old.

Storing Spices

○ Write the purchase date on each spice container. Replace the spice after 6 months to 1 year.
○ Store spices in a dark, dry, cool spot.
○ Herbs and spices keep longer in opaque containers than in bottles or jars.
○ If spice bottles are stored in a drawer with the labels obscured, write the names on the lids with a permanent marker. You can also label the lids of baby-food jars or small storage tubs containing spices.
○ You can store most spices in the fridge or freezer. This is a good option for expensive saffron. Seal tightly, since humidity may affect them.

OUTSIDE THE BOX

Small, round, interlocking plastic fishing-tackle tubs are the most convenient and efficient way to store spices. The plastic is brittle, but they are stackable, interchangeable and compact.

✦ Follow the lead of Indian cooks: Buy spices whole and grind them to order. There are good reasons to freshly grind spices:
○ Whole spices stay fresher until you need them.

○ Grinding releases aromatic oils. Grinding just before use is especially important for spices that lose their potency quickly, such as black pepper and nutmeg.
○ Grinding helps the flavor of spices blend better with your dish.

6 Ways to Grind Spices

1. Recycle an old electric coffee grinder. If you have a choice, select the espresso grind and maximum cup settings to grind spices as finely as possible.
2. Use a pepper mill to grind smaller spices such as fennel, dill, cumin and coriander seeds.
3. Whirl spices in a mini food processor.
4. Pulverize spices using a mortar and pestle.
5. Crush spices with a mallet or the side of a heavy knife. This is an easy way to release the flavor of seeds such as aniseed or fennel.
6. Crush and crumble dried herbs between your fingers.

✦ For the utmost intensity, toast spices before grinding them. Cool them completely before grinding.

Reasons to Toast Spices

○ Heat unleashes the aroma.
○ They taste better.
○ Toasting makes spices easier to grind and crush, particularly caraway and cumin seeds.

Ways to Toast Whole Spices

- Put them in a dry skillet over medium heat. Shake the skillet until wisps of smoke start to rise, 1 to 2 minutes. Remove the spices from the skillet right away, so they don't burn.
- Spices that burn easily, such as cumin, can be sealed in a foil packet, then toasted in the skillet for 5 minutes or until fragrant. (This method is also good for tiny amounts of spices.)

✧ When you double a recipe, you shouldn't necessarily double the spices. Double friendly spices such as cinnamon, but increase aggressive spices such as cloves by a half to two-thirds.

✧ How to deal with spices that clump, such as garlic or onion powder:
- Keep them in airtight jars.
- Don't try to smash a hard clump into submission. Stir in hot water or liquid from your recipe to blend it into a paste.

✧ Reasons to add some spices only at the end of the cooking time:
- Spice flavors increase in combination with acidic ingredients, and in soups and stews that are cooked low and slow. Adjust the spices when the dish is done.
- Add toasted spices toward the end so their impact is not dissipated.
- Some spices, such as paprika and cayenne pepper, scorch easily. Add these at the end and keep the heat low.
- Long exposure to heat makes some spices, such as black peppercorns and caraway seeds, bitter or acrid. Add these during the last 15 to 30 minutes.

✘ No-No

Don't shake spices over steaming pots on the stove. They will spoil faster and turn gummy.

Dry Rubs Pastes?

Dry rubs are a mix of dried herbs, spices and flavorings such as mustard powder and sugar. Add oil or vinegar to turn a dry rub into a paste. Rubs penetrate meat when it heats up and absorb escaping moisture. Pastes can act like concentrated marinades.

10 Rules for Rubs

1. To blend your own barbecue rub, start with 1 tbsp (15 mL) each sugar and salt, then add 1 tbsp (15 mL) each savory and sweet spices, in any combination. Add extras such as dry mustard or dried herbs.
2. Balance strong and mild spices.
3. Choose a theme. You can go ethnic with Cajun or jerk, or try a classic combo such as lemon-garlic.
4. Don't use too much sugar. A little adds nice color to the meat; a lot makes it stick and burn.
5. For rubs, onion and garlic powders are better than fresh. Minced onion and garlic burn.
6. Don't grind spices to a fine powder. The rub should have some texture.
7. Gently massage the rub into meat. Smear it under the skin of chicken.
8. Apply a rub in advance — 30 minutes before cooking for fish, 2 to 4 hours for steaks or chicken pieces, the night before for a roast.
9. Wrap rubbed meat in plastic and refrigerate.
10. If you find that the meat has sucked in the rub, apply more.

Uses for Leftover Rub

- Smear it onto a roast that's just out of the oven.
- Sprinkle it into scrambled eggs.
- Add a spoonful to stew or chili.
- Make flavored butter.
- Season cream cheese.
- Add it to dip.

◇ Sauté a spice paste before adding other ingredients to it, rather than stirring the paste into a dish.

Asafetida

◇ Asafetida, or stinky gum, is a plant resin. It is used, powdered, in curries. Asafetida has an overpowering, oniony, garlicky, sulfurous scent that becomes strangely appealing once you get used to it. Hence the nicknames "devil's dung" and "food of the gods." If you're shopping at an Indian grocery store, ask for hing.

♡ Healthier Eater

Asafetida is consumed alone as a remedy for flatulence and added to bean and lentil dishes to reduce their gaseous effects.

Capers

Brined Salted?

Capers come bottled in brine or dry-salted. Less common, the latter are superior in pungency and firmness.

◇ Rinse and drain capers before use.

OUTSIDE THE BOX

Capers can be fried. Dry them well and fry small batches in plenty of olive oil. It takes a few seconds for the buds to open and turn crisp. The oil ends up flavored, too. Use fried capers as a garnish, add them to salad or stir them into butter or mayonnaise.

Caper Butter

This is lip-smackingly savory and tangy. Try a dab on fish or steamed vegetables. **Makes about ¹/₂ cup (125 mL)**

Tip
Save the flavored oil for other uses.

¼ cup	olive oil	50 mL
2 tbsp	capers, rinsed, drained and patted dry	25 mL
½ cup	unsalted butter, at room temperature	125 mL

1. In a 10-inch (25 cm) skillet, heat oil over medium-high heat until shimmery. Scatter in capers and sauté for up to 30 seconds or until opened and lightly browned. Using a slotted spoon, transfer capers to a plate lined with paper towel and let drain.

2. In a small bowl, using a fork, gently stir capers into butter. Do not mash. Store in an airtight container in the fridge for up to 2 weeks.

Chili Powder

✧ The standard supermarket blend used in chili con carne is made with ground chiles, along with spices such as cumin. It is not hot. Pure chili powder is ground from specific dried chiles. The most popular type hides in plain sight under the name cayenne pepper. Others, such as chipotle, ancho and pasilla powders, are not quite as fiery.

Making Do

You can grind your own chili powder. Cut dried chiles into strips and pulverize them in a coffee or spice grinder.

OUTSIDE THE BOX

Chiles boost the flavor of chocolate. Add a pinch of cayenne pepper to hot chocolate, or ancho chili powder to cocoa cupcake batter.

✧ Is your chili con carne powder old and feeble? Stir in a bit of cayenne pepper.

Cinnamon

Cinnamon VS. Cassia?

True cinnamon (a.k.a. Ceylon cinnamon) is the bark of a small tree. Cassia is an inferior relative that is also known as Chinese cinnamon or bastard cinnamon. It may be sold simply labeled as cinnamon. When powdered, true cinnamon and cassia are hard to tell apart. Supermarket ground cinnamon is apt to be cassia.

Cloves

✧ Cloves lose their oils and get stale. Here's a test: Drop them in a glass of water. If they sink or bob upright, that's good. If they float on their sides, they're old.

✧ Stud a whole onion with cloves to season simmering sauces and stews. This way, the cloves and onion are easy to extract.

Curry Powder

Mythstake

Curry powder is not a spice; it is a blend. Authentic Indian cooking calls for a variety of individual spices, rather than generic curry powder.

Factoid Curry powder may include as many as 30 herbs and spices, but the average blend has 15.

Ⓜ is for Masala

A spice blend is called a masala. Commercial curry powder is a type of masala.

Characteristics	True Cinnamon	Cassia
Flavor	Delicate	Pungent, bittersweet
Color	Light, yellowish brown	Reddish brown
Texture	Finer, weaker, multilayered	Coarser, single layer
Strength	Crumbly, easily ground	Hard to pulverize
Shape	Tighter quill	Thick scroll, rolling in at each end

Making Do

You can make your own curry powder by toasting and grinding herbs and spices at home, then stirring them together.

Common Curry Ingredients

(All ground)
- Allspice
- Bay leaves
- Black pepper
- Cardamom
- Celery seeds
- Chiles (dried)
- Cinnamon
- Cloves
- Coriander
- Cumin
- Fennel seeds
- Fenugreek
- Garlic powder
- Ginger
- Mace
- Mustard seeds
- Nutmeg
- Poppy seeds
- Sesame seeds
- Turmeric

Five-Spice Powder

✧ Five-spice powder is an aromatic Chinese blend.

Making Do

To copy it, stir together equal amounts of ground cinnamon, cloves, fennel seeds, star anise and Szechuan peppercorns.

Mustard

Powder VS. Prepared Mustard?

Mustard powder, or dry mustard, is made of ground mustard seeds. Prepared mustard is a blend of ground mustard seeds, vinegar, water, spices, sugar, even wine.

Nigella

Mythstake

Although nigellas are called black onion seeds, they are not from onions. They come from a flowering plant that's native to Asia. Nigella has a multitude of misleading names, including black sesame, black cumin, black caraway and Roman coriander. In an Indian shop, ask for kalonji.

Nutmeg

Making Do

No need to buy a special nutmeg grater. You can scrape whole nutmeg with a rasp (Microplane) grater or a vegetable peeler.

✧ Reasons that grinding whole nutmeg yourself is not just an affectation:
- Nutmeg loses its fragrance quickly once it's ground.
- Inferior-grade nutmeg is occasionally ground and sold illegally. It may be contaminated with toxic molds.

Nutmeg VS. Mace?

The two taste and smell much alike, with good reason. Nutmeg is the seed of a tropical tree fruit. Mace is the lacy, thin, leathery seed covering. When the fruit splits open, you see the nutmeg and mace. Nutmeg is described as slightly sweeter, mace as stronger. Mace may be preferred for its lighter color.

Pepper

- ❖ Store peppercorns away from heat and moisture. Pack them in glass, leaving as little headspace as possible.

Black VS. White VS. Green?

Peppercorn berries ripen from green to red, but the color may have little relation to their final state. Black pepper is made from berries picked almost ripe, then dried until they're black and shriveled. White peppercorns are picked ripe and red. They are milder because the hulls are rubbed off to expose the naked seeds. Green peppercorns are picked unripe and soft. They are usually preserved in brine.

- ❖ Ground black pepper loses its aromatic oils quickly. It's best to buy peppercorns and invest in a quality pepper mill.

Mythstake

Pink peppercorns and Szechuan peppercorns are not from the real pepper plant. Pink peppercorns are dried berries from a type of rose bush (*Schinus molle*) or from a plant called the peppertree (*Schinus terebinthifolius*). Szechuan peppercorns are seed pods from a plant related to the prickly ash. (To release the flavor of Szechuan peppercorns, shake them in a dry small skillet over medium-low heat until they start to emit wisps of smoke.)

A Tidy Way to Measure Freshly Ground Pepper

- Grind it onto a small square of waxed paper. Form the paper into a funnel and pour the pepper into the measuring spoon.

- ❖ Add a few peppercorns to your pepper shaker for a pungent boost.

- ❖ Particular cooks prefer to use ground white pepper in a light-colored dish so no speckles show.

- ❖ Crack peppercorns with a heavy object, such as a cast-iron skillet or a mallet.

- ❖ Ways to prevent peppercorns from rolling away when you try to crush them:
  - Lay your cutting board on a rimmed baking sheet.
  - Stash the peppercorns inside a parchment packet or a zip-lock bag.

- ❖ For assertive pepper flavor, season after cooking. For mellow flavor, season before cooking.

Saffron

Factoid Stigmas from an Asian variety of crocus flowers are dried to produce saffron, the world's most expensive spice.

- ❖ Buy saffron in threads. The powdered stuff may be adulterated or stale.

A Good Sign

Look for deep, orangey-red threads. Threads with yellow are not as good quality. Yellow bits are part of the style, not the stigma.

Ways to Release the Most Color and Flavor

- Always crumble saffron before using it. Saffron is easier to crumble when it's frozen.
- Soak crumbled saffron in hot water or liquid from your recipe for a few minutes, then add this mixture to the dish.

Salt

Mined Salt VS. Sea Salt?

Salts are mined or harvested from the earth and sea. They range from plain table salt to flakes of fleur de sel. Thus, salts taste, look and feel different. Some are mild, some sulfurous.

F is for Fleur de Sel

Fleur de sel is a coarse, flaky sea salt. It is expensive. Maldon sea salt is similar.

❖ Sea salt tends to attract moisture. Keep it away from the steamy stove. Cover it tightly.

Table Salt VS. Kosher Salt?

Iodine and anti-caking agents are added to table salt. Anti-caking agents are chemical compounds with unpronounceable names that help salt flow freely. Kosher salt is additive-free and tastes better.

❖ Kosher salt is coarser and weighs less than table salt, so you can't substitute equally by volume. Measure 25% to 50% more kosher salt in place of table salt. (The amount depends on the brand of kosher salt.) Better still, go by weight when substituting.

❖ Pickling salt is coarse and free of additives that might cloud the liquid.

✗ No-No

Do not try to eat rock salt. It is unrefined. Use it as a bed for oysters or baked potatoes.

Mythstake

Salt is not organic. It keeps forever. Freshly ground salt doesn't taste any fresher. A salt grinder is good only for creating a finer texture — and it looks pretty on the table.

❖ Add ½ tsp (2 mL) uncooked rice to the salt shaker to keep the salt dry and flowing freely.

❖ Salt makes grinding and chopping easier. Add some to the mortar and pestle. Mix some into the garlic or whatever you are mincing on the cutting board.

3 Ways to Use Salt Like a Chef

1. Add salt at each stage of food preparation. The salt must penetrate for the best results.
2. Use different salts at different stages. Examples: Add kosher salt, before cooking, to the food or the water. Add smoked salt during cooking. Sprinkle on sea salt before serving.
3. Keep several types of salt in your cupboard. Cheap table salt is fine in boiling water for potatoes or pasta, for instance. When you need to sprinkle a finishing touch on a dish, reach for a pricey gourmet salt known as a finishing salt — imported, smoked or flavored.

❖ While cooking, add salt with a light hand. Oversalting firms up vegetables, toughens proteins and draws out moisture.

♡ Healthier Eater

Adding salt only at the table may defeat the purpose of cutting back. It gives food a salty top-note only. In the end, you may actually need more to get the same flavor.

❖ Add a pinch of salt to sweet dishes to enhance the sugar.

Salt Doctor

The food is oversalted.

- Ladle out the section where the salt was dumped.
- Drizzle in an acidic ingredient for balance. Try vinegar, lemon juice, buttermilk or wine.
- Add a pinch of sugar.
- Freeze the dish in portions. Add each portion to another dish.
- Add more liquid.
- Pay attention to what you're doing. When food is oversalted, Hungarians say the chef must be in love.

The food tastes saltier warm than it does cold.

- Ideally, you should adjust the salt when the dish is at body temperature.

✧ If a dish is too acidic, add salt for balance.

A Bit of Science

Salt is a preservative. It draws out moisture. The salt and liquid then form a brine that makes the surface of the food inhospitable to microorganisms.

✧ When you're packing for a picnic, prevent salt and pepper shakers from spilling by taping over the holes.

Turmeric

✗ No-No

Turmeric is bitter and unpleasant. Use it only for coloring. Halve any amount a recipe calls for.

✧ Turmeric gives supermarket curry powder its lurid yellow color. Most commercial curry powders contain too much, probably because it is a cheap filler.

Vanilla

Madagascar **VS.** Mexican **VS.** Tahitian?

Madagascar supplies the majority of the world's vanilla. Madagascar vanilla , also called Bourbon vanilla, has long, slender pods and a mild flavor. Mexican vanilla is more robust. Tahitian vanilla pods are short and plump, with a stronger, floral scent.

✧ Most of the flavor in the pod is concentrated in the seeds and the pulp surrounding them.

ⓖ is for Givre

The best beans have a frosting of vanillin crystals, called givre.

Beans **VS.** Extract?

Vanilla beans (actually, they're pods) are picked when they're dark and almost split, then dried and fermented. The beans are macerated in alcohol to make vanilla extract. Artificial vanilla extract is made with caramel coloring, synthetic vanillin and maybe a hint of real vanilla.

Ways to Use a Vanilla Bean

- Split the pod lengthwise. Scrape out the seeds by pressing the back of a knife firmly along the interior. Use the pod, seeds and pulp.
- Use the pod to infuse scalded cream or another warm liquid. Cover and let it stand for 30 minutes. Then split and scrape the pod to use the pulp.

✧ It's easier to scrape out the seeds if the bean is plump. Try to keep the pods moist by keeping them well wrapped or in an airtight container.

Ⓥ is for Vanillin

Vanillin is the chemical compound that gives vanilla its heavenly aroma. It can be synthesized.

✧ You can wrap a vanilla bean in foil, then stash it in a zip-lock bag and store at room temperature. You can also wrap it in plastic and freeze it.

♻ Waste Not

• Fill an empty vanilla extract bottle with sugar for another kick at the can.
• Don't throw out scraped or steeped pods. Extract all the flavor you can first.
• Garnish a dessert with a dry, split pod.

✧ Always add a bit of vanilla to something chocolate, from brownies to hot cocoa.

Mythstake

Vanilla seeds look like tiny black flecks. However, black flecks are no guarantee that a product was made with real vanilla beans. The flecks can be recaptured after making extract and used for effect.

Places to Stash Fresh and Used Vanilla Beans

• In a bottle of vanilla extract
• In a bottle of booze (the alcohol leaches out some of the flavor, but you end up with flavored brandy, rum or vodka)
• In sugar (the bean shrivels and hardens, but you infuse the sugar with vanilla at the same time)
• In oil, such as nut oil (drizzle the oil over fruit salad or dessert)
• In vinaigrette (vanilla cuts acidity)
• In softened butter for seafood (vanilla complements lobster)
• In the coffee tin (with ground or whole beans)
• In coffee cream
• In the tea caddy

Making Do

Substitute 1 tsp (5 mL) vanilla extract per 2-inch (5 cm) length of bean. Don't add the sensitive extract to anything while it's cooking. Wait until it's removed from the heat.

Sweeteners

 Healthier Eater

A product can contain a lot of sugar without it being listed first on the ingredient label. There are as many as 40 names for various sugars and sweeteners, and these may be split up on the label. Don't be fooled.

✧ To make honey and syrups easier to pour, zap them in the microwave for a few seconds. Do not boil. Do not microwave them in the original plastic bottle or container, since chemicals may leach from the plastic.

S **is for Sugaring**

Honey and syrups are prone to sugaring, also described as granulation or crystallization. These liquids are so saturated with sugar that the excess falls out as crystals.

Ways to Get Rid of Crystals

- Put the jar or bottle in a bowl filled with the hottest tap water.
- Heat the syrup in the microwave on High, 1 cup (250 mL) at a time and stirring every 30 seconds, for up to 2 minutes or until the crystals dissolve. Do not boil.

✧ Honey and other syrups make baked goods brown faster, so turn down the heat. Honey, maple syrup and molasses are also more acidic than granulated sugar, so you should add some baking soda.

✧ Frozen foods taste less sweet. Add more sweetener.

Master Plan
Herbal Syrup

1. Put 1 cup (250 mL) each water and granulated sugar in a small saucepan over medium heat. Stir until the sugar dissolves.
2. When the syrup comes to a simmer, add about ¼ cup (50 mL) spices or chopped herbs (try fennel or mint). Remove from heat. Cover and let steep for at least 30 minutes.
3. Strain the syrup, discarding the solids. Store it in an airtight jar or tub for up to 1 week in the fridge or 1 year in the freezer. Use it to sweeten tea or drizzle over fruit.

Agave Syrup

✧ Agave syrup is made from the nectar of a Mexican cactus. It comes in golden and blue versions, and is touted for its lower glycemic index (in relation to sugar).

✧ Agave can be used in some types of baking. Heating, however, reduces its sweetness.

Corn Syrup

✧ Corn syrup doesn't turn grainy when cold, so it's a good choice for icings and candies.

Golden **VS.** White?

Corn syrup comes in dark (golden) and light (white) versions. The latter is actually lighter or clear, rather than white, and tastes milder. Use it when you don't want to add a golden tinge to cake or icing.

Honey

✧ Honey differs according to which plants the bees visited. The color ranges from light to dark, the flavor from mellow to medicinal. The darker the honey, the more robust the flavor. Busy bees make honey by putting the nectar they collect from flowers into a honeycomb and fanning it with their wings. This honey is sold raw or pasteurized.

Types of Honey

- **Comb honey** is sold in its edible wax honeycomb, which can be chewed like gum. Liquid honey packed with honeycomb pieces is called cut comb honey or chunk honey.
- **Raw honey** is prized for compounds such as pollen and propolis, and for its antibacterial qualities. During production, it is gently strained, but not heated above the natural hive temperature. It crystallizes faster than more processed honeys and may separate.
- **Liquid honey** may be raw or heated or pasteurized. It is extracted from the honeycomb by spinning, straining or gravity, then filtered. Heating makes honey less prone to granulation.
- **Whipped or creamed honey** is evenly crystallized so it is spreadable. It is opaque with a white cast.
- **Infused honey** is flavored.

✧ Honey granulates the fastest between 50°F and 60°F (10°C and 15°C). You can freeze honey. It will not granulate below 32°F (0°C) or above 104°F (40°C). The latter, however, is not good for the quality. Do not refrigerate honey.

✧ Honey's ability to suck moisture from the air is the reason baked goods made with honey stay moist longer.

✗ **No-No**

Don't store honey in one of those cute, airy jars with drizzle sticks. Honey attracts moisture and yeast from the air, as well as insects.

♡ **Healthier Eater**

Never give honey to babies who are less than a year old. They are susceptible to botulism spores that don't normally affect us.

Master Plan
Herbal Honey

1. In a small saucepan, combine 1 cup (250 mL) honey and ¼ to ½ cup (50 to 125 mL) chopped herbs. (You could also use chopped ginger or rose petals.) Bring it to a boil over medium heat.
2. Remove the pan from the burner and let cool.
3. Repeat the boiling and cooling.
4. Boil the mixture. While it is still warm, strain the honey.
5. Store it in an airtight bottle or jar for up to a year. Use it for tea or baking.

Maple Syrup

Grade and Color

- The grade and color of maple syrup you buy depends on what you want it for. The lower the grade and darker the color, the more suitable it is for baking. It's vice versa for table syrup.
- Colors range from extra-light to medium to amber. The darker the syrup, the more distinct the flavor.
- Grade A syrup comes in light (fancy) and medium. The light syrup is made from early spring sap. The dark Grade B is made at the end of sap season.

✧ Keep unopened maple syrup in the cupboard or freezer. After opening, keep it in the fridge.

Mock Maple Syrup

This is an inexpensive alternative to maple syrup, or even store-bought maple-flavored syrups. **Makes about ¾ cup (175 mL)**

Tip
You can stretch real maple syrup by mixing it 50–50 with this mock concoction.

1 cup	packed brown sugar	250 mL
¾ cup	water	175 mL
½ tsp	cornstarch (optional)	2 mL
1 tsp	maple extract	5 mL

1. In a small saucepan, stir together brown sugar and water. Bring to a boil over medium heat. Reduce heat to low and simmer for 15 minutes or until slightly thickened.

2. In a small bowl, stir together cornstarch (if using) and maple extract until smooth. Whisk into the syrup. Continue simmering until thickened and glossy, up to 1 minute. Or simply remove from heat and stir in maple extract.

3. Pour into an airtight bottle or storage tub and refrigerate.

Maple Candy

This candy is hard, like brittle. **Makes about 12 oz (375 g)**

- **Candy thermometer**

- **8-inch (20 cm) square baking pan, lined with greased parchment paper**

Tips
Be careful not to let the syrup heat past the thread stage. If heated too long, it becomes sour and bitter.

Do not use a nonstick pan.

2 cups	pure maple syrup	500 mL

1. In a medium saucepan, heat maple syrup over medium-low heat, without stirring, until it registers 230°F (110°C) on thermometer. Let cool to 110°F (43°C), without stirring.

2. Using a sturdy hand-held electric mixer, beat syrup in pan on medium-high speed until it becomes lighter-hued and creamy-textured.

3. Scrape into the prepared pan. Let stand until cool, then score the candy or break it into pieces.

4. Store the candy in a tightly sealed box for up to a year. Exposure to air dries it out.

Making Do
- You can make imitation maple syrup at home with brown sugar and maple extract.
- You can make maple syrup candy at home.

Molasses

Sulfured **VS.** Unsulfured?

Puzzled by old recipes that call for unsulfured molasses? Sulfur dioxide was used as a preservative and clarifier, but caused allergic reactions in some consumers. If a recipe calls for unsulfured, use fancy, or light, molasses.

✧ Molasses is a byproduct of sugar refining. Juice is pressed from sugar cane, then boiled to extract sugar. The liquid residue is molasses. There are traditionally three boilings. Each time, the molasses gets stronger, darker and less sweet. Light molasses is from the first boiling, dark from the second, blackstrap from the third. These may be referred to as first, second and third molasses.

Fancy **VS.** Blackstrap?

Fancy, or light, molasses is pressed, clarified cane juice in its purest form, with the sugar intact. Blackstrap is at the other end of the scale. It is bitter, sour and pungent. Blackstrap is prized by the health-conscious for its concentrated mineral content. It is not suitable for baking or table syrup. In between is a dark molasses sometimes called cooking molasses. It may be made from the second boiling, or blended from fancy and blackstrap molasses. It makes baked goods darker and less sweet than fancy molasses.

✧ In recipes, Brits call molasses "treacle," except for blackstrap, which they call "molasses."

✧ At room temperature, light and dark molasses keep for up to 2 years, but the shelf life of blackstrap is about 3 months.

✧ Golden syrup is clarified, decolorized, evaporated cane juice.

Making Do

In a pinch, combine equal parts of corn syrup and blackstrap molasses to replace fancy (light) molasses.

Sugar

✧ Sugar is stripped and extracted from cane or beets by heating, bleaching and sifting.

Factoid Vegans don't use white granulated sugar. During processing, cane sugar is filtered through charcoal made from bones. This is not done for beet sugar, but labels are unclear and it's hard to determine which is which.

✧ Superfine sugar may be labeled "fruit sugar" or "instant dissolving sugar." Use it if you need, well, instant dissolving. It comes in handy at cocktail hour and is better for fruit and sorbet.

ⓒ is for Castor

In British cookbooks, superfine sugar is called castor sugar.

✧ To get lumps out of superfine sugar, put it into a plastic bag and work that rolling pin.

Confectioner's **VS.** Icing **VS.** Powdered Sugar?

No need to be confused. These are all the same thing. Icing sugar may also be called fondant sugar.

✗ No-No

When baking, do not use icing sugar in place of granulated or superfine sugar. It has cornstarch added to reduce caking.

✦ To get rid of lumps in icing sugar, sift it or push it through a sieve.

is for Sanding Sugar

Coarse sugar is dyed and used decoratively as sanding or pearl sugar.

Ⓛ is for Liquid Invert Sugar

This blend of glucose and fructose is used mainly in soft drinks and commercial products.

Mythstake

Sugar labeled "raw sugar" is not really raw. Real raw sugar is the dry brown crystals remaining from the evaporation of cane and beet juices. It contains impurities. Minimally refined brown sugars include golden Demerara and darker Barbados or muscovado. They are crunchy and coarse.

Ⓣ is for Turbinado

Blond turbinado is marketed as "sugar in the raw" or plantation sugar. It is processed in cylinders or turbines and steam-cleaned.

Ⓢ is for Sucanat

This name is short for sugar cane natural. Made with dehydrated cane juices, Sucanat is grainy, and light to medium brown.

Ⓙ is for Jaggery

This is made from boiled palm sap or sugar cane, and sold in cakes.

✦ Store brown sugar at room temperature in an airtight tub. When exposed to air, the molasses dries and cements together the sugar crystals.

Light Brown VS. Dark Brown?

Brown sugar, light or dark, is granulated sugar mixed with molasses. The color depends on the amount of molasses. In the past, brown sugar contained some processed raw sugar.

Mythstake

People think brown sugar is healthier than white sugar — so they eat more of it. Actually, the two have about the same calories and nutritional value. Brown sugar does have a minute amount of minerals and more moisture.

✦ To keep brown sugar moist, use a clay disc. Soak the disc in water for 20 minutes, pat it dry, then bury it in the sugar. These discs come in decorative shapes. The sugar bear is cute.

Ⓟ is for Panela

Cones, discs or blocks of brown sugar popular in Latin American cooking are known as panela or piloncillo.

Brown Sugar Doctor

It's lumpy.
- Break it up in the food processor.
- Pulverize it using a mortar and pestle.
- Add a slice of apple or bread, or damp paper towel to the container, seal it and leave it overnight.
- Stir it with a fork.

It's hard.
- Warm it in the microwave on High, for about 30 seconds per ¼ cup (50 mL). You can tuck in a slice of apple, top with damp paper towels or put a mug of water next to the sugar.
- Place it in a baking dish, sprinkle with a few drops of water and heat it in a 200°F (100°C) oven until warm.

- Put it in a bowl, cover it with wet paper towels, then plastic wrap, and let stand overnight. Pulverize it.

The softened brown sugar got hard again.

- The heat methods give faster results, but the sugar reverts to rocky consistency as it cools. The heat-free methods take a day or two, but the sugar stays soft longer.

Making Do

- If you don't have superfine sugar, whirl granulated sugar in a food processor for 30 seconds or until a powdery cloud starts to rise from the tube.
- If you don't have icing sugar, whirl 1 cup (250 mL) granulated sugar with 1 tbsp (15 mL) cornstarch in a blender until powdery. Don't bother using a food processor: The sugar remains too gritty. Also, the processor allows the powdery cloud that's kicked up to escape and make a mess.
- Make your own brown sugar by combining 1 cup (250 mL) granulated sugar with 3 to 4 tbsp (45 to 60 mL) molasses. Use a fork. Or pulse it — very gently — in a food processor.
- To turn light brown sugar into dark brown sugar, add molasses. Use 2 tsp (10 mL) molasses per 1 cup (250 mL) brown sugar.

Substitutions

- ✦ You can't substitute willy-nilly. In baked goods, sugar not only sweetens, it reacts chemically with other ingredients to create texture and color. Sugar makes dough tender and produces a golden brown crust. Solid and liquid sugars have different weights, volumes, sweetness, moisture and acidity levels. Here are rough guidelines when using substitutions for granulated sugar.

Agave Syrup

- One cup (250 mL) agave syrup is as sweet as $1\frac{1}{4}$ to $1\frac{1}{2}$ cups (300 to 375 mL) granulated sugar.
- Reduce the liquid in the recipe by about $\frac{1}{3}$ cup (75 mL) per 1 cup (250 mL) agave syrup used.
- Reduce the oven temperature by 25°F (10°C).

Corn Syrup

- One cup (250 mL) corn syrup is as sweet as $\frac{1}{2}$ cup (125 mL) granulated sugar.
- Reduce the liquid in the recipe by $\frac{1}{4}$ cup (50 mL) per 1 cup (250 mL) corn syrup.

Honey

- One cup (250 mL) honey is as sweet as $1\frac{1}{4}$ to $1\frac{1}{2}$ cups (300 to 375 mL) granulated sugar.
- Don't substitute honey for more than half of the sugar in a recipe.
- You'll have to experiment with amounts. Start by using $\frac{1}{2}$ to $\frac{2}{3}$ cup (125 to 150 mL) honey in place in place of 1 cup (250 mL) granulated sugar.
- Reduce the liquid in the recipe by 3 to 4 tbsp (45 to 60 mL) per 1 cup (250 mL) honey used.
- You may need up to 25% more flour for cookies made with honey. This will leave them drier or chewier.
- In addition to the leavening in the recipe, add $\frac{1}{2}$ tsp (2 mL) baking soda per 1 cup (250 mL) honey.
- Reduce the oven temperature by 25°F (10°C).

Maple Syrup

- One cup (250 mL) maple syrup is as sweet as $\frac{3}{4}$ cup (175 mL) granulated sugar.
- Reduce the liquid in the recipe by $\frac{1}{4}$ cup (50 mL) per 1 cup (250 mL) maple syrup.
- In addition to the leavening in the recipe, add $\frac{1}{4}$ tsp (1 mL) baking soda per 1 cup (250 mL) maple syrup.
- Reduce the oven temperature slightly.

Molasses

- One cup (250 mL) light (fancy) molasses is as sweet as ¾ cup (175 mL) sugar.
- Reduce the liquid in the recipe by ¼ cup (50 mL) per 1 cup (250 mL) molasses.
- In addition to the leavening in the recipe, add ½ tsp (2 mL) baking soda per 1 cup (250 mL) molasses.
- Reduce the oven temperature slightly.

☺ KID STUFF

- Put sugar in a salt shaker or Parmesan shaker box. Kids can shake the sugar over their cereal instead of making a mess with loose sugar and a spoon.
- If you're missing the die from a board game, use a permanent marker to put dots on a sugar cube. Don't eat it.

Ⓢ is for Stevia

This herbal product made from the sweet leaf of a shrub is 300 times sweeter than sugar. It doesn't act like sugar in cooking and is not good for baking.

Ⓧ is for Xylitol

This sugar alcohol is mainly found in gum and toothpaste.

Artificial Sweeteners

✧ Sugar is a preservative. Baked goods made with artificial sweeteners go stale faster.

Ⓐ is for Aspartame

Aspartame is 200 times sweeter than sugar but has a bitter aftertaste. Heat strips its sweetness, so don't try to bake with it.

Ⓢ is for Sucralose

The granular sugar substitute sucralose, or Splenda, is actually made from sugar. It is 600 times sweeter than granulated sugar.

8 Keys to Cooking with Sucralose

1. Sucralose works best in recipes that require sugar mainly for sweetening, such as pie fillings, sauces or muffins.
2. It is not good for recipes, such as meringue, frosting or fudge, in which sugar is used in large amounts and/or required for structure and browning. The manufacturer suggests sucralose could replace up to a quarter of the sugar in such cases.
3. Jams, puddings and custards with sucralose may be thinner or fail to set firmly.
4. For cookies, use sucralose to replace only the granulated sugar in a recipe. To help the cookies spread, flatten them with a spatula or the bottom of a glass.
5. When making muffins and quick breads with sucralose, add a couple of tablespoons (25 mL) of honey or molasses to the batter for moisture.
6. Cakes and quick breads made with sucralose may not rise as high, so switch to a pan of smaller diameter. Add ½ cup (125 mL) skim milk powder and ½ tsp (2 mL) baking soda per 1 cup (250 mL) sucralose used in the recipe.
7. Baked goods won't brown as much, so spray the top with oil before baking.
8. To compensate for a milder flavor in cakes and cookies, add ½ tsp (2 mL) vanilla extract per 1 cup (250 mL) sucralose.

Refrigerator Basics

Recipes

Dairy Products

10 Ways to Boost Calcium in Your Diet

1. Sneak skim milk powder into recipes by the spoonful.
2. Replace water with milk in oatmeal, condensed soup or whatever works.
3. Drink breakfast smoothies blended with milk or yogurt.
4. Dip fruit into yogurt.
5. Eat granola with yogurt for breakfast.
6. Favor hard cheeses over soft ones.
7. Top dishes with shredded cheese.
8. Add cheese to soup or sprinkle it on top as a garnish. My favorite is crumbled blue cheese on leek soup.

Non-dairy Options

9. Favor canned salmon over canned tuna.
10. Combine dark greens with red foods such as red bell peppers.

✧ Reasons to store sour cream, cottage cheese and yogurt tubs upside down:
- This forms a better seal, so they shouldn't go bad as fast. Try this technique for other foods in a tub.
- If you invert them occasionally, the contents are less likely to separate.

✗ No-No

Don't store cartons of milk, cream or other dairy products on a shelf in the fridge door. Keep them at the back of the fridge, where it is colder.

Butterfat

✧ Butterfat is the fatty component in dairy products. Milk and cream are classified by their levels of butterfat. Recipes may leave you scratching your head because standards (and names) vary in Canada, the U.S. and U.K.

Ballpark Butterfat Percentages

- Skim milk (traces). It is now redundantly labeled fat-free.
- Whole milk (3.25%).
- Light cream (5%).
- Half-and-half cream (10% to 18%, but typically at the lower end).
- Table cream (16% to 32%, but typically at the lower end). This may be called single cream or light cream in a recipe.
- Heavy cream (30% to 40%). Light whipping cream (30% to 36%) may be differentiated from heavy cream (more than 36%). Whipping cream is typically about 35%. Use what's available in your area.
- Double cream (48%). Some European recipes call for this. Very stiff, it's easy to overbeat and is better for piping.
- Clotted cream (55% to 60%). Sometimes called Devonshire or Devon cream, this thick, yellow cream is traditionally poured over scones. It's made by heating unpasteurized milk, letting it stand, then scooping clots of creamy fat off the top.

is for Homogenized

Homogenization prevents fat from separating out of cream as it sits. Instead, it stays finely dispersed throughout the cream.

Ways to Tinker with Butterfat

- You don't have to stock a full array of milk and cream for cooking and baking. Just do the math. Do you want table cream? Combine equal parts of whipping cream and skim milk.
- You can add melted, unsalted butter to milk to raise the butterfat. Do this only for cooking and some baking, such as cookies. It won't work in all recipes.

Formulas to Equal 1 cup (250 mL)

- Don't stock whole milk? Replace it with 15 tbsp (225 mL) skim milk and scant 1 tbsp (15 mL) butter.
- In place of half-and-half cream, use 14 tbsp (210 mL) skim milk and 2 tbsp (25 mL) butter.
- Instead of table cream, use $\frac{3}{4}$ cup (175 mL) skim milk and $\frac{1}{4}$ cup (50 mL) butter.
- To replace heavy cream, use 9 tbsp (135 mL) skim milk and 7 tbsp (105 mL) butter.

Milk

❖ Adding a pinch of salt to milk in the carton is supposed to help it stay fresh longer.

Ways to Froth Milk

- You can heat the milk before frothing. The froth will be satiny, finer and smooth. Advantage: The milk underneath is well insulated by the froth and stays steamy.
- You can froth cold milk, then heat it. In the microwave, the froth expands and expands. Advantage: The froth is thick and stable, so it holds its shape.

 **A Bit of Science**

Because it has more protein, skim milk froths better than fattier milk. Lactose-free skim milk froths the best; it has the most protein.

S is for Scalding

You can boil heavy cream, but never milk. To scald milk, heat it until small bubbles start to form around the edges and vapors start to rise from the surface. The temperature should reach 180°F (85°C), but never go over the boiling point.

❖ When heating milk, warm the saucepan first. The milk will leave a thinner film on the bottom, and be less sticky and scorch-prone. You can fill the pan with a $\frac{1}{2}$-inch (1 cm) layer of water, bring it to a boil, pour it out, then scald your milk.

Evaporated **VS.** Condensed?

Evaporated milk is condensed to half its volume before it's canned. It is sterilized with heat, which affects the milk sugar and gives it a cooked taste. Condensed milk has sugar added before it's canned. The large amount of sugar acts as a preservative. Condensed milk doesn't have to be heat-sterilized and, once opened, it keeps longer than evaporated milk.

❖ Condensed milk will thicken without cooking when you add acidic ingredients, such as citrus juice or even chocolate.

❖ Invert cans of evaporated and condensed milk in the cupboard every few weeks.

Making Do

To reconstitute evaporated milk, add an equal amount of water. Use this in place of fresh milk. It will not, however, taste fresh.

P is for Powdered Milk

Powdered milk is dried milk solids. It comes in whole milk, skim and buttermilk forms. It may be called dry milk.

- Store whole milk powder in the fridge. You can store the skim and buttermilk powders in a cool place, but they'll keep longer in the fridge.

- Reconstitute and refrigerate powdered milk a couple of hours before using it. Stir 3 to 4 tbsp (45 to 60 mL) powdered milk into 1 cup (250 mL) water. The reconstituted buttermilk is not thick.

♛ A Golden Rule

When cooking, it's better to stir or whisk milk powder with the dry ingredients in a recipe, then add the liquid.

- Lower the heat when cooking with reconstituted powdered milk. It scorches easily.

- If you're baking, don't use more than ¼ cup (50 mL) powdered milk per 1 cup (250 mL) flour.

♡ Healthier Eater

Turn skim milk powder and evaporated milk into whipped toppings. They whip up like a dream, but deflate like a nightmare, so don't let them sit in the fridge overnight. These toppings are airy rather than dense like whipped cream

Buttermilk

- Shake the buttermilk in the carton before using it.

⚛ A Bit of Science

Buttermilk used to be the liquid left after making butter. Now, buttermilk is cultured with low-fat milk and soured with friendly bacteria. Lactic acid in buttermilk and sour milk makes baked goods tender and sauces tangy.

- Buttermilk curdles more easily than other types of milk. Do not scald it.

Skim Milk Whipped Topping

Seeing skim milk whip up is a pleasant surprise. **Makes about 7 cups (1.75 L)**

Tip
Serve this as soon as possible after chilling.

¾ cup	instant skim milk powder	175 mL
Pinch	salt	Pinch
1¼ cups	cold water	300 mL
1 tbsp	freshly squeezed lemon juice	15 mL
¼ cup	confectioner's (icing) sugar	50 mL
¼ tsp	vanilla extract	1 mL

1. In a stand mixer fitted with a whisk beater, whip skim milk powder, salt, cold water and lemon juice for about 5 minutes or until stiff peaks form. Scrape the bowl. Beat in confectioner's sugar and vanilla.

2. Cover and refrigerate for 1 hour or until thoroughly chilled.

Evaporated Milk Whipped Topping

Here's another lighter alternative to whipped cream that won't break the calorie bank.
Makes about 8 cups (2 L)

Tip
This makes enough for a crowd of dieters. You can use part of a can and reduce the lemon juice.

1	can (12 oz or 370 mL) evaporated milk	1
1 tsp	freshly squeezed lemon juice	5 mL
	Confectioner's (icing) sugar	

1. Pour evaporated milk into a large bowl. Cover and freeze for about 1¼ hours or until a thin layer of ice forms on top.

2. Add lemon juice and whip for about 5 minutes (if using an electric hand mixer) or until stiff peaks form. Beat in confectioner's sugar to taste.

3. Cover and refrigerate for 1 hour or until thoroughly chilled. Use as soon as possible.

Buttermilk Substitutes
- Pour ¼ cup (50 mL) milk into ¾ cup (175 mL) plain yogurt. Shake or whisk to combine.
- Whisk together equal parts of sour cream and skim milk.
- Replace with soured milk.

Sour **VS.** Soured?
Sour milk has gone bad. Soured milk has been deliberately made acidic to use as a substitute for buttermilk. Once upon a time, raw milk would sour pleasantly if left to its own devices, but today's pasteurized milk just spoils. Adding an acid to milk makes it clabber, or thicken.

Master Plan
Soured Milk
1. Put 2 tsp (10 mL) freshly squeezed lemon juice or 1 tbsp (15 mL) cider vinegar into a measuring cup.
2. Pour in milk until it reaches the 1-cup (250 mL) mark.
3. Let the mixture stand for 5 minutes or until thickened.

Soured Milk Tips
- The milk must be at room temperature. Or it can be heated in the microwave, but briefly. Warm milk wants to separate when the acid is added.
- Lemon juice lends a buttermilk flavor. It can also make the mixture clumpier. This is fine in batters.
- Plain white vinegar tastes too bold. Use cider vinegar.
- Sour 1 cup (250 mL) milk at a time for more even consistency.
- When soured, skim, 1% and 2% milk are thinner than buttermilk. Whole milk should sour to the thickness of buttermilk.

✧ If you're using milk in place of buttermilk, replace any baking soda with the same amount of baking powder.

⚡ *Lightning Won't Strike If ...*

You freeze buttermilk. There's always some left over after baking. Frozen buttermilk does get grainy, and it separates. Shake it well after thawing and it'll be okay for baking. It's not great for other uses, such as dressings. Be warned that pancakes made with previously frozen buttermilk will be less airy.

✧ Freeze buttermilk in portions. Use small zip-lock bags. Then write to the producers and ask why they don't wake up and sell buttermilk in pints and half-pints, the way we use it.

Cream

✧ Cream needs at least 30% butterfat to whip properly. It should double in volume.

Whip It Good

✧ Three ways to help cream whip up faster and fluffier:

- Keep it cold. The fat will stay firm rather than becoming oily.
- Add ⅛ tsp (0.5 mL) freshly squeezed lemon juice per 1 cup (250 mL) cream.
- For maximum fluff, wait until you see soft peaks form and the beaters leave tracks before adding other ingredients (particularly sugar).

Ways to Keep Cream Cold

- Use a deep, narrow bowl.
- Run the coldest tap water over the bowl and beaters first.
- Chill the bowl and beaters for 30 minutes in the freezer or for 1 hour in the fridge first.
- On a hot day, nest the mixing bowl in a tub of ice.

Master Plan
Whipped Cream

1. Using an electric mixer on medium-high speed, beat cream until soft peaks form and the beaters leave tracks.
2. Add sugar or flavoring such as vanilla, reduce the speed to medium-low and continue beating until stiff peaks form.
3. Don't overdo it. Purists switch to a whisk at the end, to get stiff peaks without overbeating.

Whipped Cream Doctor

The cream looks curdled.

- It has been whipped too long.
- Gently pour in 2 tbsp (25 mL) cream per 1 cup (250 mL) cream you started with. Whisk just to smooth it out. Do not beat again.

You see buttery clumps.

- Bad news: You have reached the whipping point of no return. Good news: You are on your way to making butter. Keep going and turn your mistake into a treat. (Check out homemade butter recipes in the Butter section in Pantry Basics.)

The whipped cream weeps, especially sitting in the fridge.

- Add confectioner's (icing) sugar instead of granulated or superfine sugar when you're whipping the cream. The cornstarch in the confectioner's sugar adds stability.
- Make a hammock. Rinse and dry a triple layer of cheesecloth. Drape it across a medium bowl or plastic tub, so it sags but doesn't touch the bottom. Secure it around the rim with an elastic band. Spoon whipped cream into the hammock, then cover the bowl with plastic wrap or a lid and refrigerate it. The watery residue will drip into the bowl. Bonus: You can use this liquid in cooked dishes and sauces.
- Whipped cream won't separate if it is stabilized with gelatin.

Stabilized Whipped Cream

How come your neighbor's pies, puddings and éclairs look so perky, with their perfect dollops of cream, while yours look sad and weepy after a few hours? Don't be jealous. Do something about it. Gelatin and confectioner's (icing) sugar, which contains a bit of cornstarch, give this cream a double dose of staying power. It stays firm even after a week — although you shouldn't keep it that long. **Makes about 2$\frac{1}{2}$ cups (625 mL)**

Tip

Don't be tempted to use part of the cream to soften the gelatin. The whipped cream won't fluff up as nicely and the color will be darker.

Variations

Substitute brandy, rum or any flavored extract for the vanilla. Brandy is supposed to make the cream last longer.

Use 1$\frac{1}{2}$ tsp (7 mL) unflavored gelatin powder and 3 tbsp (45 mL) water for a super-firm version.

1 tsp	unflavored gelatin powder	5 mL
2 tbsp	cold water	25 mL
1 cup	heavy or whipping (35%) cream, chilled	250 mL
2 to 3 tbsp	confectioner's (icing) sugar	25 to 45 mL
1 tsp	vanilla extract	5 mL

1. In a small heatproof bowl, sprinkle gelatin over cold water and let stand for 5 minutes. Set the bowl in another heatproof bowl filled about halfway with boiling water. Stir the mixture until gelatin is dissolved. Remove from water and let cool to room temperature.

2. In a large bowl, beat cream to the consistency of soft custard. Continue beating while pouring in the gelatin mixture in a steady stream. Beat in sugar and vanilla until stiff peaks form.

3. Cover and refrigerate for at least 2 hours or until firm enough to pipe, or dollop it onto a dessert and refrigerate until serving.

OUTSIDE THE BOX

- For a nice tang, add $\frac{1}{4}$ cup (50 mL) full-fat sour cream per 1 cup (250 mL) whipping cream, then whip as usual.
- You can whip cream without a mixer: Pour it into a glass jar or a plastic tub and tighten the lid. Shake it for 5 minutes or until you hear clunking instead of sloshing.

Gussy It Up

For decorative cream rosettes and other shapes, beat cream until stiff peaks form, pipe the shapes onto waxed paper and freeze. Use these frozen.

♥ Healthier Eater

- Replace the cream in a recipe (if it doesn't have to be whipped). Combine 1 cup (250 mL) skim milk with 2 tsp (10 mL) cornstarch (as a substitute for table cream) or with 1 tbsp (15 mL) cornstarch (as a substitute for heavy cream). Thicken by bringing it just to the boiling point. Do not boil it.
- Cut fat by replacing some or all of the cream with evaporated milk. This works nicely in macaroni and cheese.
- You can whip half-and-half (10%) cream with unflavored gelatin powder and confectioner's (icing) sugar as an alternative to whipped cream for some uses. This technique won't work with table (18%) cream.

Lightly Whipped Light Cream

This whips up frothy, and is as thick as pourable custard but not firm enough to hold its shape. **Makes about 2 cups (500 mL)**

Tip
This was tested using half-and-half (10%) cream. Heavier cream doesn't work.

1 tsp	unflavored gelatin powder	5 mL
1 tbsp	cold water	15 mL
1 cup	half-and-half (10%) cream, divided	250 mL
1 tbsp	confectioner's (icing) sugar	15 mL
¼ tsp	vanilla extract	1 mL

1. In a tiny bowl, sprinkle gelatin over water and let stand for 5 minutes.

2. In a glass measuring cup, microwave ⅓ cup (75 mL) of the cream on High for about 45 seconds or until scalded and steamy. Do not let boil. Stir in gelatin mixture until gelatin is dissolved. Stir in the remaining cream, confectioner's sugar and vanilla. Transfer to an airtight container and refrigerate for 4 to 6 hours, stirring occasionally, until cold and set.

3. Pour mixture into a bowl. Using an electric mixer, whip on medium-high speed for 3 to 4 minutes or until the beaters leave tracks and cream is frothy. Use immediately, or cover and refrigerate for 1 hour. It will set and become moussy in the fridge.

❖ Ways to stretch and lighten powdered whipped topping mix:
- Use skim milk in place of whole milk.
- Use half skim milk, half cold water. Despite being diluted, it will be whip up just as well.
- Double the amount of milk and beat 50% longer than directed, for a reasonably firm topping.
- Make sure the milk, bowl and beaters are extremely cold. Chill them in the freezer for 30 minutes first.

 No-No
Don't use crème fraîche substitutes when making ice cream. You need the real thing.

C is for Crème Fraîche
Crème fraîche is a velvety, thickened, slightly sour cream. It has 35% to 40% butterfat. Crème fraîche can be used in place of heavy or whipped cream, sour cream or Greek yogurt. It doesn't curdle when heated. Way back when, farmers made crème fraîche by letting unpasteurized cream sit in a cool, dark place. Nowadays, it is cultured.

Making Do
- As a quick alternative to crème fraîche, use sour cream. Better, mellow the sour cream with some heavy or whipping (35%) cream. It should still be thick.
- Stir together homemade crème fraîche and leave it to thicken.

Homemade Crème Fraîche 1

Store-bought crème fraîche is expensive. You can make a reasonable substitute at home, but it won't be as rich and thick. **Makes about ¾ cup (175 mL)**

Tip

If you're worried about leaving cream out that long, you can refrigerate it after 2 hours. The result will be thinner.

½ cup	heavy or whipping (35%) cream	125 mL
¼ cup	full-fat sour cream	50 mL

1. In a small bowl, lightly whisk cream and sour cream until blended. Let stand at room temperature for about 3 hours or until thickened.

2. Transfer to an airtight container and refrigerate for at least 1 hour, until cold, or for up to 1 week.

Homemade Crème Fraîche 2

Here's another way to make a crème fraîche substitute at home. **Makes about 1 cup (250 mL)**

Tip

For food safety reasons, refrigerate this after 2 hours. The result will be thinner.

1 cup	heavy or whipping (35%) cream	250 mL
1 tbsp	freshly squeezed lemon juice	15 mL

1. In a small bowl, combine cream and lemon juice. Let stand at room temperature for 2 hours, or up to 3 hours for a thicker version.

2. Transfer to an airtight container and refrigerate for at least 1 hour, until thickened, or for up to 1 week.

Sour Cream

❖ Stir heavy or whipping (35%) cream into full-fat sour cream to thin it.

❖ How to prevent curdling when cooking with sour cream:
  • Gently stir in the sour cream at the end of the cooking time.
  • Turn the heat down low.

❖ Don't substitute low-fat sour cream in baking. It has additives for thickening.

Yogurt

❖ Make your own fruit-bottom yogurt: In a small storage tub, stir jam with chopped fresh fruit. Dollop yogurt on top.

Ⓨ is for Yogurt Cheese

This spreadable cheese is made by draining yogurt. It can be used as a low-fat substitute for cream cheese. It also makes a better base for yogurt dips, which are otherwise sloppy. Middle Eastern yogurt cheese is called labneh. It is firm enough to be rolled into balls.

Master Plan
Yogurt Cheese

1. Line a sieve with several layers of dampened cheesecloth. Place the sieve over a medium bowl. Spoon in a tubful of yogurt. Cover with plastic wrap.
2. Refrigerate and let it drain for 8 to 24 hours. The longer you leave it, the thicker it gets.
3. Gather the cheesecloth into a bundle and gently squeeze out remaining liquid. Transfer yogurt cheese to an airtight container. If desired, stir in seasonings or herbs. Cover and refrigerate for up to a week.

☰ Fast Fix

To speed draining when making yogurt cheese, put a small plate on top of the yogurt and weigh it down with a can.

✧ You can use a cheesecloth hammock to drain a smaller amount of yogurt in its original tub. Drape a triple layer of cheesecloth across the tub, so it sags but doesn't touch the bottom, and secure around the rim with an elastic band. Spoon in the yogurt, then replace the lid. Refrigerate and let it drain until it turns into yogurt cheese.

♻ Waste Not

If the yogurt you used to make yogurt cheese is organic and additive-free, you can use the drained whey in sauces and stews.

✧ Make yogurt cheese more like cream cheese: Stir in 1 tbsp (15 mL) heavy cream per $\frac{1}{4}$ cup (50 mL) dense yogurt cheese.

ⓣ is for Tzatziki

Tzatziki is a popular Greek yogurt dip. Unfortunately, too many cooks make it with straight yogurt and it ends up sloppy.

Secrets to Thick, Velvety Tzatziki

- Make yogurt cheese.
- Drain the cucumber.
- Stir in olive oil.

Greek VS. Balkan?

Balkan yogurt is processed in individual cups rather than vats. It is smoother and thicker than stirred yogurts, but nowhere near the glory of Greek yogurt. Tangy and dare we say decadent, strained Greek yogurt is stiff enough to hang from a spoon. It can be made from cow's, sheep's or goat's milk, and commonly has 5% to 10% butterfat. Greek yogurt is sold in cheese shops and ethnic specialty stores, not supermarkets.

Gussy It Up

Greek yogurt makes a heavenly dessert. Try it with honey and pistachios.

5 Ways to Prevent Yogurt-Cooking Mishaps

1. Reduce curdling. Stir in 1 tsp (5 mL) cornstarch, 2 tsp (10 mL) flour or 1 tbsp (15 mL) puréed raw potato per 1 cup (250 mL) yogurt before adding the yogurt to a hot curry or sauce.
2. If a dish with yogurt becomes grainy during cooking, stir 1 tsp (5 mL) cornstarch with 2 tsp (10 mL) water into a paste, then stir the paste into the barely simmering dish.
3. Never boil a dish that contains yogurt.
4. Whisk yogurt until it is smooth. Slowly stir it into a hot, cooked dish and remove it from the heat.
5. Incorporate yogurt by gently folding it into a cooled dish.

Tzatziki

This is thick, pungent and lip-smackingly good. Use it as a dip or as a sauce alongside grilled meat. **Makes about 2 cups (500 mL)**

Tips

I used 2% yogurt, but any kind will work.

Shred the cucumber against the large teardrop holes of a box grater.

If you push the garlic through a press, discard the tough fibers.

2 cups	plain yogurt	500 mL
1	small cucumber, peeled, seeded and shredded	1
	Salt	
2	cloves garlic, pressed, puréed or minced	2
1 tbsp	chopped fresh parsley	15 mL
1 tsp	chopped fresh mint	5 mL
	Freshly ground pepper	
2 tbsp	extra virgin olive oil	25 mL
1 tbsp	white wine vinegar	15 mL

1. Spoon yogurt into a large sieve lined with cheesecloth and set over a medium bowl. Cover with plastic wrap. Refrigerate and let drain for at least 2 hours or, preferably, overnight.

2. Place cucumber in a large sieve set over a medium bowl. Sprinkle generously with salt and toss to coat. Let drain for 30 minutes.

3. Gather the cheesecloth into a bundle and gently squeeze out remaining liquid. Transfer yogurt to a medium bowl. Discard the drained liquid.

4. Gently squeeze cucumber, then add to yogurt. Stir in garlic, parsley, mint, pepper to taste, oil and vinegar until combined. Cover and refrigerate for at least 1 hour, until chilled, or for up to 1 week.

Cheese

P is for Pasteurization

Cheeses can be made with raw or heated milk. Pasteurized milk is heated to destroy microorganisms that cause disease and hasten spoilage and fermentation.

- Most cheeses are made from pasteurized milk. Various temperature and time combinations are used.
- Raw milk goes straight from the animal to the cheese vat, or it is chilled first, then reheated during processing to no more than 104°F (40°C), which is close to the body temperature of the animal.
- Thermalized milk, also called unpasteurized or gently pasteurized, is warmed to higher temperatures. It is not heated enough to pasteurize it, but enough to kill some of the microorganisms.

Unripened VS. Ripened?

Fresh, or unripened, cheese is soft and creamy. It is made from milk that is heated and separated. The thin liquid whey is drained. The curds, or solids, are pressed. Aged, or ripened, cheese is made by curing the curds with methods ranging from heating and kneading to cutting, stretching and salting. It comes in many flavors, from mild to pungent, and different hardnesses.

Semisoft VS. Firm VS. Hard?

- Semisoft cheeses are medium-firm and moist. They are divided into categories based on the ripening method — such as unripened, interior ripened and surface ripened. Some semisoft cheeses may be smoked. Example: mozzarella.
- Firm cheeses are pressed to remove moisture. Some firm cheeses are washed and brushed, others wrapped in wax. Gases may be released before the cheese firms up, creating holes. Example: Swiss cheese.
- Hard cheeses are aged for months or years and lose most of their moisture. They are best shaved or grated. Example: Parmesan.

Factoid Purists say feta should never be made from cow's milk, just goat's or sheep's milk. Press a bit of feta between your tongue and the roof of your mouth. It should have a creamy finish. If it's grainy, almost floury, purists would suspect cow's milk was used.

M is for Mascarpone

Mascarpone is a thick, soft, slightly sweet, slightly acidic cream cheese. From half to three-quarters butterfat, it is as rich as it is expensive. Mellow mascarpone is primarily a dessert cheese. It is most famously used in tiramisu.

Mascarpone Substitutes

- In a food processor, whirl 8 oz (250 g) ricotta cheese with 1 cup (250 mL) heavy or whipping (35%) cream until blended.
- Using an electric mixer, blend equal amounts of softened block cream cheese and sour cream.
- Using an electric mixer or food processor, blend 8 oz (250 g) cream cheese with 2 tbsp (25 mL) each whipping cream and sour cream.

Mock Mascarpone

You can substitute this for mascarpone in tiramisu. **Makes about 2 cups (500 mL) or 12 oz (375 g)**

Tip

When substituting this, go by weight. In a tiramisu recipe, reduce the sugar and increase the gelatin by about a third.

8 oz	block cream cheese, softened	250 g
1/3 cup	confectioner's (icing) sugar	75 mL
3/4 cup	heavy or whipping (35%) cream	175 mL

1. In a bowl, using an electric mixer, beat cream cheese and sugar on medium speed until blended and fluffy. Increase speed to high and beat in cream until mixture is stiff.

H is for Halloumi

Halloumi is a firm, salty white cheese from Cyprus. It is traditionally made from a blend of goat's and sheep's milk. Imitations made with cow's milk are cheaper. Because halloumi has a melting point that's higher than normal for cheese, it holds its shape when heated. This makes it excellent for frying, grilling, broiling or flambéing.

❖ Slice halloumi 1/4 to 1/2 inch (0.5 to 1 cm) thick before cooking.

How to Cook Halloumi

1. Fry it. Dip halloumi in flour to create a light crust. Fry it in olive oil until golden.
2. Broil it. Drizzle halloumi with olive oil. Arrange in a single layer in a baking dish or in individual heatproof dishes. Broil until the edges are golden.
3. Grill it. Rub halloumi with olive oil. Place on the barbecue grate over medium heat, then cover and grill until golden.

❖ Do not overheat goat cheese. It will separate into a gritty, rubbery mess that can't be saved.

How to Serve Warm Halloumi

1. Squeeze lime juice over top, then drizzle with olive oil.
2. Top it with olives, capers or chopped roasted peppers.

OUTSIDE THE BOX

For an instant Brie raclette, use the barbecue. Place a small wheel of Brie on a piece of foil that's pierced with holes or on a metal grill tray. Brush the Brie with marinade or top it with salsa or roasted peppers. Cover and grill over medium heat until the edges start to bulge and the center is soft, about 15 minutes

F is for Fromage Fort

Here's a frugal way to use up all those nubs of cheese in your fridge: Make fromage fort. The name means "strong cheese." It is prepared with cheese, wine and garlic, and strengthens as it stands. It will clear your sinuses and wake up your taste buds. Because it is made with leftovers, fromage fort tastes different each time.

Fromage Fort

I used Parmesan, Brie, mozzarella, Gruyère, blue, Jack, Cheddar and goat cheeses.
Makes about 2 cups (500 mL)

Tips

Gussy this up by stirring in chopped fresh herbs or dried fruit such as cranberries.

Fromage fort is delicious spread over crackers and broiled briefly.

To jack up pasta fast, toss it with fromage fort.

4	cloves garlic	4
1 lb	leftover cheese, diced or crumbled	500 g
½ cup	dry white wine	125 mL
	Sea salt and freshly ground black pepper	

1. In a food processor fitted with a metal blade, purée garlic. Add cheese and wine; purée until fairly smooth (some texture is fine).
2. Scrape into an airtight container and season to taste with salt and pepper. Serve immediately or refrigerate for up to 2 weeks.

Factoid It's "process cheese," not "processed cheese." Process cheese is at least half cheese. "Process cheese food" contains less than half cheese.

Making Cheese at Home

✧ Cheese is made from cow's, goat's, sheep's and even buffalo's milk. The milk is coagulated and separated by adding rennet, salt or an acid. You can do this at home.

P is for Paneer

Paneer is Indian fresh cheese. It's easy to make at home. The drawback is that it takes a lot of milk to make a little paneer.

Storing Cheese

✧ Smelly, runny cheese can be delectable or horrifying. Is it well aged or past its prime?

Nine Bad Signs

- A whiff of ammonia
- Semisoft and firm cheeses that no longer feel supple or springy
- Swollen lumps or bumps on hard cheeses
- A dull interior (you should see a bit of shine)
- Tough, waxy edges or isolated waxy areas
- Yellowing and decaying at the edges of bloomy rinds (these should be velvety and white)
- Bulges in the rind
- Brittle, cracked rind
- Blue cheese that's tinged brown, yellow or pink (the veins should be only blue or green)

✧ Buy cheese in small hunks, so you don't have to store it long. Cheeses prefer high humidity and temperatures from 45°F to 60°F (7°C to 15°C). Cheesemakers have cheese caves. We have to make do with the fridge, but it's not the happiest place for cheese.

Paneer

This makes a fairly firm fresh cheese. It tastes great in curry sauce, but you could also add it to salad. **Makes about 3 oz (90 g)**

Refrigerator Basics

Cheese

Tips

Two tbsp (25 mL) white vinegar can be substituted for the lemon juice, but it adds a pungent taste.

Discard the whey, unless the milk you started with is organic and additive-free. In that case, you can use the whey for cooking.

Variation

Use goat's milk. It makes a very mild, soft cheese.

4 cups	whole milk	1 L
3 tbsp	freshly squeezed lemon juice	45 mL
	Salt	

1. In a large saucepan, bring milk to a boil over medium heat. Stir in lemon juice to separate the milk into curds and whey. Stir in salt to taste. Remove from heat, cover and let stand for 5 minutes.

2. Drain mixture in a large sieve lined with cheesecloth. Spray cold water over curds. Drain, pressing with a spatula. Gather the cheesecloth into a bundle and place in the sieve set over a bowl. Cover the bundle with a weighted plate. Refrigerate and let drain for 3 to 4 hours or until paneer is firm. Store in an airtight container in the refrigerator for up to 1 week.

Homemade Cottage Cheese

This mild-tasting fresh cheese is so simple to prepare. **Makes about 4 oz (125 g)**

Tip

You can use any type of cream.

4 cups	whole milk	1 L
1 cup	buttermilk	250 mL
2 tsp	freshly squeezed lemon juice	10 mL
1 tsp	salt	5 mL
	Cream (optional)	

1. In a large saucepan, bring milk just to a boil over medium heat. Stir in buttermilk and lemon juice to separate the mixture into curds and whey. Turn off the heat, but leave the pan on the burner for 10 minutes.

2. Drain mixture for 5 minutes in a large sieve lined with cheesecloth. Gather the cheesecloth into a bundle and place in the sieve set over a bowl. (Or tie the gathered corners of the cheesecloth around the handle of a wooden spoon and balance the spoon across the rim of a deep bowl or pot.) Refrigerate and let drain for 2 hours.

3. Crumble the fresh cheese into a bowl and sprinkle with salt. To make creamed cottage cheese, if desired, stir in cream to taste.

How to Get Rid of Mold

- You can remove a small patch of blue, green or fuzzy mold on the rind or surface of hard cheeses. Use a knife rubbed with vinegar to cut it off, cutting out at least 1 inch (2.5 cm) from around the mold. The rest of the cheese will still be good to eat. Soft cheeses that grow mold that isn't from the manufacturing process must be discarded.

- ✧ Wipe cheese dry with a paper towel before storing it.

Ways to Wrap Cheese

- In waxed paper. Secure it with an elastic band, then put it in an open plastic bag.
- In foil. Cut the name from the package and tape it to the foil.
- In cheesecloth. First dampen the cloth with salted water. Seal the wrapped cheese in an airtight container. This works best for fairly firm cheeses.

- ✧ Don't store cheese in its original plastic wrapper. It needs to breathe without drying out, getting moldy or absorbing odors.

Control Odors

- Keep cheese far from strong-smelling foods.
- Wrap each type of cheese separately, so the odors don't mingle.
- Put a small, fresh bouquet of thyme in the cheese drawer.
- For a picnic, seal cheese in a separate tub, so it doesn't make everything in the cooler smelly.

- ✧ Change the water daily for fresh mozzarella or bocconcini. Use bottled water.

7 Ways to Keep Cheese Supple

1. Store it in the cheese compartment or vegetable crisper.
2. Don't strip off the rind.
3. Rub exposed surfaces with butter.
4. Soak it in buttermilk. Do this to revive firm cheese that develops hardened, waxy edges.
5. Toss a sugar cube into the cheese compartment or a cheese container.
6. Place parchment or waxed paper over the cut surfaces.
7. Don't leave cheese lying around. Keep it away from the stove or a radiator, and out of direct sunlight. Warm cheese will sweat, run and develop rubbery patches.

Ways to Keep Feta Tender and Mellow

- Keep it in its brine or in lightly salted water.
- Store it in a boiled, cooled solution of equal parts water and skim milk. This decreases saltiness and makes the feta whiter.
- Soak it in water or skim milk for 30 minutes before consuming it.

Factoid Brie ripens from the outside in.

The Cheese Tray

✧ Serve cheese at room temperature. Remove it from the fridge 45 to 60 minutes before serving it. Exception: Cream cheese should be kept refrigerated.

Prevent Flavors from Mingling

• Arrange cheeses on a platter or board so they are not touching. In particular, keep strong cheeses away from mild ones.

• Offer a different knife, slicer or spreader for each cheese.

✧ Cover the cheese tray with a damp kitchen towel or plastic wrap so it doesn't dry out or absorb odors.

Bloomy VS. Washed?

Bloomy rinds are soft and velvety. Example: Brie. Washed rinds are rinsed with water, wine, beer or brine, and may be slightly sticky. Example: Oka.

✧ Leave on the rinds when serving cheese. They protect it, and most taste good.

✧ To soften the aggressiveness of blue cheese, mix it with butter or cream cheese. Add a splash of wine or brandy. Serve it as a spread.

❁ Waste Not

Don't throw away those rinds. Bloomy and washed rinds are edible, while tough or waxed ones (think Gouda) are not. Some inedible rinds can be tossed into simmering soups and stews, then discarded. Save the hard rinds from Parmesan. They add fine flavor to dishes, especially ones with beans and/or bitter greens.

Preparing Cheese

Tips for Cutting Cheese

• Cold cheese is easier to cut.
• Wipe the blade between each cut.
• Lightly oil the blade. It will slide through firm cheeses and cut sticky cheeses without catching.
• If cheese starts to crumble as you cut it, warm the blade by dipping it into boiling water as needed.

Making Do

Shave firm cheese with a vegetable peeler if you don't have a proper, thin cheese slicer.

✧ Blue and goat cheeses crumble better if they are frozen briefly. To crumble, chop with a knife.

Shredded VS. Grated?

Although these terms are used interchangeably, there's a difference that can affect recipes. Shredded cheese is in small slivers. This is usually done using the large teardrop holes of a box grater. Grated cheese is in granules. Rasp (Microplane) and rotary graters are best for grating. Grated cheese comes out fluffier from a rasp grater, drier from a rotary grater. Semisoft and firm cheeses are usually shredded, hard cheeses grated.

Estimated Yields

• One oz (30 g) hard cheese, such as Parmesan, yields about $\frac{1}{2}$ cup (125 mL) freshly grated, lightly packed cheese.
• Four oz (125 g) firm cheese, such as Cheddar, yields about 1 cup (250 mL) shredded, lightly packed cheese.

✧ Careful: Grated and shredded cheeses settle as they sit and dry out. That can throw off recipe amounts.

Ways to Prevent Sticking and Squashing

- Freeze firm cheese for 15 minutes before shredding it.
- Freeze the cheese grater.
- Oil the holes of a box grater inside and out. This also makes it easier to clean.

OUTSIDE THE BOX

To clean a grater, grate a raw potato after the cheese, then rinse.

How to Prevent Shredded Cheese from Clumping

1. Toss in a dried herb mixture.
2. Toss with a bit of flour.
3. Store it with a morsel of bread to absorb moisture.

✧ Give shredded mild Cheddar or cheese sauce a kick. Sprinkle in a bit of mustard powder.

✿ Waste Not

If a cheese becomes hard and waxy, you can still cook with it. Just grate and melt it.

♛ A Golden Rule

Grate your own Parmesan. It's fresher and cheaper. You can store the wedge in the freezer and grate it on demand.

✧ When using Parmesan in baking, choose shredded over finely grated. The latter is too subtle.

✧ Choose carefully between store-bought dry grated Parmesan and the kind you freshly grate at home. Different volume measurements and textures can foul up recipes. Each type has its uses. Examples: Fine, gritty Parmesan, like the kind you would find in the supermarket deli section, is best for breading. Fluffy, freshly grated Parmesan is good for oven-baked crisps. A rotary grater yields a texture that's somewhere in between.

Block VS. Deli Cream Cheese?

Beware. Recipes flop because they fail to specify block or deli cream cheese. Block is packaged like butter. Deli comes in a tub; it is fluffy and contains a lot more moisture. In most cases, cookbook authors mean block cream cheese. Clue: If the recipe calls for "cream cheese, softened," it means a block.

Ways to Soften Block Cream Cheese

- Unwrap an 8 oz (250 g) block of cream cheese. Cut it into quarters, then microwave on Medium-Low (30%) for 1 to 2 minutes.
- Put the wrapped block in a zip-lock bag. Immerse it in hot water until it is as soft as you want it.

Making Do

- If you run out of cream cheese, purée 1 cup (250 mL) creamed cottage cheese and ¼ cup (50 mL) softened butter in a food processor until smooth.
- You can prepare your own fruit-flavored cream cheese. (Pineapple and peach are popular.) Soften the cream cheese. Using an electric mixer, blend in strained puréed fruit or finely chopped soft fruit. Chill it before serving.

Eggs

7 Egg Storage Tips

1. Technically, eggs can sit at room temperature. Once upon a time, people left these perfect little packages on the counter in bowls or baskets. However, that led to the horror of the rotten egg. May you never encounter it.

2. Refrigerate! Farmers store eggs at 50°F to 55°F (10°C to 13°C) until the eggs reach the grading station.

3. Ignore the egg keeper in the fridge door. Eggs stored in the door are jostled and exposed to temperature fluctuations. Keep them in the coolest part of the fridge.

4. Ignore any uncovered egg tray that may come with the fridge. Store eggs in their carton or in a container with a lid to protect them from breaking or absorbing odors.

5. Store eggs with the wide end up, where the air pocket is. Egg farmers stack their eggs this way to keep the yolks centered. Stored small end up, the contents separate from the shell more readily and age faster.

6. Eggshells are porous. Don't store eggs near smelly foods, such as cut onions.

7. Refrigerate egg whites in an airtight container.

8. To store egg yolks, place them in an airtight container and cover them with water. This prevents gumminess and crusting. Seal the container and refrigerate it. Before using the yolks, pour off the water.

✧ Yes, eggs have expiry dates. They are stamped on the cartons or right on the shells. The sell-by or best-before date is likely a month or more after the eggs were laid or graded. Always purchase eggs before their expiry date.

Signs of Freshness

- The yolk is dome-shaped. The thin membrane surrounding the yolk is stronger when it's fresher, so it helps the yolk hold its shape.
- There is more egg white because the water in it hasn't yet evaporated.
- The white is thick and clear.
- The white adheres closely to the yolk.
- The chalazae are prominent. (Chalazae are the white bands that anchor the yolk in the center of the egg white.)
- The air cell, found at the wide end of the egg, is smaller.
- The membrane inside the shell clings.

Signs of Old Age

- The yolk breaks easily.
- The white is cloudy.
- The white spreads thin.
- The air cell is bigger. As an egg ages, it absorbs more air through its porous shell.
- The inner membrane separates easily from the shell.

✧ Is an egg stuck to the carton? Wet the egg and try to ease it out. Don't tug. If the shell is cracked, throw out the egg or cook it right away.

✤ Borrow a method from the witch trials to check the freshness of an egg. Put an egg in a bowl holding 4 inches (10 cm) of water. If it floats, it's old or even rotten. The freshest eggs sink and sit on the bottom. Older but still edible eggs sit suspended, with one end tipped up.

✤ Eggs should travel from the farm to the supermarket within 1 week.

♛ A Golden Rule

Use eggs within 3 to 5 weeks. If the sell-by or best-before date has passed, the eggs are likely still okay. If they are old, cook them ASAP.

✤ Alternate buying white and brown eggs. That way, it's easier to keep track of which ones are fresher.

Mythstakes

- No, you can't tell freshness of an egg by the color of the yolk. The color depends on the hen's diet — corn or alfalfa for an orangey yolk, wheat for a pale yellow one.
- Brown eggs are no more nutritious or tastier than white eggs. The color of the shell is determined by the breed (and color) of the hen. A Rhode Island Red will lay a brown egg. A White Leghorn will lay a white egg.
- That red spot on an egg yolk is not a sign of fertilization. Grocery store eggs are not fertilized; the hens don't get any action. A red spot may be remnants of a blood vessel that burst during the egg's development. If it bothers you, remove the spot with the tip of a knife. By the way, fertilized eggs are fine to eat. They won't develop into chicks unless a hen sits on them for several weeks.

Sizes

✤ Don't worry if some eggs in the carton look smaller. Eggs are sized by weight.

✤ The Egg Farmers of Canada use these measurements:
- **Small:** 42 to 48 g (about $1\frac{1}{2}$ oz)
- **Medium:** 49 to 55 g (about $1\frac{3}{4}$ oz)
- **Large:** 56 to 62 g (about 2 oz)
- **Extra-large:** 63 to 69 g (about $2\frac{1}{4}$ oz)
- **Jumbo:** 70 g or more (about $2\frac{1}{2}$ oz or more)

✤ The American Egg Board goes with weights per dozen, but the averages end up the same as for Canadian eggs. The American measurements per dozen:
- **Small:** 18 oz (about 510 g)
- **Medium:** 21 oz (about 595 g)
- **Large:** 24 oz (about 680 g)
- **Extra-large:** 27 oz (about 765 g)
- **Jumbo:** 30 oz (about 850 g)

✤ Eggs also come in peewee sizes, but peewees and small eggs are not generally sold in stores.

✤ Hens lay mostly medium, large and extra-large eggs. Young hens lay peewee eggs. As a hen ages, her eggs get bigger. Old hens lay jumbo eggs. Egg farmers keep flocks of various ages.

✤ Double-yolk eggs are sometimes laid by hens near the beginning or end of their reproductive lives. This is due to hormonal changes. Double-yolk eggs have a larger volume, so don't use them for baking.

♛ A Golden Rule

Though many people buy extra-large eggs, the large egg is the default in cookbooks. If a recipe doesn't specify a size, assume that you are meant to use large.

❖ When a recipe calls for a small quantity, you can substitute the same number of eggs of a different size. But avoid substituting sizes when baking. The greater the number of eggs, the greater the margin of error.

Size Substitutions

- **1 large egg:** 2 small, 1 medium or 1 extra-large
- **2 large eggs:** 3 small, 2 medium or 2 extra-large
- **3 large eggs:** 4 small, 4 medium or 3 extra-large
- **4 large eggs:** 6 small, 5 medium or 4 extra-large
- **5 large eggs:** 7 small, 6 medium or 4 extra-large

❖ Another way to substitute: Beat the eggs lightly and go by volume.

❖ If you are short one egg (but only one):
- Add ¹⁄₂ tsp (2 mL) baking powder.
- Add 1 tsp (5 mL) each cornstarch and vinegar. (Note: Cake will be denser and rise less.)
- Add 3 tbsp (45 mL) extra liquid that has been thoroughly combined with 1 tsp (5 mL) cornstarch.
- Use 2 tbsp (25 mL) mayonnaise.
- Whip ¹⁄₄ cup (50 mL) soft tofu and add it.

---

3 Volume Cues

1. The contents of 1 large egg measure almost ¹⁄₄ cup (50 mL).
2. The white accounts for 2 tbsp (25 mL). The yolk accounts for 1¹⁄₂ tbsp (22 mL).
3. To halve a recipe calling for 1 egg, beat the egg lightly, then use 2 tbsp (25 mL).

Substitutions for One Whole Egg

- Two egg whites.
- Two egg yolks and 1 tbsp (15 mL) water.

Grades

❖ Eggs may be graded AA, A and B, or A, B and C, depending on the jurisdiction. There is no difference in nutritional values, just in appearance.
- **Premium** eggs are laid by young hens at their peak. They have top-quality shells, whites and yolks. They are sold to consumers.
- **Top-grade** eggs have firm whites, centered, blemish-free yolks and small air cells. The shells are clean and free of cracks. They are sold to consumers.
- **Mid-grade** eggs are uncracked, but may have minor stains, rough shells and watery whites. They are destined for further processing or commercial baking.
- **Low-grade** eggs have watery whites and loose yolks. The shells are stained and possibly cracked or misshapen. These eggs are sold to commercial processors. They may wind up in pet foods and pharmaceuticals.

🌷 *Being Green*

- The baffling array of numbers on the cartons or the eggshells can tell you a lot. Check with the producer for help decoding them.
- What goes in comes out. Check what the hens eat.

Specialty Eggs

- Omega-3 eggs are laid by hens that are fed a diet rich in flaxseed.
- Vitamin-enhanced eggs come from hens with an enhanced diet.
- Organic eggs are produced by hens that are fed organic grains.
- Vegetarian eggs are laid by hens that are fed only plant-based foods.

3 Notes On Deciphering Codes

1. The numbers should include a code that indicates the day the eggs were washed, graded and placed in the carton. It is likely a three-digit code that represents the day of the year, from 001 to 365.
2. Stamps indicate specialty eggs, such as omega-3s. There may be numeric codes that designate organic, free-range, barn-raised and cage production.
3. Some eggs can be traced right back to the farm, using the package coding.

Free-run VS. Free-range?

Free-run eggs are produced by hens that move around the floor of the barn, and have access to nesting boxes and, perhaps, perches. Free-range hens also have outdoor runs, seasonally or all year.

C is for Cage Hens

Most commercial eggs come from cage hens. In this controversial system, hens are confined to stacked cages and the eggs roll down conveyor belts. Opponents say that the system is cruel and unnatural. Farmers counter that it prevents the hens from hurting each other, supports their instinct to cluster, reduces egg breakage and lessens contact with manure that contains bacteria.

Separating Eggs

A is for Albumen

Albumen is the fancy term for egg white. It is mostly water, with protein and minerals. Yet it can be used in so many delightful ways.

❖ Separate eggs when they are cold, then let them stand to reach room temperature. A cold egg is easier to separate; the yolk is less likely to break. However, warmer whites are easier to whip.

Efficient Ways to Separate Eggs

- Wash your hands. Cradle a cracked egg in your hand. Let the white slip through your fingers into a bowl. Scissor your fingers to break up any stubborn clumps. You'll get the most egg white this way.
- Crack the egg. Over a bowl, pass the yolk back and forth between the eggshell halves, letting the white fall into the bowl. Use the sharp edge of one shell to cut any stubborn white. Caution: Dietitians disapprove of this method. They say the contents should have as little contact as possible with the eggshell, to reduce the risk of salmonella.

❖ The chalazae, or ropy white strands, in the egg needn't be removed. However, if you are making a smooth sauce or custard, you may wish to do so. Separate the chalazae from the egg white with the tip of a knife. A thin, beaten egg mixture can be strained to remove it.

❖ You can crack an egg handily on the edge of a metal spatula.

❖ Precautions to reduce the chances of splinters, bits of stray yolk or even a rotten egg surprise:
  - Separate eggs over a smaller bowl, not your bowl of whites or batter.
  - Give an egg a sharp rap on the counter rather than the rim of the mixing bowl.

- ❖ How to get a yolk speck or eggshell splinter out of whites:
  - Scoop it out with a piece of eggshell.
  - Use a moistened, tiny corner of paper towel.
  - Grab an eggshell fragment with a serrated grapefruit spoon or the tip of a grapefruit knife.

Better Leftovers

When you're stuck with lemons, you make lemonade. But what do you make when you're stuck with leftover egg whites?

- An egg-white omelet
- Meringue kiss cookies
- Boiled icing that looks like marshmallow fluff
- Angel food cake
- Macaroons
- A higher soufflé
- Egg wash to brush on cookies or breads before baking, to make them shiny

- ❖ Egg whites are too slithery to measure evenly in small quantities. If the recipe permits it, whisk the whites a bit to break them up.

❤ Healthier Eater

You can make an egg-white substitute from flaxseeds. In a saucepan, bring ⅓ cup (175 mL) flaxseeds and 3 cups (750 mL) water to a boil over medium-high heat. Reduce heat to medium-low and simmer for 30 minutes. While it's hot, strain the mixture through a fine sieve. You should have about 1½ cups (375 mL). Let cool for immediate use, or freeze in an ice cube tray for later use. Use 2 tbsp (25 mL) to replace 1 egg white.

This substitute contains omega-3 fatty acids and is suitable for vegans, but its uses are limited. It's okay for replacing an egg or two in muffins, pancakes or cookies, but not in cakes. It won't coagulate in a hot pan like fried eggs or whip up like a meringue.

Beating Eggs

- ❖ To reach full volume, whole eggs should be at 65°F to 75°F (18°C to 24°C) before they're beaten.

- ❖ Adding a pinch of salt or sugar makes whole eggs easier to beat.

- ❖ Avoid super-fresh eggs. They don't whip properly and taste too eggy.

6 Keys to Whipping Up the Fluffiest Egg Whites

1. Bring the whites to room temperature before beating.
2. Use a deep bowl with a rounded bottom.
3. The bowl should be clean, dry and grease-free. Don't use a plastic bowl; grease tends to cling to plastic.
4. Wipe the bowl with vinegar first.
5. Use a clean copper bowl. Chemicals in the copper react well with the whites, for more volume.
6. Add ⅛ tsp (0.5 mL) cream of tartar for every 2 egg whites. Or add a squirt of lemon juice or white vinegar.

⚛ A Bit of Science

Egg whites won't whip up fluffy if there's fat in them. Fat interferes with the coagulation of the proteins. Make sure you are not using a greasy bowl. Egg whites will be fluffier when an acid, such as cream of tartar or lemon juice, is added. Acids help stabilize the foam. Don't overdo it, though: Too much acidity will prevent the proteins from coagulating during baking.

- Older, runnier whites whip up faster and more voluminously. Fresher, thicker whites create a more stable foam.

- The whites of smaller eggs are more concentrated, so they are better for whipping and meringues.

- You can warm egg whites by placing them in a small bowl set over, but not touching, very hot water.

Cooking Eggs

- Fresher eggs take longer to cook. An egg that's a day or two old may take up to 1 minute longer to steam or boil than the average egg. As an egg ages, gases leak out through the shell, changing the acidity and the time it takes the whites to solidify.

⚛ A Bit of Science

Cooking eggs is never an eggs-act science. Age and temperature are factors, as are the physics of the egg. When the contents are hidden in the shell, you have to guess at doneness. Whites and yolks coagulate at different temperatures, so it's hard to get a perfect hard-cooked or fried egg.

- If eggs are cold and you want to use them pronto for cooking or baking, immerse them in a bowl of almost-hot water for 5 to 10 minutes.

- Cook eggs at medium or low temperatures. Two consequences of cooking eggs at high temperatures:
  - It makes the whites rubbery.
  - It makes scrambled eggs weepy because the proteins contract and push out water.

- Add white vinegar or salt to simmering water for boiled or poached eggs. It firms up the eggs and thus halts oozing and spreading, and seals cracks quickly. Add 1 tsp (5 mL) vinegar per 4 cups (1 L) water.

- For frying or poaching, use eggs straight from the fridge. They hold their shape better and the yolks are less likely to break.

- When frying or poaching, don't crack an egg directly into the pan. Break it into a ramekin or heatproof cup first. Move it close to the pan and slip it in. This way, the yolk is less likely to break. This also keeps shell fragments away from the pan.

Hard-Cooked and Soft-Cooked Eggs

♛ A Golden Rule

How do you boil an egg? Don't boil it. Hard- and soft-boiled eggs should be called hard- and soft-cooked eggs because actual boiling is passé. Boiling is the worst way to cook eggs in the shell. Steeping works the best.

- Ring around the yolk: That ugly gray-green ring around the yolk of a hard-cooked egg is caused by a chemical reaction between the iron in the yolk and the sulfur in the white. The yolks of older eggs get greener. Three ways to prevent a ring:
  - Cook the egg quickly. In other words, don't heat it at a low temperature for a long time.
  - Don't overcook it. More than 20 minutes is overkill.
  - Cool it quickly under cold running water.

Master Plan
A Perfect "Boiled" Egg

1. Transfer a large egg straight from the fridge into a small saucepan. Pour in enough cold water to cover it by 1 inch (2.5 cm).
2. Heat it over high heat. When small bubbles start to rise from the bottom of the pan and the first large bubble breaks the surface around the egg, cover the pan and remove it from the heat.
3. Let stand for 12 minutes for a hard-cooked egg, or for 4 minutes for a soft-cooked egg.
4. Drain. Immediately run cold water over the egg in the pan until it is cool enough to handle. Drain.
5. If it's hard-cooked, tap the wide end on the counter. Crackle the shell and peel it off.
6. If it's soft-cooked, set it, wide end up, in an eggcup. Slice off the top with a sharp knife. You can also buy egg scissors to do this job.

❖ If an eggshell cracks during cooking, wrap it tightly with foil and carry on. This will contain the leak, not stop it.

How to Avoid Cracking

1. Never dunk a cold egg in boiling water; it's sure to crack. Eggs are less likely to crack if they are brought to a boil with the water.
2. If you want to boil eggs, avoid breakage by soaking them in warm water beforehand to reduce the temperature shock. Don't forget to reduce the cooking time.
3. Prick the wide end of the shell with a pin or an egg piercer before cooking. This gives the air inside the shell an escape route when it expands in the heat. With reduced pressure, the shell is less likely to crack.

 ## A Bit of Science

Egg producers wash eggs and thinly coat them with oil to seal the pores in the shells. This replaces the natural sealant that was washed off. We remove the coating when we boil the eggs.

❖ Hard-cooked eggs go bad faster than raw eggs. Refrigerate them for up to 1 week. You can store them peeled or in the shell.

❖ Mark an X on the shells of hard-cooked eggs before refrigerating them.

❖ To tell whether an egg is cooked or raw, spin it on a flat surface. A cooked egg spins smoothly, quickly and for a longer time. It stops quickly when you touch and release it. Because of its liquid contents, a raw egg will wobble and fail to build momentum.

Ways to Crackle the Shell

- Gently roll the egg between your palms.
- Shake the egg in the pan.

No-No

Don't roll an egg on the counter to crackle the shell. It's easy to apply too much force.

❖ To crumble hard-cooked eggs, press them through a mesh sieve.

❖ To slice eggs smoothly, dip the knife into cool water as you work.

❖ To prevent a deviled egg from rolling or wobbling, cut a thin slice off the underside.

4 Peeling Strategies

1. Fresher eggs are harder to peel. Wait for about a week before cooking fresh eggs. The shell clings tightly to the white of a hard-cooked fresh egg. It ends up with ugly pits because sections of white pull off with the shell.
2. Chill hard-cooked eggs in icy water before crackling the shells.
3. Crackle the shell. Hold the egg under cold running water. Beginning at the wide end, ease off the shell. Do this over a colander if you wish to catch fragments.
4. Instead of crackling the shell, amuse yourself by peeling off the shell to create a little hole at the small end and a silver dollar–size hole at the wide end. Puff into the hole at the small end as though you were inflating a balloon. The egg will burst out the other end. It may leave a few bits of white stuck to the shell. This is supposed to work even with fresh eggs.

Poached Eggs

OUTSIDE THE BOX

- You can poach eggs in milk, stock or even wine.
- You can poach an egg inside a greased ladle for easy extraction.
- You can poach an egg in a silicone baking cup or poaching pod (which looks like a bra cup). For faster cooking, push silicone holders down into the water or cover the saucepan. Otherwise, the eggs take a long time to cook while floating and the tops want to stay raw.

✧ The best eggs for poaching are fresh and cold. The whites are thicker, so they cling to the yolks instead of foaming and spreading. When an old egg is poached, the yolk sinks and the white floats to the surface in ragged tendrils.

Master Plan
A Poached Egg

1. Fill a deep skillet or sauté pan with 1 to 1½ inches (2.5 to 4 cm) of water. (Don't use more water or a deep saucepan; the whites will want to float upwards in tendrils.)
2. To help the egg cling together, add 1 tsp (5 mL) white vinegar or ¼ tsp (1 mL) salt per 1 cup (250 mL) water. (Vinegar works better. Salt tastes better.)
3. Bring the water to a boil, then reduce the heat so it's barely simmering. Break the egg into a heatproof ramekin. Whisk the water to create a whirlpool, which will help the whites swirl around the yolk in a tidy ring. Put the lip of the ramekin right into the water so the egg slithers in instead of plopping. Slip the egg into the center of the whirlpool. Beauty! It's like a swirling galaxy.
4. Let the egg cook for 2 to 3 minutes, until the white is opaque but the yolk is still soft. If necessary, baste the yolk with simmering water or cover the pan.
5. Using a skimmer or slotted spatula, transfer the egg to a plate. Rub the bottom of the utensil across a kitchen towel en route, so the plate doesn't get watery or the toast soggy.
6. Trim the loose, foamy whites at the edges. Gently blot the egg and plate with a paper towel.

✧ Leftover poached eggs or eggs poached for a crowd can be refrigerated, then warmed.

Holding and Reviving Poached Eggs

- Transfer them to a tub or bowl of ice water to cool. Cover and refrigerate for up to 24 hours.
- Boil water in a kettle. Drain the eggs. In the same tub or bowl, pour in enough boiling water to cover the eggs. Do this carefully — a direct hit may break a yolk. Let stand for about 2 minutes or until the eggs are warmed through.
- Alternatively, if they'll be eaten soon, put the poached eggs on a plate. Tilt it to drain the water. To reheat the eggs, use a spatula or skimmer to transfer them to gently simmering water. Remove, blot and serve.

Gussy It Up

- Make a pretty base for eggs Benedict or eggs Florentine. With a serrated cookie cutter, punch out rounds of sliced sandwich bread. Fry the rounds in clarified butter or olive oil until they're golden.
- Add zip to poached eggs on toast. Spread the bread with garlic butter.

Steamed Eggs

✧ You can steam eggs one at a time or in groups. They turn out tender and delicate.

Master Plan
A Steamed Egg

1. Crack an egg into a well-buttered ramekin.
2. Cover it loosely with a round of parchment to prevent condensed steam from making the egg too wet.
3. Place the ramekin in a steamer basket and set it over boiling water. Cover and steam for 6 to 7 minutes or until the whites are opaque but the yolks are still tender.

Fried Eggs

Customize Your Eggs

- For a crispier fried egg with lacy edges, fry it in oil rather than butter and pump up the temperature.
- For a softer fried egg, keep the temperature low and increase moisture by covering the skillet.

✧ Stop frying when the egg whites just become opaque. Cooked longer, the whites will be rubbery.

4 Ways to Fry an Egg More Evenly

An egg, sunny-side up, poses a problem: The white is still slimy when the yolk is perfectly soft. If you keep cooking to firm up the white, the yolk will be too hard. Take steps to compensate:

1. Spoon hot fat over the yolk.
2. Remove the skillet from the heat, then cover it and let stand for 1 or 2 minutes.
3. The egg white closest to the yolk tends to stay runny. Sprinkle salt or vinegar on it to encourage the proteins to coagulate.
4. One surreal gastronome separates the egg. He fries the white over low heat. When it's almost done, he puts the yolk on top and cooks it a bit longer. This requires a fresh egg with a perky, stable yolk.

Scrambled Eggs and Omelets

✧ For zip, add 1 tsp (5 mL) Dijon mustard per 4 eggs destined for scrambling or an omelet.

- ❖ Ways to cook an omelet, a frittata or scrambled eggs more evenly:
  - Start with room-temperature eggs.
  - Cover the skillet until the eggs are almost set. Quickly finish the thin, undercooked top layer under the broiler.
  - When the eggs start to set, lift the edges with a thin spatula and tilt the pan to let the uncooked egg run underneath.

Mythstake

No, salt won't make your eggs tough. Overheating and overcooking will. Add salt (and pepper) to the eggs before cooking, for the best flavor.

6 Ways to Make an Omelet Fluffier

1. Using an electric mixer on medium speed, beat room-temperature eggs with salt and pepper for 1 to 2 minutes or until they are light, thickened and frothy.
2. Separate the eggs. Whip the whites until soft peaks form, then fold them into the yolks.
3. Add about 1/2 tsp (2 mL) baking soda for every 2 to 3 eggs (you won't taste it).
4. Use lots of butter, about 2 tbsp (25 mL) per 4 eggs, in a nonstick skillet.
5. Add water to the eggs, instead of milk or cream. When the water turns to steam, it makes the eggs airy.
6. Once the bottom is set, sprinkle on the filling and slip the omelet under the broiler to set. (Use an ovenproof skillet.) Then fold over the top.

Ways to Roll an Omelet

- Fold two opposite edges toward the center. Lift one of the edges. Pulling toward the lifted edge and tilting the skillet, roll the omelet out onto a plate.
- Fold the top third of the omelet over the filling. Tilt the skillet over a plate and roll out the omelet.
- Slide the omelet flat onto a plate. Use a paper towel to manipulate it gently into a roll.
- Shake and tilt the skillet until part of the top section flips over to the center. Tilt the pan toward you to finish rolling up the omelet. Flip it onto a plate.
- On a rimmed baking sheet lined with parchment paper and brushed with oil, bake the omelet at 350°F (180°C) until set. Remove it from the oven. Lifting and peeling the parchment as you go, roll up the omelet like a jelly roll.

❖ To give an egg-white omelet a golden glow, fry it in red palm fruit oil.

❖ If an omelet sticks to the skillet as you try to slide it onto a plate, rap the handle with your fist.

F is for Frittata

A frittata is basically an open-faced omelet. Instead of a filling, ingredients are spread through the eggs. A frittata is fried until the bottom browns, then it is broiled to firm up the top.

❖ If flipping an omelet is too onerous, distribute the fillings over the top, finish the top quickly under the broiler and call the result a frittata.

Keys to Tender, Fluffy Scrambled Eggs

- Whisking in cream or milk prevents scrambled eggs from overcooking and getting tough. For fluffiness, add 1 tbsp (15 mL) cream or milk per 4 eggs. For a more substantial texture, add 1 tsp (5 mL) cream or milk per 4 eggs.
- Add an extra egg white, beaten to soft peaks — 1 white per 3 whole eggs.
- Cook eggs in butter instead of oil.
- Let the eggs sit and puff in the pan for 1 minute before stirring.
- Remove the eggs from the heat when they are three-quarters done. Stir, cover and set aside. They'll finish cooking in their own heat.

Baked Eggs

✧ The easiest way to cook eggs for a crowd: Bake them.

Master Plan
Baked Eggs

1. Generously butter ramekins or custard cups.
2. Crack an egg into each ramekin. Sprinkle it with salt and top it with a spoonful of cream. You can set ramekins on a baking sheet for easy transfer.
3. Bake the eggs at 350°F (180°C) for 12 to 15 minutes (for soft yolks) or until set as desired.

✧ Take baked eggs out of the oven earlier than you think you should (with the whites barely opaque, for instance). The ramekins retain heat and the eggs will continue to cook.

✧ You can cover each ramekin with a circle of parchment. This holds in the heat, to help cook the top part of the egg before the bottom is overcooked.

Gussy It Up

- Put creamed spinach, stewed tomato, smoked salmon or chopped cooked bacon in the baking dish, then top with the egg.
- For an edible egg cup, trim the crust off a large slice of soft sandwich bread. Butter both sides. Push it into a muffin cup or ramekin. Crack an egg into the center and bake.

Scotch Eggs

Ⓢ is for Scotch Eggs

Scotch eggs are hard-cooked eggs coated in sausage meat, then breaded and fried. They can be tricky to make.

Master Plan
Scotch Eggs

1. Put a ball of spiced ground meat (2 to 3 oz/60 to 90 g) in your palm and pat it into a circle. Center a hard-cooked egg on top. Working with moistened hands, spread and press the meat evenly around the egg.
2. Roll the egg in flour, then in lightly beaten egg, then in dry bread crumbs. (Use a spoon to turn the egg in the bread crumbs.) Even out the coating by gently rolling the egg on the work surface.
3. Deep-fry the coated egg at 350°F (180°C) until the meat is cooked and the breading is crispy.

Keys to Better Scotch Eggs

- You can spice up ground meat, preferably pork, or take a shortcut and squeeze sausage meat from its casings. Sausage meat is nice and sticky.
- Use leaner, finer-textured sausage meat. Give it a pass through the grinder at home, if you have one.
- Some cooks add Worcestershire or chili sauce to the ground meat. This tastes good, but if the mixture is too wet or thin, the coating will crack during coating and cooking.

Healthier Eater

Scotch eggs can be baked. Be forewarned: These tend to be dry and rubbery, and the coating wants to fall off.

Safer Eggs

Precautions Against Salmonella

- If you find a cracked egg or break one, cook it thoroughly as soon as possible. If the contents have been leaking, however, do not use the egg.
- Don't keep leftovers that contain raw eggs.
- You can rinse the shells with warm water, if you wish. But wait until you are ready to cook the eggs. The shells are porous.
- Scald the shell in boiling water for 5 seconds before cracking the egg.
- Wash your hands with soap and water before handling and preparing eggs.
- The very young, the elderly, pregnant women and people with chronic illnesses or weakened immune systems should avoid raw or soft-cooked eggs.
- You can buy safer eggs, liquid, frozen and dried, in cartons or packages. In some markets, pasteurized eggs in the shell are available.

✧ You can buy liquid whites only, or liquid eggs with whites and a small amount of yolk. These may have preservatives and additives, and taste different.

✧ Pasteurized egg whites take longer to whip and don't fluff up as well.

✧ Dried whole eggs can be reconstituted by backpackers hungry for scrambled eggs. Dried eggs can also be added to pancake mix, then reconstituted with water.

3 Ways to Prepare Safer Eggs

1. For an uncooked dish, coddle an egg in the shell. Put it on a large spoon or in a ladle, then dip it into boiling water for 40 seconds. Immerse it in cold water right away to stop the cooking. This type of egg won't work in baking, but will work in a dressing.

2. For mayonnaise, put yolks in a heatproof bowl. Add 1 tbsp (15 mL) water per yolk. Set the bowl over a saucepan of simmering water over low to medium heat. Beat with an electric hand mixer until the yolks froth and start to stiffen. Remove the mixture from the heat, let cool and continue with your recipe. Beware: This is very difficult to do without the yolks curdling and cooking.

3. For desserts such as mousses, make a meringue. In a heatproof bowl, stir together egg whites and 1 to 2 tbsp (15 to 25 mL) granulated sugar, 1 tsp (15 mL) water and a pinch of cream of tartar per egg white until blended. (Take your cue from the recipe. Use the smaller amount of sugar for a foamy meringue, the larger amount for a satiny one.) Place the mixture over simmering water. Beat it with an electric hand mixer on low speed until it reaches 160°F (71°C). Remove from the heat and continue beating until soft peaks form.

Dried Whites **vs.** Meringue Powder?

The dried whites are just that. Meringue powder includes other ingredients, such as cornstarch and sugar, and is used for icing or meringue. These are sold in bulk food and baking supply stores.

Chinese Marbled Eggs

Each egg is strange and lovely, with a unique webbed pattern. **Makes 12**

Tip

These are edible, but rubbery from being cooked so long. Consider them more of a conversation piece.

5 cups	water	1.25 L
3 tbsp	soy sauce	45 mL
½ tsp	salt	2 mL
3	whole star anise	3
3 tbsp	black tea leaves	45 mL
1	cinnamon stick, 4 to 6 inches (10 to 15 cm) long	1
1	large piece dried orange or tangerine peel	1
12	hard-cooked eggs in their shells	12

1. In a saucepan just large enough to accommodate a single layer of eggs immersed in the liquid, stir together water, soy sauce, salt, star anise, tea leaves, cinnamon stick and orange peel.

2. With the back of a spoon, gently tap eggshells all over to create a network of tiny cracks, but no gaping splits. Place eggs in the pan and bring to a boil over medium-high heat. Reduce heat to low, cover and simmer for 3 hours, adding more water, if necessary, to keep eggs immersed.

3. Remove from heat and let cool. Cover and let steep in refrigerator for at least 8 hours or overnight.

4. Under cold running water, gently peel eggs.

Dyeing Eggs

 Healthier Eater

You can dye eggs using natural ingredients.
Three natural solutions:

- Chopped cabbage, chopped beets or onion
  skins, water and white vinegar
- Turmeric, water and white vinegar (2 tsp/
  10 mL turmeric per 1 cup/250 mL water)
- Brewed coffee or tea and white vinegar

Master Plan
Dyed Eggs

1. Bring the dye solution to a boil. Cover,
   reduce the heat and simmer for 30 minutes.
2. Strain, discarding the solids. Return the
   liquid to the pan.
3. Add eggs. Simmer over medium-low heat
   for 30 minutes. Alternatively, soak hard-
   cooked eggs in the cooled solution for
   30 minutes, but the color will be lighter and
   perhaps mottled.
4. Transfer eggs to a rack and let them dry.
   Note: These eggs aren't good to eat.

❖ Use 2 tbsp (25 mL) white vinegar per
4 cups (1 L) liquid.

❖ If you want to eat them, keep dyed eggs in
the fridge. Food-safety rules still apply.

❖ To empty an eggshell for decorating,
prick a hole in each end with a needle.
At the wide end, gently enlarge the hole
until it is as big as, say, the tip of a baster.
Shake the egg well, wide end down
over a bowl, to empty out the contents.
Alternatively, hold the egg, wide end
down over a bowl, and blow into the hole.
Pour cool water into the shell, swish it
around, then shake it out. Let the shell
drain, wide end down, then shake it dry
again. Cover the holes with melted wax.

Soy Products

Tofu

Tofu Categories

- Silken and soft tofu are similar, but the silken type is smoother. Use either for sauces, smoothies, dips and dressings.
- Medium or regular tofu is firm and smooth. It can be crumbled and substituted for soft cheeses, such as ricotta, or cut into chunks for salads or casseroles.
- Firm and extra-firm tofus are drier and denser. They hold up well when fried or grilled.

✧ To help medium or firm tofu hold its shape, press moisture out of it. Wrap it in cheesecloth, put it in a sieve, place a weighted plate on top, and let stand for 1 hour. You can also lay a block of tofu flat between layers of cheesecloth or paper towels, then place a cast-iron skillet or a weighted baking sheet on top. To speed up the process, slice the tofu. Packaged tofu may already be pressed.

Storing Tofu

- Keep it in an airtight tub in the fridge. Change the water daily.
- Some tofu fans freeze it to make it firmer. Don't freeze soft or silken tofu.

✧ Tofu absorbs flavors. Prepare your dish ahead of time to take advantage of this.

✧ In China, tofu may be freshened by poaching it before stir-frying. To do so, cut the tofu into 1-inch (2.5 cm) cubes, poach it in a skillet of simmering water for 10 minutes, then drain and pat it dry.

✧ Pat tofu dry before using it.

Healthier Eater

- Crumble tofu on top of a pizza as a substitute for some of the greasy cheese.
- You can make "egg salad" with tofu that looks and tastes like the real thing.

Master Plan
Tofu "Egg Salad"

1. Use 2 parts extra-firm tofu and 1 part silken tofu.
2. In a food processor, purée the silken tofu, then transfer it to a bowl. Crumble in extra-firm tofu. Stir in chopped green onion, celery and fresh parsley, garlic salt, sea salt, paprika, curry power, freshly ground black pepper and ground turmeric until well mixed.
3. Refrigerate the mixture for at least 1 hour, until chilled, or for up to 2 days.

Miso

✧ Miso is an aged paste of fermented soybeans, water, salt and grain — usually rice, sometimes wheat or barley. Miso runs the gamut from beige to golden to red to brown. There are hundreds of types and brands. The Japanese match misos to different dishes. Miso also comes powdered.

✧ The simplest way to serve miso: Blend it with boiling water. Enjoy this quick, hot broth before a sushi meal.

✧ For a fancier soup, blend miso with boiling water. Add bonito flakes, finely diced tofu and kombu or wakame (seaweed).

Miso Hue Clues

- The longer the fermentation, the darker the miso. Darker miso is more pungent and tangy.
- Don't be confused. "White miso" is actually golden.
- Awase miso is a blend of red and white misos.

D is for Dashi

Dashi is a base for Japanese soup and stocks. To make a slapdash miso soup, use boiling water and dashi miso, which contains bonito (dried tuna).

Healthier Eater

Miso may be marred by MSG, so check labels.

✧ Miso can be used to flavor and lightly thicken sauces and gravies. Whisk in about 2 tbsp (25 mL) miso per 1 cup (250 mL) heated stock or even wine.

How to Prevent Clumping

Stir miso with a bit of boiling water or stock until it is loosened and smooth. Pour in the remaining liquid or add the miso slurry to your dish.

✧ Don't boil miso in a soup or stew. Always add it at the end.

Being Green

Look for brands of miso made with soybeans that are not genetically modified.

TVP

T is for TVP

Textured vegetable protein, or textured soy protein, is a ground meat substitute. The processed-food industry uses it to bulk up products. It is manufactured in chunks, flakes, granules and powder. TVP does not require refrigeration. Like tofu, it sucks up flavors.

✧ Bulk up meat with TVP. You can replace the meat in patties with up to 40% TVP, and in sausage, fish and poultry mixtures with up to 30%. This is economical and reduces fat.

Rehydrating TVP

- Add ¾ to 1 cup (175 to 250 mL) boiling water per 1 cup (250 mL) TVP flakes. Add a bit of white vinegar or freshly squeezed lemon juice to speed up the process. Combine the liquid with the TVP, then let stand for 5 to 10 minutes. You can use other liquids for added flavor.

✧ Add dried TVP to a dish to suck up liquid. If your chili, say, turns out watery, add some TVP to mop up the excess.

OUTSIDE THE BOX

You can substitute TVP for up to a third of the oatmeal in cookies. They will be drier, so add a bit more liquid.

✧ Don't eat too much TVP. It causes gas.

The Produce Department

Recipes

Fruit and Vegetable Basics

♛ A Golden Rule

Choose fruit and vegetables that feel heavy for their size. They are moist.

Mythstakes

- Frozen produce is not always inferior. It is flash-frozen right after it's picked, sealing in the nutrients. Sometimes, it is a better choice than fresh produce that has traveled far and long. It is always a better choice than canned produce, which has an unpleasant texture, loses nutrients during heat processing and tends to contain too much salt. Produce frozen in sauces and syrups is the exception. It is not as healthful as fresh produce or even plain canned produce.
- The crisper is not home sweet home for all produce. Some need a colder, drier spot, some a warmer one. Conditions at home are dire for many fruits and vegetables that find the fridge too cold and the counter too warm. They would prefer to move into a cold cellar, but not many of us have such a thing. Example: Pineapples, watermelons, cucumbers and green peppers actually like it better at around 50°F (10°C).

Natural Enemies

- Onions and potatoes help each other rot faster if stored together.
- Apples make carrots bitter. In fact, you should try to store apples separately from all other produce.
- Ethylene gas from fruit will wilt lettuce and other greens. Keep fruit and greens in separate crispers.

OUTSIDE THE BOX

Turn fruit and vegetables into fries and crisps. They make great snacks, side dishes and garnishes for salads and cheese plates.

- You can make french fries from starchy vegetables other than potatoes. Because of their natural sugars, they won't be quite as crisp.
- You can turn starchy vegetables into crisps, similar to potato chips. Parsnips, plantains, beets, rutabaga and sweet potatoes make addictive fries and crisps.
- Plantains can be salted or sprinkled with sugar. For crisps, choose yellow ones with a few spots of black — firm, but starting to sweeten.
- For fruit crisps, stick to fruit that's not too juicy, such as pears.
- Thinly slice fruit and vegetables using a mandolin. Or use a peeler to slice parsnips, carrots or other vegetables lengthwise into ribbons.
- Some cooks soak vegetable slices in cold water for 10 minutes before drying and frying them.
- Bake them in a single layer or deep-fry them. Cool them on a rack.
- They don't last long, especially in humid weather. Some crisps can be stored for up to 1 day in an airtight tub at room temperature.
- Re-crisp them in a 350°F (180°C) oven for up to 5 minutes, or put them under the broiler.

12 Tips to Safely Pick Your Own

1. Wash your hands or use a hand sanitizer before picking. Afterwards, wash your hands with soapy water.
2. If you have a sore or cut, cover it with a bandage and wear gloves.
3. Use fresh, clean baskets. Plastic bags are not recommended, especially for berries.
4. Do not use deep containers for berries and soft fruit. The produce at the bottom will get crushed.
5. Do not pick produce that is bruised, moldy, off-color or strange-smelling.
6. Use a cooler and ice packs to transport produce, especially fragile berries.
7. Pick early in the morning, in the evening or on cloudy days, when the produce is cooler. Fruit and vegetables picked in the heat, particularly berries, do not keep as well.
8. Pick only what you can use in a few days, or freeze the excess.
9. Do not eat unwashed produce in the field.
10. Do not buy unpasteurized juices on site.
11. Put freshly picked produce in the fridge as soon as possible.
12. Do not put a container from the field directly into the fridge. Transfer the produce to a clean container.

5 Storage Locations

1. The crisper is fine for artichokes, asparagus, beans, beets, broccoli, cabbage, carrots, cauliflower, celery, chiles, eggplant, green onions, greens, leeks, mushrooms, radishes, turnips and zucchini.
2. Store berries, citrus fruit, corn, melons and peas in moderately cold parts of the fridge.
3. Store apples, cherries and grapes in the coldest part of the fridge.
4. Avocados, bananas and tomatoes keep well on the counter.
5. Store garlic, onions, potatoes, shallots, sweet potatoes and winter squash in a cool, dark, dry pantry.

✦ Many fruits and vegetables, such as avocados and potatoes, are not as hardy as they look. Handle them with care.

✗ No-Nos

- Don't store produce in those thin plastic bags from the supermarket.
- Avoid washing produce in advance. This hastens decomposition. Wash it just before eating it. If you must wash it ahead of time, dry it thoroughly.

Master Plan
Baked Vegetable Chips

1. Slice vegetables thin, but not paper-thin. Slice them into ribbons if you can. They should hold their shape.
2. Toss them with oil to coat.
3. Place them in a single layer on a rimmed baking sheet lined with parchment. Sprinkle them lightly with salt and pepper.
4. Bake them at 400°F (200°C) for 10 minutes. Reduce the heat to 250°F (120°C) and bake for 1 hour. Check every 10 minutes and remove slices as they are crisped and browned. The time depends on the vegetable.
5. Cool them on a rack. The slices firm up as they cool.

Master Plan
Fried Potato or Vegetable Chips

1. Slice vegetables super-thin. Slice them into ribbons, if possible.
2. Soak them in a bowl set under cold running water. Swish until the water runs clear. Drain and dry them well to prevent clumping.
3. In a deep-fryer, heat oil to 375°F (190°C). However, you may have to fry vegetables with a high sugar content, such as sweet potato or rutabaga, at a lower temperature, such as 350°F (180°C). Test a few pieces to check.
4. Toss slices into the oil, one by one and in tiny batches to minimize sticking and clumping. Fry for 1 to 2 minutes or until the edges are golden brown.
5. Drain them on paper towels and sprinkle with salt.

✧ Use a brush to scrub produce with firm surfaces, such as cantaloupes.

✧ When produce is bruised, rot sets in quickly. Cut out the bruised part.

♥ Healthier Eater

- Long boiling leaches nutrients out of fruit and vegetables. Steaming, microwaving or stir-frying are faster, better options.
- Most of the antioxidants in produce are contained in and just below the skin. Plus, the skin has lots of fiber. Avoid peeling. Just scrub carrots, for example. Otherwise, use a very sharp peeler to shave as thin a layer as possible.
- Shop for produce several times a week, not in one efficient, weekly sweep. Fruit and vegetables start to lose their nutrients as soon as they are harvested. By the time they travel to the end of the line, they may be in sorry shape.
- Save the water from boiling vegetables. It can contain up to a third of their minerals and vitamins. Use it as a simple stock or in sauces and breads. Taste it first to make sure it is not too strong or bitter, tangy from tomatoes or sweet from carrots.

 KID STUFF

Dip cut fruit and spuds into paint and use them for kids' crafts.

✧ Once a fruit or vegetable is cut, enzymes are released that cause it to discolor. You can reduce the effect.

Ways to Stop Discoloration

- Add an acid.
- Add salt.
- Immerse produce in water, preferably running water.
- Cool produce to slow down the oxidation or deactivate the enzymes.

Ⓐ is for Acidulate

To prevent browning, you can add an acidic ingredient directly to fruit and vegetables or you can float them in an acidulated water solution. This is usually done before cooking or freezing, but the same idea applies to fruit salads.

7 Ways to Acidulate

1. As you work, toss slices or chunks into a bowl of water mixed with an acid.
2. Stir in lemon juice as you work.
3. Rub lemon juice over the cut surface of a fruit or vegetable.
4. Toss slices or chunks with citrus fruit.
5. Dip slices or chunks in lemon juice or white wine.
6. Soak cut pieces in white wine.
7. Soak fruit in its own juice (apple slices in apple juice, for example).

Acidulation Formulas

- Add 2 tbsp (25 mL) white vinegar or 3 tbsp (45 mL) lemon juice per 4 cups (1 L) water.
- For preserves, add 2 tbsp (25 mL) each salt and vinegar per 1 gallon (4 L) water.
- Dissolve 1 tsp (5 mL) ascorbic acid or citric acid in 4 cups (1 L) water or syrup.
- Sprinkle ascorbic acid over cut fruit. Use about $\frac{1}{4}$ tsp (1 mL) per 4 cups (1 L) fruit.
- Sprinkle 2 tbsp (25 mL) lemon juice onto 4 cups (1 L) cubed or sliced fruit and toss to coat.

Ascorbic VS. Citric?

Ascorbic acid and citric acid are not the same, but they are similar chemically. The former is basically vitamin C and is more commonly used to acidulate water.

- ✧ If you are cutting lots of produce at once, minimize browning by peeling it all first, coring each one (if necessary), then cutting.

- ✧ You can soak produce in acidulated water for 10 to 30 minutes. Don't leave apples and other porous produce in for longer than 15 minutes.

E is for Ethylene

Ethylene is the produce lover's friend and enemy. Ethylene is a hormone in gaseous form that is emitted by fruit and vegetables. It ripens and colors, increasing sweetness, reducing acidity and destroying chlorophyll. It also hastens spoiling. Get to know it and you can put it to work.

- ✧ Don't try to ripen fruit in a plastic bag. The humidity causes moldering.

- ✧ When ripening fruit with the help of an apple or banana, check the progress every 12 hours.

5 Ways to Speed Up Ripening

1. The brown paper bag is important equipment when tangling with ethylene. Put fruit in a brown paper bag to concentrate the gases. You can wrap each specimen in a paper towel first. Loosely crumple the top of the bag and leave it at room temperature.
2. Apples and bananas emit lots of ethylene. Store them in a bowl or bag with fruit that you want to ripen.
3. Warm a piece of fruit on a sunny windowsill or in a microwave on Medium (50%) for 15 seconds, then put it in a paper bag with a ripe apple and loosely close the bag.
4. To ripen an avocado or other fruit more quickly, bury it in a flour bin. (Make sure it's clean.)
5. Put fruit in a box and cover it with several layers of newspaper.

4 Ways to Slow Down Ripening

1. The fruit bowl is pretty enough to inspire many a still life, but it is not the best place to store a mixture of fruit. Keep apples and bananas, in particular, in solitary confinement.
2. Store produce in perforated vegetable bags so ethylene can pass through.
3. Put ripe fruit in stasis by transferring it to the fridge.
4. Ethylene wafts around in fridge crispers. Discs and bags are manufactured with a mineral that absorbs ethylene. If using discs, don't seal produce in plastic; leave the bags open.

Fruit Basics

✦ Fruits that stop ripening after picking:
- Cherries
- Citrus fruit
- Grapes
- Lychees
- Pineapples
- Pomegranates
- Raspberries
- Strawberries
- Watermelons

✦ Fruits that ripen in color, texture and juiciness, but do not get sweeter after picking:
- Apricots
- Blueberries
- Cantaloupes
- Figs
- Honeydew melons
- Nectarines
- Passion fruit
- Peaches
- Persimmons

✦ Fruits that ripen in sweetness after picking:
- Apples
- Cherimoya
- Kiwifruit
- Mangos
- Papayas
- Pears

✦ A fruit that ripens in every way after picking:
- Bananas (they are picked green)

✦ A fruit that ripens only after picking:
- Avocados

✦ Don't stack tender fruit, such as peaches, in a bowl. The ones at the bottom will bruise from the weight.

✦ Buy fruits that stop ripening after harvest at their peak of perfection. Shuttle them into the fridge. To bring out their full flavors, warm them for 1 day at room temperature before eating.

✦ Store fruits that ripen after harvest at room temperature. Most fruits of this type can go in the fridge as soon as they are ripe, but not before. If kept in the cold too long before ripening, they get mealy.

Ⓜ is for Maceration

Sugar sucks out juices by osmosis. It creates a concentrated syrup on the surface of fruit, which draws out the juices. Sometimes you want that to happen, so you toss cut fruit with sugar and let it steep in its own juices, or macerate.

✦ An alternative to maceration: If fruit is not juicy enough for pies, desserts and shortcakes, cook some of it, mash or purée it, then mix that with raw cut fruit.

✦ When peeling slippery fruit, wear a rubber glove.

✦ Ways to peel a thin-skinned fruit, such as a peach or plum:
- The fast, easy way is to strip the skin with a serrated peeler.
- The standard way is to blanch the fruit for up to 1 minute in boiling water, then spray it with cold water or dunk it in a bowl of ice water. Slip off the skin.
- An unusual way is to impale it on a fork and hold it over a gas element for a few seconds until the skin cracks. Or run a kitchen torch over the skin. Pull off the skin.

✦ Use a spoon to scoop the flesh from soft fruit such as mangos and kiwis. No need to peel.

Poaching Tips

- Poach tender, juicy fruit, such as peaches, in simple syrup with a pinch of salt.
- Firm, hard fruit, such as apples, can be poached in water or juice. You can sprinkle the drained fruit with sugar afterwards. Poaching juice can be turned into syrup. Add sugar to the pan with the juice and boil it over high heat until syrupy, then let cool to room temperature. Drizzle this syrup over fruit or make a cool drink by mixing it with club soda.
- Cook fruit as briefly as possible. Drain immediately or cool the pan to stop the cooking by putting it in a bowl of ice water.

✗ No-No

Do not eat the nut-like seeds of peaches, apricots, plums and cherries. They contain toxic compounds.

✦ You can frost fruit to use as a garnish. This is tricky, as the fruit tends to weep. Use it as soon as possible.

Master Plan
Frosted Fruit

1. Stick a piece of fruit, such as a strawberry, on a bamboo skewer. Brush it with slightly beaten egg white.
2. Roll it several times in superfine sugar.
3. Push it off the skewer. Let it dry on a rack for at least 2 hours (the time will depend on the fruit and how moist it is), until a crisp coating forms.
4. If the fruit starts to weep, roll it in sugar again and let dry.

✦ Don't steep overripe or bruised fruit in booze. It will get cloudy.

Better Leftovers

Make a fool out of overripe fruit. Coarsely mash it or chop it, then layer it in a bowl, alternating fruit with whipped cream — or yogurt, if you're watching your diet.

Vegetable Basics

✦ Soak gritty greens, lettuce and vegetables, such as broccoli and cauliflower, for 15 minutes to clean them and draw out any insects. Use a solution of 4 cups (1 L) water and 1 tbsp (15 mL) salt.

✦ When cutting starchy vegetables, such as potatoes, rinse the knife in cold water occasionally. The stickiness from the starch makes cutting harder.

✦ Slicing vegetables diagonally is not only attractive, it's practical. It exposes more surface area to the heat during cooking.

® is for Roll-Cut

Tapered veggies, such as carrots and parsnips, can be cut into pieces that are irregular but similar by employing the roll-cut. Make one cut on a 45-degree diagonal. Give the vegetable a quarter turn, rolling it toward you so you can see what you're doing. Make the next diagonal cut, turn, and so on.

✦ Ways to squeeze moisture from salted, shredded potatoes, zucchini, cucumber or cabbage:
- Twist them in a cheesecloth square or kitchen towel.
- Spin them in a salad spinner.
- Squeeze them between two plates.
- Press them in a ricer.

❖ Leave on the root ends of vegetables until you are done cutting them. This holds them together.

Keys to Cooking Vegetables

- Cook green vegetables quickly to preserve their crunch and color. Start with a large amount of vigorously boiling salted water. With lots of water in the pot, the vegetables won't slow the boil as much when they are dropped in, so the cooking time will be shorter.
- Cook root vegetables slowly. Braise or roast them to encourage the caramelization of their natural sugars. Never use a large amount of water. An exception: Use more water with carrots cut small.
- Blanch greens and firm vegetables, then spray them with cold water and drain well before sautéing, grilling or stir-frying them. This keeps them bright and helps them cook through quickly and evenly, instead of languishing in the pan.
- When cooking whole veggies, such as sweet potatoes or beets, choose specimens roughly the same size and shape, so they are ready at the same time.

Mythstake

Steaming is not necessarily better than boiling — especially short boiling. The traditional thinking is that more nutrients leach out in boiled vegetables. But some scientists say there's not much difference between the two methods. Maybe it's because steaming takes longer. Or maybe it's because most people no longer boil vegetables to death. (A certain older relative cooks them so long they fall apart when you blow on them.)

3 Ways to Give Vegetables Staying Power

1. Vegetables are automatically sprayed at the supermarket to make them glisten with appeal. Dry them before storing. The rot won't set in as fast.
2. Remove the elastic bands before storing them.
3. Cut the leaves off root vegetables when you get them home. They suck energy and moisture out of the roots. You can, however, leave 1 inch (2.5 cm) of green on top of carrots, beets, kohlrabi, rutabaga and other roots. They look prettier that way.

6 Ways to Keep Vegetables Vivid

1. Cook them in a large quantity of water.
2. Salt the cooking water. This also keeps them firmer.
3. Steam them instead of boiling them.
4. Do not add vinegar or lemon juice to the water (unless you are cooking cauliflower or turnips). They have a bleaching action.
5. Briefly spray cold water over steamed or boiled vegetables immediately after removing them from the heat. This also stops the cooking, so they won't be limp.
6. If you are preparing green beans or other green veggies ahead, cook them until they're almost done, drain them and put them in ice water to preserve their color and firmness until you are ready to reheat and eat.

- Steam fast-cooking vegetables, such as snow peas, in a colander over a pot of boiling, slower-cooking vegetables such as spuds.
- Boil two different vegetables separately, but simultaneously, in the same saucepan by wrapping them in foil. (Don't do this with acidic vegetables, which may react with the metal.) Cover the pan, as these packages float.

OUTSIDE THE BOX

- You can steam an entire head of cauliflower or a set of whole broccoli stalks with the florets facing up.
- You can make cauliflower or broccoli kebabs.

Master Plan
Cauliflower or Broccoli Kebabs

1. In boiling salted water, blanch florets for about 3 minutes or until they are softened.
2. Transfer them to a colander. Spray them with cold water until they cool down. Drain them well. Pat them dry.
3. Diagonally skewer the florets lengthwise so they stay put. Brush them with oil and seasonings.
4. Grill them on the barbecue, basting with oil, until just tender and lightly charred.

✧ Don't sauté cooked vegetables in butter to finish them. They'll develop a greasy coating. Instead, put them in a warmed bowl, add butter and toss to coat. Don't reheat vegetables in butter, either. They'll get oily.

✧ How to cut cooking odors in smelly vegetables such as cabbage, turnips, cauliflower, broccoli and Brussels sprouts:
- Cutting liberates sulfurous compounds in vegetables. A cold-water soak rinses away some of these compounds.

- There's something to be said for a slow braise. But the longer these vegetables cook, the smellier they get. Choose faster cooking methods.
- Don't overcook them.
- Stir-fry. The hot oil seals in odors.
- Add a lemon wedge or vinegar to the cooking water.
- Add a celery stalk or ½ tsp (2 mL) celery seeds to the cooking water.
- Toss a heel of bread into the pan.

✧ Carrots and other vegetables with sugary glazes lose their appealing stickiness the longer they sit. As they cool, a puddle develops and the vegetables start to get soggy. Remedies for soggy glazed vegetables:
- Set them in a sieve before serving.
- Glaze them in a very hot oven instead of on the stove. Example: Toss cut carrots with melted butter or oil, brown sugar, salt and pepper on a rimmed baking sheet. Roast them at 450°F (230°C) for about 15 minutes, tossing them once, until the bottoms are charred.
- Make a classic glossy glaze that relies on their natural sugars.

Master Plan
Glossy Carrots
(or Other Vegetables)

1. Cut carrots into coins or sticks.
2. Place them in a straight-sided saucepan that accommodates them in a single layer.
3. Fill the pan halfway with stock or salted water. A bit of butter and sugar can be added, say 1 tsp (5 mL) each per 8 oz (250 g) carrots.
4. Bring them to a boil over medium-high heat. Partially cover the pan and reduce the heat to low. Simmer until tender.
5. If the liquid hasn't evaporated, increase the heat to high and boil it off.

- It's a challenge to roast vegetables such as cauliflower and broccoli. They get rubbery, develop a leathery crust or burn before they become tender. The solution is to steam them first.

Master Plan
Roasted Vegetables

1. Toss vegetable florets or chunks with oil, salt and pepper. Do this right on a rimmed baking sheet, flipping with a spatula, instead of dirtying a bowl.
2. Cover the baking sheet with foil. Roast at 475°F (240°C) for about 10 minutes. The steam will soften the vegetables.
3. Remove the foil. Continue roasting the vegetables until the bottoms are browned (about 8 to 10 minutes for large pieces of cauliflower). Turn them over and continue roasting until the bottoms are browned (about 8 minutes for cauliflower).

- Bake stuffed peppers and tomatoes in muffin tins or ramekins that they fit snugly in. They'll hold their shape better.

- Ways to reduce sogginess in casseroles with vegetables:
  - Salt the vegetables and let them drain in a colander (about 45 minutes for zucchini).
  - Toss the vegetables in seasoned oil.
  - Arrange wet vegetables, such as tomatoes, in a single layer in a casserole.
  - Don't cover a casserole during cooking. Allow steam to escape.

♻ Waste Not

Did you go chop crazy? Refrigerate leftover chopped herbs, green onions, gingerroot, chiles, and red and green peppers in small zip-lock bags. Use them as garnishes or sprinkle them into cream soups.

4 Frozen Vegetable Cooking Tips

1. Cook frozen vegetables in as little water as possible. Better still, steam them.
2. You can cook frozen vegetables in an electric skillet. Put them in the skillet without water, cover, set the temperature to 350°F (180°C) and cook them until you see steam. Reduce the heat to 300°F (150°C) and cook them until tender.
3. Put frozen corn or peas in a sieve. Sit the sieve in boiling water for 1 or 2 minutes. Pull out the sieve, and — voila — they're ready.
4. There's no need to cook frozen corn or peas before adding them to a dish. Just rinse off the ice crystals, then add them 2 to 5 minutes before the end of the cooking time.

Better Leftovers

- Cold steamed, boiled or even roasted vegetables return to the table nicely as single-ingredient salads. Just drizzle them with dressing. Try this with asparagus, broccoli, cauliflower or green beans.
- Simmer roasted vegetables in stock, purée them and add a drizzle of cream for an intense soup.

♡ Healthier Eater

- Get kids to eat more vegetables. Hide grated vegetables in pasta and rice dishes, muffins and quick breads.
- Purée tender cooked vegetables with stock to make an unusual, healthful sauce.

No-No

Don't be tempted to reheat green vegetables in boiling water.

Better Ways to Reheat Green Vegetables

- Warm them in the microwave, but do not add water. Just cover the dish.
- Put a few tablespoons of water in a skillet over high heat, add the vegetables and toss until the water evaporates.
- Put the vegetables and a bit of water in the top of a double boiler. Cover and heat over simmering water.
- Warm them in a steamer basket. Set the basket over simmering water and cover the pan.

Veggie Doctor

The raw vegetables are limp or wilted.

- Revive them by soaking them in a 2:1 solution of water and vinegar. Or simply soak them in cold water.

The vegetables are overcooked.

- Disguise your mistake. In a food processor, purée them with a bit of cream. Stir in some butter. Sprinkle chopped herbs on top.

Foraging Rules

- If you are foraging for wild foods, such as leeks or fiddleheads, pick only part of each clump or plant. This allows them to regenerate. It can take decades for an ostrich fern to grow; taking all its fronds will kill it.
- Do not pick edible plants, such as dandelions, near busy streets, parking lots or even land alongside rural roads. They are exposed to contaminants, such as carbon monoxide, from traffic. They may be sprayed with pesticides. And a dog may have left an invisible calling card.

14 Homegrown Tips

1. Gardeners believe that some vegetables taste sweeter and are more tender if they are harvested after the first frost. A light frost is considered beneficial for turnips and Brussels sprouts. Kale and parsnips can be harvested after a hard frost.
2. Pumpkins and winter squash should be harvested when their stems start to look dry.
3. Individual garlic cloves can be planted, pointed end up. Plant large cloves to grow large bulbs.
4. To encourage more foliage, harvest herbs frequently.
5. Pinch off buds and blossoms on herbs to get bushy growth. Do not allow the plants to flower. They will devote their energy to the flowers, not the leaves you want.
6. Water herb planters with room-temperature water. Let tap water sit in the watering can for a day first, so the chlorine evaporates.
7. Dig coffee grounds into your compost. You can toss in unbleached paper coffee filters, too.
8. Pour cooled potato-cooking water onto plants.
9. Use cooled, leftover tea to water the plants.
10. Sprinkle barbecue ashes into the garden.
11. Use Popsicle sticks and a permanent marker to label potted plants.
12. Layer leftover corks on the bottom of a planter to improve drainage.
13. Bury a clean, firm sponge in the bottom of a planter to improve drainage.
14. Use a slit straw to splint a broken stem in your herb planter.

Fruit

Apples

A Good Sign

The skin is firm and smooth. Freckled areas are okay.

✧ Apples bruise easily, so handle them gently.

Reasons to Refrigerate Apples

- They ripen up to 10 times faster at room temperature. Keep apples crisp in perforated plastic bags in the fridge.
- Chilled apples taste better.

✧ Apples stay fresher in the crisper if you mist them with water once a week.

✧ One bad apple really does ruin the bunch. Toss it out.

Choosing Among Apple Varieties

✧ Consumers throw up their hands, and no wonder. There are hundreds of varieties of apples. How do you choose? By the job you want the apple to do, the texture and juiciness, the acidity (tart vs. mellow), the sweetness, how well it holds its shape and even the color. Luckily, apples are multitaskers.

Most apples are good to munch on. Crispness, juiciness and good looks are the criteria for snacking apples. Cooking apples can be divided into two groups: the ones that fall apart and the ones that hold their shape. Are you making applesauce, pie or baked apples?

Here's a list of suggestions, personal and by no means comprehensive:

Snacking

- **Top choice:** Honeycrisp. This new variety lives up to its name.
- **Popular:** Ambrosia, Braeburn, Crispin (Mutsu), Empire, Fuji, Gala, Golden Delicious, Granny Smith, Idared, Jonagold, Macoun, McIntosh, Pink Lady, Russet, Spartan.

Fruit salad or fruit plate

- **Top choice:** Golden Delicious. They don't brown much when they're cut. The yellower they are, the softer and sweeter they are.
- **Popular:** Braeburn, Cortland, Empire, Fuji, Granny Smith, Gala, Honeycrisp, Pink Lady, Red Delicious.

Baked

- **Top choice:** Granny Smith. This apple holds its shape. It's tart, so a sweet filling won't make it cloying.
- **Popular:** Braeburn, Empire, Idared, Northern Spy, Pink Lady, Rome.

Applesauce

- **Top choice:** McIntosh. It dissolves easily.
- **Popular:** Cameo, Cortland, Crispin (Mutsu), Empire, Golden Delicious, Honeycrisp, Pink Lady.

Cider

- **Top choice:** Winesap. True to its name, this apple is described as a favorite of cider makers.
- **Popular:** Empire, Jonagold, Northern Spy.

Pie

- **Top choice:** Northern Spy. "Spies for pies" is the saying. Spies are not too sweet, not too sour, and end up neither mushy nor firm. But pie makers remain divided because some like the filling chunky, others smooth, and some prefer it sweet, others tart.
- **Popular:** Baldwin, Braeburn, Cameo, Cortland, Crispin (Mutsu), Golden Delicious, Granny Smith, Gravenstein, Honeycrisp, Jonagold, Jonathan, Pink Lady, Spartan, Winesap.

Best all-purpose apple

- Granny Smith.

Least versatile apple

- Red Delicious. Sure, it has good looks going for it, but it can be bland and mealy. Never cook with Red Delicious.

- ◈ Hand-cranked apple-peeling machines leave skin at the top and bottom. Afterwards, save a bit of effort by coring the apple, then finish peeling it, instead of vice versa.

- ◈ If you miss the mark when coring an apple, cut it in half and scrape it with the corer.

Baked Apple Tips

- Here's a cool (and efficient) way to fill cored apples with brown sugar. Push the damp corer into the brown sugar. Pull it out, holding the tip, if necessary, so the sugar doesn't fall out. Push it back into the core. Tap to release the sugar.
- Use a melon baller to scoop a hole to fill with stuffing such as dried fruit, honey and spices. The baller creates a hollow without cutting down to the bottom, as a corer would do.

Applesauce Ideas

- For smooth, creamy applesauce, choose soft apples. For a chunky sauce, use a harder type.
- For intense flavor, roast the apples.
- For chunky sauce, use a potato masher instead of puréeing.
- Use unpeeled apples. The skin gives the applesauce a rosy hue.
- Add ginger.
- Stir in dried berries.
- Substitute pears for some of the apples.

Master Plan
Roasted Applesauce

1. Peel, core and quarter about 4 lbs (2 kg) apples.
2. In a large roasting pan, toss the apples with ¼ cup (50 mL) packed brown sugar and 3 tbsp (45 mL) melted butter.
3. Cover tightly and roast in a 400°F (200°C) oven for 30 to 40 minutes or until the apples are almost tender.
4. Uncover and continue roasting for 10 minutes or until the apples are tender.
5. In a food processor, purée apples to desired consistency.

Tips for Caramel and Candy Apples

- Choose tart apples to balance the sweet coating.
- Decorate the bottoms of caramel apples with toasted nuts. Besides being tasty, the nuts make the apples less likely to stick to a baking sheet or serving platter.
- After coating, place sticky caramel and candy apples on parchment, not foil.
- To loosen cooled, coated apples from a baking sheet, do not pull them by the sticks. Hold the sides and slide a spatula underneath.
- Caramel apples are best eaten the same day, as the caramel starts to sag.

Apricots

Four Good Signs

- Yields to gentle pressure at the seams.
- Heaviness.
- Fruit scent at the stem end.
- Deep golden-orange skin, especially at the stem end, the last part to ripen.

Four Bad Signs

- Soft spots (these are bruises).
- A fermented taste (the fruit is overripe).
- Green tinges in the skin.
- Wrinkling a bit when pressed (it is too ripe).

❖ To pit apricots, cut along the seams right down to the pit, then twist the halves to separate them.

Bananas

A Good Sign

Yellow bananas with tiny freckles have the fullest flavor.

A Bad Sign

A dull, gray skin indicates that a banana has been chilled or overheated.

❖ The riper the banana, the sweeter it is.

✖ No-No

If you can't break off the stem easily and the skin is hard to peel, the banana is too starchy to eat yet. It can cause upset stomach and constipation.

❖ The tiny black seeds in bananas release ripening ethylene gas.

❖ Store bananas on the counter, away from sunlight and heat.

❖ Choose slightly underripe bananas for cooking savory dishes, and use overripe ones for baking.

B is for Banana Tree

This little hanger for bananas slows down ripening by allowing air to flow around the fruit and disperse the ethylene.

⚡ Lightning Won't Strike If ...

You put a banana in the fridge. You can do this to retard ripening. Wrap the banana in foil. The skin will turn black, but the flesh will remain firm and edible.

❖ Avoid yellow- or black-skinned bananas for muffins and breads. The former are too firm, the latter too wet. Use yellow bananas with lots of freckles.

OUTSIDE THE BOX

You can add bananas to savory dishes. Example: Make Caribbean-style rice by adding a firm large banana to spiced cooked rice, along with tomatoes, onions and beans. Cut the banana in half lengthwise first, then slice it into $\frac{1}{2}$-inch (1 cm) pieces.

❖ For banana bread and muffins, use a fork to mash the bananas and stir them into a thick paste. A creamy base with small lumps is the right consistency. A potato masher leaves bananas too clumpy; a food processor leaves them too liquid.

≡ Fast Fix

Crave banana bread, but don't have any ripe bananas? You can cheat by heating firm bananas. Let them cool before mashing.

- Microwave a peeled banana on High for 20 to 30 seconds or just until you hear a sizzling sound, no longer. Otherwise, it will split and cook in the center.
- Heat a peeled banana in a 450°F (230°C) oven for 10 minutes.

- ❖ Do not pack mashed bananas into the cup when measuring.

- ❖ As soon as bananas turn too ripe to eat, freeze them for baking and smoothies.

Ways to Freeze Bananas

- In their skins.
- Coarsely mashed. Stir in 1 tbsp (15 mL) citrus juice. Seal in a zip-lock bag.

Handling Frozen Bananas

- Thaw frozen whole bananas in their skins.
- To thaw mashed bananas in a sealed zip-lock bag, place the bag in a bowl of warm water.
- Do not allow frozen bananas to thaw completely before cooking with them, as the juices are messy.
- When using frozen, thawed bananas, reduce the liquid in the recipe by up to 1 tbsp (15 mL) per banana.

♡ Healthier Eater

Turn bananas into frozen pops. They're creamy without the calories.

1. Cut each banana in half crosswise. Push a wooden stick through the straight end and into the center of each segment.
2. Hold a segment by the stick over a bowl of melted chocolate. Using a spoon, drizzle melted chocolate over the banana while twirling it to coat. You can roll the coated banana in chopped nuts or even crushed cereal or granola.
3. Place coated bananas on a plate lined with waxed paper or parchment. Freeze them until they are firm, at least 1 hour.
4. Remove them from the freezer and, if necessary, wait for 5 minutes to let them soften before eating.

Notes: Don't bother freezing bananas before coating them. The chocolate doesn't stick as well. Also, for tidier bananas, you can cut the pointy tips off the segments, coat them, then set them upright while freezing.

Factoid Hangovers are caused by dehydration and depleted potassium. Bananas have loads of potassium. They also have tryptophan, the same amino acid found in turkey that is blamed for sleepiness. Bananas are also natural antacids.

Berries

A Bad Sign

If a berry container is stained with juice, the fruit is overripe and/or bruised.

Cleaning Tender Berries

- Immerse them in cold water in the sink or a bowl, then lift them out with a skimmer.
- Dry them in a salad spinner lined with paper towels.

Ways to Store Berries

- Place them in a small sieve inside a plastic tub or bowl, to allow air circulation.
- Put them in a container lined with a paper towel. Cover them with another paper towel. If you can keep them in a single layer, that's even better.
- Refrigerate them in a colander.

- ❖ Thaw berries in the fridge. They'll hold their shape better.

Blueberries

Three Good Signs
- Cultivated blueberries are fat and purple.
- Wild blueberries are tiny and blue-black.
- The skins are smooth, with a silvery sheen called the bloom.

A Bad Sign
Reddish blueberries are not ripe.

3 Ways to Battle Mold

1. Remove berries from their containers right away, discarding any moldy ones. Mold spreads fast.
2. Wash berries just before eating or using them. They mold and spoil quickly after washing.
3. Although washing berries ahead of time is generally frowned upon, they can be treated with a 3:1 solution of water and vinegar. Vinegar destroys bacteria and mold spores. (This works for other fruit, too.) Rinse, drain and dry the berries completely before refrigerating them.

✧ It's easier to remove the stems from blueberries (or black currants) if they're frozen. Roll the frozen berries on the counter with your palm. The stems snap off.

Cranberries

Ⓑ is for Bounceberries
This is the old-fashioned moniker for cranberries. Ripe, fresh cranberries bounce. Others go splat. Growers use "bounceboards" to separate out soft or rotting berries.

White VS. Red?
Cranberries change from green to white to red as they ripen. Cranberries do not become sweeter as they redden, they become tarter. White cranberries are less acidic, so their taste is milder.

7 Ways to Greet the Festive Season with Cranberries

1. Replace the fruit in your favorite upside-down cake recipe with fresh cranberries. (You'll probably have to adjust the amount of sugar.)
2. Add dried cranberries to simmering applesauce.
3. Serve bread pudding with cranberry compote.
4. Substitute cranberry juice in popular cocktails such as margaritas.
5. Make cranberry sherbet or granita.
6. Add dried cranberries to turkey salad.
7. Sprinkle dried cranberries over mixed salad greens.

Cranberry Sauce Ideas
- Cranberries have a lot of pectin. If the sauce gets too thick, stir in orange juice or wine.
- Add $\frac{1}{4}$ tsp (1 mL) baking soda to the cranberries as they cook. You won't need to add as much sugar.
- Make the sauce with orange or apple juice instead of water.
- Add strips of orange peel.
- Add ground cinnamon and cloves.
- Use maple syrup or brown sugar instead of granulated sugar.
- Stir in vanilla extract.

Making Do

Forgot to buy or prepare cranberry sauce? You can create a replacement with berry jam, vinegar and Dijon mustard.

Alternatives to Boring Cranberry Sauce

- Salsa made with cranberries, orange juice and chopped jalapeño pepper. Freeze the cranberries for at least 1 hour before chopping; this helps them keep their texture in the food processor. Chop them coarsely. Let the salsa stand for 24 hours so flavors can meld.
- Cranberry ketchup. Simmer cranberries with onion, garlic, red wine, cider vinegar, granulated sugar, five-spice powder, hot pepper flakes and soy sauce. Purée and strain, discarding solids. For thicker ketchup, pass the mixture through a food mill instead.
- Cranberry chutney, bottled with vinegar, raisins and chopped peeled apple, plus seasonal spices such as ground allspice, ginger, cinnamon and cloves.
- Cranberry apple relish. Stir chopped cranberries with diced peeled apples, granulated sugar and a bit of marmalade to hold everything together.
- Spicy cranberry relish. Combine chopped cranberries with lime juice, shallots, cilantro, jalapeño peppers, garlic and cracked black pepper.
- Candied cranberries. Spread 1 lb (500 g) washed fresh cranberries on a greased rimmed baking sheet. Sprinkle with 2½ cups (625 mL) granulated sugar. Let stand for 1 hour. Cover the sheet with foil. Bake at 350°F (180°C), stirring occasionally, for 45 to 60 minutes or until well glazed.
- Candied orange cranberries. Stir cranberries with granulated sugar, orange juice and zest, and brandy. Spread on a greased rimmed baking sheet. Bake at 350°F (180°C), stirring occasionally, for 45 to 60 minutes.
- Roasted pearl onions with cranberries. Put onions in a baking dish, scatter lots of cranberries and granulated sugar and a bit of butter over top, then drizzle with port. Bake at 350°F (180°C) for about 45 minutes or until the onions are soft and the sauce is thick.

Mock Cranberry Sauce

This sweet, tangy concoction doesn't taste exactly like cranberry sauce, but no one will complain — or perhaps even notice. It is a fine accompaniment for roast turkey. **Makes about ¾ cup (175 mL)**

Tips

I used a mixture of strawberry and currant jam.

Toss in the dried cranberries if you have them. They will plump as the "sauce" sits.

½ cup	berry jam	125 mL
1 tsp	balsamic vinegar	5 mL
½ tsp	Dijon mustard	2 mL
2 tbsp	dried cranberries (optional)	25 mL

1. In a glass measuring cup, microwave jam on High for about 30 seconds or until warm but not boiling. Stir in vinegar and mustard until blended. Stir in cranberries (if using). Let the mixture cool and set.

Strawberries

Four Good Signs

- The berries are red right up to the hull. No white tops.
- They are firm.
- Each has a healthy green cap.
- They are fragrant — the more perfumed the berry, the better the taste.

✦ Strawberries keep for about 3 days in the fridge before they start to shrivel.

Mythstake

Bigger strawberries aren't necessarily better. Monstrous berries look impressive, but tend to be watery or spongy. The berries from your local farmer may be small, but they taste heavenly.

✦ Strawberries are absorbent. Wash them quickly in cold water, with the hull intact. Dry them before hulling.

✦ Here's a cool way to hull and core strawberries. Use a metal latte straw. Push it through from the bottom to the stem end. This leaves only a tiny hole. (A standard plastic straw is too limp to do the job.)

✦ You can add a bit of lemon juice to the wash water to clean and preserve berries.

✦ Serve strawberries at room temperature.

✦ How to enhance the flavor of strawberries:
- Weird but true: Strawberries taste good with balsamic vinegar . Add a drop to berries for shortcake.
- Before serving, squeeze orange juice over strawberries. Or, if you are sugaring them, use the juice of a lime.

Cantaloupes and Honeydew Melons

Seven Good Signs

- The melon feels heavy.
- It smells fragrant, but not cloyingly so, at the stem end.
- The skin has no blemishes.
- There's a hollow sound, rather than a dull thud, when the melon is tapped.
- The melon has a bit of give at the stem end.
- For honeydews, shake and listen for seeds and juice sloshing inside. That means they are separated from the flesh, a sign of ripeness.
- The scar at the stem end is shrunken and callused. This is a sign that the melon has matured on the vine.

Three Bad Signs

- A fermented or musky scent.
- No scent at the stem end (a sign the melon isn't ripe).
- Mold or softening at the stem end.

How to Cut a Round Melon into Wedges

1. Slice a bit off each end.
2. Place the melon upright on a cutting board. Using a sharp knife, slice off the skin in strips, top to bottom, hugging the curves of the fruit.
3. Shave off green bits on the flesh with a serrated peeler, or stick with the knife.
4. Halve the melon. Scrape out the seeds with a spoon. Cut each half into wedges.

✦ Eat melons when they're slightly cooler than room temperature.

✦ Cover cut melons with plastic, so they don't impart their odors to fridge-mates.

How to Cut Fast Melon Chunks

1. Halve the melon lengthwise and seed it.
2. Place each half cut side down. Slice off the rounded ends.
3. Turn the melon cut side up. Slice it into wedges.
4. Cut slits crosswise through the flesh of each wedge, down to the rind. Flatten the wedge. Run your knife between the skin and the flesh to liberate the chunks.

✧ Wash a melon before peeling or cutting it, so you don't transfer germs from the skin to the flesh.

Cherries

What Kind?

✧ Bing is the standard cherry. It is large, firm and sweet, with dark red skin and flesh. Rainier is an upscale cherry, sweeter than the Bing, with a yellow skin blushed with red, and yellow flesh. Red tart cherries, or sour cherries, are best for pies. They may be sold chilled and pitted in pails.

Five Good Signs

• The darker the cherries, the sweeter they are.
• Shiny skin is good. Avoid cherries with bumpy or mottled skin.
• The stems are bright green, not limp and brown.
• The cherries are taut, almost ready to burst.
• Sour cherries should be soft and juicy.

✧ Choose cherries with stems intact. Otherwise, their juices leak.

✧ Handle cherries gently. Their skins are thin and fragile.

Factoid Sweet cherries deteriorate more in 1 hour at room temperature than in 24 hours in the fridge.

✧ Cherries won't ripen from fire-engine red to mahogany after they're picked. But the brighter red ones have a longer shelf life.

✧ Toss out crushed cherries; their juice can cause fellow cherries to spoil.

✧ Wrap cherries in paper towels. You can put them in a perforated plastic bag, but don't seal it.

✧ Cherries will keep in the fridge for 3 days. Bring them to room temperature before eating, but don't leave them in a sunny spot.

✧ Remove frozen cherries from the freezer 30 minutes before using. Don't let them thaw completely.

✧ Pit cherries over an open bag.

Master Plan
Boozy Cherries

1. Wash 1 lb (500 g) cherries, but leave in the pits and stems. Put them in a 4-cup (1 L) jar with a tight lid.
2. Stir 2 cups (500 mL) brandy or kirsch with granulated sugar. Use ½ cup (125 mL) sugar for regular cherries or ¾ cup (175 mL) sugar for sour cherries.
3. Pour enough booze mixture into the jar to cover the cherries.
4. Cover the jar and keep it in a cool, dark spot for at least 1 month. After the first week, turn it upside down every day. Refrigerate it after 1 month.
5. Let steep for at least 2 months before opening.

Citrus Fruit

Three Good Signs
- Lemons have no green, limes have no yellow.
- The fruit is firm, not spongy.
- There aren't any bruises.

Mythstake
Puffy skin is not always okay on a tangerine. Extreme puffiness is a sign of old age.

✧ Citrus fruit past its prime can be frozen. Two ways to freeze it:
- Freeze it whole, then juice and zest it. To extract the most juice, thaw it to room temperature.
- Zest and juice it first. Freeze the two separately.

✧ Macerate citrus slices or wedges overnight with plenty of sugar to soften them for lemonade and desserts.

Ⓜ is for Meyer
Choose Meyer lemons for desserts. They are milder and sweeter than regular lemons, thin-skinned, rounded, with golden flesh and a hint of orange flavor. The darker the skin, the riper they are. The color ranges from deep yellow to almost orange. Look for Meyers with firm, smooth skin and no soft spots. If using a Meyer in a recipe, reduce the sugar.

OUTSIDE THE BOX
Enhance the flavor of grapefruit with heat.
- Before warming a grapefruit half, loosen the segments with a grapefruit knife.
- Spread honey or sugar on the flesh.
- Put the grapefruit under the broiler for 1 to 2 minutes or warm it in the microwave on High for 30 seconds.

Factoid Greenish bits on oranges are not necessarily a sign that they are unripe. However, some producers dye their oranges to make them more attractive.

Ⓟ is for Preserved Lemons
- Whole preserved lemons used in Middle Eastern dishes take about 1 month to steep in brine and their own juices at room temperature in an airtight jar.
- To shorten the process to 1 week, cut the lemons into wedges. Alternatively, quarter them lengthwise almost down to the base. However, it is harder to stuff and pack quartered lemons evenly into the jar.
- Use organic lemons and scrub the rinds well.
- Milder, sweeter Meyer lemons are preferred, but regular lemons work fine. Never use bottled lemon juice in the brine.
- Before making preserved lemons, pop out the stubs of the stems or slice off the stem ends.
- Some cooks flavor the brine. You can add cinnamon sticks, cloves, coriander seeds, bay leaves, cardamom pods or even tiny dried red chile peppers.
- For the safest preserved lemons, treat them as a type of pickle and pack them in sterilized mason jars.
- Once the lemons are finished curing, you may top up the jar with olive oil. Make sure the lemons remain covered in juice and oil. For optimal food safety, store the bottle in the fridge.
- Before using preserved lemons, you may blanch them for 10 seconds in boiling water to tone down the saltiness.
- The rinds are used. The pulp and any seeds can be scraped off and discarded.

B is for Blood

Blood oranges, or Moros, are less acidic than regular oranges. They are named for their ruby flesh.

✧ To get started peeling an orange or grapefruit, slip one tine of a fork into the navel and pull to make a slit. To strip off the cap, insert the tine of the fork perpendicular to the slit at the bottom and "saw" all the way around. You can obtain a strip of peel this way, too.

Three Estimates

- One orange yields 6 to 8 tbsp (90 to 120 mL) juice and 2 to 3 tbsp (25 to 45 mL) zest.
- One lemon yields about ¼ cup (50 mL) juice and 2 tbsp (25 mL) zest.
- One lime yields about 3 tbsp (45 mL) juice and 1 tbsp (15 mL) zest.

✧ Zest the fruit before you cut it and squeeze the juice. Citrus is easier to zest while the fruit is intact and easier to juice after zesting.

Zesting

Z is for Zest

Zest is not the same as citrus rind. The rind is the whole peel; the zest is the bright, thin, waxy, pebbled coating on the rind. Underneath the rind is the white spongy pith, which is bitter. Citrus flavor lies in the zest, while the tang is in the juice. If you don't like the texture of zest, strain it, if possible, but don't omit it from your recipe. Some recipes call for citrus peel; they usually mean the zest.

 Healthier Eater

- Wash the skins of citrus fruit before zesting them. Use a vegetable wash to lift off dirt, chemical residues and mold spores.
- Buy organic citrus fruit for wholesome zest.

✧ Zest citrus just before using it, to keep the aromatic oils at their peak.

✧ Grate zest very finely using a rasp (Microplane) grater. Finer zest releases more oils and is fluffier. Avoid chopping zest.

✧ Zesting shouldn't give you any trouble. But you could put the fruit in the freezer for 30 minutes to make the zest easier to strip.

✧ Zest will slide off the grater more easily if you dip the grater in cold water beforehand.

---

3 Tips for Measuring Zest

1. Grate zest over waxed paper, then roll the paper into a funnel and shake it into the measuring spoon. That's easier than trying to scoop it.
2. Zest is hard to measure. Do not pack it into the spoon.
3. Measure zest right away. It dries and settles as it sits.

✧ Round up stubborn, stray zest on the cutting board or grater with a cube of butter.

✧ Zest is full of aromatic oils. But if you don't want the texture of zest in, say, icing, you can grate it, tie it hobo-style in a single layer of cheesecloth, then bury it in the sugar for your recipe. Encourage the oils to release by rubbing your fingers against the packet in the sugar. Leave it buried for at least 15 minutes. This will gently flavor and scent the sugar.

✦ How to curl citrus strips: Shave the zest into thin strips. Loosely cover it with a damp paper towel for 15 minutes. Soaking zest in water doesn't work; this just stiffens it.

✦ To mellow or eliminate bitterness in chopped or stripped zest, briefly blanch it in boiling water. This is good to know for candy, preserves and sauces.

Ways to Handle Stripped Fruit

- Wrap it tightly in plastic to prevent drying and hardening.
- Juice it. Freeze the juice.

OUTSIDE THE BOX

Extract citrus essence by rubbing the peel with a sugar cube. Use the cube in espresso or tea. Use it within a couple of days; the fragrance slips away.

✦ Dried orange and tangerine peels are used as seasonings in Chinese cuisine. To make your own, use a vegetable peeler to shave off the zest in strips. Let them dry in the hot sun until they are hard. Transfer them to an airtight jar at room temperature. They will keep for months.

♺ Waste Not

Perfume sugar by storing it with leftover zest in a sealed container.

Juicing

✦ For best results, always use freshly squeezed juice. Bottled lemon and lime juice have additives. Exceptions: Use the bottled stuff for acidulated water and cleaning jobs.

Factoid The flesh of lime is tougher than the flesh of lemon.

✦ To squeeze a citrus wedge, stick the flesh with the tines of a fork. Twist the fork while you press the ends together.

OUTSIDE THE BOX

- Twist citrus halves or wedges in cheesecloth before squeezing, to capture the seeds and pulp. Squeeze the cheesecloth before tossing it out.
- Sturdy tongs are handy citrus reamers. Stick closed tongs in the center of a citrus half and twist. You can also squeeze from the outside with a strong pair of tongs. Or do both. Tongs with spoon-shaped ends are also handy for picking seeds out of juice. Hold them straight down.
- To squeeze lemon and lime halves in your palm, do it backwards to help trap the seeds. Hold the cut side against your palm and squeeze firmly.
- Tap a lemon or lime. Pierce the navel with a metal latte straw. (A metal skewer won't work, contrary to some advice.) Pull out the straw. Squeeze out the juice you need. Before storing the fruit in the fridge, seal the hole with duct tape or wrap the fruit in plastic.

5 Ways to Get More Juice

1. Zap the whole fruit in the microwave on High for 10 to 20 seconds, then roll it on the counter, pressing firmly with your palm.
2. Warm the whole fruit in a 300°F (150°C) oven for 3 minutes.
3. Pop it in a bowl of very hot water for 5 minutes.
4. Quarter it lengthwise, then slice the center rib from each wedge before squeezing.
5. Use a reamer instead of squeezing by hand.

Mythstake

A big lemon is not always the juiciest choice. Thin-skinned lemons are relatively juicier. Small and medium lemons tend to have thinner skins. Also, go for a smoother rind, rather than a pebbly one. Large lemons with pebbly rinds often owe their size to thicker skins, not necessarily more flesh and juice.

Cutting

✧ Ways to cut attractive citrus slices for cocktails and garnishes:

- Cut lemon and lime wedges like a bartender. Trim a bit off each end of the fruit. Quarter the fruit lengthwise. Set each wedge on its side. Using a small, sharp knife, cut off the strip of white pith running along the center. This also gets rid of a lot of seeds. With the knife, poke out any seeds you see. Finish cutting the fruit into smaller wedges.

- Cut off the ends of the fruit. Halve it at the equator. Set each half flesh side up and slice it into wedges. For little wedges, cut along the segments.
- Cut off the ends of the fruit, then halve it lengthwise. Lay each half flesh side down, then slice it into semicircles. For cocktails, put a notch in each semicircle so it can hang on the rim of a glass.
- Cut $\frac{1}{2}$ inch (1 cm) off each end of the fruit. Slice it into thin circles. If desired, cut a notch from the center to the edge in each circle, then twist it decoratively or stick it on the rim of a glass.

How to Peel and Segment Citrus Fruit

1. Roll the fruit gently with your palm to loosen the segments.
2. Cut the ends off straight. Sit the fruit on one cut end.
3. Using a very sharp paring knife, follow the contours of the peel and cut off the rind lengthwise in strips.
4. Trim any bits of pith stuck to the fruit.
5. With one hand, hold the fruit over a bowl. With the other, wield a knife to cut the membranes on both sides of each segment, all the way to the center.
6. Tease the segments apart. Drop them into the bowl.
7. Clean up each segment. Pull off loose bits of membrane. Lay the wedges on their sides and slice off pith from the center.
8. As you work, squeeze the pith and membranes over the bowl, to capture the juice, before discarding them.
9. Remove the segments from the bowl. Pour the juice through a strainer to catch seeds, pulp and debris.

✧ Getting squirted in the eye is no fun. As a preventive measure, cut three or four slits across the thin edge of a citrus wedge before squeezing it.

Coconuts

> **Factoid** The hairy brown coconut is the seed of the coconut palm. In situ, it is encased in a green pod.

Two Good Signs

• You hear liquid sloshing inside.
• You see no dustings of mold outside.

How to Crack a Coconut

1. Rinse the shell so that the debris won't muck up the juice or flesh.
2. Find the three round "eyes" at one end of the shell. Position a pick or screwdriver over one of the eyes and smack it with a hammer. Then pierce a second eye.
3. Pour out the liquid.
4. With the hammer, bang around the equator and under the eyes, to smash the shell.

✧ Before cracking a coconut, wrap it in a towel in case of flying debris.

✧ Pry the white flesh from the shell fragments with a thin, blunt knife.

✧ The thin brown crust on the flesh next to the shell is edible. If you don't want it, peel it off with a vegetable peeler.

✧ Coconut is a tough nut to crack. Heating it makes the job easier.

How to Crack a Heated Coconut

1. Put the coconut in a pan in the oven to catch any drips — though it should not be heated for so long that it cracks on its own.
2. Heat it in a 300°F (150°C) oven for 20 to 30 minutes.
3. Let it cool until you can handle it.
4. Have a bowl at the ready. Crack the shell with a hammer. As soon as a crack appears, turn the coconut and pour out the juice. This works better than it sounds.

✧ How to make the flesh easier to extract:
• Freeze, then thaw, the coconut.
• Heat the coconut.

✧ Shred the flesh in a food processor or against the second-smallest holes of a box grater.

✧ To freeze fresh coconut, grate the flesh and stir it with the liquid. For tenderness, add 1 part sugar per 8 parts coconut. You can also freeze canned or homemade coconut milk.

✧ Toast grated fresh coconut on a dry rimmed baking sheet in a 325°F (160°C) oven, stirring often, until golden.

D is for Desiccated

Dried coconut is sold at the supermarket. It may be grated, shredded or flaked, and sweetened or unsweetened. In a pinch, you can interchange these, but try to avoid it. If necessary, reduce the amount of sugar in a recipe.

✧ To substitute desiccated coconut for fresh, soak it in warm coconut milk for half an hour.

- How to toast desiccated coconut in the microwave:
  - Spread it thinly on a plate.
  - Microwave it on High, stirring it halfway through and at the end of the cooking time. About $\frac{1}{4}$ cup (50 mL) unsweetened desiccated coconut takes 2 to $2\frac{1}{2}$ minutes; the same amount of sweetened takes $1\frac{1}{2}$ to 2 minutes.

Mythstake

The clear liquid in a coconut is not the "milk." It is the juice, but is known as coconut water. Coconut milk is made with coconut flesh and hot water; you can also add the coconut juice.

Master Plan
Homemade Coconut Milk or Cream

1. Combine equal parts boiling water and smashed or shredded coconut flesh. (For whiter coconut milk, peel off the brown skin on the flesh before shredding.) If desired, stir in the coconut juice. Let stand for 1 hour.
2. Place a sieve lined with cheesecloth over a large bowl. Squeeze handfuls of coconut flesh over the sieve. Dump the flesh into the sieve. Repeat with the remaining coconut flesh. Squeeze the cheesecloth to extract as much liquid as possible. Discard the solids.
3. To make coconut cream, use 1 part water to 4 parts coconut flesh. You can supplement coconut cream with milk or cream, or start with scalded milk.
4. Use coconut milk or cream within 2 days. Keep it refrigerated in an airtight container.

- Coconut milk doesn't like high heat. Stir it in at the end of the cooking time or keep the heat moderate.

Milk VS. Cream VS. Creamed?

Commercial coconut cream is richer, denser — and harder to find. It is made from a first pressing. Coconut milk is made from a second pressing. It is widely sold, canned or powdered. Avoid the powdered kind; it is a poor cousin, thin and pallid. Creamed coconut, or cream of coconut, is a solid block at room temperature. It is sweetened.

Making Do

If you need just a bit of coconut cream, scoop the thick paste off the top of a can of coconut milk that has separated after sitting undisturbed. Note: Not all brands separate; some contain emulsifiers.

- How to turn coconut shells into decorative containers for buffets:
  - Saw off the upper third of the shell to use as a lid. You might need to bolster the base with twisted cloth or set it in a small bowl.
  - Halve the shell lengthwise.

Dried Fruit

Mythstake

Don't be fooled by brighter-colored dried fruit. It is not necessarily fresher or moister. Dried fruit naturally darkens. Organic dried apricots, for instance, are brown. Preservatives keep the standard kind orange.

- How to break up clumps of dried fruit:
  - Separate before baking by tossing it with flour from the recipe.
  - Unstick dried fruit, big or small, by warming it in the oven or microwave.

- You can soften candied peel by soaking it in hot water for 1 minute.

- Ways to make sticky, dried fruit easier to chop:
  - Put it in the freezer for half an hour.
  - Sprinkle flour on it. Use flour from the recipe.
  - Squirt it with lemon juice.
  - Butter or oil the knife, or the blade of the food processor.
  - Drop it into the food processor through the feed tube, one piece at a time.
  - Snip it with kitchen scissors. Dip the blades in hot water occasionally.

- Dried fruit, such as raisins or currants, can suck moisture from a batter. Plump them first.

- Match the soaking liquid to the fruit. Soak dried apple slices in cider, for example, or raisins in wine.

- Use the soaking liquid in the recipe, after straining it, of course.

---

4 Ways to Plump and Reconstitute Dried Fruit

1. Put the fruit into a bowl, then pour in just enough boiling water to cover it. (Or use warm wine or rum for flavor.) Let stand for 5 minutes, then strain.
2. Put it in a small bowl covered with a bit of water. Zap it in the microwave on High for 30 to 60 seconds. Let it cool.
3. Steam it over simmering water for 5 minutes or until it's tender enough to pit.
4. Rinse it, drain it and spread it out a single layer on foil. Fold the foil into a packet. Heat the fruit in a 350°F (180°C) oven until puffed — about 5 minutes for raisins, 10 for prunes.

- You can store dried fruit in the freezer.

Ideas for Date Night
- Remove the skins and pits by squeezing out the flesh at the stem end.
- Soften dates (for quick bread or sticky toffee pudding, for example) by simmering them for 5 minutes in the water from the recipe. Remove from the heat and add about 1 tsp (5 mL) baking soda per 8 oz (250 g) dates. Let the mixture cool for 15 to 30 minutes.

Honey VS. Medjool?
Honey dates are better for cooking than eating. Premium Medjool dates are good for eating and cooking. They are tender and sweet.

Seedless VS. Seeded?
Raisins are dried grapes. Seedless grapes are grown without seeds. Seeded grapes have their seeds removed. Seeded raisins are made from seeded grapes. They are larger than seedless raisins made from seedless grapes. Got that?

Figs

- Figs should ripen on the tree. They ripen from uniform green to brownish, yellowish or purplish, from the bottom of the fruit upward. They are extremely perishable and don't travel well.

Four Good Signs
- Plump, very soft flesh that yields to gentle pressure. (A firm fig is not ripe. A mushy one is overripe.)
- Taut skin. (Small slits and tears are okay.)
- A sweet scent.
- Bent stems.

Two Bad Signs
- A fermented odor (it's overripe).
- Milky sap at the stem end.

- The aperture at the base of the fig is called the eye. Varieties with closed eyes last longer.

- Store figs upright in a tub or sieve lined with a paper towel to absorb moisture and cushion the bases. Cover with plastic wrap.

- Avoid mold by keeping them in a cool, dry area.

- Ripen figs at room temperature, then put them in the fridge.

- No need to peel figs. Eat them thin skin and all.

- Dried figs should be soft, free of mold and smell mellow. Avoid hard, cracked ones.

- Improve dried figs by poaching them in juice or wine before using them.

Grapes

A Good Sign

The stem end of the cluster is green and pliable, not tough or brown.

- Don't try to wash off the coating, or bloom, on some grapes. It's a good thing.

- Serve grapes cool, rather than at room temperature.

- Before putting grapes in a fruit bowl, line it with paper towels to hinder mold.

- Should you, like Beulah, ever need to peel a grape, pour boiling water over it and let it stand for about 5 minutes, depending on the thickness of the skin. Rinse it in cold water. Pull off the skin. This is not an easy endeavor.

- Wrap a paper towel around a grape cluster and slide it into a plastic bag. Leave the bag open. Store it in the fridge.

OUTSIDE THE BOX

- Freeze grapes as a wholesome snack. (Some people roll these in sugar.)
- Sauté seedless grapes in grapeseed oil. These go nicely with pork, sausages and game meats.
- Toss grapes into a salad. (You can do the same with berries.)

- Frozen grapes can replace fresh ones in some recipes. When making preserves, there's no need to completely thaw the grapes. Thaw them in the fridge just until they're soft enough to be crushed.

Kiwifruit

- Refrigerate kiwis once they are ripe.

- The easiest way to eat a kiwi is to cut it in half at the equator and scoop the flesh with a spoon or grapefruit spoon. New Zealanders make special kiwi spoons, but they are hard to find.

- You can remove the skin with a serrated peeler.

OUTSIDE THE BOX

- To peel a kiwi, work from the inside out. Cut it in half at the equator. Insert the tip of a teaspoon between the skin and flesh. Hold the kiwi half sideways and rotate it as you press the back of the spoon against the skin.
- Some new Zealanders eat the skin. It's okay, but a bit fuzzy. Scrub it first.

Mangos

Three Good Signs

- A sweet scent, especially at the stem end. (If it smells sour, it's too old.)
- A firm texture and tight skin (not wrinkled or loose).
- Some yellow or red on the green skin.
- ✧ Ripen a mango at room temperature until it softens and the skin is no longer all green. When it's ripe, you can refrigerate it.

How to Cut a Mango

1. Cut thick lengthwise slices from either side of the large, flat pit.
2. Using the tip of a small, sharp knife, score the flesh in a crosshatch pattern. Run the knife right down to the peel, but don't cut through it.
3. Invert the peel by pushing it with your thumbs. Cut the cubes or diamonds of mango from the peel by sliding the knife between the peel and the flesh. If a mango is very ripe, you can use a grapefruit spoon to scoop the flesh. Or simply bite off chunks.
4. Cut the skin off the remaining flesh around the pit. Cut off the flesh.

Papayas

OUTSIDE THE BOX

Papaya seeds are edible. These little, round black seeds are pungent, with a peppery, mustardy flavor. Use them raw or toasted as a garnish, as you would use capers, or sprinkle them in salad. Rinse and dry them first. Toast papaya seeds on a rimmed baking sheet in a 350°F (180°C) oven for 5 to 8 minutes.

A Good Sign

It has some give. A papaya is softer than a mango.

- ✧ Mottling on the skin is okay.

Passion Fruit

Two Good Signs

- The skin is black, wrinkly, leathery and dimpled. (A smooth-skinned passion fruit has too much kick.)
- There's space between the skin and the flesh.

- ✧ To separate the seeds from passion fruit, force the pulp through a strainer.

Peaches and Nectarines

Three Good Signs

- Yielding to gentle pressure at the seams.
- Heaviness.
- A fruity scent at the stem end.

Three Bad Signs

- Soft spots. (These are bruises.)
- A fermented taste. (The fruit is overripe.)
- Green tinge on the skin. (For peaches, check the background color, not the blush. Peaches plucked green won't ripen properly.)

- ✧ When you get peaches home, remove them from the basket and sort them according to ripeness. Refrigerate the ripe ones, but let the others ripen at room temperature. Never refrigerate unripe peaches.

Freestone VS. Clingstone?

It's easy to pit freestone peaches. Clingstones arrive earlier in the season. These are sometimes called semi-freestones for better PR. Choose freestones for poaching or you'll end up mangling the peaches while cutting around the pits.

◆ To pit freestone peaches, cut along the seam down to the pit, then twist the halves to separate them.

◆ Use firm peaches for cooking.

Pears

What Kind?

- Anjou is large, yellow-green and sweet. There is also a reddish type.
- Bartlett comes in yellow and red versions.
- Bosc is firm, with russet skin, white flesh and a long neck.
- Comice has green-yellow skin that may be tinged with pink, a rounded shape, fine flesh and delicate flavor.
- Seckel is tiny, ultra-sweet, rounded, with thick reddish skin and firm flesh.
- Forelle is golden with red freckling, and is snack-sized.

- **Best fresh for snacks and salads:** Bartlett, Anjou, Comice, Seckel
- **Best baked or poached:** Bosc, Bartlett, Anjou
- **Best for baking:** Bartlett, Bosc
- **Best for preserves:** Bartlett, Seckel (avoid Comice)

Factoid Pears left too long on the tree become mealy. They should be picked before they ripen. It's best to buy immature pears and ripen them at home.

✪ Waste Not

If a pear is overripe, purée it for a cocktail or smoothie. If it is slightly underripe, bake or poach it.

5 Ripeness Tips

1. You can't depend on color to tell you when a pear is ripe. Bartletts turn from green to yellow. Some red varieties turn from dark red to bright red, but others remain dark red. Anjou, Bosc and Comice change little or not at all.
2. Pears ripen from the center out. So if a pear feels soft, it's probably too far gone. If it feels wooden and lacks sweetness, it is underripe.
3. Use the thumb test. Press the top near the stem. It should have a bit of give. Exception: Softening at the stem end is not as apparent in the Bosc because of its firm flesh.
4. Firm, green Bartletts take 4 to 6 days to ripen at room temperature. If you prefer firm pears, they are ready when they're changing from green to yellow. If you like them soft, wait another 2 to 3 days until they're a ripe, tender yellow.
5. To ripen pears faster, wrap each one in a paper towel or newspaper. Put them in a cardboard box or a bowl.

OUTSIDE THE BOX

- Core a pear from the base, using an apple corer.
- Core a pear in wedges. Cut it in half lengthwise. Lay each half cut side down. Slice off the rounded ends. Cut each half in half lengthwise. Lay each quarter on its side. Angling the knife, slice off the core.

◆ Pears stored at too low a temperature may look fine on the outside, but be brown inside.

❖ Slice off the base of a whole pear so it can stand upright while it's poaching or draining on a rack.

Ways to Make Pear Crisps

- Simmer very thin pear slices in simple syrup for 1 minute. Drain them well. Place them in a single layer on a rimmed baking sheet lined with parchment. Bake them at 200°F (100°C) for about 3 hours or until crisp.
- Thinly slice pears lengthwise. Arrange the slices in a single layer on a rimmed baking sheet lined with parchment. Sprinkle them with icing sugar. Top with parchment and another baking sheet. Dry them in a 225°F (110°C) oven for 45 minutes. Remove the top baking sheet and continue drying them in the oven until crisp. The juicier they are, the longer they'll take.

Persimmons

Fuyu VS. Hachiya?

Hachiyas have a slightly pointed base. Fuyus are squat, like many tomatoes. The eater who mixes them up will be disappointed.

❖ Hachiyas are astringent when firm, creamy when mushy. Eat them when they feel very mushy, but don't wait until they are black. The interior should be gelatinous. A Hachiya eaten too early will coat the mouth and gums thickly with tannin.

❖ Fuyus can be eaten when they're firm, like apples, but they are best when they're slightly soft — not mushy.

Pineapples

Seven Good Signs
- The crown is compact.
- The leaves are green and moist.
- A leaf in the center of the crown releases with a gentle tug. (Watch out for spikes!) If the leaf fights back, the pineapple is not ripe.
- The stem end smells sweet, not fermented.
- There's a slight give when you push on the skin.
- It feels heavy.
- The eyes (thorny studs in the skin) are protruding or weepy.

Two Bad Signs
- The skin is bruised.
- Juice is leaking from the bottom. (It's overripe.)

❖ Ripen a pineapple at room temperature. Refrigerate it once it's ripe.

❖ Save the glorious crown to decorate a fruit platter.

♻ Waste Not

Make juice with an overripe pineapple. Cut it into chunks and freeze it. Thaw it in the fridge for half an hour. Put it in a blender with cold water. Liquefy it. Strain it to remove the pulp.

❖ The brown "eyes" in the flesh run in a spiral pattern around the pineapple. You can score lightly on either side of the lines of eyes to make them easier to remove.

Ways to Excise the Eyes

- Use the V-shaped gouge in a vegetable-carving kit. Asian markets sell inexpensive kits.
- Use the tip of a vegetable peeler.

12,167 Kitchen and Cooking Secrets   **231**

Plums

✧ Plums should have a bit of hazy bloom on the skin.

✧ Store ripe plums in the fridge.

Pomegranates

✧ The color of a pomegranate rind is not an indicator of ripeness. It can vary from pink to yellowish red to crimson.

✧ Pomegranates can be kept at room temperature (out of the sun) or refrigerated.

(A) is for Aril (and for Albedo)

Pomegranate seeds are called arils. Glistening neon-red pulp surrounds the white kernels. Albedo is the spongy white cushioning inside the pomegranate. The thin, waxy "room dividers" are called the membranes.

OUTSIDE THE BOX

Arils are good in salads, soups, stews, meatballs or meatloaf, and stir-fries. They make lovely garnishes.

✧ Keep arils in an airtight tub in the fridge for a few days or freeze them.

✧ Freeze arils in a single layer on a rimmed baking sheet, then transfer them to a zip-lock bag.

✧ If you dunk it in water, you can open a pomegranate without having to take a shower afterwards.

How to Deconstruct a Pomegranate

1. Slice off the crown, say about ½ inch (1 cm) from the tip.
2. Holding the crown in a large bowl of cold water, tease out the arils underwater. Toss out the rind and pulp.
3. Score the peel of the fruit from top to bottom where you see white section dividers. The sections will be uneven.
4. Holding the fruit in the water, separate it at each score. Toss each section into the water.
5. Working underwater, section by section, use your fingers to gently tease out the arils. Discard the albedo and large pieces of membrane as you go.
6. The arils will sink and white debris will float. Swish the water. Pour off as much water as possible, along with the debris. Add more cold water, swish and drain off debris.
7. You should have fairly clean arils by now. Pour the lot through a sieve.

Grenadine VS. Pomegranate Molasses?

Grenadine is sweet pomegranate syrup. It is mixed with club soda or used to make cocktails. Pomegranate molasses is a tart, brownish red syrup used in Middle Eastern cuisine. Do not confuse the two in recipes. The "molasses" may be described as pomegranate concentrate.

- Don't try to juice a pomegranate by squeezing or reaming the halves. That's so messy. Instead, remove the arils and tie them in cheesecloth. Press the cheesecloth bundle, using tongs. Be prepared for stains.

Rhubarb

Two Good Signs

- The stalks are crisp and glossy, not limp.
- The leaves are bright green.

Considerations When Choosing Rhubarb

- Rhubarb ranges from pale green to deep red. Redder rhubarb isn't necessarily better tasting or riper.
- Stalks more than $1\frac{1}{2}$ inches (4 cm) thick may be tough and fibrous. The stalks of some green varieties, however, are still tender even if they're thick.

Field VS. Greenhouse?

Field rhubarb has a brighter color and flavor. Greenhouse, or hothouse, rhubarb is sweeter and more tender, but not as firm.

✗ No-No

Never eat rhubarb leaves. They contain toxic oxalic acid. You won't drop dead from a little bit, but you might get a stomach ache.

How to Prep Rhubarb

1. Cut off discolored spots. Trim $\frac{1}{2}$ inch (1 cm) from the base.
2. If the stalks have tough strings (like celery), or if they're thick, peel them with a vegetable peeler.
3. Use the smallest possible amount of water to cook rhubarb.
4. Don't evaporate off all the liquid. Cooked rhubarb will thicken in the fridge.

- To store rhubarb, first cut off the leaves. They draw moisture from the stalks. Then wrap single stalks in plastic. Put them in the fridge.

- Use the stalks before they become flaccid.

Master Plan
Basic Rhubarb Compote

1. Put diced or chopped rhubarb in a saucepan. Sprinkle with granulated sugar and let stand for 15 minutes. Add a tiny bit of water or, better, orange juice.
2. Bring it to a boil over high heat. Reduce the heat to low, cover and simmer, stirring frequently, for about 10 minutes or until tender.

- To make rhubarb syrup, simmer chopped rhubarb with lots of granulated sugar and a little water until it is falling apart. Press it through a sieve, capturing the syrup, Let it cool to room temperature. Store it in the fridge or freeze it.

OUTSIDE THE BOX

- Rhubarb can be used as marinade. Adding only a bit of granulated sugar to take the edge off the tartness, simmer it until very tender. Let it cool. Use it to marinate red meat or game.
- Turn rhubarb into rhubarbade. The name doesn't have much of a ring to it, but the drink tastes good. Stir rhubarb syrup into cold water or club soda, and add lime juice, if desired. Rhubarb loves ginger, so how about adding some syrup to ginger ale?

Star Fruit

C is for Carambola

Carambola is another name for star fruit.

A Good Sign

Star fruit is ripe and ready when the ridges begin to darken.

Two Parts to Trim

 You can eat the peel, but slice off the dark ridges first.
 Slice off the bitter green edges.

Tamarind

✧ Clusters of what look like giant, misshapen, brown pea pods grow on the tropical tamarind tree. Inside the pods are seeds and a brown pulp. The lip-smacking sweet-and-sour pulp is used in cooking and as a tenderizer.

✧ Tamarind is most often sold dried, in packets, and must be pressed to extract a paste. If you are lucky, you might find a bottle of pressed paste.

✧ Choose a packet of tamarind with some moisture and give, not a brick that feels like it belongs on a construction site.

Master Plan
Tamarind Paste

1. Break off a chunk, about ¼ cup (50 mL), of dried tamarind.
2. Soak it in 1 cup (250 mL) of boiling water for about 10 minutes or until softened. If it's super-dry, put it in a small saucepan with the water, then cover and simmer over low heat for 10 minutes.
3. Press it through a sieve, discarding the seeds and coarse solids.

Making Do

If you can't be bothered pressing tamarind to extract paste, substitute tamarind chutney.

✗ No-No

Don't use aluminum bowls or utensils with tamarind. They react badly with each other. Acidic ingredients can strip chemicals from metals such as aluminum, iron or copper. The food can discolor and taste metallic.

♻ Waste Not

In India, the leftover pulp was used to polish brass.

Watermelons

Factoid Watermelon is 92% water.

Six Good Signs

• The watermelon is firm, heavy and symmetrical.
• It has a creamy yellow spot, created as it sat in the field and ripened.
• The melon is smaller, thus likely to be sweeter.
• The skin is shiny and moist. You should be able to shave off a thin piece by scraping it with a fingernail.
• The stem is green and fairly dry, but not wrinkled.
• The seeds cling to the flesh.

Five Bad Signs

- Bruises.
- A white or very light green bottom.
- Mealy edges in a cut watermelon.
- White streaks in the flesh.
- A lot of white seeds, which are empty seed coats. (This is sign that the melon was picked before being completely ripe.)

Mythstakes

- You can't tell how sweet a watermelon is by the redness. You have to taste it. The sweetest watermelons are grown locally and left to ripen in the sun until the last minute. (Seedless watermelons don't seem as tasty as the ones with seeds.)
- We are told to slap a watermelon and listen for a thump. But they all thump. Instead, rap on the watermelon like you're knocking on a door. The sound should be deep and hollow.
- Icy-cold watermelon is a pleasure few of us wish to forgo. But if there's no room in the fridge, you don't have to feel guilty. Whole watermelon can spend up to 1 week at room temperature — or, better, at the ideal 55°F (13°C), if possible. It shouldn't be kept in the fridge for more than a couple of days. Once cut, though, watermelon should be wrapped and refrigerated.

✧ We are warned not to freeze watermelon; this makes it mushy and mealy. But we can make some exceptions. Two ways to enjoy frozen watermelon:

- Cut the flesh into cubes and freeze it for chills and thrills on a muggy day. Eat the cubes as is or use them to ice drinks.
- Make a slushie. Toss cubes of frozen watermelon, superfine sugar to taste, a bit of strawberry punch and mint leaves into a blender fitted with an ice-crushing blade. Blend until slushy. Drizzle with liqueur, if desired.

OUTSIDE THE BOX

You can carve a jack-o'-lantern out of a watermelon. It's easier than carving a Halloween pumpkin.

Master Plan
Watermelon Jack-o'-Lantern

1. Wear an apron. This is splashy work. Slip on gardening gloves with gripper palms.
2. Use a watermelon at room temperature; it's easier to cut.
3. Cut a thin slice from the bottom so it doesn't wobble.
4. Cut a circular lid from the top.
5. Scrape out the flesh with an ice cream scoop. Save it for eating.
6. Turn the shell upside down on a rack in the sink and let it drain briefly.
7. Set it right side up and draw a design on the rind with fine-point permanent marker.
8. Carve away.

☺ KID STUFF

- Use cookie cutters to punch out shapes, such as stars, from 1-inch (2.5 cm) slices of watermelon.
- For fat-free fun, make watermelon frozen treats. Insert wooden sticks into watermelon chunks or shapes. Place them on a baking sheet lined with foil or parchment. Freeze for about 1 hour or until firm.
- Make dippers. Cut firm watermelon into sticks. Leave the rind on one end as a handle. Dip the sticks in sweetened yogurt.

Artichokes

Three Good Signs

- The color is deep green.
- The artichoke is heavy.
- The leaves are tight and make a squeaky sound when pressed together.

◆ Brown spots on the outer leaves are okay.

◆ An artichoke lasts longer if it's wrapped in a damp paper towel and put in an unsealed plastic bag in the fridge.

Ⓒ is for Choke

The goal is to eat our way toward the heart of the artichoke, leaf by leaf. But we have to get past the choke. This is the inedible fuzzy crown on the heart.

◆ You can recognize the tender leaves by their creamy yellow base.

◆ Artichokes with purplish or reddish interior leaves and a large choke are tougher.

Artichokes VS. Baby Artichokes?

Baby artichokes are not actually babies. They're just the small ones that grow in the shadows cast by the big ones. Unlike their large siblings, baby artichokes are almost completely edible. They can be sliced and eaten raw. Some are the size of a large egg.

◆ To drain cooked artichokes, place them upside down on a rack.

Master Plan
Steamed Whole Artichokes

1. Holding an artichoke by the stem, swish it up and down in cold water to clean it.
2. Set out a large bowl of cold water. Stir in about ¼ cup (50 mL) freshly squeezed lemon juice. Do not discard the lemon halves.
3. Put on rubber gloves so you don't prick your fingers.
4. Cut off and discard the top ½ inch (1 cm), no more. Ignore recipes that tell you to trim the leaves first. The top is pinchy!
5. Rub the top with a lemon half.
6. Holding the artichoke by the stem, pull off and discard the outer layers of leaves around the bottom until you see leaves that have a tiny strip of yellowish green at the base. (For a large artichoke, trim three rows of leaves.)
7. Using scissors, trim the prickly leaf tips, one by one, rotating the artichoke as you work.
8. Slice off the stem flush with the base. Rub the base with a lemon half.
9. Use a paring knife to trim the dark green bits around the base.
10. Toss the artichoke into the bowl of lemon water. Move on to the next artichoke.
11. Arrange the artichokes upside down in a steamer basket. Steam them for 20 to 30 minutes or until they are tender.

◆ All choked up because you don't know how to consume an artichoke? The simplest way is to scrape the tender leaves with your teeth — maybe dunking them in warm, melted, salted butter or a cold dip — before reaching the heart and eating it. You can serve artichokes hot or cold.

7 Ways to Cook Baby Artichokes

1. Place them in a saucepan, cover them with water and bring to a boil. Reduce the heat, cover and simmer for 10 to 15 minutes.
2. Steam them over simmering water for 15 minutes.
3. Arrange them in a microwave-safe bowl. Add just enough water to cover the bottom of the bowl. Cover and microwave on High for 5 to 10 minutes or until tender.
4. Boil or steam them for 5 minutes or microwave them on High for 3 minutes. Drain well. Brush them with olive oil. Grill, roast or fry them until they are browned and tender.
5. Barbecue them over medium heat for 10 minutes.
6. Roast them at 425°F (220°C) for 10 minutes.
7. Halve or quarter them lengthwise. Dip them in any batter you like. Fry them at 375°F (190°C) for 3 to 5 minutes or until golden.

How to Get to the Heart of a Raw Artichoke

1. Cut off and discard the top third of the artichoke.
2. Holding the artichoke by the stem, cut off and pluck leaves until you reach the pale green heart. Trim away leaves and green bits at the base. Slice off the stem.
3. Cut the heart in half lengthwise. Scrape out the choke. Trim the heart to your satisfaction.
4. Toss it in a bowl of lemon water and move on to the next artichoke.

How to Get to the Heart of a Cooked Artichoke

1. Slice the artichoke in half lengthwise.
2. Pluck all the leaves, but don't throw them out. You can save them in the fridge and reheat them later.
3. Scrape off the choke and discard it.

OUTSIDE THE BOX

Make an artichoke cup. Steam it and fill it with cocktail shrimp, a dip or a sauce such as hollandaise. Or stuff the cup and bake it.

How to Make an Artichoke Cup

1. Slice off and discard the top quarter of the artichoke.
2. Trim the leaves with sharp tips.
3. Press down with your palm to force the leaves apart. Spread them with your fingers.
4. Use a curved grapefruit knife to cut down the center and around the heart. Don't dig too deep, though, or you'll mangle the heart.
5. Pluck out the tender center leaves as you go, until you reach the choke. (Use the tender leaves in salads.)
6. Scrape off the choke and discard it.
7. Tie kitchen string around the artichoke, so it holds its shape.
8. Steam it right side up, then let it cool. Fill it or stuff and bake it.

Is It Done?

- Poke a thin skewer into the base. There should be a little resistance.
- Tug on the tip of an inner leaf. It should pull free easily.

Lighting Won't Strike If ...

You eat the stem. It's delicious. The stem is actually an extension of the heart. Eat it straight or slice it for salad or pasta.

Master Plan
Steamed Artichoke Stems

1. Use a vegetable peeler to strip the outer skins.
2. In a saucepan, stir together water, freshly squeezed lemon juice and salt. Use 1 tsp (5 mL) lemon juice and $\frac{1}{2}$ tsp (2 mL) salt per 1 cup (250 mL) water. Simmer stems from babies for 5 minutes; simmer large stems for 15 minutes.
3. Drain the stems, reserving the liquid. Let them cool, then store them in the cooking liquid. Keep them in an airtight container in the fridge.

Asparagus

Four Good Signs
- The stalks are firm.
- The tips are compact and bright green.
- Juice seeps out when you jab a fingernail into the cut end.
- The tips are white on white asparagus. If they're purple, they've been exposed to too much sun.

Four Bad Signs
- The cut ends are dry and fibrous.
- The stalks are flaccid.
- The stalks are ridged.
- The bottoms of the stalks are dry or brown.

Factoid Purple asparagus is amusing, but it cooks up green.

3 Ways to Store Asparagus

1. Treat it like a bouquet. Cut a thin slice from the bottom of each stalk. Stand the bunch in about 1 inch (2.5 cm) of water in a jar or vase. Cover it loosely with a plastic bag. (You can do this to revive limp asparagus, too. Refrigerate it for half an hour before cooking.)
2. Wrap moist paper towel around the bottom of the bunch, then slide it into an unsealed plastic bag.
3. Store white asparagus in the darkest part of the fridge or in a paper bag. Exposure to light affects the color. The longer white asparagus is stored, the tougher it becomes.

♦ Snip off the elastic band around the bunch of asparagus. Don't pull it off — you'll injure or decapitate the delicate tips.

Mythstake

Slender doesn't mean tender. Thin and thick stalks can be equally tender, though the thick ones are meatier. Fat asparagus is not necessarily older asparagus, either. It comes from more vigorous or younger plants. Thin asparagus comes from older plants or plants grown closer together. Tenderness is linked to color rather than size: the greener, the better. Exception: white asparagus. Spears less than 1 inch (2.5 cm) in diameter are the most tender.

♦ For even cooking, use stalks of the same thickness.

Factoid **White asparagus is green asparagus that has been deprived of sunlight.**

♦ Thoroughly wash the sandy scales at the tips of the stalks.

⚡ Lightning Won't Strike If ...

You don't peel the asparagus. Fans of peeling do have their reasons, however. Some prefer to peel only the thick stalks. The frugal say peeling allows you to eat more of the spear. Unlike green asparagus, white asparagus should always be peeled.

♦ To peel an asparagus stalk, use a sharp vegetable peeler to strip the bottom half. Hold the stalk against your palm — with your fingers around the tip and the stalk extending onto your forearm. Rotate it with your fingers as you peel.

Ways to Trim Asparagus

• Snap it. Hold a spear in one hand with your thumb near the center, pointing toward the base. With your other hand as close to the bottom as possible, gently bend the base. The spear will snap at the spot where tender meets tough.

• Cut it with feeling. Cut from the bottom of the stalk an inch (2.5 cm) at a time until you feel no resistance. Some cooks believe this is less wasteful.

5 Ways to Cook Asparagus

1. In a deep, narrow asparagus pot with a basket insert. This is the best way to go.
2. In a large skillet. Lay the stalks flat, no more than two deep. Cover the bottom of the skillet with a thin layer of water. Bring it to a boil, cover and steam the asparagus.
3. In a large steaming basket over simmering water.
4. In a saucepan with 2 to 3 inches (5 to 7.5 cm) of simmering water. Bundle asparagus with kitchen string, place it upright and invert a colander over the saucepan as a steaming lid.
5. Bake or roast it.

Master Plan
Slow-Baked Asparagus

1. Pile 1 lb (500 g) asparagus into the center of a large piece of parchment.
2. Drizzle it with about 3 tbsp (45 mL) oil. Sprinkle it with salt, a tiny bit of granulated sugar and any chopped herbs.
3. Fold the parchment around it into a tight package. Secure it with kitchen string.
4. Bake it at 175°F (80°C) for 1½ to 2 hours.

- Lay the cooking pot or basket insert on its side when packing in asparagus spears. It's easier when they don't fall over.

- To blanch asparagus, tie stalks into small bundles, then drop the bundles into a large pot of boiling water. Once it returns to a boil, blanch for 1 minute. Drain. Submerge the asparagus in ice water.

> **Factoid** Whether dinner is formal or a free-for-all, it's okay to eat asparagus with your fingers.

Gussy It Up

Give packaged asparagus soup credibility by adding fresh asparagus sliced on the diagonal.

Avocados

Five Good Signs

- The avocado yields slightly when pressure is applied with the entire hand.
- It yields mainly at the narrow, stem end, where the flesh is most dense, but not much at the bulbous end.
- An indentation remains where you press with a finger.
- The skin is leathery.
- The skin pulls away from the flesh, like a pouch.

- Don't buy an avocado with the stem remnant missing. Rot tends to set in at the bit of flesh exposed by the hole.

- Though they look hardy, avocados bruise easily, leading to black pockets under the skin.

- Use this fruit like a vegetable.

- Ripen avocados at room temperature. You can refrigerate them afterwards, to slow down the process. If you refrigerate an unripe avocado, it won't ripen.

- In a hurry? Heat a not quite ripe avocado in the microwave to make it softer and edible. Zap a pitted avocado half on High for up to 1 minute.

- How to peel an avocado without crushing or mashing it:
  - If it's fairly firm, cut four slits from top to bottom. With a paring knife, grip each portion of skin at the top, then pull down.
  - If it's soft, cut it in half and remove the pit. Extract the flesh by carefully running a large spoon just under the skin and scooping. Frugally scrape the remaining flesh off the peel and pit.

- Don't try to tease out an avocado pit with a knife or spoon.

How to Efficiently Pit An Avocado

1. Cut the avocado in half.
2. Twist the halves in opposite directions to separate them.
3. Embed a sharp knife in the pit at an angle.
4. Twist the knife back and forth until the pit releases from the flesh.
5. Now the knife's stuck in the pit. Rap the pit on a cutting board. The pit will snap in half.

- The surface of mashed or cut avocado will always brown, no matter what. Just scrape off that layer before eating. You can limit the damage to the rest of the avocado by reducing exposure to the air and light, and introducing an acid.

Mythstake

Burying the pit in mashed avocado doesn't stop the flesh from oxidizing, or turning rusty brown. Only the thin layer of avocado touching the pit will stay green.

Limiting Discoloration in Mashed Avocado

- Pack it densely. Otherwise, you'll see brown tunnels at the air pockets.
- Press plastic wrap across the surface, then stretch another piece across the top of the bowl.
- Stir in some lemon or lime juice. Simply brushing the top with juice doesn't do much good.
- Stir in chopped tomato. The acidity reduces the browning.
- Make dip, such as guacamole, in small quantities and serve it soon.

- Over time, a rusty liquid separates out. You can stir it back in or pour it off.
- You can freeze avocado. The texture is fine when it's thawed, but there will be some discolored patches unless you add lemon or lime juice, about 2 tsp (10 mL) per avocado.

❖ How to store an avocado half to limit discoloration:
- Wrap it in plastic, not foil, for a tighter seal.
- Leave in the pit. Spread the flesh liberally with mayonnaise to cut off exposure to the air. (You can also use butter, which is harder to apply. Oil is a sorry substitute, as it doesn't stick well.) Then wrap it in plastic.
- Remove the pit and lay the avocado, cut side down, in a bowl or tub containing a thin layer of strongly acidulated water. Use about 1 tbsp (15 mL) lemon or lime juice per 1 cup (250 mL) water.

Guacamole

Luckily, this is so delicious, it won't sit around long enough to discolor. **Makes about 2 cups (500 mL)**

Tip
Make guacamole at serving time. It will keep at room temperature for 1 hour. If you want to refrigerate it, stir in the cilantro just before serving.

Variation
If you don't enjoy spicy food, omit the jalapeño and sprinkle in coarsely ground black pepper.

2	ripe avocados ($1\frac{1}{4}$ to $1\frac{1}{2}$ lbs/ 625 to 750 g total)	2
1	jalapeño pepper, seeded and finely chopped	1
3 tbsp	finely chopped ripe tomato	45 mL
2 tbsp	minced red onion	25 mL
1 tbsp	chopped fresh cilantro	15 mL
1 tbsp	freshly squeezed lime juice	15 mL
$\frac{1}{2}$ tsp	sea salt	2 mL

1. Cut avocados in half. Discard the pits.
2. Scoop the pulp into a medium bowl and coarsely mash with a fork. Stir in jalapeño, tomato, onion, cilantro, lime juice and salt.

❖ If you want little chunks in guacamole, mash it with a small, firm whisk instead of a fork.

Beets

Four Good Signs

- The skin is smooth.
- The "tail" isn't too frizzy.
- The beet is heavy. (Lighter beets may be spongy or dried out.)
- It's small. (A large beet may have a woody core.)

❖ No need to peel. Scrub beets and simmer gently. If you let beets cool in the cooking liquid, the skins will rub off.

♳ Waste Not

- The colorful cooking liquid can be used as a natural dye.
- Don't toss out beet greens. Use the tender greens in salads, or wash, shred and sauté them. You can cook the stems, too.

Master Plan
Prettier Roast Beets

1. Cut each beet in half at the equator.
2. Place cut sides down on a rimmed baking sheet. Drizzle with oil. Sprinkle on salt and pepper.
3. Roast at 400°F (200°C) for 20 to 30 minutes, turning the beets at halftime. When you flip them, you'll see that the pretty swirl pattern on the cut surface has been emphasized by caramelization.

❖ When cooking whole beets, leave 1 inch (2.5 cm) of the stems intact and don't cut the tips. The beets won't bleed so much.

❖ To keep a boiled beet redder and brighter, add a spoonful of vinegar to the cooking water.

OUTSIDE THE BOX

You can grate raw beets for salad. Careful: They will stain lettuce leaves. Toss them on top, instead of mixing them in. Or toss them alone with dressing.

❖ Ways to combat beet stains on your hands:
- Wear latex or other disposable gloves.
- Lightly oil your non-working hand, the one holding the beet. When you're done, wash your hands with soapy water.
- After handling beets, rub your hands with a paste made from salt or baking soda and lemon juice or vinegar.

Broccoli

Two Good Signs

- It has a fresh, not cabbagey, scent.
- The florets are compact.

Two Bad Signs

- The florets have yellow patches.
- The stem ends are dried or cracked.

❖ Broccoli will taste less bitter if you soak it for 10 minutes in cold, salted water before cutting it.

2 Ways to Cook Broccoli Evenly

1. Split the stalk into quarters and it will be ready when the florets are.
2. Deconstruct. Remove the large stems. Peel and slice them into coins $\frac{1}{4}$ to $\frac{1}{2}$ inch (0.5 to 1 cm) thick. Cook the florets and sliced stems together or separately.

❖ Choose broccoli with slender, thin-skinned stems. Otherwise, you should peel the tough skin at the bottom of the stems.

❖ To test for doneness, push a skewer through the florets into the stem at their base.

OUTSIDE THE BOX

- You can store broccoli upright in a bowl with a bit of water, like a bouquet. Cover the top with plastic.
- You can steam whole stalks of broccoli upright, too. Stand them up in 1 to 2 inches (2.5 to 5 cm) of water. Cover the pot.
- Tree silhouette shapes look cool. To make silhouettes, slice large broccoli florets, with a bit of the stalk, lengthwise. Steam the silhouettes in a single layer. Overlap them on a plate, to look like a forest.

♲ Waste Not

Small broccoli leaves can be prepared like greens. They taste like broccoli.

Broccolini

Factoid Broccolini is a hybrid. Its parents are broccoli and Chinese kale, or gai lan. It has thin, long stems topped by small florets. Sometimes it has yellow, edible flowers. Broccolini is less bitter than broccoli. It may be called baby broccoli or Asparation.

Two Good Signs
- Firm spears.
- Dark green heads with no yellowing.

❖ To prepare broccolini, trim $\frac{1}{4}$ inch (0.5 cm) from the bottom of the stems, then steam.

❖ Keep broccolini in the fridge, covered in plastic wrap.

Brussels Sprouts

Three Good Signs
- The head is compact.
- It's dark green.
- It's small. Smaller sprouts taste better.

Two Bad Signs
- The leaves are yellow, browned at the edges or wilted.
- There are blemishes.

❖ To store Brussels sprouts, wrap them loosely in a paper towel, put them inside a zip-lock bag and refrigerate them. They last for weeks, but become stronger-tasting after 3 days.

❖ How to say goodbye to soggy, bitter, pale Brussels sprouts:
- Soak them in cold, salted water for 15 minutes before cooking, to mellow them.
- Choose sprouts of a similar size for even cooking.
- Cut an X in the bottom of each sprout to channel heat to the core.
- You can halve the sprouts before cooking. Start cutting at the base, so you can see where you're going.
- Do not overcook sprouts. They will turn mushy and pallid, and smell sulfurous.

✧ Pluck and discard any damaged or yellowed outer leaves.

✧ Sprouts have multiple personalities. The core is tough, the leaves tender. The taste is bitter, yet nutty and sweet. Cooking them can be a conundrum.

OUTSIDE THE BOX

Cook the leaves and core separately:
- Slice off the base. Pluck all the loose leaves. Slice more off the base, if necessary, to get more leaves. Keep going until you get to the tight, light green core.
- Sauté the leaves for 3 minutes in browned or clarified butter. They go well with crispy bacon.
- Shred the cores.
- You can eat the cores raw in salad, like cabbage.
- Alternatively, steam or sauté the cores for 3 to 5 minutes, until tender.
- You can combine the two. Use sautéed leaves as a bed for steamed cores.

Cabbage

Four Good Signs
- It's heavy.
- The leaves are unblemished.
- There are no dried, discolored outer leaves.
- It's compact. Leaves are not separating from the stem.

✧ Smaller heads (less than 2 lbs/1 kg) are more tender.

✧ Wrap cabbage tightly in plastic and keep it in the fridge.

✧ Use cut cabbage within a couple of days. The edges turn grey.

How to Core Cabbage

1. Turn it upside down. Cut it into quarters, evenly from the base to the top.
2. Lay each quarter on its side. Use a large knife held at an angle to slice out the core from top to bottom.

How to Shred Cabbage by Hand

1. It is not necessary to core it first.
2. Cutting with the base up so you can see the core, halve the cabbage from the base to the top. Cut each half so you have four quarters.
3. Lay each quarter on its side. Holding a large knife at an angle, cut out the core.
4. Turn the quarter onto the flat edge where the core was removed. Shred by thinly slicing it crosswise.

✧ To make cabbage crispier for salad, soak chunks in ice water mixed with a spoonful of salt for 15 to 30 minutes before chopping.

Ways to Mellow Cabbage

- Soaking shredded cabbage for 1 hour before cooking makes it sweeter and milder. The firmer, nuttier, unsoaked type has character, though.
- Simmer 2 cups (500 mL) shredded green cabbage in 1 cup (250 mL) skim milk for 5 minutes, for a sweet, nutty accent.
- To make boiled cabbage more tender, add ¼ tsp (1 mL) baking soda per 4 cups (1 L) water. This also makes it greener.

❖ Ways to prevent steamed cabbage wedges from falling apart:
- Cut the head into quarters or wedges without removing the core.
- Insert a metal skewer lengthwise through each wedge. (Bamboo is not strong enough.)

⚡ Lightning Won't Strike If ...

- You eat the core of the cabbage. It is tougher, but really, it depends on your recipe and inclination.
- You don't use the whole leaf for a cabbage roll. Cut out the thick rib in a triangle, or cut straight across and favor the tender portion of the leaf. While rolling, cut off excess flaps, too, and trim and discard the thick ribs.

❖ For cabbage rolls, core the cabbage and soften the leaves to make them pliable enough to roll around the filling and less likely to tear.

❖ Pat the leaves dry before rolling them around the filling.

Ways to Soften Leaves for Cabbage Rolls

- Dunk the head, cored end down, in a pot of boiling water. Cover and boil the cabbage for 2 minutes. Put it under cold running water. Carefully pull off as many leaves as you can. Repeat.
- Core the cabbage. Freeze it overnight. Thaw it in a strainer. Pull off the leaves.
- For softer cabbage rolls, blanch leaves one at a time for 1 minute each.

OUTSIDE THE BOX

Try using savoy cabbage for stuffed cabbage. Savoy cabbage is easier to stuff because the leaves are more pliable.

❖ Red cabbage is tougher. It requires longer cooking than green cabbage.

❖ Do not use red cabbage in soups or stews. It dyes them bluish.

❖ Keep red cabbage bright purple by adding vinegar to the cooking water. Otherwise, it turns blue. Add about 1 tsp (5 mL) vinegar per 1 cup (250 mL) water. The difference is dramatic. Lemon juice, wine or apple juice will also help set the color.

ⓑ is for Bok Choy

Bok choy has crunchy white stalks and dark green leaves. It comes in full-size and baby versions. Wrap bok choy in a damp paper towel and store it in a zip-lock bag in the fridge.

❖ Instead of sticking with stir-fries, toss baby bok choy on the barbie. Grill it whole until it is heated through and has char marks. Drizzle it with oyster sauce.

ⓝ is for Napa

Napa, or Chinese cabbage, is shaped like romaine. It cooks faster and tastes lighter than standard green cabbage, and can be eaten raw or cooked. Choose tightly packed heads with no browning at the edges of the leaves. A few freckles are common. Before using, separate the leaves and wash them well.

Hungarian Cabbage Rolls

Here are some cabbage rolls with no tomato sauce in sight, just a hearty partnership with sauerkraut, smoked meat and sour cream. **Makes 8 to 10 servings**

Tips

The smoked hock is not the standard ham. Many people call it smoked pork hock, and that's how butchers and supermarkets may label it.

Sauerkraut fresh out of the barrel at a German deli is ideal, but I can make do with the bottled kind. If it is unpleasantly vinegary, rinse it.

1	large smoked ham hock (about 2 lbs/1 kg), rinsed	1
1/2 cup	long-grain white rice, rinsed	125 mL
4 oz	smoked bacon, chopped	125 g
1 1/4 lbs	ground pork	625 g
2	large eggs, lightly beaten	2
1 1/2 tsp	paprika	7 mL
1 tsp	kosher salt	5 mL
1/2 tsp	garlic powder	2 mL
1/2 tsp	dried marjoram	2 mL
1/4 tsp	freshly ground black pepper	1 mL
8 to 10	cabbage leaves, softened	8 to 10
2 lbs	sauerkraut, drained	1 kg
	Paprika	
	Freshly ground black pepper	
1	onion, chopped	1
1	large clove garlic, chopped	1
1 to 1 1/2 cups	sour cream, divided	250 to 375 mL

1. Put the hock in a deep saucepan. Add enough water to cover (about 8 cups/2 L) and bring to a boil over high heat. Reduce heat to medium-low, cover, leaving lid slightly ajar, and simmer for about 3 hours or until the meat is falling off the bone.

2. In a small saucepan, cover rice with a scant cup (250 mL) of water. Bring to a boil over medium-high heat. Reduce heat to low, cover and cook for about 15 minutes or until water is absorbed and rice is barely tender. Fluff the rice with a fork and set it aside to cool to room temperature.

3. In a small skillet, sauté bacon over medium heat until brown and crisp. Using a slotted spoon, remove to a plate lined with paper towels to drain. Drain all but 1 tbsp (15 mL) bacon grease from the skillet and set aside.

4. Drain the hock, reserving the cooking liquid. When the hock is cool enough to handle, strip the meat from the bones and discard the skin, fat and bones. Pull the lean meat into large shreds. Return the meat to the cooking liquid to keep it moist.

Tip

Skim the fat from the remaining hock cooking liquid; the liquid makes a great stock for pea soup.

5. In a large bowl, combine ground pork, eggs, $1\frac{1}{2}$ tsp (7 mL) paprika, salt, garlic powder, marjoram and $\frac{1}{4}$ tsp (1 mL) pepper. Mix in rice and bacon until just combined.

6. Place $\frac{1}{3}$ to $\frac{1}{2}$ cup (75 to 125 mL) pork filling on a cabbage leaf. Roll the leaf one turn around the filling, tuck in the sides, then finish rolling. Set it aside, seam side down. Repeat with remaining filling and cabbage leaves.

7. Spread two-thirds of the sauerkraut on the bottom of a stockpot. Top it with cabbage rolls in tight formation, seam side down. Sprinkle paprika and pepper liberally over top. Using a slotted spoon, retrieve the shredded hock meat from the cooking liquid and scatter it over the cabbage rolls.

8. In the reserved skillet, heat the bacon grease over medium heat. Sauté onion and garlic for about 5 minutes or until softened. (Do not let them brown.) Spoon over the cabbage rolls. Spread the remaining sauerkraut evenly over top.

9. Skim fat quickly from the hock cooking liquid. Ladle about 2 cups (500 mL) cooking liquid down the sides of the stockpot. Bring the pot to a boil over high heat. Reduce heat to low, cover and simmer for $1\frac{1}{2}$ hours or until cabbage rolls are tender.

10. Using a slotted spoon, transfer cabbage rolls to one or two warmed large platters. Spoon sauerkraut and shredded ham over the rolls. Sprinkle paprika generously over top.

11. In a bowl, combine $\frac{1}{4}$ cup (50 mL) of the sour cream and 2 tbsp (25 mL) of the cooking liquid from the stockpot. Drizzle decoratively over the cabbage rolls. (Save the remaining liquid for other uses, or discard it.) Serve the remaining sour cream alongside.

Carrots

Two Bad Signs

- It's a monster. Avoid carrots that are longer than 8 inches (20 cm). Bigger carrots are bitter and tougher, and tend to have woody cores. (Quarter a large carrot lengthwise, lay each quarter on its side and, with a knife held at an angle, slice off the core, if necessary.)
- It's got a green tinge. That's a sign of bitterness.

Mini Carrots **vs.** Baby Carrots?

What we may inaccurately refer to as baby carrots are actually carrots pared down to baby size. Call them mini carrots.

Two Glazed Carrot Tips

- Mini carrots are not good for glazing. Their sizes are so different that some of the wee ones inevitably get mushy.
- Add a bit of lemon juice to glazed carrots to cut the sweetness.

Ways to Keep Carrots Moist

- Store them with a bit of water in the bag.
- Strange, but carrots stay moister if you cut about ½ inch (1 cm) off the wide ends before storing them. They'll be more tender when steamed, too.

Glazed Carrot Sticks

This vintage-style recipe was inspired by long-departed Canadian cooking icon Kate Aitken. **Makes 4 servings**

Tip
Don't let these sit around after cooking; the glaze gets weepy.

Variation
You can cut the carrots into ½-inch (1 cm) coins.

4	carrots (about 1 lb/500 g total), trimmed and peeled	4
¼ cup	water	50 mL
3 tbsp	granulated sugar	45 mL
1 tbsp	unsalted butter	15 mL
1 tsp	freshly squeezed lemon juice	5 mL
½ tsp	kosher salt	2 mL
	Chopped fresh parsley	

1. Cut carrots crosswise into thirds. Halve the thin ends lengthwise. Quarter the rest lengthwise.

2. In a medium saucepan, bring carrots, water, sugar, butter, lemon juice and salt to a boil over medium-high heat. Reduce heat to medium-low, cover and cook for about 15 minutes or until carrots are glazed and almost tender.

3. Uncover the pan and increase heat to high. Cook for about 5 minutes, shaking the pan frequently, until liquid has evaporated and the carrots start to scorch.

4. Drain the carrots and transfer them to a serving dish. Sprinkle with parsley. Serve immediately.

Cauliflower

Ways to Store a Head of Cauliflower

- Wrap it tightly in plastic.
- Place it in a bowl with a bit of water in the base. Cover the top with plastic.

❖ Get rid of browned bits on the florets by scraping a scissors blade over them.

Ways to Keep Cauliflower White

- Add about ½ cup (125 mL) milk per 3 cups (750 mL) cooking water. This makes it creamy white.
- Add 1 tbsp (15 mL) lemon juice per 4 cups (1 L) cooking water. This makes it a bleached white.

OUTSIDE THE BOX

You can boil a whole head of cauliflower. Cut the base flush with the bottom of the head. Place the head in a large saucepan containing 1 inch (2.5 cm) of boiling water. Cover and steam until tender. You can also cook the cauliflower in a large steamer insert.

❖ Before cooking, soak cauliflower, head down, in cold water for 10 minutes.

❖ For intact florets, cut deeply down around the core at the base, then pull on the base and loosen the florets.

❖ To test whole cauliflower for doneness, pierce it with a skewer from top to bottom.

 Healthier Eater

The low-carb craze inspired the creation of cauliflower mashies in place of potatoes. Boil cauliflower florets in salted water until very tender. While they're hot, transfer to a food processor, along with stock, oil and seasonings. Purée until the mixture is smooth.

Gussy It Up

- Make tree-shaped silhouettes from cauliflower. Cut large florets into thin slices, leaving as much core as possible. (That way, the trees hold together and look like they have trunks). Steam them, or roast them in a single layer.
- Roasted cauliflower can look like popcorn. Serve it in popcorn boxes or bags.

Celeriac

3 Ways to Peel Celeriac

1. Cut a thin slice off the base with a sharp paring knife. Lay the celeriac on the cut end. Peel it in sections from top to bottom, hugging the curves.
2. Slice it into quarters, then peel each piece with a sharp paring knife.
3. Slice it into ½-inch (1 cm) discs, then peel around the perimeters.

A sturdy vegetable peeler will work, but it's a rough trip around the celeriac.

❖ Celeriac is dirty. Before peeling it, scrub it under running water.

❖ To prevent discoloration, soak cut celeriac briefly in water with lemon juice or vinegar.

❖ Celeriac can be eaten raw.

Four Good Signs

- Attached greens signal freshness.
- It is small. Little ones are tangier. Large ones are woody.
- The shape is symmetrical.
- Fewer gnarly roots make the celeriac easier to peel.

Three bad signs

- There's decay at the stem end.
- It's lightweight. (These are spongy.)
- It's got a green tinge.

Gussy It Up

Make celeriac ribbons for salad. Slice strips off the flesh with a vegetable peeler.

✧ If you are making a celeriac salad with mayonnaise, grate it, toss it with lemon juice and salt, then let it drain for 15 minutes before tossing it with the dressing. Otherwise, the juices will thin out the dressing.

✧ For a more delicate flavor and whiter flesh, blanch celeriac pieces for 1 to 2 minutes in boiling water with lemon juice, or simply cook it in this solution.

Celery

3 Ways to Revive Limp Celery

1. Place stalks in a bowl of cold water with some lemon juice and ice cubes. Refrigerate them for 1 hour.
2. Soak stalks in cold water with a few slices of raw potato for up to 1 hour.
3. Wrap the celery stalks in damp paper towels and stand them upright in a jug with their cut ends in cold water.

Ways to Store Celery

- In a vase, like a bouquet. Cover it with plastic.
- Wrapped in foil and placed in the crisper.

Lightning Won't Strike If ...

You don't peel off the celery strings. Chefs like to run a vegetable peeler along the stalk. But do you care enough?

OUTSIDE THE BOX

You can eat celery cooked. Steam or braise it until tender, then use the cooking liquid as the base for a creamy sauce. Celery can also be baked in a bit of stock.

♻ Waste Not

Don't toss out the celery leaves. They taste great. Use them as you would an herb. Try them in an omelet. For a fabulous flavor and fine texture, dry them in a low oven and rub them through a sieve.

Gussy It Up

Make curled celery. Slice the stalk into slivers. For weird and wild curlicues, sliver right up close to the base. For tidier slivers, slice the top few inches. Steep the celery in ice water for half an hour to encourage the curls.

Making Do

If you don't have celery, toss finely chopped cabbage with celery salt. Use about ½ tsp (2 mL) salt per 1 oz (30 g) cabbage, and omit or reduce the salt in the recipe.

Corn

 A Bit of Science

Freshness is key in corn because the sugar converts to starch after harvest. That tones down the sweetness and turns corn tough. Ideally, corn should be eaten within 24 hours after it's picked.

Five Good Signs

There's no need to wantonly rip all the husks from the supermarket corn. Look for these signs:

- Heavy ears.
- Green, tightly wrapped husks.
- Firm kernels that can be felt when pressed through the husk.
- A kernel near the tip pops when pressed.
- Silk that's moist and golden close to the husk. (It can be brown at the tip.)

E is for Ear

The ear is the whole corn. The ear is covered by cornsilk and green leaves called husks. The cob is the woody core in which the kernels are embedded. The kernels are the pulpy seeds.

✧ Don't shuck corn before storing it.

✧ To keep corn moist in its husk, swath it in a damp paper towel or put it in a wet paper bag. Place it in a plastic bag and refrigerate.

✧ If you have too much corn, blanch it for a couple of minutes, cool and refrigerate. Finish cooking it later. Or scrape the kernels from the cob and refrigerate them in an airtight container. Taking action is better than letting the corn sit, getting drier and starchier.

✧ To remove cornsilk, work from the tip to the base, opposite to the direction of growth.

Ways to Remove Cornsilk

- Use a vegetable brush or toothbrush under running water.
- Rub it off with a damp paper towel.

✧ Don't try to saw through an ear of raw corn. Embed a knife in the cob, then rap the knife and cob together on a cutting board. The cob will split.

Ways to Strip Kernels off the Cob

- Cut the ear in half. Lay a piece on its side. Slice off the kernels, hugging the curve of the cob and rotating it as you work. Go slowly and you'll see each row fall off.
- Trim the pointy tip. Set the ear on its base at an angle. Shave downwards with a sharp knife.

Tips for Stripping Kernels

- If you blanch an ear of corn for 1 to 2 minutes, the milky juices won't spurt when you cut off the kernels.
- Create less of a mess. Stand the ear in the center of a tube pan and slice downwards. The kernels drop into the pan.
- After cutting kernels off a fresh ear of corn, press along the cob with the blunt edge of the knife to extract the juices.

✧ Corn generally takes 5 to 15 minutes to cook, depending on the age and starchiness.

✧ Corn can be grilled naked or covered in foil, but is best left in the husk.

Master Plan
Grilled Corn in the Husk

1. Pull off dried, dark green husks until you get to tender, moist, light green husks. (You can save some husks to use in Step 3.) If you see the contours of kernels peeping through, you've gone too far. Snip off the cornsilk at the top. Leave the stem for a handle.
2. Soak the corn in water for 1 hour.
3. Tie the top of each ear with kitchen twine so the husks don't pull away from the kernels. If you want to get fancy, tie it with an extra strip of husk.
4. Grill over medium heat, covered, turning every 2 minutes or so, until you can see the silhouettes of the kernels, and the husks are charred and beginning to pull away from the tip to expose the kernels.
5. Strip off the husks and silk. Dip the corn in flavored butter or oil, or brush it with glaze.
6. To boost the color and create char marks, return it to the grill for 1 to 2 minutes.

Master Plan
Flavored Grilled Corn in the Husk

1. Strip the dried, dark green husks, leaving the inner, pale green husks and the stems intact. (You can save some husks to use in Step 6.)
2. Soak the corn in water for 1 hour.
3. Carefully pull back the husks on each ear to expose the kernels.
4. Rub or brush off the cornsilk under running water.
5. Pat the corn dry. Brush it generously with flavored butter or oil.
6. Pull the husks back up over the ear. Secure it at the top with kitchen string or an extra strip of husk.
7. Grill over medium heat, covered, turning every 2 minutes or so, until the husks are charred and beginning to pull away from the tip to expose the kernels.

Ways to Roast Corn

- Pull off the husks down to the tender, light green, moist layer. Trim the cornsilk at the top. Keep the stem. Secure the top with kitchen string.
- Strip and clean the corn. Brush it with flavored butter or oil. Wrap it in foil.

✧ You can make grilled corn kebabs. Slice an ear of corn into 2-inch (5 cm) segments. Make these easier to skewer by twisting a hole through the center of each with a corkscrew.

Places to Roast Corn

- In a 350°F (180°C) oven for about 30 minutes.
- In the hot embers of a campfire for 15 to 20 minutes. The corn must be wrapped in foil. Do not brush it with butter first.

Gussy It Up

Pull back the husks of cooked corn. Leave them as a cute tail or tie them into a handle.

✧ Do not microwave an ear of corn. The kernels dry out and want to pop. If you wrap it in plastic, the chemicals from the wrap can leach into the corn.

Tips for Steaming or Boiling Corn

- Remove the husks and silk. Trim the undeveloped tips. If desired, cut each ear in half crosswise.
- Insert heatproof corn holders beforehand, instead of burning your fingers afterwards.
- Steam small cobs for about 8 minutes, medium ones for 10 minutes, large ones for 12 minutes.
- Boil corn for 5 to 10 minutes, depending on its size and maturity.

Three Extras

- For added corny flavor, toss a few husks in with the boiling cobs.
- Keep corn yellow and tender. Add a spoonful of lemon juice to the cooking water.
- You can add a sugar cube or a spoonful of sugar to the cooking water to boost sweetness.

❖ You don't need to salt the water. This may make the corn tougher.

✗ No-No

Don't leave cooked corn soaking in its cooking water.

❖ To break a cooked cob in half, notch it with a heavy knife, then hold one end of the cob in each hand and snap it.

❖ How to spread butter on corn more efficiently and evenly:

- Melt it, then paint it on with a pastry brush.
- Use a buttered slice of bread to spread it.

OUTSIDE THE BOX

You can char corn kernels in a skillet for salads and salsas. Charred kernels taste great with tomato, red onion and lime accents.

1. Heat a dry medium skillet over medium-high heat.
2. Pat dry 1 cup (250 mL) fresh, uncooked corn kernels. Add them to the skillet.
3. Shake the skillet for 3 to 5 minutes or until the kernels start to make popping sounds and pick up flecks of brown.
4. Let them cool to room temperature, if necessary.

❖ Put butter on corn first, then salt, so the salt and seasonings stick.

❖ For a taste sensation, smear corn on the cob with garlic butter.

♡ Healthier Eater

Use the starch in corn kernels to thicken chowder or make creamed corn without any cream.

- After removing the kernels, scrape the cob with the back of a spreader or the blunt side of a dinner knife to capture pulp and starch.
- Shred kernels from an ear of corn against the large holes of a box grater. Place the pulp in a sieve set over a bowl, to capture the starchy juices. Three to 4 cobs yield about 1 cup (250 mL) starchy juices.
- To thicken chowder, purée a portion of the corn from the soup and stir in some starchy juices.
- To make naturally creamed corn, simmer about 2 cups (500 mL) fresh corn kernels until tender-crisp. Drain. In a saucepan, bring 1 cup (250 mL) starchy corn juices to a boil over medium heat. Reduce heat to medium-low and simmer for 2 to 3 minutes or just until thickened. Stir in the corn kernels. Serve this pronto. The sauce loses "creaminess" as time passes.

Cucumbers

Two Good Signs

- Shiny, dark green skin. (When a cuke turns yellow, it has passed the ripeness point of no return.)
- Firm ends, not withered.

Factoid Mini cucumbers are not baby cucumbers, but a separate variety.

Cucumber Vichyssoise

This family favorite incorporates a potato for richness and thickening. **Makes about 10 cups (2.5 L), or 8 to 10 servings**

Tip

Avoid heavier cream; it's too rich for this cold soup and masks the cucumber flavor.

1 tbsp	unsalted butter	15 mL
1	onion, chopped	1
1	stalk celery, diced	1
2	yellow-fleshed potatoes (3⁄4 to 1 lb/ 375 to 500 g total), peeled and diced	2
4 cups	vegetable stock	1 L
1 tsp	chopped fresh dill	5 mL
1 tsp	salt	5 mL
	Freshly ground black pepper	
2 to 3	cucumbers (about 3 lbs/1.5 kg total), peeled, seeded and diced	2 to 3
1 cup	half-and-half (10%) cream	250 mL
	Additional chopped fresh dill	

1. In a medium saucepan, melt butter over medium heat. Sauté onion and celery for about 3 minutes or until softened but not browned. Add potatoes, stock, dill, salt and pepper to taste. Increase heat to high and bring to a boil. Immediately reduce heat to low, cover and simmer for about 30 minutes or until vegetables are very soft.

2. Stir in cucumbers and bring to a boil over high heat. Reduce heat to low, cover and simmer for 10 minutes or until cucumbers are tender. Let cool for 5 minutes.

3. In a blender, working in batches, purée soup until smooth. Transfer to an airtight container and refrigerate for at least 2 hours, until very cold, or overnight.

4. Stir in cream and adjust the seasoning with salt, if desired. Serve garnished with dill.

✧ The fridge is not quite right for sensitive cucumbers. They are prone to turning limp and discoloring at temperatures below 50°F (10°C). Most people shove cucumbers into the crisper, but some dissidents believe a cool, dark place is better. I am not one — because biting into a chilled cucumber is one of life's simple pleasures.

✧ A cut cucumber will taint other foods in the fridge unless it is tightly wrapped in plastic.

✧ To seed a cucumber, halve it lengthwise. Scrape a spoon or the rounded tip of a vegetable peeler through the seed trough.

Cucumber VS. English Cucumber?

Slender English cucumbers can be eaten with the skin and seeds. Regular cucumbers have thick, waxed skin and large seeds.

❖ To crisp a cucumber for salad, thinly slice it. Place the slices in a sieve and toss them with about 1 tsp (5 mL) salt. Let stand for 30 minutes. Squeeze the slices gently with your hands to extract the liquid and salt.

☰ Fast Fix

If you don't have time to drain sliced cucumber for salad, dab the slices with a paper towel before you pour on the dressing.

❖ Serve cold soup, dips, shrimp or sake in cucumber cups.

Master Plan
Cucumber Cups

1. Choose a uniformly shaped standard cucumber.
2. Wash it. Trim the ends. Cut it into segments. Two-inch (5 cm) lengths work well for a 2¼-inch (5.5 cm) diameter cucumber.
3. You can decorate the cups by creating stripes on the skin with a vegetable peeler.
4. Using a cookie cutter, punch out a depression in the center of one cut end of each segment. Use a grapefruit spoon to finish carving a cup out of the flesh. Leave about ⅜ inch (0.75 cm) flesh at the sides and ½ inch (1 cm) at the base.
5. For drier cups, sprinkle them inside with salt, then turn them over on a rack and let them drain for 30 minutes.
6. For softer cups, marinate them for 30 minutes in a solution of ½ cup (125 mL) each white vinegar and water, 1 tbsp (15 mL) salt and ¼ tsp (1 mL) granulated sugar.

❖ Ways to make decorative cucumber rounds:
• Cut a cucumber into 1- to 2-inch (2.5 to 5 cm) lengths. Push a serrated cookie cutter through the center of each segment. Pop it out and slice it.
• Cut off the ends of an English cucumber. With the tines of a fork, score the skin from top to bottom, then slice the cucumber into rounds. You can also peel thin lengthwise strips, leaving alternating stripes of dark and light green, then slice the cucumber.

♻ Waste Not

If a cucumber is accidentally frostbitten, simmer it in stock, purée the mixture, then use it as a base for cold soup. (This is also an option for frozen greens.)

❖ Cold cucumber soup can be made without yogurt. The cucumbers are simmered in stock and puréed, then bolstered with a splash of cream.

Edamame

OUTSIDE THE BOX

You can toss cooked edamame pods with oil or melted butter, spread them on a rimmed baking sheet and roast at 350°F (180°C) for 10 to 15 minutes or until they start to brown. Do not let them get crisp.

Eggplant

Five Good Signs
• It's firm, with no soft spots.
• It's heavy.
• The skin is glossy, unbroken and soft yet taut.
• The skin springs back when pressed gently with your thumb.
• The cap is green, with a bit of stem.

Three Bad Signs

- It's got a large cap. (Eggplants with larger caps generally have more seeds and thus more bitterness.)
- There are rust-colored spots, a sign of aging.
- The seeds are large. (Larger seeds are more bitter.)

✧ Eggplant is one of those in-between vegetables that don't like the refrigerator or the counter. The flesh deteriorates faster below 50°F (10°C), but it should be kept cool. Store it in an open plastic bag along with a crumpled paper towel to absorb moisture. Keep it in the fridge crisper.

✧ Beware: Eggplant bruises easily.

Bitterness Tips

- The younger and the fresher the eggplant, the less bitter.
- Asian eggplants are less bitter than the standard large, dark purple globe eggplants. Chinese and Japanese eggplants are shaped like cucumbers, though sometimes they're curved. The Chinese type is a lighter amethyst color, and less bitter than the Japanese one.
- Peel a whole small eggplant or cube it. Dip it into a solution of 4 cups (1 L) cold water and 1 tbsp (15 mL) salt. Pat it dry, then cook it.
- Longer cooking mellows eggplant.

⚡ Lightning Won't Strike If ...

You don't get rid of the seeds. You lose a lot of eggplant that way. The bitter compounds are located in and near the seeds. After baking an eggplant, you can test the seeds first and see if they are too bitter to leave in.

Reasons to Salt Eggplant

- It prevents discoloration.
- It draws out juices that make the eggplant bitter and soggy.
- It reduces the absorbency, so the cooked eggplant will be less soggy or greasy.

How to Salt Eggplant

1. Cube it or slice it into 1-inch (2.5 cm) thick rounds.
2. Place the pieces in a large colander or sieve, or arrange them on a rack. Salt them generously. Let them drain for at least 30 minutes. (If desired, place a weighted dish on top to press the eggplant.)
3. Do not rinse or you defeat the purpose. Press the eggplant dry with a paper towel.

✧ Another way to sweat an eggplant: Slice it. Heavily salt the slices. Stack them to reassemble the eggplant. Wrap it tightly in plastic and let it stand for 30 minutes in a bowl.

✧ You can get away without salting small Chinese and Japanese eggplants.

✧ Salting eggplant makes it creamier. Unsalted eggplant is meatier.

✧ Once cut, eggplant turns brown quickly. If you are not salting eggplant, rub it with lemon juice to prevent discoloration or cook it immediately.

✧ Peeling is optional. Large eggplants, globe eggplants and white varieties have thicker skin than Chinese and Japanese eggplants.

❖ If you plan to stuff the eggplant, choose a thick-skinned one.

> **Factoid** **Eggplant is like a sponge. Bad news: It soaks up oil. Good news: It soaks up flavors.**

❖ Rinse eggplant under running water and dry it with a towel. Do not leave it in a bowl of water.

❖ Use a serrated knife to thinly slice eggplant.

❖ When frying eggplant slices, nick the skin at $\frac{1}{2}$-inch (1 cm) intervals.

Ways to Cut the Grease

- Strain fried eggplant, then pour boiling water over top.
- Precook eggplant in the microwave before frying or sautéing it.
- Grill or roast it. Brush it lightly with oil or it won't brown properly.
- Steam or bake it.

Master Plan
Steamed Eggplant

Steamed eggplant holds its shape, but the texture is creamy.

1. Cut a large eggplant lengthwise into 8 wedges.
2. Place the wedges in a 12-inch (30 cm) steamer basket. Salt them generously.
3. Steam them over 1 inch (2.5 cm) of boiling water containing 2 tbsp (25 mL) white wine vinegar. They should be tender in about 15 minutes.
4. Let them drain for 5 minutes.

Gussy It Up

- Score an eggplant from top to bottom with the tines of a fork.
- Use a vegetable peeler to create thin, alternating stripes in the peel.

❖ The flesh of baked or steamed eggplant can be scooped out, then sautéed in oil, or marinated in garlicky dressing and served at room temperature.

❖ Spice up baked eggplant: Halve the eggplant lengthwise. Score a crosshatch pattern on the surface of the flesh on each half. Rub in spices and garlic. Put the halves together and wrap them in foil. Bake.

❖ When roasting eggplant slices, cut them $\frac{1}{2}$ to $\frac{3}{4}$ inch (1 to 2 cm) thick. Any thinner and they will be dry and brittle. Thicker and they will be rubbery.

❖ For smoky flavor, blacken the skin of an eggplant as you would roasted pepper. Heat the eggplant over a flame or broil until it is charred all over. Peel it, then mash the flesh.

Fennel

❖ Tenderize fennel by trimming the stringy fibers off the bulb. Use a vegetable peeler.

❖ Get rid of the core. It's tough. Quarter the bulb lengthwise. With a knife held at an angle, slice out the core. Exception: If you're braising or roasting fennel, leave some of the core to hold the pieces together.

❖ Slice the bulb crosswise.

✪ Waste Not

Cut off the stalks and fronds where they meet the bulb, but don't toss them out. The tough stalks can be dried or used fresh to flavor stocks and sauces. The fronds can be used as an herb, fresh or dried.

Garlic

Two Good Signs

- Tight skin with a purple tinge, a sign of recent harvesting.
- Tightly packed cloves.

Two Bad Signs

- Papery skin. (The older the garlic, the more papery the skin.)
- A green shoot.

Softneck **vs.** Hardneck?

Softneck garlic is the familiar type found in grocery stores. Hardnecks have fewer and larger cloves. They are described as pungent, but not harsh, as well as juicier.

◆ Keep garlic in a cool, dry place. Do not store it next to the stove or in the fridge, which encourages mold.

◆ To separate a head quickly into cloves, set it base down and whack it with a frying pan.

◆ To peel a clove, set the thick blade of a knife over top and give it just enough of a rap to loosen the peel (no need to mash it). Cut off the root end. Slip off the skin.

⚛ A Bit of Science

Garlic must be cut or crushed to release the sulfur compound that makes it so attractive.

- For the strongest garlic flavor, expose the most juices by grating or puréeing.
- For the mildest garlic flavor, cut bigger pieces, or poach the bulbs in oil or roast them.

7 Keys to Chopping, Mincing and Puréeing

1. Mince garlic as finely as possible by switching between chopping and smearing motions with your knife.
2. Garlic jumps around when you mince it. Mince with a bit of butter or salt for traction.
3. Mince garlic by tossing it through the feed tube while the food processor is running. When making a food-processor recipe that includes garlic, switch things around. Toss in the garlic first, to mince it most effectively, then add the remaining ingredients. (This is best for gingerroot, too.)
4. After pushing garlic through a press, discard the fibrous bits. (Do the same with gingerroot.)
5. You can put a garlic clove through a press with the skin on. It will sort itself out.
6. Scrape the cup of the garlic press against the rim of a small bowl to capture the remnants.
7. You can purée garlic using a rasp (Microplane) grater. Save your fingers by impaling the clove on one tine of a fork.

Tips for Prepared Garlic

- Wait 10 minutes after chopping garlic before cooking with it. This allows the release of the maximum amount of delicious compounds. But don't leave the garlic sitting around longer than that. It loses its power.
- If you must chop garlic ahead, drizzle it with oil and stick it in the fridge.
- You can refrigerate peeled cloves, covered with oil, in an airtight jar for a day or two. Don't do this habitually.

- Ways to skin garlic without squashing the cloves:
- Microwave each clove on High for 5 to 10 seconds. Remove it as soon as you hear sizzling. (If you hear squeaking, you've left it too long and the clove is slightly cooked.) Rub the clove in a paper towel to remove the skin. Or press it gently against the counter; it should pop out of its skin. If you are microwaving more than one clove, increase the time by a few seconds.
- Put the cloves in a bowl. Pour boiling water or the hottest tap water over them to make the skins less papery. Whisk for a few seconds to loosen the skins. Rinse with cold water. Cut off the root ends and pull off the skins.
- If you have a lot of garlic to peel, put the cloves in a saucepan of cold water and bring it to a boil. Boil for 1 minute. Drain. The skins should slip off.
- You can peel garlic by rubbing it with a piece of rubber. (This also makes it easier to break a whole head into cloves.) You can buy rubber swatches and tubes designed to skin garlic. You can also try one of the rubber discs that are sold to remove jar lids.

- How to prevent garlic from browning and turning bitter:
- Keep the heat low. When adding garlic to hot oil, remove the pan from the burner and stir it in quickly.
- Avoid adding garlic to a pan on its own. If a recipe tells you to sauté the garlic first, do it for a few seconds only. Or ignore the recipe and add it to the oil with the onions.
- Juicy puréed garlic is more likely to burn. Instead of pressing it, mince garlic with a knife to create larger pieces.

 Lightning Won't Strike If ...
You fail to remove a little green sprout inside the garlic clove. It's supposed to be bitter, but you'll hardly notice it.

- How to stop garlic skins from sticking to your fingers:
- Dip each clove in cold water as you work.
- Wet your fingers in a small bowl of water.

- Dry-toasting mellows garlic and loosens the skins for easy peeling. But dry-toasted garlic doesn't become creamy, as roasted garlic does.

How to Dry-Toast Garlic

1. Put unpeeled cloves in a dry skillet over medium-high heat.
2. Toast, shaking the pan occasionally, for about 5 minutes or until the skins are golden brown.
3. Let the cloves cool on a cutting board before peeling them.

OUTSIDE THE BOX

Garlic can be barbecued. Skewer large cloves, brush them with oil, then grill them over medium heat until tender.

- To make garlic oil, heat about 6 cloves in 1 cup (250 mL) olive oil until the garlic begins to turn golden. Let the oil cool. Discard the cloves. Store the oil in an airtight jar at room temperature.

- Generally, we don't allow garlic to brown. For garlic crisps, we make an exception. Slice cloves as thinly as possible. Sauté them in olive oil over medium-low heat until they are golden brown and crisp. Garlic crisps make a wonderful garnish.

4 Ways to Roast Garlic

1. Slice ¼ to ½ inch (0.5 to 1 cm) off the top of a head of garlic to expose the cloves. Place it upright on a sheet of foil. Drizzle it with oil. Wrap the foil around the head to seal the packet. Roast at 350°F (180°C) for 45 to 60 minutes or until it is soft. You can also buy a clay garlic baking dish that holds a single head.

2. Peel the cloves from a head of garlic. Put them in a tiny ramekin or custard dish with ¼ tsp (1 mL) olive oil. Add enough water to cover the cloves, about ¼ cup (50 mL). Bake them at 400°F (200°C), stirring or turning occasionally, for about 1 hour or until the cloves are golden brown and soft. All the water should evaporate.

3. Separate a head of garlic into cloves. Cut off the stem end of each clove. Rub off any flaky skin. Put the cloves on a square of foil. Drizzle them with oil. Wrap the foil around the cloves to seal the packet. Roast them in a 350°F (180°C) oven for 30 to 45 minutes or until soft.

4. Roast a head of garlic alongside a roast beast. Diners can squeeze the cloves onto the meat, mashed potatoes or crusty bread.

✧ Reserve some minced or pressed garlic to give a dish a final kick in the butt. Say you've got a garlicky dish such as Spaghetti Aglio e Olio. Coat the pasta with plenty of garlic sautéed in olive oil. Then go in for the kill by stirring in a spoonful of the raw garlic.

Subtlest Hints of Garlic

- Spear a clove on a fork and use it to stir a dish.
- Rub the serving dish with the cut surface of a clove of garlic.

Ways to Store Roasted Garlic

- If you roasted it in foil, take what you need, crumple the top of the packet and refrigerate the rest in a sealed plastic bag.
- Mash roasted cloves with olive oil. Refrigerate the mixture in a tiny jar or freeze it in an ice cube tray.

Master Plan
Homemade Garlic Salt

1. Sprinkle ¼ cup (50 mL) kosher salt on the cutting board. Crush a garlic clove on the salt, then stir it together with the blunt edge of the knife.

2. Store the mixture in an airtight jar.

3. The clove will turn green. (Don't be alarmed.) You can toss it out after a couple of days.

✧ Squeezing roasted cloves from their papery skins is a sticky business. Keep a bowl of cold water nearby to dip your fingers into.

✧ To make roasted garlic easier to squeeze, cut the bulb in half crosswise before popping it into the oven.

✧ Keep roasted garlic on hand to flavor mashed potatoes or vinaigrette, or to smear on your morning toast if you want to repel chatty co-workers.

✧ Rubbing garlic on your skin supposedly keeps bloodsucking creatures of the night from biting — mosquitoes, that is.

 ## Waste Not

Keep the skins of squeezed, roasted cloves. Put them in a small saucepan, just cover them with water, add salt, simmer for 15 minutes and strain. This makes a tasty bit of garlic broth to add to soup or other dishes.

✥ Did you prepare something too garlicky? Adding lots of fresh, chopped parsley may counteract it.

Gingerroot

Four Good Signs

- It's firm. The knobs break off cleanly with a snap.
- It's moist. Broken knobs exude a bit of juice.
- It has a fresh aroma.
- The skin is taut. Wrinkled equals old.

Young **VS.** Old?

The longer gingerroot is left in the ground, the hotter it is, and the more pungent and fibrous. The gnarly knobs found in supermarkets are mature. Young ginger is milder, with transparent skin and pink shoots. No peeling is necessary.

Young ginger is usually found in Asian markets in the spring and summer, and is harvested before it's 9 months old.

Ways to Freeze Ginger

- Peel and slice it into coins. Place the slices in a row on a piece of plastic wrap. Wrap them tightly. Put them in a zip-lock bag. Harvest a few frozen slices at a time.
- Mince ginger in a food processor. Seal it in a freezer bag. Break off small frozen pieces as you need them.

Ways to Peel Ginger

- Scrape off the peel using the head of a teaspoon, convex side up. This is easier than fiddling with a knife or vegetable peeler.
- Cut the ginger into coins. Run a small sharp knife around the perimeter of each coin.

Ginger Extract

Use this to flavor anything from drinks to stir-fries. **Makes $\frac{1}{2}$ cup (125 mL)**

4 oz	gingerroot, coarsely chopped (about 1 cup/250 mL)	125 g
¼ cup	hottest tap water	50 mL

1. In a blender, purée ginger and water to the finest paste possible.
2. Press paste through a fine-mesh sieve. Pick up the pulp and squeeze it out with your hand, then discard pulp.
3. Store extract in an airtight container in the refrigerator for up to 2 weeks. A pasty residue will settle on the bottom. This is the most intense component of the extract. You can stir it back in or use it separately.

Storage Tips

- Gingerroot keeps best at about 50°F (10°C), but for most of us, the fridge will have to do.
- Keep it wrapped in a paper towel in an unsealed plastic bag. Change the towel if it gets moist.
- You can break a knob off and place the remainder of the root back in the fridge.

⚡ Lightning Won't Strike If ...

You don't peel ginger, especially if you're going to discard it. If you are using it to flavor a stir-fry or a stock, just wash it, slice it thin and pull out the slices after cooking. The peel makes no difference, either, if you are puréeing and straining it.

❖ A slice of gingerroot the size of a quarter yields about $\frac{1}{4}$ tsp (1 mL) chopped ginger.

❖ Chop ginger as finely as possible. It is fibrous. Smash it before mincing.

4 Ways to Preserve Ginger

1. Put a peeled knob in a jar or tub. Cover it with wine or rice vinegar. Keep it in the fridge. When you need it, slice or grate a bit, then return the rest to the jar.
2. Put a peeled knob in a jar or tub. Cover it with vodka or other liquor. You don't need to refrigerate ginger kept in alcohol.
3. Chop the ginger. Keep it covered in sherry in an airtight jar or tub.
4. Peel and freeze the ginger in a zip-lock bag. Frozen ginger is easier to grate. Return it to the freezer quickly. Never thaw it before using. It will turn dark and limp.

❖ Use ginger juice, extract and essence to flavor drinks, broths, sauces, dressings, marinades and glazes.

Ginger Syrup

Try this syrup in drinks or desserts. **Makes about 1 cup (250 mL)**

Tips

Save some time: You don't need to peel the ginger. Just scrub it before chopping.

Scrape any ginger juices from the cutting board into the pan.

1 cup	water	250 mL
$\frac{1}{2}$ cup	granulated sugar	125 mL
2 oz	gingerroot, coarsely chopped (about $\frac{1}{2}$ cup/125 mL)	60 g

1. In a small saucepan, combine water, sugar and ginger. Bring to a boil over medium-high heat. Reduce heat to medium-low and simmer for 30 minutes. Remove from heat and let stand for 1 hour.
2. Transfer to a blender and purée until smooth. Strain through a fine-mesh sieve.
3. Store syrup in an airtight container in the refrigerator for up to 2 months.

Master Plan
Ginger Juice

1. Grate a big knob of ginger into a small bowl.
2. Press the solids against the side of the bowl with the back of a rubber spatula while you tilt the bowl so juice runs off.

✧ Other ways to make ginger juice: Bundle the pulp in cheesecloth and squeeze out the juice, or push the pulp through a garlic press.

Ways to Capture Ginger Essence

- Cook with the leftover vinegar, sherry or spirits the ginger was stored in.
- Make ginger juice or buy it bottled.
- Make ginger extract.
- Make ginger syrup.

✧ Don't substitute ground ginger for fresh gingerroot.

Ways to Purée Ginger

- Cut it into coins. Cover the coins with plastic. Whack them with a mallet or heavy knife handle. Chop the ginger to break up any pieces. This purées ginger well.
- Scrape it against a Microplane grater.
- Push it through a garlic press with large holes. Use the purée and the juices, but leave the stringy fibers behind.

Crystallized VS. Preserved?

Crystallized, or candied, gingerroot is boiled in sugar water, then coated with sugar. Preserved ginger is boiled, then kept in sugar syrup. You can turn one into the other. Put candied ginger into syrup, or drain preserved ginger and roll it in sugar.

✧ Crystallized ginger should be firm but not hard, with a generous sugar coating. Avoid candied ginger that has clumped.

✧ If crystallized ginger gets too gummy while chopping, sprinkle granulated sugar on it.

✧ You can mash preserved ginger by pushing it through a garlic press.

Ways to Obtain Subtler Ginger Flavor

- Slice gingerroot into coins about the thickness of a quarter. Stir-fry with them, then discard them.
- Rub the cut edge of a small piece over food or the serving bowl.

✧ To boost the ginger flavor in a dish, use the sugar from the bag or tub of candied ginger in your recipe.

✧ To soften crystallized ginger, warm it in the top of a double boiler over simmering water for 2 to 3 minutes.

Factoid Gingerroot turns pink when it is pickled in a solution of rice vinegar, salt and sugar. The pickled ginger served with sushi is meant to clear the palate.

♲ Waste Not

Use the brine from pickled ginger to add an unusual note to sauces.

✧ In desserts, layer the ginger. For example, you can infuse cream with sliced gingerroot, add ground ginger to batter and garnish with crystallized ginger.

Green Beans

Two Good Signs

- They're thin. Slender green beans are the best.
- The stems are intact. Green beans with stems attached stay fresher and more tender.

❖ No cutting necessary: You can pinch or snap off the stem ends by hand. Please don't trim the cute squiggle at the tip.

☰ Fast Fix

Tap a handful of beans at the stem ends until they line up. Cut the lot at once.

❖ You can tie green beans into bunches for individual servings before cooking them. Use kitchen string.

Greens

❖ Fridge temperature is ideal for fresh greens such as lettuce.

Short-Term Ways to Store Greens

- Line a salad spinner bowl or colander with paper towels. Layer the greens inside, separated by paper towels. Refrigerate.
- Wrap rinsed lettuces and greens in a damp kitchen towel. Place them in the crisper.

Long-Term Ways to Store Greens

- The best way is to cut ¼ inch (0.5 cm) off the bottoms (unless, like cilantro or arugula, they have roots attached). Add an inch (2.5 cm) of water to a vase or jar. Stick the greens in like a bouquet. Loosely cover the tops with a plastic bag. You can buy herb vases for this job.
- Spread greens on a long sheet of paper towels. Roll them up. Put the roll in an unsealed zip-lock bag. Unroll it to take out the greens you need.

- Loosely roll greens in paper towels or a kitchen towel. Place them inside an unsealed plastic bag and refrigerate.
- Wrap a moist paper towel around the roots or root ends. Slip the greens into an unsealed plastic bag and refrigerate.
- Separate the leaves and store them in a covered plastic tub lined with paper towels.
- Tender greens, such as mesclun, need air. Store them in perforated vegetable bags and zip up the top. Or use a plastic bag, blow air into it and tie or seal the top. Keep them refrigerated.
- Tightly wrap sturdy greens, such as romaine or iceberg lettuce, in plastic. Store them in the fridge.

Ways to Wash Greens

- Don't mess about with a bowl. Put the greens in a sinkful of cold water and swish briskly. The dirtiest greens, such as arugula, need lots of water. The dirt falls to the bottom of the sink and the greens float. Enthusiastic rinsing also gets rid of critters. I have encountered dead flies and dehydrated beetles that made their graves among the leaves.
- You can wash a smaller amount of greens in a salad spinner. Put them in the basket, fill the spinner with cold water and swish. Lift the basket out of the water, empty the spinner and dry the greens.

Ways to Dry Greens

- Pile them in a salad spinner.
- Put them in a colander lined with paper towels. Lift the bundle and shake.
- Wrap them in a tea towel, like a hobo bundle, and whirl.

- Never wash greens until you're ready to use them.

- Pros and cons: If you cut, slice or shred greens before washing, they can be washed more thoroughly and are easier to dry. If you wash greens before cutting them, dirt has fewer places to hide and there's less to retrieve.

- Transfer greens from water to a spinner or colander using a skimmer.

- Don't dry washed greens completely if you are not using them right away. The moisture will prevent wilting.

- To refresh and crisp greens, soak them in cold water for half an hour, then wrap them in paper towels until they are completely dry. Chill them in the fridge.

- Shredded herbs and greens don't discolor as quickly as chopped ones. To shred, stack the leaves, roll them into a cigar, then slice crosswise.

- Cut off the dark green parts of escarole and frisée. They are bitter and tough. Lettuce is the opposite.

- Some greens are both tender and tough. Deconstruct beet or collard greens, kale and the like. Chop tougher stems. Shred tender greens. Sauté separately, giving stems a head start. Or blanch stems first, then sauté them with the greens.

- Excise the stems of leafy greens diagonally, right from the inside of the leaf. Don't just cut where stem meets leaf.

- Parboil wild greens, such as dandelion, dock and chicory, for 5 minutes, drain, then finish cooking them in fresh boiling water.

- Get most of the frilled, leafy greens off the tough stems of kale easily: Use a sharp knife to scrape along the stem toward the tip, liberating the leaves as you go.

OUTSIDE THE BOX

When it comes to greens, look beyond the obvious. You can cook romaine in soup, scatter arugula on pizza, toss dandelion greens with spaghetti.

Better Leftovers

Sauté leftover greens (even lettuce) in hot oil and toss them with canned beans.

Arugula

A Good Sign

Bright leaves free of spots — dark green for mature arugula, lighter green for baby arugula.

- Large arugula leaves are tougher and more pungent.

- Swap arugula for lettuce in sandwiches and salads.

- No need to cook arugula. Just wilt it briefly in the heat of a dish.

Dandelion

- The leaves, flowers and roots of the versatile dandelion are all edible. Roots are steamed or dried for tea. Flowers and leaves are used in salads. Buds and leaves are used to make wine and tea.

- The best, most tender dandelion leaves sprout in the spring before the plant flowers. After that, they become tough and bitter.

Fiddleheads

✧ People who don't like fiddlehead greens complain that they taste like ferns. That's because they are ferns. Fiddleheads are the shoots of the ostrich fern. They look like the scrollwork on a violin, hence the name.

7 Keys to Cooking Fiddleheads

1. Get rid of the papery brown skins. They are bitter. Rub the skins off using a sprayer or cold running water. Soak fiddleheads in several changes of cold water until the water is clear, not rusty brown.
2. Pull fiddleheads from the water and nip off the browned ends.
3. Government officials recommend boiling fiddleheads for 15 minutes or steaming them for 10 to 12 minutes to get rid of potential toxins, but this massacres them. Some chefs and aficionados believe 5 minutes is enough.
4. First, blanch fiddleheads in lightly salted water for 3 minutes and drain them. Then use them in a recipe or continue to cook them. Do not reuse the blanching water.
5. After blanching, you can boil fiddleheads in fresh water until tender, about 5 to 7 minutes.
6. You can steam blanched fiddleheads for 6 or 7 minutes. Steamed fiddleheads taste nuttier and have a better texture than boiled ones.
7. To roast blanched fiddleheads, toss them with oil, vinegar, salt and pepper. Sprinkle some cheese on top. Roast them at 425°F (220°C) for 6 to 8 minutes.

✧ Fiddleheads are harbingers of spring. The shoots are only coiled for a couple of weeks. They are no good to eat once they've unfurled.

Foraging Tips

- Fiddleheads grow on floodplains and wet riverbanks.
- The shoots are 2 to 3 inches (5 to 8 cm) tall.
- Snap them off at the base.
- Pick no more than a third of the fiddleheads in a specific location.

✧ To store fiddleheads, wrap them in a paper towel, then place them in a plastic bag in the fridge.

Flowers

♛ A Golden Rule

Make sure the flower is edible and has not been exposed to herbicides, pesticides or other contaminants.

- Edible flowers: roses, pansies, violets, carnations, dandelions, nasturtiums, lavender, hibiscus, marigolds, daisies, calendulas, chamomile and the flowers of some herbs (such as chives) and veggies (such as squash).
- Some flowers cause allergic reactions or have unpleasant effects (daylilies act as a laxative). Some are downright poisonous. Do your research to compile a complete list.
- Flowers to avoid: azaleas, crocus, daffodils, foxgloves, rhododendrons, oleander, lily of the valley, poinsettias and wisteria

✧ Non-edible flowers may look good, but don't use them as garnishes. A diner may eat one.

✧ Do not eat flowers from the florist. They have pesticides and dyes.

- ✧ Pick homegrown flowers in the early morning or late afternoon, when they are the most moist.

- ✧ Choose freshly opened blossoms. They should not have any spots or signs of bugs.

- ✧ Put edible flowers in a vase with water and cover the bouquet with plastic. Refrigerate the vase.

- ✧ To wash flowers, bathe them gently in salt water, then drop them in a bowl of ice water for up to a minute. Drain them on paper towels. Carefully remove the petals or parts to be consumed.

- ✧ Some parts of flowers are edible, some are not. The petals are generally good to eat. You may have to remove the stamen and pistil from whole flowers. On a rose petal, the whitish part of the petal that connects to the stem is often bitter.

- ✧ Once plucked, flowers should be used within a day. You can store petals in a perforated plastic bag in the fridge.

- ✧ You can sweeten drinks with flower sugar or sprinkle it on cakes.

Master Plan
Flower Sugar

1. Collect 2 tbsp (25 mL) tiny whole flowers or petals with a delicious scent.
2. Wash and dry them well.
3. Put ¼ cup (50 mL) granulated sugar in a zip-lock bag. If desired, work in a drop of food coloring for effect.
4. Stir in the flowers or petals. Squeeze out the air. Seal the bag.
5. Leave at room temperature for 2 days to allow the sugar to absorb the fragrance and flavor.
6. Sift the sugar. Discard the flowers or petals.

R is for Rosehip

Rosehips are the fruit, or seed pods, of roses. They can be dried for tea or made into jam. Snip off the stem and blossom ends, cut the pods lengthwise and remove the "hairy" seeds.

Master Plan
Homemade Candied Flowers

1. In a small bowl, whisk an egg white with a fork to break it up.
2. Spread superfine sugar on a large plate and put some in a small sieve.
3. Choose whole small flowers, petals or herb leaves (basil is surprisingly good).
4. Work one flower at a time. Using a small paintbrush, paint flowers with a thin coating of egg white. Lay them on the plate of sugar. Sprinkle with sugar from the sieve.
5. Lay flowers on a baking sheet lined with parchment or topped with a screen. (A splatter screen or drum sieve works.)
6. Preheat the oven to 175°F (80°C). Put the baking sheet in the oven and immediately turn off the heat. Leave it in the oven overnight or until the flowers and/or leaves are dry, turning them several times in the first few hours.

Lettuce

Ways to Clean a Head of Lettuce

- Holding the base, vigorously dunk the head up and down in a sinkful of cold water. This works best for tender, leafy lettuces.
- Cut a wedge in the base of a head of lettuce to expose the layers. Run water vigorously through the wedge. This works best with iceberg lettuce.

✦ To dry a head of lettuce, turn it upside down on a plate to drain, cover it with a kitchen towel and refrigerate it for several hours.

✦ Loosen the core of iceberg lettuce by rapping it on the counter. Then pull it out with your fingers.

Ways to Redeem Limp Lettuce

- Put the leaves in a bowl of water with ice cubes and a bit of lemon juice, or with a few slices of potato. Refrigerate them for an hour.
- Faster: Soak the leaves in ice water in a bowl or the sink for a few minutes. Spin them dry and use them immediately.

⚡ *Lightning Won't Strike If ...*

You chop or slice lettuce. Cooks are warned never to cut lettuce, just tear it. Yes, cut lettuce is more likely to wilt and go brown at the edges — but not if you eat it right away. So if you want to take the faster, easier way out, grab a knife without guilt.

How to Shred Romaine

1. Quarter it lengthwise, but keep the base intact.
2. If you wish, make another lengthwise cut in each quarter. It depends on the size of the romaine and the size of the shreds you want.
3. Shred each section crosswise. Toss out the base.

Factoid The darker the lettuce, the higher the nutrients.

Healthier Eater

- Use pliable leaves from Boston lettuce as low-calorie wraps for fillings.
- Use firm leaves from iceberg lettuce as cups for fillings.
- Some supermarkets sell bagged lettuce especially for wraps.
- Fillings can range from chicken salad to stir-fries.

OUTSIDE THE BOX

Take lettuce beyond the obvious salads.
- The French cook peas with chopped iceberg lettuce (see recipe, page 280).
- The Italians are not averse to adding chopped romaine to minestrone or *pasta e fagioli*. Lettuce adds a delightful crunch to many dishes.
- You can make cream soups using hearty greens such as romaine or escarole, instead of the usual vegetables.

Spinach

Two Good Signs

- Green leaves, with no yellowing or decayed edges.
- Moist stems.

✦ Use young spinach for salads, mature spinach for cooking. Young plants have thin, flexible stems. Thick stems are more mature.

Ways to Wilt Spinach

- In a large saucepan over medium heat, with just the water clinging to the leaves after it's washed. Stir frequently.
- In the microwave. Put it in a large bowl with about ¼ cup (50 mL) water per 1 lb (500 g) spinach. Cover, then zap it on High power.

❖ Spinach is the incredible shrinking vegetable. Wilt it in a tiny amount of water. Squeeze gently to get rid of liquid before sautéing or adding it to other dishes.

❖ Sugar subtly counters the astringency of spinach. Use about $\frac{1}{8}$ tsp (0.5 mL) granulated sugar per 1 oz (30 g) spinach.

Ways to Squeeze Water out of Spinach

- Use tongs.
- Use your hands.
- Press it between two stacked plates.
- Push it in a potato ricer.

❖ You can store spinach in an herb keeper or a makeshift vase.

Sprouts

❖ Sprouts are the germinated forms of seeds and beans. Buy crisp sprouts, with buds attached.

❖ Refrigerate sprouts in a covered colander.

OUTSIDE THE BOX

Make sprout tea sandwiches as you would watercress sandwiches.

Watercress

A Good Sign
Dark green, with no yellowing.

❖ Store watercress in a perforated plastic bag in the fridge. Wrap a damp paper towel around the stems. Watercress spoils quickly.

❖ Don't wash watercress until you're ready to use it.

❖ Pluck the leaves from the stems. Discard the stems.

OUTSIDE THE BOX

Watercress is good in curries and Asian soups.

Horseradish

❖ Peel horseradish before using it.

❖ Grate it at the last minute. Cut and exposed to air, fresh horseradish becomes pungent, then fades.

---

3 Ways to Keep Grated Horseradish Virile

1. Add an acid. (Bottled, prepared horseradish is commonly preserved with vinegar.)
2. Store it in an airtight container.
3. Stir it with schmaltz or another fat.

❖ Wear latex or other disposable gloves when working with horseradish.

❖ Store horseradish root wrapped in plastic in the refrigerator.

❖ You can freeze grated horseradish.

Jicama

❖ Store jicama in a cool, dry pantry or the vegetable crisper. Cover cut pieces with plastic.

- Jicama is shaped like a big turnip. It has thin, light brown skin and off-white, slightly translucent flesh that is the texture of an apple or water chestnut. You can eat it raw or cooked, in salads, stews, soups or stir-fries.

- Jicama doesn't discolor and stays crisp if you don't cook it too long.

Kohlrabi

- Kohlrabi can be eaten raw or cooked.

Making Do

Substitute kohlrabi for turnip.

Lemongrass

- Avoid lemongrass that is dried at the edges.

5 Keys to Prepping Lemongrass

1. Peel and discard the outer two or three layers to get to the tender core.
2. Cut off the woody stalk at the spot where the knife meets only slight resistance.
3. Cut off the tough root end.
4. You should have at least 6 inches (15 cm) of bulb. Smash it with a mallet to make it easier to cut. Slice or mince it.
5. Alternatively, get to the most tender part by smashing the bulb with a mallet until it splits. Chop with a big heavy knife. Pull out and discard any pieces that don't chop easily.

- Store lemongrass wrapped tightly in plastic in the fridge.

- The bulb is edible, but some people find it too tough. You can smash the bulb instead of chopping, then remove it from your dish before eating. Or use chopped lemongrass for flavor, then strain it out.

♻ Waste Not

- Use the tough lemongrass stalks to flavor soup, then discard them.
- Turn the stalks into barbecue skewers. First carve the bulb ends into points.

Mushrooms

Five Good Signs

- The mushroom is brown, not black.
- It's firm, without a lot of loose powder.
- It has a woodsy, earthy aroma. An ammonia odor is bad.
- The cap is dry, not slippery or slimy. Slime equals decay.
- The cap is smooth, not pitted or patchy.

- Keep mushrooms cool and dry. Keep them on a shelf in the fridge, not in the crisper.

- Store mushrooms in a paper bag. Line the bottom of the bag with a paper towel. Add mushrooms, add another paper towel, another layer of mushrooms, and so on. Fold down the top.

✘ No-No

Never store mushrooms in a plastic bag. Moisture equals mold and mush. If they came in a store package with a foam base and plastic wrap, remove them.

- Do not store mushrooms near pungent foods; they are absorbent.

✧ Mushrooms bruise easily. Do not stack other vegetables on top of them.

White VS. Button?

When they are small, white mushrooms are known as button mushrooms.

Portobello VS. Cremini?

Creminis, which look like brown button mushrooms, are baby portobellos. They graduate to portobello-hood when they're 4 inches (10 cm) wide.

✧ To clean portobellos, first tap them on the counter to loosen dirt. You don't need to scrape the dark gills.

E is for Enoki

Enokis are delicate, beige mushrooms on thin stems with tiny heads, clustered in bouquets. Before using them, cut away the base that holds them in a clump. When enokis are too old to eat, they get bitter.

G is for Gyromitra

Beware of gyromitra pretending to be morels. These copycats have the familiar webbed surface, but not the tidy cone shape of the real thing.

✧ Morels must be rinsed thoroughly to clean the interiors.

Factoid Poisonous mushrooms look a lot like their edible kin. Even fungi professors get mixed up. So don't go picking your own wild mushrooms haphazardly, unless you have a death wish.

✧ You can decorate mushroom caps: Scrape a spoke pattern into the skin on the cap before lightly cooking the mushroom. Use a skewer or a dull knife.

✧ You don't need to peel the tender skins of mushrooms, except maybe very large portobellos. But if a mushroom is old, you may be able to redeem it by stripping the skin. Use a small knife to pull off sections, starting just under the rim of the cap. Or rub the skins off with your fingers.

✧ To remove a mushroom stem, twist it carefully so you don't crack the cap. Or slice it off flush with the gills.

✧ Most modern mushrooms require only a thin trim off the stem. But shiitake stems are too tough to eat.

⚡ Lightning Won't Strike If ...

You wash mushrooms. Yes, they are like sponges, but you don't have to fuss with dainty brushes. You can rinse them quickly. Any residual water will evaporate in the pan. Just don't leave them soaking.

✧ Mushrooms tend to release so much liquid, they steam instead of sear. To brown them better, use your largest skillet, or sauté them in batches until the liquid evaporates. Keep the heat high.

✧ Add a spoonful of lemon juice to the butter or oil when frying mushrooms, to keep them lustrous and firm.

✧ You've heard of grilled portobellos. You can also grill button, cremini or shiitake mushrooms if you skewer them. Make sure the skewer runs through the center of the cap and stem.

✧ Save mushroom trimmings, even the tough shiitake stems, for stock. Rinse them before using.

❖ The liquid released by mushrooms is a great flavoring agent. Exception: Over-the-hill, slippery brown mushrooms exude the most liquid, but it tastes bad.

Ways to Capture Mushroom Liquid

- Steam mushrooms over the tiniest amount of water. Afterwards, reduce the liquid.
- When you are frying mushrooms, pour the liquid out of the skillet before it evaporates, then carry on cooking.
- Save the liquid used to soak dried mushrooms.

Dried Mushrooms

❖ Break dried mushrooms to help them hydrate faster.

How to Dry Your Own Mushrooms

1. Wash and pat dry some small, fresh mushrooms.
2. Place them on a screen or thread them onto a string. Set or hang them in a shady, airy place. Let them dry for up to 1 week.
3. When they are dry, wrinkled and hard, pack them in an airtight glass jar or plastic container.

OUTSIDE THE BOX

You can grind dry mushrooms into powder for an intense molecular gastronomy hit. Use a spice grinder. Sprinkle the powder over mashed potatoes, add it to mushroom soup or sprinkle some into an olive oil dip.

Golden Seared Mushrooms

Mushroom lovers will waste no time digging into this dish. **Makes 4 side servings**

Tips

I used creminis, shiitakes and king oyster mushrooms.

You can serve this as a side dish or spoon the mushrooms over rice or pasta as part of a vegetarian meal.

2 tbsp	canola or olive oil	25 mL
8 oz	mixed mushrooms, sliced ¼ to ⅜ inch (0.5 to 0.75 cm) thick	250 g
	Kosher salt	

1. In a 12-inch (30 cm) skillet, heat oil over medium-high heat until it is shimmery. Add mushrooms in a single layer. Sprinkle salt to taste evenly over top. Sear the mushrooms, without stirring, until the bottoms are browned, 2 to 3 minutes.

2. Turn the mushrooms with a spatula. Sear the mushrooms, without stirring, for 30 seconds.

3. Stir-fry the mushrooms, using the spatula, for 30 seconds. The bottom of the pan should be dry and the mushrooms should start to sound squeaky.

4. Remove them to a platter and serve them immediately.

* Soak dried mushrooms in the smallest possible amount of water. Pour the water through a sieve to strain out the grit before using it.

P is for Porcini

Porcinis, or çepes, are usually sold dried. If you ever come across a fresh one, remember that they tend to harbor worms. As insurance, you can heat fresh porcini in a 175°F (80°C) oven for 30 minutes or steam them for 5 minutes. Any worms should crawl out and die. But the concept turns the stomach.

* Don't add raw mushrooms to quiches and casseroles. They will get soggy. Sauté them first.

Truffles

* The truffle is an underground fungus. Once you smell one, you'll know why gourmands covet them. Bonus: That heady scent permeates any food the truffle makes contact with while awaiting consumption. Truffles come in black and white varieties. The most prestigious is the French Perigord black truffle. White truffles are milder.

* Rub or peel off the rough skin of black truffles. Wipe the white ones. Save the trimmings for seasonings and garnishes.

* Truffles can be cooked or eaten raw. Shave, grate or mince them.

* The longer a truffle sits, the more moisture it loses. The more moisture, the more flavor. Use a truffle within 2 to 3 days. Or freeze it.

* Read labels. Some truffle oils are chemically flavored. Some products just contain truffle aroma.

---

6 Ways to Get More from a Fresh Truffle

1. Use it to flavor oil.
2. Bury it in rice. If a fresh truffle is packed in rice when you buy it, save the rice.
3. Leave it in a sealed container with eggs in the fridge for a couple of days. The essence will seep through their porous shells.
4. Refrigerate it overnight in a jar with an unwrapped stick of butter.
5. Store it in brandy or sherry overnight or longer. Use the spirits for cooking.
6. Slice it thinly. Arrange the slices on any type of food in a tub with a tight lid and leave it overnight.

Okra

Three Good Signs
* It has bright green, velvety skin.
* The pods have a bit of give, but snap easily at the tips.
* There are no black or brown spots.

* Younger pods are choice. Look for okra that's no more than 4 inches (10 cm) long.

* Before cooking, rinse okra to rub off the fuzz. Dry it well.

Ways to Store Okra in the Fridge
* In a paper bag
* Wrapped in a paper towel and placed in a perforated plastic bag

✦ Okra takes 5 to 10 minutes to boil, sauté, steam or microwave.

⑤ is for Slime Mucilage

That's what botanists call the slick, clear juices that seep from the okra seeds. No wonder okra is the vegetable we love to hate. The slime is a fine thickener, but we'd rather do without it. We can't get rid of it entirely, but we can reduce it. Just keep chanting: Okra is okay.

---

6 Slime-Busting Techniques

1. Leave the pods whole. Trim no more than a tiny slice from the stem end and perhaps the tip. Don't pierce the pods. Options: Drizzle them with oil and roast them at a high temperature. Pickle them. Dust them with cornmeal and fry them. Steam them to make them creamy, not gummy.

2. Use the least amount of water. Okra cooked by a watery method releases more mucilage. Fry rather than steam. Steam rather than boil.

3. Cook the pods rapidly until just tender. That way, not as many juices are released. If you are adding okra to a dish, add it during the last 10 minutes of cooking time.

4. If you slice okra, sear the pieces over high heat to create a seal of sorts.

5. Acidity cuts slime. Options: Roast okra until it's crispy, then squeeze lime juice over top and season with a spice blend. Cut okra into $\frac{1}{2}$-inch (1 cm) circles and sauté it with diced tomatoes.

6. For a soup, stew or casserole that will be cooked a long time, cut up okra and allow it to release its slime. It will blend in. In gumbos that require thickening, this is a good thing.

Olives

Green VS. Black?

- Olives change from green to black as they ripen, and their skins turn from smooth to wrinkly.
- Green olives are harvested before they are ripe.
- Brown or wine-colored olives are in transition.
- Natural black olives are harvested ripe or close to it.
- Unnaturally black olives are ripened artificially and quickly with a lye or alkaline treatment, then packed in brine and sterilized. Voila, canned olives. Unnatural black olives may be coated with herbs to compensate for the flavor that was stripped out of them.

Brine VS. Salt VS. Oil?

Brined olives are soaked in a salt-water solution. Sometimes vinegar is added. Salt-cured, or dry-cured, olives are packed in salt, then may be plumped in oil. They are wrinkly and assertive. Oil-cured olives are soaked in olive oil. There are also water-cured olives, simply soaked in daily changes of water, and lye-cured ones.

✦ Reasons to store salty, wrinkled black olives in olive oil:
- It mellows their bitterness.
- It plumps them.
- You can use the oil later for salad dressing.

How to Replenish or Replace Brine

1. Rinse olives in cold water. Drain.
2. Stir together a solution of 1 tbsp (15 mL) white vinegar and $1\frac{1}{2}$ tsp (7 mL) kosher salt per 1 cup (250 mL) water.
3. Put the olives in a clean tub. Pour in enough solution to cover them. Put on a tight lid. These olives will be mellow.

❖ Black olives are softer and easier to pit than green ones.

---

5 Ways to Pit an Olive

1. Rap it sharply and quickly with the broad blade of a knife.
2. Cover it with waxed paper and press gently with a rolling pin.
3. Press it with the bottom of a small glass.
4. Press down with your thumb until you can feel the pit. This works for black olives only.
5. A cherry pitter works on some olives.

Onions

Fresh VS. Storage?

Fresh onions are harvested early. Milder, moister and sweeter, they are good consumed raw. Storage onions are harvested late, stored in climate-controlled barns and sold year-round. They are pungent and beg to be cooked.

> **Factoid** Freshly cut onions are antibacterial, but only for the first 10 minutes.

What Kind?

- **Yellow:** The all-purpose workhorse of the onion family
- **White:** Firmer, not as pungent, a staple in Hispanic cooking
- **Spanish:** Large, round and sweeter
- **Bermuda:** Mild, can be yellow, white or reddish
- **Red:** Assertive, but good raw, and turns an unappealing blue when cooked (counter this chemical reaction with a splash of vinegar)

- **Shallot:** Small clove with a tight brown skin, for cooking, but kinder and gentler
- **Cipollini:** Small, flat white onion, good in stews and condiments
- **Pearl:** Immature onion, can be yellow, white or red, looks cute (also sold pickled for cocktails)

Ⓥ is for Vidalia

The Vidalia is but one of many sweet onions. Its popular cousins include the Maui and Walla Walla. Large and mild, these are ideal to eat raw in sandwiches and salads.

Three Good Signs

- The onion is firm, dry and heavy.
- The skin is papery and brittle.
- There's no green sprout.

---

4 Ways to Make Onions Easier to Strip

1. Cut a slit in the skin from top to bottom, then pull the edges sideways.
2. Cover and microwave an onion for a few seconds. Beware: An onion can explode if it overdoses on microwaves.
3. Treat whole onions, shallots, cipollini and pearl onions to a boiling-water plunge, then immediately spray them with cold water.
4. Stick a peeled onion under cold running water to rub off the clingy membrane.

Sprouts VS. Chives?

Onion sprouts are sprouted from onion seeds. They're good in sandwiches and salads.
The stalks of the chive plant are used as an oniony herb.

Storage Tips

- Most storage onions keep best in a cool, dry, dark spot. Keep them well ventilated in a basket in the pantry. Avoid plastic bags.
- Sweet onions, however, spoil quickly — particularly if they touch each other. Keep them separate. Store each one in a brown paper bag in the crisper.
- Keep shallots at room temperature for the short term. Otherwise, refrigerate them.
- To store a cut onion, rub the cut surface with butter. It will keep longer and reek less. Wrap the onion hunk in plastic or toss it in a zip-lock bag.

Two Ways to Finely Chop Onions
Chef-style

- Halve an onion lengthwise. Start at the root end so you can see where you are going. You want enough root on each half to hold it together. Pull off the skin.
- Place each half face down on a cutting board. Trim the top end. Press down on the onion with your palm. Make three or more cuts parallel to the cutting board, from the top to the root end. Don't cut all the way through.
- Make a series of vertical cuts along the grain, leaving the root end intact.
- Slice crosswise from top to base. Discard the root end.

A fast alternative

- Trim the root and tip of the onion.
- Cut it in half lengthwise.
- Place each half face down on a cutting board.
- Thinly slice it crosswise.
- Press down with your palm so that the onion slices fan out in overlapping semicircles.
- Slice lengthwise.

- For onion rings, cut $\frac{1}{8}$-inch (3 mm) thick circles crosswise. Separate them into rings. (Set aside small or broken slices for another use.) Before coating, drain the rings on paper towels.

- You can grate onions against the medium teardrop holes of a box grater. This is a technique used in Indian cuisine.

☼ A Bit of Science

Cutting or chewing an onion creates a chemical reaction that forms a sulfur compound. The liberated gases react with the salty tears in your eyes to form a stinging, sulfurous acid. No wonder you weep! The older the onion, the more you cry. Yellow cooking onions have the most sulfur. On the plus side, it's all those nasty chemicals that make an onion taste so good.

- For oniony flavor without the onions, use onion juice. In your food processor, chop an onion with a bit of water. Drain it in a sieve, pushing out the juices.

- Onions are more likely to be bitter or harsh if they're cooked over high heat.

Customized Cooking

- If you want soft, translucent onions, cover the pan and sweat them over low heat.
- If you want golden or caramelized onions, uncover the pan and turn the heat to medium-low heat.
- If you want browned or fried onions, turn the heat to medium or medium-high.

- How to stop sautéed onions from overbrowning:
- Add $\frac{1}{4}$ cup (50 mL) water to the pan and stir until it evaporates.
- Cover the pan to introduce steam.

12 Ways to Hold Back the Tears

1. Best: Shield your eyes. Wear squash goggles, a diver's mask, swim goggles, a welding mask, construction safety glasses. I've seen onion goggles in kitchen stores. Contact lenses and glasses help.
2. Refrigerate the onion for at least 1 hour or freeze it for 15 minutes before cutting it. Cold subdues the substance that seeps while you weep.
3. Peel the onion, cut it in half and soak it in cold water for 10 minutes before cutting it. The onion will taste milder, too.
4. Drop the onion into boiling water for about 10 seconds, drain and refrigerate it, then cut it.
5. Cut an onion under the overhead stove vent, going full blast, to disperse the gases.
6. Plug in a portable fan next to your cutting board. The ceiling fan doesn't work.
7. Brush the cutting board with white vinegar beforehand.
8. The root end is where the sulfurous compounds are most heavily concentrated. Keep it intact until the last minute.
9. Use a super-sharp knife. Fewer juices will be released.
10. Use a chopper. It's quicker and the base contains the fumes for a while.
11. Briefly pulse the onion in a food processor, so you don't have to get up close and personal with the fumes.
12. Work quickly.

A Strange Method That Helps a Bit

- Hold a wooden match between your teeth. (Please don't light it.)

Inconvenient Remedies

- Chop the onion coarsely. The finer the cut, the more pungent the onion.
- Chop under cold running water.
- Blanch the onion in boiling water for 1 minute, spray it with cold water, then cut it. The outside layer will cook.
- Boil or steam the onion until it is cooked, then cut it.
- Mop up the juices from the onion halves and your cutting board.
- Hold your breath, lean back and turn your face away. When you have to catch a breath, do so only through your mouth.
- Cut out the root in a cone shape.
- Dice lots of onions often. This is supposed to build up a resistance.

Grilled Onion Tips

- Grilled onions tend to burn before they get soft enough. Give them a head start. Blanch a whole onion for 2 minutes in boiling water, let it cool, then slice it. Or zap 1-inch (2.5 cm) slices for 1 minute in the microwave on High power.
- Slice onions for the grill $3/4$ to 1 inch (2 to 2.5 cm) thick.
- Keep grilled onions intact. Skewer thick slices like lollipops.

✧ To keep a whole onion from falling apart while it's cooking, leave on the root end. If cooked long enough, however, the onion will collapse and even dissolve.

✧ Ghastly supermarket fried onions, or "toppers," taste like chemicals. Asian markets sell better fried onions. The best, however, are homemade. A variation: crispy shallots.

✧ Ways to make onions mild and/or crispy for sandwiches, salads and garnishes:
- Soak a whole onion in ice water for 5 to 10 minutes before cutting it.
- Soak sliced or chopped onions in cool water for an hour.
- Soak an onion in milk for an hour.
- Put cut onions into a strainer. Dip them in a bowlful of cold water with vinegar. Swish. Strain.
- Thinly slice an onion, place it in a colander, salt it liberally and let it drain for 15 minutes. Squeeze the onion to extract the liquid, or pat it dry.
- Pour boiling water over an onion. Let it stand for an hour. Drain. Revive it in ice water for 5 minutes.

Master Plan
Crispy Shallots

1. Cut shallots crosswise into ⅛- to ¼-inch (0.25 to 0.5 cm) thick slices.
2. Deep-fry them for 3 to 5 minutes or until they are golden brown.
3. Drain them on paper towels. Spread them out on a baking sheet until they are cool and crisp.
4. Sprinkle them with salt before using.

✧ For uniform cooking of a whole onion, cut an X into the root end.

✧ You can draw out harsh juices and reduce bitterness by soaking or salting an onion.

Green Onions

Green Onion VS. Scallion?

There's a whole family of mild onions with white bulbs and long green stalks. Green onions are immature, with a small, rounded bulb. If left to develop further, they become spring onions, or bulb onions. These look like mammoth green onions. Scallions are a specific variety of immature onion, with a straight, narrow bulb. Bunching onions, or Welsh onions, are not bulbous and grow in tight clusters.

Ways to Store Green Onions

- They last longer in the fridge if you take off the elastic band. Store them loosely in a plastic bag.
- Stand them like a bouquet, root ends down, in a thin layer of water. Cover the tops with a plastic bag and refrigerate them. Change the water occasionally. Bouquet onions are less likely to wither.

How to Make a Decorative Green-Onion Brush

1. Cut off the root end.
2. Cut slits in the white part, lengthwise and close together, up to about 1 inch (2.5 cm) away from the green part.
3. Cut off most of the green part.
4. Immerse the onion in ice water for at least 15 minutes.

- ❖ Ways to chop green onions without little circles rolling all over the place:
  - Before cutting, smash and flatten them with the blunt edge of the knife.
  - First, slit the white section lengthwise.

Leeks

Three Good Signs
- The bottom of the bulb is flat. A rounded bottom may indicate old age.
- The stem is white.
- The leaves are bluish-green and have no yellow edges.

❖ Before using a leek, trim the roots and wilted green ends.

✪ Waste Not
- Get more leek goodness by trimming the green leaves judiciously. Rotating the leek as you slice, cut off one leaf and one layer at a time. Cut just where dark green meets light green, then where light green meets white. All the tender white and light green parts will be longer.
- Tie the trimmed green tops of leeks into a bundle and use them in stock, alone or as part of a bouquet garni.

❖ Be fanatical about cleaning leeks. They are notoriously dirty, with clots of clay clinging between the layers. Two ways to clean a leek:
  - Starting at the root end, slice the leek in half lengthwise. Fan out the layers and rinse and rub them under running water. Shake the layers, then pull them back together.
  - Chop or thinly slice the leek. Put it in a sinkful of cold water. Swish vigorously. The dirt will fall to the bottom. Skim the chopped leek from the surface.

Leek VS. Ramp?

A leek looks like a giant scallion with coarse leaves, but it's no good raw. A ramp is a wild leek. It's small and slender, and has a garlicky accent.

❖ Before storing a leek, trim bruised and damaged leaves. Wrap it loosely in a damp paper towel. Place it in an unsealed plastic bag. Refrigerate.

Parsley Root and Parsnips

❖ Parsley root is astringent, and offers a bonus: a head of flat-leaf parsley. Parsnips are creamy and sweet.

Three Good Signs
- Firmness.
- No blemishes.
- Perky green tops on parsley root.

❖ Refrigerate both types in a plastic bag in the crisper.

Ways to Prevent Discoloration
- Add lemon juice and salt to the cooking water.
- Do not peel them, just scrub.

Tips on Parsley Root Greens
- Separate the greens from the roots. Store the roots in a plastic bag in the fridge. Store the greens like a bouquet, in a vase or jar with 1 inch (2.5 cm) of water at the bottom. Cover the tops with plastic, then put the vase in the fridge.
- The greens are a type of parsley, but have tougher stems. You can use them as you would regular parsley.

- Parsnips can have woody cores, especially if they're large or old. Quarter a parsnip lengthwise. Lay it on its side. With a knife held at an angle, slice off the core.

- Parsnips are more tapered than carrots. For even cooking, cut off the thin end of each, then cut the thick end into similar-sized pieces.

- Ways to make oven parsnips less rubbery:
  - Blanch them for 1 minute before roasting them.
  - Bake them wrapped in foil.
  - Cover the roasting pan with foil for the first 10 minutes.

- Parsnips are sweeter and crisper in the fall and winter.

Peas

A Bad Sign

If you see the bulging outline of the seeds within the pod, the peas are too mature or the pod is withering. The peas are apt to be tough and fibrous.

OUTSIDE THE BOX

Very little moisture is needed to cook peas. They will even cook in the liquid leaking from lettuce, a fact we can take advantage of.

Peas and Lettuce

The lettuce leaks moisture to the peas and adds a pleasing, contrasting crunch. **Makes 6 side servings**

Variations

Omit the butter and use all oil.

You can substitute a romaine heart for the iceberg lettuce.

To make this with fresh peas, stir them in along with the lettuce until they are coated with oil. Cover and cook, stirring once, until the lettuce wilts, about 1 minute. Uncover and cook until most of moisture has evaporated and peas are tender, about 5 minutes.

1 tbsp	extra virgin olive oil	15 mL
1 tbsp	unsalted butter	15 mL
3	cloves garlic, minced	3
¼ tsp	hot pepper flakes	1 mL
1	small head iceberg lettuce, coarsely chopped	1
3 cups	frozen green peas, rinsed	750 mL
½ tsp	kosher salt	2 mL
¼ tsp	granulated sugar	1 mL

1. In a 10-inch (25 cm) sauté pan, heat oil and butter over medium heat until hot. Remove from heat. Stir in garlic and hot pepper flakes. Stir constantly for 20 to 30 seconds or until garlic is golden. Do not let it brown.

2. Stir in lettuce until it is coated with oil. Cover and cook over medium heat, stirring once, until it wilts, about 1 minute.

3. Stir in peas. Cook, uncovered, until most of moisture has evaporated and peas are tender, 2 to 3 minutes. Stir in salt and sugar.

- When boiling shelled green peas, toss in a few pods for flavor.

- Snap peas should live up to their name and give a distinct snap when broken.

- With snap peas, bigger is not better and length does not matter.

How to Get Rid of Tough, Thin Strings in Snow Peas

1. Using a small knife, grab the tip and pull out the string along the spine (the edge where the little peas are attached).
2. Pull toward the center. If the whole string doesn't pull off, flip the pod and pull from the other end.
3. Repeat along the other edge.

Peppers

Factoid Green bell peppers ripen into red ones. Yellow and orange bells are stages along the way. The redder, the sweeter.

- Cut peppers with the fleshy side up. It offers less resistance.

- Go stuff a pepper. But first, blanch the prepped pepper shell in boiling water, spray it with cold water and drain it.

Prettier Stuffed Peppers

- As an alternative to hollowing out a pepper, cut it lengthwise and leave on the stem.
- Use the top of a bell pepper as a cap. Do not overcook the cap.

How to Cut a Bell Pepper Efficiently

1. Slice off the rounded cap and base.
2. Slit the center section from top to bottom, making a vertical cut next to, but not along, one of the seams.
3. Press against the interior with your knife to unroll the pepper, slicing out the veins and seeds as you go.
4. Scrape out any white pulp you missed.
5. You'll end up with a rectangle. Cut it into segments. Dice or slice the segments.
6. Discarding the stem, chop the cap, then the base.

P is for Poblano

Poblanos are dark green and bell-shaped, but smaller than bell peppers. They are on the edge of hot.

- Roasted peppers are overdone if you see an ashy hue on the black, charred parts.

- Peppers char more evenly under the broiler if they are cut in half lengthwise.

OUTSIDE THE BOX

- To remove the skin, you can blister a chile, such as a jalapeño pepper, in hot oil. Pierce the stem with a fork. Immerse it in hot oil until the skin bubbles up. Peel it under cold water. This technique takes off a thin layer of skin and cooks the chile a bit. Larger bell peppers can go in the deep-fryer for the same effect.
- You can skin peppers with the assistance of a kitchen torch.

How to Blister a Pepper with a Kitchen Torch

1. Ram a carving fork into the base and blast away with the torch. Work methodically to ensure even coverage. Blister the base last.
2. This method burns off only a thin layer of skin. The pepper itself stays firm.
3. Scrape the skin off with the blunt edge of a knife or rub it off with a paper towel.
4. Rinse the pepper.

How to Peel a Roasted Pepper

1. Put a hot roasted pepper in a paper bag or a bowl covered with plastic, to sweat and cool. The steam lifts the skin.
2. Rinse it under cold running water.
3. Pull off the peel with your fingers.
4. Scrape off any tough sections of peel with a small, sharp knife.
5. Pull out the core. Scrape out loose seeds with wet fingers, a pastry brush or a paper towel.

✦ If you have a gas stove, you can char peppers over the flame. Stick one on a carving fork and rotate it.

✦ Ways to make peeling roasted peppers less of a sticky, messy job:
- Keep dipping your fingers into cold water in a bowl set next to your cutting board.
- Pull off the skin under cold running water.

♻ Waste Not
Save the smoky juices from roasted peppers to flavor soups, dressings and sauces.

✦ You can freeze roasted peppers in zip-lock bags. Break off pieces as you need them. Or thaw the lot in warm water.

C is for Capsaicin
Capsaicin is the compound that makes chiles hot.

⚛ A Bit of Science
When we consume chiles, capsaicin alerts the pain receptors in our bodies. In response, our brains produce feel-good endorphins. So that's why we love chiles. In fact, the more we eat, the more we want.

S is for Scoville
The heat of chiles is measured in Scoville units, from 0 for the sweet bell pepper to 15,000,000 for pure capsaicin. The Cubanelle is a mere 800, the jalapeño about 5,000, the habanero about 300,000. The hottest chile in the world is the Indian bhut jolokia, or ghost chile, with a rating of up to 1,000,000 units.

Heat Tests
- Sniff. If your nose stings, use the pepper cautiously.
- Take a lick.
- Eat a seed.
- Check the color and size. If comparing two peppers of the same type, the smaller, brighter one is probably hotter.

✦ To control spiciness, remove and reserve the veins. Chop them and add them to your dish in stages. Testing is better than guessing.

✦ To remove the seeds from a whole chile with minimal cutting (say you want to stuff a jalapeño), cut off the stem end and rotate a vegetable peeler inside. Tap out stray seeds and bits of vein. Run water into the chile. Drain and invert it on a rack to dry.

Mythstake

The heat of a chile is not mainly in the seeds. It's in the spongy veins. Thick veins are hotter than fine ones. The seeds are the second-hottest part. The stem end of the chile is hotter than the tip.

3 Ways to Minimize the Heat of a Chile

1. Cut it in half lengthwise, scrape out the seeds, then some or all of the veins. Rinse the chile under cold running water.
2. Discard the seeds and veins. Soak the chile in cold, salted water for an hour.
3. Use less.

Ⓒ is for Chipotle

Chipotles are smoked jalapeños. They are widely available canned in tomatoey adobo sauce.

✧ To reduce the heat in canned chipotles, gently split them and rub the seeds off the flesh.

✧ How to keep capsaicin off your hands when cutting chiles:
- Wear latex or other disposable gloves.
- Rub oil over your hands so they won't absorb the oily capsaicin.

A Bit of Science

Don't bother drinking water to quell the heat from a chile. Water just spreads the oily capsaicin around in your mouth. Beer won't do it, either. Capsaicin is soluble in alcohol, but it has to be hard liquor — and plenty of it. A protein, however, will coat the mouth, forming a barrier between nerve receptors and the capsaicin. This is called "unbinding."

8 Ways to Put Out the Fire in Your Mouth

1. Drink milk.
2. Eat yogurt. There's a reason Indians serve a yogurt dip called raita and a yogurt drink called lassi.
3. Eat ice cream. The cold is soothing, too.
4. Eat cheese.
5. Eat bread, potatoes or rice. The starch mops up the oil.
6. Suck on a lemon.
7. Drink tomato juice.
8. Drink room-temperature sugar water.

✧ Be careful not to touch your eyes after handling chiles.

Factoid You can raise your tolerance for spicy food. Start slowly, eating peppers with a mild sting, such as poblanos. Graduate to the strong stuff. Eat a bit more each time.

How to Reconstitute a Dried Chile

1. Cut off the stem.
2. Cut a slit along the side of the pod.
3. Shake out the seeds.
4. Put the chile in a bowl. Cover it with boiling water. Soak it for 15 to 20 minutes.
5. Drain, reserving the liquid.
6. Chop the chile or purée it with some soaking liquid. Or scrape the pulp from the skin and stir in some soaking liquid to make a paste.

The leftover soaking liquid from a dry chile can give chili con carne quite a kick.

Plantains

✦ The plantain is the banana's complicated cousin. Plantains come in green, yellow and brown versions, with varying degrees of spottiness along the road to ripeness and beyond. To cooks, the plantain is not one vegetable but three. Your recipe will determine which type to buy. It is a given, however, that you will not be eating your plantains raw.

Three Types

• Green plantains are firm and astringent.
• Yellow plantains are starchy and slightly sweet. The ones with black speckles are sometimes called amarillos.
• Brown-black plantains are mushy and sweet.

✦ Ripen plantains at room temperature. Plan ahead. This takes time.

✦ Plantain skins are thicker and harder than banana skins. The blacker they are, the easier to peel. You should pull off the peel around the plantain, not from top to bottom like a banana peel.

✦ The greener a plantain, the longer it takes to cook. It takes about 10 minutes to boil a peeled yellow one.

✦ Ways to cook plantains without peeling:
• Cut off the ends. Slit the peel along one seam. Place the plantain in a saucepan. Cover it with salted water by 2 inches (5 cm). Boil for 10 to 20 minutes.
• Wash the plantain well. Bake it at 350°F (180°C) for about an hour.

8 A-Peeling Tips

1. Trim each end. Using a small, sharp knife, slit two seams at opposite sides of the plantain.
2. Soften the peel by placing the plantain in a large bowl filled with hot water, or 4 cups (1 L) cold water with 1 tsp (5 mL) salt. Let it soak for 5 minutes.
3. Moisten your hands. Rub them with salt to prevent stickiness.
4. Using your fingers or the tip of a knife, pry and tease off the skin along one slit. Continue to push the peel away from you in segments.
5. You can make peeling easier by cutting a plantain into 2-inch (5 cm) segments.
6. Beware: Sharp edges of the peel can give you nasty, shallow slashes, similar to paper cuts. You can wear gloves, if you wish.
7. If you're peeling firm plantains, part of the skin may cling to the flesh after the peel is removed. Shave these bits off.
8. Remove all the strands of sticky membrane left from the peel. They turn gray during cooking.

✦ Test a cooked plantain by piercing it with a fork. It should be tender, but still firm in the center.

✦ For the smoothest mashed plantains, mash while they're hot.

✦ Plantains are often double-cooked in the tropics — boiled, then fried, for example.

✦ Peeled green plantains fry up moister if you soak them first. Immerse them in cold, salted water for 15 to 20 minutes. Pat dry.

Potatoes

✧ The ideal world for potatoes would be well-ventilated, cool and dark. Potatoes keep best at about 45°F to 50°F (7°C to 10°C) — awkward for the average consumer. Try the basement.

✧ Don't store spuds in plastic. Use a heavy paper bag. It's airy and dark. Or keep them in a basket in a dark pantry.

✧ Separate withered or sprouted specimens from the pack. If one goes bad, it taints the others. And the smell!

What Kind?

• Russets are the starchiest potatoes. They have thick skins. They are best for baking, frying and mashing. They'll crumble in soups and stews.

• Waxy red and white potatoes have a firm, smooth texture and thin skin. They hold their shape. Roast them or use them in soup, stew, potato salad, scalloped potatoes and casseroles. They make limp, soggy fries and gummy mashed potatoes.

• Yellow-fleshed potatoes are the most versatile, with a medium amount of starch. They work in almost anything. If you mash them, they will be creamy rather than fluffy. If you fry them, they will be a bit limp.

• New potatoes are harvested early. They are low in starch. The skin is thin and flaky, the flavor subtle. You can boil, roast or smash them.

✧ When in doubt, choose by shape. Oval spuds are best for baking and mashing, round spuds for roasting and boiling, long spuds for mashing, baking and frying.

 No-No

Cut out potato sprouts. They are toxic.

 A Bit of Science

When it's heated, starch sucks up water and swells. Some potatoes are high in starch and low in moisture. Others are the opposite. When cooked, the starchy spuds become mealy or fluffy, and fall apart. The moist ones become gummy or waxy, and hold their shape.

5 Reasons for Discolorations

1. Black spots under the skin are bruises. Cut them off. And handle potatoes more gently.
2. The starches turn to sugar when the potatoes are too cold, which causes dark spots and softening. However, a couple of days in a warmer climate and they revert back.
3. An ugly brown center in a spud is called hollowheart. Rapid growth or sudden temperature changes cause it. Hollowheart is harmless. Just cut it out.
4. Greenish bits are caused by exposure to light. Cut them off. They are bitter and contain a toxin. The green compound is called solanine.
5. The grayish hue on the exterior after cooking is caused by a chemical reaction involving iron in the potatoes. Add lemon juice or vinegar to the cooking water to prevent it.

✧ For a thicker stew, use two types of potatoes. Waxy potatoes will hold their shape. Russets will fall apart and thicken the sauce. Use a 3:1 ratio of waxy to russet.

✧ Potatoes can be peeled and left in cold water for a couple of hours, no longer. If they have begun to turn brown, whiten them by adding 1 tbsp (15 mL) skim milk per 1 cup (250 mL) soaking water.

✧ To cure flaccid raw spuds, soak them in ice water for 15 to 30 minutes before peeling them.

✧ Before slicing or dicing a potato, cut a thin strip from one side. You'll have a flat surface to rest it on, so the spud won't roll around.

Better Leftovers

- Redeem a leftover cooked whole potato: Cut the potato in half, brush it with oil and grill it, cut side down, until it is warm. Top it with cheese and place it under the broiler.
- "French fry" soggy, day-old baked spuds: Cut them into 1/4-inch (0.5 cm) slices. Cover the bottom of a large skillet with a thin layer of oil. Heat it on medium until it shimmers. Add the potato slices in a single layer, working in batches. Fry them, turning once, until a golden brown crust forms. Transfer them to paper towels to drain.
- To reheat french fries, refresh them with a quick dip in hot oil in the deep-fryer. You can redeem any limp, soggy potatoes the same way.

✧ Spin-dry raw french fries or cubed potatoes in a salad spinner.

☼♡ Healthier Eater

You can "grease" a baking sheet, griddle or barbecue grate with a piece of cut, raw potato. This will even work on stainless steel.

♲ Waste Not

Save leftover potato cooking liquid for baking or for thickening soups, stews or gravies. The starchiest water comes from russets.

Boiled Potatoes

✧ To cut down on scum in the cooking water, rinse spuds, peeled or unpeeled, before boiling them.

✧ Add just enough water to cover whole potatoes, no more.

Is It Done?

- Drain potatoes when they are easily pierced with a skewer but offer a hint of resistance.
- Potatoes that look shaggy or cracked are overcooked, and no doubt waterlogged and tasteless.

✧ Don't wait until the potatoes cool down. Hot potatoes are easier to peel.

OUTSIDE THE BOX

- Boil whole potatoes in a puddle. Place them in a single layer in a saucepan. Add enough water to come three-quarters of the way up the sides. Bring them to a boil over high heat. Reduce the heat to medium-low. Cover the pan and simmer the potatoes until tender, about 30 minutes.
- Steam potatoes in a single layer over simmering water. This will take about 45 minutes.

✦ Peeling cooked, whole potatoes can be a sticky business. Keep a bowl of cold water beside the cutting board and dip the knife and your hands into it frequently.

✦ Potatoes boiled in their jackets are less watery, have an earthier flavor and retain more nutrients.

Ways to Protect Your Hands

- Wear rubber gloves when peeling a hot potato.
- Spear the potato with a sturdy fork and use that as a holder.

 Lightning Won't Strike If ...

You don't boil potatoes in their jackets. Sometimes we have to give in to the gods of speed and convenience. In that case, we'll peel them, cube them and boil them fast. And save ourselves the awkwardness of playing hot-potato as we struggle with the peels.

✦ To remove rösti potatoes intact from the pan, first slide a long offset spatula around the edges and underneath.

✦ Always finish cooked potatoes by steaming them dry. They'll be fluffier. Two ways to steam potatoes dry:
- Turn off the burner. Return the drained potatoes to the pan and let them sit on the burner for a minute.
- Shake drained potatoes in the hot pan over low heat for a minute.

♥ Healthier Eater

- Most of the nutrients in potatoes are just below the skin. If you're in a hurry, but want to make a concession to healthful eating, cut them into chunks but leave the skins on. And you can make potato salad with unpeeled mini potatoes.
- Flavor boiled potatoes without fat. Cut them into halves, quarters or chunks. Add a spice blend, such as Cajun seasoning, to the cooking water.. Or add garlic cloves, halved lengthwise. One clove garlic per 1 lb (500 g) potatoes should do it.
- Lighten potato salad by using a mixture of light mayonnaise and yogurt for the dressing.

Potato Salad Techniques

- If you're boiling potatoes in their jackets for salad, buy large ones to cut down on peeling time.
- Let potatoes cool before dicing them and they'll hold their shape better. Don't wait too long, though, or they will discolor.
- For better absorption, you can toss potatoes in dressing while they are still warm (unless mayonnaise is involved).

✗ No-No

Don't use cold, leftover boiled potatoes for salad. The dressing won't redeem them.

Mashed Potatoes

Master Plan
Perfect, Simple Mashies

1. Simmer whole potatoes or peeled cubes in salted water until just tender when pierced with a fork. Drain.
2. Turn off the burner. Return the potatoes to the pan. Set them on the burner for a minute, or, for peeled potatoes, until the bottom of the pan is covered by a starchy film.
3. Peel the potatoes, if necessary. Push the hot potatoes through a ricer. To take a shortcut: Cut unpeeled potatoes in half. One at a time, put them into the ricer, skin side up, and press. The flesh goes through; the skin stays behind. Scrape out the skin.
4. Put milk, butter and salt in a microwave-safe cup. Zap it on High just until the butter melts. Be careful; if overheated, the milk curdles.
5. Drizzle the milk mixture over the potatoes a bit at a time as you stir them with a fork.
6. Adjust the salt.

⚛ A Bit of Science

When potatoes are boiled, the starch granules swell. Aggressive mashing breaks the granules, liberates too much starch and turns the potatoes into a gluey paste.

Mashing Tools

- The ricer is ideal. Pushing potatoes through a ricer ruptures fewer starch cells.
- Next best: Some people swear by a food mill. It works in a similar fashion to a ricer, but is more awkward to use.
- If you want to whip the potatoes, use a mixer on low speed.
- A hand-held potato masher makes lumpy mashies unless you really apply the elbow grease — a bad thing. To limit the damage, use an up-and-down motion; don't smush sideways. A flat masher with a grid pattern or holes like the ricer's is better than a zigzag one.

9 Tricks for Perfect Mashed Potatoes

1. Use the right type of potato. Russets are ideal. Moist, waxy potatoes are never a good choice.
2. If you are finicky, try this parboiling technique: Heat potatoes for 20 minutes in water that's below a simmer. Add cold water if the cooking liquid starts to bubble. Drain and let them cool. When you are ready to mash, simmer the potatoes in fresh water until they are tender. Parboiling and cooling firms up the starch. So when you break the granules, the potatoes don't get gummy.
3. Simmer potatoes gently. Vigorous boiling ruptures starch granules.
4. Let drained spuds sit on the burner for a minute to allow excess steam to evaporate. Then they can absorb the milk and butter better.
5. Mash potatoes while they are hot.
6. Mash as gently and briefly as possible. Don't take a long time to mix in the milk and butter.
7. Warm the milk and melt the butter. Never add either cold. Some cooks prefer to add the butter first; this is supposed to coat the grains and make the mashies creamier. Others prefer to add the milk first; this is supposed to make the lightest mashies. However, it's convenient and effective to melt the butter right in the milk.
8. Add the salt to the milk instead of the potatoes. This means less mixing. You can also use salted butter.
9. Use a fork, not a wooden spoon, to stir in the milk, butter and salt.

♔ A Golden Rule

Never use a food processor or hand blender to make mashed potatoes unless you enjoy eating glue.

Fluffy VS. Dense?

Some people like their mashed potatoes fluffy. Some like them dense and creamy.

- For fluffier, whiter mashies, use russet potatoes, mash for a shorter time, add less milk and butter, and stir lightly.
- For denser mashies with a buttery glow, use yellow-fleshed potatoes, mash for a longer time, add more butter, use cream instead of milk, and stir well.
- Can't make up your mind? Mix russets and Yukon golds.

♦ Routes to earthier-tasting mashed potatoes:
- Cook the potatoes whole in the microwave.
- Bake the potatoes (in foil to keep the skin soft).

♦ Microwaved and baked potatoes are drier, so mash the flesh with extra milk and butter. The texture will be coarser.

♡ Healthier Eater

- Use olive oil instead of butter.
- Pass on the butter. Stir in buttermilk or yogurt instead.
- Use skim milk or stock.
- Add creamy evaporated milk, instead of milk and butter.
- Save some of the starchy cooking water. Add some if your mashed potatoes are too stiff and you don't want to add more milk or butter. Or simply add cooking water instead of milk and butter. The potatoes will be fluffy, with a thin flavor.
- Vegans can add soy margarine along with rice milk or soy milk.

Mashed Potato Doctor

Too much liquid was added by accident.

- Add dried potato flakes or granules to the hot potatoes and give them a minute to swell. Never, ever, use this dreadful product as it's intended — to make instant mashed potatoes.

There isn't enough to go around.

- If you didn't guess who was coming to dinner, quickly microwave some baking potatoes, scoop out the flesh, push it through the ricer and add it to your bowl of mashies.

You ran out of potatoes.

- Serve bread or rice.

Gussy It Up

- Boil the potatoes in vegetable or meat stock.
- Instead of using milk, add tang with sour cream or crème fraîche.
- Pour in warmed, thick cream, instead of milk and butter.
- Use browned butter.
- Drizzle mashed potatoes with roasted nut oil.
- Splash in white wine.
- Crumble saffron into the warmed milk, to add a golden hue.
- Add chopped sage to potatoes served with chicken.
- Make horseradish mashies for roast beast. Beat in a spoonful of horseradish. It's a tasty surprise.
- Stir in hummus and garnish with cilantro.
- Stir in peanut butter instead of butter.
- Make mashies garlicky. Stir in mashed roasted garlic. Or chop the cloves from a head of garlic, simmer them in cream until very tender, then strain the cream and stir it into the potatoes. Or boil the potatoes with chopped garlic (or onion).
- Belgian stoemp is a dish that combines mashed potatoes with vegetables such as carrots.
- For colcannon, cooked cabbage is added to mashed potatoes.

- Don't stir in the butter. Create a pond of melted butter in a well in the center of the mashed potatoes. Sprinkle chopped green onions over top, and you've got Irish Champ.
- Eat your veggies. Stir in corn kernels, chopped fennel, braised celeriac or sliced mushrooms. Put caramelized onions on top or stir them in.
- Add sweet potato to boost the flavor, color and nutrients. Use 1 sweet potato (about 1 lb/500 g) per 2 to 3 lbs (1 to 1.5 kg) spuds.
- Get back to your roots. Mix in mashed roasted parsnips, turnips or rutabaga.
- Add Cheddar, blue cheese or goat cheese. Use mascarpone or deli cream cheese instead of butter and milk.
- Enrich mashed potatoes with egg yolks.
- Sprinkle bacon bits on top.
- Make the mashies rustic. If you're not using russets, leave the skins on and mash by hand. Or roast new potatoes in their skins and mash them.

Better Leftovers

Combine flour or bread crumbs and egg with cold mashed potatoes. Form into patties and fry them up as potato pancakes.

✧ For mashed potatoes in advance, make a casserole. Mash potatoes with lots of soft deli cream cheese and sour cream. The mixture must be rich. Put it in a casserole dish, cover and refrigerate. Heat it through in a 375°F (190°C) oven.

✧ The starch in potatoes firms up, or gels, in the fridge. So it's hopeless trying to return mashed potatoes to their former glory. This is especially problematic for cooks who are trying to make as much of a big holiday meal in advance as possible. Two ways to avoid reheating:
- Keep mashed potatoes warm in the top section of a double boiler over simmering water. Pour a thin layer of warm milk or cream over top. Cover the pan with some foil, then the lid. If you don't have a double boiler, set a heatproof bowl over a saucepan.
- Put mashed potatoes in a greased, heatproof serving dish. Cover them with a thin layer of cream. Hold them in a 200°F (100°C) oven. The cream will become thick and golden.

Mashed **VS.** Smashed?

Mashed potatoes are good. Smashed potatoes are better. They are a cross between mashed and roasted potatoes.

Master Plan
Smashed Potatoes

1. Toss about 16 mini potatoes with 1 tbsp (15 mL) oil and salt to taste. A mixture of red and white potatoes is colorful. (You could use regular waxy or yellow potatoes, too.)
2. Roast them in a 400°F (200°C) oven until soft and browned, about 40 minutes.
3. In a large bowl, smash them with fresh basil, chopped garlic, freshly ground black pepper and a goodly amount of olive oil. Use a sturdy fork or whisk and press just until each spud pops open.

Roasted Potatoes

✧ To roast potato wedges, cut a potato into 8 wedges. Toss them with some oil and seasonings. Roast them on a rimmed baking sheet at 425°F (220°C), turning once, for 10 to 15 minutes.

⚡ Fast Fix

Give roast potatoes a head start. Simmer peeled chunks in salted water until they are almost cooked. Drain, then briefly dry them on the burner to evaporate moisture. Arrange them on a rimmed baking sheet, drizzle them with plenty of oil and roast them in a 450°F (230°C) oven until crisp on the outside.

Better Leftovers

Give whole, waxy boiled potatoes a golden brown, crusty exterior. Melt a bit of butter with olive oil in a baking dish. Add the potatoes, turning them to coat. Roast in a 450°F (230°C) oven, uncovered, turning occasionally. Mini potatoes take 30 minutes, regular ones 45 minutes. You can make these from scratch, too.

Roasted Potato Doctor

The potatoes are leathery.

- Next time, use plenty of oil.
- Potatoes roasted alongside meat tend to get leathery. First, parboil them for 5 minutes or steam them until partially tender. Alternatively, you can put them in the oven after the meat has been cooking for a while, or remove them early.

The potatoes are soggy.

- Roast them in a very hot oven, for a crispy crust and a tender interior.
- Before roasting, scratch ridges on the surface of the potatoes so oil can penetrate and make them crispier.
- Crisp them up in a dry skillet over high heat.

Baked Potatoes

✧ Pierce the skin of a baking potato with a fork to let steam escape.

✧ Bake directly on the rack in the center of the oven.

✧ Draw moisture out of baking potatoes by laying them on a bed of rock salt during cooking.

✧ Play with baking times to suit your schedule and complement whatever else is in the oven. Three possibilities:
- 40 to 50 minutes at 425°F (220°C)
- 50 to 60 minutes at 375°F (190°C)
- 75 to 85 minutes at 325°F (160°C)

✧ The higher the temperature, the crustier the skin.

6 Ways to Speed Up a Baked Potato

1. Poke a metal skewer through it. This can halve the baking time. It also releases steam, making the potato fluffier.
2. Cut the potato in half. On the cut surface of each half, make 4 diagonal cuts about 1/2 inch (1 cm) deep, then 3 cuts to form a grid. Drizzle oil into a baking dish just large enough to hold the pieces. Liberally sprinkle salt and pepper into the oil. Place the potatoes in the dish, cut side down. Slide them around to coat them. Bake at 400°F (200°C) until tender (about 40 minutes, depending on size and shape).
3. Wrap a potato in foil to bake it partway. Unwrap it to finish baking. Don't keep potatoes in foil for the entire baking time; that steams them.
4. Kick-start a potato in the microwave. Prick holes in it and microwave it for 3 minutes on High. Finish it in a 425°F (220°C) oven for 30 to 45 minutes, depending on size.
5. "Bake" it in the microwave. Pierce the potato. Wrap it in a paper towel. Turn it halfway through cooking. If you're making more than one, choose similar shapes and sizes, and arrange them on the turntable in a spoke pattern, pointing the narrower ends toward the center. Times on High for medium potatoes: 4 to 6 minutes for 1 potato, 6 to 8 minutes for 2 potatoes, 8 to 12 minutes for 3 potatoes.
6. Set one or more spuds on end in a muffin tin. Bake.

Is It Done?

✧ Squeeze the baked potato with tongs. It should yield.

✧ Cut an X in the top of a baked potato rather than a slit. When it's done, squeeze the top and bottom of the X toward the center to push out the flesh.

✧ Pierce a whole potato with a skewer before microwaving it. Otherwise, it may explode.

Master Plan
Potato Skins

1. Wrap a pierced, large potato in a paper towel. Microwave on High until it is just soft.
2. Slice the potato in half. Scoop out the flesh.
3. Stir the flesh with your stuffing tidbits, plus butter and milk.
4. Stuff the filling into the shells.
5. Bake them at 400°F (200°C) until heated through.
6. Serve them topped with dollops of sour cream.

French Fries

☼ A Bit of Science

When potatoes are fried, water is pulled from the interior while starch on the exterior expands and dries the surface. The surface develops a crusty seal that prevents it from absorbing fat. The goal is a thin, brittle, golden brown crust and creamy, soft, hot interior.

Cutting Options

● For standard fries, cut ³⁄₈-inch (0.75 cm) sticks.
● For crispy frites, cut ¼-inch (0.5 cm) sticks.
● Avoid wedges; they cook unevenly.
● Use a mandolin to make crinkle cuts.
● French-fry techniques also work with small potato balls.

✧ Some french-fry fans go through elaborate preparations involving hours of soaking, tinkering with the oil and precise timing. But simplicity works fine.

Master Plan
Perfect Simple Fries

1. Use large russets. The starchy texture and sub shape are ideal.
2. Cut ¼- to ³⁄₈-inch (0.5 to 0.75 cm) sticks. Uniform pieces are a must. If necessary, pull out the dreaded mandolin. If you don't have one, cut each potato into a block, then slice it into sticks. It's better to peel the potatoes; the skin gets leathery in hot oil.
3. Blanch the potatoes in boiling water or soak them in cold water.
4. Drain and dry well. To do so, wrap the potato sticks in a kitchen towel.
5. Heat the oil to 300°F (150°C). Fry the sticks for 3 to 5 minutes or until they are tender when poked with a skewer, the color is still blond, but the ends are beginning to brown. Shake the basket or pan if you see any clumping.
6. Drain the fries on paper towels layered several sheets thick. Let them cool for at least an hour. Or wrap them in paper towels, seal them in a zip-lock bag and freeze them. (Do not thaw them before frying again; just increase the time.)
7. Just before you want to eat, heat the oil to 375°F (190°C) and fry them for 3 to 4 minutes or until golden brown. Do not overbrown them or they will be bitter.
8. Drain them on a rack set over paper towels, not directly on the towels. Pat the tops dry with a paper towel.
9. Salt the fries immediately, while they are glistening, so the salt will stick. For spicy fries, sprinkle with a seasoning blend such as Tex-Mex.
10. Serve the fries hot, with ketchup or flavored mayonnaise.

Top French-Fry Secrets
Get rid of surface starch.

- Soak raw potato sticks in cold running water, swishing occasionally, until it runs clear. This is simple and effective.
- Another option: Blanch raw potato sticks in boiling water for 1 minute, then drain. Blanching creates fast food–style fries that remain crisper when cooled.
- Dry the spuds well. If the starch granules suck up water clinging to the surface, they won't dry and seal the potatoes, and thus the fries will suck up grease.

Fry in two stages.

- The stages are sometimes called par-fry and shock-fry.
- Potatoes are par-fried to evaporate water and cooked until just tender.
- They are shock-fried to make them crisp and golden.
- Extending the frying job into two stages sounds like a pain, but it actually makes life easier. You can leave par-fried potatoes lying around or grab some from the freezer, then finish them in minutes and serve them hot.

Let them rest.

- Let the potatoes cool after you par-fry. French-fry fans swear by different amounts of time, from 20 minutes to 24 hours.
- Par-fried potatoes can stay on the counter or go in the fridge or freezer.
- Frozen french fries turn out the least greasy, though they spit and bubble furiously when returned to the oil.

Fry in small batches.

- Dunking too many potatoes at once drops the temperature of the hot oil — and fries get soggy.
- Use twice as much oil as potatoes to avoid overcrowding in the pan or deep-fryer.

Embellishments

- To give french fries a crispy coating, you can dust them with cornstarch. Soak the raw potato sticks in cold water. Pat them dry. Toss them with cornstarch, then transfer them to a wire rack and let stand for 20 minutes to develop a thin film. The resulting fries are very crispy. The cornstarch sucks up some of the surface moisture and forms a protective coating. Use about 1 tbsp (15 mL) cornstarch per 1 lb (500 g) potato sticks.
- For browner fries, refrigerate whole potatoes for up to 2 hours before cutting and frying them. Par-fry at 350°F (180°C) or shock-fry at 400°F (200°C). Chilling brings out sugars that caramelize on the surface. But the crust may also become leathery.

- ✧ Use corn or peanut oil. Lard and shortening used to be favorites, but people don't want to use them anymore. Some cooks embellish by adding bacon grease to the oil.

- ✧ To transfer potatoes quickly into the hot oil with less splashing, pour them from a paper bag.

- ✧ Once out of the hot oil, fries contract and suck up some of the oil on their surfaces. Immediately drain them on a rack and blot them with a paper towel.

Warming Tips

- Keep french fries or home fries warm on a rack set on a rimmed baking sheet in a 200°F (100°C) oven.
- Never cover french fries to keep them warm. They'll get flabby and sad.

Alternatives to a Deep-Fryer

- Use a deep pot and a large sieve or skimmer with a long handle. The pan should have at least 4 inches (10 cm) of clearance above the oil. It bubbles up when you add the potatoes.
- Use a large electric skillet. The heating control is ideal.
- Use a large cast-iron skillet. It holds heat evenly. But is it deep enough?

◆ For best results, check oil temperatures with a deep-fry or instant-read thermometer.

◆ Other signs that the oil is hot enough:
- Toss in a potato stick. For par-frying, it should sink to the bottom of the pot, become surrounded by bubbles, then bob to the surface within 15 to 20 seconds.
- For shock-frying, it should be surrounded by rapidly dancing bubbles and bob to the surface within 2 seconds.

◆ If you don't want to make two-stage fries, you can still get good results. For super-crispy, single-stage fries, the ¼-inch (0.5 cm) sticks are a good choice.

Master Plan
Crunchy One-Stage Fries

1. Cut a large russet potato into ¼-inch (0.5 cm) sticks. Rinse them in cold water. Dry them well.
2. Put the potato sticks in a deep 10-inch (25 cm) skillet or sauté pan. Add 1¼ cups (300 mL) vegetable oil. They should be almost covered by oil and almost in a single layer.
3. Heat the pan over medium heat until the spuds develop a pale blond crust, about 20 minutes. Carefully shake the pan during the first 5 minutes to break up any clumps, then do not disturb them for the next 10 minutes while they are limp and breakable.

4. Increase the heat to medium-high. Move the potatoes around constantly with a metal spatula for the next 5 minutes or until they are golden brown.
5. Drain, salt and enjoy.

Master Plan
Commercial-Style One-Stage Fries

1. In a large bowl or tub, soak potato sticks in cold water for a couple of hours. Or swish them in cold running water until the water runs clear, about half an hour. Drain them.
2. Soak the sticks in a solution of 1 tbsp (15 mL) granulated sugar per 1 cup (250 mL) cold water for 15 minutes. Drain and dry well.
3. Heat oil to 375°F (190°C), then add sticks and fry them for 8 to 10 minutes or until they are tender and a gorgeous golden yellow.

Master Plan
Greek Fries

1. Cut potatoes into ½- to ¾-inch (1 to 2 cm) sticks. Rinse, drain and pat dry.
2. Into a large skillet, pour olive oil to 1-inch (2.5 cm) depth. Heat it over medium heat until it is shimmery.
3. Reduce the heat to low. Working in batches, add a single layer of sticks and fry, covered, until they start to turn golden. Remove the lid. Increase the heat to high. Fry, turning frequently, for about 5 minutes or until they are golden brown.
4. Drain the potatoes. Place them on a serving platter. Sprinkle them with salt, dried oregano and crumbled kefalotyri cheese. Ignore recipes that tell you to drizzle lemon juice on top. This will make the fries soggy.

Master Plan
Perfect Home Fries

1. Cut unpeeled potatoes into ½-inch (1 cm) cubes.
2. Boil them for 5 minutes or until they are almost tender. Drain them well.

3. Spread them on a rimmed baking sheet and let cool to room temperature.

4. Choose a cast-iron or stainless-steel skillet that will accommodate them in a single, uncrowded layer (don't use a nonstick skillet).

5. Heat a generous amount of oil over medium-high heat until it is shimmery.

6. Add the potatoes and fry until they are crusty and brown, but not mushy. Use a small spatula to toss and turn the potatoes without crushing them.

7. Drain them on paper towels.

Master Plan
Great Oven Fries

1. Cut a russet potato into 10 to 12 wedges. Leave on the skin, if desired.

2. For speed, soak the wedges in warm water until it becomes cloudy with starch. For a thinner crust on the fries, soak the wedges for 1 hour in cold water, or rinse them under cold running water until it runs clear. Dry them well.

3. Alas, the best oven fries are not diet fries. Toss the wedges with salt, freshly ground black pepper and enough oil to coat them — at least 1/4 cup (50 mL) — or they'll be leathery. Spread them out on a rimmed baking sheet.

4. Cover them with foil. Bake them on the lowest rack in a 475°F (240°C) oven for 5 minutes.

5. Remove the foil. Roast the potatoes until the bottoms are golden brown and spots appear on the tops, 15 to 20 minutes.

6. Turn the wedges. Rotate the pan. Bake the wedges until they are crisp and uniformly brown, 10 to 15 minutes.

7. Drain them on paper towels. Sprinkle them with more salt and pepper. Or boost the flavor with Tex-Mex spice blend, garlic salt or curry powder. Do not add such seasonings during baking. They will scorch.

✧ If you use a small amount of oil for oven fries, sprinkle salt and pepper over the baking sheet to reduce sticking.

☀ Healthier Eater

You can make crispy McDonald's-style fries in the oven.

1. Cut a peeled large russet potato into 1/4-inch (0.5 cm) sticks. Measure out 8 oz (250 g) and set the rest aside for other uses.

2. Blanch the sticks in boiling water for about 2 minutes. Drain, then let them cool for 5 minutes.

3. Toss the sticks with 1 tsp (5 mL) vegetable oil and salt to taste. Place them on a rimmed baking sheet in a single layer, not touching.

4. Roast them at 400°F (200°C), turning them halfway through, for 20 to 25 minutes or until crisp and golden brown.

5. Sprinkle them with more salt, if desired.

Pumpkins

♻ Waste Not

• Cute little pie pumpkins are best for cooking. However, you needn't throw out the trimmings from the Halloween pumpkin. Cook them.

• Don't throw out large seeds from the jack-o'-lantern. Wash them, spread them out to dry on a rimmed baking sheet and leave them overnight. Toss them with oil, then roast in a 250°F (120°C) oven until golden. Sprinkle with salt.

• You can toast the seeds of any squash. Soft, tender seeds from acorn squash and its brethren can be eaten whole. Unlike pumpkin seeds, they require no shelling. To toast them quickly, toss them with oil on a rimmed baking sheet (turning with a spatula) and roast them at 400°F (200°C) for 5 minutes.

✧ Before cooking pumpkin, scrape out the seeds and fibers.

✧ Grate pumpkin for fast, even cooking. Peel it. Cut it into eighths. Shred pieces in a food processor or against the large holes of a box grater.

✧ Use cooked pumpkin in salads or as a side dish.

Master Plan
Homemade Pumpkin Purée

1. Steam, boil or, for more intense flavor, roast pumpkin until it is very soft but not mushy.
2. Peel it. Push the flesh through a ricer or food mill, or pulse it in the food processor.
3. Freeze it in portions for use in pies. Or flavor it with butter and spices and serve it hot, as a side dish.
4. One lb (500 g) flesh yields about 1 cup (250 mL) purée.

✧ Homemade pumpkin purée can be frozen. Thaw it before using.

✧ Homemade pumpkin purée is more watery than the canned kind. Drain it in a sieve for half an hour before using it. Even then, you may have to adjust your recipe.

ⓟ is for Pepitas

Hulled pumpkin seeds are called pepitas. You can buy them in bulk food and health food stores.

Rapini

♲ Waste Not

When cooking rapini, don't discard the stems.

✧ To cook rapini more evenly, split the stems with a sharp knife. Split thicker ones several times.

Sea Vegetables

✧ Sea vegetables sound more appetizing than seaweed. Seaweed is algae, not plants or weeds. Seaweed is divided by color: Greens grow along the shore, browns at mid-depth, reds in the deepest water. Although most North Americans are repelled by seaweed, it is fabulously nutritious and a natural source of savory glutamates that whet the appetite. Nori, dulse, kombu, wakame, arame, hijiki and Irish moss are among the best-known sea vegetables.

✧ Harvesting your own seaweed is a cottage industry in some small seaside towns. Never use specimens washed up on shore. The smell should warn you — they are rotting.

✧ Dried seaweed, with its high salt and mineral content, can be pulverized and used as a seasoning.

Ⓝ is for Nori

Sushi has made nori famous. Also known as laver, nori is prepared from *Porphyra*, a red algae. Processed nori is dried and pressed into papery sheets, then usually toasted or roasted. It is a dark, purplish green.

✧ Nori has to be toasted for sushi.

✧ You can snip nori into strips for a garnish, or crumble and stir it into cooked foods.

Ⓘ is for Irish Moss

A jelly extracted from Irish moss is the basis for carrageenan, a widespread commercial thickener that emulsifies and mimics fat in low-fat products and gelatin in jelly desserts. It's used in ice cream. Do-it-yourselfers put it in anything from chowder to cream pie. Irish moss gives food a texture reminiscent of processed foods and a faint whiff of seaweed.

✧ To use it as a thickener, substitute Irish moss jelly for some of the liquid in your recipe.

Calculations

- ¼ oz (7 g) dried Irish moss is about ¼ cup (50 mL).
- The jelly from ¼ to ½ oz (7 to 14 g) Irish moss will set about 4 cups (1 L) liquid, depending on the thickness of the liquid. Note: Acidic ingredients thin out the jelly.
- ¼ cup (50 mL) Irish moss boiled with 1 cup (250 mL) water yields about ⅓ cup (75 mL) jelly.

Master Plan
Irish Moss Jelly

1. Soak dried Irish moss in cold water for 15 minutes. Drain it.
2. Put the moss in a saucepan with fresh water. Bring it to a boil over high heat, then reduce the heat to medium-low and simmer until the liquid thickens and the moss looks molten. This can take 5 to 15 minutes, depending on the amounts.
3. Strain the moss through a sieve, pressing and stirring the solids to extract the jelly. Discard the solids.

✧ Health food stores sell Irish moss, usually dried but sometimes powdered.

Squash

Winter VS. Summer?

Summer squash are immature, with soft skin and a short shelf life. They are well represented by the zucchini. Winter squash, such as acorn, butternut and hubbard, are mature, with thick, tough skin and seeds, and survive long storage. There are many types, some looking like they arrived from outer space.

Two Good Signs

- It's heavy. The weight comes from moisture. Old ones are dried up.
- There are no moist patches on the skin. These are a sign of internal decay.

✦ Don't refrigerate winter squashes. They find temperatures below 50°F (10°C) inhospitable. Store them in a cool, dry place, like the basement, for several months. Exception: Store cut squash in the fridge. Wrap it tightly in plastic.

✦ Cutting and skinning hard, unyielding squash is a recipe for scary accidents. Cut a sliver off the bottom first, to balance it.

Techniques for Cutting Tough Squash

- Insert the knife, then rap the squash against the cutting board or hit the knife with a rubber mallet. Don't try to force the knife in all at once.
- Don't cut it. Drop it onto a hard surface, such as a stone patio, so it shatters.

✦ Microwave a large piece of squash for 5 minutes on Defrost, to make it easier to peel and dice. Use a vegetable peeler.

✦ You can save trouble by peeling squash after cooking it. Keep it whole or cut it. Remove the seeds and fiber. Then boil, steam or bake it. Scoop the pulp from the rind. Mash or purée it.

♡ Healthier Eater

Replace pasta with spaghetti squash. When it's cooked, use a fork to pull out the strands of flesh. It's easiest to microwave. Prick it with a knife, microwave it on High for 5 or 6 minutes per 1 lb (500 g), then let it stand for 5 minutes before cutting.

✦ Smaller squash are less bitter, more tender.

✦ Wash the rind of a winter squash before cutting or cooking it.

3 Ways to Cook Squash with the Rind

1. Simmer or steam chunks until they are tender.
2. Place chunks in a baking dish with a bit of water, cover and bake at 325°F (160°C) until tender. Or place halves cut side down in a baking dish filled with $\frac{1}{4}$ to $\frac{1}{2}$ inch (0.5 to 1 cm) of water. Bake them at 375°F (190°C) until tender and easy to peel.
3. Pierce a whole squash all over with a fork or metal skewer. Bake it at 350°F (180°C) until it softens.

Sunchokes

✦ Although they are known as Jerusalem artichokes, these tubers have nothing to do with Jerusalem or artichokes. Sunchokes are related to sunflowers. They have brown skin and are knobby, like ginger.

Five Bad Signs

- Soft flesh.
- Wrinkles.
- Bruises.
- Green spots.
- Sprouts.

✦ Sunchokes can be eaten raw or boiled, like potatoes, until tender-firm.

✦ You can peel them or simply scrub them. Blanching will make them easier to peel.

F is for Fartichoke

The sunchoke is fearfully described as the "fartichoke" for its ability to produce flatulence so intense that you couldn't pay some people to eat it. On the plus side, sunchokes are full of beneficial fiber.

✧ How to reduce the sunchoke's gas production:
- If you grow your own, harvest them after the frost has killed the tops.
- Keep them in cold storage for 1 month.
- In an unscientific test, sunchokes long-simmered for soup caused the least gas. Roasted sunchokes caused the most. Blanched, firm sunchokes were in between.
- Take Beano — a lot of it — before eating sunchokes.

Sweet Potatoes

Sweet Potato VS. Yam?

The two aren't related except in the minds of people who use the terms interchangeably. The yam is a tropical tuber that can grow several feet long. Its flesh is off-white to purple, and starchier than that of the sweet potato. Its bark-like skin is white to dark brown. It must be peeled, since the skin contains crystals that irritate the digestive system.

The confusion seems to have originated when deep orange sweet potatoes were dubbed yams to set them apart from cousins with pale yellow flesh. The orange sweet potato is the most common, although there is a type with purple flesh.

B is for Boniato

Pale sweet potatoes, set apart by the name boniato, have thinner yellow skin and yellow flesh, are not as sweet, and are fluffier when cooked, somewhat like baked potatoes, with a chestnut accent.

A Good Sign

A wrinkle-free skin.

✧ Store sweet potatoes in a dry, dark place, ideally at 55°F (13°C). Do not refrigerate them.

✧ Handle sweet potatoes carefully to prevent bruising. They are not as rough and tough as they look.

✧ Anything you'd do to a potato, you can do to a sweet potato.

✧ The skin is leathery when baked. Rub the sweet potato with oil to soften the skin beforehand. Or wrap it in foil.

Is It Done?
- Squeeze the sweet potato with tongs. It should yield.

✧ You can cut off a piece of sweet potato and it will scab over with a new, rough surface. Leave it that way until you are ready to cook it. (This works for potatoes, too.)

Gussy It Up

Drizzle sweet potatoes with maple syrup.

Tomatoes

Four Good Signs
- The color is an even, bright red. It's ripe.
- The flesh yields slightly when pressed.
- The stems are green, not shriveled or browned.
- The tomato has a garden aroma at the stem end. Smelling helps with heirloom tomatoes that are green, yellow, zebra-striped — anything but red.

- Buy tomatoes at different stages of ripeness. They go from firm green, to green with streaks of red, to red with patches of green, to red. Some varieties ripen from the bottom to the top, so green at the top is okay. They will ripen on the counter or in a fruit bowl.

- Tomatoes need light and warmth to ripen. To slow down ripening, set them upside down, at room temperature, out of direct sunlight.

✗ No-No

Never refrigerate tomatoes. They get mealy. Keep them at room temperature.

- Optimal storage temperatures are 55°F to 60°F (13°C to 16°C) for ripe tomatoes, 57°F to 68°F (14°C to 20°C) for unripe tomatoes.

- Leave the stem on. Air enters and moisture escapes from the stem end. Also, the scar is an invitation to mold and bacteria. Store tomatoes scar side down.

- The "shoulders" are the softest part and bruise the most easily. Don't stack tomatoes in piles.

- To firm up soft, overripe tomatoes, immerse them in a bowl of ice water in the fridge for an hour.

- While scorching or peeling a tomato, stick a fork in the stem end and use it as a holder.

- Three ways to blanch a load of tomatoes:
  - Tie them first in a large piece of cheesecloth.
  - Put them in a basket or sieve. Plunge them into boiling water.
  - Use a pasta pot with an insert.

5 Ways to Skin a Tomato

1. Use a serrated peeler.
2. Cut a small X into the base. Plunge the tomato into boiling water for 15 to 30 seconds. (Longer times cook part of the tomato and you'll end up ripping off part of the flesh along with the skin.) Drain. Plunge the tomato into icy water or spray it. Pull off the skin in strips.
3. Put the tomato in a bowl and cover it with boiling water. Microwave it on High for 15 to 20 seconds. Plunge it into icy water. Peel it. Do this one tomato at a time.
4. Hold the tomato over a gas flame or blister the skin with a kitchen torch. When the skin turns yellowish and dull, dunk the tomato in icy water. Peel it.
5. Roast the tomato at 400°F (200°C) until the skin splits, about 10 minutes. You can slice off the stem end and set the tomato on a rack before roasting it.

Factoid Most of the tomato's flavor is in the seeds and the jellied pulp that surrounds them. It pays to keep the juices after seeding a tomato.

- To make cut tomatoes less juicy, toss them with salt, let them stand for half an hour in the bowl of a salad spinner, then spin. Pour off the juices.

✪ Waste Not

- You can use tomato juices in marinades or as a substitute for lemon juice. To concentrate the juices, strain them and reduce them in a small saucepan on the stove.
- If your tomatoes are too wet, you can reduce the juices and return them to your dish along with the flesh, instead of discarding them.
- Seeds are okay in sauces. You don't have to get rid of them.

✧ For less soggy sandwiches, blot a slice of tomato on a paper towel before adding it to the filling.

3 Ways to Seed a Tomato

1. Best: Halve the tomato at the equator. Use your thumb to gouge out pockets of seeds.
2. Core and cut the tomato lengthwise into 4 wedges. With a grapefruit spoon, scrape the pulp from each wedge. Use your thumb to rub off any leftover seeds.
3. Squeezing is a popular method, although it mangles the poor tomato. Instead of cutting it at the equator, you can slice off the stem end and squeeze the tomato.

✧ When coring tomatoes, cut out and discard a cone-shaped plug from the "navel" at the stem end.

✧ Tomatoes sliced from the north to south poles stay firmer than ones sliced at the equators.

5 Ways to Crush or Purée Tomatoes

1. For quick puréed tomatoes, toss chunks, skin, seeds and all, into a blender or food processor. Pulse only. If you see foam, you've gone too far. Too watery? Strain it.
2. Use a ricer to purée canned or fresh peeled ripe tomatoes. Use the larger holes for the fresh ones, if you have the option.
3. Indian matrons associated with the film *Bend It Like Beckham* had it going on when they insisted that canned tomatoes be grated against the large holes of a box grater. This produces a better texture than a machine.
4. You can coarsely crush tomatoes with a pastry blender.
5. The easiest way to "chop" canned tomatoes: Scoop each tomato from the can, then squash it by hand as you add it to the pot.

How to Make a Tomato Cup

1. Cut a thin slice off the base, so the tomato sits level and stable.
2. Cut off the top quarter. Scoop out the pulp with a grapefruit knife. Scrape the shell out gently with a grapefruit spoon. Leave the walls $\frac{1}{4}$ to $\frac{1}{2}$ inch (0.5 to 1 cm) thick.
3. Lightly salt the cavity.
4. Set the tomato upside down on a rack and let it drain for 15 minutes. It will hold its shape better.

♡ Healthier Eater

Fill a tomato cup with tuna salad or healthy grains.

My Gazpacho

This is so refreshing when local tomatoes are at their peak. **Makes about 10 cups (2.5 L), or 8 to 10 servings**

Tips

I use V8 for the vegetable cocktail.

You can substitute 1 tsp (5 mL) dried tarragon for the fresh.

2½ to 3 lbs	ripe tomatoes, peeled and coarsely chopped	1.25 to 1.5 kg
2	cloves garlic, coarsely chopped	2
1½	large cucumbers (about 1½ lbs/750 g), peeled, seeded and cut into ¼- to ½-inch (0.5 to 1 cm) dice, divided	1½
1	jalapeño pepper, seeded, deveined if desired and coarsely chopped	1
1 cup	coarsely chopped red onion	250 mL
2 to 3 cups	vegetable cocktail	500 to 750 mL
½ cup	red or white wine	125 mL
¼ cup	red wine vinegar	50 mL
2 tbsp	chopped fresh parsley	25 mL
1 tbsp	chopped fresh tarragon	15 mL
2 tbsp	extra virgin olive oil	25 mL
1 tsp	sea salt	5 mL
½ tsp	freshly ground black pepper	2 mL
3 dashes	Worcestershire sauce	3 dashes
1	small green or yellow bell pepper, cut into ¼-inch (0.5 cm) dice	1
	Hot pepper sauce	

1. In a large bowl, combine tomatoes, garlic, two-thirds of the cucumbers, jalapeño and red onion. Stir in 2 cups (500 mL) of the vegetable cocktail. Let stand for at least 2 hours or cover and refrigerate overnight.

2. Drain juices and reserve. Purée the solids in a blender. Return them to the bowl. Add the reserved juices. Add wine, vinegar, parsley, tarragon, oil, salt, pepper and Worcestershire sauce. Stir in bell pepper and the remaining cucumber.

3. Cover and refrigerate for at least 2 hours or overnight. Add some or all of the remaining vegetable cocktail to adjust the consistency. Add hot pepper sauce to taste. Adjust the salt.

Tips for Baking Stuffed Tomatoes

- Bake them in muffin tins to help them hold their shape.
- Chill the tomato cups in the fridge beforehand, so they don't end up too mushy.

- ❖ Roast tomatoes (and other wet veggies) on a rack set over a lined rimmed baking sheet.

Gussy It Up

- Smear pesto on sliced tomatoes. Sprinkle them with grated Parmesan. Broil.
- Barbecue tomatoes. Cut them at the equator or thickly slice them. Brush them lightly with garlic oil. Grill them cut side down. Sprinkle them with herbs and grated Parmesan before serving.

- ❖ It's easier to empty a can of tomato paste if you cut the lid off at both ends.

Making Do

If you don't have canned tomato juice for cooking, thin some tomato paste with water.

Red VS. Green Tomatoes?

Green tomatoes are unripened, garden-variety tomatoes, not a special breed. Tomatoes ripen from the inside out, so green ones may have pink centers. Green tomatoes are prized for their tart flavor.

Ripening Tips for Green-Tomato Lovers

- Immature green tomatoes will never ripen. Mature ones have a slightly yellowish tinge or pink blush, and have developed a gelatinous interior.
- If they are mature, green tomatoes will transition to red, so use them immediately.
- Keep ripening tomatoes away from green ones; there's a ripening chain reaction.

- Hours of warmth, not sunlight, ripen green tomatoes. If you don't want them to ripen, store them in a cool location, but not a cold one.
- If you want your green tomatoes to ripen, put them in a jar or bag with a banana or an apple. Keep it in a warm spot, but out of the sunlight. Or arrange the tomatoes close to each other in a single layer in a cardboard box.
- You can uproot the whole plant and hang it upside down.
- Pick green tomatoes before the frost sets in.

- ❖ Before frying green tomatoes, soak the slices in cold water for 5 minutes. To counter tartness, add sugar to the coating, about 2 tbsp (25 mL) per 1 cup (250 mL) flour and cornmeal mixture.

♡ Healthier Eater

Green tomatoes don't have to be fried.
- They are firm, so they grill nicely.
- They can be chopped to add tang to a salad.
- Make them into pickles.
- Put them on pizza.

- ❖ Make your own marinated sun-dried tomatoes:
  - In a heatproof bowl, plump dried tomatoes by pouring in enough boiling water to cover them and soak for 15 minutes. Drain well.
  - Place in an airtight tub or jar. Add 5 parts olive oil and 1 part white wine vinegar.
  - Refrigerate, making sure the tomatoes are always covered in oil. These keep for months.

- ❖ For a kick, add sun-dried tomatoes to fresh or frozen tomatoes that will be cooked and puréed for a creamy soup or sauce.

Turnips and Rutabaga

Turnip VS. Rutabaga?

The two are often confused, though they don't look alike. Rutabagas are thought to be a cross between a cabbage and a turnip. Sometimes, they're called swedes or neeps. The rutabaga's usually yellow flesh is denser and creamier in texture than that of its smaller relative, the turnip. Turnips have white skin with a purple blush. They are not waxed. Rutabagas are heavily waxed. Both are bittersweet.

✧ Store turnips and rutabagas in a cool, dry spot, or in the fridge. A waxed rutabaga will keep for a couple of months.

OUTSIDE THE BOX

- You can eat turnips raw or shredded — the younger and smaller, the better.
- There's no need to peel small or medium turnips.

✧ Select turnips that feel heavy. Old, bitter ones are spongy.

Three Good Signs

- Smooth surface.
- Bright cream and purple hues, not faded.
- Smaller size (larger ones have woody cores).

♲ Waste Not

Don't throw away turnip greens. They can be sautéed or used in soups and stews.

✧ Rutabagas are hard to peel. First slice off the top, then cut the rutabaga into pieces, then peel. It's easier to peel a rutabaga with a Y-shaped peeler.

✧ Rutabagas can be mashed like potatoes.

Water Chestnuts

✧ Canned water chestnuts will keep for several weeks after being opened if you put them in a tub and cover them with cold water. Change the water every day or so.

Yuca

✧ Yuca is a starchy tuber that's also known as cassava, manioc or tapioca root. The flesh contains an acid that decomposes into cyanide, in low levels. Heating destroys the problem.

Master Plan
Boiled Yuca

1. Cut peeled yuca into 3-inch (7.5 cm) segments. Put them in a saucepan and cover them with cold water. Add 1 tsp (5 mL) lemon juice, to bleach them, and ½ tsp (2 mL) salt.
2. Bring the water to a boil over medium-high heat. Reduce the heat to medium-low, cover and simmer until cracks appear in the centers of the segments, about 15 minutes.
3. Add 1 cup (250 mL) cold water. This tenderizes the pieces of yuca.
4. Increase the heat to medium-high and return the water to a boil. Reduce the heat to medium-low, cover and simmer for 5 to 10 minutes or until the centers start to split and the flesh is tender, but not mushy. Remove the smaller pieces as they are done.
5. Drain. Pull off and discard the layers on the surface that look like parchment.
6. Cut each segment in half lengthwise. Pull out and discard the stringy, fibrous cores.
7. Cut the flesh into 1-inch (2.5 cm) chunks or mash it.

✤ Yuca should be firm and shiny. Use it within a couple of days. Aged yuca will surprise and disgust you with rotten, mushy patches lurking beneath the skin.

✤ Yuca's thick brown skin looks like bark. Underneath the skin is a pink layer that must also be peeled off.

Zucchini

Two Good Signs

- The skin is smooth and thin. You should be able to easily scrape it off with a fingernail. Pitting is a sign of old age.
- It's small. Those monsters left in the garden are bitter and watery. Choose zucchini that's less than 6 inches (15 cm) long.

♛ A Golden Rule

Always extract water from zucchini before cooking it.

Factoid Zucchini is the moistest vegetable — about 95% water. When cooked, it gets waterlogged in its own juices.

✤ Some fanatical cooks insist on always removing the seeds and core. This should be optional with smaller zucchini, but it does help with large ones.

11 Ways to Prevent a Soggy Mess

1. Slice zucchini into ultra-thin circles or matchsticks or, better still, shred it. The thinner and smaller the pieces, the better and faster they drain.

2. Put cut zucchini in a strainer, toss it liberally with salt and let it drain. Drain slices for 30 minutes or shreds for 5 minutes.

3. Press the zucchini dry using paper towels or wring it in a kitchen towel to squeeze out liquid.

4. Toss zucchini with olive oil before sautéing it. Shreds tossed with oil don't clump as much.

5. Cook zucchini over medium-high heat with plenty of oil.

6. Cook zucchini in batches, arranging it in a single layer to allow moisture to evaporate quickly.

7. Let zucchini brown on the bottom before flipping it.

8. Don't stir zucchini with a wooden spoon. Flip and toss it with a spatula.

9. You could use a grill pan to let the water run off.

10. Grill zucchini. Cut it in half lengthwise. Brush it with oil and sprinkle it with a spice blend. Grill it, oiled side down, over medium heat until it is tender but not limp, and charred with grill marks.

11. If using zucchini in a casserole, always sauté or grill it first.

Herbs

◆ When cooking, add herbs in stages. Add dried or woodier herbs at the beginning of the cooking time. Add fresh herbs during the last 15 minutes.

◆ To wash herbs, hold them by their stems and swish them in cold water. Dry them in a salad spinner or blot with paper towels.

◆ Make sure herbs are completely dry before chopping them. You don't want a paste.

◆ Herbs can be softened by scalding them. Put them in a colander, then pour boiling water over top. Drain. Squeeze them dry in a paper towel.

◆ No need to laboriously strip the leaves from herbs such as cilantro, parsley, oregano or mint. You can mince them tender stems and all.

◆ Use only the leaves of thyme, rosemary, tarragon and basil.

◆ Tear off herb sprigs or leaves just before using them.

How to Pluck Leaves

1. Pull backward along the stalk with your thumb and index finger.
2. For parsley and cilantro, in particular, run a fork up along the stalk, with your thumb helping. Comb through the stalk with the fork.

◆ For better traction, sprinkle salt over herbs, such as mint or basil, before chopping them.

Ways to Store Herbs

• They survive best in an herb vase, makeshift or commercial, with 1 inch (2.5 cm) of water in the base and a plastic covering. The herbs will last for several weeks, rather than days, in a vase in the fridge.
• Tie a damp paper towel around the root ends and place the herbs in an unsealed plastic bag in the crisper.

4 Keys to Using an Herb Vase

1. Trim about ¼ inch (0.5 cm) from the stem ends, just like you'd trim fresh flowers, before putting them in the vase. Exception: herbs, such as cilantro, sold with roots intact.
2. Do not submerge leaves. The vase will get swampy. Pluck leaves close to the bottom.
3. Change the water every couple of days.
4. Keep herb vases on a shelf in the fridge door. There's less chance of spillage and the herbs won't be shocked by the cold walls of the fridge.

 No-No

Leaving herbs in vases at room temperature is useless.

Types of Commercial Herb Vases

- A simpler vase works best: This type has a short base and ring above it to support the stems. Cover the top with a plastic produce bag from the supermarket and loosely tie it at the base.
- Sealed plastic tubs are less successful, but still work well. One variety is a clear plastic tub with a base and top that screw together. Another is a flattened tub that snaps together at the sides and sits in a separate base.

- ❖ To mince herbs, use a chef's knife like you would a mezzaluna (a half-moon cutter). Hold the handle of the knife in one hand, the tip in the other, then chop with a rocking motion.

- ❖ Don't try to chop damp herbs in the food processor. When they are perfectly dry, however, you can process them in large quantities. Use the pulse function and keep stopping to scrape down the sides.

Making Do

If you run out of fresh mint, basil or oregano, mix chopped fresh parsley with the corresponding dried herb.

- ❖ For herb garnishes, fry basil or mint leaves, or parsley or cilantro sprigs in olive oil until they are crisp. Or make herb fritters by dipping the leaves in seasoned flour before frying them.

OUTSIDE THE BOX

- Toss whole leaves of fresh herbs into salad as a green. Basil and mint work well.
- You can use fresh herbs in flower arrangements for a nice scent.

Preserving Herbs

Watery VS. Oily?

- Aromatic oils in the leaves give staying power to oily herbs. These hold up in the heat of cooking. They are also okay dried. Examples: thyme, rosemary, marjoram, oregano.
- Watery herbs have a fleeting essence. These are best used as fresh garnishes, or added right at the end of the cooking time. They are no good dried. These herbs keep best frozen in stock or preserved in oil. Examples: chives, parsley, tarragon, chervil, cilantro.

4 Ways to Dry Herbs

1. Hang a tied bundle of stalks upside down in a warm, but not humid, spot with good circulation, away from direct sunlight.
2. Place herbs in a single layer on a screen. Prop the screen up to allow air circulation. You can use an old window screen, a splatter screen or a drum sieve.
3. For faster dried herbs, strip the leaves from their stems. Place the leaves in a paper bag. Close it with a clothespin. Leave the bag in a warm spot for up to 10 days, until the herbs crumble easily.
4. For instant dried herbs, use the microwave to make small quantities only. Place about 5 sprigs between two paper towels on the turntable. Zap them on High for 2 to 3 minutes. Check them, then give them an extra 30 seconds if they need it. Warning: This weakens the flavor.

- Before drying garden herbs, you can wash them in a solution of 1 cup (250 mL) water and 1 tbsp (15 mL) baking soda. This is supposed to make them dry faster and stay greener.

✖ No-No

Do not dry herbs in the oven. The heat dries up some of the aromatic oils.

- Test herbs for dryness before storing them in airtight jars: Put a sample in a jar. Cover it tightly and let it stand for a few hours. If you see any condensation or discoloration, the herbs are not dry enough.

---

3 Ways to Add Dried Herbs to Dishes

1. Crumble them first.
2. Soak them in some liquid from the recipe, such as stock, milk or wine, for 15 minutes.
3. Stir them into hot butter or oil beforehand.

- Subbing dried herbs for fresh ones is not a straight exchange. Some are stronger than others. It depends on their essential oils and moisture content. Generally, use a quarter to a third of the amount of fresh herbs called for in the recipe. But you'll have to taste, to be sure.

- You can preserve herbs in salt. In a small container, alternate ¼-inch (0.5 cm) layers of kosher salt and chopped fresh herbs, beginning and ending with the salt. Cover and store at room temperature. The herbs should remain green. A bonus: herb salt. If the salt looks damp, air it by removing the lid.

Ways to Preserve Herbs in Oil

- Watery herbs can be chopped and mixed with a bit of oil. When you store them, make sure there is always a layer of oil on top. They will last in an airtight container in the fridge for a couple of weeks this way.
- Make a thick herb paste with oil and freeze it. Break off chunks when you need to flavor pasta or soup.
- Wilted or limp herbs can be turned into herb oil for dressings and the like. Make sure the herbs are completely dry. Purée them in a food processor with oil. Refrigerate for up to 2 weeks.

Tips for Frozen Herbs

- You can freeze herbs by the stalk and just snap off the amount you need. Freeze the stalk on a plate, then transfer it to a zip-lock bag once it's firm.
- Freezing chopped parsley, cilantro and other watery herbs in stock or water prevents freezer burn. Use ⅓ cup (75 mL) liquid per 1 cup (250 mL) chopped herbs. Break off chunks as you need them. You can also freeze the mixture in ice cube trays.
- Another way to freeze leafy herbs, such as basil or mint, is in a roll. Spread a single layer of clean, dry leaves on waxed paper. Carefully roll up the paper. Put the roll in a zip-lock bag and freeze it. You can unroll the paper to take the number of leaves you need.
- Use frozen herbs without defrosting them.

Potent Pesto

I like to make plenty of this intense pesto when the garden basil is blooming out of control. **Makes about 2 cups (500 mL)**

Tips

Make sure the basil is completely dry. After rinsing it, you can whirl it in a salad spinner or dab it with paper towels. Then let it air-dry.

Toast the pine nuts in a dry large skillet over medium heat until golden and fragrant.

Don't use pre-grated cheese; it may make the pesto gritty.

8	cloves garlic	8
2 oz	basil leaves	60 g
1 cup	freshly grated Parmigiano-Reggiano cheese	250 mL
⅔ cup	pine nuts, toasted	150 mL
½ tsp	kosher salt	2 mL
¾ to 1 cup	extra virgin olive oil	175 to 250 mL

1. In a food processor fitted with the steel blade, with the motor running, drop garlic through the feed tube and process until minced. Add basil and pulse to mince. Add cheese, pine nuts and salt. Pulse until nuts are finely chopped.

2. With the motor running, gradually pour oil through the feed tube in a steady stream, adding just enough to reach the desired texture.

Basil

✧ Sensitive basil is the hardest herb to store fresh. It goes limp in plastic and swampy in an herb vase. It doesn't like the cold, and decays rapidly. Use it up quickly.

✧ Some cooks add a small, waxy boiled potato to pesto to cut any bitterness.

✧ Exposure to air turns pesto brown. It can be frozen instead.

Bay Leaves

✧ Bruise fresh bay leaves by holding them at the tapered ends and twisting in opposite directions. This releases their potency.

Chives

✧ Chives don't freeze well. To improve their texture, blanch them for 10 seconds, then plunge them into ice water for 1 minute. Dry them well. Place them in small zip-lock bags and freeze.

Cilantro

♻ Waste Not

Cilantro roots offer a burst of flavor and hold up in cooking. Don't throw them out.

Lovage

✧ Lovage is an herb that tastes like celery. It's hard to find. As an alternative, mix parsley with celery leaves in equal proportions.

Parsley

Curly **VS.** Flat-leaf?

Curly parsley is easy to chop and holds up better, but it's more astringent than flat-leaf, or Italian, parsley. The curly kind has a firmer texture for Middle Eastern salads.

Master Plan
Deep-Fried Parsley

1. Wash 1 cup (250 mL) curly parsley sprigs. Dry them well.
2. In a skillet, heat 2 inches (5 cm) of olive oil over medium heat until shimmery.
3. Fry the parsley until it stops hissing and becomes crisp. This takes a few seconds. If it's too limp, the oil wasn't hot enough. If it's olive green, the oil was too hot. Adjust the temperature.

Rosemary

✧ Gardeners say you can plant rosemary stalks. Cut the base of the stem at an angle. Strip off the bottom leaves. Put the stalk in potting soil in a small pot. Dampen it with water. Seal the pot in a zip-lock bag. Place it on a windowsill out of direct sunlight. Once it begins to grow, remove the bag.

✧ Add a hint of smoky rosemary by putting stalks on the grill underneath the meat.

✧ Rosemary stalks make good skewers for barbecue kebabs or cheese. Refrigerate the assembled kebabs or cheese skewers overnight for a bolder rosemary flavor.

✧ No need to wrap rosemary stalks in a moist paper towel or keep them in water. A plastic bag will do fine. Rosemary is very hardy.

Thyme

✧ Dry thyme in whole sprigs. Rub the sprigs between your palms over meat or a casserole.

⚡ Lightning Won't Strike If ...

You don't bother pulling the leaves off the tip of a sprig of thyme. Save some aggravation.

Meat and Seafood

Recipes

Meat Basics

(P) is for Primal

An animal is split lengthwise into two halves — like the proverbial sides of beef. Such a big hunk of meat is unmanageable, so each side is cut into sections called primal cuts. From these primal cuts come the retail cuts that consumers encounter. A retail cut comes from a single muscle (such as the tenderloin) or a cross section of several muscles (such as the T-bone).

❖ The same cut of meat can have different names, depending on where your recipe came from. You may encounter American, Canadian, British and French names. The actual cuts that are available in your area may differ, too.

(D) is for Dry Aging

There's a thin line between aging and rotting. Meat is left hanging in cool temperatures. As it ages, bacteria break down the proteins and the surface gets dry and crusty, but the meat doesn't decay. It gets more tender and tasty. Well-aged meat is more expensive. The longer it hangs, the more moisture is lost — evaporating potential profits.

❖ Larger cuts of meat can be kept longer in the fridge and freezer.

❖ Count the storage time from the packaging date or purchase date.

Five Bad Signs of Spoilage

- Bad odor.
- Slimy coating.
- Stickiness or tackiness.
- Discoloration (there may be grey, brown or purple patches on the flesh or skin, or spots where the bone meets the flesh).
- Flabby, puffy flesh.

❖ Meat needs some ventilation. Wrap it loosely. Exception: If it's vacuum-packed, leave it that way.

❖ To open vacuum-packed meat without getting the juices everywhere, slash a large X on top.

❖ Avoid meat packages with lots of liquid sloshing around.

The Meat Locker: A Finicky Storage Guide

Type	Fridge	Freezer
Ground meat	1 to 2 days	2 to 3 months
Liver and organ meats	1 to 2 days	2 to 3 months
Stewing meat	2 days	3 to 6 months
Ribs	2 days	3 to 6 months
Steaks	3 days	6 to 9 months
Roasts	3 days	9 to 12 months
Cooked meat	3 to 4 days	2 to 3 months
Cold cuts	3 to 4 days	Don't freeze

- ❖ Reasons to always rinse meat (and fish) before cooking:
  - It's psychologically satisfying. Although rinsing doesn't kill bacteria, it gets rid of the coating that makes one imagine all those germs seething on the surface.
  - It cuts down odors.
  - It makes slippery flesh easier to handle.
  - It rinses off bone dust (a gritty white paste).

- ❖ Instead of just rinsing with water, raw meat can be refreshed with vinegar, then sprayed with water.

How Much?
- Allot $\frac{1}{4}$ lb (125 g) boneless meat per serving.
- Allot up to 1 lb (500 g) bone-in meat per serving.

Cutting Raw Meat

Ⓑ is for Butchery
Butchery is the art of separating large cuts of meat around and across the bones, and along delineated lines of fat and gristle. You, too, can use these lines as a guide, whether you are cutting stewing beef or carving chicken.

♛ A Golden Rule
When you're carving, watch where you're going. Expose the joint, then cut the actual bone. Slash and hack in stages.

- ❖ When trimming slippery fat and connective tissue, stay safe. Always push the knife blade away from your body.

Ⓢ is for Silverskin
The silverskin is a shiny, fairly thin, opaque membrane. It is tough, it doesn't dissolve and it distorts the shape of the meat as it roasts. So cooks don't like it. We encounter silverskin on tenderloins in particular.

How to Remove Silverskin
1. Slide the tip of a sharp knife under the silverskin, but leave both ends attached.
2. Start sawing in one direction until you reach the end.
3. Grab the loose end with a paper towel. Pull it taut.
4. Finish the job by sawing toward the other end.

Ⓕ is for Frenched
A rack of lamb, rib roast or pork roast is frenched when the ends of the bones are neatly stripped of fat, gristle and bits of meat. The best way to french is to get your butcher to do it. But you can do it at home. For a fancy presentation, frenched meat is curved into a crown shape. You can also French individual lamb, pork or rib chops.

How to French Meat at Home
1. Note where the loin starts to taper off. That's where you slice straight in, down to the bone, to create a neat border.
2. Cut along the bones, between each pair of ribs, down to the border.
3. Pull and peel away hunks of meat and fat from the bones. Use a paper towel for grip.
4. Scrape off the membranes from each bone.

- ❖ Reasons to firm up meat in the freezer:
  - To debone it
  - To thinly shave it
  - To evenly slice it
  - To cut it into neat cubes
  - To grind it
  - To trim small, slippery patches of fat and connective tissue

Tenderizing Meat

8 Ways to Tenderize Meat

1. Pound it with a mallet or a heavy skillet to break down the tough fibers.
2. Score the surface.
3. Grind it.
4. Marinate it.
5. Add fat. Smear butter or oil over it, insert strips of firm fat into the meat, lay bacon over top or baste frequently.
6. Use commercial tenderizer. Note: It is supposed to shorten the cooking time, but it mars the flavor. To apply tenderizer efficiently, prick the meat all over with a fork. Use about 1 tsp (5 mL) tenderizer per 1 lb (500 g) meat. The enzyme in the tenderizer springs into action as the meat warms up.
7. Don't cook meat past medium-rare.
8. Add moisture. To tenderize ground meat (especially the leaner kind) being fried in a skillet until no longer pink, add 1/2 cup (125 mL) water per 1 lb (500 g) meat, stirring until the water evaporates.

✦ How to reduce sticking and mangling when pounding meat:
- Sandwich delicate meat, such as chicken breast, between sheets of oiled parchment paper. This keeps the mallet cleaner, too.
- Put the meat in a thick plastic bag. Note: The bag will be ruined.
- Moisten a spiked mallet if you are using it directly on the meat.
- Wet the meat slightly.

⚡ Lightning Won't Strike If ...

You salt meat before cooking. It'll taste better. People are afraid to salt for fear of drawing out juices. But the salt would have to sit on the meat for a long time to have an impact. If you do salt too far in advance, beads of moisture appear on the surface. This can prevent browning. Pat the meat dry before searing or grilling it.

Cooking Meat

A Bit of Science

In response to heat, muscle fibers contract, squeezing out moisture. Meat turns opaque, shrinks and becomes denser. By the time it reaches 170°F (77°C), or well-done, most of the liquid has been released and the meat is leathery. However, if a tough cut is cooked to well-done in moist heat, the connective tissues dissolve and proteins gelatinize. The meat is tender.

Mythstake

Expensive cuts of beef are more tender, but not tastier. Tougher, cheaper cuts actually have more flavor.
- Hard-working muscles, or locomotive muscles — such as the shoulder, the rear portion of the hip and legs — are tougher. Tough cuts take longer to cook and require wet heat. Long cooking breaks down the connective tissue.
- Supporting muscles, or suspension muscles — such as the back and loin — are tender. Tender cuts taste milder. They do well with dry heat.

Wet **VS.** Dry?

Wet-heat methods include stewing, braising, poaching and cooking in casseroles or slow cookers. Dry-heat methods include roasting, grilling, searing, sautéing and deep-frying.

✧ To cook meat faster and more evenly, some people prefer to let it come to room temperature (or close to it) beforehand. They don't leave it out for longer than 2 hours. However, experts say the food-safety risks outweigh the benefits. They say meat should be kept refrigerated until just before cooking.

✧ Cook large cuts at lower heat for a longer time, to give the exterior time to brown while the interior cooks through. Turn the heat up on small, thinner cuts, to create a brown crust before the interior gets overcooked.

✧ Any meat cooked on the bone tastes better.

✧ Blood makes bone marrow turn gray when it's hot. To remove blood, soak bones in salty water for several hours in the fridge.

Signs It's Time to Turn the Meat

- You see blood and juices beading on top.
- The bottom of the meat stops sticking to the pan or grill grate.

5 Fat Tips

1. Fat equals flavor. The more marbled the meat, the more tender and tasty. In fact, the meat-grading system is based on marbling, or fat content, not quality.
2. Though pork is thought of as more fatty, beef is actually more marbled. So you can cut the cap of fat from that beef, but leave some fat on the pork to moisten it.
3. Slit the fat along the edge of a steak or chop before searing or grilling it. The fat shrinks faster than the flesh and causes the meat to curl up. Slit the fat at 2-inch (5 cm) intervals.
4. Use the melted fat in a grill pan to baste meat as you sear it.
5. Before searing or grilling, it's more efficient to rub the meat with oil, rather than oiling the pan or grate.

✧ Let grilled, roasted or seared meat rest after removing it from the heat. The resting time depends on the size of the meat. Braised or stewed meat doesn't need to rest.

Reasons to Let Meat Rest

- The juices get redistributed and reabsorbed. Your meat will be juicier.
- The fibers relax. Your meat will be more tender.
- The meat finishes cooking.

Estimated Resting Times

- 5 to 10 minutes for steaks and chops
- 20 minutes for roasts and whole birds
- 30 minutes for a mammoth roast or turkey

✧ Tent resting meat with foil. Do not wrap it tightly; you don't want steam.

Veal Marsala

Here's a meal that takes longer to describe than to cook. For maximum tenderness, the thin veal is barely seared. Surprisingly, the small amount serves four, maybe because the meat is pounded thin. **Makes 4 servings**

- **Preheat oven to 200°F (100°C)**

Tips

Don't use a nonstick skillet. The meat won't crust properly.

Though it's not a traditional ingredient, the lemon juice brightens the final result.

12 oz	veal scaloppini (thinly pounded veal cutlets)	375 g
	All-purpose flour	
	Salt and freshly ground black pepper	
5 tbsp	extra virgin olive oil, divided	75 mL
2	cloves garlic, minced	2
1	large shallot, minced	1
4 oz	button mushrooms, sliced	125 g
¼ cup	Marsala	50 mL
¼ cup	beef stock	50 mL
Pinch	ground nutmeg	Pinch
1 tsp	freshly squeezed lemon juice	5 mL

1. Dust veal with flour. Sprinkle salt and pepper on both sides.

2. In a large skillet, heat 2 tbsp (25 mL) of the oil over medium-high heat until shimmery. Sear veal, in three batches, for about 1 minute per side, turning it as soon as you see blood seeping on top and the bottom is browned and releases from the pan. Add 1 tbsp (15 mL) oil to the pan between each batch, and reduce heat to medium if the browned bits stuck to the pan threaten to burn. (You'll need them later.) Transfer the veal to a heatproof dish. Place it, uncovered, in the oven to keep warm.

3. Add the remaining oil to the skillet and heat over medium heat until shimmery. Sauté garlic and shallot for 20 to 30 seconds or until fragrant. Add mushrooms and sauté for 2 minutes or until mushrooms are golden and start to release liquid. Stir in Marsala. Stir in stock, scraping up browned bits in the pan. Stir in nutmeg and season to taste with salt and pepper. Simmer for 2 minutes or until slightly thickened.

4. Dip each veal cutlet in the pan to coat both sides. Place veal on a large serving platter. Scrape sauce over top. Drizzle with lemon juice.

❖ Don't put sweet or fatty sauces on meat until the end of the cooking time unless you like burnt offerings.

Better Leftovers

Make a boiled beef dinner on day one, then turn it into soup on day two. Simmer chuck roast for long hours in water or stock, along with herbs, carrots, celery, onion, turnips, leeks, tomatoes and potatoes. If desired, add cabbage and parsnips 30 minutes before the end of the cooking time. Serve the beef sliced, with veggies and a bit of the broth ladled on top, and horseradish on the side. The next day, focus on the broth. You can do the same with poached chicken.

Roasting Meat

Factoid A roast with a bone is supposed to cook relatively faster than a boneless roast because the bones conduct heat.

Roasting Tips

- The best pan for roasting has low sides and a rack to raise the meat up, allowing hot, dry air to circulate.
- Set the pan on a lower rack so that the meat itself sits in the center of the oven.
- Use a heavy pan that can move from oven to stovetop. It will be easier to make gravy when the time comes.
- For even cooking, rotate the pan 180 degrees every half-hour.

♻ Waste Not

You can freeze the juices and fats from a roast for gravy or Yorkshire pudding another day.

8 Ways to Preserve Drippings

1. Grease the pan to prevent juices from sticking and burning.
2. To reduce evaporation, use a pan just big enough to hold the hunk of meat.
3. Put meat trimmings in the bottom of the pan.
4. Cover the bottom of the roasting pan with moist onion slices or carrots.
5. Don't use a rack. Drippings are less apt to evaporate or burn.
6. Pour $\frac{1}{2}$ cup (125 mL) water, stock or wine into the pan, so the juices won't scorch. You'll be on your way to better gravy. Pour in liquid as needed. Don't add it enthusiastically. You'll steam the meat and prevent browning. Add more only if the drippings are sticking and scorching.
7. If you're roasting poultry, tilt the bird and pour the juices out of the cavity halfway through the cooking time.
8. At the end of roasting time, pour off the fat from the pan, add stock or wine and scrape the browned bits from the bottom of the pan.

❖ Don't cover a roast with foil while it's in the oven. The meat steams rather than roasts, and it toughens.

❖ Make a roast prettier by scoring diagonal slashes on the presentation side. Make them shallow; you don't want to lose too many juices.

❖ To create a golden brown crust or crisp skin, start roasting at a high heat, then turn down the oven.

Alternatives to a Rack

- Set the roast on bones. Later, simmer the bones for stock.
- Kill two birds by roasting meat on top of the potatoes that will be served with it.
- Create a bed of celery stalks, carrots or other root vegetables, thickly sliced onions, or even oranges or lemons. Toss on any wing tips. The bed will flavor the meat and the pan juices, and prevent sticking. The vegetables end up pallid and soft. Blast them under the broiler before serving, if desired.
- You can roast pork tenderloin or strips of beef loin by hanging them in the oven. Use drapery hooks to hang the meat from the top rack. Place a drip pan underneath. Roast strips, about 8 inches (20 cm) by 2 inches (5 cm), for up to 1 hour at 400°F (200°C).

- ✧ Not everyone is a fan of adding vegetables to the roasting pan with the meat. The veggies stand accused of releasing steam that interferes with browning. If you want to roast meat and vegetables all at once, they may be better off in separate pans. That way, the vegetables can be removed before they overcook.

✖ No-No

Don't baste a roast until a crust has formed on the meat.

- ✧ Roast meat fat side up. Deliberately leave a thin layer of fat on the meat to baste it as it cooks.

- ✧ When roasting tenderloin, tuck under a couple of inches of the thin, pointy end to create an even thickness. Secure it with kitchen string.

- ✧ Roasting very slowly at a low temperature, say 200°F (100°C), gives meat a rosy hue from center to edge, instead of leaving a swath of pink surrounded by overcooked grayish brown. It also cuts moisture loss.

Tips for Low, Slow Roasting

- The meat won't develop a lovely brown crust. So sear it before it goes in the oven.
- The timing is difficult. One guesstimate is that roasting at 200°F (100°C) takes at least twice as long as at 350°F (180°C).
- The temperature of slow-roasted meat doesn't continue to rise as much as regular roasted meat does when it is resting. Figure on it rising no more than 5°F (3°C).
- Slow-roasting does wondrous things for meat, but it is frowned upon by food-safety experts. They worry that bacteria won't be killed before multiplying to dangerous levels. One compromise is to start roasting at 500°F (260°C) for 20 minutes to blast the germs, then reduce the heat to 275°F (140°C) and slow-roast.

- ✧ Remove any string or netting on roasted meat while it's still in the pan, so any seasonings and crusty bits fall into the pan juices.

3 Ways to Turn and Transfer a Hot Roast

1. Protect your hands with thick rubber gloves, oven mitts or silicone holders. Be careful not to touch hot metal.
2. Stick a large carving fork or the handle of a large wooden spoon inside the cavity of poultry.
3. Place a length of cheesecloth in the pan or on the rack, leaving the ends draped over the rim, then set the roast or bird on top. When the time comes, turn the cheesecloth into a sling and lift.

✦ If you want to serve a big roast beast dinner in a shorter time, cook two smaller roasts instead of one large one.

> **Factoid** Three roasts in an oven will take longer to cook than one because they absorb more heat.

✦ To keep a roast hot for 1 to 2 hours, wrap it in foil, then in newspaper for insulation.

Judging Doneness

✦ The food-safety folks would have it done to shoe leather, while chefs play the odds. Governments, marketing boards and cookbook authors add their voices to the mix. So what temperature should meat be cooked to? The charts are all over the place, depending on who's doing the recommending. Another variable: Is that the temperature at which you pull the meat from the heat, or does it account for resting time?

Here's a list of temperature ranges that play the averages:

- **Rare:** 120°F to 130°F (49°C to 54°C)
- **Medium-rare:** 130°F to 140°F (54°C to 60°C).
- **Medium:** 140°F to 150°F (60°C to 66°C)
- **Medium-well:** 150°F to 160°F (66°C to 71°C)
- **Well-done:** 160°F to 170°F (71°C to 77°C)

🅱 is for Blue

It was once chic and daring to order steak or tenderloin "blue." Seared black outside, bloody inside, blue meat is in the 115°F to 120°F (46°C to 49°C) range. Blue meat is chewy.

Is It Done?

- Beef, veal and lamb are best cooked to rare or medium-rare, except for ground meat, which must be well-done.
- Poultry must be cooked to well-done, white and dark meat to 165°F (74°C) and ground poultry to 170°F (77°C).
- Pork is best cooked to medium, but ground pork and sausage must be well-done.

Mythstake

There's no need to cook the heck out of a cut of pork. It is done when you see a hint of pink in the center, rosy but no longer shiny. Well-done pork is dry and tough. In the past, fear of trichinosis led to overcooking.

🆃 is for Trichinosis

Trichinosis is a disease caused by roundworms found in undercooked meat, particularly pork. It has become rare in North America. These parasitic roundworms are destroyed at 137°F (58°C). To ensure a safe margin (and palatable meat), some experts recommend cooking pork to at least medium (150°F/65°C) or medium-well (160°F/71°C). Others still say pork should be cooked to well-done (170°F/77°C), strictly as insurance.

✦ As meat rests, it continues to cook in its residual heat and the internal temperature rises a few notches. We need to take this into account. Otherwise, meat can end up overcooked.

Residual Heat Guidelines

- The temperature of meat generally rises 5°F to 10°F (3°C to 6°C) as it rests.
- Large beef and pork roasts can rise from 10°F to 15°F (6°C to 8°C).
- The cavity in whole poultry lets heat escape quickly. The temperature may rise less than 5°F (3°C).

6 Tips for Taking Temperatures

1. Don't let the thermometer touch bone. Bones are hotter than meat.
2. Insert the thermometer into the thickest, deepest part of the meat.
3. Take readings in two or three different parts of the beast. (Do the same with ground-meat mixtures, casseroles and egg dishes.)
4. For thin foods, such as burgers or chops, insert the thermometer horizontally through one side until the end of the probe is at the center.
5. For poultry, insert the thermometer into the thigh, parallel to the bone. There's no need to test the breast because it cooks before the thigh.
6. The pop-up guide that comes with a turkey is just that — a guide. Verify doneness with an instant-read thermometer.

❖ You can guesstimate how long meat will take to cook. Four time guidelines:
- **Steak:** Per 1 inch (2.5 cm) thickness, allow 8 minutes for rare, 10 minutes for medium-rare and 12 minutes for medium, plus a resting time of 5 minutes.
- **Roast beef, veal or lamb:** Per 1 lb (500 g), allow 20 minutes for medium-rare and 25 minutes for medium.
- **Roast pork:** Per 1 lb (500 g), allow 25 minutes for medium.
- **Roast poultry:** Per 1 lb (500 g), allow 15 minutes for bigger birds and 20 minutes for chicken.

❖ Stuffed birds and roasts take longer to cook, about 5 to 10 extra minutes per 1 lb (500 g).

OUTSIDE THE BOX

Here's a funny, low-tech way to test for doneness: Insert a metal skewer into the meat, then touch the tip to your cheek or hand. If it's uncomfortably hot, the meat is well-done. Older ladies may employ this method with the holiday bird.

Judging Doneness Visually

Rare
- Interior about three-quarters red.
- Red juices, not readily released.

Medium-rare
- Interior half red.
- Red juices, beginning to bead on the surface of grilled or seared meat.

Medium
- Interior one-quarter pink.
- Pink juices, beginning to turn brown.

Well-done
- Interior brown, gray or beige throughout.
- Juices run clear.

✘ No-No

Don't maul meat with a knife to test the juices. Prick it with a skewer, infrequently and only if absolutely necessary for your peace of mind.

❖ For braises, stews and soups, skewer the meat with a fork. If the fork grips, the meat is not ready. If it slides out easily, the meat is done.

❖ You can test doneness by pressing meat with your finger:
- Rare feels squishy, like an unflexed muscle.
- Medium-rare yields to pressure, but the dent immediately springs back.
- Medium feels firm but springy.
- Well-done feels hot and hard.

❖ For poultry, prick the thickest part of the thigh to test the juices.

✧ Cooks have all kinds of tricks to judge doneness, particularly those steak fans who hover over the barbecue. They like to use body parts for comparisons:

Comparing meat by pressing the ball of your thumb
- **Rare:** Keep your hand loose.
- **Medium:** Make a loose fist.
- **Well-done:** Make a tight fist or flex your palm.

Comparing meat by flexing your fingers
- **Rare:** Touch your thumb to your index finger. Press the ball of your thumb.
- **Medium-rare:** Touch your thumb to your middle finger. Press the ball of your thumb.
- **Medium:** Touch your thumb to your ring finger. Press the ball of your thumb.
- **Well-done:** Touch your thumb to your pinkie. Press the ball of your thumb.

Comparing meat to your face
- **Rare** feels like your cheek or earlobe.
- **Medium** feels like the tip of your nose.
- **Well-done** feels like your chin.

Cutting Cooked Meat

Ⓖ is for Grain

The grain is the pattern formed by long, parallel muscle fibers. The grain changes in different parts of the meat. Why do you care? Because you should always slice meat against the grain. Slashing across the muscle fibers, rather than along them, makes a cut easier to chew.

✧ Catch the juices of a roast, turkey or steak by slicing it on a cutting board that has a built-in trough. Or improvise by setting a flat cutting board in a rimmed baking sheet.

✧ Shred hot cooked meat with two forks. This was perfected by pulled-pork fanciers, but it works with poultry and beef, too.

Reheating Meat

✧ Avoid reheating meat. It gets rubbery and dry. If you must reheat, do so only until the meat is barely warm. Avoid the microwave.

5 Better Ways to Reheat Meat

1. Thinly slice it, arrange it on individual serving plates, then pour super-hot gravy over top.
2. Dip it in hot stock.
3. Wrap it in foil and heat it in a 200°F (100°C) oven.
4. Stack it with a lettuce leaf between each slice. Heat the pile in a 200°F (100°C) oven.
5. Steam it in a basket over simmering water. Steaming is particularly good for lean meat that dries out, chicken or turkey breast.

Ground Meat

✧ Before grinding meat at home, cut it into chunks and freeze it just until it is firm, not solid. The job will be quicker and tidier.

Using a Meat Grinder

- Always use a pusher to cram meat into the grinder. If you don't have an official pusher, use a wooden spoon, never your fingers.
- For a finer, smoother mix, you can put meat through the grinder twice. The second time, you can freeze the meat briefly again. Exception: Grind fatty meat just once.
- Use cold, wet hands to extract sticky ground meat from the plates of the grinder.

Understanding Labels

✧ Ground beef is labeled according to maximum fat content and, sometimes, the type of beef used.

- In the U.S., regular ground beef is up to 30% fat, lean is up to 22%, extra-lean is up to 15%. Ground chuck is 15% to 20% fat, ground round 10% to 15%, ground sirloin 8% to 10%.
- In Canada, regular ground beef is up to 30% fat, medium is up to 23%, lean is up to 17%, extra-lean is up to 10%.

✧ To refrigerate ground meat safely, pat it into a pile no more than 2 inches (5 cm) thick before wrapping, so the cold can penetrate it quickly.

Keep It Clean

Before washing the meat grinder, run a piece of bread or a small chunk of raw potato through it.

ⓒ is for Crumbles

You can buy cheaper, fattier ground beef and cut the fat by making crumbles. The crumbles can be used in pasta sauce, chili, tacos and casseroles. Pan-fry regular ground beef until it is well-done. In a fine strainer, drain it well. Rinse it well with hot water. Shake the strainer to drain it well.

Making Do

If you don't have a meat grinder, use a food processor.

How to Grind Meat in a Food Processor

1. Freeze the meat until it is firm but still pliable, 15 to 30 minutes. Otherwise, it will become pasty.
2. Pulse to chop the meat. For an even grind, use a scraper to move the meat around between pulses.
3. Spread the meat out on a cutting board. Pull out stringy bits of connective tissue, bits of gristle and chunks of fat. Luckily, some of that gets wrapped around the blade, so you don't have to deal with it.

Mythstake

No, ground beef that looks brown has not gone bad. The color changes with exposure to the air. It goes from purplish when first cut, to red, to brownish red. The surface may be brown, while the center remains red. If the meat is brown or gray all the way through, it is spoiling.

- Break up partially frozen ground meat by digging at the edges with a fork, then breaking off clumps.

4 Ways to Make Ground Meat Tender

1. Add water. It evaporates during cooking.
2. Add some ground pork, particularly with lean ground beef.
3. Mix it loosely. Don't compact it densely into balls, patties or meatloaf. It shrinks and tightens in the heat.
4. Avoid overly enthusiastic mixing when adding ingredients.

Healthier Eater

You can cut fat, boost fiber, save money and extend the number of servings by padding and bulking up ground meat. Just don't add too much filler. If you do, your patties, meatballs and meatloaves will either fall apart or become rubbery.

Fillers for Ground Meat

- Quick-cooking oats. Use 1 part oats per 8 parts meat. Oats create the best texture.
- Fresh, whole-grain bread crumbs. Use 1 part bread crumbs per 4 parts meat.
- Canned, mashed beans. Use 1 part beans per 4 parts meat.
- Cottage cheese. Use 1 part cottage cheese per 4 parts meat.
- Grated potato. Use 1 part potato per 3 parts meat.
- Grated apple. Use 1 part apple per 4 parts meat. This complements ground pork.
- Lightly crumbled corn flakes cereal. For bouncy meatballs, use 2 oz (60 g), or about 1 cup (250 mL), corn flakes per 1 lb (500 g) ground beef. Mix in 1 egg, 2 tbsp (25 mL) ketchup and ½ tsp (2 mL) salt.
- Cooked grains. Couscous, bulgur and barley have potential as fillers.
- Grated vegetables. These can be used to moisten, as well as to stretch, lean ground beef.

- When mixing ground meat for meatballs or meatloaf, avoid overmixing. First, stir together the egg, liquid, spices and bread crumbs. Pour this mixture evenly over the meat, then combine.

OUTSIDE THE BOX

You can brown ground beef in the microwave. Put it in a plastic colander set over a microwave-safe dish. Cover it with vented, microwave-safe plastic wrap. Microwave it on High for 4 to 5 minutes per pound (500 g), stirring twice.

♻ Waste Not

If you want to keep the juices of cooked ground meat, drain it in a sieve over a bowl. Pour the juices into a clear measuring cup. Let them stand for 5 minutes. Suck the fat off the top with a baster and discard it. Return the juices to your dish for a hit of beefy flavor.

Burgers

Mixing Your Own Grind

- Try a blend of chuck roast (for juiciness) and sirloin steak (for red-meat flavor). Cut the meat into strips, toss it with salt and refrigerate overnight before grinding.
- A ruddy cut, such as flank steak, will be too lean unless you supplement it with fat. Add suet or well-marbled, boneless short ribs to the mix.

11 Keys to Making the Best Burgers

1. A juicy burger is not diet food. Use ground beef that is at least 20% fat.

2. Moisten. Add 1 tbsp (15 mL) ice-cold water or stock per 1 lb (500 g) ground meat. Or moisten both sides of each patty with cold water before grilling or broiling.

3. Burger enthusiasts frown upon unnecessary binders, such as egg and bread crumbs. If you are nervous about burgers falling apart, 1 egg per 1 lb (500 g) ground meat is the limit.

4. Gently press the meat into patties ¾ inch (2 cm) thick. Dampen your hands so the meat doesn't stick.

5. Help the burgers hold their shape. Refrigerate them while the barbecue is preheating, or at least 15 minutes. Better still, put the patties in the freezer for 15 minutes. Add some cooking time for chilled burgers.

6. Professional barbecue-circuit guys like to create a crust, called the "bark," on burgers. To create a crust, coat the patties with a paste made of mustard and barbecue rub, then spray on oil to prevent sticking.

7. Push an indent into the center of each patty with your thumb or the base of a juice glass. Burgers swell in the center while they're cooking.

8. Grill over medium heat with the lid closed.

9. Do not turn a burger before its time. If you do, it will crumble.

10. Quit that constant flipping and pressing with the spatula. It squeezes out the juices. Turn a burger once.

11. To add cheese, place a slice on each patty for the last minute of cooking. Close the lid to melt it. If you are using a skillet, put the lid on.

OUTSIDE THE BOX

For faster cooking, use a skewer to create a hole about ¼ inch (0.5 cm) in diameter through the center of each burger. The holes will close up during cooking.

Tips for Marinating Burgers

- Place the patties in a baking dish in a single layer.
- Use creative or theme marinades, such as jerk sauce.
- Pour the marinade over top. Lift the patties with a spatula to let the marinade run underneath.
- Thirty minutes is enough time to marinate.

❖ Burgers cooked on an indoor contact grill hold their shape better.

Meatballs

♛ A Golden Rule

Don't overmix or overcook. Meatballs should be springy, and firm enough to hold their shape, but tender.

✘ No-Nos

- Avoid extra-lean ground meat. It makes dry, tough meatballs.
- Don't put raw meatballs in soup or sauce unless you want the dish to get greasy and taste bad. Cook the meatballs first, until they are barely done.

For quick meatballs, squeeze sausages from their casings and roll the meat.

Making Do

You can use matzo meal instead of bread crumbs.

---

6 Ways to Make Meatballs Lighter and Juicier

1. Add ground veal and/or pork to the beef.
2. Soak bread crumbs in water, milk or even oil, then squeeze out the excess liquid before adding them to the ground meat.
3. Some cooks swear by a splash of soda water.
4. Add chopped bacon or pancetta.
5. Stir in ricotta.
6. Add grated potato or cooked rice.

❖ Ways to divide a meatball mixture into equal amounts:
- Form the meat into a log. Cut off equal slices.
- Weigh the mixture, then divide by the number of meatballs you want. Toss each clump of meat on the scale to check. You don't have to be fanatically precise. This is easier if you work in grams.

What Size?

- **Cocktail meatballs:** ¾-inch (2 cm) diameter
- **Soup or pasta meatballs:** 1-inch (2.5 cm) diameter
- **Sandwich meatballs:** 2-inch (5 cm) diameter

❖ Two times to refrigerate the meat for half an hour:
- After mixing. The meatballs will be easier to roll.
- Before cooking. The meatballs will be less likely to fall apart.

How to Roll Meatballs

1. Use a disher or ice cream scoop to pick up the meatball mixture.
2. Make a master meatball to copy. Meatballs are smaller than you think.
3. To prevent sticking, form meatballs with moistened hands. Set a bowl of water beside you as you work.
4. To coat meatballs as lightly as possible, don't roll them in flour. Instead, put the flour on a large plate and press your palms into it before rolling each meatball.

❖ Cook your meatballs for the minimum amount of time — just until there is no hint of pink visible in the center. They will be tough if you overcook them.

Frying Meatballs

- For meatballs that are crispy outside, tender inside, roll them in flour or crumbs before frying.
- Turn meatballs just once when frying, or gently shake the pan.
- Fried meatballs toughen as they cool, especially if they've been coated.

❖ Test one meatball first. Cook it, then cut it in half and taste it. Check the cooking time, saltiness, firmness and doneness.

≡ *Fast Fix*
Make quick sliders by slipping meatballs into mini buns. Hold them together with decorative toothpicks.

How Many Meatballs?

Diameter	Weight per meatball	Meatballs per 1 lb (500 g) meat
1 inch (2.5 cm)	½ oz (15 g)	30 to 32
1¼ inches (3 cm)	¾ oz (20 g)	21 to 22
1½ inches (4 cm)	1 oz (30 g)	15 to 16
2 inches (5 cm)	2 oz (60 g)	7 to 8

Alternatives to Frying

Bake meatballs.

- Baking tends to dry them out, but they do cook more evenly.
- Arrange meatballs on a well-oiled rack over a rimmed baking sheet.
- As they bake, suck up the drippings with a turkey baster.
- There's no need to turn the meatballs.

Grill meatballs (tricky).

- Adding extra binder, such as egg or bread crumbs, makes them less likely to crumble.
- Make them large. Go for the 2-inch (5 cm) size.
- Oil both the meatballs and the grate.
- Grill over indirect medium heat until the meatballs have set enough to turn. Turn and grill them until they are almost done. Move them over direct heat to brown.
- You can skewer round meatballs for the grill. Or pat the meat mixture around skewers, cigar-style, the way it's done in India and the Middle East.

Double-cook meatballs.

- Pan-fry the meatballs to brown and develop flavor. Drain them.
- Then bake them for even cooking.

Steam meatballs (moist).

- Chinese cooks steam meatballs mixed with sticky rice.
- Line the steamer with lettuce leaves so the meatballs don't stick.

"Steam-fry" meatballs without oil (works well).

- Brown meatballs in a nonstick skillet over medium heat.

- Add a thin layer of water. Cover and cook the meatballs through.
- Uncover the skillet to evaporate the moisture and finish the meatballs in their own fat.

✧ You can bake meatballs from the frozen state. Or thaw them in the fridge first, but not all jumbled together. Cook them while they're cold and firm.

3 Ways to Freeze Meatballs

1. Freeze the seasoned meat mixture, then thaw and form it into balls.
2. Freeze raw meatballs on a rimmed baking sheet until they're firm, then pop them into a zip-lock bag.
3. Cook meatballs until they are almost done, freeze them on a rimmed baking sheet, then transfer them to a zip-lock bag.

Meatloaf

✧ For even distribution and less mixing, first toss the meat with the dry ingredients. Combine the wet ingredients separately. Toss them with the meat mixture only until it's moistened.

Benefits of Different Ground Meats

 Meatloaf should be juicy. It should also hold its shape, so it's easy to cut. Mix different meats to get it right.

- Beef provides holding power and strong flavor. Give it the largest proportion.
- Pork contributes juiciness.
- Veal makes meatloaf tender and lighter.
- Poultry is lower in fat and calories, but compacts a lot.

Healthier Eater

If you are making meatloaf with ground chicken or turkey, compensate by using lots of binder. Otherwise, it will be too dense.

Meatloaf Extras

- Binder lightens meatloaf. Try fresh bread crumbs or cracker crumbs. Soak them before adding them. They'll blend better.
- Sauté chopped onions before adding them. Otherwise, you'll end up with crunchy bits.
- Add milk, sour cream, yogurt or cottage cheese to moisten the meatloaf.

✘ No-No

Don't glaze the top of the meatloaf until it's almost done.

◇ Finish the glaze by putting the meatloaf under the broiler.

≣ Fast Fix

Halfway through the cooking time, drain the fat, cut the meatloaf into 8 slices in the loaf pan and pour sauce over the top. The meat will cook faster and the sauce gets into the crevices.

◇ Meatloaf may be done and still look pink inside thanks to the nitrates in onions, celery or bell peppers, or red or brown sauces. Check for doneness with an instant-read thermometer.

Ways to Make Pan Meatloaf

Use a loaf pan.

- Cons: The sides don't brown and the loaf ends up swimming in fat.
- A glass loaf pan is better because it lets you check on the color.
- Line the pan with a parchment sling to make the loaf easier to pull out.
- To suck up grease, put a slice of bread at each end of the loaf and/or use a baster to siphon off fat as it cooks.
- Line the pan with a strip of bacon to prevent sticking.

Use a perforated pan.

- Pans with perforated bottoms and lids are marketed for the barbecue.
- You can pierce holes through the bottom of an old metal loaf pan or a disposable aluminum one.
- Place the perforated pan on a rack on a rimmed baking sheet. This automatically drains the meat.

Use a tart pan with a removable bottom.

- The grease will leak out. Put the pan on a rack on a rimmed baking sheet.
- Cut the meatloaf into wedges, like a pie.

Use a ring mold or tube pan.

- If the tube pan has a removable bottom, put it on a rack on a rimmed baking sheet.
- A ring loaf tends to break during removal unless you let it cool a bit first.
- For a retro laugh, fill the center of the ring with peas or corn, pack mashies around the outside and drizzle chili sauce over the meat. Horrors!

Use a muffin tin.

- Make individual meat loaves.
- Heap a $\frac{1}{4}$-cup (50 mL) scoop into each muffin cup. Press gently to flatten the meat.

4 Ways to Make Free-Form Meatloaf

1. Mound it on a rimmed baking sheet. The sides will brown nicely. This tends to look like a giant hamburger, a good thing or bad thing depending on your tastes.
2. Form it into a giant patty and grill it. Flip it using the base of a springform pan, a metal pizza paddle or a rimless baking sheet.
3. Mound it on a broiler pan, on the slotted rack over the drip pan. This allows the fat to drain.
4. Put the meatloaf mixture into oiled ramekins. Invert the meat onto a rimmed baking sheet to make individual meatloaves.

Gussy It Up

- Surprise eaters and make your meatloaf slices more attractive by arranging a smoked sausage and hard-cooked eggs lengthwise through the center of the loaf.
- Try an ethnic theme. Prepare Asian meatloaf with panko, sesame oil, ginger and soy sauce, then glaze it with hoisin sauce. Or add chunks of feta to lamb meatloaf.
- Make it seasonal — say turkey meatloaf with cranberry glaze.
- Vary the meat. Put chunks of ham in a chicken meatloaf. Squeeze some spicy sausage meat into the mix.
- Run mozzarella cheese strings through the center. Four should do it.
- Add grated carrots or potatoes, chopped tomatoes or chopped cooked mushrooms or spinach.
- Add shredded apples or applesauce.
- Add cooked white or wild rice.
- Use cheese crackers instead of bread crumbs.

- Top the loaf with bacon strips or add chopped bacon to the meat mixture.
- Add pesto.
- Add spice blends such as Cajun or Tex-Mex.
- Serve meatloaf with tomato gravy instead of ketchup.
- Play with the glaze. Think honey mustard for turkey meatloaf. South African bobotie has a layer of custard on top.
- Wrap meatloaf in pastry, the Scandinavian way. They use sour cream pastry, but you can cheat with crescent roll dough.

OUTSIDE THE BOX

- Meatloaf is good in cold sandwiches. You can also use it to mimic a hot Italian sandwich. Put a slice of meatloaf on a crusty Italian roll, top with mozzarella and roasted peppers, then broil it until the cheese is molten.
- Roll the meatloaf mixture around a filling, instead of forming it into a rectangle. You can use a comfort food cheese-and-mashed-potato center. (Make the mashies dense.) Or try an Italian meatloaf filled with prosciutto, provolone and pine nuts.

Master Plan
Rolled Meatloaf

1. Place the meat mixture on plastic wrap.
2. Pat to flatten it into a rectangle.
3. Top it with fillings.
4. Use the edge of the plastic wrap to help you roll up the meat from one short end.
5. Pinch the meat together to seal along the edges, then pat the ends flat.

✧ Let meatloaf stand, tented with foil, for 15 to 30 minutes before serving. Otherwise, it will fall apart when you slice it.

Sausages

✧ There's a wide world of sausages. They may be fresh or cured, cooked or not, smoked or not, dried or not.

Tips on Sausage Fillings

● Leave some fat in the meat for sausages or they will be tough and bland. Sausages are not diet food.

● Sauté onion, garlic and peppers before adding them to the ground meat. Otherwise, they will be too hard.

● Taste-test homemade sausage mixture before you start to stuff the casings. Fry a spoonful in a small skillet over medium-high heat until it is no longer pink. Taste and adjust the salt and other seasonings.

ⓒ is for Casings

There are many kinds of sausage casings. Some are edible; others are not. Natural casings are made from intestines, notably those from hogs. Casings are not widely available. Supermarkets that make their own sausages will often sell casings without fanfare. You have to ask for them. Go to the butcher's counter. Some butchers' shops also sell casings.

♲ Waste Not

To get the remnants out of a sausage tube, remove it with the casing still attached. With the handle of a wooden spoon, push the meat through and into the casing.

Making Do

You can fill sausage casing with a piping bag, but it's awkward. Use short lengths of casing and a large, round piping tip. Stick the tip into the end of a casing, then squeeze the bag.

✧ After stuffing the casings, refrigerate the sausages for an hour to firm them up.

8 Keys to Working with Hog Casings

1. Casings are normally packed in salt. Before using them, soak them under cold running water for 30 to 60 minutes. Or soak them in several changes of water.

2. Flush each casing before filling it. Hold one end under the tip of the faucet and run cold water through the casing for several minutes.

3. Drain each casing by pinching it between your index and middle fingers and squeezing it down the entire length.

4. You'll need about 2 feet (60 cm) of casings per 1 lb (500 g) sausage mixture.

5. Work with a reasonable length of casing — say no more than 3 feet (1 m).

6. You can loosely tie one end of the casing with a short length of kitchen string before filling it. Don't knot the casing or you'll get a giant air bubble.

7. Don't overfill the casing or it will split.

8. Leftover casings can be tossed with salt, then wrapped and refrozen.

✧ Reasons to put sausage under cold running water for a minute:

● This makes it easier to squeeze uncooked sausage from its casing.

● The skin of a dried sausage will pull off more readily.

✧ How to make a sausage less likely to split or extrude from its casing while cooking:

● Pierce it lightly with a fork before cooking. Some do say, however, that the loss of juices will make it less tender.

● Dip it for 10 to 20 seconds in water just brought to a boil. Blot before frying.

Lamb, Garlic and Rosemary Sausages

Homemade sausages are more wholesome. At least you know what's in them.
Makes 10 links, each 5 to 6 inches (12.5 to 15 cm) long

- **Sausage casings**

Tip

You can vary the meat and the seasonings to come up with your own creations.

2 tbsp	extra virgin olive oil	25 mL
1	onion, finely chopped	1
4	cloves garlic, minced	4
1 tbsp	chopped fresh rosemary	15 mL
1 tsp	hot pepper flakes	5 mL
1 tsp	kosher salt	5 mL
½ tsp	coarsely ground black pepper	2 mL
2 lbs	boneless lamb shoulder, trimmed and ground	1 kg

1. In a medium skillet, heat oil over medium heat. Sauté onion for 3 to 4 minutes or until softened. Add garlic and sauté for 2 to 3 minutes or until the mixture turns golden. Do not brown. Stir in rosemary, hot pepper flakes, salt and black pepper. Let cool to room temperature.

2. In a large bowl, combine lamb and onion mixture, blending well.

3. Stuff the lamb mixture into casings. Refrigerate for 1 hour.

4. Meanwhile, preheat barbecue grill to medium-high.

5. Place the sausages over indirect heat on the grill. Close the lid and grill, turning occasionally, for about 5 minutes per side or until just cooked through.

How to Fill a Casing

1. Fit a sausage funnel, or tube, over the end of a meat grinder.
2. Grease the outside of the tube with shortening. The casing will slide off more easily as it fills.
3. Pull the end of the casing over the tube. Pull the whole casing onto the tube like a stocking, wrinkling and gathering it.
4. As the meat extrudes into the casing, the casing will slowly pull off the tube on its own. Make sure it isn't twisted, and support the casing as it fills.
5. Massage the casing every once in a while to evenly pack the filling and squeeze out air bubbles. Pierce stubborn air pockets with a needle or a toothpick.
6. As it fills, twist the casing at 5- to 6-inch (13 to 15 cm) intervals to create sausage links. Leave about 1 inch (2.5 cm) between each link. (The twists are apt to unravel, but create a space as a marker. You can twist them again at the same spots.)

✧ Ways to help sausages brown more evenly:
- Dip them in boiling water before cooking.
- Roll them in flour before frying. Careful: They will develop a soft crust if they sit around too long.

✧ Cook sausages over low heat or grill them over indirect heat. Turn them frequently until they are browned and just cooked through.

OUTSIDE THE BOX

- Sausages are easier to turn in a skillet or on the barbecue if you skewer pairs together like the base of a raft. Use two skewers, one at each end, and keep the sausages well separated.
- You can form a sausage mixture into patties, then grill or fry them, instead of stuffing it into casings. You can do this with the bits left in the grinder or when you run out of casings.

✧ Grilled sausages stay plumper than fried ones.

✧ Pan-fried sausages won't turn out so leathery if you add water to the skillet. Prick them, add $1/2$ cup (125 mL) water to the skillet and fry the sausages until the water evaporates. Then shake the sausages in the pan to finish browning. Turn them frequently.

Beef

- ❖ Buy chuck, brisket and shank for stews, pot roasts, burgers, sausages and chili.

- ❖ Leave some fat and connective tissues on stewing beef. They melt into tender deliciousness after long cooking, and enrich stews.

- ❖ Beef shank is the best meat for goulash and soup. Cut out the small bone in the center and trim the marbled beef, but leave some connective tissue.

💗 Healthier Eater

From the round come the leanest cuts of beef. These must be braised or marinated. The round (hip) includes the sirloin tip, eye of round, outside round and inside round.

Beef Doctor

The steak is undercooked.
- Slice it in half horizontally, then sear it in a skillet. It has to be at least 1 inch (2.5 cm) thick for this remedy.

The roast is undercooked.
- Cut off a thick slice and sear it like a steak in a pan or on a grill.

Brisket and Corned Beef

Point Cut VS. Flat Cut?

Brisket is a delicious, inexpensive meat that is sold in two parts. The front cut, or point cut, is thicker, with an irregular shape and more fat. It is also cheaper than the even bottom part known as the first cut, or flat cut.

- ❖ Tie a brisket before braising, so it doesn't fall apart.

- ❖ Let brisket cool in its own liquid for half an hour after removing it from the oven.

- ❖ To reheat brisket, slice it, arrange it in overlapping circles in a pan, then warm it in its own sauce in the oven.

- ❖ It's easier to slice brisket neatly when it's cold. This holds true for corned beef too.

♻ Waste Not
Save the cooking liquid from corned beef and use it as a soup base.

- ❖ If you're cooking corned beef in a boil-in bag, scrub off the store price label and pierce the bag.

- ❖ Corned beef tends to dry out. After it cools, refrigerate it in its cooking liquid.

- ❖ Recommendations from fussy fans of corned-beef hash:
  - The meat has to be shredded, not chopped.
  - It must be "real" corned beef, not the canned stuff.

- ❖ Reasons to chill canned corned beef and luncheon meat:
  - It slides out of the can more easily.
  - It will slice without breaking.

Beautiful Pot Roast with Marsala

This is comfort food and a festive dinner wrapped in one. Share it with close friends and family. **Makes 6 to 8 servings**

- **Preheat oven to 325°F (160°C)**

- **Large stovetop-safe roasting pan with a lid**

3 to 4 lb	boneless beef shoulder blade roast	1.5 to 2 kg
¼ cup	all-purpose flour	50 mL
1½ tsp	kosher salt, divided	7 mL
¾ tsp	freshly ground black pepper, divided	3 mL
¼ cup	vegetable oil	50 mL
1	small carrot, finely chopped	1
1	stalk celery, finely chopped	1
1	leek (white and light green parts only), finely chopped	1
1	clove garlic, minced	1
1 cup	water	250 mL
½ cup	beef stock	125 mL
½ cup	Marsala	125 mL
1	can (28 oz/796 mL) tomatoes, coarsely chopped, with juice	1
1	bay leaf	1
½ tsp	dried rosemary	2 mL
¼ tsp	dried thyme	1 mL
6 to 8	small potatoes, peeled and halved	6 to 8
3 to 4	carrots, cut into 3-inch (7.5 cm) lengths, thick sections split lengthwise	3 to 4
3 to 4	stalks celery, cut into 3-inch (7.5 cm) lengths	3 to 4
3 to 4	small onions, peeled	3 to 4
1 tbsp	balsamic vinegar	15 mL
	Chopped fresh parsley	

1. Coat roast lightly in flour. Sprinkle with ½ tsp (2 mL) each salt and pepper. Reserve the excess flour.

2. In a large roasting pan over two burners, heat oil over medium-high heat. Brown the roast on all sides. Do not pierce it. Remove it to a large plate.

Variations

Use red wine or dry port instead of Marsala.

You can purée the sauce with the solids (remove the bay leaf first). This is less wasteful and creates a thicker, more rustic sauce.

3. Reduce heat to medium-low. Add chopped carrot, celery, leek and garlic. Sauté for 3 to 5 minutes or until softened. Pour in water, stock, Marsala and tomatoes. Increase heat to medium. Scrape the pan as you bring the liquid to a boil. Stir in the remaining salt and pepper, bay leaf, rosemary and thyme.

4. Add the roast and its juices, turning to coat. Bring it just to a boil. Immediately cover the pan with foil, then a tight lid. Roast in preheated oven for $1\frac{1}{2}$ hours. Turn the roast over. Add the halved potatoes and carrot segments. Cover the pan with the foil and lid. Roast for 45 minutes.

5. Add the celery segments and onions. Cover the pan with the foil and lid. Roast for 45 minutes. Test the tenderness of the vegetables. Cover the pan with the foil and lid. Roast for 15 to 30 minutes or until the vegetables are tender. Remove the roast to a cutting board. Tent it with foil. Let it rest for at least 15 minutes.

6. Meanwhile, use tongs to remove the potatoes, carrots, celery and onions to a large bowl. Cover with foil.

7. Strain the sauce through a large sieve lined with cheesecloth. Push on the solids, then fold up the sides of the cloth and squeeze to extract liquid. Discard the solids. Skim excess fat from the liquid. Transfer it to a medium saucepan. Bring it to a boil over medium-high heat. Reduce heat to medium-low and simmer until the sauce is slightly thicker, about 5 minutes. Stir in balsamic vinegar. Remove from heat and cover.

8. Thinly slice meat across the grain. Place it on a large platter. Surround it with some of the reserved vegetables. Drizzle with some of the sauce and garnish with parsley. Serve the remaining vegetables in a separate dish. Serve the remaining sauce in individual gravy boats.

Pot Roast

8 Tips for Perfect Pot Roast

1. Cook pot roast in a small amount of liquid. It should come halfway up the sides of the roast. To minimize the amount of liquid, the pot should be just slightly bigger than the roast.
2. Cover the pot with foil, then secure the lid so the evaporated liquid falls back into the pot.
3. Never let a pot roast rise above a simmer or the liquid will be too cloudy.
4. You can make pot roast in a clear baking dish to keep an eye on it and ensure that it doesn't boil.
5. Turn the roast over halfway through the cooking time.
6. To shine and thicken the cooking liquid, strain and degrease it. Transfer it to a saucepan. Bring it to a boil on medium-high heat. Reduce the heat to medium-low and simmer it for about 5 minutes. You now have a sauce. Do this while the roast rests, tented with foil.
7. To exquisitely finish the sauce, stir in a bit of balsamic vinegar.
8. To adapt a pot roast recipe for a slow cooker, reduce the liquid by half.

Roast Beef

OUTSIDE THE BOX

A Scandinavian method for roast beef gives the meat a break right in the middle of cooking. This is a trick to give the roast an even color throughout. It seems to work.

Master Plan
Evenly Colored Sirloin Roast

1. Marinate a sirloin roast.
2. Roast it at 350°F (180°C) for 40 minutes.
3. Remove it from the oven. Turn it over. Let it stand, uncovered, for 20 minutes.
4. Reduce the oven temperature to 300°F (150°C). Roast the meat until a thermometer inserted into the thickest part registers 135°F (57°C) for medium-rare or 145°F (63°C) for medium, about 30 minutes.
5. Let the roast rest, uncovered, for 20 minutes before serving.

Roast Beef Tenderness Scale

1. Tenderloin
2. Prime rib
3. Rib eye
4. Strip loin
5. Top sirloin
6. Sirloin tip
7. Inside round
8. Outside round
9. Eye of round

Ways to Slice Prime Rib

- If you want to serve some pieces on the bone, cut 1-inch (2.5 cm) slices between each pair of bones. Every second slice will be boneless.
- If you're not into chewing on bones, get rid of them before carving the roast by sliding a knife along the meaty side of the ribs close to the bone. Separate the entire loin (the oval part) before slicing.
- If you want to carve just the meat as you go, point the ribs down, slice under the first rib to loosen the meat, then cut slices from the loin part of the roast. Repeat the process when you reach the next rib.

Steak

What Kind?

- Rib eyes are from the rib section. T-bones, porterhouses, strip loins and tenderloins are from the loin. Strip loins are generally considered to have the best balance between tenderness and taste. Tenderloin is the most tender, but it's bland.

- Salt steak before grilling or searing it. This encourages browning and crust formation.

- Make pepper steak more mellow. Use cracked white and pink peppercorns along with the black ones. Rub the steak with oil or mustard first, to help the pepper cling better.

- Carve a heart-shaped filet mignon for your loved one: If the filet is surrounded by a bacon strip, remove it. Put the filet in the freezer just until it firms up (for neater cutting). Using a small, sharp knife, carefully cut a slit through the meat, from the top center to about a third of the way down. Gently spread the sections to form the top of the heart. Cut each side at a slight angle to form the point at the bottom of the heart. Don't carve too deeply; keep as much meat as possible. Save the shavings to cook and snack on later.

✖ No-No

Don't cook steak above medium-rare. When overcooked, steak gets leathery.

Pork

✧ A side of pork is split into four primal cuts: shoulder (including the front leg), loin (actually the back), belly and ham (the hind leg).

● Loin cuts are prime. They are lean. Cook them on high, dry heat.

● Shoulder cuts are cheap and fatty. Treat them to long, slow cooking, and you'll be rewarded with pulled pork. They also make fine sausage meat.

● Belly cuts are the most fatty and most flavorful. They include bacon and ribs.

Trotters **VS.** Hocks?

Trotters are the feet. Hocks are the shanks just above the feet. They can be braised or smoked.

Larding **VS.** Barding?

When you insert tiny chunks or strips of pork fat into a lean roast, you are larding it. A lardoire is a needle designed for that purpose. When you lay strips of fat over a lean roast, you are barding it. Bacon strips are perfect. Caul fat, a lacy abdominal lining, is also used for barding.

Suckling Pig

✧ If you want to serve a suckling pig with an apple in its mouth, stuff a block of wood into the mouth to hold it open during roasting. Insert the apple when the pig is on the platter.

✧ While roasting suckling pig, shield the ears and tail with foil.

Tenderloin

✧ A supermarket pork tenderloin is usually 12 oz to 1 lb (375 to 500 g).

✧ To cook a larger amount of tenderloin, tie two together with kitchen string and cook them like a larger roast, or cook a pair side by side.

Chops

Is It Fresh?

✧ Look for reddish pink chops, with no dark spots on the fat. Grayish is not good.

✧ Thick pork chops are more tender and less likely to overcook.

✧ Make the fat on pork chops extra-crispy: Rub it with baking soda before searing the chops. Careful: If you use too much, it will taste soapy.

Ham

Fresh **VS.** Cured?

True hams are made from the hind leg of the pig. The upper thigh is the butt; it is meatier. The lower end is the shank. Fresh ham is actually a pork roast. Cured ham may simply be cured with salt or in brine, or cured and smoked. Lengthy aging may follow. Milder hams are not smoked. At the opposite end is the country ham, such as Smithfield — dry-cured and very salty.

✧ Cured hams don't require cooking or heating, but they look so festive when served hot and glazed. Getting them that way without drying them out is the trick.

Ways to Glaze Heated Ham

- Brush on the glaze. Increase the oven temperature to 400°F (200°C). Heat the ham until the glaze looks sticky and golden brown.
- If the ham is smaller or in thick slices, brush on the glaze and stick it under the broiler.

3 Ways to Heat a Whole Cured Ham

1. Put it on a rack in a roasting pan. Pour a thin layer of water in the bottom. Cover the pan tightly with foil. Roast it in a 325°F (160°C) oven for about 15 minutes a pound, or until a meat thermometer inserted into the thickest part registers 140°F (60°C).
2. If the ham is spiral-sliced, place it cut side down on a large swatch of heavy foil. Wrap the foil over the ham completely and tightly. Bake it at 300°F (150°C) for about 15 minutes a pound, or until a meat thermometer inserted into the thickest part registers 140°F (60°C).
3. Warm ham in a slow cooker — if it fits. Pour the glaze, along with 1 cup (250 mL) stock, water or cola, into the cooker. Put in the ham and replace the lid. Heat it on Low. This will take all day, but the ham should be very moist.

✗ No-No

Do not try to grill a large ham. It will dry out too much.

♻ Waste Not

Save prosciutto ends and rinds for soup.

⚡ Lightning Won't Strike If ...

You freeze the ham leftovers. It is said that the definition of eternity is two people and a ham. Unfortunately, all those leftovers get spongy when they're frozen. If your fridge is overflowing with the remnants of a spiral-cut holiday ham, and you are desperate, toss it in the freezer anyway. When the time comes, thaw and grind it. Use it to supplement the ground beef in meatloaf.

Gussy It Up

To decorate a ham, evenly score the surface in a diamond pattern. Apply the glaze. Stick a clove in at each intersection. Heat.

Two Ham Imitators

- The picnic ham is cut from the front leg. Never mind the name — it's actually a roast. It is smoked and ham-like, but requires longer cooking. It is also fattier, bonier and cheaper.
- A smoked butt may be called a cottage ham. It's very fatty.

> **Factoid** That rainbow you see on ham and cold cuts is caused by light hitting a film of fat.

Ribs

Spareribs Back Ribs?

Spareribs (also called side ribs) come from the belly. They are larger, meatier, fattier, less tender and cheaper than the back ribs from the loin.

⑤ is for Skirt

Ask the butcher to slice off the skirt, if he or she hasn't done it already. Or cut it off yourself. This is the floppy flap of skin at the end of the rack. It can be marinated and grilled separately.

❖ Trim off the cellophane-like membrane on the bony side of a rack of ribs. It makes ribs taste too porky. Loosen it by cutting a small slit with a knife, then prying it up with your finger. Get rid of any large hunks of hard fat.

❖ If you substitute spareribs for back ribs in a recipe, adjust the time. Spareribs take almost twice as long to cook.

♛ A Golden Rule

Always cook ribs low and slow.

❖ Four ways to give ribs a head start before grilling or roasting:
- Steam them on a rack in a roasting pan in a 325°F (160°C) oven, $1\frac{3}{4}$ to 2 hours for spareribs.
- Lay them in a rimmed baking sheet. Pour in about 2 cups (500 mL) water. Cover the sheet tightly with foil. Bake at 325°F (160°C) until the ribs are almost tender.
- Seal them in a foil packet with about $\frac{1}{2}$ cup (125 mL) liquid. Bake at 325°F (160°C) until almost tender.
- Bake them in a 325°F (160°C) oven directly on the oven rack, with a drip pan filled with water on the rack below.

❖ An added touch: Steam ribs using beer or apple juice.

✖ No-No

If you want joylessly dry, bland ribs, parboil them before grilling or roasting. Sure, parboiling dissolves some of the fat and mellows the porky flavor. But it sucks out flavor.

Ways to Finish Ribs

- Grill them over medium-low heat, 20 to 25 minutes for spareribs. Brush them frequently with sauce or glaze, and turn to prevent charring.
- Put them under the broiler to brown.

Pulled Pork

Ⓑ is for Butt

The butt is prime territory for all who love pulled pork. Never mind the name — it is actually cut from the shoulder.

❖ For pulled pork that dissolves into silky, moist threads, roast a pork shoulder at a low temperature all day. It can take 8 hours.

3 Finishing Touches

1. Wrap the roast in foil and place it in a paper bag for an hour. Remove any crisp skin first.
2. Use your hands and two forks to pull the pork into shreds 1 to 2 inches (2.5 to 5 cm) long and $\frac{1}{8}$ to $\frac{1}{4}$ inch (0.25 to 0.5 cm) thick. Pull the pork while it's hot. Wear rubber gloves.
3. To keep pulled pork hot and moist, stir in the traditional spicy vinegar sauce, cover the pork with foil and return it to the warm barbecue or oven.

OUTSIDE THE BOX

Make Carolina-style pulled pork with a Cuban accent. Instead of vinegar sauce, use a mojo made with sour orange juice and garlic.

Crackling

- Choose a shoulder roast with a thick rind. You'll get less shrinkage, plus a bonus in the form of crackling, or crispy skin.

- To optimize the crackling on a roast, score the skin and rub it with salt. Let it dry in the fridge for 30 minutes before roasting.

- If the crackling on your roast is not crisp enough, cut it off and scrape off the soft fat. Roast the crackling on a rack on a rimmed baking sheet in a hot oven for 10 minutes.

Master Plan
Crackling on Its Own

1. Remove the skin from a shoulder roast. Trim as much excess fat from the underside as possible. It tends to curl, so cut slits at the edges, about 1 inch (2.5 cm) long.
2. Rub the skin with olive oil and salt.
3. Place it on a rack set over a baking dish to catch the drippings. Roast it at 400°F (200°C) for 20 minutes. Reduce the heat to 350°F (180°C) and roast until it is crisp.
4. You can put a pork roast in the baking dish underneath the crackling and let the drippings baste it. Once the crackling is crisp, remove it from the oven, reduce the heat to 300°F (150°C) and continue roasting the pork.

- Crackling softens as it sits. Give it some air. Do not store in a sealed tub.

- Restore crackling to its former glory by heating it, in the microwave even, until it sizzles. Parts puff up like pork rinds.

- To make homemade pork rinds, first soften the thicker sections of crackling by boiling them. Cut the skin into strips and deep-fry them. They puff.

Bacon

Fab Fats

- Bacon is cured, smoked belly fat that's striped with meat.
- Fatback is cut from the back. It is used in Southern cooking and soul food.
- Salt pork is cured fat. It can come from various parts of the animal.
- Lardo is cured pork fat taken from directly under the skin. This Italian delicacy may be consumed as antipasto or used as a substitute for pancetta in cooking.

- Do not keep bacon in a plastic bag. It gets slimy.

- Store a slab of bacon wrapped in a kitchen towel in the fridge.

7 Ways to Separate Sticky Strips of Bacon

1. Keep the package rolled up. Secure it with an elastic band. Before opening the package, roll it on the counter.
2. Pull off two or three strips at once, then separate them.
3. Loosen strips by microwaving them for 20 to 30 seconds on High.
4. Dip a metal spatula repeatedly in the hottest tap water, then use it to pry off slices of frozen bacon. This is still hard work, but the slices will separate if you worry at the edges.
5. Freeze strips individually on a baking sheet, then pack them in plastic bags. You don't have to thaw frozen bacon before cooking it.
6. Accordion the strips in a piece of parchment paper before freezing.
7. Cook the strips, then freeze them.

Alternative Ways to Make Bacon

- Drape it across the top oven rack. Put a drip pan underneath. Bake it at 350°F (180°C) until crispy. To keep it warm, turn off the oven.
- Arrange bacon strips on a rimmed baking sheet. Place another baking sheet on top to keep the strips flat as they cook. Bake at 375°F (190°C) until they are almost crisp, 18 to 20 minutes. Drain them. Transfer them to a clean baking sheet and return them to the oven for about 5 minutes or until they crisp up.

Easier Ways to Chop Bacon

- Using scissors, cut from cold or frozen strips directly into the skillet.
- Freeze the bacon for 15 minutes before chopping.

✧ You can cook bacon ahead of time. Refrigerate or freeze it. Reheat it on a paper towel in the microwave.

✧ Briefly microwave a bacon strip before wrapping it around a filet mignon. It is more likely to crisp up when you cook the filet. Secure the strip with toothpicks.

♻ Waste Not

- Save bacon rinds. Toss them into soups and stews. Discard them before serving the dish.
- Use the bacon fat. Otherwise you are only consuming a quarter of what you paid for. Fry green tomatoes in it. Give fried eggs a hit of bacon flavor. Store bacon fat in a sealed container in the fridge.

Canadian VS. Peameal?

Lean Canadian bacon, or back bacon, has little in common with the standard breakfast strips. It is the eye of the loin. Though it's not from the same neighborhood as ham, you can treat it like ham. Its sibling, peameal bacon, is made from the same cut, but is pickled or cured in brine, then rolled in cornmeal.

Lamb

Is It Fresh?

✧ Choose lamb that's pink and springy, not ruddy.

🄵 is for Fell

The fell is the papery membrane that covers the fat on lamb. Some cooks blame the fell for a gamy taste and take it off. Others say it holds large cuts together and should be kept on. I vote for trimming it, along with large hunks of fat. Don't go overboard; leave a thin coating of fat on the lamb.

✘ No-Nos

• Avoid cooking lamb beyond medium-rare.

• Do not use leg of lamb for stews or curries, with your mind on less fat. It gets way too dry. Buy shoulder instead. It's cheaper and tastier, but fatty. Trim it.

✧ Slow-roasting makes lamb exceptionally tender and uniformly cooked.

✧ You can unroll a tied, boneless leg of lamb, then roast or grill it flat, to cater to a range of tastes. The thickest bits will be rare, the thinnest ones medium. Do not cook the lamb well-done.

Master Plan
Slow-Roasted Lamb

1. Marinate the lamb.
2. Bring it to room temperature on a rack in a shallow roasting pan.
3. Preheat the oven to 450°F (230°C). Set the lamb in the lower third of the oven. Immediately reduce the temperature to 250°F (120°C).
4. Roast until it is medium-rare.

✧ To roast an unrolled leg flat, lay it on a rack in a roasting pan. Pour about $\frac{1}{2}$ cup (125 mL) wine into the pan.

Master Plan
Herb-Crusted Lamb

Use egg yolks to glue an herb crust on a leg of lamb:

1. Stir together herbes de Provence and plenty of minced garlic.
2. After marinating the lamb, pat it dry. Sprinkle it with salt and pepper. Brush it liberally with egg yolks.
3. Press the herb mixture all over the lamb. Refrigerate it for about 1 hour or until the crust is set.
4. Roast it on a rack.

Game and Organ Meats

B is for Boar

Wild boar is leaner than pork — a lot leaner. The meat is ruddy.

6 Ways to Keep Boar Moist

1. Use a marinade.
2. Cook it in sauce.
3. Baste it frequently.
4. Wrap roasts in several layers of foil.
5. Add water, stock or wine to chops as they bake.
6. Do not roast at a temperature higher than 325°F (160°C).

C is for Cervids

As members of the *Cervidae* family, farm-raised deer and elk are marketed as cervids — perhaps so it won't seem like we're eating Bambi. The meat is lean, with no marbling. Elk, for instance, has only 5% fat. Caribou are related. Unlike animals in the wild that consume pine needles and the like, farmed cervids don't have a gamy taste.

✧ To minimize drying, cook cervid meat either low and slow, or quickly on high, dry heat, to no more than medium-rare.

✧ The lean meat contains lots of water, so freeze it quickly and thaw it slowly to prevent moisture loss.

✧ If using ground venison or elk for sausages, add some ground pork and bacon for juiciness.

Foods That Complement Cervid Meat

- Fruity sauces, such as blueberry
- Rich gravies
- Dried fruit
- Jellies
- Juniper berries

V is for Variety Meats

That's the innocuous name for innards, organs and bits and bobs such as sweetbreads (pancreas and thymus glands), brains, kidneys, livers, testicles, tripe, bony appendages (such as oxtails or pigs' knuckles), muscles (such as hearts and tongues) and even beef cheeks.

✧ Variety meats are highly perishable. Use them at once.

✧ Soak sweetbreads and brains for 1 hour in lots of changes of cold water to release the blood.

✧ Before cooking sweetbreads, blanch them in water with lemon juice.

♛ A Golden Rule

Don't overcook liver. Some people hate it because they've never had properly cooked liver. Overcooked liver is rubbery. Tender liver is delightful.

OUTSIDE THE BOX

Liver and bacon are pals. Put a different spin on the friendship by frying liver in bacon grease.

How to Improve Liver

1. Gently dig your fingers into raw liver to pull out the veins or strings of connective tissue.
2. Soak liver in a milk bath for 1 hour, to mellow the bloody, iron-rich flavor.
3. If you are frying liver, dust it with a light coating of flour and sprinkle it with salt. Don't use a lot of oil.
4. Cook liver over medium heat until it is barely done, with a thin line of pink in the center. It will finish cooking as it sits in the serving dish. A slice of calves' liver that's $\frac{1}{4}$ inch (0.5 cm) thick takes about $1\frac{1}{2}$ minutes per side.

F is for Foie Gras

Foie gras is duck or goose liver, swollen and fatty from the birds being force-fed during the last few weeks of their lives. The custom can be traced back to ancient Egypt. Foie gras is a controversial food. Opponents say force-feeding is cruel. Producers note that geese and ducks in the wild naturally gorge before migrations.

A Good Sign

Choose foie gras that is yellowish, with only a bit of give.

A Golden Rule

Foie gras should melt in your mouth, not in the pan. If you don't cook it quickly, your gourmet food dollars will dissolve along with it.

Master Plan
Seared Foie Gras

1. Because the cooking time is so short, let foie gras come to room temperature before cooking, to help it along.
2. Separate the two lobes. Press your fingers into each lobe to extract veins and sinew.
3. Slice foie gras $\frac{3}{4}$ inch (2 cm) thick. To make it easier to cut neatly, warm the knife under tap water first.
4. Lightly score a crosshatch pattern on both sides of each slice to allow heat to penetrate. Dust the slices with flour.
5. Heat a skillet over high heat. Add a drizzle of oil.
6. Sear the foie gras about 30 seconds per side or until a brown crust forms. Pay attention, or half of your foie gras will melt before you notice.

Poultry

White VS. Dark?

White meat is dry, dark meat is fatty. White meat cooks faster. By the time the leg is done, the breast is dry. Herein lies the conundrum that plagues cooks grappling with poultry.

The Challenges of Cooking a Whole Bird

- The temperature must rise to 165°F (74°C) in order to kill bacteria.
- At 155°F (68°C), the breast is past its prime. But the leg must be cooked to 165°F (74°C) or it will be chewy.
- The stuffing has to reach a safe temperature of 165°F (74°C), but it doesn't cook as fast as the bird.
- Wait, there are two more complications: The bird is an architectural nightmare of thick and thin pieces. The skin should be crispy, not soggy.

How to Cut Poultry

1. Cut the skin to expose the joint.
2. Cut the flesh at the joint to expose the bone.
3. Bend the joint backwards to separate it.
4. Cut through the joint.

❖ To slice a breast more attractively, pull it off the bones first. Loosen it by sticking a dull, round-tipped knife between the bones and meat. Pull off the meat with your fingers.

10 Ways to Help Poultry Cook More Evenly

1. Chill it, breast down, on ice packs for an hour before cooking, to give the dark meat a head start.
2. Mutilate the creature by cutting deep slashes in the drumsticks and thighs. This reduces the cooking time. (It works for other meats on the bone, too.)
3. Tent the white meat with foil. Fold it triple thick and butter one side. Cover the entire breast — for the first hour of cooking for chicken, or until the thighs start to brown for turkey.
4. Cover the breast with cheesecloth that has been dampened with ice-cold water.
5. Spray the breast with cold water periodically as the bird cooks.
6. Cram stuffing under the skin of the breast to insulate the meat.
7. Truss the bird into a compact dome.
8. Cook it from frozen. Because the breast is larger, it will take longer to thaw and longer to cook. (Exception: Do not cook poultry from frozen in a slow cooker or microwave.)
9. If there's room, point the legs toward the back of the oven, where it's hotter, and the breast toward the front.
10. Deconstruct. The late Julia Child believed that was the only way to deal with duck, for instance. She cooked the breast, legs and skin separately.

Remedies for Dryness

- Smear butter or oil between the skin and breast meat. Press down on the skin to smooth and distribute it. As an added touch, make that herb butter.
- Cover the breast with oil-soaked cheesecloth. Remove it half an hour before the bird is done so the breast can brown.
- Lay bacon strips over the breast.

- ◇ To apply rub or make room for stuffing under the bird's skin, insinuate your finger under a flap of skin near the neck and tear the thin membranes in a windshield-wiper motion. If you are squeamish, use a spoon held convex side up.

- ◇ Finish poultry, especially gamy goose or duck, with a glaze. Brush on warmed cranberry or apple jelly once the bird is out of the oven.

- ◇ If you are roasting small fowl, such as squabs and quail, brown them in a skillet first. The short cooking time in the oven doesn't allow for adequate browning.

Remedies for Dry, Overcooked Poultry

- Slice it. Spread out the slices on a microwave-safe dish. Cover them with stock, then add a pat of butter. Microwave on High just until warm. Transfer the meat and its juices to a heatproof platter. Place it in a 250°F (120°C) oven for 10 minutes.
- Brush it all over with a barbecue or Asian sauce to moisten it.

Being Green

Free-range chickens take longer to grow and are older when they're processed. Organic and free-range turkeys are not necessarily tastier. The toughest turkey I ever cooked was free-range.

S is for Spatchcock

Butterfly a chicken lengthwise. Voila, you've spatchcocked it. Do the same with any bird. You can carry on and split the bird in half by cutting through the breast. It's easiest to cut through the breast from the inside, so you can see all the bones.

How to Spatchcock

1. Start at the neck on one side of the backbone. It's easier than starting at the tail end. Cut along the backbone to the tail end. Then grip the tail as you cut in the other direction along the other side of the backbone. (Set aside the backbone for stock.)

2. Push on the sides to expose the interior of the bird. Remove the breastbone, also known as the keel bone. To do so, cut a short, lengthwise slit through the centre of the gristle and flesh at the top of the bird, between the sets of ribs. Press on the two sides to pop out the breastbone. Attached to it is a long piece of cartilage, which extends down the centre of the bird toward the tail. You can use your fingers to tease out the cartilage or cut along either side of it.

3. A shortcut: Don't bother removing the breastbone. Flip the bird over. Flatten it by pressing on the breast until you hear bones snapping.

4. Use scissors or a sharp knife to trim flaps of skin or fat.

5. You can skewer the bird to hold it firmly for marinating or grilling. Push a bamboo skewer diagonally through the flesh of one breast and the opposite thigh. Repeat with a second skewer to form an X.

Chicken

- ❖ Chickens are rated by age and weight. These indicate how they should be cooked. So do their names. The older the chicken, the tougher the meat and the stronger the flavor. Here's a general pecking order, starting with the youngest and smallest:
  - Broiler
  - Broiler/fryer
  - Roaster
  - Capon (large, castrated male with tender, light meat)
  - Rooster (mature male with coarse, dark meat)
  - Stewing/baking hen
  - Fowl
  - Old hen

ⓒ is for Cornish

A Cornish hen is a breed of chicken. A Cornish game hen is an immature Cornish chicken, or a hybrid bred tiny, with lots of white meat. It is the two-bite brownie of the chicken world. It is considered a broiler/fryer.

- ❖ If the tip of the breastbone bends easily, the bird is young.

- ❖ On the off chance that you get a bird to pluck, remember that the old method of scalding the chicken in boiling water to loosen the feathers has been discredited. It turns the skin blotchy and dissolves fat that otherwise makes the flesh juicy.

Plucking Tips

- Hang and chill a bird to make it easier to pluck the big, coarse feathers.
- To get rid of down, give the chicken a Brazilian. Smear it with wax, let it cool and pull.
- Use a kitchen torch to singe off remaining feathers.

Four Good Signs

- Moist skin.
- Soft legs and feet.
- Bright eyes.
- Red comb.

Factoid Birds slaughtered by hand are less likely to get blood clotting, which toughens the meat.

ⓣ is for Trussing

When you tie a chicken into a neat, tight package, you are trussing it. Pros: Binding the wings and legs against the body prevents the tips from drying and scorching, and creates a more even shape for cooking. Cons: The skin won't be as crispy. Trussing also slows down the cooking of the legs, which we may not want.

To Truss a Chicken...
With one string

- Place the chicken, breast side up, with the neck end closest to you.
- Slide a 3-foot (1 m) length of kitchen string under the tail.
- Cross the string over the tops of the drumsticks at the tips. Cross it under the drumstick tips and pull them together tightly.
- Pull the string along the sides of the chicken, around the thighs and over the wings.
- Flip the chicken over.
- Tightly knot the ends above the wing joints. Twist the wing tips and tuck them against the back. Tuck the tips under the string.

In a crisscross

- Twist the wing tips and tuck them against the back.
- Place the chicken, breast side up, with the legs toward you.

- Slide a 4-foot (1.2 m) length of kitchen string under the chicken at the wings.
- Cross the string over the breast to create an X. Draw the ends down above the thighs.
- Cross the string under the chicken. Draw it up near the tail.
- Tie the string around the tips of the drumsticks to seal the cavity.

Upside down

- Twist the wing tips and tuck them against the back.
- Place the chicken, breast side up, with the legs pointing away from you.
- Loop a 3-foot (1 m) length of kitchen string under and over the tips of the drumsticks.
- Cross the string, loop it under the tips, then pull to draw the legs together.
- Pull the string up the body, over the thighs and wings.
- Turn the chicken over. Tie the string across the crook of the wings.

The lazy way

- Tie together the legs.
- Twist the wing tips and tuck them against the back.

Securing the legs

- Slit the skin at the sides of the cavity. Cross the drumsticks and stuff their tips into the slits.
- Alternatively, twist a large, straightened paper clip around the tips of the drumsticks to hold them together.

Or Not to Truss...

- Use a V-shaped rack to hold the poultry snugly, so you don't have to truss it.

- ✧ Once you know how to carve a raw chicken, you'll figure out how to carve a cooked one. And you can expand your repertoire to other poultry.

- ✧ To tease off raw chicken skin and membrane, rub it with a terrycloth towel.

How to Cut Up a Raw Chicken

1. Slice the skin and flesh between the thigh and breast to expose the leg joint.
2. Turning the chicken as you work, carve a semicircle through the skin and flesh around the "bum."
3. Bend back the thigh to pop the joint. Cut through the joint.
4. Repeat with the other leg.
5. Cut each leg into thigh and drumstick, guided by the line of fat between them.
6. Bend the lower back section back and up to unhinge it. Cut it off and set it aside for stock.
7. Snip off the wing tips with scissors and set them aside for stock.
8. Cut around each wing joint, through the skin and flesh, to expose the joint. Bend it back to separate it, if necessary. Cut through the joint.
9. Cut each wing into a wingette and drumette.
10. Push down on the breast to loosen it and snap the bones.
11. Turn the chicken upside down. With poultry shears, cut along both sides of the backbone, and set it aside for stock.
12. Turn the chicken breast side up. Slice through the skin and flesh along the center line until you meet resistance. Push the knife down hard to snap through the bone.
13. Turn each breast so you can see the inside. Cut away any loose bones. Slip the knife under the ribs and saw them off. Set the bones aside for stock.
14. Turn each breast right side up. Cut it in half diagonally to get two sections of roughly the same weight. Do so by pushing down with the knife to snap through the bones. You could also use scissors or poultry shears.

♻ Waste Not

Use up the giblets. You can save them for stock (except for the liver). Finely chop the heart and gizzard, and stir them into gravy. Sauté the liver, chop it and add it to stuffing. Or treat your cat or dog.

✦ Leave the skin on a chicken breast. It will be juicier. The fat in the skin bastes the chicken. You can pull off the skin before you eat the meat.

How to Butterfly a Boneless Breast

1. Start at the top, thick end of the triangle, with the pointed end facing away from you.
2. Hold your palm across the top. Slicing parallel to the counter, cut partway through the center. Leave no more than 1 inch (2.5 cm) attached at one edge.
3. Open the two flaps like a book. Pound to flatten the meat, or roll it, or stuff it.

Ⓣ is for Tenders

Chicken tenders are the long strips of filet on the underside of the breasts. A tender is easy to remove. Just hold the breast down on the counter and pull off the strip with your fingers.

Reasons to Remove the Tenders

- You can save them for delicate chicken fingers.
- The breasts will be easier to pound flat.
- The meat will cook more evenly.

✦ Red food dye is the secret behind the vibrant color of chicken tikka masala and tandoori chicken. You can get a gentler effect with paprika. Just don't expose it to the heat for a long time.

✦ You can microwave chicken pieces, but the outcome will be disappointing.

Tips for Microwaving Chicken

- Remove the skin, as it will not crisp.
- Place the meat on a plastic rack so it won't boil in its own juices.
- Arrange the pieces with the thickest parts at the outside and the thinner parts toward the center.
- Drape parchment over the top to prevent spattering and distribute heat.
- Tent the cooked chicken and let it rest for 15 minutes before serving.

✦ To have chicken on hand for salads and sandwiches, poach a whole chicken, cool, skin and strip. Bonus: leftover stock.

How to Get Barbecue Flavor in the Oven

1. Marinate chicken pieces, adding a few drops of liquid smoke to the marinade.
2. Place the meat directly on the middle oven rack, with a drip pan on the rack below. Roast it until it is nearly done.
3. Baste both sides of the meat with the marinade.
4. Raise the rack up under the broiler. Broil the meat for about 5 minutes per side or until the juices run clear. Careful, it burns quickly.

Mythstake

Pink near the bone is sometimes mistaken for undercooked meat. Pigment from bone marrow can seep into the surrounding tissue, especially in frozen or young birds. If the meat is raw, it will also be rubbery and shiny. Check for doneness with a thermometer.

Poached Chicken Tips

- Use stock instead of water to intensify the flavor.
- Tint the bird by adding soy sauce to the liquid.
- Poach it breast side down. It will cook faster.
- You don't have to simmer the chicken the whole time. A Chinese method: Simmer the chicken, covered, over medium-low heat for 15 minutes, then turn off the heat and let the pot sit on the burner for 30 minutes. Turn the chicken, cover and let it sit for 15 minutes. This works with a 3- to 3½-lb (1.5 to 1.75 kg) chicken.
- You can freeze the poaching liquid and reuse it. This liquid gets stronger each time.

Ⓦ is for White Cut

Poached chicken tends to become spongy and bland. To firm it up, Chinese cooks use a technique called white cut. As soon as the chicken is done, it is plunged into ice water for 15 minutes, then returned to the stock. This is used for other types of simmered meat, too

♡ Healthier Eater

To make creamier-tasting butter chicken without adding a lot of butter, use sour cream instead of yogurt in the sauce.

- Grill boneless, skinless chicken thighs smooth side down at first. There's less chance of the meat sticking and ripping. Don't forget to unfold flaps of meat onto the grate.

⚡ Lightning Won't Strike If ...

You dice the cooked chicken. Purists like to shred chicken, saying it is tastier and more tender. But diced chicken looks neater and has a better texture.

Roast Chicken

- Don't forget to salt the cavity of the chicken. It's more effective than salting the skin, or even under the skin.

5 Ways to Prep a Chicken Before Roasting

1. Soak it in flavored brine.
2. Rinse the chicken, then dry it well, inside and out, so it steams less.
3. Rub it all over with oil, then sprinkle it with salt and pepper, inside and out. Avoid barbecue rubs; they scorch.
4. Inject it all over with marinade (like a barbecue injection).
5. Arrange fresh herbs, such as sage leaves, attractively under the skin.

Ways to Perfume the Meat

- Fill the cavity with half a lemon, a cut onion, an herb bundle and/or garlic cloves. (Eat the roasted garlic later in mashed potatoes or on crusty bread.)
- Insert a ramekin of spiced wine into the cavity.

- Always preheat the roasting pan and the rack. The chicken should sizzle when you put it in.

- Chicken cooked at higher temperatures is juicier. Start with a quick blast at 450°F (230°C) for 10 to 15 minutes, then reduce the heat to 375°F (190°C) and baste every 10 minutes. The opposite works, too.

- Roast stuffed chicken at a lower temperature, such as 325°F (160°C). This allows the stuffing to reach a safe temperature before the chicken overcooks.

- Start roasting the chicken on its side. Flip it onto its other side. Then finish roasting it breast side up. Some cooks start the chicken on its breast, but that's too much of a hassle. Loosen the chicken from the rack with a spatula.

Master Plan
Restless Roast Chicken

1. Place a chicken on its side in a V-rack set in a roasting pan. Roast at 375°F (190°C) for 15 minutes.
2. Turn the chicken onto its other side. Roast for 15 minutes.
3. Turn the chicken breast side up. Crank the heat up to 450°F (230°C). Roast until the juices run clear.

Master Plan
Remarkably Fast Roast Chicken

This chicken is very tender, but has a pale back.
1. Rub oil all over the chicken. Sprinkle it with salt and pepper, inside and out.
2. Preheat a cast-iron skillet in a 450°F (230°C) oven.
3. Place the chicken in the skillet. Roast it for 30 to 45 minutes or until the juices run clear. At halftime, lift it on a fork to pour the bloody juices out of the cavity.

- Although a small cadre says it's a waste to baste, most of us find it essential and satisfying.

Alternative Ways to Baste
- Use hot chicken stock. You'll have more drippings later.
- Use the chicken's own fat. Pull out clumps of fat before roasting the bird. Render it in a skillet over medium-low heat.

- Brush the chicken with a mixture of 1 part melted butter and 1 part maple, corn or cane syrup. Do this a couple of times. It browns but, strangely, doesn't scorch.

How to Extract More Drippings

1. Halfway through the cooking time, insert a carving fork into the cavity, tilt the chicken and pour the bloody juices into the pan.
2. Slash the skin between the thighs and the breast, and tilt the chicken.

Master Plan
Quickest Roast Chicken

1. Halve the chicken lengthwise. Cut off the wing tips for a prettier presentation.
2. Preheat a large cast-iron pan in a 400°F (200°C) oven.
3. Place the chicken halves side by side in the pan. Keep them skin side up so the skin will baste the meat.
4. Place a weight on top of the chicken.
5. Roast the chicken until the juices run clear, about 20 minutes.

Ways to Weight Chicken Halves

- Put a cast-iron pan on top of them.
- Press them with bricks wrapped in foil.
- Place them between two rimmed baking sheets. Put bricks or weights on the top sheet.

Vertical Roasting Tips
- Put the roaster in a baking dish or aluminum baking pan that's large enough to catch the drippings.
- Secure the wings at the back.

- Make beer can chicken on the barbecue. Shove the upright chicken over a tall opened beer can. Or use a commercial "beer can" roaster.
- For super-crispy chicken, use a vertical roaster. With the roaster in its cavity, the chicken stands upright in the oven and fat runs down it. Roast at 400°F (200°C).

6 Ways to Make the Skin Crispier

1. Salt the bird and refrigerate it, uncovered, for at least 2 hours or up to 48 hours.
2. Coat the chicken with melted butter or oil. To brown it even more, sprinkle 1 tsp (5 mL) granulated sugar over top.
3. Put the chicken in at 450°F (230°C), then immediately reduce the heat to 350°F (180°C).
4. Roast the chicken in an open pan.
5. Place the chicken so it sits close to the top element.
6. Turn the chicken from up to down and from one side to the other in the roasting pan, to expose more areas of the skin. Beware: This leaves rack marks.

P is for Peking Duck

Fans of crispy skin should take note of the methods employed for Peking duck. Air is pumped under the skin to separate it from the flesh, the bird is blanched in boiling water, the skin is coated with molasses, honey or sugar syrup, the duck is hung until the skin is firm and dry, and finally it is roasted while hung by the neck.

✧ The crispiest roast chicken is unstuffed.

✧ You can roast chicken on a plank on the barbecue.

✧ You can cook two birds at once, each with a different stuffing or flavoring.

The Best Way to Roast a Chicken

- Don't roast it. Grill it on a rotisserie or spit.

✧ You can brush roast chicken with a glaze during the last 10 minutes of cooking time.

Fried Chicken

✧ For fried chicken, everyone has a secret recipe. There seem to be as many recipes as there are cooks. We can, however, all agree on certain givens: The crust and skin are fused and crispy. The flesh is silky. The real thing has a bone to gnaw on. And it tastes good cold at a picnic.

Top Tips for Getting Started

- Start with air-chilled chicken. It contains less water. Trim the excess fat and skin. If you want to maximize gnawing, use chicken parts with the backbone intact. They also happen to be cheaper.
- Kill two birds, so to speak, by marinating the chicken in buttermilk brine for at least 2 hours or overnight. It's well worth the time. It makes the flesh super-tender and slippery.
- Pat the chicken dry and let it air on a rack in the fridge for up to 2 hours. Air-drying before coating makes a lighter, flakier crust. Air-drying after coating makes a heartier, harder crust.

Brine VS. Marinade?

Brining in a salt solution is not common for fried chicken, but marinating it in buttermilk is. They are both worthwhile. Luckily, the two steps can be condensed into one.

- Liberally season both the marinade and the flour coating.
- A dash of hot pepper sauce (such as Tabasco) is de rigueur in the buttermilk marinade.

Optional Marinade Ingredients

- Black pepper
- Soy sauce (for color)
- Beer
- Chopped herbs, sprigs of tarragon or thyme
- Paprika
- Chopped onion
- Garlic cloves
- Mustard

Top Tips for Coating

- Seasoned flour can't be beat. Not that people haven't tried to top it. Personal tastes vary from the thick crumb breading made by Hungarian grandmothers to

11 Top Frying Tips

1. Always use fresh fat. Some Southern cooks swear by the clean taste of shortening, but it contains unhealthy trans fats. Stick to a neutral oil with a high smoke point, such as peanut or corn oil. If you want to compromise, use half oil, half shortening.

2. Fill the skillet with 1 to 2 inches (2.5 to 5 cm) oil.

3. Shake off excess flour before dunking chicken in the hot oil.

4. Start with the skin side down for maximum crispness.

5. The cold chicken immediately lowers the temperature of the oil and starts sucking it up. So start off at 375°F (190°C). When the chicken starts to look lively, after no more than 5 minutes, reduce the heat to 350°F (180°C). Each piece should be surrounded by a border of small bubbles as it fries.

6. It's fine to cook the chicken uncovered. There's less chance of steam making the crust rubbery. However, keeping the lid on can cut frying time and reduce spattering.

7. Fry the pieces in batches. Do not crowd the pan or the temperature of the oil will drop and your chicken will be soggy.

8. Between batches, use a slotted spoon to removed browned bits. Better still, pour the oil through a sieve, wipe the pan and reheat the oil to 375°F (190°C).

9. Use two skillets if you can: one for breasts and wings, the other for thighs and drumsticks. Dark meat takes longer to cook. Or simply remove the white cuts earlier.

10. Southerners are fond of cast iron, but an electric skillet works best. The temperature control makes it easier to maintain the proper heat. A deep fryer does the same, but overcrowds the chicken.

11. Fried chicken takes about 30 minutes. However, the timing will vary depending on the stove, the heat of the oil, the type of fat, the size of the pieces and the coating. Fry the chicken until it is golden brown on both sides and the juices run clear. Turn the pieces occasionally. Remove smaller pieces as they are done.

the parchment-thin crust encountered at the Southern church social. Alternative coatings include panko, corn flake crumbs and melba toast crumbs.

- Add cornstarch to the coating. This makes the crust sturdy and crispy.
- Use white pepper. Black specks make diners nervous.
- Paprika adds a rosy glow. You can use chili powder instead. Save cayenne pepper or hot sauce for the marinade.
- Double-bound coating is the most tenacious. Dip the chicken in seasoned flour, then in egg whisked with a bit of milk or water, then again in the flour. Let it stand for a few minutes until it looks doughy. (Single-bound coating omits the first step.)

Coating Disappointments

- A coating made with self-rising flour falls off more readily after frying. All-purpose flour with baking powder added is thicker. Use neither.
- A 1:1 mixture of flour and corn flour is too gritty.
- Old Bay Seasoning and poultry seasoning in the flour turn the coating a weird brown color and, despite their promise, taste funny on fried chicken.
- Adding baking soda and a bit of buttermilk to the egg wash is supposed to keep the coating crisp as it cools, but there's no discernible difference.

❖ Drain the chicken on a rack set on a rimmed baking sheet. Keep it warm in a 200°F (100°C) oven.

❖ Serve country gravy on the side, not over the chicken, as it makes the coating soggy.

Gussy It Up
Some cooks add bacon fat to the oil for a smoky accent.

❖ Cornmeal crust is a delicious alternative to seasoned flour, and it doesn't need double-binding. However, it seems to work better on chicken nuggets than fried chicken pieces.

Master Plan
Cornmeal Crust for Chicken Nuggets

1. For every pound (500 g) of boneless chicken, stir together 1/4 cup (50 mL) each fine cornmeal and all-purpose flour, and 1 tsp (5 mL) each kosher salt, freshly ground black pepper and paprika.
2. Cut chicken into nuggets. Dip them into buttermilk, then into the cornmeal mixture.
3. Fry the chicken. Drain it on paper towels.

♥ Healthier Eater

There's nothing like the real thing. But a satisfying crunch is still a possibility in "oven-fried" chicken.

- The skin gets rubbery. Just remove it.
- Coat the chicken with a mixture of egg and mustard, then dip it in crumbs.
- Melba toast crumbs are a good choice. Corn flake crumbs are popular.
- You need a hot oven. Crank it up to 400°F (200°C).
- Bake the chicken on an oiled rack over a rimmed baking sheet. This allows air to circulate.

OUTSIDE THE BOX

Oven chicken that is par-fried before it's baked has a crunchy skin and tastes good cold. Fry the chicken pieces in oil heated to 375°F (190°C) for 3 to 4 minutes on each side or until they are browned. Transfer them to a rack on a rimmed baking sheet. Bake them at 400°F (200°C), 15 to 20 minutes for white meat, 20 to 25 minutes for dark meat.

Fried Chicken

I got the idea for buttermilk brine from Cook's Illustrated, *a fount of knowledge.* **Makes 6 to 10 servings**

- **Rimmed baking sheet, with a rack set inside**

- **Electric skillet**

Variation

The seasoned flour mixture makes about 1⅓ cups (325 mL). If you want to use this mixture without brining the chicken, increase the salt to 1 tbsp (15 mL).

Buttermilk Brine

6 cups	buttermilk	1.5 L
½ cup	kosher salt	125 mL
¼ cup	granulated sugar	50 mL
2	bay leaves, crumbled	2
2 dashes	hot pepper sauce (such as Tabasco)	2 dashes

Chicken

3½ lbs	chicken, cut into 12 pieces	1.75 kg
1 cup	all-purpose flour	250 mL
¼ cup	cornstarch	50 mL
1 tbsp	paprika	15 mL
1 tsp	kosher salt	5 mL
1 tsp	freshly ground white pepper	5 mL
2	large eggs	2
2 tbsp	milk	25 mL
	Peanut oil	

1. *Brine:* In a large bowl or a strong zip-lock bag, combine buttermilk, salt, sugar, bay leaves and hot pepper sauce.

2. *Chicken:* Add chicken to brine and turn to coat. Cover or seal and refrigerate for at least 2 hours or overnight.

3. Remove chicken from brine, discarding brine. Place chicken in a single layer on the rack over the baking sheet. Refrigerate, uncovered, for 1 to 2 hours.

4. In a wide, shallow bowl, using a fork, stir together flour, cornstarch, paprika, salt and pepper. In another wide bowl, lightly beat eggs and milk. Dip each chicken piece in seasoned flour, turning to coat. Shake off the excess. Dip the chicken in the egg, turning to coat it well. Let the excess drip off. Coat with seasoned flour. Return the chicken to the rack. Discard any excess flour and egg mixtures.

5. In an electric skillet, heat 1 to 2 inches (2.5 to 5 cm) of oil to 375°F (190°C). Add half the chicken pieces, skin side down. (Do not overcrowd the pan.) Cover the pan. Fry the chicken for 5 minutes. Reduce the heat to 350°F (180°C). Fry the chicken, covered, for 15 minutes. Remove the lid and fry, turning chicken occasionally, for 5 to 15 minutes or until golden brown all over.

6. Meanwhile, preheat the oven to 200°F (100°C). Place a clean wire rack on the rimmed baking sheet. Remove pieces as they are done, beginning with wingettes and drumettes, then white meat, then dark meat. The chicken is done when the juices run clear and the temperature is at least 165°F (74°C). Put the cooked chicken on the rack and keep it warm in the oven.

≡Fast Fix

Some cooks just dip the chicken in buttermilk, then in seasoned flour, then put it straight into the hot fat.

Chicken Wings

Drumette VS. Wingette?

After the tips of the chicken wings are cut off, the rest of the wing is cut into two sections. The wingette is the flat part. The drumette is the meaty base. They each have their fans.

◆ A dozen wings weigh about 2 lbs (1 kg). The tips account for about 4 oz (125 g).

Routes to Crispier Wings

- Air-dry them. After marinating, pat them dry and refrigerate before cooking.
- Coat them. In a large bowl, whisk 1 egg white with 2 tbsp (25 mL) cornstarch for every 2 lbs (1 kg) wings. You can add cayenne pepper and 1 tsp (15 mL) freshly squeezed lemon juice. Toss the wings with the coating before cooking.
- Sprinkle them with sesame seeds before cooking.

Tips for Spicy Wing Lovers

- Toss the raw wings with lots of hot sauce or you won't notice the heat after they're grilled.
- Paint hot sauce on the wings before serving them.

◆ You can parboil wings if you're in a big hurry. They lose some taste and texture, but they're passable. Bonus: You can keep the liquid for stock.

Master Plan
Express Chicken Wings

1. Put wingettes and drumettes in a large saucepan. Add just enough water to cover them. Sprinkle in salt. Bring to a boil over medium-high heat.
2. Reduce the heat to medium-low. Simmer for 10 minutes.
3. Drain the wings. Pat them dry.
4. Toss the wings with a sauce, such as honey garlic, but don't overdo it or they will burn.
5. Grill the wings over medium heat, basting occasionally with the sauce, for about 15 minutes.

◆ Keep chicken wings hot. Serve them on a metal platter that has been warmed in the oven.

Turkey

◆ Use a fresh turkey within 2 days of purchase.

◆ Remove the giblets and store them separately. Don't forget them inside the bird when you roast it. Apparently, a lot of people do. If that happens to you, just pull out the bag and carry on roasting. The turkey is still good to eat.

Turkey Thawing Tips

- It's best to thaw turkey in the fridge. Experts say you should allot about 5 hours per pound (500 g). That's 2 days for a bird up to 10 lbs (4.5 kg), 4 days for a bird up to 20 lbs (9 kg). Thaw the turkey, breast side up, in its plastic wrapper.
- Turkey can be thawed in cold water. Experts say you should allot 30 to 60 minutes per pound (500 g). Keep the turkey in its plastic wrapper. Immerse it breast side down. Change the water every 30 to 60 minutes. The surface of the turkey must remain cold.
- Never thaw a turkey at room temperature. If you are running out of time, roast the turkey from frozen.

Reasons to Roast a Turkey from Frozen

- There's no need to worry about germy drips.
- You don't have to find thawing space in the fridge.
- There are lots of drippings for gravy.

Reasons Not to Roast a Turkey from Frozen

- You can't stuff it.
- The extremities become leathery.

How to Roast a Frozen Turkey

1. Place it on a rack in a shallow roasting pan in a 325°F (160°C) oven.
2. Roast a 12-lb (5 kg) turkey for 3 hours. If necessary, cover the wing tips with foil.
3. Pull out the giblet bag, finally. Tilt the bird to drain the juices from the cavity into the pan.
4. Continue roasting for 2 hours, or until the juices run clear.

How to Roast a Commercial Frozen Stuffed Turkey

1. Never defrost.
2. Rinse the turkey under warm running water for a minute.
3. Remove the plastic wrapping and the giblet package.
4. Place the bird on a rack in a shallow roasting pan. Brush it with oil. Shield the exposed stuffing with foil.
5. After roasting for the time and temperature recommended on the package, check for doneness. A brand-name, frozen stuffed turkey from the supermarket may take about 5 hours.
6. Remove the turkey from the oven and tent it loosely with foil.

Emergency Turkey Technique

- If your bird can wait no longer to be cooked, but the dinner has been put off, roast it as you normally would, but preferably without stuffing.
- Once it's done, wrap the turkey in thick foil and refrigerate. If it is stuffed, scrape out all the stuffing first and reserve it separately. If it's not stuffed, make stuffing separately.
- When the time comes, reheat the turkey at 450°F (230°C). The internal temperature should reach 165°F (74°C). Do not overheat the turkey or it will get rubbery. Reheat any stuffing separately.
- Serve it with very hot gravy.

◇ Ways to prep fresh or thawed turkey before roasting:
- Brine the turkey overnight.
- Air-dry it in the fridge for at least 8 hours.
- Let it stand for 1 hour at room temperature before putting it in the oven.

Risotto with Turkey, Arugula, Pepper and Olives

This is a colorful solution to dealing with the remains of the day. **Makes 4 servings**

- **Rimmed baking sheet, with a rack set inside**

- **Electric skillet**

Variation

You can, of course, use chicken.

3 cups	chicken stock (approx.)	750 mL
2 tbsp	extra virgin olive oil	25 mL
1	onion, finely chopped	1
2	cloves garlic, minced	2
1	orange bell pepper, finely chopped	1
1 cup	Arborio rice	250 mL
1/2 cup	white wine	125 mL
1 oz	Parmesan cheese, freshly grated	30 g
1/2 tsp	kosher salt	2 mL
1/4 tsp	freshly ground black pepper	1 mL
2 cups	chopped arugula leaves	500 mL
2 cups	diced cooked turkey	500 mL
20	whole black olives	20

1. In a small saucepan, heat stock over medium-high heat until very hot. Reduce heat to low and leave it on the burner.

2. In a wide saucepan, heat oil over medium heat until shimmery. Sauté onion for 3 to 5 minutes or until softened. Stir in garlic and bell pepper. Sauté for 1 minute. Add rice and cook, stirring to coat it with oil, for 1 minute. Add wine and stir gently until it is absorbed.

3. Add stock, about 1/2 cup (125 mL) at a time, stirring gently but thoroughly until it is absorbed. Do not add more stock until the previous amount is absorbed. Adjust the heat to maintain a gentle simmer. Keep adding stock until the rice is creamy and tender but still al dente. This should take about 20 minutes. You may not need all the stock.

4. Remove from heat and stir in Parmesan, salt and pepper. Stir in arugula and turkey. The heat will wilt the arugula and warm the turkey.

5. Transfer risotto to a serving platter. Scatter olives over top.

✦ You can place a slice of buttered bread, buttered side down, under a turkey to keep the bird from sticking to the rack.

6 Safety Tips

1. Don't start cooking a turkey in one place and finish it in another.
2. Never cook a turkey overnight at a low, low temperature.
3. Do not try to stuff and freeze fresh turkey. Commercial pre-stuffed turkeys are "blast frozen."
4. Do not barbecue a stuffed turkey. The heat is too uneven to cook the stuffing safely.
5. Don't leave cooked turkey at room temperature for more than 2 hours. Strip the meat from the bones. Separate it into small containers so it cools quickly in the fridge.
6. Reheat leftovers to at least 165°F (74°C).

✦ When the turkey is two-thirds cooked, tent the breast with foil.

✦ If you have a lot of white-meat fans, roast a turkey breast alongside the bird if there's room in the oven, or cook it the day before if there isn't.

✦ Start checking for doneness half an hour before your guesstimated finish time.

Ways to Free Up the Oven

• Barbecue the turkey.
• Deep-fry the turkey. Always do this outdoors, in case of flare-ups, and use oil with a high smoke point.

OUTSIDE THE BOX

For a non-traditional Thanksgiving, cook turkey the day before, then transform the meat into a variety of sandwiches, pot pies, curries, enchiladas and salads for the big dinner.

Better Leftovers

• Keep the meat, stuffing and gravy in separate containers. They will last longer without spoiling.
• Toss your holiday dinner into the blender. Make stock from the turkey carcass. Strain out and strip the bones. Briefly simmer the stock with the leftover root vegetables. Purée the mixture until it is creamy. Pour in a dash of cream, if you wish. Add chunks of turkey. Voila, cream of turkey soup.
• Serve leftover turkey on pizza. Pair it with a mild cheese that won't overpower it. With some sliced Brussels sprouts on the pizza, it would be funny.

Duck and Goose

✦ Ducks have a heavy skeleton and lots of fat, so plan on serving up to 1½ lbs (750 g) per person.

✦ While it's roasting, prick the duck or goose to allow fat to escape and coat the skin.

✦ Roast duck slowly and remove the fat every 15 minutes. You can siphon off the fat with a turkey baster. Freeze the delicious fat for other uses.

✦ Duck can be steamed before roasting. This makes the skin extra-crispy.

Fish

◇ Fish monikers have multiplied until there are more than enough to go around — like the miracle of the loaves and fishes. There are scientific names, colloquial names and marketing names, and they're mixed up in cookbooks from around the world. Patagonian toothfish, for instance, does not sound as tasty as Chilean sea bass, but they are one and the same. The image of slimehead was rehabilitated by renaming it orange roughy.

◇ If you are unfamiliar with the fish recommended in a recipe, substitute another with similar characteristics. Three questions to narrow down the choice:

• Is it a flat fish (like flounder) or a round fish (like cod)?
• Is it lean or fatty?
• Is the flesh white and mild-tasting, or dark or deeply colored and assertive?

Mythstake

Wild equals organic, but organic doesn't equal wild. Fish labeled "organic" are farmed. Organic fish are farmed with better aquaculture techniques and eco-friendliness. They may be fed natural foods, raised without pesticides or swim in uncrowded pens. If fish are wild, they are labeled so. Wildness is no guarantee of purity. Expensive wild fish can have chemicals or mercury concentrated in their flesh.

🌱 Being Green

• Choose ethical seafood. Questions to ask: Where is it from? Is it farmed or wild? If it is farmed, is it organic? If it is wild, how and where was it caught?
• You can go online to find updated lists of endangered and contaminated species. Check seafoodwatch.org, edf.org, seafoodchoices.com or seachoice.org.
• Assume shrimp and salmon are farmed unless they're labeled "wild."

◇ Fresh seafood is not always better. It may be held in icy seawater for several days. In landlocked areas, frozen seafood is the fresher option. Seafood may be flash-frozen on the trawler. Shellfish, such as shrimp, spoil so quickly that they are always frozen. Most of the seafood at fish counters is thawed.

Seven Good Signs

• Shiny, bulging, clear eyes with black pupils.
• Luminous skin.
• Shiny scales that adhere firmly.
• Translucent flesh.
• Flesh that springs back if pressed.
• An ocean scent.
• A newly caught fish is supposed to float.

Eight Bad Signs

• Fishy or ammonia odors, especially around the gills or belly.
• Sunken eyes.
• White patches on the skin (signs of dehydration or contact burns from ice).
• Brown gills (gills age from red to pink to gray to brown).
• Mushy or watery flesh.
• Flesh with browned edges.
• Flesh that is starting to flake or gape.
• Swollen abdomen.

❖ Use fish within 2 days after buying it.

❖ Two reasons never to buy marinated raw fish fillets at the seafood counter:
  ● Marinades conceal decay.
  ● Fish shouldn't be marinated for a long time.

No-No

Don't place fish directly on crushed ice.

Ways to Store Fish

- Put it in a zip-lock bag. Place it in a bowl of ice or a bowl filled with ice packs.
- Put it in a strainer. Cover it with a towel. Put crushed ice on top. Set the strainer in a larger bowl to catch the drippings.
- To store large whole fish or sections, wrap them in a damp cloth, then in plastic and refrigerate.

❖ Expect to lose about half the weight of a whole fish once it is beheaded, gutted and filleted.

Fish Scaling Tips

- First cut off the sharp fins so you don't get poked.
- It's easier to scale a wet fish than a dry one.
- Get a grip. Grab the fish at the base of the tail. Hold it with a cloth if it's slippery.
- Strip the scales, working from tail to head.
- Use the blunt edge of a knife, a scraper, a hard brush or a vegetable peeler.
- Wear gloves. Scales can cause tiny cuts.
- Hold the fish under running water or use a sprayer to rinse off the scales.
- Rub your hands all over the fish to check for any missed spots.

❖ Always gut a fish before storing it. The entrails decay faster than the flesh.

How to Skin a Fish Fillet

1. Use a flexible knife. At the tail end, make a slit between the skin and the flesh.
2. Lay the fish skin side down.
3. Push the knife flat toward the work surface while moving it from side to side. At the same time, hang on to the skin and pull it taut with your other hand.

🅟 is for Pin Bones

These small, soft bones run the length of a fillet. You can see the white ends. You can feel the bones. Run your finger along the middle seam of a whole fillet or along the inner edge on the thicker side of a fillet that has been halved lengthwise. You can pluck out the pin bones after cooking, but doing so beforehand will increase your dining pleasure.

- Pluck out pin bones with tweezers, small needle-nose pliers or clamps.
- To make pin bones jut out for easy spotting and removal, drape a whole fillet, inside facing up, over an inverted bowl.

✖ No-No

Do not bathe or immerse fish in vinegar to get rid of the smell. It can "cook" the surface flesh. You can, however, refresh fish by pouring vinegar over it and rinsing immediately.

❖ If you want to give a firm fish fillet a spice rub, score the surface in a crosshatch pattern about $\frac{1}{4}$ inch (0.5 cm) deep. Smear the rub into the cuts. Cover the fillet with plastic. Marinate for 30 minutes.

7 Ways to Refresh Fish and Minimize Fishy Flavors

1. Soak it in cold, salted water.
2. Thaw or soak it in skim milk.
3. Soak it in buttermilk for 15 to 30 minutes.
4. Soak it in a lemony milk solution for 15 to 30 minutes. Use 1 tsp (5 mL) lemon juice per 1 cup (250 mL) milk.
5. Squeeze lemon or lime juice over the raw fish. Rub it on lightly.
6. Some people freeze fish in citrusy soda pop, such as 7UP, to get rid of fishy odors.
7. Use chopped ginger, garlic or onions in the dish.

Cooking Fish

◇ Allot 4 to 6 oz (125 to 175 g) fish fillets or 8 oz (250 g) whole fish per person.

◇ For two servings, halve a large fish fillet lengthwise along the center seam, not crosswise.

◇ Slash a whole fish to allow heat to penetrate the flesh and cook the thicker parts. This also stops the skin from bursting.

> **Factoid** There's a saying that fish should swim three times — in water, then oil, then wine.

◇ If you're cooking a fillet in the oven or microwave, tuck under the thin tail end to even out the thickness. For a tidier seam, cut halfway through the flesh near the tail end before folding it under the fillet.

◇ If you want to keep the skin on a barbecued fillet, grill it skin side up.

♛ A Golden Rule

Cook large fish at a lower temperature than smaller fish. The goal is to give the interior time to cook through before the exterior is too brown or flaky.

◇ Fast, high heat can squeeze proteins and cause coagulation. A sign of coagulation: a soft, patchy, white coating on the fish.

◇ Roast fish at 350°F (180°C) or less. Place it on a rack so it doesn't sit in the juices.

◇ To braise fish in a skillet, place a circle of parchment or foil directly, but loosely, over the top.

◇ Sear skinless fish fillets with the smooth (exterior) side down. It releases more moisture.

◇ If a large, pan-fried fish is browning too much, finish it in a 375°F (190°C) oven.

How to Double-Glaze

Give fish a golden glow with a double dose of glaze.

1. In a small saucepan, stir together a glaze. Example: orange juice, honey and puréed ginger. Simmer until it is reduced.
2. Brush the glaze over the fish.
3. Bake the fish, basting it generously.
4. When the fish is barely cooked through, remove it from the oven and brush it with the glaze.
5. Place the fish under the broiler to turn up the shine.

- ❖ Ways to stop a fish fillet from curling up during cooking:
- Score the skin to help it stay flat.
- Use a razor to cut shallow slashes across the skin.
- Remove the skin.
- Press on it firmly with a spatula for the first 30 seconds of cooking.

- ❖ You can brown fish that has been baked or grilled in foil or parchment. Open the packet and push any vegetables or fruit (such as onions or lemon slices) off the top of the fish to the side. Put the fish under the broiler until it starts to brown, about 5 minutes.

Keys to Poaching Fish

- Put small fish into simmering poaching liquid. Otherwise, the flesh will be cooked before the liquid simmers. Start large fish in cold liquid. Otherwise, the exterior will be overcooked by the time the center is done.
- Don't boil the poaching liquid. Do not immerse cold fish in boiling liquid. The skin will burst.
- The water should barely simmer. It should be just shivering.
- If the poaching liquid doesn't cover the fish, baste the top frequently.
- Do not cool fish in its poaching liquid. It will be overcooked and waterlogged.
- It's easier to remove the skin and trim poached fish while it's still warm.

12 Ways to Counter Flaking and Breaking

1. Cook fish in an attractive dish that can go straight to the table. The less it is transferred, the less likely cooked fish is to fall apart.
2. Why turn it? That's when a fillet falls apart, particularly on the barbecue. Fillets are often thin enough to cook through without being flipped. Certainly don't bother turning fish that's less than $\frac{1}{4}$ inch (0.5 cm) thick. You can grill a fillet, skin side down, until it is opaque.
3. If you turn fish in a pan or on the grill, use two spatulas.
4. Fry or grill a fillet with the skin on, to help it hold its shape.
5. Flour the fish. For quick, pan-fried fish fillets, dredge them in seasoned flour.
6. If fish starts to stick, shake the pan back and forth, instead of trying to loosen the fish with a spatula.
7. If the fish refuses to loosen, don't force the matter. Reduce the heat and wait until the fish is ready to release.
8. If a fish sticks, let the bottom get crispy and baste the top with hot oil.
9. Barbecue a whole fish without turning it. Cut three or four crosswise slashes about 1 inch (2.5 cm) apart and $\frac{1}{2}$ inch (1 cm) deep on each side. Rub the fish, inside and out, with a paste of herbs, spices and oil. Cover it with plastic and marinate it briefly before grilling. Make sure the lid is down.
10. Oil the fish before putting it on the grill.
11. Use a big, two-pronged fork with a long handle to poke between the bars of the grate and under the fish, to loosen and lift it occasionally.
12. Don't attempt to grill delicate fish such as sole fillets. Choose firm and/or oily fish such as snapper or salmon.

Court Bouillon

This should be enough to poach a 2-lb (1 kg) fish, though the size of the poacher is a factor. **Makes about 12 cups (3 L)**

Tips

If you want to be tidier, tie the spices and herbs in cheesecloth.

Poach fish for about 5 minutes per pound (500 g). Start counting when the liquid returns to a simmer.

10 cups	water	2.5 L
½ cup	white wine	125 mL
3	lemon slices	3
1	small carrot, coarsely chopped	1
1	small stalk celery (including leaves), coarsely chopped	1
½	small onion, halved	½
5	whole black peppercorns	5
2	whole cloves	2
1	small bay leaf	1
1	parsley sprig	1
1	dill sprig	1
1 tbsp	sea salt	15 mL
1 tsp	fresh thyme	5 mL

1. In a fish poacher, combine water, wine, lemon, carrot, celery, onion, peppercorns, cloves, bay leaf, parsley, dill, salt and thyme. Bring to a boil over high heat. Reduce heat to medium-low. Cover and simmer for 15 minutes.

❖ How to make steamed or poached fish easier to handle:
- A large fish can be a slippery customer. Wrap it in cheesecloth, leaving the ends long. Use the cloth as a sling to transfer the fish to and from the steamer or poacher.
- Poach or steam fish on a rack that you can lift and transfer.

ⓒ is for Court Bouillon

Court bouillon is a poaching solution for fish. It usually contains salted cold water, white wine or lemon juice, a bouquet garni (dill is a good addition), chopped vegetables (such as onions or fennel) and sometimes lemon or lime slices.

♻ Waste Not

- Used court bouillon can be turned into fish stock, if it's powerful enough.
- You can strain poaching liquid, reduce it greatly and turn it into sauce by whisking in some butter or cream.

Gussy It Up

Add a decorative touch to poached fish. Cut vegetables, such as carrots, into fancy shapes and soften them in the court bouillon while the fish is cooking. Arrange the vegetables over and around the finished fish on the platter.

Making Do

You can steam fish on a rack in a poaching or roasting pan. You can poach fish in a roasting pan.

How to Remove the Skin from a Cooked Fish Fillet

1. Put the fish on a plate, skin side down. Let it cool slightly.
2. Insert a thin spatula between the flesh and the skin, and lift the fillet. Use your fingers to help separate the skin from the fillet. Start from the thin end and work in small sections.

How to Bone and Fillet a Whole Cooked Fish

1. Slit along the backbone from top to bottom.
2. Separate and pull off the top fillet by running a spoon or butter knife between the flesh and the backbone, from head to tail.
3. The bones will be laid out in front of you. Grab the tail. Gently pull it up toward the head, working slowly so that you don't leave bones behind.
4. Discard the head. With tweezers, pull out the pin bones and any stray bones.

3 Ways to Keep Fish Warm

1. Place a whole fish on a serving platter in a 200°F (100°C) oven with the door ajar.
2. Place fillets on a serving platter. Cover them with a damp, warm cloth or paper towel.
3. Smooth waxed paper over a fillet. The waxed paper keeps it quite hot and it doesn't dry out. You can put it in a 175°F (90°C) oven, but it's not necessary.

♻ Waste Not

Before throwing out the head of a whole cooked fish, peel back the skin and remove the tiny cheeks, likely boomerang-shaped. The tender flesh is a delicacy.

Judging Doneness

♛ A Golden Rule

Fish is done to medium when the juices have gone from transparent to white, and the flesh from translucent to opaque, and from firm to flaky.
'

Is It Done?

- Cook most fish to medium (140°F to 150°F/60°C to 66°C). Examples: catfish, cod, flounder, grouper, haddock, halibut, mackerel, monkfish, red snapper, sea bass, sole, swordfish, tilapia, trout.
- Cook salmon, arctic char and swordfish to no more than medium-rare (130°F to 140°F/54°C to 60°C) so it doesn't become dry. The flesh should just be turning opaque, but still have a thin, translucent section in the center. The center will turn opaque in the residual heat.
- Cook fresh tuna just to the bottom end of rare. The surface should be browned, the center warm and raw.

- ✧ Use a slim, instant-read thermometer to check the temperature of fish.

- ✧ Remove fish from the heat just before it's done. Residual heat will finish the job. Note, however, that the cavity in a whole fish lets heat escape. Its temperature may rise less than 5°F (3°C).

- ✧ A fish is overcooked if the flesh is so flaky that it falls apart and so dry that there are no juices.

✧ Allow at least 6 to 8 minutes of cooking time per inch (2.5 cm) of thickness.

Ways to Check Temperatures

- For a whole fish, slide a thermometer into the thickest part, ensuring the probe doesn't touch the spine.
- For a fish steak or fillet, slide a thermometer through the side at the thickest part and aim toward the center.

4 Ways to Test Doneness

1. Twist a fork gently into the flesh to test for flakiness.
2. Stick a toothpick into the thickest part to see if it comes out clean.
3. Push a metal skewer into the thickest part. Touch the tip to your skin. It should feel warm but not uncomfortably hot.
4. Slide a thin spatula into the flesh near the dorsal fin of a whole fish to check if the flesh is opaque or shiny.

Anchovies

Anchovies **VS.** Boquerones?

Anchovies are tiny fresh fish, of course, but we encounter them preserved, usually in salt. Boquerones are fresh anchovies marinated in vinegar and oil. They are also known as white anchovies, because they are bleached, or sometimes as collioures. Use salty anchovies in cooking. Use boquerones in salads or on tapas and antipasto platters.

✧ It's easier to chop anchovies before soaking them.

✧ Before using a salted anchovy, rinse, drain and pat it dry. Some cooks soak them in water, white wine or milk for 10 to 15 minutes. This also plumps them.

OUTSIDE THE BOX

Use a bit of chopped anchovy as seasoning. Try it in egg salad or dip.

Caviar

Caviar **VS.** Roe?

Technically, the name "caviar" is reserved for the wildly expensive, salted, unfertilized eggs of sturgeon. The eggs must be harvested while the fish is alive. Types of caviar are named after sturgeon breeds such as beluga, osetra and sevruga. Wild sturgeon is endangered. Eggs from other fish are known as roe or fish eggs, or qualifiers are added to the name, such as "lumpfish caviar."

✧ Inferior caviar or roe is dyed red or black to disguise its unattractive color. To absorb the excess dye, spread fish eggs over several sheets of paper towel. You can rinse them in a small sieve under cold running water, too.

✧ Fish eggs spoil quickly. Always serve them over ice.

ⓒ is for Caviar Spoon

Traditionally, caviar is served with a spoon made of mother-of-pearl, glass, bone or even wood. Anything but metal — there is a myth that metal will react with acids in the caviar or cause oxidation. Maybe there is one good reason to avoid metal: You don't want to crush the delicate fish eggs.

✧ How to take a caviar shot: Put a small spoonful in the web of your thumb, lick it off, then wash it down with a gulp of vodka.

Salmon

Being Green

The good news: Farmed salmon is cheaper. The bad news: Crowding makes the fish prone to diseases and parasites. Fish pellets used as feed promote the concentration of chemicals, such as PCBs and mercury, in the flesh of the salmon. Waste from the pens pollutes the surrounding waters. Farmed salmon are fed dye to make them pretty; the color can be customized.

✧ Atlantic salmon have been fished almost to extinction. If you see a sign saying, "Atlantic salmon," the fish are farmed.

3 Steps to Crispy Salmon Skin

1. In a nonstick skillet, heat a thin layer of oil over high heat until it shimmers.
2. Add a fillet, skin side down, and shake the pan. Fry the fillet until the edges of the skin begin to brown.
3. Reduce the heat to medium-low and fry, shaking the pan occasionally. Remove the fillet when the flesh is just done and the skin is crispy.

Healthier Eater

Mashing the bones with the salmon in the can adds enough calcium to equal the amount in a small glass of milk.

Salt Cod

A Good Sign

A creamy color with no dark spots.

✧ The bigger the cod, the better. It has thicker back and loin pieces, which are the best cuts.

✧ Buyer beware: Some products passed off as salt cod are actually whitefish such as pollock.

Keys to Soaking Salt Cod

• Salt cod must be soaked for 2 to 3 days before cooking.
• Cover salt cod generously with cold water. Soak it in the refrigerator until it is just pleasantly salty, changing the water at least twice a day, but preferably every couple of hours.
• You can soak cod under cold running water, but the fish is perishable, so refrigeration is better. Keep it covered.
• For milder, softer cod, soak it in milk for 4 to 6 hours after its water bath.

Ways to Speed Up Soaking

• Cut the cod into large chunks.
• Separate the flesh into thin flaps and meatier fillets. Soak them separately.
• Poach salt cod for 5 minutes, then soak it in cold water. Rinse and repeat several times.

✧ Is the cod ready to cook? Chew a tiny piece. If the saltiness is overwhelming, continue soaking.

- Desalted cod deteriorates quickly. Refrigerate it and use as soon as possible. Or freeze it.

- You can poach salt cod in an olive-oil bath in the oven.

Ways to Cook Salt Cod

- Simmer it in water or milk over medium-low heat for 5 to 10 minutes.
- Cover it with water and bring it to a boil. Remove the pan from the heat, cover and let it stand for 5 to 10 minutes.
- Bake it, covered with foil, for 5 to 10 minutes at 325°F (160°C).

- Poaching in milk adds flavor and reduces saltiness.

- For full flavor, simmer cod with the skin on.

- Remove the skin and bones from salt cod after simmering. It's easier. Or buy the more expensive boneless, skinless fillets.

- To flake it, bring soaked salt cod to a boil in court bouillon and simmer it for 30 minutes. Drain, skin and bone it. Pull the flesh apart with your fingers.

Skate

- Unlike other fish, fresh skate may have a whiff of ammonia if it wasn't put on ice or dressed immediately after being caught. Skate has a lot of urea in its blood and skin. After death, the urea breaks down into ammonia.

- If skate has a slight ammonia odor, soak it in lemon water, brine or milk for half an hour.

- If skate has a heavy ammonia odor, it is not fresh enough to eat. (Shark is the same.)

Smelt

- You don't need to pull the bones out of smelt before cooking it.

- To enjoy a fried smelt, open it like a book, pull out the backbone from top to tail like a zipper, and pop the steamy white flesh in your mouth.

Snapper

Snapper VS. Red Snapper?

There are many species called snapper, but only a few are red snapper. Some species are so alike, they differ only in the number of fins. Real red snapper has a distinctive red iris. Depending on the jurisdiction, other fish (such as a similar type of Pacific rockfish) may be officially marketed as red snapper. Real red snapper tends to be sold whole, while similar snappers are sold as fillets.

Tuna

Keys to Searing Fresh Tuna

- Thoroughly pat it dry or it will steam instead of sear.
- Don't overcrowd the skillet. Steaming can overcook the sides and change the color.
- Check the side to see if it's done. You should see a line of pink along the center.

- Strips of darker meat running through tuna steaks are edible but strong-tasting. You can cut them out, but you don't have to.

Being Green

Buy "dolphin-safe" canned tuna. Precautions are taken so that dolphins aren't caught in the nets.

A is for Albacore

Several varieties of tuna are canned. Mild-tasting albacore is the most expensive. Skipjack and bluefin are tangy; yellowfin falls in between. Bonito is the fattiest and tastes strongest.

Chunks VS. Flakes?

Canned tuna comes in solid (or fancy), chunk and flaked versions. The larger the chunks, the pricier the tuna. For pasta salads and the like, use the solid. For casseroles or sandwich fillings, use the chunk. You're breaking it up anyway, so why pay extra?

- Solid has large chunks or consists of one large piece.
- Chunk has smaller chunks and some flakes.
- Flaked has small pieces. It is mushy and comes from undesirable parts of the tuna.

Oil VS. Water?

- Canned tuna may be packed in vegetable oil or olive oil. The price tag on the latter may surprise you. Oil-packed tuna is best eaten as is, or in salads or pan bagnat (a sandwich).
- Health-conscious consumers prefer water-packed tuna. It is drier (and less flavorful).

Light VS. Dark?

Canned tuna ranges from white to light to dark. Dark canned tuna suffers from a fishy, metallic accent.

- Canned tuna made from albacore is labeled "white." Solid white consists of one large loin piece or large chunks of it.
- "Light" is generally from skipjack and/or yellowfin and/or bluefin.
- If the can isn't labeled "white" or "light," it may be bonito.

✧ Don't squeeze out the water or oil by pressing hard on the lid of the can. This crushes the tuna. Your tuna salad will be pasty. Drain the contents of the can in a colander. Your tuna salad will be toothsome.

Gussy It Up

- Perk up a tuna sandwich by combining cream cheese with the tuna.
- For a kid, fold in a couple of spoonfuls of green relish along with the mayo.
- Add chopped celery, green onions or even shredded carrots for crunch.

Crustaceans

✗ No-Nos

- Do not hold live crustaceans in a bucket of chlorinated tap water. Lobsters need running, aerated salt water or they'll swell up. But they can live out of the water for a day or two.
- Stressed crustaceans supposedly have pasty flesh. Keep them calm. Don't recreate the scene from *Annie Hall*.

⚛ A Bit of Science

The salinity of seawater is 32 to 35 parts per thousand. So if you were very finicky and wanted to mix an approximation, you would use 35 g salt per kilogram distilled water. In volume equivalents, that would be about 3 tbsp (45 mL) plus 1 tsp (50 mL) salt and 4 cups (1 L) distilled water. Aquarium shops also sell sea-brine mixes.

How to Store Live Lobsters and Crabs

1. Place them in a large container. Cover them with damp newspaper or long sheets of dampened paper towel.
2. Place them over ice, but not directly on it.
3. Keep them refrigerated. The cold anesthetizes them.

✴ Waste Not

- When dismantling crustaceans, save the juices, clumps of tomalley and coagulated white blood and proteins inside the carapace for sauce or soup.
- Extract flavor from crushed lobster shells and shrimp shells. Simmer them in white wine, then strain out the solids and boil the liquid until it's reduced. Add the liquid to seafood dishes.

Tips for Crab Cakes and Lobster Cakes

- They hold together better if the flesh is dry. Do not squeeze out excess moisture with your hands. Spread out the flesh and pat it dry with a paper towel. Or give it a blast under the broiler.
- Extend crab cakes and lobster cakes with whitefish. Dry the whitefish under the broiler for about 1 minute until it flakes.
- Add crunch and a bit of structure by coating them with panko before frying.

5 Tips for Extracting the Flesh

1. A three-pronged approach — cracker, scissors, pick — is the most efficient way to get at lobster or crab meat.
2. To remove the meat from a big claw, hit the pincer end sharply with the side of a mallet. The shell should split lengthwise. Pull out the small serrated pincer, twist it backward and sideways, then pull it straight out.
3. You can crack the hardest parts of crab and lobster legs with a mallet or rolling pin. Use a heavy metal rolling pin, not a wooden one, which can suck in odors. Crack judiciously, or juices will fly out and the flesh will be squashed.
4. To get at small pieces, snip through the sides of the shell with scissors.
5. You can run a rolling pin over thin legs to push out the meat. You can extrude it with a seafood pick. Or you can gnaw on a leg and suck out the flesh.

Healthier Eater

You can bake crab cakes and lobster cakes instead of frying them.

- Dip the patties in a 1:1 flour and cornmeal mixture.
- Flatten them slightly. Place them on a baking sheet brushed with oil. Drizzle the tops with melted butter or oil.
- Bake them at 450°F (230°C), turning once, until crispy, say 15 minutes.

⑤ is for Surimi

When whitefish such as pollock is pressed and steamed into shapes to mimic crab and lobster, it is called surimi. This surimi comes in leg and flake styles. It's best used in salads or sushi, not as a replacement in actual crab and lobster dishes.

Crab

✧ Subdue a live crab by grabbing its two back legs like a handle. It will stop struggling.

✧ Start deconstructing a whole cooked crab by pulling off the legs and the claws. Make sure you pull out the knuckles. If you don't, start digging. The sockets contain a lot of meat.

ⓐ is for Apron

The apron is a segment of shell folded up across the crab's belly. You can tell a crab's gender by the apron. The male, or jimmy, has a narrow, penis-shaped apron. An immature female, or sally or she-crab, has a triangular apron. A mature female, or sook, has a domed one.

✧ The male crab has bigger claws and more of the prized white meat. The female has a bigger body.

✧ To remove a crab's shell, begin by popping off the apron — and the intestinal vein that comes along with it. Pry it up and pull it toward the tail end of the crab.

ⓓ is for Dead Man's Fingers

This is a fanciful name for the spongy, feathery gills. The devil is another name for them. You will see the gills when you pull off the crab's carapace, or top shell. They are inedible. Cut them and/or pull them out.

ⓜ is for Mustard

Do not throw out this soft yellow fat. It is good to eat.

♺ Waste Not

Snip the lower, or small, leg sections into pieces for stock or shellfish butter.

✧ A soft-shell crab is freshly molted, with a flexible carapace. This is a seasonal treat. You eat it whole — most of it, anyway. Preparing a live one is gruesome. Tenderhearted cooks can buy frozen soft-shell crabs.

How to Prep a Soft-Shell Crab

1. Clean the crab with cold water.
2. Using sharp scissors, cut off the face, straight across the top. Your aim is to remove the eye and mouth parts. If you see a small sac behind the eye cavity, pull it out.
3. Pull off and discard the apron and intestinal vein. It should be clean. Crabs don't eat when they are molting.
4. Peel back the carapace to expose the gills on either side. Pull them out. Straighten the carapace.
5. Rinse the crab well.
6. Cook the crab right away. It decomposes quickly.

✧ Pick over canned crabmeat to remove stray bits of shell. To make these easier to find, drop a spoonful of crabmeat onto a metal plate or baking sheet. If it splats, it contains no bits of shell. If it makes a tapping noise, sort through it.

Lobster

✧ Female lobsters are considered more tender and tasty. The flesh of the male stays firmer when it's boiled.

4 Ways to Tell the Sex of a Lobster

1. Look at the first set of appendages near the top of the tail. The female's are soft and feathery, the male's hard and bony.
2. The female's tail is wider, particularly at the top, where it joins the body.
3. The female has a rectangular shield between the second pair of walking legs.
4. The female contains coral, a packed, bright red roe. It is edible.

Two Good Signs

• When you pick the lobster up, it spreads out aggressively, throws back its claws and tucks its tail under. A lobster should be lively.
• If you straighten the tail, it curls again, rather than hanging limply.

Two Bad Signs

• A lobster that has algae growing on it has been hanging around for a long time in a tank.
• Avoid lobsters that weigh more than 3 lbs (1.5 kg). They're tough buggers.

Wanted: Alive, Not Dead

• A lobster has a primitive nervous system. Even scientists have trouble figuring out just when a lobster is dead. It may be moribund. After death, a lobster rapidly begins to putrefy and liquefy, and the flesh turns bitter. Cooking a lobster live is the only way to ensure freshness. In other words, its expiry time is the expiry date.

Factoid A live lobster may look like a tank, but it's fragile. The shell will crack if you drop it and a claw will snap if you pull on it. A lobster can die of blood loss. One lobster scientist treats his subjects like "fine china."

✧ How to tell if a lobster was alive when it went into the pot: The tail is tucked. If you straighten it, the tail should roll back. A live lobster curls its tail when it is plunged into boiling water.

Mythstake

Lobsters do not scream when they hit the boiling water. They have no voice boxes. That whistling sound is air expanding in the shell.

Factoid A cooked lobster turns red because the blue and yellow pigments in the mottled shell give way to the red pigments, which are plentiful but masked until the heat releases them.

5 Ways to Calm Your Victim

1. The most humane way to kill a lobster is by dropping it into a large pot of boiling water. It's slow torture to put a lobster in cold water and bring it to a boil.
2. Some people freeze lobster before boiling it, but that adds another nasty temperature change for the crustacean to endure. Refrigerating it, to slow its metabolism, is fine.
3. Strangely, you can pacify a lobster before popping it into the boiling water. Rub the top of its head or stroke the inside of its tail from abdomen to flippers. It should relax its claws and let its tail hang. (The tail also hangs when you hold the creature vertically.)
4. Put lobsters in the pot one at a time. The more you add, the longer it takes the water to return to a full boil and the slower the death.
5. Some theorize you should put the lobster in head first and upside down. This is supposed to disorient it, so it thrashes less when plunked into the boiling water.

Head VS. Belly?

Lobsters are traditionally put into boiling water head first because that's where the brain is. Another theory says belly first may be better, because there is a large nerve along the abdomen that radiates out toward the legs. Lobster fishermen just chuck in the crustaceans any which way.

Head First or Tail First?

- If you're cooking one lobster, put it in head first. There's less splashing.
- If you have more than one, plunge them in tail first. The tails curl up, so you can arrange them vertically in the pot.

◇ Gruesome techniques for cooks who don't want boiled lobster:
- Stab it through the brain. This is hit or miss, because the brain is barely a bundle of nerves smaller than a pea, just behind the eyes. You need steely nerves and maybe a cruel streak for this one. A test subject with its head neatly split in two kept moving around for 5 minutes.
- Twist off the bottom half while the live lobster struggles.
- Whack the lobster into pieces with a cleaver.
- Give it a slow death by steaming. Put it in a steamer basket over $\frac{1}{2}$ cup (125 mL) white wine. If the wine runs dry, add another $\frac{1}{2}$ cup (125 mL). Some crustacean lovers say steamed lobster is sweeter and more delicate.

How to Kill a Live Lobster with a Knife

1. Hold it firmly by the carapace at the tail, pressed straight against the cutting board.
2. Find your starting point near the delineation in the carapace between the head and the abdomen, in the center, aligned between the eyes. This is about 2 inches (5 cm) past the eyes.
3. With the tip of your knife at the starting point, cut directly down to the board, then continue cutting toward the antennae, right between the eyes. This splits the head in half. You can line up your aim: Conveniently, there is a line along the center of the shell that you can follow.

A Kinder Alternative

- Toss the lobster into boiling water for only 1 minute, just to kill it.

✧ Give your lobster a cold bath under the faucet before cooking it.

Factoid A lobster's blood is light gray with a bluish tint. It is sometimes described as orange, green or light pink; the color changes upon exposure to air. When cooked, it turns into a white gel. That's what you see coating the carapace of a cooked lobster.

Master Plan
Boiled Lobster

1. Fill a large pot with enough water to generously cover the lobster. Put on the lid and bring it to a boil. Add $\frac{1}{2}$ cup (125 mL) sea salt per 1 gallon (4 L) water.

2. Holding the carapace firmly in one hand and, snipping with scissors in the other, cut the elastic bands off the claws. Always keep the claws pointed away from you and your fingers out of their reach.

3. Immediately plunge the creature into the boiling water. Put the lid on. Wait for the water to return to a full boil. Reduce the heat to medium-low. Keep the pot covered. The cooking time will depend on the size. Guesstimate: 8 to 12 minutes. When it's done, the antennae should pull out easily.

4. Meanwhile, fill the sink or a large tub with ice water. Stir in $\frac{1}{3}$ cup (75 mL) sea salt per 1 gallon (4 L) water.

5. Plunge the lobster into the ice bath and leave it for 10 minutes. This will "fringe," or loosen, the flesh from the shell.

6. If you want hot lobster, skip the bath. Just rinse it with cold water and let it stand for 5 minutes before serving it.

✧ Lobster cooking times are all over the map, but most recommendations are too long. There are a lot of overcooked, chewy lobsters out there.

Lobster Boiling-Time Estimates

- **1 lb (500 g):** 5 to 7 minutes
- **1$\frac{1}{4}$ lbs (625 g):** 8 to 10 minutes
- **1$\frac{1}{2}$ lbs (750 g):** 10 to 12 minutes
- **2 lbs (1 kg):** 12 to 15 minutes.

✧ If steaming a lobster, reduce cooking time by a couple of minutes, as steam is hotter than boiling water.

✧ If you plan to dismantle the crustacean and continue to cook the meat in a sauce or another dish, boil a 1$\frac{1}{4}$- to 1$\frac{1}{2}$-lb (625 to 750 g) lobster for just 5 minutes.

Gussy It Up

- To add briny flavor, some people toss a strand of seaweed into the cooking water.
- You can cook lobster in seawater, as seaside residents do. But algal scum tends to rise to the top of the pot, and there may be a strong seaweed odor.
- Add white wine to the cooking water.
- Boil the lobster in court bouillon.

How to Serve Warm Lobster on the Half Shell

1. Rip off the claws.
2. Discard the antennae.
3. Flip the lobster onto its back. Draw a knife down the center from head to tail.
4. Remove and discard inedible parts: the stomach, spongy gills, the intestinal vein that runs through the middle of the top side of the tail. Leave the coral and tomalley.
5. Serve the claws alongside.

❖ For more fastidious guests, slice lobster in half lengthwise and serve it warm with clarified butter. However, purists say it loses a lot of juices this way, plus it should be served cold with a squirt of lemon only.

How to Consume a Whole Lobster

- Use your hands, assisted by the cracker and pick, not the other way around. Bend and snap limbs in the opposite direction to the articulation of the joint.

Claws

- Tear off each claw at the body.
- Tear the stems from the claws.
- Suck the juices out of each claw by tilting your head back, placing the torn end of the claw to your mouth and snapping the pincer off. This is called a lobster shooter.
- Crack the claws and extract the flesh.
- Crack or break the stems into sections at the joints. Pick out the flesh.

Tail

- With one hand, hold the lobster across the carapace. With the other hand, firmly grab the tail. Twist and pull back to snap off the tail.
- Hold the tail with the swimmerets on the underside facing you. Interlace your fingers around the back of the shell, cradling it. Push with your palms until you hear crackling. Unlace your fingers. Using thumb pressure on both sides, push outwards on the shell, section by section, until it breaks away from the flesh.
- Extract the tail meat. Pinch together the two strips of flesh sticking up at the top of the tail and pull them down like a zipper. This should reveal the intestinal vein, which may be clear, gray or green. It's not poisonous, but it's unappetizing, so pull it out.

- If you have a female, the compact red stuff inside the tail is roe. It's considered an aphrodisiac.
- Don't forget the flippers. Pull them off the end of the tail shell. To get at the flesh, use a pick, or scrape each flipper with your teeth.

Body

- Position the carapace with the dangly little walking legs facing you. Push your thumb (nail facing down) into the body cavity and place two fingers in the middle of the belly. Pull the leg section up and off. Set it aside.
- The carapace is filled with tomalley, the delicacy otherwise known as the green stuff. Scrape it out and eat it now, later or not at all.
- Underneath the tomalley, on the lower carapace, is a butterfly-shaped piece of sweet, tender meat. This is the lobster's filet mignon.
- Eat any other tidbits you find in the carapace. Just don't dig too deep into the head.

Legs

- Go back to the leg section you tore off. Pressing with your thumbs, twist and rip it apart into two sections with four legs each, if you can.
- Twist off each leg and set it aside. Pick the flesh out of each leg socket.
- Break each leg into sections at the joints. Squeeze out the meat with your fingers, or gnaw and suck to extract it.
- Discard the remainder of the carapace, filled with the nasty, gray, feathery gills.

> **Factoid** The large, dominant claw is called the crusher and the smaller one is called the pincer. Lobsters can be right- or left-handed, so to speak.

is for Tomalley

Though not technically correct, the pasty green tomalley is often described as the lobster's liver. It is a gland or organ.

OUTSIDE THE BOX

- Smear tomalley on rounds of toast, crisp them under the broiler and use them as croutons for soups or salads.
- Make tomalley bruschetta. Sauté tomalley in butter with herbs and spices. Smear this on slices of baguette. Top it with chopped tomato.

✧ Frozen, thawed lobster tails tend to curl when they are cooked or grilled. Keep them straight by sliding a small metal skewer between the membrane and the flesh on the underside.

Storage Tips

- Store a boiled lobster belly up to preserve the juices. Refrigerate it in a covered container for up to 2 days.
- Shucked lobster meat can be refrigerated for 3 days or frozen.
- To freeze a whole cooked lobster, place it in a zip-lock bag and cover it with salt water.

Shrimp

✧ Shrimp is sold flash-frozen or thawed. It's better to buy it frozen. Defrosted shrimp become mushy. Defrost shrimp the same day you cook it.

Two Bad Signs

- An ammonia odor.
- Loose shells. (Shells loosen as the flesh dries and shrinks.)

✧ Shrimp cooked in the shell have more flavor.

✧ Shrimp is usually sold minus the head because that's the first part to decay. If you are served whole shrimp — in the Caribbean, say — you can join the diehards who believe sucking the juices from the head is sublime.

🌱 *Being Green*

Chances are your shrimp was farmed and imported. Farmed shrimp are bred for thicker, sturdier shells. Their flesh is less delicate. Beware of pond-raised shrimp from developing countries, which may be polluted with medications and chemicals. Wild shrimp are caught in factory vessels that freeze their catch at sea.

Count Matters

✧ Go by the count per pound (500 g) rather than the size description. The smaller the count, the larger the shrimp. Example: Jumbo may be 16 to 20 per 1 lb (500 g). Size descriptions vary too much. Every retailer wants to call his shrimp large.

How to Shell Shrimp

1. Pull off the legs like you are opening a zipper.
2. Tease off the shell from top to bottom.
3. Hold the tip of the tail and tug gently to extract the shrimp completely.

 is for Vein

The vein running along the shrimp's back is the intestinal tract. It may be clear, gray or black. The vein is less likely to be gritty if the shrimp is farmed. Don't worry if you accidentally eat the vein. It is harmless. Nowadays, most shrimp is sold deveined. But if you have to do the job yourself, it's a simple matter.

How to Devein Shrimp

1. Use a small, sharp knife to make a shallow slit along the back.
2. With the tip of the knife, lift and pull out the thin vein. Or use a toothpick.

✧ Cook shrimp quickly or they will become rubbery.

Factoid Cold-water shrimp, or northern shrimp, start out as males, then undergo a sex change in midlife.

✧ To boil shrimp, toss them into boiling salted water. They should be done by the time the water returns to a boil. Drain. Rinse with cold water.

Is It Done?

- Cook shrimp until the body curls and the flesh changes from translucent gray to pastel pink.
- Remove it from the heat while the flesh is slightly clear in the center. It will finish cooking in the residual heat.
- Shrimp curled into a tight circle is overcooked.

Shrimp VS. Prawn?

The two terms are used interchangeably. In North America, we may call a large shrimp a prawn. But technically, they are not the same. The prawn is a small freshwater crustacean with claws. It looks like a cross between a shrimp and a lobster, or like a crayfish. It may be called a Dublin Bay prawn, langoustine or scampi.

Mollusks

✧ It's an open-and-shut case for bivalves. Before you cook a clam, mussel or oyster, the shell should be closed tight or snap shut when you give it a rap. After you cook it, it should be open. So contrary! Exception: Steamer clams don't close firmly.

✧ To test the liveliness of a geoduck, touch the siphon that sticks out of the shell. It should move.

✧ Choose bivalves with undamaged shells.

✗ No-Nos
- Do not store shellfish in a sealed container or plastic bag. They will suffocate.
- Do not store shellfish in fresh, chlorinated water.

✧ Keep shellfish in a bowl or tub covered with a damp towel or damp newspapers. You can add ice, if you wish. Refrigerate.

✧ If you store bivalves crowded or weighed down gently, they are less likely to open and spill their juices.

✧ Scrub bivalves under cold running water just before shucking or cooking them. Hold one in your palm; scrub it with a brush. Flip and scrub. Then scrub along the edges of the shell opening and the hinge. You don't want grit to fall into a shucked oyster, for instance.

✧ To cook clams and mussels, sauté them in a skillet, then cover and steam them. After 5 minutes, check their progress frequently, removing bivalves as they open. Discard any that don't open.

✧ Sieve fresh "liquor," or cooking liquid, from shellfish.

Ways to Strain
- Line a sieve with cheesecloth. Dampen the cheesecloth first, so it doesn't suck up the liquor, or cooking liquid.
- For the finest filtering, use a hard mesh coffee filter.

♻ Waste Not
If you are not using the "liquor," or cooking liquid, immediately, freeze it for soup or stock.

✧ Clams or oysters are usually steadied and baked on a bed of coarse salt. But the salt can stray into the shells. You could lay them on lemon slices, instead.

Clams

Hard VS. Soft Shell?
The latter group includes clams called steamers, razors and geoducks. The term "soft-shell" is a misnomer. The shells are thinner or more brittle, but are not actually soft. They have a little spout that prevents them from closing fully.

P is for Purging
Clams live buried in sand. Soft-shell clams, such as steamers, cannot close tightly, so they are likely to contain sand. Purging is the process of soaking them in salt water, perhaps with cornmeal added. Purging is supposed to whiten the flesh, clean out the sand and cause the clams to eject dark stomach contents.

❖ There's usually no need to purge store-bought shellfish, except for soft-shell clams. Ask the fishmonger.

6 Keys to Purging

1. Soak clams in a tub of seawater or a solution of 3 to 4 tbsp (45 to 50 mL) kosher or sea salt per 4 cups (1 L) cold tap water.
2. Set clams on a small rack in the tub so they don't sit in any grit they expel.
3. Soak the clams for at least 2 hours. Change the water frequently — about every 30 minutes — because the clams use up the oxygen.
4. If you want to leave the clams soaking overnight, soak them in a very large washtub.
5. Cornmeal can be added to the water to purge the dark stomach contents. The clams supposedly feed on the cornmeal. Use ⅓ cup (75 mL) cornmeal per 4 cups (1 L) water. Oatmeal is an alternative.
6. Rinse the clams under cold running water.

❖ Some people soak clams in fresh water to try to make them less salty. This could kill them.

Mussels

Mussel Tests
- Push the top and bottom shells in opposite directions. They all have some give, but if the mussel is dead, its shell should open. Discard any that do.
- Shake the mussels. If they sound sloshy or feel heavy, they may be filled with mud.

B is for Beard

The mussel uses its "beard" to cling to rocks or posts. Pulling it out injures the mussel, but must be done. Do so just before cooking.

Ways to Remove the Beard

- Grab it with a dry paper towel and give it a sharp yank, jerking it toward the hinge end. Pull in the other direction and you may rip out some flesh.
- Clip the beard with scissors.

❖ You can purge mussels the same way you purge clams.

❖ Mussels don't necessarily snap shut pronto when their shells are rapped. They may be the most fearless of the bivalves. I have seen honey mussels in the sink fanning their shells open and closed.

H is for Honey Mussel

This new type from British Columbia will make a mussel lover out of you if you aren't one already. Honey mussels are plump and golden.

Oysters

A Good Sign
Deep cups, suggesting a plump creature inside.

A Bad Sign
Broken shells. (Discard these damaged oysters.)

Oyster Grades
- Fancy or Choice grade oysters have rounded shells with deeply cupped bottoms.
- Standard oysters have longer, more irregular shells, with cups that aren't as deep.
- Commercial oysters have uneven shells and are flatter. They are more likely to be sold shucked.

❖ Shucking aids for the desperate or the clumsy:

- Before shucking, put oysters in a 400°F (200°C) oven for 1 minute. (Don't leave them in longer, as some recommend. They will be unpleasantly warm.) Dunk them briefly in ice water.

- Strange, but it's easier to shuck oysters if they've been soaked in club soda for 5 minutes.

❖ Professional shuckers dab oysters with a cloth first, to get rid of slipperiness.

❖ Wear a gardening glove or rubber glove on the hand holding the oyster to prevent cuts while shucking.

Which Side Is Up?

- The flatter part of the shell is the top. The hinge where the two shells meet is slightly skewed toward the top. The rounded cup is the bottom.

How to Shuck an Oyster

1. Place the oyster, cup side down, on a cutting board or shucking board. Special boards are sold in kitchenware stores. Steady the oyster by pressing a kitchen towel against one end.

2. Pick up a shucking knife with a broad handle and a short, heavy blade. Pry it into the hinge. Twist to pop the hinge. Keep the oyster level to prevent the juices from spilling.

3. Sweep the blade of the shucking knife along the top shell to release the meat.

4. Remove the top shell. Run the knife under the flesh to separate it from the bottom shell.

OUTSIDE THE BOX

Get the shucking started. Use the pointed tip of a church key can opener to pop the hinge. It works well.

ⓛ is for Liquor

The oyster juices are called the liquor. Preserve as much as you can.

- Don't shuck oysters on top of a towel. It will wick up the liquor.
- After shucking, scrape the juices from the cutting board into a strainer set over a bowl.
- Shuck oysters on a board in a rimmed baking sheet, to capture more liquor. Or use a cutting board with a trough.
- If shucked oysters seem gritty, rinse them with a bit of cold water. Strain the water and add it to the liquor.
- Oysters produce another round of liquor if you drink or rinse off the first round.
- Return the liquor to the oysters on the half shell. If you are cooking the oysters, spoon the liquor into the sauce.
- When buying shucked oysters, look for liquor that is clear, not cloudy. It should have a pleasant scent.

❖ If an oyster is muddy inside, you can transfer the meat and liquor to a small bowl, scrub the shell, rinse the meat if necessary and replace it, strain the liquor and spoon it over the meat.

❖ To serve raw oysters on the half shell, place them on a bed of cracked ice, rather than coarse salt, which gets into the oysters. Or use a bed of seaweed.

❖ If you must cook an oyster, it should barely be heated. Overcook an oyster and it will shrivel to nothing.

- Raw oysters should not be swallowed whole. That would be a waste. Chew them to savor the flavor.
- Oysters are not poisonous in the months without the letter R. The prohibition dates back to the days before refrigeration. It is also related to algal blooms that occur in the summer and can lead to shellfish poisoning. You can eat oysters in months that don't contain the letter R, but you may not want to. Oysters spawn in the summer, which makes the flesh soft and bland.

✧ Oysters from cold waters take longer to mature, and taste better. Inferior oysters from warm waters are better when cooked or eaten with condiments.

Storage Tips

- Oysters are remarkably hardy. East Coast fishermen would pile them in their basements all summer. However, we prefer refrigeration.
- Place oysters, cup side down, in a tub. Cover them with a damp kitchen cloth, seaweed or wet newspapers.
- They can be stored for up to 3 weeks, but start to taste stale in 3 days.
- Store shucked oysters in an airtight container, pushed down into a bowl of ice.
- To freeze shucked oysters, place them in an airtight tub, covered in their juices.

No-No

Do not freeze oysters in their shells.

Scallops

Sea VS. Bay?

Sea scallops are the big ones that can be seared. Bay scallops are the small ones. They are best used in stir-fries, sautés or soups. Diver scallops, large and hand-harvested, are scarce.

Three Bad Signs

- Dried or dark edges.
- White patches. (These are a sign of freezer burn or contact burns from ice.)
- A sharp or pungent scent. (Scallops should smell like the sea.)

Dry VS. Wet?

Scallops may be soaked in water with a preservative called sodium tripolyphosphate, so they don't lose moisture and plumpness en route to the customer (and the weigh scale). When you try to sear them, they just steam and stew. Look for dry-packed or chemical-free scallops. They are sweet and firm when seared.

- Wet scallops are sometimes white, but not necessarily so. It depends on how much chemical has been added to the water to bleach them. They may sit in a milky liquid. Their texture is rubbery.
- Dry scallops have various hues, such as pink, pastel orange or ivory. They feel more slippery.
- Often, dry scallops will be labeled "dry" and wet ones will simply be labeled "scallops." So, if the label doesn't say it's a dry scallop, it probably isn't. Ask your fishmonger.

✧ How to make scallop dishes less watery:
- Buy dry scallops.
- Rinse scallops quickly and pat them dry. Don't leave them sitting in water.
- Frozen scallops are particularly watery. If making scallops in sauce, first cook the scallops separately, at a higher heat.

❖ If you're finicky, you can pull off the little flap of muscle on the rim of the scallop. It is a bit tougher.

Tips for Searing Scallops

- Dry them well. Pat them dry or even refrigerate them overnight.
- Use high heat.
- You don't want to boil or steam them in any liquid that is released. To minimize liquid and enhance browning, add scallops to the pan one or two at a time. Use a wider pan to hasten evaporation.
- Scallops should be barely cooked. Sear them for 30 to 60 seconds.

❖ For more golden scallops, slice each one in half, into coins.

Cephalopods

Octopus

✧ Octopuses weighing more than 2½ lbs (1.25 kg) and squid longer than 8 inches (20 cm) are apt to be tough.

✧ Discard the tips of the tentacles.

✧ You can clean slime and dirt from octopus by rolling it in rice bran. Rub the bran all over the body and the tentacles. Run your fingers along each tentacle to scrub the suckers. Rinse off the bran under cold running water.

3 Ways to Tenderize Octopuses

1. Greek fishermen pound them on rocks by the sea. You, too, should pound them. Try whacking them with a meat mallet or slapping them against the sink.
2. Blanch them before cooking.
3. Rub them with meat tenderizer.

Squid

C is for Calamari

Squid tastes better when it is called calamari. That's the Italian name for this mollusk.

✧ Remove the red membrane on squid. You can rub it off, or blanch the squid for 1 to 2 minutes, then plunge it into cold water.

✧ Avoid gutting and cleaning squid yourself. It's messy and smells bad.

How to Clean Squid (If You Have To)

Check out the squid's head. It has large eyes and a mouth with a hard beak. Ten tentacles surround the mouth.
1. Cut through the tentacles.
2. Squeeze the beak, pull it out and throw it away.
3. The mantle is the elongated body above the head. Feel inside the mantle for the pen, a quill-shaped piece of chitin.
4. Pull out the quill and, along with it, the guts and the ink sac. Keep the ink if you wish. It is a delicacy. It is sometimes used in seafood pasta.
5. Rinse the tentacles and the body, inside and out, under cold running water. If desired, slice the body into squid rings.

✧ When buying cleaned squid, you'll still have to pull out the pen, rinse the gelatinous coating out of the tube and rub off hard bits of chitin from the tentacles.

A Good Sign

Shiny ivory flesh with speckles.

Illex **VS.** Loligo?

There are two types of squid. The illex is larger and coarser. The long-finned loligo is preferred.

♛ A Golden Rule

Squid should be cooked for either a short time or a long time. Anything in between and it gets rubbery. Follow the 2/20 rule: Use high heat for no more than 2 minutes or cook it for at least 20 minutes.

Liquid Assets

Beverage Basics

❖ How to prevent icy drinks from being watered down:
- Put lemonade ice cubes in lemonade, and so on.
- Use frozen whole berries, instead of ice cubes.
- Use ice cubes made with coffee and tea.

❖ To frost a glass, wet it with cold water and put it in the freezer for 30 minutes.

♻ Waste Not

Flat cola can be put to many good uses.
- Use it as a meat tenderizer.
- Braise or bake with it.
- It's tasty in barbecue sauce.
- It shines up metal and strips rust fairly well.
- Pour it down the drain to clean the pipes.
- Rub it on hair to remove chewing gum.

Juice VS. Cider?

Cider is the unfiltered juice of pressed fruit. Juice is filtered. Cider may be fermented. In that case, it is called hard cider.

❖ How to speed-thaw frozen juice concentrate:
- Smash it with a potato masher or pastry blender.
- Shake or whisk it with warm water.

❖ For the thickest smoothies, start with frozen fruit and frozen yogurt. Dice leftover fruit, especially the ripe stuff that's about to go off, and stash it in the freezer.

❖ To create a pretty, layered smoothie, pour in some juice, then pour in the smoothie, slowly and carefully, over the back of a spoon.

❖ Mix drinks from a powder or concentrate without creating sludge. Start with a quarter of the water, then add the powder or concentrate. Stir until it dissolves. Add the rest of the water.

Gussy It Up

For a Middle Eastern accent, add orange blossom water to lemonade. Try about 1 tbsp (15 mL) orange blossom water per 1 cup (250 mL) lemonade.

❖ Drinks stay hotter in a deep, narrow cup.

❖ Swizzle sticks for hot chocolate, coffee, tea or creamy cocktails:
- Cinnamon sticks
- Candy canes

♡ Healthier Eater

- Beware of a juice labeled "drink." It may not have any real juice in it.
- Toss a fresh banana into your smoothie for creaminess. Then you can get away with using skim milk or fat-free yogurt.
- Finish your meal before plugging in the kettle. The polyphenols in coffee and tea prevent the body's absorption of iron.

Better Leftovers

- Refrigerate leftover tea or coffee to use for iced lattes or iced tea.
- Save strong coffee or tea to cook with. Use it to replace some or all of the water in recipes from cake to brisket. Save the drinks in sealed containers in the fridge. This is not, however, a license to use up stale tea or burnt coffee languishing in the bottom of the pot.

Water

> **Factoid** Avoid heartburn by drinking lots of water with meals and throughout the day to dilute stomach acid.

❖ Refrigerate bottled water after it is opened. Bacteria in the water can multiply at room temperature.

❖ Freeze water in bottles for picnics or road trips. It'll be nice and cold when you get there.

🌱 *Being Green*

A large percentage of commercial bottled waters, plain and flavored, start out as tap water. Switch to tap water and a filter jug. Carry your home-filtered water in insulated, reusable plastic or metal bottles. This cuts down on waste from disposable plastic water bottles.

❖ Start hot drinks with fresh, cold water. Cold water tastes better because it contains more oxygen.

Soft **Vs.** Hard?

Hard water is high in minerals such as calcium and magnesium. Soft water is the opposite. The hardness of water is expressed in gpg, or grains per gallon. Hard water is not harmful to drink, but it can affect cooking and shorten the working life of appliances such as dishwashers.

❖ Is your water hard? Phone your municipality and ask. That's the easiest way to check. You can also get professional testing kits.

Signs of Hard Water

- Toothpaste doesn't froth well and soap doesn't lather well. Because you have to use more soap, scum builds up and coats sinks and other washing areas.
- The dishes and laundry don't seem to get clean enough. Dishes have a lot of water spots and kitchen towels remain dingy.
- Mineral deposits (mainly calcium) appear as a white crust on faucets, strainers, spray attachments and showerheads, as well as rings in sinks.
- Rust-colored stains appear on fixtures and silverware.
- Dirt builds up quickly on porcelain and fixtures. This is because dirt adheres more to the rough coating formed by mineral deposits.
- The hot-water pressure is lower than the cold-water pressure.

❖ To soften hard water, boil it for 15 minutes, cover it and let stand for 24 hours. Skim any scum off the surface.

👑 A Golden Rule

Every bartender knows this one: If you want a drink to taste fresh, you need fresh ice. Old ice tastes stale or metallic, and it smells funny.

Ways to Keep Ice Fresh

- Buy an ice cube tray with a snap closure.
- Wrap your ice cube tray in heavy plastic.
- Store an open box of baking soda next to the ice cube tray.
- Once ice is frozen, pop the cubes out of the tray. Stash them in a sturdy zip-lock bag.

7 Ways to Decorate Ice Cubes for Cocktails, Lemonade and Cold Drinks

1. Freeze shredded mint or a tiny mint leaf in each ice cube.
2. Add whole berries.
3. Add tiny, decorative cross-sections of lime wedges.
4. Freeze a small edible flower in each ice cube.
5. Add a tiny herb sprig.
6. Pop in a pitted fresh cherry or maraschino.
7. Freeze an olive in an ice cube for a cold martini. Petite Spanish arbequin olives are cute.

◇ To crush ice, place it in a heavy plastic bag, a canvas bag or a cotton bread bag, or cover it with a clean kitchen towel, then smash it with a meat mallet or hammer.

◇ You can make a rainbow array of ice cubes by adding drops of food coloring to the water.

◇ If you use a lot of ice cubes, shake them out of the tray and into a plastic storage tub with a tight lid. You can also recycle a large plastic ice cream tub with a lid for this purpose.

Coffee

❖ Store coffee — beans or ground — in an airtight container in a cool place.

Coffee Bean Pointers

- For the freshest coffee, grind your own beans.
- Green coffee beans keep the longest, but they have to be roasted, as well as ground. There are machines that do both. Next best and more practical: roasted beans. They keep for a couple of weeks.
- Roasted beans create carbon-dioxide gas and should be vented. Open the container once a day to vent.
- If you're keeping whole beans for longer than 2 weeks, wrap them in plastic or put them in an airtight container, leaving no headspace, and freeze them.
- You can grind frozen beans.

Ways to Keep Ground Coffee Fresh

Once it's ground, coffee stays in prime condition for only a couple of days.

- If you don't want to fuss with grinding beans every day, grind a small batch, freeze it, then thaw only the amount you need for a few minutes at room temperature before brewing. Beware: Grinding before freezing makes coffee go stale faster because it exposes a large surface area to the elements.
- If you buy coffee already ground, transfer it from the store bag after opening it. Keep ground coffee in a container that is preferably opaque as well as airtight. If your coffee is in clear glass, keep it in a dark cupboard.

✖ No-Nos

- Do not refreeze thawed beans.
- Do not store whole beans in the fridge. It's not cold enough to make much of a difference in freshness, and their flavors mingle with those of other foods.

Keys to Brewed Coffee

- Use 1 to 2 tbsp (15 to 25 mL) ground coffee per 8 oz (250 mL) serving.
- Don't pour vigorously boiling water over the coffee. This strips the aromatic compounds. Wait until the water settles down to an optimal temperature of about 200°F (100°C).

❖ In an emergency, you can reuse a paper coffee filter. Dump out the grounds and rinse the filter carefully with cold water. Don't make a habit of this.

Coffee Doctor

The coffee is bitter.

- Clean the coffee machine. Bitter oils from the beans linger.
- Don't let brewed coffee sit on the burner all day. It's better to let it cool, then zap it in the microwave to reheat it.
- Add salt to the brew. Use about $\frac{1}{8}$ tsp (0.5 mL) salt per 4 cups (1 L) brewed coffee.
- To keep espresso mellow, some baristas never let the first little drizzle run into the cups.

The coffee tastes acidic or tainted.

- To reduce the acidity, add a pinch of baking soda to brewed coffee.
- Avoid metal or plastic containers. They can mar the taste.

There are grounds in the coffee.

- Wet the paper coffee filter. It will stick to the funnel, so it won't flop over.

✧ To clean a burnt coffee pot, warm it, then add ice cubes and salt. Swirl, then rinse.

C is for Crema

The brown foam on the surface of espresso is the crema. Avoid whole milk in lattes. It competes with the crema. Many baristas favor 2%.

✧ When making espresso, tamp coarser grinds more firmly than fine grinds.

✧ Instead of fussing with steamed milk for cappuccino, use a manual frother. You can get a pump-action model or a little battery-operated, hand-held whisk. They don't cost much.

✧ You can add ground coffee to barbecue rubs and pastes, particularly for steak. Use fresh coffee, not exhausted grounds.

Master Plan
Cold-Brewed Iced Coffee

1. Put medium-ground coffee into a French press coffee maker, then add cold water. Use 1 oz (30 g), or about 6 tbsp (90 mL), ground coffee per 2 cups (500 mL) water.
2. Stir to submerge the grounds.
3. Put on the lid. Let the mixture "brew" for 12 to 24 hours.
4. Press down the plunger. Pour out the coffee base.
5. To make iced coffee, use 3 parts coffee base, 2 parts water and 1 part milk, then add sugar to taste. Pour it into a glass filled with ice cubes.

F is for Freeze-Drying

Choose freeze-dried instant coffee. It is made by freezing coffee, then removing the ice. A cheaper method involves spraying dry, concentrated coffee from a tower inside a hot-air chamber. The water evaporates as the drops fall. The heat harms the essential oils that make coffee smell and taste so good.

✧ Instant coffee tastes less harsh if it is simmered over low heat for 2 minutes.

Gussy It Up

Infuse the coffee cream for a special klatsch.

- Add a cinnamon stick, crushed cardamom, a vanilla bean or a chunk of crystallized ginger to half-and-half (10%) cream. Cover and refrigerate it overnight.
- You can flavor heavy or whipping (35%) cream the same way, then whip it to soft peaks. Let guests dollop it into their coffee cups.

✧ How to make instant coffee and espresso granules smoother for use in cakes and desserts:
  Crush the granules into a powder with the side of a knife.
  Stir them into a paste with some of the liquid from the recipe.

Tea

Categories of Tea

- White tea is made from the youngest leaves, which are dried but barely processed. It is subtle, as fans would say, or weak, as critics might complain.
- Green tea is made from leaves that are dried after they're harvested. They may be given a shot of steam, but they're not left to "ferment." Green tea has the most antioxidants of any type of tea. Matcha is the powdered leaf.
- Black tea is made from leaves that are dried and "fermented." That's the term commonly used, but it's inaccurate. Actually, the leaves are left to oxidize and turn black.
- In between the green and black teas are oolong and Pu-erh. Oolong is not allowed to oxidize for as long as black tea. Pu-erh is made from a tea plant that has large, brown leaves. It may be classified as a green or black tea, depending on the processing. The leaves are compressed into "cakes" and may be double-fermented, or naturally ripened, and aged for years.
- Rooibos, like other herbal teas, is not made from the tea plant. It is also known as red tea.

Bag VS. Loose Leaf?

Leaf size is a big factor in grading tea. Broken leaves lose essential oils. Mainstream tea bags are filled with broken leaves. Some of the tiniest broken leaves, called dust or fannings, end up in tea bags. Loose tea is made with larger, higher-quality leaves. It has a longer shelf life.

- Hot water doesn't circulate well around leaves that are stuffed into a bag. This can be a problem with loose tea stuffed into a tea ball, too.

Tea Ball Tips

- Reserve a tea ball for a single serving only. The leaves need room to unfurl and swirl.
- Don't fill a tea ball more than half full.

- Standing increases the bitterness of tannins. Brew tea in small amounts, and drink it right away.

- Tea is mainly water, so don't skimp on the water quality. It is an especially important factor in delicate green and white teas.

Water Options

- Use fresh water, not water that has been previously boiled or has sat around in the kettle. Let the faucet run for a minute before filling the kettle.
- Brew tea with spring water.

Teapot and Teacup Tips

- Preheat the teapot or cups by swishing boiling water in them.
- Avoid aluminum or plastic pots and cups. They taint the taste of green tea.
- A transparent glass teapot lets you monitor the color and strength of your tea.

- Do not pour water at a rolling boil over tea leaves. They'll get cooked and taste stale. Different water temperatures are recommended for different teas.

Temperature Estimates for Brewing Tea

- Black and herbal teas: 210°F (99°C). Bring the water to a boil. After the kettle switches off, wait a few seconds before pouring.
- Oolong: 195°F (91°C). Bring the water to a boil. After the kettle switches off, leave it for 1 minute before pouring.
- White and green teas: 180°F (82°C). Bring the water to a boil. After the kettle switches off, leave it for 1 to 3 minutes, or until steam drifts sideways rather than rising.

✧ Use 1 tea bag per 1 to 2 cups (250 to 500 mL) water. Use 1 tsp (5 mL) loose tea per 1 cup (250 mL) water, plus 1 tsp (5 mL) for the pot.

F is for Flushing

You can condition tea leaves before steeping them by "flushing." Pour a bit of hot water over the tea leaves, swirl, then drain them.

✧ Steeping time depends on the variety of tea, the size of the leaves, and whether they are loose or in bags. Loose tea is steeped longer. Be careful. Long steeping brings out the astringent tannins.

Estimated Steeping Times

- White and green teas: 1 to 3 minutes
- Oolong: 2 to 4 minutes
- Black and herbal teas: 3 to 5 minutes

✧ If you are using a tea bag, squeeze it against the side of the cup for 2 seconds. Stir the tea once. Squeeze the bag for 2 more seconds, then discard it.

✧ If you are using tea leaves, stir the tea just before serving. This circulates the essential oils in the leaves. Asians invented a bamboo whisk for the job. Strain the leaves immediately.

How to Reduce Caffeine

This also reduces the flavor, but doesn't weaken the tea as much as you'd think.

1. Steep the bag or leaves for 30 seconds. Pour off the water.
2. Add fresh boiled water and steep as usual.

✧ Don't use cream in tea. Milk, preferably lower-fat, is best.

✧ The optimum amount of milk per 1 cup (250 mL) tea is considered to be 1 tbsp (15 mL).

Gussy It Up

You can subtly scent and flavor tea by putting a dried orange rind, a cinnamon stick, whole cloves or a vanilla bean into the tea caddy.

♛ A Golden Rule

Think double strength, not double length, when brewing iced tea. Ice dilutes the tea and the cold tempers it, so it doesn't seem as strong. Increasing steeping time, on the other hand, increases bitterness. An exception: When alcohol is added, brew regular-strength tea. Alcohol makes strong tea taste bitter.

A Bit of Science

- Add hot tea to cold milk, not the other way around. This heats the milk gradually, and makes the tea less bitter. Pouring cold milk into hot tea denatures the proteins and may cause a bit of curdling.
- Hot water can hold more tannins than cold water. As tea cools, especially if it cools quickly, tannins fall out of the solution. Plus, they react with the caffeine in the tea. That's why ice tea becomes cloudy.

5 Ways to Make Iced Tea Less Cloudy

1. Steep the tea for a shorter time.
2. Let it cool to room temperature before refrigerating it.
3. Use bottled or distilled water to brew it, especially if your tap water is hard.
4. Add an acidic ingredient, such as lemon juice.
5. If your iced tea is already cloudy, stir in some boiling water.

✧ Iced tea cools faster if you brew it with a small portion of the water from the recipe, say 1 cup (250 mL). When it's steeped, top it up with cold water.

Gussy It Up

• Start with flavored teas — from mint to mango.
• Add fruit and juice. Examples: orange juice and lime slices, pomegranate juice and cherries, kiwi juice and strawberries.
• Add ginger ale.
• Sweeten it with honey or maple syrup.
• Garnish it with fresh herbs (mint being the most obvious, or lavender sprigs).

OUTSIDE THE BOX

• Sweeten and flavor hot or iced tea with jelly. Try mint, grape or apple jelly. I enjoyed some tea with Sauvignon Blanc jelly.
• Pour grenadine or a concentrated syrup made with lime, sorrel or passion fruit, or even ginger beer, into hot or iced tea.
• Drop a hard candy into hot tea instead of sugar.

✗ No-No

Never reuse tea bags. You wouldn't reuse coffee grounds ... I hope.

Options for Cooking with Tea Leaves

• You can cut open tea bags and use the leaves inside.
• Use a spice grinder to powder the leaves.
• Smoky lapsang souchong leaves are great crumbled into spice rubs.
• Put tea-leaf powder on edamame or other vegetables. Smoky tea, salt and oil are a great combo.
• Sprinkle green tea leaves into stir-fries.
• Infuse butter for cooking by melting it, adding tea leaves, steeping for up to 15 minutes, straining and chilling.
• Mix tea leaves in with the wood chips in the barbecue smoker.
• Add matcha powder to custard.

Options for Cooking with Brewed Tea

• Substitute tea for some or all of the water when cooking rice.
• Steep white tea up for to 10 minutes in chicken stock, then strain and use the stock.
• Use tea to make vinaigrette.
• Poach pears or other fruit in tea.
• Chai is a fabulous flavor in desserts and truffles.
• Soak a duck in tea brine before cooking.
• Make a green-tea marinade for seafood.
• Strong brewed tea is a marinade that tenderizes.

✧ Tea for cooking is brewed differently. Minimize astringency or bitterness by steeping tea in lukewarm spring water for half an hour. Steep green tea in cold water.

Spirits

Proof VS. ABV?

Proof is a measure of alcohol content. To find out the amount of alcohol in a beverage, divide the proof by half. Thus, 100 proof is 50% alcohol. Maximum proof is, of course, 200. Proof is now considered obsolete and inaccurate. The modern alternative is ABV, which stands for "alcohol by volume." The alcohol content is stated as a percentage of the total liquid. So 50 ABV indicates 50% alcohol.

✧ When tasting wine or spirits, sniff first. If your sense of smell becomes overwhelmed, sniff a body part, then go back to the glass.

✧ Rub a glass of aged spirits with your hand to warm the contents before drinking.

✧ Younger rum is felt more on the roof of the mouth. Older rum is felt in all parts of the mouth. The finest rum coats the mouth smoothly but doesn't clear the sinuses. Like Scotch, fine aged rum can be drunk straight.

✧ Swish the glass and check the teardrops forming on the sides. The older the rum, the thicker the teardrops. Eight-year-old rum coats the glass.

OUTSIDE THE BOX

Beer and cider tenderize meat, dough and batters.

A Bit of Science

Alcohol has a lower boiling point than water. So most of the alcohol — but not all — evaporates in cooked dishes.

Cooking with Alcohol

● As a dish cooks, the flavor of the spirits intensifies and concentrates. So use decent brands that you would actually drink. And be sparing.

● Careful. Long cooking times and high temperatures evaporate not only alcohol, but its flavor.

Cocktails

Ⓢ is for Simple Syrup

This is a cocktail staple. It's also great to have on hand for lemon-or-other-ades. Simple syrup is also used in desserts, for poaching, glazing and making frosting.

• To prepare simple syrup, boil equal parts of water and granulated sugar over medium-high heat for 5 minutes. Let it cool. Store it in a container or squirt bottle in the fridge; it will keep for months. Caution: It can go moldy at room temperature.

• To prevent crystallization, add a spoon of corn syrup to the mixture.

• For the longest-lasting simple syrup, add a spoonful of lemon juice or a pinch of cream of tartar and simmer the mixture for 20 minutes. Or use 2 parts sugar to 1 part water and boil the mixture for 5 minutes. Or add a spoonful of vodka to the mixture after you take it off the heat.

• You can make flavored simple syrup by using liquids other than water, from coffee to fruit juice. Or add a dash of flavor extract.

♻ Waste Not

Use the squeezed rind of a fresh lime or lemon to wet the rim of a glass.

How to Rim a Cocktail Glass

1. Cool the glass. Put it under cold running water or stick in the fridge or freezer.
2. Swab the rim generously with lemon or lime. You can use a slice, a wedge or even juice.
3. Dip the rim $\frac{1}{4}$ inch (0.5 cm) down into confectioner's (icing) sugar or superfine sugar, a spice blend or a commercial rimming mixture.
4. Tap the glass to remove the excess.
5. Pour the drink into the glass without disturbing the sugared rim.

Gussy It Up

Instead of sugar, dip the rim of the glass in coarse salt, finely grated chocolate or shredded coconut. Pour in the drink carefully.

✧ If you hold a flame to the rind of a citrus wedge, the oil in the zest will briefly flare. This can add a subtle caramel flavor to your cocktail.

℗ is for Piña Colada

Puerto Rico is the home of the piña colada. At one of the bars that claims to have invented it, a blend of pineapple juice, coconut cream, rum and water is frozen until it's almost solid. Then it is blended into a cocktail. This treatment would be great for many cocktail mixtures.

✧ If a cocktail blend, alcoholic or nonalcoholic, freezes solid (accidentally or on purpose), let it thaw at room temperature for 15 minutes, then break it into chunks and toss them into the blender.

Punch

How to Carve a Punch Bowl (or Buffet Bowl) out of Ice

1. Get a 50-lb (23 kg) block of ice. Chip out a depression with a hammer and chisel.
2. Set a 3-quart (3 L) metal bowl in the depression. Fill the bowl with boiling water. (Don't spill any onto the surrounding ice.)
3. Stir the water. The heat will melt the ice. Pour the cooled water out of the bowl.
4. Repeat steps 2 and 3 until you have a large depression.
5. Set the block on a waterproof tray.
6. Surround it with flowers or greenery.

✧ Let punch or sangria mixtures stand for 1 hour before serving to let the flavors blend.

Gussy It Up

Serve sangria or punch in a watermelon bowl. Cut a thin slice off the bottom of a round watermelon to give it stability. Halve the melon, then scoop the flesh from the trimmed half. You could put some of the fruit in the punch. Eat the rest later.

✧ Add only half the ice to a punch, then add the rest when the punch is half drunk. (You know what I mean.) Otherwise, the ice melts and dilutes the drink.

♻ Waste Not

• Freeze leftover punch in ice cube trays.
• After the party, transform the remains of an alcoholic punch or sangria into a sherbet or granita, using an ice cream machine.

⑤ is for Sangria

Sangria is a punch made with red wine, liquor and fruit. Sangria is the Spanish word for "bleeding."

✧ Use a robust Spanish wine for sangria, in honor of its roots.

Master Plan
Sangria

1. Pour a 750-mL bottle of red wine (a reasonable quality, please) into the punch bowl.
2. Add ½ cup (125 mL) brandy, rum or Grand Marnier.
3. Add 2 cups (500 mL) juice.
4. Add 2 cups (500 mL) frozen fruit, diced, sliced or chopped, or whole fresh fruit such as berries or grapes.
5. Just before serving, add soda water to taste.

✧ Freeze grapes and fruit and citrus slices, then add them to punch.

Wine

ⓣ is for Terroir

Growing regions are defined by their particular terroir, a term that refers to the topography, soil, temperature, rainfall and other climate factors. Terroir is commonly linked to wine, but it is also relevant to coffee, chocolate and even the wheat that winds up in our bread flour.

Wine Storage Tips

- Store wine at 45°F to 65°F (7°C to 18°C). The ideal is 50°F to 53°F (10°C to 12°C).
- Put the wine in a dark but airy place, such as a ventilated closet.
- Lay the bottles on their sides to keep the corks moist.
- Temperature fluctuations of no more than 5°F (3°C) once a year and humidity higher than 50% are optimal. The ideal humidity is 75%. That's why connoisseurs store their bottles in wine cellars and special cabinets.
- If you are moving, thickly wrap bottles of wine in newspaper and let them rest for 1 month in their new home before opening them.

✘ No-Nos

- Don't store wine bottles in the kitchen. They don't like the shifting temperatures and bright lights.
- Don't store wine bottles near the laundry room. They don't like the heat and vibrations.

✧ As a general rule, serve wine at no warmer than room temperature.

Serving-Temperature Guidelines

- Dry red wines: 57°F to 68°F (14°C to 20°C)
- Light red wines, dry whites and rosés: 50°F to 54°F (10°C to 12°C)
- Dessert wines: 46°F (8°C)
- Sparkling wines: 41°F to 43°F (5°C to 6°C)

⚡ Lightning Won't Strike If ...

You serve red wine cold. It can be chilled or at room temperature or somewhere in between. A vin ordinaire, or hearty peasant wine, is a likelier candidate for chilling. As for rosés, they are best chilled.

✧ To chill wine quickly, wrap a damp kitchen towel around the bottle and put it in the freezer for 15 to 30 minutes.

Wine-Tasting Tips

- Aerate the wine by sucking it into your mouth through slightly parted lips.
- Turn the wine over in your mouth, as though you're chewing it.

✘ No-No

Don't shake the bottle and pop the cork on champagne like a wild thing. You'll put someone's eye out, as Mama would say. And it's a waste of good bubbly.

How to Open Champagne

1. Hold the neck of the bottle with one hand.
2. Point the cork away from you (and onlookers).
3. Ease out the cork with your other hand, twisting it step by step, until it pops decorously.

ⓑ is for Breathing

Letting wine breathe unleashes its flavors and aromas. Set an uncorked bottle upright for a few hours before serving. Or decant the wine about 1 hour before serving. (You don't always have to decant it.)

✦ Don't leave wine languishing in a decanter. Return it to the bottle and put the cork back in.

Mythstakes

- Never mind the cliché about the guy who put away a bottle in his basement back in 1980. Wine gets old. For most ordinary vintages, after a year or two the wine is past its prime. It won't get better over time. As for fruit wine, it should be consumed while it's young, say less than a year after purchase.
- "Red wine with meat, white wine with fish" is not a rule set in stone.

✦ Fend off wine drips the way sommeliers do. As you finish pouring, give the bottle a slight twist and lift the neck.

Better Guidelines to Matching Wine with Food

- Match the weight of the wine and the food — light wine with a delicate dish, full-bodied wine with a hearty dish.
- Match the wine region with the nationality of the dish. Drink a Barbera or Sangiovese, for example, with Italian ragu.
- Serve slightly sweeter wines with spicy food, such as curries or Tex-Mex dishes.
- With dessert, serve a wine that's sweeter than the sweets, or it will taste sharp, even sour.

✦ If you are serving a variety of wines at a meal, party or tasting, serve younger wine before older, light before robust, dry before sweet.

Foods That Wine Clashes With

- Tart salad dressing (balsamic is the only vinegar that harmonizes with wine)
- Curry
- Onions
- Garlic

♲ Waste Not

Save leftover wine for cooking. Store it in small bottles, preferably screw-tops, in the fridge. The less air it's exposed to, the better.

✦ To keep the fizz in an opened bottle of champagne, hang the handle of a metal spoon down the neck of the bottle and refrigerate it.

Recorking Options

- Moisten the cork with a bit of wine before pushing it back into the bottle. Push it in deep. You can pull it out with a corkscrew again, if necessary.
- Want to replace a cork that no longer fits? Soften it by soaking it in hot water.

6 Keys to Testing Wine in a Restaurant Without Feeling Intimidated

1. When the waiter brings you the wine to examine, there's no need to feel sheepish. It's not done to put you on the spot or examine your wine-tasting credentials. She just wants to make sure that it's the right wine and that it tastes fine or meets your expectations.

2. The label is presented so you can confirm that this is the wine you ordered. No need for comment. A nod will do.

3. You may be offered the cork. Just check that it's not dry. Or put it down and ignore it.

4. A glass is offered to the person who is considered the "host," but anyone can taste the wine. First sniff it, then swish a bit around in your mouth.

5. If you encounter these smells, send the wine back: vinegar (acidic), prune (oxidized), dank basement (mold).

6. If the wine tastes musty or rusty, send it back.

Tips for Bringing Your Own Wine to a Restaurant

- Carry the wine gently, especially a fine one, and hold it upright. You don't want to shake up the sediment. (The same thing goes for transporting wine to a party.)
- If you think you stirred it up en route, ask the server to decant it.
- Expect a corkage fee.
- You can take home an unfinished bottle, so don't feel compelled to get drunk. Restos have special recorking machines.

Cooking with Wine

- The cooking wine should be reasonably priced. It doesn't have to be expensive or mature. Heat highlights unpleasant qualities in wine, but also does away with the nuances of the good stuff.
- You can cook with a fine wine that's been sitting around too long.
- Opt for white wine that's acidic rather than sweet. Choose a red wine that's mild rather than tannic. Avoid oaky wines.
- Replace some of the liquid in a recipe with wine, rather than adding the wine as an extra.
- Wine intensifies saltiness, so use less salt when adding wine.
- For tenderizing, add wine at the beginning of cooking. For a flavor boost, add it near the end, or use it to deglaze the pan.
- Add wine before adding ingredients (such as eggs, milk or butter) that may curdle or separate. Cook the wine slightly. Add the sensitive ingredients after taking the pan off the burner. Do not reheat; keep the dish warm in the top section of a double boiler.
- Wine (especially fortified wine, such as sherry or Marsala) can be reduced to add distinctive flavor without too much liquid. Swirl in the reduced wine at the end of cooking.
- Fruit wine can be reduced by boiling until thickened, then used as a sauce for desserts or ice cream. Over medium-high heat, 1 cup (250 mL) wine reduces to 1 tbsp (15 mL) sauce in about 12 minutes. For a sweeter version, stir in some granulated sugar before reducing the wine.
- When using dealcoholized wine, add a dash of lemon juice or wine vinegar to cut any sweetness.

♛ A Golden Rule

No dumping, please. If you wouldn't drink it, don't cook with it.

Substitutions for Cooking Wine

- Stock
- Watered-down wine vinegar
- Dry sherry
- Brandy
- White vermouth
- Beer
- Mirin (Asian cooking wine)
- Fruit juice (particularly apple, orange or pineapple)
- Cider (hard or not)
- Watered-down white grape juice
- Verjus

ⓥ is for Verjus

Verjus (or verjuice) is an extremely expensive juice made from seedless, unripened, unfermented grapes. It has been used in French cuisine since the Middle Ages. Acidic but fruity, its flavor lies between white wine and fine wine vinegar, so it can be substituted for either. Verjus is sold in exclusive gourmet food shops.

Beer

Ale VS. Lager?

Beer can be divided into two broad categories: ale and lager. These are distinguished by brewing techniques, temperatures and yeast characteristics.

Characteristics of Ale

- Yeast ferments at warmer temperatures (60°F to 75°F/16°C to 24°C).
- Ferments at the top of the tank.
- Ferments faster.
- Higher alcohol content than lager.
- Tastes robust and complex, with fruity tones.

- After fermentation, aged for a few weeks at 40°F to 55°F (4°C to 13°C).
- Associated with Great Britain.
- Available in a wide variety of types, from pale ale to stout to wheat beer.
- Best consumed cool, at 50°F (10°C) or warmer, rather than cold.
- Harder to pair with foods.

Characteristics of Lager

- Yeast ferments at cooler temperatures, sometimes just above freezing, but typically from 46°F to 55°F (8°C to 13°C).
- Ferments closer to the bottom of the tank than ale.
- Ferments slowly.
- After fermentation, aged for a few months, generally at 32°F to 45°F (0°C to 7°C).
- Has less residual sweetness than ale.
- Tastes smooth, clean, and lighter and simpler than ale.
- Originated in Bavaria and is associated with Europe.
- Types include pilsner, Oktoberfest, bock and well-known brand names such as Heineken.
- Best consumed cold, but purists say lagers lose their flavor when colder than 38°F (3°C).
- Can be served with a wide variety of foods.

✧ Dry beers have a lower sugar content.

✧ Ice beers are brewed for a higher alcohol content and smoother taste. The "ice" part refers to the icy filtration system.

✧ The definition of a light beer varies from country to country. It may be based on alcohol content or calories, or both.

- Beer can be matched with food as you would match wine with food, with ales acting as red wines and lagers standing in for white wines.

Matching Beer with Food

- Choose beer that originated in the same country as the dish.
- The darker the food, the darker the beer should be.
- Darker beers go well with roast beef and game. These beers get their color from dark malts.

- Spicier food can stand up to more bitter beers. These beers get their bitterness from hops.

- When measuring beer for cooking, let the foam settle down first.

♻ Waste Not

Store leftover beer tightly covered in the fridge. Pour it into stews and batters. Or use it to rinse your hair.

Cooking Techniques

Recipe Basics

Collecting Recipes

✦ Stick to a system. Loose recipes or photocopies in three-ring binders are simple and convenient. So are computer files you can print out on demand.

Criteria to Fulfill

● You can add notes to the recipes.
● You can sort your collection into categories.
● You can expand it easily.
● You can alter the order.
● You can refer to a single recipe while you're cooking.
● You can see a recipe without squinting (which rules out those recipe cards with the smudged, itty-bitty writing).

OUTSIDE THE BOX

• Store recipes in a photo album (the binder style with removable pages). The plastic covering on the pages protects the recipes from food stains, and preserves delicate newspaper and magazine clippings.
• Cover the cookbook page you are using with press-and-seal plastic wrap to protect it from spills.

✦ Put sticky notes in food magazines, so you don't have to go flipping for the recipes you want. Photocopy them when you are ready to cook.

⚡ Lightning Won't Strike If ...

You write in a cookbook. Note the date and changes you've made to the ingredients or method, or you will forget them. But if you are like me and tinker extravagantly, the pages will begin to look like Sanskrit. So I make photocopies. It's easy to scribble changes onto a copy, and the cookbook doesn't get splattered with food. You can also scan recipes from a cookbook and print them.

5 Ways to View a Loose Recipe While You're Cooking

1. Tape it to a cupboard door.
2. Clip it to a pant hanger and dangle it on a knob.
3. Secure it to a hanger with clothespins and hang that on a knob.
4. Stick it to the fridge with a magnet.
5. Shove it in a cheap, freestanding picture frame.

✦ When giving a food gift, attach a copy of the recipe.

Following Recipes

✦ When a recipe offers metric and imperial amounts, don't cherry-pick from both lists. Stick to one or the other.

♛ Golden Rules

- Read a recipe from beginning to end before you even lift a knife. This sounds like a no-brainer, but it's amazing how often folks in the throes of cooking suddenly realize they are missing an ingredient or can't understand the method.
- The fewer the ingredients in a dish, the finer their quality should be.
- Prep the ingredients before you start cooking.
- Set the timer for a few minutes less than the recipe calls for. It's easier to deal with undercooking than overcooking.
- Live in the moment when you're in the kitchen. A watched pot may never boil, as the saying goes, but an unwatched pot seems to boil over immediately.

Ⓜ is for Mise en Place

The concept of mise en place always reminds me of the acquaintance who said she liked a particular recipe simply because she managed to keep up with all the chopping, measuring, stirring and pouring on the go. People who lurch from task to task become frazzled, get poor results and eventually abandon the kitchen. They think they can't cook! Mise en place is the cure. This French term means "setting in place," or having all the ingredients prepped, measured and set out in little bowls, and all the necessary equipment laid out, before you start cooking. Then see how stress-free cooking can be.

✧ If part of a recipe involves long cooking, the ingredients can be prepped one section at a time. Look for the word "meanwhile" as your cue.

✧ A recipe can't be indefinitely doubled or quadrupled, or halved. Most problematic when changing batch sizes are soups, stews and other wet dishes, and stir-fries.

Tips for the Organized Cook

- When prepping, put a discard plate next to the cutting board. Peel directly over it. Tip trimmings into the garbage or the kitchen compost pail when you're done.
- Hook a plastic grocery bag over the handle of a cupboard or drawer for garbage.
- Stick metric conversion charts, meat-cooking temperature lists, equivalency tables and the like to the inside of a cupboard door for fast reference.

✧ Your kitchen is almost as unique as you are. Ovens and stovetops vary from home to home. Pans vary from shiny metal to glass. Even mixers vary. So rely on clues in recipes, such as "until fluffy" or "golden brown," rather than slavishly sticking to cooking times.

Pan Size Tips

- Don't switch skillet or pan sizes indiscriminately. This will affect the cooking time and evenness. Measure the diameter across the top, not the bottom, to find out what size you've got there.
- Try to use the size and type of baking dish the recipe calls for. If you don't have the right size, measure the volume of a substitute. Using a measuring cup, fill the dish almost to the rim with water. However, the surface area of the food that's exposed to heat also plays a big part in the baking time.

♡ Healthier Eater

All that sampling adds up, and pads you up. After cooking dinner, you may feel like you've already eaten an entire meal. If you're watching your weight, chew gum while cooking.

Developing Recipes

Ways to Kick-Start Your Creativity

- Learn the basic techniques for risottos, stews, curries, stir-fries, omelets, crêpes, pizza — whatever you enjoy. Then start playing with ingredients and amounts.
- Be open to accidents. Take the fridge challenge: Open the door, check what's inside, then mix and match to make a meal. (No extra shopping is allowed.)
- Adapt new recipes to your home and your taste. Jot down changes you discover in the first test batches. When you find a good recipe, tweak it until it's perfect.
- Cook often, for better or worse. Salvage good ideas from failed recipes or save only the good parts of ridiculously complicated recipes.
- Copy commercial dishes that you enjoy. They'll taste sort of the same, but without the chemical life support. (I enjoy homemade Rice-a-Roni.)

How to Copy a Pasta Salad from the Supermarket Deli Counter

1. Spread it out on a flat plate and list every ingredient you spot. Note them in order of priority in the dish.
2. Taste for invisible spices, vinegars and oils.
3. Prepare a manageable amount of the main ingredient. Add and subtract the other ingredients until you come close to a match.

❖ While you are eating a dish you adore at a restaurant, jot down tasting notes. They'll jog your memory when you try to recreate the recipe.

❖ Don't get discouraged. New recipes usually have to be tested and tweaked multiple times.

Measuring

✧ Measure twice, cut once: This carpentry adage works for cooks, too.

Cup **VS.** Dry Measure?

Measuring properly is crucial for baking. It doesn't hurt with cooking, either. Dry measures are stand-alone cups of specific sizes, usually nested. Use a dry measure for flour, sugar or any other dry ingredient that tends to settle. A glass or plastic measuring cup with a spout is meant for liquids, chopped food and large pieces of dry food, such as pasta. It's okay to measure rice with either.

Mythstake

The fluid ounces marked on the side of a measuring cup are not necessarily the same as ounces. The first is a measure of volume, the second a measure of weight. Water will be in the ballpark either way, but other foods vary.

✧ Hold a measuring cup at eye level to check the amount.

✧ If the recipe writer is kind, she will state whether ingredients are "packed" into a measuring cup. They're usually not. So don't pack, or cram, a cup or dry measure. Brown sugar is the exception. It is always packed. Push it down firmly into a dry measure; unmolded, it should gently hold the shape of the cup.

✧ Work with two sets of measuring spoons, one for wet ingredients, one for dry.

✗ No-Nos

• Don't use dry measures as scoops. Spoon the ingredient into the measure, then level the top with a knife or scraper. If you were to scoop 1 cup (250 mL) flour, for instance, it could weigh 1 oz (30 g) more. That adds up in baking. The more flour the recipe calls for, the more the error compounds.

• Don't keep shaking a dry measure or rapping it on the counter. Its contents will settle and the volume will be off.

• Never measure ingredients over the mixing bowl or pan. Your hand will inevitably slip.

4 Sizing Techniques

1. Mark a few sample measurements at the edge of your cutting board. That way, you can assess the diameter of a rum ball or the thickness of a tomato slice without pulling out the tape measure. Use a fine-point permanent marker or cut notches. The marker will eventually fade in the wash.

2. The distance from the tip of the pinkie finger to the first knuckle is about 1 inch (2.5 cm). From the tip of the thumb to the first knuckle, it's about $1\frac{1}{4}$ inches (3 cm). That'll give you a rough guide.

3. Use the metal tip of a measuring tape to poke a mark indicating where to cut.

4. When sizing anything from meatballs to truffles, create a master to copy, so everything ends up more or less the same.

- Old eyes find it difficult to read numbers on measuring spoons, especially the odd sizes. You can paint the engravings with red nail polish, then sand it flush with a nail buffer.

- The visually impaired use brightly colored measuring cups and spoons, preferably a different color for each size. You don't have to be visually impaired to take advantage of this idea.

- To measure drops or pour a tiny stream of liquid, hold a toothpick across the top of a small bottle, carefully tilt the bottle and allow the liquid to run along the toothpick.

- When measuring honey, molasses, syrup, mustard, ketchup, barbecue sauce or anything viscous and sticky, spray the spoon or cup with oil first. The sticky stuff will slide off. If you have to measure oil for the recipe, do that first. You could also run hot water over the cup or spoon before measuring, though that doesn't work as well as the oil.

- A pinch is about $\frac{1}{16}$ tsp (0.25 mL), but don't sweat it. A little more or less isn't going to make a difference. If you feel better measuring, fill a $\frac{1}{8}$ tsp (0.5 mL) measure halfway.

Weight and Volume Equivalents

Ingredient	Volume	Weight
Water or stock	1 cup (250 mL)	8 oz (250 g)
Fruit juice or wine	1 cup (250 mL)	$8\frac{1}{2}$ oz (265 g)
Milk, cream, evaporated milk, plain yogurt	1 cup (250 mL)	$8\frac{1}{2}$ oz (265 g)
Sweetened condensed milk	1 cup (250 mL)	11 oz (330 g)
White all-purpose flour, bread flour	1 cup (250 mL)	5 oz (150 g)
Cake-and-pastry flour	1 cup (250 mL)	4 oz (125 g)
Whole wheat flour	1 cup (250 mL)	$5\frac{1}{2}$ oz (165 g)
Cornstarch	1 cup (250 mL)	4 oz (125 g)
Granulated white sugar	1 cup (250 mL)	7 oz (210 g)
Brown sugar	1 cup (250 mL)	8 oz (250 g)
Confectioner's (icing) sugar	1 cup (250 mL)	4 oz (125 g)
Honey, corn syrup, maple syrup	1 cup (250 mL)	12 oz (375 g)
Molasses	1 cup (250 mL)	11 oz (330 g)
Butter	1 cup (250 mL)	8 oz (250 g)
Shortening	1 cup (250 mL)	7 oz (210 g)
Oil	1 cup (250 mL)	$7\frac{1}{2}$ oz (225 g)
Whole eggs (out of the shell)	1 cup (250 mL)	8 oz (250 g)
Large egg white	1	1 oz (30 g)
Large egg yolk	1	$\frac{2}{3}$ oz (20 g)

Ingredient	Volume	Weight
Shredded semisoft cheese (Cheddar, Swiss, mozzarella)	1 cup (250 mL)	4 oz (125 g)
Grated hard cheese (Parmesan, Romano)	1 cup (250 mL)	4 oz (125 g)
Pasta (macaroni)	1 cup (250 mL)	4 oz (125 g)
Rice (long-grain white or brown)	1 cup (250 mL)	$6\frac{1}{2}$ oz (190 g)
Dry bread crumbs	1 cup (250 mL)	$5\frac{1}{2}$ oz (165 g)
Chopped onions	1 cup (250 mL)	5 oz (150 g)
Herb leaves (basil, parsley)	1 cup (250 mL)	$1\frac{1}{2}$ oz (45 g)
Whole almonds	1 cup (250 mL)	5 oz (150 g)
Walnut and pecan halves	1 cup (250 mL)	$3\frac{1}{2}$ oz (105 g)
Slivered or chopped nuts	1 cup (250 mL)	4 oz (125 g)
Raisins	1 cup (250 mL)	6 oz (175 g)
Chocolate chips	1 cup (250 mL)	6 oz (175 g)
Cocoa powder	1 cup (250 mL)	$3\frac{1}{4}$ oz (100 g)
Peanut butter	1 cup (250 mL)	10 oz (300 g)
Ketchup, mustard, barbecue sauce	1 cup (250 mL)	10 oz (300 g)
Mayonnaise	1 cup (250 mL)	8 oz (250 g)

❖ Measuring by weight, rather than volume, is more common outside North America. Two advantages of measuring by weight:

  • It is more accurate than measuring by volume. Flour and sugar settle. The volume of cheese differs depending on how finely it is grated and how dry it is. Chopped herbs and greens may be packed more tightly into a cup than the recipe writer intended. Nuts go up or down in volume depending on how coarsely they are chopped. Semisolids, such as peanut butter, are messy. When you weigh the ingredients, you get better, more consistent results with baked goods.

  • It is more efficient than measuring by volume. You can start with one bowl on the scale and reset to zero after adding each ingredient — no intermediate measuring and dirtying of cups.

❖ When weighing food packaged in a thin, light wrapper, such as butter, you can leave the wrapper on so you won't have to wipe the scale.

❖ When weighing loose food, place a piece of waxed paper or parchment on the scale. You won't have to wipe the scale. Plus, you can roll the paper into a funnel to transfer the food.

❖ To convert recipes, write weights next to the volume measures on recipe ingredient lists.

Adjusting for Altitude

⚛ A Bit of Science

At higher altitudes, there's less air pressure, and the air is thinner and drier. Water comes to a boil at a lower temperature. At sea level, the boiling point of water is 212°F (100°C). It decreases by about 2°F (1°C) for every 1,000 feet (305 m) of altitude. This takes its toll in the kitchen. For cooks, the great divide is 3,000 feet (914 m). That's generally where you require adjustments in cooking times, temperatures and techniques. But you can see some effects at 2,000 feet (610 m).

Effects of High Altitude

- Gases and steam expand more, so dough and batter rise faster and higher.
- Food heats up faster, but it may not become hot enough or it may remain undercooked.
- Food takes longer to cook because the temperature is lower. (Water can't heat beyond its boiling point.)
- Liquids evaporate faster and in greater amounts, so mixtures become more concentrated or drier. They brown less.

✧ The following are examples only. Get specific information for your area. Start with the smallest adjustments and experiment. Use a food thermometer.

Baking at High Altitudes

✧ Sensitive baked goods, especially cakes, suffer the most at high altitudes.

✧ If cakes rise too high, they collapse, overflow the pan or end up coarse. Adjust the leavener, sugar, liquid and fat.

9 General Adjustments

1. Don't whip egg whites until they are stiff. Beat them to soft peaks.
2. Reduce the baking soda and baking powder.
3. Reduce the yeast.
4. Don't let yeast dough double in size.
5. Reduce the sugar. It can become too concentrated and weaken the structure of cakes, muffins and cookies.
6. Increase the liquid.
7. Substitute extra-large eggs for large eggs in a recipe, for moisture and structure. Or use more eggs.
8. Reduce the fat.
9. Increase oven temperatures. In a hotter oven, baked goods firm up faster. The goal is to attain a firm structure before they over-expand. This also browns the crust better.

✧ Cake adjustments, to be started one at a time and in this order:
- For each teaspoon (5 mL) of baking soda or baking powder, decrease the amount by about $1/8$ tsp (0.5 mL) at 3,000 feet (914 m) and by $1/4$ tsp (1 mL) at 10,000 feet (3,048 m).
- For each cup (250 mL) of sugar, decrease the amount by up to 1 tbsp (15 mL) at 3,000 feet (914 m) and by 3 tbsp (45 mL) at 10,000 feet (3,048 m).
- For each cup (250 mL) of liquid, increase the amount by up to 2 tbsp (25 mL) at 3,000 feet (914 m) or by $1/4$ cup (50 mL) at 10,000 feet (3,048 m).

Other Remedies

- Increase the baking temperature by 15°F to 25°F (8°C to 14°C).
- Reduce the fat by 1 to 2 tbsp (15 to 25 mL).
- Add an egg for moisture and structure.
- Reduce the flour by 1 to 4 tbsp (15 to 50 mL).

Keys to High-Altitude Angel and Sponge Cakes

- Beat egg whites to soft peaks that fall over, not stiff ones that hold their shape.
- Use less sugar.
- Add flour.
- Raise the oven temperature.

Remedies for Biscuits, Muffins and Quick Breads

- Decrease the sugar and fat by 2 to 4 tbsp (25 to 50 mL) each per 1 cup (250 mL) that the recipe calls for.
- If they taste bitter, reduce the baking soda or baking powder by $1/8$ tsp (0.5 mL) per 1 tsp (5 mL) that the recipe calls for. At 5,000 feet (1,524 m), use no more than 1 tsp (5 mL) baking powder or $1/2$ tsp (2 mL) baking soda per 1 cup (250 mL) flour. This applies to cookies, too.
- To combat dryness and improve texture, replace some or all of the liquid with buttermilk, sour cream or yogurt.

- ✧ Adjust pies by adding a bit more liquid to the crust and filling.

Fixes for Cookies That Spread Too Much

- Reduce the sugar or fat by an eighth to a fourth.
- Increase the flour and liquid by an eighth to a fourth.

- ✧ Popovers may puff too rapidly, then collapse. Increase the number of eggs and reduce the fat.

Adjustments for Yeast Dough That Rises Too Quickly

- Decrease the yeast by a third to a half.
- Add a bit more salt. The yeast doesn't like it.
- Let the dough rise twice and punch it down twice, not once, before shaping it. This develops flavor.
- Watch the dough carefully. It should barely double in size.
- If you're making sweet bread, cut the amount of sugar, which softens dough and makes it more prone to collapsing.
- Increase the baking temperature by 25°F to 50°F (14°C to 28°C) to help the bread form a crust quickly. The crust contains the over-exuberant dough and prevents over-rising.

Making Sweets at High Altitudes

- ✧ Sweets made with boiled sugar syrup, such as candy, fudge and frosting, are affected by evaporation at high altitudes. They become hard or grainy. Cook syrup to a lower temperature.

Calculations for Cooking Syrup

- Subtract the boiling point of water at your altitude from the boiling point of water at sea level. Example: 212°F minus 202°F = 10°F (100°C minus 94°C = 6°C).
- Subtract this difference from the final temperature at which the recipe says you should remove your syrup from the heat. Example: If the recipe says to cook the syrup to 250°F (120°C), cook it to 240°F (114°C).

- ✧ Instead of just relying on a thermometer, you can use tests that call for dropping syrup into cold water and assessing what stage (such as soft-ball or hard-ball) it's at.

♦ Above 5,000 feet (1,524 m), there are problems with custards, puddings and creamy pie fillings that are thickened with cornstarch. In the top of a double boiler, they don't get hot enough to allow the cornstarch to thicken properly. You'll have to use direct heat.

Cooking at High Altitudes

♦ Cooking with wet heat or liquid is a problem because water can't rise beyond its boiling temperature (without help). For grilling and roasting, you can simply crank up the oven or barbecue temperatures, although food may turn out dry.

Adjustments for an Electric Skillet

- Increase the cooking temperature by about 25°F (14°C).
- Keep vents closed to retain steam.
- Keep the lid on.
- Keep checking and add liquid if necessary.

Slow Cooker Adjustments

- Food safety is a concern if your dish doesn't reach bacteria-busting temperatures within 2 hours. Start food on High for the first hour, then you can turn the cooker to Low.
- Allow longer cooking times.
- Don't remove the lid during cooking.

Deep-Frying

♦ As a general guide for deep-frying, lower the temperature of the fat by about 3°F (2°C) for every 1,000 feet (305 m) above sea level. With food from doughnuts to fried chicken, the exterior may brown before the interior is done because the moisture inside the food doesn't get steamy enough.

10 General Adjustments

1. Increase cooking times by 5% to 10% per 1,000 feet (305 m) of altitude. Watch for quick evaporation and scorching.
2. Cook meat up to 25% longer at 5,000 feet (1,524 m).
3. Cover pans on the stove to preserve heat and reduce evaporation. Create a tighter seal by putting foil over the pan, then put on the lid.
4. When baking a casserole, increase the oven temperature and/or add cooking time.
5. Use fattier meat. Leaner meat has a higher water content, so it's more prone to evaporation and thus drying out.
6. Add more liquid. Opt for braising and stewing over roasting or broiling.
7. When roasting, baste frequently and add time to compensate for opening the oven door and lowering the temperature.
8. Rely more on a food thermometer to check if something is done.
9. Blanch veggies for the freezer for 2 minutes longer at 5,000 feet (1,524 m).
10. Microwaving may take less time because of rapid evaporation. Use slightly less than the maximum recommended time. Exceptions: Meat and dense or dry foods such as rice or pasta.

Pressure Cooker Adjustments

❖ A pressure cooker is essential equipment at high altitudes. It increases pressure, thus raising the boiling temperature for faster, more thorough cooking. But even pressure cookers require adjustments. Check with the manufacturer for specific instructions. Here are some guidelines:

● Increase the pressure by $\frac{1}{2}$ lb (250 g) for every 1,000 feet (305 m) above sea level.

● If you can't increase the pressure enough, increase the cooking time by 5% for every 1,000 feet (305 m) above sea level, but only starting at 2,000 feet (610 m).

● Watch the time carefully when using a pressure cooker. Foods cook faster. Five minutes in a pressure cooker can be like 10 or 15 in a saucepan.

Making Preserves at High Altitudes

❖ Use gel tests and sheet tests, as well as timing, for jams and jellies.

❖ Fruit and pickles may not be thoroughly processed in a boiling-water canner. Check with the manufacturer to determine how much you will need to increase the processing time at your altitude.

❖ Low-acid foods always require a steam pressure canner. At high altitudes, increase the pressure but not the processing time. Check with the manufacturer.

Thickening

L is for Liaison

A liaison is a thickener or binder. Liaisons used in cooking range from flour to blood.

✧ Starches should be cooked or mixed into a paste before they're added to a dish, or lumps will result. Blend starches with cool water before stirring them into a hot liquid. That goes for flour, cornstarch, arrowroot and tapioca starch.

S is for Slurry

A slurry is a watery paste. To thicken with a slurry, mix 1 part starch (such as flour or cornstarch) with 2 parts cold water (or stock or wine). Shake the slurry in a jar or tub. For gravy, whisk it into hot stock and drippings.

Flour

✧ The simplest way to thicken with flour is to whisk cold slurry into a hot sauce or soup. Use about 2 tbsp (25 mL) flour per 1 cup (250 mL) liquid.

R is for Roux

A roux is a paste of 1 part flour and 1 part fat (usually butter or oil) that is stirred over low heat, and cooked until it's anywhere from beige to Cajun-style brown. It has a nutty flavor. The browner the roux, the weaker its thickening power.

B is for Beurre Manié

Beurre manié is a gummy paste made with flour and butter (or other saturated fat). Knead together equal amounts of flour and softened butter. Form it into small balls. You can make beurre manié with cornstarch and butter to prevent a floury taste.

9 Keys to Making Roux

1. Cook roux for at least 5 minutes to get rid of the raw flour taste. Whisk constantly until it has a pink tinge.
2. If you are adding paprika or minced garlic, stir it in after removing the cooked roux from the heat. Paprika and garlic are prone to burning.
3. Dilute roux before adding it to your dish. Or add enough liquid to the roux to make a sauce.
4. Remove roux from the heat while you gradually whisk in a liquid such as stock, wine or milk. Then return the roux to the heat to thicken.
5. Use about 2 tbsp (25 mL) roux to thicken 1 cup (250 mL) liquid.
6. Make roux sauces a bit thinner than your desired result. They thicken as they cool.
7. Roux is often added to soup to give it a pleasing heft and velvety texture. A roux made with 1 tbsp (15 mL) each of flour and fat should thicken 3 cups (750 mL) soup. Whisk a ladleful of warm soup into the roux, then add it to the soup pot — you'll get fewer lumps.
8. You can make roux in advance and store it in the fridge.
9. You can freeze roux in an ice cube tray or dollop large spoonfuls onto a rimmed baking sheet. When they're frozen, transfer them to a zip-lock bag.

Beurre Manié Tips

- Drop beurre manié into hot liquid and stir. Let it simmer for a couple of minutes, but do not boil it.
- Use about 2 tbsp (25 mL) beurre manié per 1 cup (250 mL) liquid.
- You can add beurre manié to a briefly cooled soup in a blender and pulse them together.

Precautions

- Flour reaches its maximum thickness just below boiling temperature. Boiling will make a sauce bound with flour thinner and wetter. So will heating the sauce for a long time after adding the thickener.
- Whisking or stirring too vigorously will reduce flour's thickening power. So if a sauce bound by flour is too thick, there's no need to add water — just whisk hard.
- Avoid adding lemon juice or vinegar to a sauce thickened with flour until it is removed from the heat. Otherwise, it will get thinner.

✧ To intensify flavor, toast flour before using it as a thickener. Do not let it get too dark or it will be bitter.

Ways to Toast Flour

- Pour it onto a rimmed baking sheet, then shake the sheet to spread it out. Toast it in a 300°F (150°C) oven until it turns golden, about 30 minutes. Shake or stir it occasionally.
- Toast it in a dry skillet over medium heat, scraping from the sides and bottom, until the flour is golden, about 5 minutes.
- If you are making a roast, add some flour to a small baking dish and stick it in the oven next to the meat. Leave it until it is browned and nutty. Use it for your gravy.

✧ Soups, sauces or gravies thickened with flour curdle when frozen and reheated. Use cornstarch or tapioca instead.

Cornstarch

✧ Cornstarch makes sauces glossy and opaque.

✧ When substituting, use half as much cornstarch as you would flour. Use 1 tbsp (15 mL) cornstarch to thicken 1 cup (250 mL) liquid.

How to Thicken with Cornstarch

1. Create a slurry with cornstarch and water, stock or wine.
2. Slurry separates as it sits. Give it a big stir before adding it to a warm liquid.
3. Bring the mixture to a boil, but immediately reduce the heat and simmer for no longer than 30 to 60 seconds.

Precautions

- Boiling too long causes cornstarch to lose its thickening power.
- Don't overbeat mixtures with cornstarch. This causes thinning.

Arrowroot

✧ Arrowroot is a particularly pure starch obtained from the roots of a tropical plant. It is clear and tasteless when cooked.

✧ Use 2 tsp (10 mL) arrowroot to thicken 1 cup (250 mL) liquid.

✧ Just as soon as an arrowroot mixture thickens, take it off the heat.

Substitutions

- Substitute 1 tsp (5 mL) arrowroot per 1 tbsp (15 mL) flour.
- Substitute 2 tsp (10 mL) arrowroot per 1 tbsp (15 mL) cornstarch.

✧ Arrowroot thickens at a lower temperature than flour or cornstarch, so it's a good choice for custardy sauces that aren't allowed to boil.

Tapioca

✧ Tapioca is made from cassava, or yuca. It is best known for the pudding named after it. Tapioca is also recommended for thickening sauces and pie fillings.

How to Make a Clear Glaze for Desserts

1. Stir tapioca flour with juice in a small saucepan. Use about 2 tsp (10 mL) tapioca flour per 1 cup (250 mL) juice.
2. Bring it to the boiling point, but do not let it boil or it will get stringy.
3. Remove it from the heat and let it stand for 2 minutes. The mixture will be thin and milky at first, then clear.
4. Stir. Wait for 2 minutes and stir again.
5. Let it cool for 10 minutes. It should be thick enough. Brush or spread it on your dessert.

Pearl VS. Instant VS. Flour?

Pearl tapioca is used mainly for puddings. It may be cracked into granular, or instant, tapioca for speedier cooking. Soak pearl tapioca for 1 hour before using it. Add water to tapioca in a 2:1 ratio. If the water is not absorbed, the pearls are too old. Tapioca flour, or tapioca starch, is powdery.

✧ For firm tapioca pudding, don't use as much milk as the package says. Use 2 cups (500 mL) whole milk, 3 tbsp (45 mL) granular tapioca and 1 large egg.

✧ Use tapioca flour as you would use cornstarch, and in the same amount.

Potato Starch

✧ Potato starch, or potato flour, is made from cooked, dried, ground potatoes. Use about 1 tbsp (15 mL) to thicken 1 cup (250 mL) liquid.

✧ Substitute 1 tbsp (15 mL) potato starch per 2 tbsp (25 mL) all-purpose flour.

✧ To avoid lumps, stir potato starch with softened butter before adding the liquid.

✧ When using potato starch, don't heat it past a simmer. It doesn't thicken properly at temperatures higher than 175°F (80°C). You can add it at the very end of the cooking time.

✧ Cooked potatoes, diced or mashed, mainly thicken by adding bulk.

OUTSIDE THE BOX

- You can thicken applesauce or squash purée with instant mashed potato flakes or granules. Use about 1 tsp (5 mL) per 1 cup (250 mL) sauce or purée. You can't taste it.
- You can thicken with the natural starch of raw potato. Stir puréed raw potato directly into your dish or harvest the starch from a shredded raw potato.

How to Harvest Wet Potato Starch

1. Shred peeled raw potatoes.
2. Put them in a cheesecloth bundle. Wring out as much liquid as possible into a small bowl. (Save the potatoes for other uses if desired.)
3. Stick the bowl in the freezer for 1 minute.
4. Pour off the liquid on top, leaving the sludgy potato starch at the bottom. It will be a small amount. Scrape it out and use it as a thickener.

Rice

✧ Rice flour is used to thicken sauces and desserts.

OUTSIDE THE BOX

Cambodians use raw rice as a thickener. On a rimmed baking sheet, toast ½ cup (125 mL) raw rice at 350°F (180°C) for 15 minutes. Once it has cooled, pulverize it in a spice grinder. To use it, stir it directly into boiling liquid. The sauce or soup will remain a bit granular. Push it through a sieve for a smoother result.

♻ Waste Not

To add bulk to a dish, purée leftover rice with stock, then stir it in.

Other Options

✧ Whisk in heavy cream, sour cream, yogurt or crème fraîche to thicken sauces, particularly cold ones.

Classic Thickeners

- Add an egg yolk to soup or sauce. To prevent curdling, beat a spoonful of cream or sherry with the yolk before whisking it in. Do not allow the mixture to boil.
- Blood may be traditional, but it's a turnoff. Blood should be combined with a couple of spoonfuls of vinegar to prevent it from clotting, then stored in the fridge for no longer than 2 days. Strain it and stir it into a sauce just before serving. It may be simmered but not boiled.
- Adding wine and cold butter to warm pan juices is a classic way to create a rich sauce, particularly for fish. This is not for calorie counters. You'll need a 1:1 ratio of butter and wine.

How to Thicken with Butter

1. Deglaze the pan with its juices by pouring in wine.
2. Remove the pan from the heat. Stir in cold cubes of butter one at a time. They should spiral in the wine before they melt.
3. Do not return the sauce to a boil or it will separate.

🄵 is for Filé

Filé powder is a thickener associated with gumbos. It is made from dried sassafras leaves. Sensitive filé becomes stringy if it's cooked. Stir it in after removing the pot from the burner or sprinkle it on at the table, then stir.

✗ No-No

Do not use okra and filé in the same dish. That's a recipe for a gummy gumbo.

❤ Healthier Eater

- Purée vegetables left over from making stock, then use the purée to thicken soups, sauces, gravies and stews.
- Beans, lentils and other legumes provide thickening power.
- Quick-cooking oats, wheat germ, quinoa flakes and pearl barley add fiber and bulk. For a more homogeneous texture, purée the mixture in a blender.
- Use evaporated skim milk as a fat-free thickener.

✦ Not recommended, but tried-and-true thickeners: Canned condensed cream of mushroom, chicken or celery soups are commonly used by college kids and desperate housewives. Eat at your own risk.

OUTSIDE THE BOX

- You can thicken pan drippings or sauces by whisking in softened gelatin.
- To thicken a sauce quickly as it simmers, toss in a large raw pasta noodle, such as lasagna or manicotti, to suck up some liquid. Then discard it.

Brining

❖ Brining is the process of plumping and flavoring meat in a salt-water solution. Cooks swear by it for cooking juicy roasts and birds. Soaking in plain water will moisten a chicken, for example, but won't tenderize it. Salt aids in the retention of the water, so less moisture is lost during cooking. Why doesn't the salt suck out moisture? Because of its concentration and the length of time the meat is soaked.

6 Brining Options

1. Meats that don't have enough marbling to bathe them in tender juices are the best candidates for brining.
2. Brine large, lean cuts of meat that will be cooked to medium and beyond.
3. Poultry and pork are popular choices. Do not brine frozen, self-basting turkeys injected with fat, or kosher poultry.
4. Seafood benefits from brining. Brine whole fish or shrimp.
5. Beef and lamb are never brined. They are fattier and cooked (hopefully) just to medium-rare.
6. If you will be smoking meat, brine it first.

Brine Qualifications
- It should taste salty, but shouldn't leave you gagging.
- It should be salty enough to make an egg bob, or even float.

❖ Formulas are all over the place. My favorite: 4 cups (1 L) water, $\frac{1}{3}$ cup (75 mL) kosher salt and $1\frac{1}{2}$ tbsp (22 mL) granulated sugar. Three hours in this brine is perfect for a whole chicken. You can up the salt to $\frac{1}{2}$ cup (125 mL) and the sugar to 2 tbsp (25 mL).

How to Mix Brine

1. Boil a small portion of the water. Dissolve the salt and sugar in it.
2. Add any herbs and garlic at the same time, to coax out their essences. Seasonings are too weak in cold water.
3. Add the rest of the water — cold.

❖ Another option: Brew spices and herbs as a strong tea, let them cool, then add them to the brine.

Basic Brine Ingredients
- Tap water is fine for brine.
- I prefer kosher salt. Many brine recipes call for table salt because the strength of kosher salt varies and sea salt is too expensive. If substituting table salt for kosher, cut the amount by a third to a half.
- Sugar counters the saltiness. But it is optional. In brine recipes, you may see a range from zero to $\frac{1}{3}$ cup (75 mL) granulated sugar per 1 quart (1 L) liquid or an amount equaling 25% to 100% of the salt used. Omit the sugar or stick to a small amount if the meat must roast for a long time, as it can cause too much browning.

Gussy It Up

- Most cooks use water because they don't want to pour money down the drain along with the used brine. But you can replace some or all of the water with any liquid you fancy: cider (for pork), wine, beer, fruit juice, soda pop, coffee, tea, vinegar or buttermilk. Try white cranberry juice in the brine for turkey.
- You could use a seasoned salt mixture. Or add some soy sauce and reduce the salt.
- Any type of sugar or syrup is fine: brown sugar, honey, maple syrup, even molasses.
- Flavorings define the brine. They can range from crushed garlic to vanilla extract. Toss in a spoonful of a spice rub or blend. Try Worcestershire sauce or chopped ginger. Add heat with smoky chipotles or other peppers.
- Herb stalks are good additions, as are peppercorns, whole cloves, juniper berries and cinnamon sticks.
- Try cut fruit or vegetables such as lemon, onion, gingerroot and jalapeño. Or use citrus zest.

✧ Be careful with acidic brine containing vinegar or citrus juice. It tenderizes, but it can also turn meat to mush. Reduce the brining time.

How Much?

- Guesstimate about 1 quart (1 L) brine per 1 lb (500 g) meat.
- If you want to figure it out exactly, put the meat in the brining container and cover it liberally with water. Remove the meat and measure the water.

✧ Salt helps hold bacteria at bay, but brining is safest and works best when the meat is cold. Soak it in the fridge.

✧ Submerge the meat by weighing it down with a large plate or a foil-wrapped brick.

✧ Brining can be messy and gobble up a lot of fridge space. Use a container that just holds the meat and brine, preferably one with a lid.

Being Green

Recycle buckets from commercial food products for brining. The lids prevent sloshing and the handles are handy for lugging a heavy hunk of meat. You have to clean them well, though. Examples:

- A 10-lb (4.5 kg) sour cherry tub is the perfect size for brining a standing chicken. These tubs appear in some supermarkets for a couple of weeks in the summer.
- Large plastic ice cream tubs will work.

More Brining Containers

- Try a soup pot or a large Dutch oven.
- For smaller pieces of meat, use plastic storage tubs.
- Zip-lock bags can be used. Double them up.
- You can brine in a picnic cooler with ice packs. It will have to be disinfected afterwards.
- If there's no room in the fridge for a brined turkey, double two heavy garbage bags and put them in a cooler. Put the turkey in the bags. Pour in the brine. Press air out of the bags. Close each bag separately and tightly. Keep the turkey cold and submerged with lots of ice packs, changing the packs as required.

✗ No-Nos

- Never put meat in warm brine. Brine should cool to at least room temperature before it is used.
- Never brine in an aluminum or cast-iron container.
- Do not reuse brine.

How Long?

- Do not overdo it. Brining meat too long will make it unpleasantly salty. Brine for at least half an hour, but don't let most meats languish for more than 8 hours.
- You needn't be subtle or strict about the times. The strength of the brine and the density of the meat play a part. Guesstimate 1 to 2 hours per 1 lb (500 g) meat, or 30 minutes per 1 lb (500 g) seafood.
- Determine times by the size or weight per hunk, not the total weight of all the pieces.
- The math is not linear, so you'll have to experiment.

10 Timing Suggestions

1. **Whole chicken:** 3 hours
2. **Bone-in chicken parts:** 1½ hours
3. **Boneless chicken parts:** 1 hour
4. **Cornish hen:** 1 to 2 hours
5. **Whole turkey:** 12 to 24 hours
6. **Pork chops:** 1 hour
7. **Pork roast:** 2 hours
8. **Spareribs:** 2 hours
9. **Pork shoulder:** 24 hours
10. **Shrimp:** 30 minutes

✧ Though brining makes chicken tender, it makes shrimp firmer.

✧ After brining, rinse the meat thoroughly in the sink under cold running water, using a sprayer if you have one.

✧ Brining makes the skin of poultry less crisp. So add the extra step of air-drying the bird, uncovered, for several hours or even overnight in the fridge. Do this on a rack to allow air circulation.

✧ The pan juices of brined birds are salty, so beware of using them for gravy. Make a separate gravy and add pan juices, bit by bit, at the end.

Alternatives to Brining

- In France, some cooks simmer poultry in salted water before roasting it.
- Buy kosher birds. They are already salted.

Ⓓ is for Dry-Brining

This simpler variation involves rubbing meat with salt and letting it sit. The meat essentially brines in its own juices. Since there isn't as much liquid, the skin gets crisper in the oven. Some cooks actually bury the meat in salt.

How to Dry-Brine

1. Massage salt generously all over the meat. If you are salting poultry, rub salt under the skin and don't forget the cavity.
2. Wrap the meat in plastic. Let it sit in the fridge. Double or triple the brining time. Dry brining takes longer because the meat dries out at first.
3. Rinse the meat well in cold water.

Marinating

Acid VS. Oil?

Marinades tenderize and flavorize. An acid is used for the former, an oil for the latter. A marinade need not have both. And it need not be a liquid. You can marinate in a spice paste.

✧ A marinade won't penetrate much beyond the surface, so marinating for tenderness is a dubious endeavor.

Options When Tenderizing Is Your Main Goal

- Up the acid ante.
- Stick to tougher, fibrous cuts, such as flank steak.
- Use thinner cuts or cube meat into small pieces.
- To pierce or not to pierce? Meat, particularly a thick roast, is sometimes poked full of holes to allow a marinade to penetrate and increase tenderness. The downside: This may defeat the purpose, as more juices will be lost during cooking.

Common Marinade Ingredients

(Ranging in acidity from high to low)
- Lime juice
- Lemon juice
- Wine vinegar
- Orange juice
- Wine
- Tomato juice
- Beer
- Buttermilk
- Yogurt

✧ If your marinade is very acidic, marinate meat for no longer than 2 hours, unless you want it to be gray or mushy.

✧ Soak chicken in milk or buttermilk. The lactic acid makes it tender.

✧ In Indian cuisine, meat is marinated in yogurt and spices. The natural acids in yogurt are not as aggressive as those in vinegar.

OUTSIDE THE BOX

- Natural enzymes in figs, kiwifruit, pineapples and even papayas can tenderize meat. For a fat-free marinade, purée the fruit and spread the paste over the meat. Let it marinate for half an hour — no longer, or the meat will turn to mush. These enzymes are powerful. You can tone them down by adding the purée to a regular marinade base.
- Cola marinates. Make a cocktail-themed marinade by adding rum. Other distinctive sodas, such as Dr. Pepper, can also be used.

♲ Waste Not

Put leftover dill pickle juice to work as a marinade. It imparts a slight dill flavor, but is not unpleasant.

☰ Fast Fixes

- For a basic marinade, stir together oil, vinegar and a dried spice blend.
- Use bottled salad dressing as a quick marinade. You can be frugal and combine the dregs from several bottles.

How Much?

- You don't need a lot of marinade. Use about ½ cup (125 mL) per 1 lb (500 g) boneless meat or other food.
- Use the least amount of marinade by putting the food in a container just large enough to hold it. For the best coverage, marinate in a zip-lock bag. The food can be massaged and turned.

How Long?

- Chicken soaks up marinade faster than pork or beef. Marinate chicken for up to 6 hours, or 2 to 4 hours if it's skinless. Marinate pork or beef for up to 8 hours.
- Marinate fish for no longer than 30 minutes. If the marinade includes citrus juice, cut the time to 20 minutes. The acidity begins to "cook" the flesh.

- ✧ Marinated meat and fish cook faster. Marinating overnight can cut the cooking time by up to a third.

- ✧ You can freeze meat in its marinade or a spice paste, which is particularly useful when preparing for a camping trip. Make the marinade stronger and thicker, because the juices from the thawing meat will dilute it.

Marinade **VS.** Rub?

Marinades are wet. Rubs are dry. Use a marinade on lean meat, a rub on fatty meat.

- ✧ "Marinate" a roast neatly in a spice rub. Press it in with your fingers, cover the roast with plastic wrap and refrigerate it for 1 to 2 hours.

- ✧ If you're squeamish, wear disposable gloves to rub spice blends into meat.

❶ is for Injector

Injecting marinade deep into the flesh is an alternative to long marination. An injector is a big syringe. The needle is thick, with a relatively large hole at the tip. Originally, veterinary syringes were used; that's where the idea came from.

10 Injector Tips

1. Use a thin sauce that contains no solids, or buy one marketed for injectors. You can dilute a sauce or marinade for use in the injector.
2. Push the plunger down slowly at the same time as you gradually pull the injector out of the meat. This distributes the marinade more evenly.
3. Cut the meat before injecting it, not after.
4. Inject chops and steaks at 1- or 2-inch (2.5 to 5 cm) intervals across the top. If the cut is thick, turn it over and inject the other side.
5. Inject poultry in the thighs, drumsticks and breasts.
6. You can use the same hole to inject at different angles.
7. Avoid contaminating the jar of marinade. Don't keep dipping the needle into it as you work. Pour the marinade you need into a narrow cup or glass, then dip into that.
8. Injecting is messy. If the marinade is fairly sweet, wipe drips off the surface of the meat or they will scorch.
9. You can brush leftover marinade over meat near the end of the cooking time. First, boil the marinade for 5 to 10 minutes.
10. To clean the injector, use it to suck up and squirt out hot, soapy water several times. Then drop the components into the water. Swish and rinse well.

✧ Marinades with thick herbs and minced garlic, ginger and onion will burn on the surface of meat. Scrape them off thoroughly with a butter knife before roasting or grilling.

✧ With raw meat sitting in them for hours, marinades are full of bacteria. Take precautions not to cross-contaminate.

Safety Tips

● Don't brush a used marinade over meat that's almost cooked. Use it only if the meat will be on the heat long enough to kill the germs.

● Throw out leftover marinade or boil it for 5 to 10 minutes before using it for basting or dipping.

● If you want to turn marinade into sauce or dip, it's better to reserve a portion of the unused mixture, rather than boiling the marinade that the meat sat in.

● Don't save a used marinade. It shouldn't live to marinate another day.

Breading and Battering

B is for Bound

If you're in a hurry, you might dip wet meat in crumbs or flour before frying it. But if you want the coating to stick, you want bound breading. So take three steps: Dust it in flour. Dunk it in egg wash. Dip it in crumbs, seasoned flour or cornmeal.

Coating Tips

- Start with meat or fish that has been patted dry. Strange, but the coating will stick better.
- Blend seasoned flour and breading mixtures by stirring them with a fork.
- After dusting the meat, shake off the flour so the food is not too doughy.
- The coating will go on more evenly if the egg is loosened. (Add a spoonful of water or milk to the egg and whisk with a fork just to break up the gel. The egg shouldn't be frothy.)
- The neatest, most efficient way to coat is to put the crumbs in a plastic bag. Toss the food into the bag. Blow air into the bag, then twist the top closed and shake.
- Transfer breaded food to a rack, not a plate. Let it dry for at least 15 minutes. This sets the coating, making it less likely to fall off, and dries it, so it doesn't steam when plopped into hot oil. Avoid refrigeration. Cold food lowers the oil temperature. If the food doesn't develop a crust quickly, it sucks up more grease.
- Shake off any loose coating before frying, so bits don't fall into the hot oil and burn.
- To reduce all the globbing on your fingers when you're breading, use one hand for wet ingredients, the other for dry ones.

- Some cooks pierce food with a fork in an attempt to make the breading stick better. You might lose juices that way.
- Coat the food just before cooking. Otherwise, the breading gets moist and wants to peel away.

Gussy It Up

Add dry, grated Parmesan to bread crumbs for a savory coating.

✧ Remember that breading absorbs fat. Use tasty olive oil or clarified butter if you won't be frying over high heat for a long time.

✧ Flip breaded meat with a spatula or two rather than tongs, which might tear the breading.

The Batter Balancing Act

- The thinner the batter, the crispier the coating. The crispier the coating, the more fragile — and the more likely to fall off.

✧ Is the fritter batter thick enough? Take a big spoonful and pour. It should land in successive splats, not flow in a broad band. Batter for fish, however, should be the consistency of house paint — not too thick.

✧ Use chickpea flour, or besan, to make a batter for onion rings that won't fall off. Mix 1½ cups (375 mL) chickpea flour, ½ cup (125 mL) milk and 1 tsp (5 mL) salt. For a thinner batter, add another 2 tbsp (25 mL) of milk.

For a makeshift fritter batter, combine buttermilk pancake mix and beer.

✧ When coating fish, meat, vegetables or fruit in batter, it's easier to pick them up with a spoon that's been dipped in hot fat.

Tempura Tips

- The lightest, yet clingiest tempura batter has equal amounts of flour and cornstarch, along with baking soda and club soda.
- To keep tempura batter icy cold (a good thing), whisk two ice cubes in with it just before using. They won't melt much when you use icy water in the batter.

5 Routes to Better Batter for Fritters

1. Substitute club soda or beer for the water.
2. Add a spoonful of baking powder to the batter before using it.
3. Add about 1 tsp (5 mL) granulated sugar per 1 cup (250 mL) batter. This makes it browner.
4. Beat batter until it's very smooth, then refrigerate it for at least 2 hours to let the flour suck up the liquid. It will be less rubbery.
5. Adding extra egg yolks helps prevent grease from penetrating the fritters when they are frying.

Boiling and Steaming

Boiling and Simmering

Simmer VS. Boil?

When small bubbles rise to the surface and barely break, the water is simmering. The term "gentle simmer" is redundant. Shivering is a step below simmering; the water barely ripples. A simmer is en route to a full boil, when big bubbles pop to the surface and small bubbles cling to the sides of the pan. Keep the heat cranked up and you're headed toward a rolling boil. This boil is so exuberant that it tries to escape the pot and doesn't stop bubbling when you stir it.

✘ No-No

Don't boil a dish any longer than briefly. Remember the adage: "A stew spoiled is a stew boiled." That goes for most foods. Boiling deteriorates odors and aromas. Simmering helps preserve them.

✧ To test whether a tightly covered dish in the oven is simmering or boiling, put a small covered baking dish of very hot tap water next to it. Check whether it boils.

✧ A watched pot never boils. A covered pot boils faster.

⚡ Lightning Won't Strike If ...

You add salt to water when you put it on the stove. Normally, we are warned that salted water takes longer to boil. True. But the difference is negligible. Some experts say it takes a full ounce (30 g) salt per quart (1 L) water to raise the boiling point by 1°F. If you want to feel efficient, wait to add the salt. Otherwise, don't lose sleep over it.

✧ By raising the boiling point, salt also helps food cook faster. Sugar also raises the boiling point. That's why preserves bubble so furiously.

✧ If you are told to boil something for X amount of time, start timing when the liquid returns to a boil.

✧ Toss green vegetables into boiling water. Start slow-cooking root vegetables in cold water and bring it to a boil. This prevents them from getting mushy on the surface.

> **Ways to Prevent Boil-Overs**
>
> • Rub the inside of the pan with oil.
> • Lay a wooden spoon across the top of the pan. Exception: This doesn't work for milk.

✧ Easy ways for food to enter and exit boiling water:
  ○ Scoop it with a skimmer.
  ○ Lower and raise it in a wire basket, like the one hiding in your deep-fryer.
  ○ Don't save that pasta pot with an inset only for pasta.
  ○ Dip small items in and out with a long-handled sieve.

Blanching

Ⓑ is for Blanching

Blanching is a quick dip in boiling water — not long enough to cook the food. Anything can be blanched, but the technique is most often used with fruit and vegetables.

5 Reasons to Blanch

1. To set bright colors.
2. To soften food. (Some foods need blanching before they're grilled, so they won't char before being cooked through. Root vegetables should be blanched before roasting, so they don't get leathery.)
3. To halt the work of enzymes that cause browning and decay. (This is necessary for freezing and preserving.)
4. To loosen tender skins so they can be slipped off.
5. To reduce bitterness. (Turnips, celeriac and other roots will become mellower.)

◆ When blanching, use 3 quarts (3 L) water per 1 lb (500 g) produce.

◆ Vigorously boil the water over medium-high heat.

◆ Add the produce, cover and wait for the water to return to a boil, then start timing. If the water takes longer than 1 minute to return to a boil, the heat isn't high enough or you put too much produce in the pot.

◆ When blanching several different vegetables in succession, save the water and save time and energy. Skim out the vegetables instead of draining the saucepan.

◆ You can blanch with steam, but only small amounts. Steam in one layer, no more than 1 lb (500 g) at a time. Begin timing when steam starts to emerge from under the lid. Shake the steamer basket or insert a couple of times.

◆ Cool blanched produce quickly, to stop the cooking and keep the color vivid.

Ways to Hasten Cooling

- Immediately dunk vegetables in ice water.
- Spray them with cold water.
- Spread them across a rack or cutting board set over the sink.

Poaching

 is for Poaching

Food cooked in simmering water is poached. Delicacy is the key. Your poaching liquid should never come to a boil or you'll make a mess.

◆ When poaching small items, add them to simmering water. When poaching a large item, such as a whole chicken, put it in the pot with cold water, then bring the water to a simmer.

Steaming

◆ Mind that gap. Two inches (5 cm) is the magic number. Put at least that depth of water in the saucepan and keep the food in the steamer at least that high above the water.

◆ Don't crowd food in the steamer. Give the steam room to circulate.

◆ Steam food over wine, stock or spiced water, as opposed to plain water. Moisture from the food mingles with the liquid. When you're done, save the liquid as a base for sauce or soup.

◆ When adding water to a steamer, first bring it to a boil in a kettle.

> **Factoid** Steaming doesn't extract flavor the way boiling does. It doesn't add flavor the way grilling or frying does.

✦ If you are worried that the food in the steamer will get wet when you're adding liquid to the pan, put a small funnel alongside the food, then pour the liquid through the funnel.

✦ If your steamer basket has a tight fit or is hard to lift out of the base, make a sling before you start. Crisscross two folded kitchen towels in an X on the rack, letting the ends hang over the pot rim. Place the steamer basket on top, then put on the lid. Drape the ends of the towels over the lid.

✦ If the food you are steaming is piled so high that you can't put a lid on it, create a foil dome. If you're using a double boiler–style steamer, tuck the edges of the foil under the rim of the base pan.

✦ Line a bamboo steamer with a lettuce leaf or cabbage leaf, as Chinese cooks do. The leaf prevents sticking and shields delicate food from direct blasts of steam.

♺ Waste Not

Foods that release juices, such as chicken, can be placed on a rack over a pie plate inside the steamer. Use the captured juices in sauce.

✦ Avoid lifting the lid while steaming. This lowers the temperature and prolongs the cooking time.

Making Do

A round metal cake rack in a pot with a tight-fitting lid can serve as a steamer.

♡ Healthier Eater

You can steam a whole chicken instead of roasting it. Smear oil and spices over the chicken. Refrigerate it for 30 minutes. Steam the chicken over simmering wine. This takes 45 to 60 minutes.

Braising and Stewing

Braise **VS.** Stew?

Braising and stewing both involve cooking in liquid. Smaller pieces of meat are stewed, larger cuts braised. For braising, start with enough liquid to come halfway up the sides of the meat. For stewing, start with enough liquid to barely cover the meat.

◈ Stew tastes better when the meat is browned first. Coat the meat lightly with flour before browning it. The color will be better and the flour will thicken the stew.

◈ You can add a spoonful of vinegar to stew to tenderize the meat.

✗ No-No

Never let a stew or pot roast boil vigorously. It makes the liquid cloudy and greasy, and the meat dry. When braising and stewing tough cuts, keep the temperature well below the boiling point.

Ways to Defat Stew

- After removing it from the heat, let the stew stand for 5 minutes before serving. This allows the fat to rise to the surface so you can skim it.
- Separate the solids from the liquid. Refrigerate them separately overnight. Skim the congealed fat off the liquid. Return the liquid to the solids, then reheat the stew.

◈ Make stew or curry the old-fashioned way, with bone-in chunks of meat. The bones intensify the flavor and are great to chew. Two caveats: Shards of bone may fall off as the meat becomes tender. Bone-in stews are awkward to eat, so if the Queen's coming to dine, use boneless meat.

◈ Stew always tastes better the next day. Try to make it in advance.

ⓒ is for Couscoussière

A couscoussière is a Middle Eastern double-tiered stewing pot. Stew is cooked on the bottom, and the steam from it rises to cook granules of couscous above. If you don't have a couscoussière, try a colander lined with cheesecloth set over a stew pot. Make sure the liquid from the stew doesn't touch the couscous.

◈ Indian curries start with an aromatic spice sludge sautéed in oil. This base is ready when the oil separates out from the spice paste. Then you can add your meat and coconut milk or yogurt. The method is similar for sofrito, the base for Hispanic stews.

Better Leftovers

Bored with leftover stew?
- Turn it into a hearty soup by adding stock and perhaps pasta or rice.
- Add tomato sauce and serve it over sturdy pasta such as rigatoni.

Frying

6 Reasons to Preheat a Pan

1. When the oil is added, it thins and spreads better, preventing food from sticking in spots.
2. It allows you to use less oil.
3. It evens out hot spots in the pan that would cause food to burn and stick.
4. It gives you more control over the heating of the oil.
5. The oil is less likely to burn because it is not heated for so long.
6. It helps ensure that the oil will be at a high enough temperature when the food hits the pan.

❖ Preheat over medium-high heat and wait for the signs that the pan is ready:
- The rim is almost too hot to touch.
- The sides seem hot when you put your hand close to the pan.
- A knob of butter bubbles briskly when added to the pan.
- Water sprinkled in the pan forms balls that dance and roll around.

❖ Frying is simply cooking in hot grease, which can reach much higher temperatures than boiling water. You can fry in oil, lard, shortening and sometimes butter.

 A Bit of Science

Steam escapes from food faster than the oil entering it, and a crust is quickly formed. Verdict: crispy. Oil enters food faster than the steam can escape, and an adequate crust fails to form. Verdict: greasy. When frying, the oil has to be hot enough to bring the liquid in the food to the boiling point almost instantly. Immediate bubbling and the release of vapor are good signs. But, if the oil is too hot, the surface of the food will burn before the center is cooked.

Temperature Tips
- The proper frying temperature is usually 350°F to 375°F (180°C to 190°C).
- A shorter cooking time at a higher temperature is better. But you have to factor in the surface area of the food.
- Small items, such as tempura vegetables, are quick to cook and form a crust before they absorb too much oil. These can be fried at high temperatures.
- Larger items have to be fried at a lower temperature to ensure that they cook through, but they may get soggy in the meantime.
- Fried food should be browned outside and tender inside, within the time range given in the recipe. Always fry a test sample before you start, then make temperature and perhaps time adjustments.

Ways to Fry

- **Deep-fry:** Immerse the food in oil.
- **Pan-fry:** Use enough oil to reach about halfway up the sides of the food.
- **Shallow-fry:** Use enough oil to reach about a third of the way up the sides of the food. It shouldn't float in the oil.
- **Sauté:** Cook in a small amount of oil in a wide, shallow pan over medium-high heat, stirring frequently. *Sauter* means "to jump" in French.
- **Stir-fry:** Cook in a small amount of oil over high heat while stirring constantly.

✗ No-No

Never wait until the oil is smoking; that means it is decomposing and could soon catch on fire.

✧ Butter burns easily. If you want to fry in it, keep the heat down, cut it half and half with oil, or use clarified butter.

Ways to Guesstimate if Your Oil Is Hot Enough

- Hold your hand about 3 inches (7.5 cm) above the oil. You should feel the heat vapors.
- A drop of water should sizzle and evaporate in it.
- A pinch of flour should sizzle and brown.
- A 1-inch (2.5 cm) cube of bread should immediately bubble, dance around and begin to brown. If the bread takes longer than 60 seconds to brown, the temperature is too low.
- Touch the handle of a wooden spoon to the bottom of the pan. Bubbles should surround it immediately.
- In a skillet, the oil shimmers and the surface appears to have rivulets moving through it.

Ways to Reduce Splattering

- Set a splatter screen on top of the skillet to keep your stove clean. Avoid burns by holding the screen like a shield when you're turning hot food.
- You can lay a paper towel over the splatter screen to absorb grease.
- When shallow-frying meat, sprinkle salt liberally into the pan with the oil beforehand.

Making Do

- A large, fine-mesh sieve can be pressed into action as a splatter guard.
- Turn a colander upside down over a skillet to catch splatters.

✧ Just before shallow-frying, some cooks wash down the hot pan by pouring in more oil than they need, then pouring out the excess. This is done to prevent the food from browning instantly.

✧ When you fry food, particularly breaded items in batches, the loose particles in the grease start to burn. Alas, you must strain the oil and wipe the skillet between batches, or use fresh oil each time. To wipe a hot skillet, hold a paper towel with tongs.

✧ Reheat fried and battered foods on a rack in a 350°F (180°C) oven, never the microwave.

OUTSIDE THE BOX

You can drain fried foods on a brown paper bag instead of paper towels. They won't stick as much and will end up crispier. Paper towels, however, sop up more grease.

8 Ways to Cut the Grease

1. Ironically, the more oil, the less greasy the food. That's because adding food doesn't lower the temperature as much when there's plenty of hot oil. In a deep-fryer, food should tumble freely.

2. Fry in small batches. Crowding lowers the temperature of the oil. It also creates too much steam, which the heat must then busily vaporize before it can crisp the food. Bonus: Food cooks more evenly in a roomy pan.

3. Many cooks prefer to bring food to room temperature before frying or even sautéing it. Food straight from the fridge cools the oil. However, experts say food is safer if kept refrigerated until just before cooking.

4. The food should be dry. Besides creating unwanted steam, damp food causes the oil to splatter. It can burn you and it makes a mess.

5. The richer the dough, the more fat it soaks up. Too much butter or sugar can result in a greasy doughnut. A rich batter for onion rings can slide off.

6. Use a skimmer to remove food from hot oil. It scoops up way less fat than a slotted spoon does.

7. Drain fried food on a rack set over a baking sheet lined with paper towels. Pat the tops dry with paper towels.

8. Keep fried food warm in a 200°F (100°C) oven. Otherwise, it cools and gets soggy.

Deep-Frying

✧ Deep-fry in oils that have high smoke points. Don't try to deep-fry in butter.

✧ To heat a large amount of oil faster, cover the pan with a lid.

✧ It's difficult to regulate the heat in a pan to keep the temperature in the right range, especially for deep-frying. Electric stoves can be especially maddening. Always try to use a deep-fryer or electric skillet with temperature controls.

Making Do

You can deep-fry in a wok. It requires less oil yet offers a large surface area. Put it on a back burner for safety.

✧ If you are deep-frying in a pot, fill it no more than halfway with oil. The grease bubbles up, especially when moist foods (such as potatoes) are added. If you're pan-frying, fill the skillet no more than 2 inches (5 cm) from the top.

Stir-Frying

✧ Everything happens at once when you stir-fry. All the work is done up front, but the actual cooking is fast. If you are not prepared, you can become hopelessly muddled and frazzled.

Keys to Prepping a Stir-Fry

• Have all the ingredients cut, measured and set out before you turn on the stove.
• Cut the ingredients into small, uniform pieces so they cook quickly and evenly.
• Blanch any vegetables that have to be cooked for a long time. Also, if you want to stir-fry food cut into larger pieces, you may have to blanch it beforehand.
• Make any sauces in advance.

✧ To halve a stir-fry, halve the solid ingredients, but reduce the liquids by just a quarter.

◆ Don't overfill the wok or the heat won't be intense enough. Brown meat in batches, if necessary, and return it to the pan later. If you have to double the recipe, make the stir-fry twice, then combine the batches.

◆ Stir-fry over medium-high heat and turn the food with a tossing motion. Toss with a small, short-handled spatula, rather than a wooden spoon.

4 Stages in Stir-Frying

1. **Explode:** Add oil to a very hot wok over medium-high heat and swirl. Toss seasonings, such as minced garlic, ginger and chile, in the oil for a few seconds for an explosion of flavor.
2. **Sear:** Scatter in the main ingredients. Toss and flip until they are softened.
3. **Steam:** Add the sauce. Cover the pan. Reduce the heat to low or medium-low. Simmer for 1 to 4 minutes or until you hear crackling noises that indicate the liquid has almost evaporated.
4. **Finish:** Thicken the stir-fry with a cornstarch slurry. Dash in sesame oil and/or chile oil. There should be very little liquid left in the pan.

Ⓥ is for Velveting

Give chicken, pork and seafood that silky, slippery texture you enjoy in stir-fries at Chinese restaurants. A Chinese technique called velveting is the secret.

Master Plan
Velveting Meat or Seafood

1. Put 1 lb (500 g) diced boneless chicken, pork, fish or whole shrimp in a bowl. Toss it with 1 tbsp (15 mL) sherry and ½ tsp (2 mL) salt. Lightly whisk 1 large egg white just to break the gel. Stir it into the mixture. Stir in 1 tbsp (15 mL) each cornstarch and oil, just until the meat or seafood is smoothly and evenly coated.
2. Refrigerate the mixture for 30 minutes.
3. In a large saucepan, stir 1 quart (1 L) water with 1 tbsp (15 mL) oil, then bring it to a simmer. Scatter in the meat or seafood, stirring to separate it.
4. Drain the saucepan as soon as the meat starts to turn white, the fish becomes opaque or the shrimp starts to curl. This can take a few seconds. Do not cook them.
5. Add the meat or seafood to your stir-fry as usual.

◆ You can also velvet in oil at 275°F (140°C), but the food will be greasy.

◆ You can velvet a little while in advance, say 1 to 2 hours. Cover and refrigerate the velveted meat or seafood. Exception: Don't refrigerate meat that has been velveted in oil; it will harden. Prep it right away.

Ⓢ is for Slippery Coating

A technique similar to velveting is called slippery coating. It's used with tougher cuts of beef. Follow the velveting instructions, but omit the egg white.

Searing and Browning

Ⓜ is for Maillard Reactions

Foods release liquid as they cook. In meat, the liquid is mainly water with sugars and proteins. Over high heat and in the presence of fat, the liquid evaporates, while the sugars and proteins undergo chemical reactions to create compounds that taste and smell great. These are called Maillard reactions. They apply to meat and other foods.

Reasons We Love Browning

- The brown crust that forms on meat tastes intense.
- Browning leaves caramelized juices stuck to the bottom of the pan, waiting to be lifted with wine and scraped to make a sauce or glaze.

Mythstake

No, the crust doesn't seal in or trap juices. If that were true, the pan wouldn't fill with drippings. When you sear meat over high heat, it actually loses more juices than it would at lower temperatures. But higher heat is desirable because the meat tastes fabulous when it browns.

✦ To encourage Maillard reactions, sear meat briefly over high heat. Once a crust forms, turn down the heat so the meat can finish cooking without burning.

✦ Brown food in small batches over high or medium-high heat. Overcrowding causes too much steam, lowers the temperature and leaves meat gray rather than brown. On the other hand, a pan shouldn't be so empty that the juices spread thin and burn.

✦ Wipe meat dry before searing, especially marinated meat. You don't want it to steam.

5 Ways to Deal with a Sticking Situation

1. Rub meat or fish all over with oil.
2. Shake the pan frequently.
3. If meat or fish sticks to the pan, don't try to turn it forcefully. It will release when the proteins on the surface are seared.
4. If food is burning and you can't wait, remove the pan from the heat and put on the lid for about 30 seconds. The steam should loosen it.
5. Cold food sticks more. Some cooks let meat or fish stand for at least 10 minutes at room temperature after removing it from the fridge. However, food safety experts frown on this practice.

✦ Always brown meat before stewing it or making pot roast. The meat will not only taste better, it will shrink, so you won't need as much cooking liquid.

✦ To sear steaks, chops or other meat in a cast-iron skillet, heat the dry skillet over high or medium-high until it is smoking hot. Thinly sprinkle salt over the bottom of the skillet. Drop in the meat. Sear it for about 3 minutes or until you see juices beading on the surface and you can turn it.

Grilling and Smoking

Grill **VS.** Barbecue?

Technically speaking, the two are different, but you will be forgiven for using the terms indiscriminately. Grilling refers to cooking food over direct, close heat, usually at high temperatures, for a short time. Barbecuing is low and slow. Smoke is involved, sometimes a pit, and many hours pass. The result is called barbecue — the noun.

❖ Number one barbecue mistake: impatience. You don't walk away from a pan on the stove. So why would you wander off to watch TV or manicure your nails while your food's on the barbie? Barbecue times are unreliable because the equipment and outside temperatures vary. Hovering is recommended.

❖ Number two barbecue mistake: impatience. Cooking too fast at too high a heat will result in burnt offerings.

❖ Number three barbecue mistake: impatience. Overcrowding doesn't pay off. Use no more than three-quarters of the grill surface at once. On a large barbecue, follow the three-burner rule: one on low, one on medium, one on high, so you can shuffle food around.

✘ No-No

Don't grill meat over a direct flame generated by wood or charcoal. Wait until you have embers.

❖ For grilling, stick to steaks and chops that are 1 to 2 inches (2.5 to 5 cm) thick. Even 2 inches (5 cm) is pushing it.

Some Like It Hotter

❖ Hold your palm just over the grate, or at about the same distance above the coals or flame that the food will be cooking. How long can you stand it?

- **Less than 1 second:** The grill is very hot, above 500°F (260°C).
- **1 to 2 seconds:** The grill is hot, 400°F to 500°F (200°C to 260°C).
- **3 to 4 seconds:** The grill is medium, 350°F to 375°F (180°C to 190°C).
- **5 seconds:** The grill is medium-low, 325°F to 350°F (160°C to 180°C).
- **6 or more seconds:** The grill is low, 300°F (150°C) or less.

❖ Here's another test: Think of a memorable four-syllable word such as bar-be-cue-ing. If you can pronounce it once while holding your hand just over the grate, it's high heat. If you can pronounce it twice, it's medium. Three times, it's low.

❖ Charcoal turns from black to gray with a red glow under the ash. Four charcoal readings:

- **Too hot:** bright red coals licked by flame
- **Hot:** red coals covered with light ash
- **Medium:** red coals completely covered by ash
- **Low:** red glow barely visible under thick ash

❖ Oil the grate liberally after it's hot. Do it sooner and it just burns off.

✘ No-No

Don't oil the grate with butter. It scorches.

3 Ways to Superheat

1. Fire up the barbecue. Scrape the grate. Invert a cast-iron pan or disposable aluminum dish on the grate. Close the lid on the barbecue for 5 minutes or until it reaches the maximum or desired temperature. Remove the pan. Quickly grease the superheated grate and add your fish or meat.
2. Large pieces of meat, such as roasts and bone-in chicken breasts, can be loosely covered with a piece of foil before you close the lid. This traps heat against the meat and helps it cook more evenly.
3. You can grill veggies with a colander inverted over them. This allows steam to escape, but still concentrates the heat.

Ways to Grease the Grate

- Generously oil the food instead of the grate. This works best.
- Use a barbecue brush, not tongs, to smear the grate with an oiled paper towel or commercial wipe. The brush really grabs and grips it.
- Hold a piece of trimmed fat or bacon with tongs. Rub it over the grate.
- Remove the grate and spray it with a fine mist of vegetable oil. Never spray into the fire.

Covered or Uncovered?

- You can leave the lid open if the meat is thinner than your palm. Otherwise, close the lid. This is especially important when grilling over indirect heat or smoking (the meat, not you).

Direct VS. Indirect?

If a large piece of meat will take longer than 30 minutes to cook, opt for indirect heat. Turn off one burner and put the meat on that. Keep the other burners going. Close the lid.

Making Do

- If you only have one burner, but need indirect heat, try this: Preheat the barbecue to high. Reduce the heat to low and line half the rack with a double thickness of heavy foil. Put the food on the foil.
- If you don't have a barbecue tray for smaller foods, shape one from heavy-duty foil with holes poked in it with a skewer.
- Create high and low heat zones on a charcoal barbecue by piling the coals to one side.

Low and Slow VS. Hot and Fast?

Grill hot and fast with steaks, chops and fish. Barbecue low and slow with tough, large cuts, such as pork shoulder or a whole bird.

❖ T-bone or porterhouse steaks have strip loin on one side of the bone and delicate tenderloin on the other side. Position the meat so the tenderloin faces the cooler side of the grill.

❖ If flare-ups are causing burnt spots on steak, trim the fat around the edges. You'll still have the marbling in the steak for juiciness and flavor.

X No-No

Don't flip out. Frequent flipping disturbs heat distribution, causes sticking, encourages juices to drip out, prevents a nice crust from forming and interferes with caramelization. So there!

Tips for Flipping

- Flip steak or chops just once. Or if you must have a classic grill-mark pattern, flip no more than three times.
- Use tongs, not prongs, to flip meat on the barbecue, so juices don't escape.
- Don't fret over sticking. The meat will signal when it's ready to be flipped. A crust forms and it releases from the grate.

How to Get Grill Marks

1. Oil a steak or chop (or other food). Sear it for 1 minute on high heat. Do not cover it.
2. Flip it over, placing it at the same angle, and grill it for 1 minute
3. Turn it at a 45-degree angle and complete half the grilling time.
4. Flip it over, placing it at the same angle, then grill it until done. This will give you a crisscross pattern, more prominent on one side.

- Pat marinated meat all over with a paper towel to dry it before grilling.

- For a lovely glow, spray meat instead of basting it. Save money and stir up your own spray. Use a good-quality spray bottle that mists rather than squirts. Just make sure the mixture is not too sweet or thick, or it may clog the nozzle.

Components of Barbecue Spray

- Start with apple or other juices, vinegar or lemon juice. Dark vinegars, such as raspberry or balsamic, give a darker sheen without burning.
- Add about 1 tbsp (15 mL) maple syrup, honey or packed brown sugar per 1 cup (250 mL) liquid.
- Add salt and pepper, spices and seasonings such as garlic powder.

- Brush on barbecue sauce during the last 15 minutes of cooking time and watch the meat carefully to make sure it doesn't scorch.

- Brush on a sweet glaze about 1 minute before you remove meat from the grill. Or paint it on after the meat rests.

- Meats smeared with rubs that have a high sugar content should be cooked over low or indirect heat only.

- Reasons to grill chicken pieces starting skin side up:
  - They don't stick as much.
  - Fat from the skin bastes the meat.
  - The bones warm up faster and transmit heat to the meat above.
  - Flare-ups are reduced.
  - The skin on wings is less likely to tear.

- When you turn chicken pieces skin side down, reduce the heat to low.

A Better Way to Grill Sausages

- Wrap them in foil and grill them over indirect heat until they are almost cooked. Remove the foil and place the sausages directly over the flame. They are less likely to char this way.

Grilled Banana Tips

- In Polynesia, they grill miniature bananas. These finger bananas are sold in supermarkets here.
- Dip bananas in coconut milk, then roll them in sugar to coat. A coarse sugar, such as turbinado, gives a nice crunch, but suffers in the tidiness department.
- Grill bananas over medium-low heat, rolling them frequently, until they are browned all over but not mushy.

T is for Tandoor

Tandoori chicken is prepared in a tandoor, a barrel-shaped clay oven, over a super-hot charcoal fire. The juices drip down and the smoke drifts up. The characteristic red color of the chicken has nothing to do with the oven and everything to do with red food dye — or the natural way, with paprika or cayenne pepper.

Master Plan
Mock Tandoori Chicken on the Barbecue

1. Marinate the chicken overnight in heavily spiced yogurt (with red dye, if desired).
2. Start grilling at medium heat to prevent burning. Keep the lid closed.
3. Turn the chicken occasionally and baste it with leftover marinade.
4. When the chicken is just about cooked, increase the heat to high to char the surface and dry the meat. There should be no uncooked marinade left on the surface.
5. Before serving, brush the meat lightly with melted butter and squeeze lime juice over it.

◇ For superior ribs, grill them on the rotisserie instead of laying them on the grate. Skewer them accordion-style.

◇ When grilling vegetables, cut them thick, say ¾ to 1 inch (2 to 2.5 cm).

Ways to Cook Kebabs More Uniformly

- Skewer the meat and vegetables separately, although that's not as decorative.
- Parboil firm vegetables, such as peppers, before skewering them with the meat, so they'll take the same amount of time to cook.
- Leave air space between the items. Heat needs to reach into the crevices.

Meat Kebab Tips

- To cook meat more, space the cubes farther apart. To cook meat less, press the cubes closer together.
- If the meat is lean and dry, insert bits of trimmed fat between the cubes.
- When molding ground meat to skewers for Indian and Middle Eastern kebabs, keep your hands moist. Rotate the skewer as you work to spread the mixture evenly. Squeeze gently.

Skewer Ideas

- Soak wooden skewers for 30 to 60 minutes beforehand, so they don't burn on the barbecue.
- Have bamboo skewers presoaked and ready to go. Soak them for at least half an hour, gather them into a bundle, shake off moisture, put them in a plastic bag and freeze them. The frozen skewers stick together a bit, but are easy to separate.
- Buy flat skewers; they don't roll.
- Prevent round skewers from rolling by creating a ladder. Use two skewers and pierce large pieces of food as the rungs.
- Use rosemary stalks as skewers. Pick long, thick, sturdy stalks. Remove all the leaves except the sprigs at the top. Trim the bottoms at a sharp angle. Push the tips into the food. Do not lift kebabs using rosemary skewers. Use tongs.

Hot **VS.** Cold Smoking?

Temperatures are kept below 100°F (38°C) for cold smoking. This is done commercially. Hot smoking also cooks the meat. It's generally done at temperatures up to 200°F (100°C). But you can add smoke to meat at higher temperatures on the barbecue.

◆ For big, dark flavor, nothing beats a full-sized smoker. But you can dabble with smoky goodness.

Making Do

• Get a smoker tube or box, fill it with wood chips, place it next to or under your meat and vegetables, then close the barbecue lid.

• Generally, wood chips should be soaked first. Submerge them in cold water for 30 to 60 minutes, then drain. However, you can use dry chips for meat that cooks quickly.

• If you don't have a smoker tube or box, spread 2 cups (500 mL) of soaked wood chips on one side of a long piece of heavy-duty foil. Mix in some dry wood chips. Fold the foil over and crimp the edges. Poke holes in the top and bottom with a fork.

• Ad-lib by poking holes in a used soda pop or beer can. Stuff wood chips in through the top.

• You can wrap a chunk of untreated hardwood with perforated foil instead of using wood chips. This smokes well.

Types of Wood

- **Alder:** Light (traditional for salmon)
- **Almond:** Nutty, sweet
- **Black walnut:** Heavy, bitter
- **Citrus:** Light, fruity, lemon or orange
- **Fruitwood:** Sweet, mild, apple or cherry
- **Grapevines:** Fruity, very smoky (use sparingly)
- **Hickory:** Strong
- **Maple:** Sweet
- **Mesquite:** Strongest, burns hot and fast (use for short bursts of grilling)
- **Oak:** Strong (most versatile hardwood)
- **Pecan:** Nutty, sweet

Recommended Wood Pairings

- For fish, try alder.
- For poultry, try alder, fruitwood, grapevines or maple.
- For pork, try fruitwood or maple.
- For beef and lamb, try hickory or oak.

7 Winter Grilling Tips

1. Pull the barbecue into an area protected from the wind, but never in a garage or enclosed space.

2. Keep the barbecue at least 10 feet (3 m) away from the house or garage.

3. Wipe snow off the barbecue before preheating it. Otherwise, the snow melts around the equipment, refreezes and creates a skating rink.

4. Preheat the barbecue for longer in the winter. Five summer minutes equal 15 to 20 winter minutes.

5. In the freezing cold, handle the control knobs gently. They get brittle and can snap off.

6. Buy a barbecue light or keep the equipment near a strong porch light. It gets dark so early.

7. Choose meat that requires as little hovering as possible so you don't freeze your butt off.

♻ Waste Not

Use nutshells instead of wood chips. You'll need lots.

Gussy It Up

You can soak wood chips in juice for a bit of extra aroma. This can be expensive.

◆ Always close the barbecue lid when smoking with wood chips. Otherwise, what's the point?

◆ Barbecue shops, big-box stores and some supermarkets sell wood chips. Different types impart different flavors.

◆ Planks offer grillers another way to smoke. So planks for the memories.

How to Plank-Grill

1. Soak planks for at least 1 hour, but preferably overnight, before using. Weigh down each plank to keep it immersed. You can use a jumbo can of tomatoes to do so.
2. Preheat the barbecue to high. Put the plank on the grate, close the lid and leave it there until it begins to crackle and smoke, about 5 minutes.
3. Brush the top with oil, then lay the food on it.
4. Close the lid and keep it that way as much as possible.
5. Keep an eye on the barbecue to make sure the plank hasn't caught fire. If it has, spray it with water.

♛ A Golden Rule

Never, ever, make do with treated wood, which has chemicals in it. Buy special barbecue planks.

Lightning Won't Strike If ...

You reuse a plank. If it's in good shape, you can recycle it, especially if you're making something small and quick-to-cook, such as shrimp. Don't forget to soak the plank. Keep using it until it gets too small and charred.

Better Leftovers

Make planked mashies. Mix day-old mashed potatoes with lots of sour cream or soft cheese, then stir in spices. Mound the mixture on a plank. Drizzle it with butter. Close the lid and grill until it's heated through and the surface is golden.

Making Do

For an impromptu charcoal barbecue, stack two sets of bricks as a base. Lay a grate or rack on top.

Other Ways to Smoke

- Cheat with some bottled liquid smoke from the supermarket. Add it to marinades and sauces. Or rub it over meat. Use it in small doses.
- You can smoke chicken in a pan or wok.

Master Plan
Smoked Stovetop Chicken

1. Cover the bottom of a wok or pan (avoid nonstick) with two layers of foil that hang over the rim.
2. Sprinkle the bottom with equal amounts of tea leaves and raw rice, and some sugar.
3. Place a steamer basket on top. Add chicken that has been steamed until it's almost cooked. You can use a whole chicken or pieces.
4. Put on the lid. Fold the foil ends over the lid. Cover the lid with more foil. Place the wok over medium-high heat and smoke for 15 to 30 minutes, depending on the size.

✧ Keep a spray bottle of water next to the barbecue in case of flare-ups. However, charcoal is cooled by water. You don't want that. An alternative: Throw on salt or sand to deaden flames and smoke.

✧ You can use a cast-iron pan on the barbecue.

✧ If the oven goes on the fritz, roast in the barbecue. Just don't use a good, shiny pan.

✧ Did you know there's a battery in the gas barbecue ignition? If the ignition fails, don't reach for a wand lighter. Unscrew the knob and check the battery. It may simply be dead.

Ⓓ is for Drip Pan

A drip pan is placed beneath the meat so fat doesn't drip directly onto the flames, causing a messy conflagration. It's mandatory for barbecued chicken or roasts that take a long time, or rotisserie grilling.

- You don't need an official drip pan. An aluminum roasting, lasagna or pie pan will do. Save your old ones from the supermarket. Toss them out when you're done — no scrubbing.
- For rotisserie cooking, place the drip pan on the grate directly under the meat.
- If you are grilling on the grate, place the drip pan under the grate, directly over the flame.
- Add water to the pan so the drippings don't burn or flare. With the lid down, the steaming drip pan also moistens the meat.
- For grilling over indirect heat, place the drip pan on one side of the barbecue. Preheat the barbecue to medium. Turn off the flame on the drip pan side. Place the meat on the rack over the drip pan.

✧ Always close the valve at the fuel tank before turning off the controls. Don't leave the controls in the open position.

Barbecue Maintenance Techniques

- Turn the gunk on the grate to ash right after grilling by cranking the heat to high and closing the lid for 5 minutes. (Careful: You'll be a fuel hog if you forget to turn it off.)
- If you have an old gas barbecue with permanent briquettes, turn them over and run the barbecue on high for 5 minutes to strip them.
- When preheating the barbecue, place a large piece of foil over the grate. It lifts the crud. You can reuse the foil a couple of times.
- Lay newspaper sections soaked in vinegar on the warm (not hot) grate. Leave them for 1 hour, then lift them off and scrape the grate.
- To make a scoop for the ashes in a charcoal barbecue, cut one corner off the bottom of a large plastic jug. Hold it by the handle.
- Loosen gunk by leaving the grates lying on the grass overnight. The grass enzymes and dew will work on them. Pick them up early in the morning and scrape.

Camping Techniques

✘ No-No

Never, ever burn charcoal in an enclosed tent, cabin or garage. This causes carbon-monoxide poisoning.

Campfire Cooking Tips

- Cooking over a fire is not as easy as it looks. Be patient. Wait for embers. Avoid direct flames.
- Coat the outside of the pan with a thin layer of dishwashing liquid. The soot will be easier to clean off.
- Wire netting called hardware cloth can be spread over the campfire grate to turn it into a grill.

🄷 is for Hobo Pack

A hobo is a homeless wanderer. I doubt hobos carried heavy-duty foil. Still, food wrapped in a foil packet and cooked over a campfire is called a hobo pack. Campers like hobo packs because they can cook a complete meal in one package.

Making Do

- Mark the outside of a plastic drinking cup with measurements in permanent marker so it can double as a measuring cup.
- Drill a few holes through the lid of an old pot to turn it into a pasta strainer.
- A thin, flexible cutting board can do triple duty. You can also use it as a funnel or fan the fire with it.

- ✦ Save on cleanup by using cheap, uncoated, disposable paper plates, then tossing them in the fire.

- ✦ If water is scarce, scorch cookware and utensils in the fire to sterilize them.

Ways to Keep Your Cool

- Freeze as much food as possible ahead of time. Frozen packages act like ice packs in the cooler and seem to thaw just in time.
- You can use a northern lake as a cooler at night. Seal food in zip-lock bags and immerse them. Or dunk your beer to keep it cool.
- Put the cooler in the shade with a blanket or thick towel over it.

4 Ways to Make Camping Bread

1. Spread a sliced baguette with flavored butter, wrap it in foil and freeze it for the trip.
2. Bring frozen bread dough. When it's thawed, pull it into pieces and fry them.
3. Buy biscuit dough. Twist it around the tip of a long stick, then pat it in place. Cook it above the campfire for 15 to 20 minutes.
4. Make your own dough at home. In a sturdy zip-lock bag, shake together 1½ cups (375 mL) all-purpose flour, ½ tsp (2 mL) salt and ¼ tsp (1 mL) baking soda. Add 2 tbsp (25 mL) cold butter. Seal the bag and massage the mixture until it resembles coarse crumbs. At the campsite, massage in about ½ cup (125 mL) cold water to make a firm dough. Cook it the same way as the biscuit dough, on sticks over the fire.

◆ Double-seal raw meat and fish in plastic bags, so their juices won't drip onto other foods in the cooler.

◆ Bring along a fondue pot to make easy desserts such as fruit dipped in chocolate sauce. You can buy an inexpensive mini pot that runs on candle power.

Keys to Roasting Marshmallows

● Don't stick them in the campfire until they burst into flame and blacken. Patiently turn them above a flame or glowing embers until they puff dramatically. The exterior should be brown and chewy, the interior molten.

● If a marshmallow catches on fire, don't shake it vigorously to douse the flame. It can go flying off the end of the stick and burn someone.

Miscellaneous Techniques

Seasoning

✦ Opposites attract. Add a pinch of salt to something sweet, a pinch of sugar to something savory or acidic.

Remedies for a Dish That's Too Sweet

- Stir in citrus juice.
- Sprinkle in salt.
- Add a dash of alcohol.

Ways to Deal with Over-Salted Soup or Stew

- Add 1 thinly sliced potato per 1 quart (1 L) soup or stew. Discard the slices at the end of the cooking time. The potato will suck up some of the salt, but don't expect miracles.
- Stir in vinegar and sugar in ½-tsp (2 mL) increments, sampling as you go.

Maximizing Your Sense of Taste

A Bit of Science

There are five components of taste — sweet, sour, salty, bitter and umami — or, possibly, six. The sixth is described as "pepper." It is a tingling sensation, not an actual response to pepper.

U is for Umami

Umami is hard to describe. It is a savory quality found in glutamates. Seaweed, fermented foods, aged foods, wine, mushrooms, soy sauce and miso are rich in umami. The cheap route to umami is MSG.

M is for MSG

That's the acronym for monosodium glutamate. MSG comes in the form of fine white crystals. It is produced from glutens. MSG is used widely as a flavor enhancer in processed foods and is considered a bane by many patrons of Chinese restaurants. Reactions to MSG include flushing, dizziness and headache.

✦ To cook a dish that intrigues the palate, make sure it incorporates at least three of the components of taste.

Factoid Our taste buds perform at maximum efficiency with foods in the 72°F to 105°F (22°C to 41°C) range.

Temperature and Taste

- Cold foods, such as ice cream and potato salad, require more salt, pepper, sugar and other seasonings. Taste food once it's cold and make adjustments.
- Hot food may seem less acidic.

✦ The sense of smell is closely linked to taste. You can't have the other without the one. If your nose becomes desensitized after hours of cooking, stick your head out the window or step outdoors for a few cleansing breaths. Food will taste better.

Understanding Temperature

Water Temperatures
- **Lukewarm:** 85°F to 105°F (30°C to 41°C)
- **Warm to hot:** 110°F to 120°F (43°C to 49°C)
- **Hottest tap water:** 130°F to 135°F (54°C to 57°C)
- **Slow simmer:** 130°F to 135°F (54°C to 57°C)
- **Poach:** 160°F to 180°F (71°C to 82°C)
- **Simmer (little bubbles):** 185°F to 200°F (85°C to 100°C)
- **Slow boil (movement and large bubbles):** 205°F (96°C)
- **Rolling boil (bubbling vigorously and steaming):** 212°F (100°C)

✧ A test: Stick your finger in the water and try to count to 10. You should be able to if it's warm, but not if it's hot.

✧ When measuring hot food, first warm the thermometer under hot tap water. Insert it into the food near the center of the pan, but do not touch the bottom.

✧ A good general rule: Start with ingredients at room temperature.

® is for Residual Heat
Funny how the temperature of food continues to rise after it is removed from the heat. It finishes cooking in the residual heat. Meat suddenly flips from medium-rare to medium. Blanched vegetables keep steaming unless they're sprayed with cold water. To avoid overcooking, we must make allowances for residual heat.

≣ Fast Fix
If something is too hot, cool it quickly by tossing or pouring it from one large metal bowl to another.

✧ Start with cold water. Hot water can cause proteins to coagulate, so they seize up and fail to release their flavors. Plus, it picks up more minerals from the pipes.

Mythstake
Room temperature ain't what it used to be. Once upon a time, our homes were cooler and we wore sweaters and fuzzy slippers to compensate. Now we bask in central heating. References to room temperature in recipes can mislead us. Is that modern, standard 70°F (21°C), or slightly cooler?

"Room Temperature" Considerations
- Though a recipe may call for egg whites at room temperature, some sources cite 65°F (18°C) as the optimal temperature for whipping them.
- Butter at modern room temperature may be too soft for baking. It, too, is considered best at about 65°F (18°C). The butter should be pliable and easy to dent, but hold its shape firmly. Butter that's too soft provides less leavening and causes dough or batter to spread.
- Wine drinkers are also affected. Red wine at modern room temperature is actually too warm.

Making Dips and Spreads

✧ Give dips and spreads at least 2 hours in the fridge after preparing them. But don't serve them chilled. Leave them at room temperature for a few minutes.

✧ Add nuts or fresh herbs at the last minute so they don't get soggy or discolored.

Two Transformations

- To turn a spread into a dip, thin it with sour cream, cream, olive or nut oil, or lemon juice.
- To turn a dip into a spread, thicken it with cream cheese or mayonnaise.

Ways to Make Better Layered Mexican Dip

- Strain the salsa to prevent it from weeping.
- Stir shredded firm cheese, such as Monterey Jack, into a cream cheese base to hold it together.

Ways to Gussy Up Your Guac

- Char a jalapeño or serrano pepper instead of just mincing it.
- Use a smoked soft chipotle chile in adobo sauce.

 No-No

Double-dipping.

Emulsifying

✦ Like a reverend presiding at a marriage of opposites, an emulsifier dissolves in both fat and water, and thus unites them in an emulsion. In cooking, this is handy. Emulsifying is not to be confused with thickening, though they do go together.

✦ Like many marriages, the emulsion may fail at the outset, or eventually, when fat and water once again go their separate ways. Mayonnaise can have a stable marriage, while vinaigrette is notoriously fickle.

✦ For a proper emulsion, you need patience. The fat should be beaten almost drop by drop into the liquid.

✦ There's a limit to how much fat you can beat in. Add too much and the emulsion comes apart.

✦ It's easier to emulsify a liquid that's acidic.

✦ Besides the gibberishy additives noted on product labels, natural emulsifiers include egg yolks (lecithin), mustard (in the mucilage from the seeds), carrageenan (derived from Irish moss seaweed) and soybeans.

✦ The fresher the egg, the better it will emulsify a sauce.

✦ When binding a sauce with an egg, add a pinch of flour.

Whipping

✦ Egg whites and heavy cream are whipped to soft, medium or stiff peaks.
- **Soft peaks:** Flop over. Look rounded rather than spiky. Fall softly from the beaters.
- **Medium peaks:** Tips curl over when the beaters are lifted. Beaters leave lines and swirls.
- **Stiff peaks:** Firm. Hang from the beaters without falling. In the case of meringue and whipped cream, but not necessarily plain egg whites, stiff peaks stand up when the beaters are turned upside down.

Working with Dyes

✧ Synthetic food colorings come in water-based form, gels and pastes. Water-based dyes are the most common, but the least concentrated. The pastes are the hardest to find.

5 Tips for Using Gel Dye

1. It's worth going to a cake-decorating shop to buy gels. They come in more colors, even black. You can mix custom colors.
2. Don't confuse gel dye with the thin gels sold in squeeze tubes for writing messages. The latter are made with royal icing.
3. Use a toothpick to scoop gel dye, but do not double-dip. Any dough or other food that winds up in the dye can get moldy.
4. Start with a tiny amount and build up the color, from pastel to dark.
5. If the dye dries up, add a drop of glycerin (sold in drugstores and cake-decorating shops).

Remedies for Stains

- Wear disposable gloves to avoid staining your hands.
- Wipe stains off counters or cutting boards with a mild bleach solution, then soapy water. Wipe right away; don't wait until you are finished the job.
- If a stain sets, you may be able to buff it off with sandpaper or an emery board.

☰ Fast Fix

Don't have food dye? Mix cold-drink powder and icing sugar. Careful, you don't need much powder. The mixture will look pastel, but the finished color will be bright. You can use it for icing. The taste will be tangy.

Factoid Synthetic food dyes have been blamed for ailments ranging from allergies to hyperactivity to cancer. Governments regulate synthetic food dyes, but if in doubt, it's wise to use them sparingly or not at all.

✧ Good news: Many foods can be used as natural dyes. Bad news: The final colors are subtle and pastel, and hard to control. They are not concentrated. You will be disappointed if you expect vivid hues from natural dyes.

Colors from Nature

- **Red:** Beets, paprika, cranberries, pomegranates, tomato paste
- **Green:** Spinach, algae
- **Blue/purple:** Red cabbage, blueberries, lavender flowers, red onion skins
- **Yellow:** Annatto (achiote seed), saffron, turmeric, mustard
- **Gold/brown:** Onion skins, coffee, tea, chili powder, cumin, soy sauce

✧ To extract color from natural ingredients, chop or tear them, then simmer them for 30 minutes in the smallest possible amount of boiling water. To intensify the dye mixture, add white vinegar to the water. Use about 2 tbsp (25 mL) vinegar per 4 cups (1 L) liquid.

✧ Many fruit juices and edible flowers come in lovely, strong colors.

✧ You don't need to use the actual beet — the skin works fine. Eat the beet.

Reducing

✦ We reduce by evaporation, to intensify and thicken stock, tomato sauce, pan juices or whatever we place over high heat.

✦ Season after reducing, rather than before. Otherwise, your dish will be too salty or overpowering.

✦ When reducing a liquid, you don't have to guess. Start by measuring the amount, boil it down, then check your progress by pouring it back into the measuring cup.

OUTSIDE THE BOX

Use a wooden spoon as a measuring stick when reducing liquid.
- If the recipe says to reduce the liquid to, say, 1/2 cup (125 mL): Pour 1/2 cup (125 mL) water into a saucepan. Stand the handle of the spoon in the water. Mark the water level with a notch. Empty the pan. Proceed to reduce your liquid until it boils down to the notch.
- If the recipe tells you to reduce the liquid by half: Stand the handle of the spoon in the liquid in a saucepan. Mark the level of the liquid. Remove the spoon and make a notch halfway down from your mark. Proceed to reduce the liquid down to the notch.

Broiling

✦ For easier cleanup, always line the bottom of the broiling pan with foil or parchment and spray the top with oil.

✦ Lay slices of stale bread over the bottom of a broiling pan to suck up dripping fat and prevent smoking.

Using a Bain-Marie

✦ A bain-marie is a hot-water bath. It cushions delicate desserts, particularly eggy ones, and other culinary creations in an even, steady temperature and adds moisture to the oven. A bain-marie is not complicated just because it has a French name. You need no official equipment.

How to Cook in a Bain-Marie

1. Set ramekins, custard cups or a baking dish inside a larger pan, which you can call the bain-marie. A lasagna pan works nicely as a bain-marie because the sides aren't too high, so air can still circulate.
2. To prevent jiggling and jostling, line the bottom of the bain-marie with a terry-cloth towel. Or set your dishes on a rack.
3. Add boiling or very hot tap water to the bain-marie. It should reach no higher than halfway up the sides of the dishes inside. If it's too high, it will bubble up into the dishes.

Safety Tips

- You can burn yourself with sloshing water. Instead of dropping dishes into the filled bain-marie, pour the water in around them. Use a watering can or kettle.
- When you are ready to remove the dishes, suck out some of the steamy water with a turkey baster.
- Another remedy is to set a barbecue tray in the bain-marie and put the dishes on that. Just lift the handles of the tray when you are ready to empty the bain-marie.
- You can use preserves jar lifters to extract ramekins from a bain-marie.

Making a Bouquet Garni

✧ A bouquet garni is a bundle of herbs and spices, usually used to flavor soups and stews. It is usually wrapped in cheesecloth or tied with twine, so it can be discarded intact. No need for fishing. But if you're making stock, why bother? It's going to be strained anyway.

4 Ways to Make a Bouquet Garni

1. Place herbs and spices on a square of cheesecloth. Tie it into a hobo bundle, opposite corner to corner.
2. Use the cheesecloth, but twist the corners together and tie them with one end of a long piece of kitchen string. Tie the other end to the pot handle so you can pull the bundle out easily.
3. Put herbs and spices in a tea ball. If the chain's long enough, it can be hooked over the side of the pot.
4. Tightly bundle stalks of fresh herbs or leek leaves, fold them over a few times and tie them with kitchen string.

Using Collars

✧ Use a collar to extend the height of a baking dish.

✧ Cut a sheet of parchment or foil that is 2 inches (5 cm) longer than the circumference of your dish, so it will overlap. Fold it in half lengthwise, twice. Secure it with the open ends down.

✧ A collar is easier to secure if you lay the dish on its side. Unfortunately, it has to be empty.

4 Uses for a Collar

1. Collars are used most notably for soufflés.
2. Put a collar around a cake to secure a glaze or filling while it sets.
3. Trick the eye with a mousse that looks like a soufflé. Tie a collar on the dish. Pile the mousse high. When it's set, remove the collar.
4. Add depth to a baking pan by inserting a collar.

Ways to Secure the Collar

• Tie kitchen string around it.
• Snap a thick elastic band over it.

Ways to Secure the Overlapping Ends

• Butter them and press them together.
• Use a large paper clip.

How to Make a Reverse Collar to Add Depth to a Cake Pan

1. Cut a sheet of parchment that is 2 inches (5 cm) longer than the circumference of the pan, so it will overlap. Fold it lengthwise, several times, until it's about 3 inches (8 cm) wide.
2. Butter one side of the strip. Line it around the inside of the pan with the buttered side facing in and the open ends at the bottom.
3. Pour in the batter.

Cooking en Papillote

✦ Food baked in an oiled parchment paper package is prepared "en papillote." At the table, the package is slit and dinner is served. (Papillote is also the term given to the frilly white paper hats that decorate the protruding bones of rib roasts.)

✦ You could use a foil package to cook en papillote and call it a hobo pack, but that would be less refined. The foil seals more tightly and you end up steaming the food. The looser parchment works somewhere in the realm between roasting and steaming.

✦ Cut the parchment twice the size of the food.

Using a Sling

✦ Whenever you have to lift food from a pan in one piece, use a sling. Line the pan with a sheet of parchment that's long enough to hang over the side.

Advantages of a Sling

● It helps you lift out awkward or heavy bars, sticky loaves, brownies, cakes, polenta, meatloaves and firm casseroles.
● It prevents sticking.
● The food is easier to cut, since you wind up with one, tidy block.

✦ To make it easier to remove a sling from underneath food, start with two overlapping pieces of parchment. Push one side of, say, a cake away from you as you pull out a section of parchment toward you. Repeat on the other side.

✦ If the food is not sticky, you can cut right on top of the sling instead of removing it.

Making Do

Use foil for a sling. Fold it to the proper width for the pan, and spray it with vegetable oil.

Cooking for One or Two

Keys to Cooking for Singles or Couples

Think small
● Not all recipes can be reduced. Look for small-batch recipes.

Shop small
● Buy from bulk bins. The irony is that you can get the smallest amounts there.

Cook small
● Cook lasagna in a loaf pan.
● Make meatloaf in muffin tins.
● Bake cakes in mini Bundt pans or make cupcakes.
● Use small disposable aluminum pie plates and pans if you don't have the right size.

Eat small
● Roast Cornish hens.
● Buy small cuts, such as lamb chops, or cut a rack of lamb into "Popsicles."
● Make fancy sandwiches.
● Put pizza toppings on pita rounds.
● Have breakfast for dinner. Enjoy added touches, such as smoked salmon, on poached eggs.

✦ If you're halving a recipe that calls for one egg, lightly beat the egg in a measuring cup, then pour out half. Use the rest the next day.

✦ Make full recipes and freeze the leftovers. Don't go overboard. One bored couple I know would make a big pot of something or other, then eat it for the whole week.

Dealing with Burnt Food

❖ Turn a burnt casserole, lasagna or other solid food upside down. Eat the part that falls out.

5 Ways to Disguise a Burnt or Smoky Flavor

1. Squeeze in some lemon juice.
2. Add sliced onion.
3. Stir in Worcestershire or barbecue sauce, or another bold sauce.
4. Add a bit of sugar.
5. Stir in peanut butter.

❖ If a dish burns, quickly plunk the base of the pan into a sinkful of cold water to stop the cooking. Pour the food into a fresh pan, being careful not to disturb the scorched food sticking to the bottom.

Heating Casseroles

Keep It Clean

After filling a casserole dish, wipe the exposed surfaces. This small step will reduce burnt spots and make the dish easier to clean.

Tips for Heating a Casserole

- Add 15 minutes to the cooking time if you've made the casserole ahead and refrigerated it.
- To reheat a casserole, put it in the oven straight from the fridge (for food-safety reasons). Start it in a cold oven, so the baking dish doesn't crack, then set the oven to 325°F (160°C).
- When reheating, pour about $\frac{1}{4}$ cup (50 mL) liquid over the casserole.

Dealing with Leftovers

❖ When I open the fridge, I see the makings of a meal. When my husband and kids open the fridge, they see a mysterious jumble — and complain there's nothing to eat. Keep a list of leftovers on the fridge and freezer doors, and what should be done with them.

❖ Two ways to reheat leftovers containing custardy or creamy ingredients that are prone to curdling:
- In a bain-marie in the oven
- In the top of a double boiler

❖ Food-safety experts recommend reheating leftovers to 165°F (74°C).

❖ Many dishes taste better the day after they're made. Let soup, stew, pasta sauce and chili con carne sit overnight in the fridge before serving.

Classic Dishes

Recipes

Pancakes, Crêpes and Latkes

OUTSIDE THE BOX

Instead of serving scrambled eggs on or with toast, use a whole-wheat waffle as a plate. If desired, melt cheese on it first or lay a slice of smoked salmon over it.

Pancakes

✧ Don't keep pancake batter overnight. The baking powder will get tired. If you want that much of a head start, combine the dry and wet ingredients separately, then stir them together the next morning.

✧ Use a nonstick pan. Brush the pan lightly with butter or oil just to add flavor. Don't overgrease the griddle. The pancakes will fry instead of browning evenly. If you are worried about sticking or want extra buttery flavor, you can generously grease the griddle, heat it, then swab it before pouring on the batter.

8 Keys to Fluffy Pancakes

1. Zealous blending makes pancakes tough and dense. Avoid overbeating. Combine the liquid and dry ingredients separately. Add wet to dry. Stir just until the flour is moistened, and be quick about it. Ignore small lumps. They are okay.

2. Let the batter stand after mixing. This gives the flour a chance to puff up from the moisture. Leave the batter for at least 5 to 10 minutes, or refrigerate it for up to 3 hours. (This doesn't apply to pancakes raised with yeast or whipped egg whites.)

3. Use half milk, half yogurt. Skim and non-fat are okay. This combination works better than buttermilk, which, in turn, works better than using only milk.

4. Add melted butter. It interferes with the gluten in flour that can cause toughness.

Add 1 tbsp (15 mL) melted butter for every 2 cups (500 mL) batter.

5. You can mix the yolks with the batter. Whip the egg whites to soft peaks, then fold them in.

6. Use batter at room temperature.

7. Skimp on the berries. The fewer the blueberries, the puffier the pancake. Don't mix blueberries into the batter. Sprinkle a few onto each pancake as soon as the batter is poured. This makes the pancakes prettier and easier to flip.

8. Use all-purpose flour. Pancakes made with whole grain flours are tasty, but are apt to fall flat. Add some all-purpose flour to lighten them. For buckwheat pancakes, add at least 1 part all-purpose flour for every 2 to 3 parts buckwheat flour.

- If you're making pancakes intended for the freezer, stir in about $\frac{1}{2}$ tsp (2 mL) white vinegar per 1 cup (250 mL) batter. They won't be as rubbery.

- Sandwich pancakes between parchment squares before freezing them.

Places to Defrost and Reheat Pancakes
- On a warm griddle.
- Under the broiler.
- In the microwave.
- In a toaster oven.

☼♥ Healthier Eater
- You can replace the liquid in the batter with club soda.
- Make fat-free pancakes. Use egg whites instead of whole eggs. Choose skim milk or fat-free yogurt.

- Preheat the griddle or pan to 375°F (190°C). Batter will stick to a cold pan.

- The griddle is ready when water drops sizzle, dance and evaporate. If water evaporates instantly, it is too hot. If the water boils quietly, it is not hot enough.

- Stick to about $\frac{1}{4}$ cup (50 mL) batter for each 3-inch (7.5 cm) diameter pancake. If they're too big, pancakes cook unevenly. Plus you'll see flying batter when you try to turn them.

- Cook one test pancake, then adjust the consistency of the batter, if necessary.

Signs That a Pancake Is Ready to Be Flipped
- The edges look dry.
- The surface is covered in little bubbles, but they haven't burst yet.
- The bottom is golden brown.

- Before scooping, you can dip the ladle in milk or cold water as needed to help the batter flow off it more smoothly.

Ways to Make Rounder Pancakes
- Pour the batter from a pitcher.
- Use a squeezable jar with a large nozzle and aim straight down at the griddle.
- Pour the batter from the tip of a large spoon, not from the side.
- Pour the batter into a zip-lock bag, then seal it. Cut off one corner and direct the flow onto the griddle.

- To flip a pancake more easily, bolster it at one side with a small, flat knife or an offset spatula while slipping a wide spatula underneath it.

- If you want old-fashioned crispy edges on your pancakes, use a cast-iron skillet instead of a nonstick griddle and fry them in plenty of oil.

- To keep pancakes warm while cooking in batches, lay them on a rack on a rimmed baking sheet in a 200°F (100°C) oven.

OUTSIDE THE BOX
Forget the stereotype. Try not to stack pancakes. If you must, here's a weird tip: Stack them with facecloths layered in between. Otherwise, the ones on the bottom get steamed.

- The second side of a pancake will never brown as nicely as the first. Serve pancakes with the browned side up and the speckled side down.

Finishing Touches

- Warm the maple syrup before pouring it over the pancakes.
- Melt butter or serve it in precut, room-temperature cubes.

Gussy It Up

- Even if it's nonstick, rub the griddle with butter or a slice of bacon to add flavor.
- For extras, think beyond chocolate chips and blueberries.
- Add muesli, granola, wheat germ or bran flakes to the wet ingredients. Let the mixture stand for half an hour before making the batter.
- Add dried fruit and toasted nuts. Stir in the dried fruit, then let the batter stand for 5 minutes. The fruit is absorbent, so adjust the amount of liquid, if necessary. Add the nuts at the last minute.
- For a festive, seasonal touch, stir ground ginger and crystallized ginger into the batter.
- Another festive touch: Add pumpkin purée to the batter, then sprinkle on dried cranberries when the pancakes are cooking.
- For sauce, purée and strain berries, then add maple syrup. (Blackberries are a wonderful choice.)
- Top pancakes with sliced fruit and custard sauce.
- Make smoother chocolate pancake batter by whisking cocoa powder and a bit of warm milk into a paste. Whisk this paste into the rest of the liquid.
- Use coconut milk instead of milk.
- Substitute apple cider for the milk. (The resulting pancakes will be flatter, with a rosy tint.) You could also add chopped dried apple.

♻ Waste Not

Turn leftover jam into pancake syrup. Combine 3 to 4 tbsp (45 to 60 mL) jam with 1 tbsp (15 mL) each water and unsalted butter. Warm it in the microwave. If you want a smooth syrup, heat the jam with the water first and strain it. Then stir in the butter.

4 Ways to Have Fun with Pancakes

1. Use a squeeze bottle to squirt batter onto the griddle in patterns. Kids love eating their own initials. You can also squeeze out holiday shapes, such as hearts, Christmas bells or bunny heads (add chocolate chips for eyes). Squeeze an outline, then fill it in with batter.
2. Stamp pancakes with designs. Stir about $\frac{1}{3}$ cup (75 mL) of the batter with enough cocoa powder to turn it dark brown. Pour or squeeze the brown batter onto the griddle in the shape of a small initial or a design. (Remember that it will be a mirror image when it's served.) Let it set for a few seconds, then ladle the plain batter over top. Cook as usual, then flip.
3. Make pancake lasagna or torte. Stuff whipped cream, syrup and fruit between stacked pancakes.
4. Prepare a colorful breakfast. Add a few drops of food dye to the pancake batter. Use several colors for a rainbow stack.

French Toast

- For every 3 slices of standard sandwich bread, whisk together 2 large eggs, $\frac{1}{4}$ cup (50 mL) milk and $\frac{1}{4}$ tsp (1 mL) salt. You can soak French toast in a baking dish or on a rimmed baking sheet. Pour the egg mixture into the dish. Lay the bread in the mixture, push it down and soak briefly. Flip and soak again, if necessary.

Crêpes

◆ Unlike pancake batter, crêpe batter should be smooth and thin, about the consistency of heavy cream. Small lumps are no good because the crêpes must be smooth and thin, too.

◆ Don't bother pushing crêpe batter through a sieve to get rid of lumps, as some cooks do. Just mix it in a blender. Start with the liquid ingredients, then add the flour. Blend for 30 seconds. Scrape down the sides. Blend in the melted butter for 30 seconds.

◆ Refrigerate the batter before using it, for 1 to 2 hours (optimal) or up to 2 days. Crêpes are light and sturdy, rather than rubbery, when the flour is given a chance to suck up the moisture.

◆ Thin crêpe batter with club soda or beer. Beer makes the most tender crêpes, but it's best for savory creations. Club soda is better than water.

✖ No-No

Don't bother adding beer or club soda when you first make the batter. It goes flat as the batter sits. Add it when you are ready to cook.

◆ Freeze crêpe batter in 1- to 2-cup (250 to 500 mL) portions. Thaw it in the fridge.

◆ For a 10-inch (25 cm) crêpe, use about ¼ cup (50 mL) batter.

Temperature Cues

- Cook crêpes over medium-low or medium heat.
- Always preheat the pan. If it's not hot enough, the batter flows around aimlessly. The batter should set as soon as it hits the pan.

Making Do

You can make crêpes in a medium, nonstick skillet. However, a crêpe pan (which has a shallow rim) or a crêpe maker (a drum-shaped appliance) makes the job easier.

◆ Before making each crêpe, brush the pan with melted butter or oil. Keep it in a small bowl beside the stove. Wipe off any excess butter between crêpes; it scorches.

🫶 Healthier Eater

If you don't want to use butter or oil, the crêpe will turn out fine in a dry, nonstick pan. You can also omit butter from the batter and end up with reasonably good crêpes.

Crêpe-Cooking Techniques

- Everything happens suddenly when you pour the batter into the pan. It helps to lift the pan from the heat after pouring. Work quickly to swirl the batter to the edges before it sets, tilting and rotating the pan. Then put it back on the burner.
- If there's a gap in the crêpe, quickly add some batter. Tilt the pan, or use a long offset spatula to smear batter over any holes.
- If you accidentally pour in too much batter, tilt the pan and pour it back into the bowl.

◆ Both the batter and the crêpes are very forgiving. Dry edges are the biggest problem. Two ways to prevent them:
- Don't skimp on the batter and try to make the crêpes paper-thin. Eking out the batter toward the edges makes them lacy.
- Don't overcook a crêpe. Cook it for about 1 minute or until the top looks dry, rather than shiny, and the bottom is golden but not crispy. Flip it and cook for 30 seconds or until it is just set.

✧ The first crêpe is never great. Even pros make a tester, then assess. You may have to adjust the flour or water, or the temperature.

Ways to Make Mini Crêpes

- Pour 1 tbsp (15 mL) batter into the skillet. Swirl, then spread it from the center outward with the back of a teaspoon into a circle about 4 inches (10 cm) in diameter.
- For thicker crêpes for hors d'oeuvres, whisk in an extra 1 tbsp (15 mL) flour per 1 cup (250 mL) batter. Make 2-inch (5 cm) crêpes by pouring in 1 tsp (5 mL) batter for each one and letting it spread naturally.

3 Ways to Flip a Crêpe

1. The best flipping tool is a long, thin offset spatula.
2. If you have no nerves left in your fingertips (like the chefs who keep sticking their fingers in hot food, then complain of numbness), use two hands to grab the nearest edge of the crêpe, then pull it up and over, using a circular motion.
3. Toss it in the air, if you dare. Loosen the crêpe by shaking the pan and lift an edge slightly, if necessary. Push the pan away from you as you lift it and the crêpe up into the air, then back toward you in a circular route. You have to commit to this or it won't work. The crêpe must be tossed high enough to flip over.

✧ Loosen a crêpe by rapping the pan against the stovetop.

✧ Sweet crêpes and cocoa crêpes are stickier, more apt to tear or scorch, and prone to crispy edges. Use lower heat. To loosen them, shake the pan or gently pry up the edges with a spatula.

Ways to Keep Crêpes Warm

- Stack them on a heatproof plate over a bowl of barely simmering water.
- Stack them on a baking sheet lined with parchment. Crêpes stick to metal, but not really to each other. Loosely cover them with foil or a sheet of parchment. Keep them warm in a 200°F (100°C) oven.

Ways to Make Crêpes in Advance

- Cool them before wrapping, so beads of moisture don't attack them. You can cool crêpes on a rack.
- If you are making them just a bit early, say an hour, you can wrap finished crêpes in plastic and leave them on the counter.
- If you are holding them for a long time, stack them sandwiched between parchment squares. Cover the pile with plastic wrap. Put it in a round airtight tub. Store the tub in the fridge or freezer.

✧ The second side of a crêpe is spotty and less attractive. Use that for the filling. As you stack crêpes, you can slip them out of the pan onto a dish, then invert them.

✧ Fridge and freezer crêpes are both okay when reheated, but frozen ones are tougher at the edges.

Cocoa Crêpes Suzette

Suzettes are boozy and showy. Using cocoa crêpes gives them a modern twist. **Makes 8 servings**

Tips

Use a good-looking skillet (it will be your serving dish). Don't use a nonstick one.

Serve crêpes suzettes with ice cream.

Variation

For a classic version, simply use regular crêpes.

½ cup	unsalted butter	125 mL
¼ cup	granulated sugar	50 mL
	Finely grated zest of 2 oranges	
	Juice of 2 oranges (about ½ cup/125 mL)	
8	warm Cocoa Crêpes (see variation, page 459)	8
¼ cup	brandy	50 mL
¼ cup	orange-flavored liqueur	50 mL
2 tbsp	turbinado sugar	25 mL

1. In a 12-inch (30 cm) skillet, melt butter over medium heat. Stir in granulated sugar, orange zest and orange juice. Let it bubble until syrupy and thickened, about 3 minutes. Remove from heat.

2. Fold each crêpe into quarters. Place crêpes in a pleasing, overlapping pattern in the skillet. Spoon the orange mixture evenly over top.

3. In a measuring cup, combine brandy and liqueur. Warm in the microwave on High for 30 seconds. Drizzle evenly over crêpes. Sprinkle turbinado sugar over top.

4. Tilting the pan away from you, use a barbecue lighter or long match to ignite the booze. Return pan to medium heat and shake until the flames subside.

Multiple Personality Crêpes

This basic batter is just right, making crêpes that are thin and tender, yet sturdy. **Makes about 2 cups (500 mL) batter or 8 crêpes (10 inches/25 cm in diameter)**

- **10-inch (25 cm) nonstick crêpe pan**

Tip

This batter works nicely with 2 tbsp (25 mL) butter. However, you can add up to 3 tbsp (45 mL) butter for richness. Or go the opposite route and use no butter at all.

Variations

Crêpes Sucrées: Add 3 tbsp (45 mL) granulated sugar to the batter. Make these for dessert crêpes.

Cocoa Crêpes: Add 2 tbsp (25 mL) sifted unsweetened cocoa powder and 3 tbsp (45 mL) granulated sugar to the batter.

Tomato Crêpes: Add 2 tbsp (25 mL) tomato paste to the batter.

Pesto Crêpes: Add 1 tbsp (15 mL) pesto to the batter and reduce the butter to 1 tbsp (15 mL).

Buckwheat Crêpes: Use ½ cup (125 mL) buckwheat flour and ½ cup (125 mL) all-purpose flour. Add an extra 2 tbsp (25 mL) club soda or beer.

1 cup	2% milk	250 mL
2	large eggs	2
¼ tsp	salt	1 mL
1 cup	all-purpose flour	250 mL
2 tbsp	unsalted butter, melted	25 mL
¼ cup	club soda or beer	50 mL
	Melted butter	

1. Put milk, eggs and salt in a blender. Top with flour. Blend on high speed for 30 seconds. Scrape the sides. Add 2 tbsp (25 mL) butter. Blend for 30 seconds or until smooth.

2. Scrape the batter into a large airtight container. Refrigerate for at least 1 hour or for up to 2 days. When ready to cook, whisk in club soda.

3. Heat the crêpe pan over medium heat. Brush it lightly with melted butter. Lift the pan up from the burner. Ladle in about ¼ cup (50 mL) batter. Tilt and swirl to coax the batter to coat the bottom of pan thinly but adequately. Pour any excess back into the container. Cook the crêpe for about 1 minute or until the bottom is golden and the top looks dry. Flip it with a large offset spatula. Cook it for 30 seconds. Slide it onto a platter. Repeat with the remaining batter.

✗ No-No

You may come across a suggestion to warm refrigerated or frozen crêpes by sticking them in a plastic bag and microwaving. Ignore that. Chemicals can leach into the food if the plastic is not microwave-safe.

Latkes

❖ Use russet potatoes for latkes; they have the least moisture. Yukon golds are second choice. Don't use waxy potatoes.

Crispier VS. Denser?

Shredding the potatoes makes latkes light and lacy. Finer grating results in dense, firmer, smoother latkes. To each his own, but I say the thin shreds of potato obtained using the large holes of a box grater are the perfect texture.

6 Ways to Minimize Discoloration and Browning

1. Keep peeled potatoes in a bowl of cold water before shredding them.
2. Some cooks blanch the potatoes before shredding them. This removes surface starch, so the latke mixture needs more flour.
3. Shred the potatoes into a bowl of cold water.
4. After shredding, place the potatoes in a sieve and rinse them with cold water.
5. Don't wait for the potatoes to drain. Squeeze out the water.
6. For every 4 large potatoes, add 2 tbsp (25 mL) lemon juice or a vitamin C tablet dissolved in 2 tbsp (25 mL) water to a bowl. Put in the shredded potatoes and toss. Then add the remaining ingredients.

❖ Work quickly. Once cut, the potatoes turn brown fast.

❖ Always drain the potatoes. As you shred them, you can toss them into a sieve in the sink, then transfer them to a kitchen towel or large piece of cheesecloth. Or shred them directly onto the towel or cheesecloth. Twist the cloth to wring out as much liquid as possible.

Ingredient Tips

- Latke purists use only potatoes, egg and salt.
- Matzo meal may be added as a binder. For the crispiest latkes, add as little matzo meal as you can get away with, say 1 to 2 tbsp (15 to 25 mL) per 1 lb (500 g) potatoes.
- Add 1 egg per 1 lb (500 g) potatoes.

Gussy It Up

- Shred some onion against the box grater along with the potatoes.
- Add finely shredded celeriac.
- Add chopped herbs, from dill to chives to parsley.
- Add coarsely ground black pepper.
- Add a dry cheese that stands up to the heat, such as grated Parmesan or crumbled halloumi.
- Make hors d'oeuvres. Put smoked salmon or caviar on top of mini latkes.

OUTSIDE THE BOX

Make latkes with sweet potatoes, parsnips, carrots or zucchini. Peppery cabbage makes very good latkes. Don't forget to salt and drain the vegetables. If you don't want to get that drastic, mix some of these vegetables with the potatoes.

- It's tricky to cook latkes thoroughly before they become too brown. Use an electric skillet for even heat.

- Stir the latke mixture before frying each batch. The liquid separates out. Toward the end, scoop with a slotted spoon, leaving excess liquid behind.

- After scooping, flatten latkes in the skillet by tapping the tops with the edge of a spatula, rather than pressing down.

- Avoid splattering and breakage by flipping latkes with two short-handled spatulas. Hold one at a 45-degree angle in the pan while you push the latke against it with the other spatula. Turn it and lower it back into the oil.

- Latkes can be held in a 250°F (120°C) oven on a rack over a baking sheet lined with paper towels. Dab the grease off the top.

Latke Doctor

The latkes fall apart.

- Don't shred the potatoes too coarsely.
- Add another egg.
- Add (more) matzo meal.

The latkes aren't crisp and firm.

- Shred the potatoes more finely.
- Dry the shredded potatoes better.
- If you salt the spuds while they are draining, the latkes will have super-crispy edges.
- Don't stack or cover latkes. They'll get soggy.

No-No

If you need to warm latkes, don't attempt to refry them.

How to Warm Latkes

1. Place latkes on a rack in a 350°F (180°C) oven. Cover them with foil.
2. Heat until they are barely warm.
3. Place them under the broiler to crisp.

Salads and Dressings

✦ Prep a salad French-style — without wilting your lettuce or diluting your dressing. Start by putting chopped tomatoes, cucumbers, bell peppers or other vegetables in a big salad bowl. Add the dressing. Leave it to marinate and macerate at room temperature for a couple of hours. You can lightly rest the greens on top. Toss the salad when you're ready to eat.

ⓒ is for Chapon

To give salad a hint of garlic, make a chapon. Rub a dry crust of bread with the cut side of a split garlic clove. Place the bread in the bowl with your salad. Add dressing and toss. Discard the chapon.

✦ Rubbing the inside of your salad bowl with a cut piece of garlic is a subtle, but appreciated, touch. If the bowl is wooden, so much the better.

How to Mold and Stack a Mixed Salad

1. Use greens that aren't too chunky. Toss them lightly with dressing.
2. Pat them gently into a plastic tub, ramekin or ring mold. Don't stack them too tall.
3. Invert them onto a plate or remove the ring.

✦ Caesar salad can be finger food. That's how it started out. Take it back to its roots by serving the romaine leaves whole, coated with dressing.

OUTSIDE THE BOX

Forget trying to stab those leaves with a fork. Salad is way easier to eat with chopsticks.

✦ Roughly handled greens crack and get more wilted when they meet the dressing. When using two or three types of greens, toss the tougher ones first, then add the delicate ones.

✦ You'll need 2 to 3 tbsp (25 to 45 mL) dressing per 1-cup (250 mL) serving of greens. If the dressing is a thin vinaigrette, you can coat the greens with less. If the dressing is thick, you may need more.

✦ The dressing never seems salty enough once it's on the lettuce. Sprinkle the salad with salt before tossing.

✦ When you're making a warm salad, the greens should be slightly wilted but still crisp. For best results, toss only half the greens (such as spinach) with warm dressing. Then add the other half.

Ⓥ is for Vinaigrette

A vinaigrette is a basic oil-and-vinegar dressing. Simple vinaigrette begins with 3 parts oil, 1 part vinegar, and salt and pepper. Then you play with the proportions and ingredients.

✖ No-No

Never use harsh white vinegar. Use wine or other milder vinegars. Still, some vinegars are stronger than others. For example, you'll want to use less cider vinegar, more rice vinegar.

4 Ideas for Dressing Salad Evenly

1. The greens must be completely dry or the dressing will not coat them properly. If the lettuce in the salad bowl is still slightly wet, toss it with a cotton kitchen towel or two paper towels in your hands.
2. Transfer dressed salad gently from one bowl to another. Or put two bowls together and invert them a few times.
3. Pour dressing all around down the sides of the bowl, not over the greens. Toss from the sides in.
4. If you add the oil before the vinegar, the vinegar slides off the greens. If you add the vinegar first, the greens tend to wilt. Compromise when dressing a salad free-form. Condition the greens with a bit of the oil, toss with the vinegar and seasonings, then the rest of the oil.

✧ Always add at least a pinch of sugar to vinaigrette, to blunt the edge.

Ways to Thicken and Emulsify

• A spoonful of mustard is the traditional way to hold oil and vinegar together.
• A pressed clove of garlic does the job.
• An egg yolk or heavy cream does, too, although technically, your dressing will then no longer be a vinaigrette. If using cream, let the dressing stand for 10 minutes. The acidity thickens it.

✧ To check a dressing accurately, don't use the tip of your tongue on a spoon. Dip a piece of lettuce into it.

Lightning Won't Strike If ...

You shake vinaigrette in a tub or bottle. Traditionally, the vinegar, mustard and spices are whisked in a bowl, then the oil is whisked in as you slowly drizzle it into the bowl. This helps the mixture emulsify. But vinaigrette separates quickly anyway, and you can always shake it before using.

Ways to Emulsify Efficiently

• Combine the oil, vinegar and mustard, then put the mixture in the freezer for 5 minutes before blending.
• Store your vinegar in the fridge.
• Add the vinaigrette ingredients to a jar with an ice cube. Shake it well, then remove the ice.

3 Ways to Boost Flavor

1. Blend vinegar with the salt first, so it dissolves properly.
2. Soak chopped garlic and fresh herbs in the vinegar for 15 minutes before adding the oil.
3. For a strong garlic flavor, use a fork to mash a clove of garlic against the bottom of your salad bowl, along with salt and other seasonings. Whisk in the vinegar, then the oil. This is a classic way to make dressing, perfected by Caesar salad fanciers.

♲ Waste Not

• Use a bit of puréed fresh tomato as a base for vinaigrette. Add a nut oil, garlic and herbs. It may need a splash of vinegar and dash of sugar.
• Use the oil from marinated artichoke hearts and marinated mushrooms to make dressing.

You don't have to use vinegar. You can make a citronette or even a vinette, so to speak.

- Let's call a vinaigrette made with citrus juice a "citronette." Try lemon, lime or even grapefruit juice. You may need less oil. Start with 2 parts oil to 1 part lemon juice, for example.
- You can use wine instead of vinegar. Start this vinette with a 1:1 ratio of wine and oil. I once reduced a whole bottle of Gewürtztraminer to ½ cup (125 mL), cooled it and whisked in honey, Dijon mustard, salt, chile flakes and oil. Excellent! You don't have to go that crazy. Simmer your wine until it's reduced by at least half, though.

✦ Vinaigrette is not just for salads. Drizzle it on meat, fish or vegetables. Balsamico complements liver. Sun-dried tomato vinaigrette is great on grilled chicken. To warm it up, pour the vinegar into the pan juices, then whisk in oil.

Gussy It Up

- Add chopped sun-dried tomatoes or olives.
- Make Asian vinaigrette with rice vinegar and sesame and peanut oils.
- Make herb vinaigrette. Using a mortar and pestle, pound fresh herbs and salt into a paste. Transfer to a bowl, if necessary. Whisk in vinegar, then gradually whisk in oil.

♡ Healthier Eater

- Reduce the ratio of oil to vinegar to 2:1, or lower. Adjust with broth, wine or juice so the dressing won't be so sharp. Just before serving, thicken by shaking the dressing with an ice cube, then remove the ice. Toss the salad just before serving; with less oil in the dressing, the greens will go limp faster.
- Lighten up by mixing salsa and water with a bit of oil. Purée or leave it chunky.
- Reduce calories and fat by combining 2 parts creamy dressing with 1 to 2 parts fat-free yogurt, or 2 parts vinaigrette with 1 part sweet juice, cider or stock. This works fine with bottled dressings.
- Serve the dressing separately. Save calories by dipping your fork into the dressing, then into the greens.

Lime Pistachio Citronette

This is lovely on greens with crabmeat and/or tropical fruit. **Makes about ¾ cup (175 mL)**

Tips

Roasted pistachio oil is sold in gourmet food shops. It is expensive.

You can also shake the ingredients in a tub instead of whisking them.

3 tbsp	freshly squeezed lime juice	45 mL
2 tbsp	heavy or whipping (35%) cream	25 mL
1	clove garlic, pressed	1
1 tsp	granulated sugar	5 mL
¼ tsp	sea salt	1 mL
½ cup	roasted pistachio oil	125 mL

1. In a bowl, whisk lime juice, cream, garlic, sugar and salt. Let stand for 10 minutes to thicken a bit.
2. Whisk or shake in pistachio oil.

Sandwiches

❖ When salting a sandwich, sprinkle the salt on the butter or mayonnaise rather than on the tomato or other vegetables. The salt sticks better and is more even.

❖ Stave off sogginess in cucumber or tomato sandwiches. Drain the sliced vegetables for 1 hour in advance. You can add salt to draw out the moisture.

❖ For thick Italian sandwiches and subs, pull out some of the bread in the center to make room for fillings.

♻ Waste Not

Don't bother spreading the filling to the edges of a sandwich that's destined to be crustless.

☺ KID STUFF

Prepare open-faced sandwiches with faces. Stuffed olives make good eyes. Use sprouts for the hair.

Wraps

❖ When making a wrap, spread the tortilla or flatbread with a thin layer of cream cheese first, to glue on the other fillings.

Ways to Avert Leaks

• Put the filling on a soft lettuce leaf.
• Roll the wrap in paper to catch any drips.

OUTSIDE THE BOX

Pocket pitas tear and leak. Avert the mess by turning a pocket pita into a wrap.

How to Turn a Pocket Pita into a Wrap

1. Use only the freshest pita or heat it in the microwave — otherwise, it may tear.
2. Lay the pita with the bottom side facing up. Create a semicircular flap: Using a blunt knife, coax and tear the edges of the pita to separate the pocket halfway down each side.
3. Put the filling into the remaining pocket.
4. Tuck the flap over the filling, then push to secure it under the filling.
5. Roll the pita to close it. Wrap it in parchment or a napkin.

How to Roll a Tidy Wrap in Paper

1. Place the filling vertically, no more than a couple of inches (5 cm) wide. Leave a 1-inch (2.5 cm) gap at the top and a couple of inches (5 cm) at the bottom.
2. Fold up the bottom third over the filling.
3. Fold the left side over the filling.
4. Turn up the tortilla at the bottom right at a 45-degree angle.
5. Fold the right side of the wrap over the filling.
6. Turn the wrap seam side down on a napkin or a square of waxed paper. The paper should reach halfway up the tortilla, with the rest lying below.
7. Roll the paper on the left side over the wrap. Flip up the bottom of the paper. Finish rolling the paper around the wrap.

Finger Sandwiches

Bread Tips for Canapés, Tea Sandwiches and Pinwheels

- Use resilient, fine-textured bread.
- Thinly slice the bread. Freezing it just until it has firmed up will help. Day-old bread is also easier to slice.
- Make shorter work of pinwheels and cutouts by slicing the crusts off the whole loaf to make a rectangular box. Then slice the box lengthwise rather than crosswise.
- To make pinwheel sandwiches easier to roll, flatten the bread slightly with a rolling pin. Spread on the filling, then roll tightly, starting along the short edge. To firm up the roll before slicing it into tidy pinwheels, wrap it tightly in plastic and refrigerate it for 30 minutes.
- Tea sandwiches look more interesting if you use white bread on one side and whole wheat bread on the other.
- Slice with a long serrated knife.

✧ Go the extra mile. Decorate the cut edges of round or triangular tea sandwiches.

How to Decorate Cut Edges

1. Spread a thin layer of mayonnaise on a sheet of waxed paper.
2. Sprinkle finely chopped parsley or nuts on another sheet of waxed paper.
3. Lightly coat the edges of the sandwiches in mayo by running them across the paper.
4. Roll or dip them in the parsley or nuts.

✧ To speed up the job of buttering bread for party sandwiches, smear with a pastry brush. Use butter that is very soft but not melted.

✧ Use cookie cutters to cut sandwich shapes. Do this after filling the sandwiches, rather than cutting shapes from plain bread. You can make star-shaped sandwiches for the birthday girl or hearts for your valentine. Punch out fish shapes for tuna and salmon salad sandwiches.

OUTSIDE THE BOX

Make a sandwich loaf that looks like a layer cake.

1. Cut layers horizontally through a crustless loaf.
2. Spread filling between the layers.
3. Wrap the loaf in foil. Refrigerate until it is fairly firm.
4. Spread cream cheese "icing" over the surface. You can use food coloring to dye the "icing," and pipe rosettes and/or a message on top.

Grilled Cheese Sandwiches

✧ How to keep the bread from burning before the cheese gets oozy:
- Keep the heat medium to low.
- Use thickly sliced bread.

X No-No

Avoid coarse, rustic bread or bread with too many air pockets.

✧ For a crispier exterior and slightly herbal flavor, brush the bread with olive oil instead of soft butter.

7 Cheesy Tips

1. Use stronger cheeses that melt well, such as Cheddar, fontina, Gruyère or Swiss. Avoid bland cheeses.
2. Don't pile on the cheese. It won't melt properly.
3. Slice the cheese thinly to promote melting, but don't shred it. Shredded cheese is harder to distribute evenly and gets messy at the edges of a sandwich.
4. An exception: If you want to use process cheese, buy the thick slices.
5. Bookend fillings, such as tapenade or chopped artichokes, between two layers of cheese, not against the bread. The sandwich sticks together better when the cheese is glued to the bread.
6. As an added touch, stir some dry grated Parmesan into the softened butter you'll smear on the outsides of the bread. You can also embellish with flavored butter.
7. Don't cook the sandwich for too long. If the cheese melts too much, it exudes grease.

Healthier Eater

- For lighter grilled cheese, spray the bread with oil instead of smearing butter on the outsides. Use low heat only.
- You don't need to oil or butter the insides of the bread. That's too greasy with the cheese.

✧ You can assemble grilled cheese sandwiches in advance. Place them on a baking sheet or platter. Separate the layers with waxed paper so the butter doesn't stick. Cover the lot with plastic wrap and refrigerate.

Ways to Cook Grilled Cheese

- For crispy, golden grilled cheese sandwiches, use a hot, dry skillet. A cast-iron pan works best.
- An electric skillet offers reliable, even heat.
- Panini presses are popular. Purists, however, don't want grill marks on their grilled cheese. Luckily, some presses come with interchangeable flat plates.
- An old-fashioned sandwich machine will melt the cheese, seal the edges and divide the sandwich into two triangles. But it only works with a specific size of sliced, squarish bread.

✧ Apply some weight (but nothing too heavy, please) to grilled cheese. Pushing the bread firmly against the heated surface promotes even browning and gets rid of any air pockets in the filling.

Ways to Press the Sandwich

- Push down gently with a spatula.
- Cover it with another pan.
- Top it with a brick wrapped in foil.
- Put a plate on top, then place a can on that.

✧ Grilled cheese sandwiches will stay warm for up to an hour if you immediately wrap each one in foil. Keep them huddled together.

✧ The sandwiches get soggy as they sit. To re-crisp, heat them directly on an oven rack under the broiler.

Panini

✧ A panino is an Italian sandwich with meat and cheese stuffed into crusty bread or a roll. Make more than one and you have panini. But nowadays, we use "panini" to refer to sandwiches that are grilled in a double-sided panini press. As for the filling, anything goes.

✧ Stick to firmer, less oozy cheeses when using a panini press. If you cook panini for too long at too high a temperature, or use too much pressure, the cheese seeps out.

✧ Let panini sit a minute before cutting. They'll be less oozy.

Making Do

You can prepare a panini-style sandwich without a press.

1. Heat a couple of spoonfuls of oil in a skillet over medium-low heat.
2. Put your sandwich in upside down. Weight it down with a small skillet.
3. Cook until the sandwich is slightly flattened and the side touching the skillet is golden brown.
4. Flip it and replace the weight. Cook until the sandwich is golden brown on the bottom and the cheese has started to melt.

Sauces

❖ The world of sauces is a wide one. If you're into classifying, you can sort them by use, by the base, by how they are made or by whether they are hot or cold. Any flavored liquid, paste, purée or wet mixture that accompanies a dish is a sauce.

❖ How to prevent lumps, thinning or separation in warm sauces:
- Don't use high heat.
- Remove the sauce from the heat before adding new ingredients.
- Don't cover the sauce. Steam falls in from the lid and dilutes it. Plus, it may get too hot and curdle.
- Don't replace heavy or whipping (35%) cream directly with milk, half-and-half (10%) cream or yogurt. Heavy cream can be boiled. Lower-fat dairy products will curdle without the help of flour or another starch as a binder.
- Don't add flour, cornstarch or other thickeners directly. Combine the thickener with cold water to make a slurry, then gradually whisk that in.
- Add wine, lemon juice or other acidic ingredients before adding eggs and/or cream.
- When serving sauce with grilled or seared meat, make it very thick, as the meat's juices will dilute it.
- If a sauce can be reheated, do it over gentle heat or in the top of a double boiler over simmering water. Add a bit of liquid.

❖ Keep sauce warm in an insulated bottle or coffee jug. This is a good way to hold sensitive sauces that don't reheat well, such as hollandaise.

❖ Sauces (sweet and savory) and custards thickened with egg yolks are sensitive. They will curdle if provoked. Some precautions:
- Never let them boil. Use a double boiler to moderate the temperature.
- Temper the eggs. Whisk them in a bowl while slowly pouring in part of the hot liquid from the recipe. Then whisk the egg mixture into the pan.
- Whisk cream into the yolks before you temper them.
- Add cornstarch. It not only thickens, it prevents curdling.

Sauce Doctor

The sauce is threatening to separate.
- Stir in warm water, cream or a thickener, such as cornstarch paste.

The sauce is curdling.
- Immediately remove it from the heat and plunge the pan into cold water.
- Add a few ice cubes.
- Whisk vigorously.

The sauce is lumpy.
- Purée it in the blender.
- Push it through a sieve.
- Shake it in a bottle.
- Beat it with a mixer.

Matching the Alcohol to the Sauce
- Use dry white wine in sauces for fish or white meat.
- Use dry red wine in sauces for red meat.
- Use rum, brandy, sherry, Marsala or port in sauces for game and lamb.
- Use sherry, Marsala, sweet wines, rum, brandy, port or fruit liqueur in dessert sauces.

Old-Fashioned Green Beans in Mustard Sauce

Here's a vintage dish. These green beans are tangy, rich and strangely delicious — cold or hot. The sauce is bound with both egg and flour. **Makes 8 servings**

Tip

Use the thin, dark green specimens sometimes labeled "French beans."

1 lb	thin green beans, trimmed	500 g
¾ cup	skim milk	175 mL
1 tbsp	all-purpose flour	15 mL
1 tbsp	cider vinegar	15 mL
1 tsp	kosher salt	5 mL
1 tsp	dry mustard	5 mL
	Freshly ground black pepper	
1	large egg	1
1 tbsp	unsalted butter	15 mL
4	large green onions, thinly sliced	4
	Chopped fresh parsley	

1. In the top of a double boiler over simmering water, steam beans, stirring occasionally, for 10 to 12 minutes or until tender. Drain well.

2. Meanwhile, in a medium saucepan over medium heat, scald milk until steamy. Do not boil it. Remove from heat.

3. In a medium bowl, stir flour, vinegar, salt, mustard and pepper to taste into a paste. Whisk in egg until the mixture is smooth.

4. Whisk the vinegar mixture into the milk. Return to medium heat and whisk until smooth and thickened, about 2 minutes. Remove from heat. Whisk in butter until it melts.

5. Transfer beans to a large serving bowl. Stir in green onions. Pour sauce over top. Garnish with parsley.

 Waste Not

Swish wine around in an emptied bottle of pasta sauce (or other sauce) to extract the remnants. Stir them into the sauce in the pan. Heat until the sauce is slightly reduced.

A Bit of Science

A skin forms on sauces, puddings and custards when protein separates out of dairy products.

6 Remedies for the Skin

1. Use cake/pastry flour. It has less protein.
2. Press plastic wrap directly on the surface.
3. Cover the surface with dampened waxed paper.
4. While the sauce, pudding or custard is hot, rub the top with a stick of butter.
5. Pour a thin layer of sherry or oil over the surface before refrigerating.
6. Get rid of the skin by gently reheating a sauce, then straining it.

Béchamel Sauce

❖ Béchamel is white sauce made with flour and milk. It is the base for many creamy sauces. A velouté is similar, but made with stock.

❖ The magic numbers for béchamel are one, two, three. For every 1 cup (250 mL) milk, use 1 tbsp (15 mL) flour for a thin sauce, 2 tbsp (25 mL) flour for a medium sauce, 3 tbsp (45 mL) flour for a thick sauce. The flour is stirred with 2 tbsp (25 mL) butter over low heat to form a roux, then the milk is whisked in.

Gussy It Up

You can flavor béchamel by steeping a bay leaf and a small onion studded with three whole cloves in milk for 30 minutes. Warm the milk first. Cover the pan, but don't let it sit on the burner.

❖ Instead of cooking béchamel over low heat on the stove after the milk is whisked in, you can finish simmering it in a 350°F (180°C) oven for about 20 minutes.

Cheese Sauce

❖ For the easiest cheese sauce, stir shredded or grated cheese into béchamel (white sauce made with butter, flour and milk).

Categories of Cheeses

- Moist, young cheeses make the sauce creamy and velvety.
- Hard cheeses, such as Parmesan, and mature cheeses, such as aged Cheddar, tend to make the sauce gritty, but add sharpness.

❖ Experiment by blending cheeses.

♻ Waste Not

Use up the odds and ends of leftover cheeses in your fridge by turning them into sauce.

❖ Hard cheeses should be finely grated and added before the softer cheeses. Softer cheeses can be shredded or cubed.

❖ Always reduce the heat before stirring in cheese and keep it low. Otherwise, the cheese can become gritty or separate into oily strings.

Cheese Sauce Doctor

The sauce doesn't want to smooth out.
- Stir in a spoonful of lemon juice.
- Add a flour or cornstarch slurry.
- Add liquid.

Tomato Sauce

❖ Turn tomato sauce into a rose sauce by drizzling in some cream.

Tomato Sauce Doctor

The sauce is too thin.

- Reduce it by simmering it, uncovered, for a long time over low heat.
- If you're in a hurry, add a couple of spoonfuls of dry bread crumbs.

The sauce is too acidic.

- Strain out tomato skins and seeds beforehand.
- Roast the tomatoes.
- Add a spoonful of granulated sugar to the sauce.
- Add grated or chopped carrots.
- Add a pinch of baking soda.

These remedies work for other tomato dishes, too.

Gussy It Up

You can improve canned tomato sauce by adding your own touches:

- Cubed eggplant
- Zucchini slices
- Slivered fresh herbs
- Spinach leaves
- Baby clams
- Wild mushrooms
- Chunks of hot sausage
- Whole roasted garlic cloves
- A spoonful of pesto
- Diced carrot, green bell pepper or fennel

Mayonnaise, Hollandaise and Béarnaise

Mayonnaise VS. Hollandaise VS. Béarnaise?

All three members of the "aise" family are emulsions made with egg yolks, an acid and a slowly incorporated fat. Mayonnaise is cold and made with oil. (When garlic is added, it becomes aioli.) Hollandaise and béarnaise are warm sauces made with butter. Hollandaise starts with lemon juice. Béarnaise starts with reduced vinegar. Tarragon, shallots and white wine round it out.

✧ When making "aises," have all the ingredients and the bowl at room temperature. You can warm the bowl by rinsing it with hot water.

✧ If working by hand, whisk vinegar or lemon juice with the egg yolks before whisking in oil or butter. The yolks coat the fat droplets and suspend them in the liquid. They can do their job best when there in full force from the start.

✧ Add the fat drop by drop. Whisk with one hand while you add the fat with the other. Your aim is to separate the oil into tiny droplets.

Finicky Ways to Add Fat Drop by Drop

- Hold a small, dripping ladle in one hand over the bowl to add the fat gradually.
- Use a baster to drip in the fat.

The Better Way

- Go electric. A blender or food processor works great. Add the fat with the motor running. Even Julia Child stooped to making mayonnaise in a machine. She preferred a food processor over a blender, because it is easier to scrape out.

How to Use a Blender or Food Processor

1. Pulse the yolks, lemon juice and seasonings a couple of times. (For hollandaise, they should be whisked together and warmed first.)
2. While the motor is running on high speed, slowly and evenly drizzle in the oil or melted butter.
3. Once all the fat has been added, blend the mixture until it is smooth and thick, about 30 seconds.

Whole-Grain Mustard Hollandaise

I marveled at this combination at the Ritz-Carlton hotel in San Francisco. It was served alongside a hearty breakfast of eggs and corned beef hash. Here's my take on it. If you omit the mustard, you can use this as a master hollandaise recipe. **Makes about 2 cups (500 mL)**

Tip

Want to play with it? Replace the lemon juice with orange juice. Add herbs or cracked peppercorns instead of mustard.

3	large egg yolks	3
2 tbsp	freshly squeezed lemon juice	25 mL
1 tbsp	cold water	15 mL
1 cup	unsalted butter, melted, cooled	250 mL
1 tbsp	whole-grain mustard	15 mL
	Kosher salt	

1. In a heatproof bowl or the top of a double boiler, whisk together yolks, lemon juice and water. Place over simmering water. Whisk constantly until the mixture is light-colored and thickened, about 2 minutes.

2. Remove from heat. Very gradually, drop by drop, whisk in butter until hollandaise is fluffy and thick. Whisk in mustard and salt. Use immediately.

❖ Let melted butter cool for 5 to 10 minutes before using it. The yolks may curdle if the butter is too hot.

❖ Purists use clarified butter in their hollandaise and its more complex cousin, béarnaise.

♻ Waste Not
To stretch mayonnaise, add 2 tsp (10 mL) water per 1 cup (250 mL) mayonnaise.

❖ Serve hollandaise and béarnaise sauces warm, not hot.

Gussy It Up
Make mayonnaise with gourmet nut oil or substitute flavored vinegar or orange juice for the lemon juice.

⩦ Fast Fixes
• Instead of using fresh tarragon, start béarnaise with tarragon vinegar. Or add chopped fresh tarragon at the end instead of boiling it with the vinegar, then straining it out.
• I have known Philistines to pour warmed process-cheese spread, instead of hollandaise, over eggs Benedict. You didn't hear it here.

❖ Ways to make bottled mayonnaise taste home-style:
  • Whisk in 2 tbsp (25 mL) extra virgin olive oil or a premium unrefined oil.
  • Whisk in homemade mayo ingredients. For every 1/4 cup (50 mL) bottled mayonnaise, stir in 1 tsp (5 mL) each lemon juice and Dijon mustard, plus salt and pepper to taste. Slowly whisk in 1 tbsp (15 mL) oil.
  • Whisk in some sour cream.

MHB Doctor

The mayonnaise is bitter.

- Mellow it with $\frac{1}{2}$ tsp (2 mL) granulated sugar.
- Don't use olive oil. It becomes bitter when blended into homemade mayonnaise. If you want the flavor of olive oil, start mixing in vegetable oil until a stable emulsion is formed. Stir in some olive oil with a wooden spoon.

The mayonnaise is dark.

- Add a bit of liquid.

There are little lumps in the hollandaise or béarnaise.

- The eggs have scrambled. Next time, keep the heat low.
- Make it in a double boiler.
- Get out the strainer.

The hollandaise or béarnaise looks oily at the edges.

- It's about to break, or separate. Remove the pan quickly from the burner and whisk like a madman until the mixture is cooled and smooth.
- The temperature is too high. Turn it down.

The hollandaise or béarnaise doesn't want to bind.

- The weather is too humid. Try using clarified butter.

The mayonnaise, hollandaise or béarnaise breaks or curdles.

Who knows what happened! It's been overheated. It was overbeaten. The ingredients were too cold. There wasn't enough liquid or acid. The fat was added too quickly, or there was too much fat. Lack of water can cause separation, another reason to use low heat. Try one of the following remedies:

- Start with a simple remedy: water. Pour the sauce into a blender, add a small spoonful of cold water and blend on high speed. Or add the water quickly with an electric mixer.
- Another simple remedy is cold. Pour the sauce into a chilled bowl and whisk. Then return it to the pan and reheat.
- Put a spoonful of cold water, lemon juice, vinegar or cream, 1 egg yolk, or a yolk blended with any of the above liquids in a large bowl. Whisk the ruined sauce into it, not the other way around. Work gradually. Add small amounts and whisk vigorously. No one will be the wiser.
- Stir cold water, lemon juice or an egg yolk into the sad sauce and warm it over low heat while whisking.
- Let the inevitable happen. Wait until the oil and water separate. Pour off the oil. Beat it in again, drop by drop.

The leftover hollandaise or béarnaise has solidified in the fridge.

- You can coax it into pourable form. Fill a large metal bowl halfway with hot tap water. Put the sauce in a smaller metal bowl, then set it in the hot water. Let it stand for 5 minutes. Stir and repeat until smooth.

  Careful: If it gets too warm, it separates. If that happens, use the same remedies you would for broken sauce, above.

✧ You can use condensed milk to make "magic mayonnaise." This vintage recipe was used as a dressing for coleslaw, thickly sliced tomatoes and potato salad, and in salmon or tuna sandwich fillings. It is very sweet and sour for modern tastes, but still has its fans. It's prepared in a large jar, but if you don't want the exercise, switch to a blender.

Master Plan
Magic Mock Mayonnaise

1. In a large jar, combine a 14-oz or 300 mL can of sweetened condensed milk, $\frac{1}{2}$ cup (125 mL) each cider vinegar and vegetable oil, 1 large egg, 2 tsp (10 mL) dry mustard, 1 tsp (5 mL) salt and a pinch of cayenne pepper.
2. Shake the jar vigorously for 2 to 5 minutes or until the mixture is fluffy.
3. Refrigerate it for 1 hour before serving.

Glaze

Fast Fixes

A glaze can be the simplest of sauces. Two fast glazes:

- After searing meat, pour wine or stock into the pan. Deglaze by scraping up the brown bits from the bottom of the pan. Reduce the liquid until syrupy, then drizzle it over the meat. Or paint on the glaze. This is lovely on chicken.
- Reduce stock by at least half, until it is syrupy enough to coat a spoon. Drizzle, brush or paint it on meat or fish. It takes 10 to 15 minutes over medium heat to reduce 1 cup (250 mL) beef stock to an intense, salty tablespoon (15 mL).

D is for Demi-Glace

Demi-glace is a big production. It begins with espagnole sauce, a rich, dark brown concoction that includes sautéed vegetables, veal or beef stock and tomato paste. Brown stock (traditionally veal, but perhaps beef) is added to the espagnole sauce. The mixture is reduced until thick and shiny, and is boosted with Madeira or sherry. Luckily, you can buy demi-glace. Go to a butcher shop or specialty food store. Avoid demi-glace powder in a packet.

Jus

OUTSIDE THE BOX

Thicken pan juices with the starchy cooking water from potatoes or pasta.

✧ Enhanced juices made from drippings are called the jus. When roast beef is served with this thin sauce, we say it is "au jus." Its thickened cousin is gravy.

Fast Fix

Make an easy sauce from drippings. Heat the drippings in a saucepan over medium-high heat. Add beef or chicken stock. Scrape up the browned bits stuck to the pan.

- Serve this as is for meat "au jus."
- Thicken it by simmering until it is reduced to a glaze.
- Thicken it by adding a cornstarch slurry. Stir over the heat until it comes to a boil.
- If you wish, strain the sauce.

How to Make Jus

1. Pour drippings into a fat separator.
2. Pour about 1 cup (250 mL) red wine into the roasting pan. Heat it over medium-high heat. Scrape up the browned bits stuck to the pan as it comes to a boil.
3. Reduce the heat to medium. Boil until it is reduced by half.
4. Strain the mixture through a sieve lined with damp cheesecloth. Press on the solids with a wooden spoon to extract juices. Gather the cheesecloth into a bundle and squeeze out the juices. Discard the solids.
5. Add salt and pepper to the jus. Add any non-fat drippings from the separator.
6. When the beef is sliced, drizzle jus over it.

Another Fast Fix

Add cream to pan juices to make a quick sauce for seared chicken, chops or cutlets. Bring the cream to a boil, then stir in some Dijon mustard or fresh chopped herbs.

Gravy

✧ Cook giblet stock for gravy the day before. It will save time. Plus, you can peel off the fat and use it to start the gravy.

✧ To hasten the separation of pan juices, pour them into a gravy separator, heatproof glass measuring cup or zip-lock bag. Plunge the container or bag into ice water. The fat will rise quickly to the surface.

✧ More fat than juice in the pan? Tip the pan and use a baster to siphon off juices from beneath the floating fat. Pour out the fat. Return the juices to the pan. Supplement with stock and/or wine.

✧ Develop flavor in gravy by simmering pan juices for half an hour over low heat. Add stock or wine, if necessary. Add the thickener at the end.

3 Ways to Thicken Gravy

1. Start a roux by stirring flour into the fatty drippings in the pan over the heat, then add stock and juices (separated out earlier and saved after slicing the meat). For stronger gravy, cook the roux until it is dark brown.
2. In a jar, shake flour with cold water. Drizzle the mixture into the hot pan juices while whisking.
3. Whisk cornstarch slurry into the pan juices.

✗ No-No

Do not use drippings from lamb to make gravy. They're too strong-tasting.

Gravy Doctor

Whoa, it's lumpy!
• Pulse it in the blender, push it through a strainer, or both.
• Next time, add the stock very slowly while you whisk.
• Next time, blend the flour or cornstarch thoroughly with the water.

The gravy is too salty.
• Try adding a few cubes of toast for 2 to 3 minutes.

There isn't enough gravy to go around.
• Add stock, plus flour or cornstarch slurry.

☰ Fast Fixes

• In a saucepan, bring commercial chicken or beef stock to a boil over medium-high heat. In a jar, shake flour with cold water to make a slurry. Whisk the slurry into the stock.
• Add pan juices and meat juices to pre-thickened brown sauce.

OUTSIDE THE BOX

Darken gravy with brewed coffee or cola for an interesting flavor.

Gussy It Up

• Add wine, sherry, port or cider to gravy.
• Whisk a spoonful of whipping cream into gravy to make it velvety. You can also whisk cream to thicken it slightly before stirring it into gravy.
• Wake up gravy with roasted garlic.
• Dash in some balsamic vinegar.

✪ Waste Not

• Give your gravy another boost. After slicing the meat, scrape the juices on the cutting board into the gravy. Do the same with juices from the serving platter.
• Create gravy from the bones of barbecued chicken or roast turkey.

Bone Gravy

You can eat your chicken and have more gravy, too. Here's how gravy lovers can get another fix. **Makes about 4 cups (1 L)**

- **Preheat oven to 400°F (200°C)**

- **Shallow roasting pan**

Tips

Exactitude is not required for the bones.

Scrape and save the juices from the cutting board after carving your bird and from the serving platter; keep them in an airtight tub in the fridge for up to 3 days.

The bottom part of a broiling pan is just the right size for roasting the bones.

This makes a thin gravy. You can up the cornstarch to ¼ cup (50 mL) to thicken it.

Variations

You can substitute a guesstimated equivalent of roasted turkey bones.

If you don't have Marsala, add sherry, white wine (double the amount) or even a couple of dashes of Worcestershire sauce.

	Bones from 1 roasted or barbecued chicken	
1	onion, coarsely chopped	1
4 cups	water	1 L
3 tbsp	cornstarch	45 mL
6 tbsp	cold chicken stock	90 mL
1 tbsp	Marsala	15 mL
	Juices left from cutting chicken (optional)	
	Salt and freshly ground black pepper	

1. Put the bones in a single layer in a stovetop-safe roasting pan. Add the onion. Roast in preheated oven for 20 minutes.

2. Put the pan on a burner. Add water. Bring to a boil over medium-high heat, scraping up any browned bits. Reduce heat to medium and boil for 5 minutes. Strain, discarding bones and onion. Return liquid to the pan.

3. In a small bowl, stir together cornstarch and stock. Stir it into the liquid.

4. Bring the mixture to a boil over medium heat, stirring constantly. Boil briefly, just until thickened. Remove from heat. Stir in Marsala and chicken juices (if using). Season to taste with salt and pepper.

Browning

✧ Also known as browning sauce or caramel coloring, this dark liquid is basically sugar, boiled until almost black. Funny, it is not sweet at all. Browning is used drop by drop, so a bottle may last longer than you do.

Two Uses for Browning
- Add a dash to pallid gravy or other sauces.
- Brush it on microwaved or pale foods to deepen the color and shine.

✧ Bottled commercial browning contains caramel, water, salt and glucose solids. It is thicker, darker and not at all bitter in comparison to homemade efforts. But you can make your own.

Master Plan
Caramel Coloring

1. In a skillet, over medium heat, melt 1 cup (250 mL) granulated sugar without stirring. Simmer until it is dark brown. There should still be a hint of sweetness in it. If cooked until almost black, it will be too bitter to use.
2. Remove it from the heat and let stand for 5 minutes or until it resembles molasses and starts to develop a crust.
3. One spoonful at a time, slowly stir in ¼ cup (50 mL) of the hottest tap water.
4. Let it cool, stirring occasionally. Add another 1 or 2 tbsp (15 or 25 mL) water if the mixture is too thick or threatens to solidify.

Fondues

✧ Don't try to prepare fondue in the fondue pot. Slowly melt a cheese mixture in a saucepan on the stove. Gently melt chocolate with some cream in a microwave-safe bowl in the microwave. Then pour the cheese or chocolate mixture into the fondue pot.

✧ Don't eat off the fondue fork. That way, you won't transfer germs into the communal pot. Use the dinner fork to push tidbits onto your plate.

✧ If you don't have enough fondue forks, offer diners long bamboo skewers.

Cheese Fondue

Fondue Cheese Tips

- Stick with fairly firm cheeses, such as Emmental or Gruyère.
- If you want to add a bit of semisoft or soft cheese, stir it in after melting the firm cheese.
- Some cooks soak fontina or other cheeses in milk for a couple of hours beforehand to tenderize them.
- You can add more cheese to the pot on the table, but do it slowly. Let one batch melt completely before adding more. It should be shredded, not in chunks.
- Don't let it boil.
- It's traditional to stir in a figure-eight pattern. This is supposed to prevent excess evaporation.
- If the cheese mixture thickens, add tiny amounts of white wine.

♛ A Golden Rule

Eat slowly and keep the heat low.

✧ When you cube the bread, try to make sure each piece has a bit of crust. It's less likely to slip off the fondue fork that way.

✧ Rub the fondue pot with a cut piece of garlic before you start.

✧ Use cornstarch to keep the cheese mixture from separating.

Ways to Add Cornstarch

- Dissolve cornstarch in enough cold white wine, kirsch, beer or whatever alcohol you are using to make a slurry. Whisk that into the cheese mixture.
- Toss the cornstarch with the shredded cheese before melting it with liquid.
- If the cheese mixture separates or gets clumpy while you're eating, take a break. Stir $\frac{1}{2}$ tsp (2 mL) cornstarch into 1 tbsp (15 mL) wine. Warm it slightly. Add it to the pot. Stir it slowly to smooth everything out.

® is for Religieuse

The browned cheese crusted at the bottom of the fondue pot is good to eat. The Swiss consider it a delicacy. Fondue lovers call it "la religieuse," or the nun. Nurture la religieuse by leaving a thin coating of cheese on the bottom of the pot when you are done. Lower the flame and let the coating brown. Scrape it off, divide it into pieces and enjoy.

Play around with the cheese, the alcohol and the dippers — and you've got yourself a post-millennial fondue.

- Kirsch (cherry brandy) is a traditional ingredient, but you can add any fruity liquor. Ponder which fruit you might enjoy on a cheese platter. Apple, pear and grape (grappa) come to mind.
- Use Cheddar cheese and pair it with beer or cider instead of wine. So hearty!
- Add goat cheese for tang.
- Make a Mexican fondue by stirring together tomato sauce, shredded cheese (try Monterey Jack), minced jalapeño pepper and chili powder. Dip in tortilla chips and veggies, such as green bell pepper strips.
- For a simpler Tex-Mex effect, stir minced jalapeño pepper or salsa into the cheese sauce.
- Offer cooked shrimp to dip in the cheese.
- Try wedges of tart Granny Smith apple or firm Bosc pear as dippers.
- Reintroduce cauliflower to its old friend, the cheese sauce, in the form of fondue. First soften it slightly in a steamer. Other steamed vegetables work, too, such as broccoli-stem coins or long green beans.

Ⓡ is for Raclette

Not content with just the fondue, the cheese-loving Swiss decided to melt raclette cheese (once upon a time in an open fire and now in a machine), scrape it onto plates and serve it with boiled potatoes, cornichons, dried meats and other delicacies. Thank you.

Making Do

You can enjoy a cheese fondue without the equipment.

- Melt cheese with wine and kirsch in an ovenproof dish. Whisk in a cornstarch slurry. Serve it at the table with crusty bread, pickles, pickled onions or salad.
- Make Welsh rabbit, or rarebit. Made with melted Cheddar and ale, this British dish is usually served on toast. But you can dip, too. The Brits like tomatoes alongside. Wise choice.
- Serve a round of cheese raclette-style. You can melt it in the oven or on the grill, then slash open the top.

Stock and Oil Fondues

✧ Pieces of meat or fish can be cooked in hot stock or oil in a fondue pot. Sometimes they are battered first.

✗ No-No

Don't bother with an oil fondue. It's messy and dangerous, and there are food-safety and cross-contamination issues with raw meat. In my thoughtless youth, I once stripped the varnish from a tabletop when some oil swept into the flame and turned into a fireball. My fellow guests were highly entertained.

Keys to Quick Cooking

- Cut meat, fish and vegetables into thin, even slices or small cubes.
- Use only tender meat that cooks quickly or small bits of seafood. Shrimp is a good choice.

✧ Once the dippers are gone, add quick-cooking Asian noodles to the stock in a fondue, toss in a handful of bean sprouts and enjoy a soup course.

Dessert Fondue

⋽ *Fast Fixes*

- Turn supermarket fudge sauce or caramel sauce into a fondue. Heat it with cream. Try strawberries with the chocolate or sliced apples with the caramel.
- Prepare caramel fondue by heating chopped caramels with cream.

Fondue **VS.** Fountain?

Chocolate fondues are passé now that we can get our kicks with chocolate fountains. A fountain cascades a steady stream of warm chocolate.

Fountain Tips

- You're supposed to allot about 1 lb (500 g) chocolate for every 10 people at the fountain. But they go crazy. Four oz (125 g) per person is more realistic.
- Never try to run the fountain without thinning the melted chocolate with a neutral oil (or a fragrant nut oil if you are rich). Consult the instruction booklet for amounts.
- Place the fountain on a bare counter or tabletop, or set a large plastic mat under it. The chocolate inevitably splatters as people help themselves.
- Post a guard to slap the hands of potential double-dippers.

Dippers for a Chocolate Fountain or Fondue

- Strawberries are beautiful, for sure, but there's more in the fruit department. Try chunks of banana, pineapple and kiwifruit.
- Take the cake — pound or angel.
- Check out ladyfingers and soft cookies.
- Make or buy some crispy rice squares. Cut them into cubes.
- Marshmallows are good, but there can be s'more to them: Put out graham crackers to sandwich them in after dipping.

Stocks

Stock VS. Broth?

A stock is a soup base. A broth is a clear soup. Of course, a broth can be used as a stock. The boundaries are blurred. But if you want to get picky, a stock is long-simmered with bones. (A brown stock is made with roasted bones.) Broth is made with meat and bone. But cancel that — either can be vegetarian. Bouillon is a broth or a concentrated brown stock, depending on its purpose. A consommé is clarified bouillon, possibly reduced with a bit of sherry, served hot or cold.

6 Ways To Make Stock Intense

1. Start with good ingredients.
2. Don't skimp. The winner of a Jewish chicken soup contest in New York had the right idea when she made stock from chicken bones, then simmered a whole chicken in the stock along with vegetables.
3. Don't add too much water. It should barely cover the meat and vegetables. It's better to thin a concentrated stock than to reduce a thin one.
4. Roast and caramelize bones and vegetables.
5. Braise chicken backs and other bony bits for an hour in a small amount of water beforehand.
6. Reduce the stock after defatting and clarifying it.

♜ Two Golden Rules

- Don't turn your stock into a garbage dump. The fresher the ingredients, the better the stock. Avoid dubious meat or distressed vegetables. They can be a bit past their prime, but not old, bruised or smelly.
- Water is the major ingredient in stock, so it should be good. Start with cold water, preferably filtered or bottled.

Reasons to Start with Cold Water

- Proteins won't tighten or firm up, so flavor is easier to extract from them.
- Blood dissolves more readily, so it can rise up later in the foam that is skimmed. When heated, blood proteins form particles that can cloud the stock and taint the flavor.
- Particles remain larger and less evenly suspended. When the water is heated, they are more likely to rise to the surface, rather than remaining dispersed. So the stock isn't as cloudy.

♦ Some cooks soak bones and vegetables in cold water for an hour before setting the pot on the stove. They say the resulting stock is tastier and the cold water draws out more blood. It's hard to gauge.

♦ When making fish stock, soak the heads and bones in cold water for a couple of hours to extract the blood, which turns the stock gray. Change the water before cooking.

♦ For meat stock, add no more than twice as much water as solids. For vegetable stocks, add $1\frac{1}{2}$ to 2 times as much water as solids.

♻ Waste Not

When you buy poultry, immediately pull out the giblets and freeze them. Once you collect enough, prepare stock.

Ⓒ is for Collagen

Collagen is the protein in connective tissue and bones. It dissolves into gelatin, giving stock its silky richness. Bones high in collagen are best for stock. Younger animals have more collagen; that's why veal bones are choice.

✧ Cut or break bones into pieces no larger than 4 inches (10 cm).

✧ For brown stock, roast meaty bones at 400°F (200°C), turning them every 10 minutes, for 30 minutes or until they are darkened. Drain the fat.

♡ Healthier Eater

Adding 1 tbsp (15 mL) vinegar to stock is supposed to extract a tiny bit more calcium from the bones. The vinegar leaves a hint of sourness, though.

Tips for Adding Vegetables

- You don't have to peel vegetables for stock, or even peel garlic. Just rinse or scrub.
- Avoid assertive broccoli, cabbage, turnips, beets, asparagus, rutabaga, eggplant and cauliflower.
- Coarsely chop or crush raw vegetables to extract the most flavor. You can use a food processor.
- Roast vegetables to give the stock more depth. Or sauté them in butter first.

✧ Simmer stock slowly and for as long as possible. Beef and veal stock need 6 to 8 hours, chicken stock 3 to 4 hours, fish and vegetable stock 1 hour.

✧ Simmer stock partially covered so it doesn't evaporate too quickly.

✧ At the start, season lightly with kosher salt. Add salt to taste at the end. Stock reduces and intensifies. The goal is a barely salted stock.

✧ You can attempt to rescue oversalted stock by adding a thinly sliced potato. Simmer until it is translucent.

♻ Waste Not

- Save fish bones and shrimp shells in the freezer for stock. Ask for the heads, too. Shrimp heads have the most flavor.
- Save your fresh vegetable trimmings for the stockpot, like real chefs do — ends of tomatoes, carrot peels, mushroom stems, leek stalks, even ginger peel.

OUTSIDE THE BOX

- A pasta pot insert or a wire basket from a deep fryer can be pressed into service for stock. Once the stock is done, you can lift out the solids.
- Add onion or tomato skins to give the stock a glow. Or add an onion with just the papery part of the peel stripped off.

▤ Fast Fixes

- Make stock in a pressure cooker. It will be cloudier, though.
- Canned or packaged stock saves time but is too strong. Get more bang for your buck — and better flavor — by diluting it from a quarter to a half with cold water.

✧ Make any savory dish better by replacing the water with homemade stock. Don't forget to reduce the salt in the recipe.

✧ Whenever possible, cook with reduced-sodium stock (homemade or purchased). You'll have more control over the amount of salt in your dish.

- For small portions, you can freeze stock in a muffin tin, or in an ice cube tray. Once the pieces are frozen, transfer them to a zip-lock bag.

6 Ways to Make Stock Less Cloudy

1. Start stock with cold ingredients in cold water.
2. Never let stock boil. A riotous boil churns up fat and proteins, and mixes the rising scum back into the liquid. Bring the stock barely to a boil, then lower the heat right away, so it simmers. The surface should bubble only gently. Fanatics keep the heat low by putting bricks on the burner. A double boiler would work, although these are normally too small for stock.
3. Once stock comes to a simmer, skim the foam from the surface, then wipe the edge of the pot. Simmer for half an hour before adding vegetables, and skim several times.
4. Don't stir too much.
5. Don't add potatoes or other starchy vegetables. The soup will not only be murky, it will spoil faster.
6. When straining the stock, don't push on the solids with a heavy spoon. Instead, tap the edge of the strainer or lift and shift the solids.

Clarifying Stock

- Strain stock thoroughly through a sieve lined with cheesecloth. Lift and shake the cheesecloth to get the last bit of liquid out. Put the solids in the compost bin.

S is for Scum

Meat and seafood release proteins and fat. The proteins tangle up and rise to the top of the stock in the form of foam.

C is for Clarifying

Once stock is cooked, it is clarified to remove sediment and impurities. That involves capturing the unwanted particles and straining the liquid.

- Once the solids are strained out, simmer the stock for 5 minutes.
- For each quart (1 L) of stock, lightly beat 1 egg white. Drizzle the egg white over the top of the soup and throw in the crumpled eggshells. Simmer for 5 minutes; do not allow the soup to boil.
- A thick, crusty foam will rise to the top. Remove the pot from the burner and let it stand for up to an hour. Push the foam to one side. Carefully ladle the soup through a sieve lined with wet cheesecloth. Don't pour it.
- Some cooks recommend throwing just the eggshells in, but they don't work as well on their own.

Defatting Stock

Slow Ways to Defat

- Defatting is simplest when you have patience: Refrigerate, congeal, peel. This also leaves a layer of fat as a protective coating until you are ready to use the stock.
- Place waxed paper on the surface of the stock. Refrigerate until the fat solidifies. Peel off the paper with the fat stuck to it.

The Best Way to Defat Hot Stock in a Hurry

- Pour it into a large zip-lock bag. Shove it into the freezer, standing upright, not on its side. The fat should start to congeal in 15 to 30 minutes. Cut a piece off one bottom corner, then pour out the stock and leave the fat behind.

Decent Ways to Defat Hot Stock in a Hurry

- Let the stock stand for a few minutes without disturbing it, so the fat can rise, settle and start to congeal. While the stock is still hot, swirl a large metal spoon from the center outward, then spoon off the fat at the edges.
- Toss zip-lock bags filled with ice cubes or ice packs into the stock. Fat will congeal on them. This is messy.
- Use the insulated container from your ice cream maker (which should always be sitting in the freezer awaiting your whims). Ladle stock into the container, then ladle off congealed clumps of fat that float to the surface. Or, if you have a large pot of stock, toss the frozen container into it.

Fiddly Ways to Defat Hot Stock

- Use a baster to suction grease off the surface. Squeeze the fat into a discard bowl and the stock back into the pot.
- Ladle stock into a gravy separator. Pour off the fat. Repeat.
- Run a fat mop over the top. It's a messy job. (A fat mop looks like a miniature mop with plastic strands.)
- Swirl a pastry brush over the top. Brush the captured fat up the sides of the pot. Squeeze out the brush.
- Lay a sheet of paper towel over the top and immediately pull it up and off.
- Wrap an ice cube in a paper towel and skim it over the stock. The fat congeals on the paper, but the paper and ice have to be changed frequently.

A Strange Way to Defat Hot Stock

- Add a cold lettuce leaf to the stock to absorb fat, then discard it.

- ✧ Leave a bit of fat in chicken stock to make it silky. Remove all the fat from beef and veal stock to make it light.

- ✧ Most stock-defatting techniques work on stews and sauces, too.

- ✧ Stock is allowed to boil once it's clarified and all the fat is removed. Now is the time to reduce it, if you wish.

Cooling Stock

6 Ways to Cool Stock Faster

1. Set the pot in an ice bath.
2. Place the pot on a rack in the sink. Fill the sink with cold water.
3. Transfer the stock to smaller, shallow containers.
4. Submerge a zip-lock bag filled with ice cubes in the stock.
5. Freeze water in a very clean pop bottle or storage tub, then dunk it in the stock.
6. Pour the stock into a cold metal bowl or container. Or pour the stock back and forth from one metal container to another.

Safety Tips

- Don't refrigerate hot stock. This endangers other foods by heating up adjacent items or the fridge as a whole.
- Don't leave stock to cool at room temperature.

- ✧ These cooling techniques also help cool creamy soup. Chill it faster so you can serve it sooner.

Soups

4 Ways to Avert Murkiness

1. For clear chicken or beef soup, leave super-thin egg noodles on the side. To serve, dole a big spoonful of noodles into each bowl, then ladle steamy hot soup over the top, the Hungarian way. No soggy noodles, no cloudy soup.

2. If you're putting pasta or rice into your soup, cook it separately until it is barely tender. (You can rinse it, too, if desired.) It will finish cooking once it joins the soup. The starches won't cloud the broth.

3. If you're making soup with a ham bone, simmer the bone in water first, with chunks of vegetables. Scrape the meat off the bone and return it to the soup. You'll find all the fatty tidbits floating on top. Skim them off and give them to the dog. Then carry on making the soup.

4. When adding cooked meat, such as shredded leftover turkey, to soup, do it at the end of the cooking time and heat just until warmed through.

Fast Fix

When making beef soup in a hurry with leaner beef, add gelatin to mimic the richness extracted from long-simmered beef bones. Add about 1 tbsp (15 mL) gelatin powder per 8 cups (2 L) liquid.

✧ Avoid burns when puréeing hot soup in the blender: Hold a wadded towel over the lid before turning on the blender.

✧ To mellow soup that is over-seasoned, stir in a bit of butter.

✧ To thicken chowder or other hearty soups neatly and efficiently, drain them. Thicken the stock, then stir the solids back in.

✧ You can use a variety of starches and grains to boost soup stock. These amounts will give 1 cup (250 mL) of soup a slightly thicker body:
- $1\frac{1}{2}$ tsp (7 mL) flour
- 1 tsp (5 mL) cornstarch, arrowroot or tapioca flour
- 1 tbsp (15 mL) quick-cooking oats or wheat germ
- 1 to 2 tbsp (15 to 25 mL) quinoa flakes
- 1 tbsp (15 mL) pearl barley
- 1 tbsp (15 mL) toasted ground rice
- $\frac{1}{4}$ cup (50 mL) puréed, cooked rice
- 3 tbsp (45 mL) mashed potatoes
- 1 tbsp (15 mL) grated raw potato
- 2 tbsp (25 mL) instant mashed potato flakes

✧ When serving cold soup, chill the bowls.

☺ KID STUFF

To cool a bowl of soup for a kid, stir in an ice cube.

Gussy It Up

- Stir or swirl pesto into soup.
- Whisk heavy or whipping (35%) cream until slightly thickened. Stir in finely chopped herbs. Drizzle it over soup just before serving, for a burst of freshness. You could also use sour cream.

- Alternatives to crumbled crackers and croutons as garnishes:
  - Toasted nuts
  - Corn chips or tortilla chips
  - Shredded carrot or other vegetables
  - Bacon bits

Chowder

- A chowder is a thick seafood or corn soup.

- The seafood in chowders and other fish soups cooks at different rates. Cook each type of seafood separately in the stock just until it is done. Scoop it out with a skimmer and reserve it in a bowl. Cook the soup base and vegetables. Then add the seafood and its juices.

Creamy Soups

- Reserve some tips or tiny florets to garnish creamy, puréed asparagus, cauliflower or broccoli soups. Blanch the tips and florets for tenderness.

- For a smoother cream soup, push it through a fine sieve.

Ways to Protect Cream Soup

- After adding cream, butter or eggs, never let the soup boil.
- Cook or reheat cream soup in the top of a double boiler over simmering water. You can also reheat in the microwave on Medium (50%), stirring frequently. Anything but direct heat.

B is for Bisque

A bisque is a silky smooth cream soup based on shellfish.

V is for Vichyssoise

Vichyssoise is a cold creamy soup made with potatoes.

- Cold cream soup tastes better when made with lighter cream. Whipping cream forms a greasy coating in the mouth.

- Before adding cream to cold soup, chill the soup base for at least 2 hours.

♡ Healthier Eater

After a stint in the freezer, baked or boiled spuds are crumbly, waterlogged and mealy, and mashed potatoes are barely passable. Leftover frozen vegetables are soggy and rubbery. Save them anyway. They're great for preparing creamy soup without cream. You don't even have to thaw them, so they're a fast route to soup.

- Add frozen potatoes to stock along with fresh or leftover frozen vegetables. Simmer until tender, then purée. Serve it warm. Or, to make a healthful sort of vichyssoise, chill the soup. You could add a splash of skim milk before serving.
- Mix and match whatever happens to be in the freezer. What you end up with is usually a pleasant surprise.

Other Ways to Thicken Soup Without Cream

- Purée some of the solids, such as beans or vegetables, then return them to the soup. Or use an immersion blender to partially purée bean soup to thicken it.
- Stir in a cornstarch slurry or use a flour roux.
- Stir in mashed potatoes and purée with an immersion blender. If you are in a hurry and your soup isn't creamy enough, microwave a potato and scoop out the pulp.

Onion Soup

✧ Comté is the traditional and best cheese for onion soup. It is creamy, rather than rubbery, and the top gets crunchy under the broiler. If you can't find any, use Emmental.

✧ Cook the onions until they are caramelized and very soft. Do not brown or crisp them.

OUTSIDE THE BOX

Onion soup can be topped with a mound of croutons instead of a baguette circle — making it easier to break through into the soup. I witnessed this convenient sacrilege in a Paris bistro.

✧ Let onion soup cool, then refrigerate it overnight to mature and mellow. The next day, warm the soup, add the toppings and set the bowls under the broiler.

Egg Drop Soup

How to Add Egg Drops to Clear Soup

1. Add 1 egg for every 2 cups (500 mL) stock.
2. Bring stock to a simmer.
3. Break an egg into a cup. Whisk it with a fork just to combine the yolk and the white.
4. Hold the cup about 5 inches (13 cm) above the surface of the stock.
5. Very slowly pour the egg into the stock in a fine stream. At the same time, swish the fork in wide circles on the surface of the stock to catch the egg and separate it into threads.

Dumplings

A Bit of Science

Dumplings, plain or filled, including ravioli, perogies and wontons, sink to the bottom of the pot at first. Once their starch granules swell, they are no longer denser than the simmering water and thus float to the top.

Dumpling Cooking Tips

- Use plenty of water and don't crowd the pan.
- Do not heat the water past a simmer.
- Once the dumplings float to the top, put the lid on so steam can help cook them.

Is It Done?

- Dumplings swim on top of the simmering water.
- Dumplings look puffed.
- A toothpick inserted in the center comes out clean (except for any filling).

✧ You can steam dumplings in an egg poacher or steamer basket.

✧ After draining, set dumplings on a greased baking sheet so they don't stick together.

Better Leftovers

- Steamed Chinese dumplings, including wontons, harden in the fridge. Turn them into outstanding soup. Warm the dumplings in simmering chicken stock. Add a few dashes of soy sauce and chile oil. Garnish with chopped green onion.
- Make another delicious soup by adding leftover ravioli, including any tomato sauce clinging to it, to a saucepan of hot stock. Stir in hearty greens. Sprinkle grated Parmesan over the top when serving.

♻ Waste Not

Use the cooking water from meat or fish dumplings and wontons as a basis for stock. You can put leftover dumplings in it afterwards and add other ingredients to make soup.

Wontons

Ways to Seal Wontons (and Egg-Roll Wrappers)

- Run a moistened finger around the edges of the dough. Gently press the seams together.
- For a firmer seal, stir water and cornstarch to make a slurry, not a paste. Dip your fingers in, then paint it around the perimeter of the dough. Press to seal. Keep a tiny bowl of water beside you as you work, to clean your fingers.

Making Do

Wonton wrappers can be pressed into service to make ravioli.

Matzo Balls

Sinkers Floaters?

In the world of matzo balls lovers, floaters are the lovely, fluffy, desirable kind that, well, float. Dense sinkers are frowned upon — although some folks secretly prefer them.

♛ A Golden Rule

Don't firmly roll or pack matzo balls. They'll be hard. Be quick and casual, and you'll be rewarded with puffy matzo balls.

Master Plan
Matzo Balls

1. Bring a large pot of boiling salted water to a simmer.
2. Drop each matzo ball into the water right after you quickly shape it. Don't build up a stockpile.
3. If a ball sticks to the bottom of the pan, nudge it with a wooden spoon.
4. Don't crowd the pan. Make the balls in batches, if necessary.
5. Once all the matzo balls are in the pan, keep the lid on. Don't keep checking on them. If you do, the steam will subside, the heat decrease and the balls sink.
6. Simmer them for 35 to 40 minutes. They should rise to the top of the pot and puff dramatically.
7. With a slotted spoon, transfer them, one at a time, to simmering chicken soup.
8. Serve the soup right away. Or simmer the matzo balls for up to half an hour in the soup to make them extra-light and tasty. Keep the temperature as low as possible; the water should be barely moving.

Keys to Forming Matzo Balls

- Dampen your hands.
- Scoop a heaping tablespoon of batter. Use your index and middle finger to flick the batter onto your palm.
- Don't try to form perfect spheres. Coax the batter into a ball, more or less, by tossing it from palm to palm, with your fingers extended. If necessary, loosen it by flicking at it with your thumb.

✗ No-No

Don't cook matzo balls in the chicken soup. It will get cloudy.

❖ Though a pure matzo ball is perfect in its simplicity, cooks are not averse to experimentation. The only caveat: Don't add anything that may drastically change the texture or consistency.

Gussy It Up

- Add minced or dried onion.
- Add puréed garlic or ginger.
- Try minced parsley, dill or marjoram.
- Stir in tomato paste.
- Add coarsely ground black pepper.
- Try Vegeta. Beloved by old European soup makers, the original Vegeta is a blend of spices, dried vegetables and the dreaded MSG. (Vegeta also makes a no-MSG version now.)

❖ Store matzo balls in chicken soup in the fridge. (They'll probably turn into sinkers.)

❖ Reheat matzo balls in the soup. Bring it to a simmer only.

❖ You can freeze matzo balls. After cooking them, transfer them to a baking sheet. Freeze until firm, then transfer into zip-lock bags.

Soufflés

8 Ways to Prevent a Soufflé from Falling Flat

1. Overbeaten egg whites can cause a collapse. Beat the whites until they are glossy and firm, not grainy and dry-looking. To stabilize the whites, you can add a bit of cream of tartar while whipping.
2. A soufflé needs to climb the sides of the baking dish. Butter the dish well to prevent sticking. Coat the bottom and sides with bread crumbs, granulated sugar, flour or dry grated cheese for grip.
3. For a high, airy soufflé, bake the mixture immediately.
4. Start with a hot oven. A soufflé is most delicate before a crust has formed around the air bubbles. Start it at 400°F (200°C), so the eggs can quickly rise, solidify and hold their shape. Reduce the heat to 375°F (190°C) to finish cooking.
5. Bake a soufflé on the lower rack. This reduces heat from above that can evaporate too much of the steam that gives the soufflé its lift.
6. Don't open the oven door. This introduces colder air that may stop evaporation and cause the soufflé to deflate. If the soufflé firms up before the vapor rises again, it will remain flat.
7. Don't slam the oven door. This may release or disturb the gases in the soufflé.
8. Make a cheese or chocolate soufflé. They are the most stable.

Mythstake

Actually, a soufflé is not terribly fragile. It is surprisingly easy to make, forgiving and even sturdy. You can dig right into it, and if you discover it's undercooked, pop it back into the oven. A soufflé will sink after you remove it from the oven, but you don't have to tiptoe around while it's baking.

✦ If you don't want to fuss with a collar, fill the soufflé dish no more than three-quarters full. If you want drama, fill the dish higher to create a crown.

How to Create a Crown

1. Prevent the soufflé from running over by attaching a collar to the top of the dish. Make it with parchment or foil, and butter it.
2. To prevent sticking, run your finger between the batter and dish all around the rim.
3. Use a small rubber spatula to run a groove 1 to 2 inches (2.5 to 5 cm) deep around the top, about 1 inch (2.5 cm) in from the rim.

✦ To make a dessert soufflé, start with thick custard, add flavorings and fold in the whipped egg whites. When it's done, poke a small hole in the center with a spoon and pour in custard, caramel or chocolate sauce, or a splash of liqueur.

Manchego and Smoked Paprika Soufflé

This is not as smooth as soufflés made with softer, moister cheeses, but you'll enjoy the smoky Spanish accent. **Makes 4 servings**

- **Preheat oven to 400°F (200°C)**

- **6-cup (1.5 L) round casserole dish or soufflé dish**

- **Kitchen string (optional)**

Variation

File this as a basic cheese soufflé recipe: Use the same amounts and technique, but play with the ingredients. Use any combination of cheese and spices. Emmental or Gruyère and cracked black peppercorns are a good basic combo.

7 tbsp	unsalted butter, divided	105 mL
	Dry bread crumbs	
½ cup + 2 tbsp	all-purpose flour	150 mL
1¼ cups	2% milk	300 mL
3	large egg yolks	3
1½ tsp	smoked paprika	7 mL
1 tsp	kosher salt	5 mL
	Freshly ground black pepper	
5 oz	manchego cheese, finely shredded	150 g
6	large egg whites	6

1. Grease casserole dish with 1 tbsp (15 mL) of the butter and sprinkle with bread crumbs to coat evenly, shaking out excess. Cut parchment paper or foil to create a collar that extends above the dish by at least 3 inches (7.5 cm); wrap around the dish and secure with string. Set aside.

2. In a saucepan, melt remaining butter over medium-low heat. Stir in flour. Cook, stirring constantly, for 2 minutes or until the mixture starts to turn golden. Gradually whisk in milk. Bring to a simmer, whisking constantly; simmer for 1 to 2 minutes or until thick. Remove from heat.

3. In a large bowl, lightly whisk egg yolks. Gradually whisk in some of milk mixture to temper the yolks. Whisk in the remaining milk mixture. Stir in paprika, salt and pepper to taste. Stir in cheese.

4. In another large bowl, using an electric mixer, beat egg whites to firm peaks. Do not overbeat. Gently fold one-quarter of the egg whites into the cheese mixture. Carefully fold in the remaining whites.

5. Pour batter into prepared dish. Run your finger in the batter all around the rim. Using a spatula or spoon, run a groove 1 to 2 inches (2.5 to 5 cm) deep around the top, about 1 inch (2.5 cm) in from the rim.

6. Place the dish in the lower third of preheated oven. Bake for 15 minutes, then reduce heat to 375°F (190°C). Bake for 20 to 30 minutes or until the soufflé rises high and develops a golden brown crust.

- To make a savory soufflé, start with a thick béchamel sauce, stir in spices and cheese, then fold in whipped egg whites.

Is It Done?

- It's hard to tell when a soufflé is cooked. Look for the signs.
  - It doesn't jiggle much when you move it. On the other hand, if it doesn't jiggle at all, it's overcooked.
  - The top is golden and feels firm.
  - A skewer inserted down to the bottom in the center doesn't come out wet. But if it comes out bone dry, the soufflé is overcooked.
  - It doesn't weep when you cut into it.
  - If it's wildly undercooked, it falls dramatically when you pull it out of the oven.
  - You can push back the top with a knife and take a peek inside. If it looks soft, but not raw and runny, it's done.

Stuffings

♕ A Golden Rule

Dire warnings from public-health officials about the dangers of stuffing are matched only by the lackadaisical reaction from cooks who love it. If you are willing to follow one rule, let it be this: Heat stuffing until it reaches 165°F (74°C).

Ways to Dry Cubed Bread for Stuffing

- Leave it overnight on a baking sheet.
- Set it in a 200°F (100°C) oven for a few minutes.

✧ Stuffed birds have fewer juices. The stuffing absorbs them. Start with stuffing that seems a bit dry.

✧ If cornbread stuffing is too rich, use half cornbread, half white bread.

Stuffing Estimates

- Allow about ¾ cup (175 mL) of stuffing per pound (500 g) of bird for the cavity, plus extra for stuffing under the skin of the breast.
- Stuffing expands. Stuff the cavity about three-quarters full.

9 Other Safety Tips

1. Never stuff poultry, pork or other meat or fish ahead of time. Ideally, make the stuffing just before you are ready to cook.
2. If stuffing is refrigerated, let it come to room temperature. This will help it reach a safe temperature before a big bird is done.
3. The stuffing should not be hot when you use it. Hot stuffing heats up the cavity in a raw chicken or turkey, making it more inviting to bacteria.
4. Pack the stuffing loosely. Dense stuffing is not only unappealing, it may prevent the interior of a bird from getting hot enough to kill germs.
5. Stuffing can be removed from the heat when it reaches 160°F (71°C), covered and allowed to reach 165°F (74°C) with residual heat.
6. Remove all the stuffing just before or during carving. Refrigerate it immediately after the meal.
7. You can bake stuffing and poultry separately. Heat the stuffing in the microwave on High until it's steaming. Transfer it into the cavity of the bird for the final 30 minutes of roasting time. It's awkward, but the bird cooks faster and the risk of food poisoning is reduced.
8. Stuffing takes longer to reach a safe temperature than the bird does, so you risk overcooking the breast. One solution: Remove the finished bird from the oven. Scoop the stuffing into a baking dish. Pop it back into the oven while the bird rests.
9. Freeze cooked stuffing. Reheat it without thawing.

✧ More stuffing locations for those who can't get enough:

* Cram it under the skin of the breast.
* Sew the long flap of neck skin into a stuffing pouch.

Ways to Secure Stuffing

* Put a large piece of cheesecloth in the cavity of your bird. Leave the ends hanging out past the opening. Stuff the creature. Tie together the corners of the cheesecloth. After roasting, tug on the ends and pull out the stuffing in one go. Beauty!
* Pull the tail up. Sew the opening closed with a needle and thread.
* Create a closed door with a slice of firm, toasted bread.
* Cover the opening with a square of foil or folded parchment. This also prevents the stuffing from scorching.
* Pierce the skin and crisscross metal or bamboo skewers across the opening.

✧ Stuffing makes overcooking more likely. It slows interior cooking, which leads to longer oven times and dry meat. If the meat is your priority, cook the stuffing separately.

Cooking Stuffing Separately

* You can bake stuffing in a buttered foil packet or a greased, covered baking dish. Bake it at 350°F (180°C) for 20 minutes. Open the foil or uncover the baking dish. Bake until the top starts to brown, 10 to 15 minutes.
* If you want the stuffing moist, keep the dish covered. Uncover it earlier if you like a crisp top.
* For the crispiest stuffing, bake personal portions in muffin tins.
* Add an extra 2 tsp (10 mL) each butter and stock per 1 cup (250 mL) stuffing.

Better Leftovers

First there's the big meal, then come the big leftovers. The stuffing can be recycled in soup, along with the turkey.

Master Plan
Stuffing Soup

1. Break up the carcass and simmer it for 1 hour. Use as little water as possible — say about 10 cups (2.5 L) for a former 15-lb (7 kg) turkey.
2. Remove and discard the carcass. Strain the stock, then add leftover stuffing and a chopped onion. Simmer for 15 minutes.
3. Add diced fresh vegetables such as carrots. Simmer until they are tender.
4. If desired, add strips of diced, leftover turkey meat.

Macaroni and Cheese

✧ Macaroni and cheese requires a lot more sauce and cheese than you might think. Use cheese and raw pasta in equal amounts, by weight.

OUTSIDE THE BOX

You can make overnight mac and cheese starting with raw or almost raw pasta. It is super-rich if you use cream. Also, getting the texture and timing right is difficult. After baking, the pasta must be tender and most of the liquid absorbed.

Overnight Mac and Cheese

This is the strangest way to make macaroni and cheese. It is extremely creamy, but not very cheesy. Though not to everyone's taste, the recipe is widely disseminated. Paris chef Guy Savoy is credited with creating it. Chicago chef Grant Achatz makes a macaroni and Cheddar that can be left overnight, but he soaks the parboiled pasta in milk, not cream. Then there are the ordinary home cooks who, for many years, have been soaking raw macaroni overnight in canned soup mix and cheese before baking. **Makes 6 servings**

- **8-inch (20 cm) square baking dish**

8 oz	macaroni	250 g
2 cups	heavy or whipping (35%) cream	500 mL
1¼ cups	skim milk	300 mL
4 oz	Gruyère cheese, shredded, divided	125 g
	Salt and freshly ground black pepper	

1. In a pot of boiling salted water, cook macaroni for 4 minutes. Drain, cool it under cold running water, then drain thoroughly.

2. In a large bowl, combine macaroni, cream, milk, half the Gruyère and salt and pepper to taste. Tightly cover and refrigerate for at least 24 hours or up to 2 days.

3. Transfer the mixture to the baking dish. Let it come to room temperature. Meanwhile, preheat oven to 400°F (200°C).

4. Sprinkle the remaining Gruyère on top. Bake for about 30 minutes or until macaroni is tender and top is golden brown. Let stand for 15 minutes to absorb the remaining cream.

❖ You can't just stir together pasta and cheese. It separates in the oven. You wind up with dry pasta bathed in grease. Start with a béchamel, or white sauce, and stir the cheese into it.

❖ Keep macaroni and cheese creamy by baking it in a deep dish. Make it crusty by baking it in a wider, shallow dish.

More Ways to Cut the Creaminess

- The sauce thickens in the oven because the pasta sucks it up. Start with fairly thin sauce.
- Replace some or all of the milk with stock.
- Add Dijon or dry mustard to the sauce.

❖ Some cooks prefer to bind the macaroni and cheese with a custard-style sauce, but it curdles in the oven. How to prevent curdling:

- Use custardy sauces for stovetop macaroni and cheese only.
- Combine the eggs with evaporated milk or cream.

Gussy It Up

- Play with the noodles: Find interesting shapes.
- Play with the cheese: Use four cheeses. Include Gorgonzola or blue cheese for a kick. Use cheese with chiles or flavored cheese.
- Play with the sauce: Add a bit of tomato or Worcestershire sauce.
- Play with themes: Go south of the border with roasted poblano chiles and cilantro, or simply add Tex-Mex spice blend. Add smoked Spanish paprika. Go English with peas and parsley. Cross into retro Beefaroni territory by adding cooked ground beef.
- Play with the toppings: Try crushed Ritz crackers. For a crunchier topping, use panko. For an extra hit of cheese, sprinkle on a mixture of bread crumbs, butter and grated

Parmesan, then stick the dish under the broiler until crispy.

- Play with the extras: Add tidbits such as diced ham, smoked chicken or chorizo. Try flaked tuna or crumbled bacon. Stir in tiny broccoli florets, halved grape tomatoes, chopped green onions or whole cloves of roasted garlic.

Fast Fixes

- Process cheese, or American cheese, is the cheap, easy key to macaroni and cheese. It won't clump or get grainy when it melts. If you can stand the taste, simply mix it with cooked pasta.
- Stir together mac and cheese on the stove. Top it with bread crumbs or shredded cheese. Quickly brown it under the broiler.

Pot Pies

❖ Cut the raw dough generously to allow for shrinkage.

❖ Shield the underside of the dough from the steamy filling. Brush it with lightly beaten egg white.

❖ If your pot pie has a top crust only, give it something to cling to, so it doesn't shrink away from the sides. Roll strips of dough between your palms. Line the rim of the baking dish with the strips. Drape the top crust over the baking dish. Don't stretch it. Press the crust into the strips to create a seal. This works best on a baking dish with a flat rim. It also works well with top-crust-only fruit pies.

❖ Steam makes pot pie crusts soggy. Cheat. Heat the filling separately in a baking dish. Cut a pastry round a bit larger than the dish, to allow for shrinkage, then bake it. Set the pastry on top of the filling.

Better Leftovers

Turn stew into an instant pot pie. Cover the top with biscuit dough or pie pastry and bake.

Shepherd's Pie

3 Ways to Liven Up Bland Shepherd's Pie

1. Add parsnips or sweet potato to the mashed spud topping.
2. Use lamb instead of ground beef.
3. Add Guinness to the filling.

Quiche

✧ Before pouring the filling into the crust, place the pie plate on a baking sheet lined with foil. This will make transfers in and out of the oven easier, and will help with any cleanup.

✧ For a creamy texture, take the quiche out of the oven while the center is still slightly jiggly.

Ways to Avoid a Soggy Quiche

- Sauté or precook the vegetables, drain them well and pat them dry beforehand.
- Prebake the empty pie shell on high heat for 5 minutes before filling it. You can sprinkle some shredded cheese evenly into the shell beforehand to help seal it.
- Use whole milk or cream. Skim or light milk will make the quiche watery, and may even prevent it from setting properly; as a result, you might overbake the quiche because it doesn't look done.

OUTSIDE THE BOX

Make crustless quiche. Cook the filling in a well-buttered pie plate or individual ramekins.

Pizza

> **Factoid** Don't call it pizza pie. That's redundant. Pizza means "tomato pie" in Italian.

Standard Pizza Diameters
- **Small:** 11 inches (28 cm)
- **Medium:** 14 inches (35 cm)
- **Large:** 16 inches (40 cm)
- **Extra-large:** 18 inches (45 cm)

How Much?
- ✧ About 8 oz (250 g) of pizza dough is enough for a personal 9-inch (23 cm) pizza. One lb (500 g) of pizza dough makes a 12- to 14-inch (30 to 35 cm) pizza round or square, depending on how thin the crust is.

- ✧ Use an oven temperature of 450°F to 500°F (220°C to 260°C) and bake the pizza on the lowest rack. This makes the crust crispier.

Pizza Dough

- ✧ Use bread flour for pizza dough. It is made like bread dough, minus the second rise. Crispy and chewy, but not leathery, is the goal. Purists swear by Italian flour classified as 00 (finely milled). The flour should be at room temperature.

Tap Water **VS.** Spring Water?
Tap water gives pizza distinctive local flavor, according to proud pizza lovers in Chicago or New York. Others swear only spring water will do. In reality, the type you use will make no discernible difference.

Machines for Mixing Pizza Dough
- In a heavy-duty stand mixer with the paddle attachment, first blend the dough until it's cohesive but still ragged. Switch to the dough hook and knead on low speed for 5 minutes. The dough should climb up the hook.
- Make dough in a food processor with a plastic blade. Never use the metal blade. Pulse until the dough is smooth. Turn it out onto the counter and briefly knead it.
- Delegate the job to a bread machine.

- ✧ When the dough is mixed, pinch off a piece and feel it. Then make adjustments.

- ✧ A textured work surface is better than a smooth surface when kneading and stretching pizza dough. A granite counter is considered ideal.

- ✧ Refrigerate pizza dough overnight. It is less likely to tear, and makes a tangy, chewy crust.

- ✧ Pizza dough lasts up to a week in the fridge if left untouched. It can be punched down four times before the yeast is exhausted. Freezing the dough is more reliable.

- ✧ Whole wheat flour is too robust to go it alone in a pizza crust. Use at least 1 part white flour to 2 parts whole wheat flour. For grilled pizza, which is harder to handle, 4 parts white flour to 1 part whole wheat flour is recommended.

- Make double the amount of pizza dough you need and freeze half in individual portions. Defrost it in the fridge.

6 Keys to Stretching Pizza Dough

1. Plop the dough into a big bowl of flour. Pat and squeeze the perimeter to form a disc. Transfer it to a work surface dusted with flour.
2. Make a round of dough rather than an amoeba shape. Pinch the perimeter flat with both thumbs. Walk your fingers from the center to the north, south, east and west, to flatten and enlarge the circle. Turn the dough as you go. Repeat as needed.
3. For a thinner crust, hold the dough in the center with your palm and pull it outwards as you would pull taffy, to the north, south, east and west. Rotate the dough as you work. Repeat as needed.
4. Lift the dough periodically while you're stretching it, to make sure it's not sticking.
5. Cold dough is hard to stretch and doesn't bake properly. Let dough come to about 65°F (18°C) before using it.
6. If dough starts to resist stretching as you are kneading it, dust it with flour. If it's still stubborn, cover it with a damp kitchen towel and let it rest for 5 minutes.

- If the dough is divided, cover the piece you aren't stretching with a damp kitchen towel. (Do the same with bread dough.)

Extras
- Add a couple of spoonfuls of cornmeal to the dough. This makes it easier to handle, especially for the grill.
- Add 2 tbsp (25 mL) dry milk powder per 1 cup (250 mL) water. This creates a thicker crust with a crispy surface (albeit softer than a thin-crust pizza).

Gussy It Up
- You can add coarse spice blends, such as Tex-Mex seasoning, to pizza dough.
- To make garlic pizza dough, first heat minced garlic and the oil from the recipe in a small saucepan. Do not let the garlic brown. Let the mixture cool before using it in the recipe.
- With a rolling pin, press a bit of shredded cheese, some spices and minced fresh herbs into the dough. Use firm herbs, such as rosemary.
- Enhance the dough for a dessert pizza with honey and cinnamon.

OUTSIDE THE BOX
- You can stretch pizza dough over the bottom of a large bowl. Drape it, let it rest, then pull it down from the center. Rotate the bowl as you work.
- For a dessert pizza, you can dust the work surface with cinnamon sugar instead of flour before stretching the dough.

- If you need to transport stretched pizza dough across the kitchen, drape it over your forearm.

P is for Peel
A pizza peel is a paddle with a long handle. Use it to transfer your pizza into and out of the oven. If you love pizza, you'll need one. Buy a peel that's at least big enough for a large pizza.

Making Do

In a pinch, use a rimless baking sheet or the bottom of a jelly roll pan as a peel.

Pizza Peel Techniques

- To transfer the dough, lay a large flap over your knuckles and quickly turn the dough over and onto the peel.
- Add toppings to the pizza after transferring it to the pizza peel, not before.
- If the peel has a long handle, rest your forearm along it as a bolster.
- To coax a pizza into the oven, hold the peel firmly at the hilt and insert it deep into the oven. Give the peel a sharp jerk to make sure the dough is not sticking as you start to slide it into the oven. Tilt and shake the peel slightly to release the dough.
- To center pizza on a baking stone, jerk the peel back a couple of times.

- ❖ Cornmeal, flour or semolina can be sprinkled onto the peel first, to prevent the dough from sticking. But they cause gritty or burnt spots on the bottom of the crust. A better idea: Put a square of parchment on the peel.

Reasons to Use Parchment

- It can be used as a sizing guide. Just mark the diameter you're aiming for on the parchment, turn it over and stretch the dough on top of it. Then pull the parchment onto the peel. Reshape the dough, if necessary.
- Pizza on parchment is easy to slide into and out of the oven.
- If you wish, you can tug on it and slide it out once the crust firms up in the oven. The parchment does tend to brown at the edges, but I prefer to leave it in because one tug at the corner is all it takes to slide the pizza out of the oven and onto a cutting board.

- It keeps the pizza stone cleaner.
- You don't have to worry about whether your peel is wood or metal. Dough sticks less to a traditional wooden peel. But aluminum peels with wooden handles are also available.

- ❖ For dessert pizza, top the crust with about $\frac{1}{2}$ cup (125 mL) shredded mozzarella. It helps stop the crust from puffing as it prebakes, but doesn't influence the flavor.

- ❖ For a thicker pizza crust, stretch the dough to the desired diameter, cover it and let it rise for 30 to 45 minutes.

4 Steps to a Thin Crust

1. On a lightly floured work surface, knead the dough for 1 minute. Shape it into a disc about 1 inch (2.5 cm) thick. Place it on parchment.
2. Starting from the center, press out quickly with the heels of your hands, rotating the dough as you go, to create an even shape. Keep going until the dough is about $\frac{1}{2}$ inch (1 cm) thick. Generously dust it with flour as needed.
3. Rest one palm on the surface of the dough. With your other hand, lift one quadrant of the dough and gently pull it outward. Repeat, rotating the dough as you work, until it is $\frac{1}{8}$ to $\frac{1}{4}$ inch (0.25 to 0.5 cm) thick.
4. To finish, press with the edge of your hand to form a slight rim around the perimeter. Bake ASAP.

Advice on Using a Rolling Pin

- Finger-shaping the dough, the Neapolitan way, is best. You won't catch the Naples pizza guys with rolling pins in their hands. A rolling pin presses out air and leaves uneven patches. The patches become bruises or freckles on the crust.
- Having said that, using a rolling pin may be the only way to stretch a crust super-thin.
- A rolling pin is often used for drier, thinner New York–style crusts — although tossing is the preferred method.
- To use a rolling pin, first flour the top of the dough. Press the dough into a circle, then start rolling. Do not roll over the edges; keep them thicker than the center. Pick the dough up and turn it over several times to stretch it.

OUTSIDE THE BOX

To make extra-thin pizza crust, some cooks roll the dough through a pasta machine.

❖ Your pizza needn't be round. Instead of wrestling with the dough, try a Middle Eastern oval or a big-eater rectangle. A rough-hewn crust has its own attractions, particularly if it has grill marks.

❖ Determined to toss pizza dough? Start small. Balance the dough by putting the knuckles of both hands under the center. Maneuver a few short rotations. Work your way up to higher, bolder, circular tosses, using the same motion.

Fast Fix

Use whole-grain pitas as crusts for personal pizzas. For a thin crust, use scissors to cut a pocket pita into two circles. For a thicker crust, use a Greek-style pita (without a pocket).

How to Shape Deep-Dish Pizza

1. Use a 10-inch (25 cm) cast-iron skillet and a pliable cornmeal dough.
2. Lightly sprinkle cornmeal in the skillet.
3. Put a 12-inch (30 cm) round of dough into the skillet. Press the edges against the sides of the skillet to make the dough look like a pie shell. Pinch around the top to even out the rim.
4. For a thicker crust, let the dough rise for 20 minutes before filling it.
5. For a thinner crust, fill and bake it right away.

How to Transform a Pizza Recipe into Calzones

1. For each calzone, use an 8-inch (20 cm) round of dough.
2. Spread the toppings over half the dough.
3. Fold the top over to create a semicircle. Pinch the edges closed by pressing with the tines of a fork.
4. Rub the top with olive oil.
5. Transfer to a preheated pizza stone or directly onto an oven rack. Bake at 400°F (200°C) for 20 to 30 minutes.

C is for Conditioning

A pizza crust may be conditioned, or smeared with an oil mixture, before the toppings go on. Conditioning assists in browning, combats sogginess and adds deliciousness. The jury is still out on this one, but some aficionados swear that conditioning prevents toppings from sliding off. A sample conditioner: Combine 2 tbsp (25 mL) extra virgin olive oil, 1 pressed garlic clove and $\frac{1}{2}$ tsp (2 mL) granulated sugar. Lightly brush the mixture onto the dough, right to the edges.

Toppings

Matching Dough and Toppings

- Use denser whole wheat dough with lighter toppings, such as vegetables.
- Use lighter white dough for meaty or thick toppings.

◆ Reasons to leave a $\frac{1}{2}$-inch (1 cm) border when you spread sauce and toppings on pizza:
- The border makes a slice easier to hold.
- It helps prevent melted cheese from drooling over the sides.

◆ To spread sauce on pizza dough, use the bottom of a ladle, swirling it outward from the center.

Ⓢ is for San Marzano

The San Marzano is the preferred tomato for pizza. It's a type of plum tomato originally grown in volcanic soil near Naples. It's thick-skinned, with a flavor described as bittersweet. You can buy canned San Marzanos in some supermarkets.

Master Plan
Intense Pizza Sauce Without Opening a Can

1. Use 8 chopped fresh plum tomatoes, $\frac{1}{2}$ cup (125 mL) extra virgin olive oil, lots of minced garlic and dried oregano.
2. Cook in a 10-inch (25 cm) skillet to encourage evaporation. Stirring and breaking up the tomatoes occasionally, keep the mixture screaming over high heat until it is concentrated, 10 to 15 minutes.
3. Remove the skillet from the heat when the tomatoes are soft and caramelized, and the oil is starting to separate out.
4. Season with salt and pepper.

Keys to Cheese

- You don't need as much cheese on a pizza as you might think. You just have to grate instead of shred. Grated cheese goes further.
- Grate the cheese in a food processor fitted with the large-grate metal disc.
- Grated cheese won't clump if you toss it with dried herbs. It also tastes better and you wind up using less. Add 1 tbsp (15 mL) of any Italian herb blend per 1 lb (500 g) cheese.

◆ When putting chicken or another lean meat on pizza, position it under the cheese, so it doesn't dry out. Use chicken breast rather than dark meat. It's lean, so it's a better match with the rich cheese.

◆ Sauté onions and peppers before putting them on a pizza, or they won't cook enough.

OUTSIDE THE BOX

For a nifty presentation, lightly press two ropes of dough in an X across the top of a dough round. Put separate toppings in each section instead of mixing them up. I have seen this technique used on traditional *quattro stagione* (four seasons) pizzas.

◆ Sprinkle fresh herbs on pizza only after it comes out of the oven. They will stick to the cheese yet remain vibrant and uplifting.

Pesto Tips

- Brush pesto or oil over the exposed edges of pizza if it comes out of the oven looking dry.
- To make a plain pesto pizza, bake the crust first, then slather it with pesto. The pine nuts and basil are too sensitive to survive the high heat.

Pizza Margherita

My version of an Italian classic. Margherita proves you don't need a loaded pizza to hit the mark. **Makes 1 medium pizza**

- **Pizza stone**

Tips

I used Neapolitan-style dough, made with bread flour and olive oil.

Pizza Margherita is traditionally made with buffalo mozzarella, but is just as good with fresh cow's milk mozzarella, or fiore de latte. Fresh mozzarella is soft and white, and sits in whey. The yellow rubbery balls of more aged mozzarella won't do.

The cheese melts and drips. Don't put it too close to the edge of the crust.

Variation

It's hard to make a pizza Margherita with perfect circles of fresh mozzarella. If you want to take a stab at it, bake the pizza without the cheese. Turn off the heat. Arrange the mozzarella circles on top. Return the pizza to the oven just until the cheese barely melts. This can take less than a minute. Carefully remove the pizza from the oven; you don't want the cheese to shift. It may do so despite your best efforts.

Herbed Conditioning Oil

2 tbsp	extra virgin olive oil	25 mL
1½ tsp	kosher salt	7 mL
¼ tsp	dried oregano	1 mL
⅛ tsp	freshly ground black pepper	0.5 mL
2	cloves garlic, minced	2

Pizza

1 lb	pizza dough	500 g
8 oz	fresh mozzarella cheese ball, drained, sliced ¼ inch (0.5 cm) thick and patted dry	250 g
2	plum (Roma) tomatoes (about 8 oz/250 g total), sliced ¼ inch (0.5 cm) thick	2
10	large basil leaves, torn	10

1. Place the pizza stone in the oven. Preheat the oven to 500°F (260°C). Heat the stone for 30 to 60 minutes.

2. *Herbed conditioning oil:* In a small bowl, stir together oil, salt, oregano, pepper and garlic. Set aside.

3. *Pizza:* Stretch dough to a 12-inch (30 cm) round or square. Brush conditioning oil right to the edges of the dough. Arrange mozzarella evenly over the top, then the tomatoes.

4. Bake for about 12 minutes or until the bottom is golden brown and the cheese bubbles and spreads. Remove from oven. Scatter basil over top. Let cool for 5 minutes before cutting.

❖ A crust baked on its own, or with only a thin layer of herbed oil or sauce, will bubble up. Prick it all over with a fork beforehand. Check it often as it bakes, and pierce large bubbles with a sharp knife or skewer.

Cooking Pizza

Stone VS. Screen?

Bake pizza on a terra-cotta or ceramic stone. A pizza screen is a perforated metal sheet. It's an inferior alternative. Even cooking directly on an oven rack is better.

Advantages of a Pizza Stone

- It creates even heat in the oven.
- It transfers heat to the pizza.
- It browns the crust uniformly.
- It makes the crust crispier by absorbing moisture.

Pizza Stone Tips

- Buy the largest stone that will fit in your oven, so you can make big pizzas. It should be at least $1/2$ inch (1 cm) thick.
- Make sure your stone is flat. Raised edges make it harder to slide the pizza on and off.
- A rectangular stone is handier than a round one.
- Preheat the stone in the oven for 30 to 60 minutes before baking. When the pizza is done, let the stone cool in the oven.

Making Do

Unglazed tiles can be substituted for pizza stones. However, this hardly seems necessary now that the stones are so easy to find.

❖ A crust baked on a pizza screen is not as crispy and chewy. If you want to use a screen, oil it to stop the dough from sticking.

✿ Waste Not

You can recycle a pizza screen as a grilling pan on the barbecue.

Pizza Doctor

I tore a hole in the dough.
- Pinch it closed. Cornmeal and whole wheat doughs tear more easily.

The crust is chewy.
- You made the dough too sticky. Next time, add a bit more flour or use less water.

The crust is like cardboard.
- You left the dough too dry and crumbly. You can adjust dough by adding 1 spoonful of water at a time. Humidity in the air will affect the amount of water you need.

The crust is tough.
- Too much kneading toughens the crust because it builds gluten. Pizza dough should be as soft as a baby's butt, and a bit sticky.

The crust is burnt.
- A pizza doesn't take long at 500°F (260°C). Pull it out when the crust is golden brown and the toppings are sizzling, say 10 to 15 minutes.
- To see if the bottom of the crust is done, lift one edge with a long metal spatula.

The pizza is soggy.
- Toppings with a lot of moisture should be added last.
- Don't top a pizza with raw mushrooms. They're too wet. Sauté sliced mushrooms in oil over medium-high heat until they are browned and their liquid has evaporated. But do not cook them until they are limp and dark.
- Drain sliced fresh tomatoes before putting them on pizza.
- If you have a lot of wet toppings, such as ricotta and spinach, lower the oven temperature by 25°F (10°C) and increase the baking time. Or bake the pizza at 500°F (260°C) on the top rack for 10 minutes, then slide it onto a preheated stone on the second rack from the bottom.

- After taking it out of the oven, wait for 5 minutes before slicing homemade pizza. The cheese won't ooze as much.

- Cut your creation with a pizza wheel. The rolling blade should be at least 4 inches (10 cm) in diameter.

- You can reheat pizza in a dry, nonstick skillet or cast-iron pan over low heat. The crust will stay crisp and the toppings are less likely to dry out.

No-Nos

- Do not cover a cooked pizza with foil to keep it warm. It will get soggy. A better alternative: Bake pizza 1 to 2 hours ahead, then briefly reheat it in a 500°F (260°C) oven.
- Reheating pizza in the microwave makes the crust too soft and chewy.

Grilling Pizza

- You can grill crusts ahead of time. Wrap each one in plastic and refrigerate it for up to 3 days. Or freeze it for up to a month.

---

8 Steps to Grilled Pizza

1. Press out each round of dough just before putting it on the grill. It can get sticky sitting around on the counter, especially on a hot, humid day.

2. Lightly oil a flat metal tray or the bottom of a rimmed baking sheet, then sprinkle it with cornmeal. (Or use a metal pizza peel if you have one.) Gently fold the dough in half, place it on the tray and unfold it. It's easier to slide dough onto the grill from a metal tray than from a wooden pizza peel, which can scorch.

3. If you're grilling thicker pizza dough, use a lower heat to allow the interior to cook before the outside burns.

4. Grill the crust, but don't turn it. Once it is set, lift to check for a golden brown color and grill marks.

5. You don't need to pop any bubbles on top. The browned side will become the top of your pizza.

6. Flip the crust by gripping it in the middle with long tongs. Place the pizza over indirect heat. Add the toppings. Keep them light.

7. Close the lid and grill until the bottom has browned and the toppings are bubbly.

8. After grilling, you can crisp the toppings under the broiler.

Global Cuisine

Falafels

✧ Raw chickpeas are the key to better falafels. Soak them for 12 to 24 hours before puréeing.

✗ No-Nos

• Don't try to cook the soaked, raw chickpeas before puréeing them with the rest of the ingredients.

• Do not use canned chickpeas. Your falafels will be mushy and fall apart.

✧ Avoid those green falafels. Add chopped parsley and/or cilantro only after puréeing the main ingredients, then blend briefly. Your falafels should be yellow with green flecks.

✧ Add baking soda to the falafel mixture for lightness. Use about 1 tsp (5 mL) baking soda for every 8 oz (250 g) dried chickpeas you start with.

✧ Let the mixture stand for 30 to 45 minutes to dry a bit before frying.

✧ The ideal falafel mixture is soft, but should hold its shape in the hot oil.

✧ Make it easier to pat the soft mixture into discs: Put a dollop onto a square of waxed paper, then pat it into shape with your fingers.

✧ Poke an indent into the center of the disc with your pinkie. The falafel will cook more evenly.

Tahini Sauce

Tahini sauce is essential for falafels. You can also use it to moisten vegetable wraps.
Makes about 1 cup (250 mL)

Tips

Tahini is sesame seed paste. It is sold in many supermarkets.

You can substitute cilantro for the parsley.

3	cloves garlic	3
½ cup	tahini	125 mL
⅓ cup	freshly squeezed lemon juice	75 mL
¼ cup	extra virgin olive oil	50 mL
¼ cup	warm water	50 mL
2 tbsp	chopped fresh parsley	25 mL
½ tsp	kosher salt	2 mL
½ tsp	ground cumin	2 mL

1. In a food processor, mince garlic. Add tahini, lemon juice, oil, water, parsley, salt and cumin. Blend until smooth and thick.

Falafel Patties

Put hot patties in pita pockets. Drizzle them with tahini sauce. Stuff the pockets with shredded lettuce, thinly sliced red onion, chopped tomato and diced cucumber. Finish with a dash of hot sauce. Yum! **Makes about 26 patties**

- **13- by 9-inch (33 by 23 cm) baking dish**

Tip

Falafel patties don't hold up well. Serve them hot, and immediately.

8 oz	dried chickpeas (about 1¼ cups/300 mL)	250 g
3	large cloves garlic, quartered	3
1	onion, diced	1
2 tsp	kosher salt	10 mL
1 tsp	baking soda	5 mL
1 tsp	ground cumin	5 mL
1 tsp	ground coriander	5 mL
¼ tsp	freshly ground black pepper	1 mL
⅛ tsp	cayenne pepper	0.5 mL
¼ cup	packed fresh parsley leaves	50 mL
¼ cup	packed fresh cilantro leaves	50 mL
	Vegetable oil	

1. In a large bowl, cover chickpeas generously with water. Soak for 12 to 24 hours. Drain well.

2. In a food processor, finely chop chickpeas. Add garlic, onion, salt, baking soda, cumin, coriander, black pepper and cayenne. Purée until smooth, about 1 minute. Scrape the bowl. Add parsley and cilantro. Process briefly, until the mixture is flecked with chopped herbs.

3. Spread the purée in the baking dish. Let stand for 30 to 45 minutes. Meanwhile, preheat oven to 200°F (100°C).

4. For each falafel patty, scoop 2 tbsp (25 mL) purée onto a square of waxed paper. Shape it with your fingers into a 2-inch (5 cm) disc. Flip it onto a large sheet of waxed paper. Poke an indent in the center with your pinkie.

5. Heat a deep fryer to 350°F (180°C). (Alternatively, fill a deep, wide pan with 1 to 2 inches/2.5 to 5 cm of oil and heat over medium heat until a candy/deep-fry thermometer registers 350°F/180°C or the oil is very shimmery.) Test a patty by frying it until browned and crunchy, turning as needed, about 2 minutes. If the oil is too hot, reduce heat to 325°F (160°C).

6. Fry 4 to 6 patties at a time. Transfer them to a heatproof platter or baking sheet lined with paper towels. Keep the batches warm in the oven.

Sushi

✧ Use only sushi rice. Other types won't work. The rice has to stick properly.

✘ No-No

Don't substitute orange or red roe from the supermarket for the Japanese orange tobiko, or flying-fish roe.

✧ Japanese shops sell long rolls of imitation crab, or surimi, that match the length of a sheet of nori.

✧ Japanese shops sell toasted sesame seeds for sushi, as well as black sesame seeds and mixed beige and black seeds. Otherwise, you can toast your own.

✧ Cut sushi (maki rolls) using a small, sharp knife moistened with cold water.

Sushi Rice

A few small touches transform plain rice into a savory base for maki, nigiri and other types of sushi. **Makes about 8 cups (2 L)**

Tips

The flavor should be subtle.

Some cooks use seasoned rice vinegar instead of adding sugar and salt separately.

2 cups	sushi rice	500 mL
	Salt	
½ cup	unseasoned rice vinegar	125 mL
3 tbsp	granulated sugar	45 mL
1 tbsp	sea salt	15 mL

1. Rinse rice very well in cold water and drain. Put rice in a medium saucepan and add about 2½ cups (625 mL) cold water and salt to taste. Let stand for 1 hour.

2. Bring the rice mixture to a boil over medium-high heat. Reduce heat to low. Cover and simmer for 12 to 15 minutes or until water is absorbed. Cover the pan with a clean kitchen towel, then the lid. Let stand for 10 minutes.

3. In a small microwave-safe bowl, stir together vinegar, sugar and salt. Heat it in the microwave on High for 30 seconds or just until warm.

4. Spread the rice on a baking sheet. Drizzle the vinegar mixture over top. Using a thin metal spatula with a short handle, gently mix with folding and scooping motions. Do not stab or crush. While mixing, fan the mixture or enlist a helper to do it. Mix until the vinegar is absorbed and the rice has cooled, about 5 minutes. It should be moist and shiny, not mushy.

Master Plan
Sushi Rolls (Maki)

1. Place a sushi mat on a large cutting board. Put a medium bowl of cold water next to the board.

2. Lay one sheet of toasted nori horizontally on the mat, with the smoother, shiny side down. In this position, the perforated lines on the nori will be vertical.

3. Dump prepared sushi rice onto the nori. You'll need 1 to 1¼ cups (250 to 300 mL).

4. Moisten your fingers. Spread the rice over the nori, patting it down gently. Spread it all the way to the east, west and south edges, but leave a ¼-inch (0.5 cm) gap at the north end. Keep moistening your fingers; the rice should be very sticky.

5. Place fillings horizontally across the nori, starting almost at the center. Arrange each filling in a single line.

6. With the help of the sushi mat, fold and tuck the south edge of the nori over the fillings. Before you start rolling, run your fingers from the center out to the edges, to shape an even cylinder. Finish rolling.

7. Starting at the north end, roll the sushi mat around the filled nori. Press and squeeze along the length to create a firm roll.

8. Remove the roll from the mat. Slice off the ends if they're ragged or if the filling protrudes. Cut each roll in half crosswise, then cut each half crosswise into 4 slices.

Tacos and Tortillas

✧ Hard taco shells are easier to fill if you perch them upright between the cups on an overturned muffin tin. Some oven racks have the right spacing to hold them, too.

✘ No-No
Don't substitute wheat tortillas for corn tortillas in a recipe. They are very different.

✧ Line a hard taco with lettuce before putting in the filling. If (or rather when) the taco cracks, the filling won't leak or fall out.

✧ When serving taco salad in a tortilla bowl, line the bottom with lettuce leaves before adding the beef chili, so it doesn't soak through. Top the chili with grated cheese and garnishes such as chopped red onions and sliced avocado. No need for salad dressing.

♡ Healthier Eater
Enjoy salad in a tortilla bowl without breaking the calorie bank. Normally the bowls are fried. Make baked bowls instead.

• Brush large wheat tortillas with vegetable oil on both sides. Sprinkle them with salt and pepper. Press the bottoms into large custard cups. Bake them on the second rack from the bottom in a 400°F (200°C) oven until crispy, about 10 minutes.

• Place a whole wheat tortilla over a deep, narrow bowl. Ruffle the edges as you gently push it into the bowl. Bake it at 350°F (180°C) for 15 to 20 minutes or until the edges and bottom are golden brown. (This will cook faster, but less evenly, at a higher temperature.)

• Make an unbaked bowl. Microwave an 8-inch (20 cm) flour tortilla on High until it softens, about 15 seconds. Drape it over a small, inverted bowl, no more than 4 inches (10 cm) in diameter. Let it cool, then loosen it and set it upright on a rack.

✧ You can replace tart shells with sweet tortilla shells. Use small wheat tortillas. Lightly coat one side of each tortilla with oil. Sprinkle on sugar and cinnamon. Press the tortillas, oil side up, into muffin tins and flute to fit. Bake at 375°F (190°C) for about 10 minutes or until crisp and golden. Let them cool before adding fruit and ice cream or other fillings.

Better Leftovers

Turn corn tortillas into tortilla chips.

1. Cut 6-inch (15 cm) tortillas into 8 wedges each. Or cut larger tortillas into 1-inch (2.5 cm) strips.
2. In a large skillet, heat ¼ inch (0.5 cm) of oil over medium-high heat until it is shimmery.
3. Fry the wedges or strips for 30 to 60 seconds or until they start to turn golden. Do not brown them.
4. Drain them on paper towels.

Ways to Warm Corn Tortillas

- Wrap them in a damp paper towel, then in foil, and heat in a 300°F (150°C) oven.
- Wrap them in a damp kitchen towel and microwave them.
- Wrap a stack in a clean kitchen towel. Place in a steamer over simmering water. Steam for 1 minute. Let stand for 10 minutes.
- Warm them in a hot, dry skillet for about 30 seconds per side.
- To make corn tortillas more pliable for filling, Mexicans soften them by dipping them into hot oil in a skillet. It's less fatty and messy to spray or brush each tortilla with oil, then bake it at 300°F (150°C) for 2 minutes. Better still: Zap each one in the microwave on High for 20 to 30 seconds.

OUTSIDE THE BOX

Turn a flour tortilla into a makeshift Mexican crêpe. Fill it with tropical fruit, whipped cream and dulce de leche (milk caramel).

Ways to Warm Flour Tortillas

- Stack them in a parchment packet or wrapped in a damp towel. Microwave, seam side down. Microwave 4 large tortillas on High for 1 minute.
- To revive a single large tortilla, roll it up in a damp paper towel and microwave on High for 20 seconds.

♻ Waste Not

Garnish salads with the broken corn tortilla chips left in the bottom of the bag.

Yorkshire Pudding

♛ A Golden Rule

Cold batter, hot pan.

Batter Tips

- It should be the consistency of heavy cream, no thicker, not like whipped cream.
- Use whole or 2% milk.
- Refrigerate the batter until the roast is ready. The batter can be made the night before and kept cold in the fridge.
- Transfer the batter to a pitcher for fast pouring.

◆ Individual Yorkshire puddings are the best. Make them in a muffin tin or ¾-cup (175 mL) ramekins set on a rimmed baking sheet.

◆ Once the roast is removed from the oven, make Yorkshire pudding using the drippings. Use about 1 tsp (5 mL) drippings per muffin cup or ramekin. Heat the drippings until they sizzle.

- ◇ Fill each muffin cup or ramekin between half and three-quarters. The intense heat causes the puddings to rise dramatically. They don't (or shouldn't) fall much after they are removed from the oven.

- ◇ Once the Yorkshire puddings are cooked, pierce them with the tip of a sharp knife to release the steam that can make them soggy.

- ◇ They should really be served hot from the oven, but can be kept warm at 200°F (100°C) for 15 minutes.

- ◇ Old-fashioned Yorkshire pudding is made in the roasting pan. Heat the pan with drippings in a 400°F (200°C) oven for 5 minutes or until you hear sizzling. Pour in the cold batter. Bake until the pudding has risen and browned.

Yorkshire Puddings

Fab! These high-rise puddings have a crusty brown exterior with characteristic double peaks, and a soft, chewy interior with a large air cavity. **Makes 18 puddings**

- **18 muffin cups**

Tip

Make these while the roast rests, tented in foil.

Variation

If you don't have drippings or even a roast, substitute flavorful oil.

2 cups	all-purpose flour	500 mL
1 tsp	kosher salt	5 mL
	Freshly ground black pepper	
4	large eggs	4
2 1/2 cups	milk, divided	625 mL
6 tbsp	roast beef drippings	90 mL

1. In a large bowl, whisk together flour, salt and pepper to taste. Make a well in the center. Add eggs and 1/2 cup (125 mL) of the milk. Whisk into a paste, gradually pulling flour in from the edges. Whisk in the remaining milk until batter is the consistency of heavy cream. Cover and refrigerate for several hours or overnight. The batter should be very cold.

2. Preheat oven to 400°F (200°C). Using a pastry brush, grease muffin cups with drippings. Spoon 1 tsp (5 mL) drippings into each cup. Heat in the oven for 5 minutes or until sizzling.

3. Immediately pour in cold batter, filling each cup half to three-quarters full. Bake for 25 to 30 minutes or until puddings are browned and puffed.

Baked Goods and Sweets

Recipes

Baking Basics

Greasing and Dusting Pans

✧ It's best to grease a pan with shortening or oil. Butter has a lot of moisture and is prone to scorching. Breads and cakes stick more readily to it. If you want to use butter, apply plenty.

✧ Grease pans liberally. The grease should be visible.

✧ To grease a pan evenly, paint on the grease with a pastry brush rather than smearing it.

ⓢ is for Super-Greasing

If you are in a dire, sticky situation, super-grease that pan or mold. Brush it liberally with softened (not melted) butter or shortening. Refrigerate or freeze the pan until the fat is solid. Brush with more softened butter or shortening, or oil. Put the pan into the fridge or freezer until the butter is firm. When baking, you'll have to compensate for the cold pan by adding time.

✧ When spraying muffin tins or baking dishes with oil, lay them on the open door of your dishwasher. It's less messy.

✧ If you don't like the white residue from flour, dust pans with bread crumbs, sugar or cocoa powder.

✧ Dust greased pans with flour over your flour container or a sheet of waxed paper. Dump out the excess flour in the pan. Rap the pan to loosen extra flour. Use the paper to funnel the flour back into the container.

✧ Spray paper baking cups with oil to make them easier to peel off muffins or cupcakes. Avoid nonstick paper cups; they don't cling at all.

Keeping Your Cool

✧ Cold hands are not helpful in romance, but they're an asset in the kitchen. Butter and chocolate, for example, melt at close to body temperature. Keep hands especially cold when working with pie pastry, biscuit dough and truffles (not to mention meatballs and burger patties).

✧ Dry your chilled hands well before proceeding with the recipe.

Ways to Keep Your Hands Cold

- Rub an ice cube over your palms.
- Run cold water over your hands.
- Press your hands against an ice pack.

Ways to Create a Cool Work Surface

- Use a marble or granite slab. It's the ideal surface for rolling out pie pastry, making candy or working with chocolate. Stick protective pads on the underside, if you wish.
- Set a baking sheet loaded with ice on the counter until the surface is cold.
- Put a large cutting board in the freezer.

- ❖ Store your rolling pin and pastry cloth in the freezer. This also keeps odors at bay. (Pastry cloth becomes embedded with dough and starts to smell stale or rancid.)

Ingredients for Baked Goods

- ❖ Bake with bottled water if your tap water is hard, minerally or strong-tasting.

- ❖ Flour can vary by 20% in its ability to absorb moisture. So a recipe may not work out quite the same from one day to the next. On a damp day, the flour will absorb less liquid from the recipe.

Balancing Flour and Water

- If a range is given in the recipe, start with the smallest amount of flour and add gradually.

Lower-Fat Brownies

These dense, chewy brownies can compete with the best of them. **Makes 18 bars**

- **Preheat oven to 350°F (180°C)**

- **13- by 9-inch (33 by 23 cm) baking pan, greased and floured**

Tips

Don't use century-old prunes; they should be plump.

Buy pitted prunes and purée them in a food processor.

Variations

Use ½ cup (125 mL) unsweetened applesauce instead of the prune purée. These specimens will be moister and cake-like, not as dense as regular brownies.

You can add walnut pieces; stir them into the batter at the end.

1 cup	all-purpose flour	250 mL
¾ cup	unsweetened cocoa powder	175 mL
2 tsp	baking powder	10 mL
½ cup	unsalted butter, at room temperature	125 mL
1 cup	granulated sugar	250 mL
1 cup	packed brown sugar	250 mL
½ cup	packed prune purée (about 4 oz/125 g)	125 mL
3	large eggs	3
2 tsp	vanilla extract	10 mL

1. In a medium bowl, sift together flour, cocoa and baking powder. Set aside.

2. In a large bowl, using an electric mixer, beat butter on medium speed until fluffy. Add granulated and brown sugars; beat until blended and light. Beat in prune purée. Beat in eggs, one at a time. Beat in vanilla. Scrape sides of bowl. Add flour mixture. Beat on low speed just until blended (batter will be very thick).

3. Scrape batter into prepared pan. Spread with a spatula, smoothing top. Bake in preheated oven for 25 to 30 minutes or until a tester inserted in the center comes out almost clean. (The center will still feel a bit soft.) Let cool completely in pan on a wire rack before cutting.

- Don't add all the water from a recipe. Mix, test and add the final amount at the end, if necessary.
- Add any extra liquid 1 tbsp (15 mL) at a time.
- It's better to add less water than to add more flour.
- Generally, you add water only until the flour mixture is no longer sticky and pulls away from the sides of the bowl.
- Err on the side of softness over dryness.

✧ Don't forget to add a pinch of salt to pie fillings and pastries to bring out the sweetness.

✧ To distribute salt more evenly without excessive mixing, dissolve it in the water, milk or other liquid from the recipe.

Ⓢ is for Short Pastry

Puzzled when you come across this term? It's the old-fashioned description for pastry that has fat added to the flour to "shorten" the gluten strands or masses, in pursuit of tenderness.

Healthier Eater

You can replace up to half the butter in a recipe with mashed or puréed fruit.

Fruit Fillers

- Prune purée
- Applesauce
- Mashed bananas
- Puréed figs
- Puréed dried dates

✧ Peel plums for dumplings, cobblers and other sweets. The peel is bitter. You can leave the skins on peaches and apricots.

Leaveners

✧ There's more than one way to get a rise out of breads, cakes, muffins, quick breads, biscuits and popovers, but it all comes down to gas and steam. Baking soda, baking powder and yeast create gases. Baked goods also get a lift from the air bubbles captured in whipped egg whites and creamed butter, and the steam from melting fat and moist dough. The oven's heat sets the batter or dough around the air pockets.

Baking Soda and Baking Powder

Baking Soda VS. Baking Powder?

Baking soda is the same bicarbonate of soda that goes fizz, fizz to get rid of your stomach ache. It is alkaline. Activated by moisture and an acid, it produces carbon dioxide bubbles.

Baking powder is a blend of baking soda, an acid or two and starch (usually cornstarch) to absorb any moisture that might cause premature activation. Single-acting baking powder (gone from the modern picture) needs only moisture to enthusiastically go to work. Double-acting baking powder releases some gases when moisture is added, but waits for heat before finishing the job. The bubbles get bigger in the oven.

- Don't be cavalier. Use whichever one the recipe specifies.
- Recipes with acidic ingredients, such as buttermilk, lemon juice, vinegar, cream of tartar, fruit or even molasses, are fine with baking soda.
- Baking powder supplies the acid for recipes that don't have any, or enough.
- Sometimes a recipe calls for both. Chocolate and honey, for instance, are acidic, but perhaps not enough.

✧ Bake batter containing baking soda right away. It gets feeble. Batter with double-acting baking powder can sit for a few hours.

✗ No-No

Never dip a moist spoon into baking powder or baking soda.

- ✦ Signs you've used too much baking powder or baking soda:
  - There's a bad, soapy taste.
  - Gas bubbles get too big, rise to the top of the batter and burst. Your creation falls flat.
  - Cherries and raspberries turn blue.
  - Sunflower seeds go green.
  - Blueberries turn greenish in the batter.

Freshness Tests

- Stir 1 tsp (5 mL) baking soda into 2 tbsp (25 mL) white vinegar. It should bubble delightfully.
- Test baking powder by adding 1 tsp (5 mL) to ⅓ cup (75 mL) hot water. It should immediately fizz and foam.
- ✦ If either is sluggish or moribund, throw it away.

- ✦ Baking soda has a shelf life of either a couple of years or eternity, depending on what source you believe. Baking powder keeps for up to 1 year.

- ✦ After you open the baking powder can or tub, write the date on it. Test it after 6 months.

is for Hartshorn

You might stumble across this precursor of baking powder in an historic recipe. It was ground from antlers, hence the name. You may also encounter it as "baking ammonia." The name is apt. It is reputed to give baked goods a nasty ammonia odor unless they are small and stay in the oven for a long time.

- ✦ Replace hartshorn with a 1:1 mixture of baking powder and baking soda.

Making Do

If you don't have baking powder, sift together 2 parts cream of tartar with 1 part each baking soda and cornstarch. Or use baking soda and add some vinegar or lemon juice to your recipe.

Yeast

It's Alive!

- ✦ Yeast is alive. Give it sugar or starch, and it will eat. Offer it moisture and warmth, and it will grow. In return, it produces the carbon dioxide, alcohol and acids that make dough rise and taste good.

Types of Yeast

- **Fresh yeast:** The pros love fresh compressed yeast, or cake yeast. But it is so perishable it must be used within 2 days. Moist, tan-colored and crumbly, it can be cut with a wire cheese slicer.
- **Active dry yeast:** Here's your supermarket yeast. Dehydrated and dormant, it is in the form of granules waiting to be awakened with water.
- **Instant yeast:** It's not really instant, but it is quick. Also known as rapid-rise, this yeast comes in smaller granules, with a bit of ascorbic acid. By eliminating the first rise, it halves the total rising time. Instant yeast is popular with the bread machine gang.
- **Wild yeast:** If you're making sourdough, you may stalk the elusive wild yeast, but not with a butterfly net. Spores are captured from the air via a sloppy, loose dough, or "starter." It must be fed and nurtured, and is sensitive to high heat and drafts. A starter can take months to become strong and stable.
- **Brewer's yeast:** This deactivated yeast is eaten for nutrition, rather than used for leavening. It is sold in health food stores. The brown type is supposed to be more bitter than the yellow type.

⚛ A Bit of Science

Kneading develops gluten strands in dough. The gluten captures the gas from the yeast in pockets, so the dough rises evenly. As long as they get food and oxygen, the yeast cells divide, multiply and produce more gas. If the temperature dips below 1°F (17°C), the yeast goes dormant. Once the oven hits 130°F to 140°F (54°C to 60°C), the yeast cells die.

❖ A single pouch of active dry yeast weighs $\frac{1}{4}$ oz (7 g) and contains about $2\frac{1}{2}$ tsp (12 mL). Use it in place of a 0.6-oz (17 g) cake of yeast.

Ⓟ is for Proofing

Active dry yeast must prove itself worthy of merging with the dough.

- Sprinkle yeast into water with a bit of sugar. Let the mixture stand for 5 minutes. It should become smooth and beige, with a topping of foam. Then it's ready to go into your dough.
- If you don't want to use sugar, the yeast will accept a sprinkling of flour.
- You can use milk instead of the water, though the yeast tends to clump in it.
- In some bread recipes, yeast is proofed in a thick "sponge" with some of the flour from the recipe. It should bubble within 10 minutes.

❖ Proof yeast in lukewarm to warm water, between say 105°F (41°C) and 110°F (43°C). One finicky chef mixes 2 parts cold tap water with 1 part boiling water to get the temperature right. You needn't be so obsessive. Just splash some on your wrist or stick your finger in it. The water should feel barely warm.

❖ Instant yeast mixed with dry ingredients can stand warmer water of up to 120°F (49°C). It should not feel uncomfortable.

❖ Store yeast in the fridge or freezer. Let it come to room temperature before using.

Factoid Once yeast is stirred into water, it must be fed with sugar or flour within 15 minutes or it will die.

Freshness Tips

- Always note the expiry date on the package.
- If you want to check your stash, here's a formal test: Dissolve 1 tsp (5 mL) granulated sugar in $\frac{1}{2}$ cup (125 mL) lukewarm water. Sprinkle in 1 packet of yeast. The mixture should develop a gnarly head of foam and slowly reach the 1-cup (250 mL) mark. If there are no signs of life within 10 minutes, throw the yeast out.
- Try the potato test: Sprinkle a packet of yeast into lukewarm potato cooking water (it's rich with starch). Wait for 5 to 10 minutes. If the yeast clumps and the water stays clear, discard the yeast.
- To revive tired yeast, cook a chopped potato in unsalted water until tender. Combine $\frac{1}{4}$ cup (50 mL) of the warm cooking water, 1 tsp (5 mL) granulated sugar and 1 packet of yeast. Let it stand for up to 15 minutes. If it bubbles and doubles, use it.

❖ Two $\frac{1}{4}$-oz (7 g) packets of yeast should raise dough made with 4 cups (1 L) flour in $1\frac{1}{2}$ to 2 hours.

Mixing

❖ Think ahead and save yourself some work. When preparing cookie dough or pie pastry, make a double batch and freeze the extra.

Tactics When Kneading or Handling Dough

- Dust your hands with flour. But if the dough is sticky, oil your hands.
- For easier cleanup, wear disposable gloves. This is especially handy when dealing with sticky dough.

Ways to Hasten Mixing and Prevent Overbeating

- Before mixing batter or dough for cakes and pastries, let eggs, butter and milk come to room temperature.
- Lightly whisk eggs beforehand instead of cracking them directly into the mixing bowl.

✧ Rotate the bowl as you scrape batter. Hold the spatula perpendicular to the sides of the bowl.

ⓒ is for Creaming

Butter and sugar are creamed, or whipped together and aerated. The term is a bit of a misnomer because the result should be fluffy and light-colored, rather than creamy or dense.

Creaming Tips

- The butter and sugar should be at room temperature.
- Take the extra step of beating the butter for a minute, to fluff it, before adding the sugar.
- Many cakes and cookies get off to a bad start because the butter and sugar are not creamed for long enough. Keep the mixer going for 5 to 10 minutes.

≡Fast Fixes

- If it's a hot day and/or the butter is too soft, compensate by standing the mixing bowl in a pan of cold water.

- If the butter is not quite soft enough, warm the sugar in the microwave. Heat 1 cup (250 mL) granulated sugar on High, stirring every 30 seconds, for about 2 minutes or until it is barely warm. Do not let the sugar melt.

Causes of Curdled Batter

- Adding cold eggs to the creamed butter and sugar. They harden the butter.
- Adding the eggs too quickly. Blend them in one at a time.
- Beating too quickly.

✧ Blend eggs one at a time into creamed butter and sugar. It's faster to dump them in all at once, but the extra beating makes cakes lighter and cookies chewier.

✧ Don't worry about the curdling. Your batter will survive. If you wish, smooth it out by beating in a bit of flour from the recipe.

How to Beat Egg Yolks with Sugar

1. Beat the yolks until they are light yellow.
2. Add the sugar gradually, while the mixer is going.
3. Beat until the mixture is pale yellow and thick enough to hold its shape briefly. A dollop dropped from a spoon should clump before settling.

✧ To reach their full volume, eggs or yolks on their own should be beaten for 5 minutes. Don't get impatient and add other ingredients too soon.

ⓕ is for Folding

Folding is not stirring. It's lifting, scooping and turning. The object is to carefully blend whipped cream or egg whites, or any light ingredient, into a heavier batter without losing too much air.

Folding Tips

- Always add light to heavy. Fold whipped cream and egg whites into the batter, not vice versa.
- Lighten the batter first by folding in a quarter of the cream or egg. Then fold in the remainder.
- Fold until no white streaks remain.
- Whip egg whites and cream to medium peaks rather than stiff ones. They will be easier to fold in and thus less likely to deflate.

4 Ways to Fold

1. Cut through the center of the batter with a big rubber spatula. Bring the bottom up to the top in a wavelike motion. Give the bowl a quarter turn and repeat.
2. Using a rubber spatula, scrape down the sides of the bowl toward the center. Drag some batter up from the bottom and flip it over the top. Repeat while turning the bowl.
3. Revolve a large round whisk through the batter. Be slow and gentle.
4. Scoop and turn the batter with your hands.

✘ No-Nos

- Don't bang the bowl on the counter or rap on the sides when folding.
- Don't whisk or stir energetically when folding.

Adding Dried Fruit or Nuts to Dough

- To prevent clumping, dust them with flour.
- To prevent sinking, warm the dried fruit or lightly toast the nuts, then dust them with flour.
- Use flour from the recipe.

- In baking, thawed berries, particularly blueberries, add too much liquid and streak the batter. Four ways to avoid singing the blue-batter blues:
- Alternate layers of batter and blueberries, instead of stirring them together. The berry layer should be a smattering, not thick.
- Avoid releasing the juices. Don't crush the berries as you stir.
- Don't thaw berries before using them. (These will still make baked goods a bit gummy.)
- Toss berries with some of the flour from the recipe.

Rolling

- Sprinkle the work surface lightly with flour. Too much flour will make your pastry or dough tough. Use as little flour as possible on your hands and the work surface. The less flour, the lighter the pastry.

- You can sprinkle confectioner's (icing) sugar on the work surface instead of flour.

- Draw a circle or square on parchment as a sizing guide/template when rolling out pie pastry or cookie dough, spreading brittle or caramel, or preparing meringue. To make it easier to see, outline the shape using a permanent marker. Turn the parchment so the marked side is down.

- Roll out dough from the center outward. Keep lifting it and giving it quarter turns. Slide it around so it doesn't stick. Exception: If the dough is very soft, just rotate the direction of the rolling pin.

✘ No-No

Hot water cooks and sets sticky dough on counters, bowls and utensils. Wash them in cold water. Soak, if necessary.

Best Ways to Roll Out Pastry or Dough Without Sticking

- On top of plastic wrap or sandwiched between two sheets. Waxed paper and parchment work, too, but transfer crinkle marks to the dough.
- On a pastry cloth (cotton canvas) rubbed with flour.
- On a silicone mat.

✧ Dampen the counter to prevent plastic wrap, waxed paper or parchment from sliding while you roll out dough.

✧ Using plastic wrap or paper makes it easy to transfer rolled dough. If you are using a top sheet, peel it off. Flip the dough into a pie plate or pan. Peel off the remaining sheet.

✧ Because of pressure from the rolling pin, dough sticks more firmly to the bottom sheet of plastic or paper than to the top sheet. To make it easier to lift off cookie or pastry cutouts, first flip the rolled dough and peel off the sheet. Then cut your shapes.

Ways to Clean a Pastry Cloth

- Run a scraper over it, then shake out the flour.
- Soak it for several hours in cold water. Scrape, then air-dry. You may want to iron it. Don't launder a pastry cloth with detergent or put it in the dryer.
- You don't have to wash a pastry cloth after each use.

✧ Maintain even pressure when rolling. There's a tendency to press harder at the edges, which makes them thinner. Ease up on the pin just before you reach an edge.

 No-No

Don't use a rolling pin with handles. It hampers your sense of touch, making you more apt to press too hard.

OUTSIDE THE BOX

Use two wooden slats to help you roll out pie and cookie dough more evenly. Lay the slats at opposite sides of the dough and use them like railway tracks, rolling the pin over top. The slats should be about 1/8 inch (3 mm) thick. Rulers make good slats.

✧ After rolling, sweep excess flour off the dough with a pastry brush.

Mythstake

Silicone rolling pins and silicone sleeves for metal rolling pins don't live up to their hype. They are not stick-proof. Silicone is a bit less sticky than bare wood. But I still recommend sticking (pardon the pun) to a classic wooden pin with tapered ends. All those French pastry chefs can't be wrong.

Ways to Make a Wooden Rolling Pin Less Sticky

- Cover it with a stockinette. This thin, knit cotton sleeve works well, but does leave a minute pattern on the dough.
- Swathe it in plastic wrap.
- Put it in the freezer for a minute.
- Rub flour all over it.

✧ Moisten your fingers to smooth cracks in pastry or dough.

Filling Pans

👑 Two Golden Rules

- Use the proper pan size.
- Do not overfill the pan. If batter or dough rises above the rim and has nothing to grip, it will collapse.

Tips for Filling Pans

- Generally, plan to fill a pan or muffin cup one-half to three-quarters.
- Fill a cake pan no less than halfway but no more than two-thirds.
- For quick breads in loaf pans, fill to 1 inch (2.5 cm) below the rim.

Making Do

You can reduce the baking area of a pan. Fold heavy-duty foil to create a divider. Fill the excess area with dried beans, raw rice or pie weights.

Dividing Batter, Dough or Pastry

- ✧ Use a weigh scale to divide evenly.
- If you have to dole batter evenly into two pans, don't pour it into and out of measuring cups. This reduces the volume and creates a delay en route to the oven. Put each pan on a scale and pour in equal weights of batter.
- Eyeball dough or pastry, then cut it in half. Tweak, by pinching off bits, until they weigh the same.
- Make the arithmetic easier by weighing in grams.

Ways to Scoop Batter for Cookies and Muffins

- Use a disher with a spring release.
- Use an ice cream scoop.
- Use two spoons, not one. Scrape them against each other.

- ✧ Help the dough co-operate: Spray scoops or spoons with oil. Or dip them into cold water.

- ✧ How to even out and smooth thick batter before baking:
  - Shake and tilt the pan gently. Run a moistened rubber spatula over the top.
  - Lightly press damp fingers across the surface.
  - Lay a sheet of plastic wrap over the batter and smooth it out with your fingers. Press gently along the edges, particularly at the corners. Peel off the plastic. A thin layer of batter will stick to it, but that's okay.

8 Cutting-Edge Tips

1. Dip the cutter in flour each time you punch out a shape in cookie or biscuit dough.
2. When cutting fondant or marzipan, oil the cutter or dip it in icing sugar.
3. For sharp edges on rolled dough, use a scraper to press against each side or to cut it cleanly.
4. A scraper is a good tool for scoring pastry and thick bars.
5. For cleaner cuts, first chill brownies, blondies and other rich bars.
6. Use a spatula to lift cutouts or transfer pastry or dough, so they hold their shape. Lightly oil the spatula.
7. You can cleanly slice firm dough, such as biscotti dough, with an electric knife.
8. To cut sticky cakes and meringues without tearing, butter the knife.

Glazes and Washes

❖ Use a wide pastry brush to apply glazes and washes to breads, pastries, cookies and biscuits. For a softer crust, apply after baking, while the bread or pastry is still warm. For a crunchier crust, apply before baking.

❖ If the baking time is long, brush on the glaze near the end — the last 10 minutes, for example.

✖ No-No

Add glazes and washes to the top of the pastry only. Don't let any run down the sides. They cement the pastry to the pan. The pastry will struggle to break free and rise. This is especially important for delicate choux and puff pastries, and biscuits.

🄴 is for Egg Wash

Egg wash is brushed on breads and pastries to create a golden glow. To make it, whisk 1 egg with 1 tbsp (15 mL) water or milk and a pinch of salt.

Egg Wash Tips

- Whisk just to break up the egg; it needn't be foamy. The salt makes the egg wash smoother and thinner — no white globs.
- For a browner glaze, use just the yolk. Careful: It tends to burn and crust.
- For a lighter, firmer, glossier glaze, use just the egg white.
- For a lovely glow, whisk an egg white with milk. Apply it at the end of the baking time — the last 15 minutes, say.
- For extra sheen, brush pastry with egg wash, let it dry, then apply a second coat before baking.
- For bread and rolls, lightly brush on the egg wash before slashing. Otherwise, the egg is likely to seal the slashes, which are necessary for rising.

- Use egg wash to glue toppings securely onto dough and pastry.

10 Other Finishes

1. Milk and cream turn golden.
2. A mixture of custard powder and milk turns matte yellow and tends to burn.
3. Vinegar gives a mild sheen. Brush it on during the last few minutes of baking.
4. Salted water adds crispness and a bit of shine.
5. Melted butter makes crusts golden and soft.
6. Oil creates shine.
7. Cornstarch creates some crunch. Cook a slurry of cornstarch and water until translucent, then brush it on.
8. Soy powder and water is a vegan option.
9. Sugar syrup makes crusts shiny and crisp. It tends to burn. Brush it on after baking only.
10. Honey or corn syrup makes crusts soft and sticky. Brush it on after baking only.

❖ Sprinkle granulated or coarse sugar on top of a glaze. Try crunchy turbinado. Beware of burning.

♻ Waste Not

Shake out an empty jar of jam by adding a bit of water. Turn the mixture into a glaze.

OUTSIDE THE BOX

Make an easy glaze for cookies and cakes by stirring 1 part softened ice cream with 3 parts icing sugar. Refrigerate it for a couple of hours after spreading. It sets firm, but not hard.

Master Plan
Simple Glaze for Fruit Tarts

1. Pick a jam, any jam. In a small saucepan, stir ½ cup (125 mL) jam with 1 tbsp (15 mL) water.
2. Over high heat, bring it just to a boil.
3. Strain. It should be as thick as maple syrup. If it's too thin, reduce it over medium heat. If it's too thick, add more water.
4. Use the glaze hot on uncooked fruit.
5. Use the glaze cool on hot fruit. Brush it on the fruit and the edges of the pastry when the tart comes out of the oven. Brush again when the pastry has cooled.

❖ For a golden brown glaze on fruit in an open or free-form pie, cover uncooked fruit (such as plums) with thinly sliced sheets of butter, then sprinkle liberally with granulated sugar. Bake at 325°F (160°C) until the pastry is golden.

Baking

❖ Fumbling with a springform pan? Put the base on the counter. Place the rim over it. Close the clasp. It will catch and snap up the base. Pick it up and push down on the base.

❖ Cheap, thin baking sheets allow the bottoms of baked goods to brown too much and encourage cookies to spread. Double them up for insulation.

Baking Sheet **VS.** Jelly Roll Pan?

A baking sheet is flat. A jelly roll pan has short sides. Since no one makes jelly rolls much anymore, this pan is often referred to as a rimmed baking sheet.

❖ Reasons to fill unused cups in muffin tins halfway with water:
- It evens the heat. Otherwise, the metal will draw heat away from the batter.
- It moistens the oven.
- It protects the bakeware.

❖ Bake rich, sweet dough at no higher than 350°F (180°C), so it doesn't brown too quickly.

❖ Stop opening that oven door. The temperature drops each time you do it. This can turn your cake into a flop. Switch on the oven light and peer through the window, especially near the beginning of the baking time.

Halftime Activities
- Rotate baking pans from rack to rack and from back to front. Ovens have hot spots. Plus, the back of the oven is hotter.
- Slide a spatula underneath pastries to unstick them and to prevent scorch spots or uneven edges.

Mythstake

No, a toothpick inserted near the center of a cake, muffin or quick bread should not come out clean. This is the traditional test for doneness, but actually, a few moist crumbs are okay. Baked goods will continue to firm up as they sit. A dry tester is a sign of a dry, overcooked cake.

❖ They sell official cake testers, but a toothpick or a thin skewer works fine.

Cooling and Finishing

✧ Cool baked goods on a rack to let air circulate. This prevents a buildup of steam, which causes soggy bottoms. It also prevents overheating (and overcooking) on the bottom.

✧ To cool a cake, loaf or Bundt pan upside down without squishing its contents, balance it on the rim of a large colander.

✧ How to make it easier to extract the bottom of a springform pan from a tart or cheesecake:
- Use the pan with the bottom upside down — that is, rim facing down.
- Line it with a circle of parchment.

✧ Use a spray bottle to mist cake layers or other pastries with liqueur. It moistens lightly and evenly.

✧ To ice cupcakes, tea cakes and cookies, turn them upside down and dip the tops into glaze, ganache or soft icing. Rotate them as you turn them upright, then set them on a rack.

✧ Keep the surface of cream pies and iced cakes pristine. Instead of wrapping them in plastic or foil, invert a large bowl over them.

✧ Remedies for a fruit dessert with an unappealing color:
- Brush it with jam.
- Sprinkle sugar over top. Caramelize it under the broiler or with kitchen torch.

Bread

Yeast Dough

✧ Flour that's a couple of months old makes better bread than fresh flour. The dough is more elastic.

✧ Whole wheat flour and non-wheat flours, such as rye, must be mixed with bread flour or the loaf won't be light enough. Light rye, for example, may be just a quarter rye flour.

✧ Whole wheat bread dough ferments more quickly, and is softer and moister.

Making Do

You can use all-purpose flour instead of bread flour. It has less gluten, so there's less need to knead.

✧ Too much sugar is too much of a good thing for yeast, too. Sweet yeast dough takes longer to rise.

✧ You can use natural sweeteners other than sugar. Yeast enjoys honey, molasses and malt extract. But yeast will starve if you try to fool it with artificial sweeteners.

✧ Salt inhibits and even kills yeast. Always add salt to bread dough, because it bolsters the gluten, but never in direct contact with the yeast. Add salt to the flour rather than the yeast liquid.

✗ No-No

Don't use coarse salt in the dough. You can, however, sprinkle it on top of the loaf.

8 Alterations

1. To make white bread more rustic, substitute ¼ cup (50 mL) whole wheat, rye or barley flour for the same amount of white, unbleached bread flour in a recipe.
2. For a softer crust and crumb, replace ¼ cup (50 mL) of the water in a recipe with the same amount of milk. For better volume and less of a yeasty flavor, scald and cool the milk before using it.
3. For a tangy, moist loaf with a fine crumb, replace ¼ cup (50 mL) of the water in the recipe with buttermilk or yogurt.
4. You can use white wine instead of water in bread, but not for proofing the yeast.
5. Add flavor to bread dough by using stock instead of water.
6. Go for potato bread. Potato cooking water speeds up the yeast and makes bread coarser and moister. You can also add mashed potatoes to the dough in small amounts. Bakers may get the potato effect by adding ½ cup (125 mL) instant mashed potato flakes per 6 cups (1.5 L) flour.
7. Add 1 tbsp (15 mL) cocoa powder to the dough for a pleasing color in rye and wheat breads.
8. Give bread more rising and staying power by using about 1 tsp (5 mL) malt powder per loaf.

⚛ A Bit of Science

Fat coats the gluten strands. This allows the strands to stretch more easily. It also makes it harder for the yeast to consume the flour. Fermentation is slowed and the loaf ends up more tender and cake-like. Too much fat, however, makes dough crumbly. Use unsalted butter, a neutral vegetable oil or olive oil.

✧ Generally speaking, yeast dough should be a mite soft and sticky after mixing, but smooth and elastic after kneading. However, dough can range from moist to stiff, depending on what you are making. Refer to the recipe. It should say how soft or wet the dough ought to be.

✧ Err on the side of soft dough.

✧ In hot, humid weather, use a bit less liquid in the dough.

Master Plan
Yeast Dough by Hand

1. Make a well in the center of the flour mixture. Pour in the proofed yeast liquid.
2. Use a wooden spoon to gradually sweep the flour from the sides of the bowl into the well.
3. As you mix, you create a shaggy mass that begins to come away from the sides of the bowl and form a ball. Add the remaining liquid ingredients, as needed, during this process.
4. The dough should be soft and not too dry. The dough is too dry if it gathers into a ball but crumbly clumps remain at the bottom of the bowl. In that case, add 1 tsp (5 mL) water to the dry bits, stir them into a paste, then blend them with the rest of the dough while kneading.

Master Plan
Yeast Dough in a Stand Mixer

1. Place the proofed yeast liquid or starter in the bowl. Using the paddle, mix in half the flour mixture on low speed.
2. Mix in the remaining liquid ingredients to form a loose batter.
3. Switch to the dough hook. With the machine running on low speed, gradually add the remaining flour mixture. Mix until the dough pulls away from the sides of the bowl.
4. Increase the speed to medium. Let the machine knead the dough for 5 to 10 minutes or until it is smooth and elastic. Avoid the temptation to switch to low speed.
5. Turn out the dough onto a lightly floured surface. Briefly knead by hand, to shape it into a ball.

Master Plan
Yeast Dough in a Food Processor

1. Insert the plastic dough blade. Don't use the metal blade; it heats up too much.
2. Put the dry ingredients in the bowl. Pulse to blend.
3. With the machine running, pour in the proofed yeast liquid and half of the remaining liquid ingredients. Or add the starter.
4. With the machine running, continue adding liquid ingredients and blend until the dough starts to form a ball.
5. Let the dough rest for 5 minutes.
6. Turn out the dough onto a lightly floured surface. Knead by hand until it is smooth and elastic, about 10 minutes.

Ⓐ is for Autolyse

Cover the mixed bread dough with plastic wrap and let it rest for 20 minutes before kneading. This rest is called the autolyse. It allows the gluten strands to align and the flour to suck up moisture.

Benefits of the Autolyse

- The kneading time is shortened.
- The dough is easier to shape.
- The texture of the loaf improves.
- The bread tastes better.

L is for Lángos

Transform bread or pizza dough into Hungarian lángos. Flatten a chunk of dough into an amoeba-shaped disc. Slash a couple of slits in the center, cutting all the way through if desired. Deep-fry the disc in a skillet. Eat it while it's hot. But first, rub it with cut garlic, then salt it generously. You can use store-bought dough.

≡ Fast Fix

Make dinner rolls with store-bought bread or pizza dough. Roll pieces of dough into ropes. Tie each rope into a loose knot. Put the knots on a baking sheet. Brush them with flavored butter. Bake at 375°F (190°C) for 20 to 25 minutes or until golden brown.

Starters

Sponge Starter

✧ Breads made with a sponge starter are considered superior, lighter and less yeasty.

Adapting a Recipe to Start with a Sponge

• Instead of proofing active dry yeast in water, mix some of the flour, water and yeast into a thick batter. Cover it lightly and let it ferment at room temperature for at least 2 hours or for up to 5 days. The sponge is ready once it bubbles.

How to Use a Sponge

1. Pour it into the well in the flour mixture. Draw in enough flour from the sides to form a soft paste.
2. Cover the bowl. Let the paste stand for a few minutes, until frothy and slightly expanded. Then continue mixing and knead as usual.

Sourdough Starter

S is for Sourdough

Sourdough is a yeast culture that's kept alive in a starter. The starter is added to bread dough as a leavener. Starter constantly ferments. It is home to bacteria that produce lactic acid, which gives sourdough bread its tang. Just as wild yeast varies according to locale, so does sourdough.

5 Keys to Creating Sourdough Starter

1. You are more likely to succeed in the summer. The ideal temperature for the dough and water is 75°F (24°C).
2. Begin with organic unbleached flour, distilled water and sterilized equipment. (You can loosen up once the starter is stable.)
3. Keep the starter in a wide-mouth jar or a bowl. Don't use a metal container. Cover it loosely, not airtight.
4. Frequent feedings liven up a starter. Feed a starter at room temperature one to three times a day. Remove about 1 cup (250 mL) starter, then stir in $\frac{1}{2}$ cup (125 mL) water and $\frac{1}{2}$ to $\frac{3}{4}$ cup (125 to 175 mL) flour. Don't worry about lumps. They dissolve as the yeast eats.
5. Maintain a spongy, not creamy, consistency. You can refrigerate the starter after making your first loaf of sourdough bread.

H is for Hooch

The alcohol that forms on sourdough starter is called hooch. This liquid can range from gold to dark brown. Stir it back in or pour it off. Hooch is harmless.

Three Good Signs

- Bubble holes.
- A sour, yeasty odor.
- A grayish color is okay.

Three Bad Signs

- Pink or orange streaks or patches.
- A foul odor.
- A bold yellow color.

Easier Ways to Create Sourdough Starter

- Borrow some from a friend — hence its common name "friendship starter."
- Buy starter in a packet.
- Cheat by adding a bit of active dry yeast to your culture.

✧ Keep starter in the fridge to slow it down. Feed it once a week.

Cleaning the Jar or Bowl

✧ Pour out the starter. Wash and sterilize the bowl. Return all but 1 cup (250 mL) starter to the bowl and feed it. Leave it at room temperature for 8 to 12 hours or until frothy. Refrigerate. Some people clean the container occasionally. Others do this each time they use the starter.

✧ Before using sourdough starter, feed it, then let it come to room temperature and bubble.

Factoid San Francisco miners used to sleep holding close their sourdough "mothers," or starters, to keep the yeast warm.

"Old Dough"

ⓞ is for Old Dough

So-called "old dough" is sometimes used as a starter. This dates back to the days when cooks would pinch off a wee hunk of bread dough and save it for the next loaf.

✧ To make not-so-old old dough, sprinkle $\frac{1}{2}$ tsp (2 mL) yeast into $\frac{1}{4}$ cup (50 mL) lukewarm water. Let it stand for about 5 minutes or until foamy. Mix in $\frac{1}{4}$ cup (50 mL) flour to make a stiff dough. Knead for 10 minutes. Let it rise for 3 hours. Divide it into two pieces. Use one piece per loaf of bread.

Kneading

Reasons for Kneading

- It pulls apart and rearranges the gluten strands that give bread its fine texture.
- It distributes the yeast.
- It breaks down starches to feed the yeast.
- It distributes the pockets of carbon dioxide gas.

✖ No-No

It may feel satisfying to slap the dough around, but quick, light kneading is better, even for hearty bread.

✧ It's easier to knead yeast dough on a cold surface. It remains firmer. This is also supposed to help the gluten develop.

✧ Firm yeast dough should stick to the counter yet pull away cleanly when you tug on it. If it suddenly turns sticky, add another dusting of flour to the work surface.

✧ To test whether the dough has too much flour on it, slap the ball of dough. Your palm should come away clean.

How to Knead by Hand

1. Lightly flour your hands. Throw a few pinches of flour, not a handful, onto the work surface.
2. Pat the dough into a ball.
3. Fold the dough toward you with one hand. Push it away from you with the heel of your other hand.
4. Give the dough a quarter turn.
5. Repeat Steps 3 and 4. You can get into a rhythm by alternating hands. (Some people prefer to use both hands at once if there's a lot of dough.)
6. Knead for about 10 minutes, or even up to 20 minutes (depending on the recipe and the amount of dough). The dough should feel firm, smooth, elastic and springy.

Avoid Drying Out the Dough

- Sprinkle as little flour as possible on the work surface.
- Use some of the flour from your recipe when kneading. Hold back a bit when mixing the dough.
- When working with wet dough, use a scraper to push and turn it slowly instead of relying on adding flour. The dough should get less sticky as you knead.

Adjustments

- If the dough seems wetter than the recipe says it should be, knead in 1 tbsp (15 mL) flour at a time.
- If the dough is so stiff it is hard to knead, add 1 tsp (5 mL) liquid at a time.

◆ Add coarse ingredients, such as nuts, at the end of the kneading time. Flatten the dough to about 1 inch (2.5 cm) thick. Sprinkle nuts over half the surface. Fold dough over the nuts. Knead for 2 to 4 minutes to distribute the nuts.

◆ You can use a stand mixer or food processor to blend and knead dough. Overworking or overheating the dough is the danger with these machines.

Ways to Lightly Moisten Dough While Kneading

- Smear your hands with buttermilk, milk or water. Run them over the surface of the dough.
- Mist the dough with water using a spray bottle.

◆ Precautions when using a food processor:
- Avoid high speeds.
- The dough may overheat if the machine mixes it for more than 30 seconds at a time. Make friends with the pulse button.
- Use slightly cooler water in the dough to make up for the heat generated by the machine.
- Work in batches, if necessary. At the end, knead the balls of dough into one hunk.

◆ A stand mixer with a dough hook kneads more efficiently than you can do it by hand. Plus you don't have to add extra flour to prevent sticking. The hook is particularly good for firm dough and dough with eggs or other extras.

◆ How to tell when you have kneaded long enough:
- The baby's bottom test: The dough should feel like one.
- The press test: Press the dough with your fingertip. It should indent and spring back, pronto.
- The windowpane test: With both hands, stretch a piece of dough as thinly as possible. It should stretch almost until translucent without breaking. Getting dough to this stage is difficult.

- After kneading, let dough rest for 10 to 15 minutes before trying to roll or stretch it. If it starts to resist while rolling or stretching, cover it with a damp kitchen towel and let it rest for 5 minutes.

Rising

Fermentation VS. Proofing VS. Oven Spring?

Bread dough rises not once, not twice, but three times. The first rise, after the kneading, is called fermentation. The second rise, after the shaping, is called proofing. The third rise, in the oven, is called oven spring. Sometimes, yet another rise is added between the fermentation and proofing, to build flavor or to compensate for overly fast rising at high altitudes.

- Dough rises faster on a hot, humid day, slower on a cold, dry day.

- Whole wheat and sweet doughs take longer to rise. Sweet dough may require the encouragement of 25% more yeast.

- You can slow down rising by using cooler liquid.

- You can let dough rise in the fridge, albeit slowly. Chill it for at least 8 hours. Or dough can be slowed down in the fridge after the first rise and the punch down. In either case, coat it with oil and put it in a covered bowl.

- Dough kept refrigerated for more than a week will become too exhausted to work.

- Before using refrigerated dough, let it sit on the counter for at least 30 minutes or until it returns to room temperature.

- If you make a lot of bread at once, mark each bowl to indicate what stage the dough is at.

X No-Nos

- Proof dough in a glass or plastic bowl, not a metal one. Metal conducts heat. Parts of the dough may rise more than others, say if one side of the bowl is closer to the stove. Some bakers believe metal bowls and spoons also react with the yeast.
- Don't stash dough in a large zip-lock bag in the fridge. The dough can outgrow it and actually burst a hole in the bag. If you have a supersize plastic bag, go for it. Grease the bag first.
- Avoid baking pans that are too big. The shaped dough likes support while rising. Make sure it touches all the sides of the pan.

Fermentation (the First Rise)

- Roll the dough into a ball before setting it aside to rise. This relaxes it and eventually makes shaping easier.

- Coat the dough with oil to prevent sticking and crustiness.

Ways to Coat the Dough

- Roll it around in a greased bowl.
- Spray the dough with oil, then roll it around in a bowl.

- Cover the dough with plastic wrap rather than a towel. The wrap keeps it moister.

14 Warm Ideas for Dough

1. Make it with warmed flour. Heat the flour in a large stainless-steel bowl in a 200°F (100°C) oven until warm. Stir if there's a lot. Do not allow the flour to get hot or brown.

2. Cover the bowl of dough with plastic wrap. Zap a damp kitchen towel in the microwave on High for 30 seconds. Place it over the bowl.

3. Rest the bowl of dough on a rack set over a bowl of warm water.

4. Put the bowl on a hot water bottle covered with a towel.

5. Put the bowl on an electric warming pad.

6. Heat the oven for less than a minute and turn it off. It should be barely warm. Put in the dough.

7. Tuck the bowl of dough into a gas oven (with a pilot light).

8. Leave the bowl in the oven with the light turned on.

9. Put a bowl of boiling water on the floor of the oven. Place the bowl of dough on a rack above it.

10. Warm an empty dishwasher on the dry cycle for a minute. Put in the bowl of dough.

11. Set the bowl near a radiator — but never on it.

12. Fill a sink with warm water. Put the bowl of dough in it.

13. Fill an insulated cooler with warm water. Put the bowl in it and close the lid.

14. Warm up the microwave by bringing a bowl of water to a boil. Exchange it for the bowl of dough. Close the door.

Reasons to Cover Rising Dough

- To prevent a crust from forming. A crust inhibits rising. Plus, crusty bits get mixed into the dough when it's shaped. If you find crusty bits, cut them off.
- Yeast doesn't like drafts.

◆ Let the dough double in bulk. This should take $1\frac{1}{2}$ to 2 hours at room temperature. Whole wheat breads, sweetened breads and breads with added egg or fat take longer.

◆ A sizeable contingent of home cooks prefers to let dough rise quicker in a warm spot. Between 75°F (24°C) and 85°F (29°C) is considered optimal. Once temperatures get higher than that, the dough attracts undesirable bacteria and ferments quickly. It will taste and smell bad. It may become bitter or stickier.

◆ If you're making heavy, whole-grain bread, let it rise to three-quarters the bulk. If it doubles, it may collapse.

Mythstake

Bread doesn't have to rise in a warm place. Many bakers prefer a long, cool rise. They say it improves taste and texture. However, this can take all day. Room temperature is the best compromise. But if your bread-making is interrupted, don't be afraid to stick the dough in the fridge.

✘ No-Nos

Don't add extra yeast to speed things up, or let the dough more than double. You might think you are getting more of a good thing, but you are actually setting the bread up for failure. It will need some rising power in reserve when it hits the oven.

Is It Done?

- Press your fingertip into the dough. If the dent slowly springs back, but not completely, it is ready.
- If it springs back right away, the dough is not ready.
- If the dent remains, the dough is over-risen.

Punching Down

Reasons to Punch Down Dough

- It redistributes heat that builds up during fermentation.
- It breaks up yeast colonies and sends them off to discover new food depots and create more gas.
- It adds oxygen for the yeast.
- It evens out gas pockets.
- It forces out carbon dioxide and prevents over-rising.

- ✧ You don't have to be Mike Tyson and go 10 rounds with the dough. Be quick and efficient, not forceful.

How to Punch Down Dough

1. Press a fist down into the center of the dough.
2. Pull the bottom of the dough from the back over the center.
3. Pull the bottom of the dough from the front over the center.
4. Turn the dough upside down.

- ✧ A punched loaf has a finer, tighter crumb, like that of sandwich bread. For a coarser, chewier loaf, like rustic bread, turn and fold the dough instead of punching it down.

Steps after the Punch Down

- It may (or may not) be followed by a (quick) second kneading.

- Cover the dough with plastic wrap and give it a 10- to 15-minute nap.
- Chafing.

ⓒ is for Chafing

After the punch down, oddly shaped dough is tucked into a tight round. Gently cup your hands around the dough. Rotate it as you drag it around the counter and press down against the sides. This is called chafing. It's supposed to align the gluten strands and hold the gases better.

Dividing and Shaping

- ✧ When dividing dough for loaves or rolls, cut it rather than pinching bits off.

- ✧ For uniform rolls and loaves, weigh the dough, do the arithmetic, then divide it.

- ✧ After dividing, let the dough relax for 10 minutes. If it tightens up while you're shaping it, let it rest for 5 minutes.

- ✧ Be gentle. Don't wrestle dough into submission and be obsessive-compulsive about shaping it.

Ways to Shape a Sandwich Loaf

- Roll out the dough into a rectangle. Roll it up like a jelly roll, from one short end.
- Press the dough into a rectangle, with the long ends vertical on the work surface. Fold it into thirds like a business letter. From the top, roll the dough toward you into a cylinder. Roll your hands along the cylinder to elongate it. Fold the ends under slightly, if necessary.

- ✧ Place shaped dough into the pan seam side down. Cover it with plastic and let it rise slightly above the top of the pan.

Ways to Shape a Boule

- Flatten the dough into a disc. Pull the dough up from the sides to form a hobo pack. Turn the dough over and smooth it into a ball.
- Dust a kitchen towel with flour. Use it to line an 8-inch (20 cm) basket. Add the dough and let it rise. Lift out the dough and transfer it to a baking sheet.

How to Shape an Oval Loaf

- Shape the dough into a ball. Put your palms on top and gently rock the dough until the ends taper.

✧ To make a traditional indentation in an oval loaf or roll, press a wooden spoon across the center.

How to Make a Ring

- Shape the dough into a disc. Punch a hole through the center. With your fingers on the inside edges, push the dough outward. Apply even pressure to create a hole about 6 inches (15 cm) in diameter.

> **Factoid** Bread was originally made in a ring shape so it could be carried in the loop of one's arm.

How to Make a Braid

- Divide the dough into three pieces. Roll each piece into a 16-inch (40 cm) rope. Line up the ropes. Start at the middle and braid toward you. Press together the ends and tuck them under. Turn the dough and braid toward you. Press together the ends and tuck them under.

Ways to Shape a Long Loaf or Baguette

- Roll the dough into a tight cylinder. Put your hands, one over the other, at the center. Rock the dough back and forth while applying pressure and pulling your hands apart.
- Flatten the dough into a disc. From the right and the left, fold it into thirds like a business letter. Press along the seams. Press indentations across the top and stretch the dough slightly to flatten it. Flip the dough seam side down. Press toward the ends with your palms and roll the dough back and forth until it reaches the shape and length you want.

How to Make Round Rolls

- Cup your palm over a piece of dough and roll it around the counter until it's round.

How to Make Knots and Twists

- Take a piece of dough about the size of a lemon. Roll it into a rope by rubbing it against the counter with your palm. Tie the rope into a knot. Or twist two ropes of dough around each other.

✧ When rolling strips of dough that have to be a certain length — for pretzels, say — mark the work surface with masking tape.

> **Factoid** Bagels are boiled before baking to give them a dense crumb and shiny, chewy crust.

No-No

Avoid putting cubed cheese in bread dough. Your cheese bread will end up with holes where the cubes melted.

Ways to Make Bagel Rings

- Roll the dough into a rope. Press the ends together.
- Form the dough into a ball. Poke a hole through the center with your index finger. Twirl the ring around the index finger of one hand and the thumb of the other, with the tips joined. Keep twirling until the hole is about a third of the diameter of the bagel.

Ways to Make Filled Bread

- Cut the dough into two pieces. Form each into a disc. Distribute the filling over one disc, leaving a small border. Top with the second disc. Pinch the edges together.
- Form the dough into a rectangle. Spread the fillings over top. Starting at one short end, roll up the dough like a jelly roll.

5 Fillings for Bread

1. A paste of chopped herbs and olive oil
2. Chopped sun-dried tomatoes
3. Shredded cheese
4. Sunflower, pumpkin or sesame seeds
5. Chopped dried fruit and nuts

Proofing (the Second Rise)

✧ After the loaves or rolls are shaped, they are covered and left to rise again. The dough should rise to $1\frac{1}{2}$ to 2 times its original bulk.

✧ Proofing generally takes 45 to 60 minutes at room temperature, or half to a third of the time of the first rise.

Is It Done?

- Gently press your finger into the dough. It should be spongy, not firm.
- The indentation should slowly fill in.

Slashing

✧ Reasons to slash loaves and rolls just before baking:
- Rising steam is trapped as the crust forms, unless given an escape route.
- It allows the bread to expand in the oven without cracking.
- Gas escapes randomly from unslashed bread, making the top less attractive.
- Free-form breads with slashes rise better.
- It prevents holes and blistering under the crust.
- It's decorative.

✧ Deeper slashes create more crust to enjoy.

Slashing Bread How-Tos

- Slash it quickly or the dough will snag and become ragged.
- Prevent deflation. Use a razor blade or scalpel for the cleanest cuts.
- For deep cuts, as much as three-quarters of the depth of the dough, you can use scissors.
- To create a crown on a loaf, use scissors to snip a crisscross in the top of the dough.
- Instead of slashing, you can poke holes in the top of the dough with a pick.

Oven Spring (the Third Rise)

 A Bit of Science

Bread continues to rise in a hot oven. In a final burst of gorging, the yeast creates carbon dioxide and alcohol even faster. The heat makes the gases expand. The alcohol evaporates and makes bigger bubbles. The moisture in the dough turns to steam, which adds to the rise. Evaporation, along with natural sugars in the dough, creates a firm, golden crust.

Temperature Tips

- The optimal temperature for bread dough before it goes into the oven is 75°F (24°C).
- Baking bread rises the most during its first 20 minutes in the oven. Don't open the door just to peek, as this lowers the temperature and shocks the bread. If you are opening the door to mist the oven, open it partially and spray quickly.
- Fast warming encourages the yeast to speed up its activities and spurs faster evaporation before the crust contains all the gases. Set the oven to 400°F (200°C) for the first 15 minutes, then reduce the heat to 350°F (180°C).
- If the temperature is too high, the crust solidifies before the gases inflate the bread.
- If the temperature is too low, the bread inflates too much before the crust is formed, then collapses. Also, not enough moisture evaporates.

Baking Stone Tips

- Bake bread directly on a preheated baking stone. Stones radiate steady heat and help retain moisture.
- As an alternative, line the bottom rack with unglazed ceramic tiles, leaving 2 inches (5 cm) of space all around them to allow air circulation.
- For free-form loaves, you can sprinkle cornmeal lightly over the stone. (Or sprinkle it on a baking sheet.)

Making Do

If you don't have a baking stone, transfer free-form-breads or flatbreads from a baking sheet directly onto the lower rack once they have firmed up.

- Bake bread on a lower oven rack to slow down the development of a crust.

Pan Tips

- Grease the loaf pan.
- Using an aluminum pan results in a lighter-colored loaf.
- If baking in two pans at once, separate them to allow air to circulate.
- You can bake rolls in a muffin tin.

Reasons to Apply Steam to the Oven

- At first, it softens the crust to let the dough rise quickly to its maximum glory. Bakers call this "accelerated spring."
- It helps a thin, crispy crust form.

Ways to Apply Steam to the Oven

- The best way is to mist the walls 8 to 10 times after placing the loaf in the oven. Repeat twice during the first 10 minutes of cooking time. Avoid spraying the oven light, heating coils and fan.
- You can put a wide dish filled with ice cubes on the oven floor while preheating. Put the loaf in the oven before the ice has completely melted. When the cubes are melted, remove the dish. This should happen within 15 to 20 minutes.

Is It Done?

- Test with a thermometer inserted in the center of the loaf, or look for other signs.
- A sandwich loaf reaches 195°F to 200°F (91°C to 100°C).
- A rustic loaf reaches 200°F to 210°F (100°C to 105°C).
- A whole-grain loaf reaches 210°F (105°C).
- A sweet bread reaches 200°F (100°C).
- The loaf shrinks from the sides of the pan.

- The crust is golden brown.
- The loaf feels firm but not hard.
- The bottom (not the top) sounds hollow when tapped. If the bread's not done, you can return it to the oven and continue baking.

Bread Doctor

The dough is threatening to rise too high above the pan.

- Put it in the oven early.
- Use a smaller pan next time.

The dough collapsed in the oven.

- It was allowed to rise too much. Next time, punch it down again rather than risking collapse.

There are large holes in the loaf.

- The gases weren't distributed. Knead the dough longer next time.

The crust is broken at the sides.

- Don't set the oven too hot.
- Add moisture to the dough next time. It was too stiff.

The bread is streaked.

- Add the fat before the flour instead of near the end of the mixing time. The flour absorbs fat in streaks and globs.
- Don't let the top of the dough get crusty. Cover it.
- Flour was left on the bread before the second rise. Use melted butter or oil when shaping the loaves. You can rub it on your hands beforehand.
- The mixing and kneading were insufficient.
- The dough was pinched, rather than cut, when shaping.

The bottom is soggy.

- Remove the bread from a loaf pan ASAP.
- Let the bread cool on a wire rack to allow air to circulate.
- Place the loaf on its side while it's cooling.

Three symptoms of under-rising:

- Dark crust with blisters.
- Dense texture.

- Cracks on the sides. (The loaf expanded too much in the oven and burst after the crust formed.)

Five symptoms of over-rising:

- Sour taste.
- Heavy yeasty flavor.
- Heaviness.
- Sunken center.
- Coarse, porous texture.

The Crust

◆ If the crust is getting too brown as the bread is baking, cover it loosely with foil or parchment.

Ways to Create a Crispier Crust

- Brush or spray the dough with water.
- Brush the dough with egg wash.
- Brush or spray it with salty water when the bread is half baked.
- Brush a finished loaf with butter or oil, then return it to the oven for 5 minutes.
- Shape the dough into a ring, baguette or braid with two, not three, twisted ropes.

◆ The sweeter the dough, the more golden the crust.

◆ Dust dough with flour to give it a golden finish. Scatter the flour through a sieve.

Ways to Create a Softer Crust

- Brush the top of the dough with milk.
- Brush the top with melted butter or oil after removing the bread from the oven.
- Cover the bread with a kitchen towel for 5 minutes after taking it out of the oven.

Gussy It Up

- Potential toppings: cracked wheat, bran flakes, rolled oats, sugar, paprika or other spices, coarse salt, cornmeal, poppy seeds, sunflower seeds, fresh or dried herbs.
- For drama, press an entire herb sprig, such as rosemary, into the top of a loaf.

Using a Bread Machine

✧ Follow the manual and always add ingredients in the order listed.

✧ You can open the lid or door during mixing and kneading, but not during rising and baking.

Mythstake

It's a machine, yes, but that doesn't prevent you from customizing and tinkering. Check the dough about 10 minutes into the kneading cycle. If it's too soft, add flour 1 tbsp (15 mL) at a time. If it's stiff, add water 1 tsp (5 mL) at a time.

✧ Reasons to remove the loaf from the pan before it is cool:
- To prevent a soggy crust.
- To remove the paddle. If you wait, it will be lodged too firmly into the bottom of the loaf.

Adapting Regular Recipes to the Bread Machine

- Add ingredients in the order listed in the manual, not the recipe.
- For free-form loaves or rolls, use the Dough setting and finish in the oven.
- If the recipe has a sponge starter, use instant yeast instead.

Important Features to Look For in a Bread Machine

- A horizontal loaf shape (upright loaves are too awkward to slice)
- Settings for 1- and $1\frac{1}{2}$-lb (500 and 750 g) loaves
- Two kneading bars (they handle the dough much better than just one)
- A delay timer — essential for fresh, hot bread in the morning

Slicing, Storing and Serving

✧ Before slicing, let freshly baked bread sit until it is cool enough to handle.

✧ Use a serrated knife to slice bread.

✧ If fresh bread is too hard to slice, shove it in the freezer for a few minutes.

✧ To make bread cubes for croutons and stuffing, freeze bread slices until just firm, then stack and cut them. The cubes will be even and not squashed. Work fast, as bread thaws quickly.

✧ Avoid becoming one of the many North Americans who are driven to emergency rooms by bagel injuries. Instead of standing a bagel on its side, place it flat on a cutting board, put your palm on top to steady it, then saw through it parallel to the counter. Or buy a bagel cutter, which works like a guillotine.

✧ Keep rolls warmer for longer. Serve them in a bread basket lined with foil. Cover the top with a cloth napkin.

✧ The true test of fresh biscuits and bread: Are they good when they're cold? (They're always good warm.)

✦ To keep freshly baked flatbreads soft and moist, stack them and cover the lot with a kitchen towel.

Ways to Refresh Stale or Frozen Bread

- Spray it with water, wrap it in foil and warm it in a 400°F (200°C) oven for 10 to 15 minutes. Let it cool before unwrapping if you prefer a softer crust.
- Dip the loaf in water or brush it with milk. Put it directly on the rack in a 350°F (180°C) oven. A frozen loaf will take about 15 minutes.
- Wrap it in damp paper towels. Microwave it on High for 30 seconds or less.

Making Do

Use a heel of bread as a disposable spoon rest.

OUTSIDE THE BOX

Love *pain au chocolat*? Improvise by preparing it like grilled cheese. Butter two slices of challah or a halved croissant, outside and in. Sprinkle a generous layer of finely chopped chocolate over one slice. If desired, sprinkle on some sugar. Top with the second slice. Place it in a heavy skillet over medium heat to toast the bread and melt the chocolate. Weigh it down or press with a spatula.

♻ Waste Not

- Turn day-old bread into Melba toast. Remove the crusts. Flatten each slice with a rolling pin. Bake in a 200°F (100°C) oven until golden brown. Let cool.
- Turn stale pitas into crackers to go with dips or salads. Separate a 7-inch (18 cm) pocket

10 Keys to Keeping Bread Fresh

1. Condensation is an invitation to mold. Cool bread completely before wrapping it. Avoid airtight bags.
2. Paper bags promote crisp crusts, plastic bags soft crusts. But forget them. You'll get better results from plain, thick, white cotton drawstring bags. If a loaf gets moldy, banish spores and the off-putting scent by washing the bag in cold water with a hint of mild, unscented soap.
3. If you don't have cotton bags, wrap your loaves in clean, cotton kitchen towels.
4. Unlike other breads, pitas and flatbreads keep better in plastic bags.
5. Place a stalk of celery in the bread box or bin. Replace it when it goes limp.
6. To prevent mold, wipe the bread box with vinegar. Air it out before storing the bread.
7. Wash the bread box once a week with baking soda and water, and dry it well.
8. Keep bread at room temperature or in the freezer, but not in the fridge, which dries it out too much.
9. To freeze bread, wrap it in plastic end to end, then wrap another piece of plastic around the loaf. Place it in a plastic bag, press out the air and seal it. Or wrap it in foil. Thaw it in the plastic to preserve moisture.
10. The best way to keep pitas fresh is to freeze them immediately. To thaw, spray them with water and warm them in a toaster oven. Or wrap one in a clean kitchen towel or paper towel, then microwave it on High for 20 to 30 seconds.

pita into two circles. Cut each circle into 6 triangles. Brush with garlic-herb butter and sprinkle with salt. Broil on the top oven rack for 3 to 4 minutes or until golden and crispy. No need to turn them.

Garlic Bread

Master Plan
Garlic Bread

1. Slice a loaf of bread crosswise, but not all the way through. Leave the bottom crust intact.
2. Smear garlic butter liberally over the slices, both sides.
3. Place the loaf lengthwise on a piece of foil. Pull the foil over the ends and up the sides, leaving part of the top exposed to become crunchy.
4. For an even crunchier top, smear some garlic butter over the crust.
5. Heat in a 350°F (180°C) oven until warm, about 20 minutes.

❤ Healthier Eater
For lower-fat garlic bread, spray or brush a slice of crusty bread with olive oil, sprinkle on garlic salt and broil it.

⫶Fast Fix
Make garlic toast like Hungarians do. Butter a slice of rye toast. Rub a cut garlic clove all over it.

Toast

◆ Food scientists at the University of Leeds came up with the formula for a perfect piece of toast:
- The butter should be about $\frac{1}{17}$th the thickness of the bread.
- The bread should be toasted to at least 248°F (120°C).
- The butter should be smeared straight from the fridge, applied unevenly, within 2 minutes of the bread popping out of the toaster.

◆ Keep day-old bread in the freezer and use it for morning toast. No need to thaw it.

◆ Stale bread toasts up better than fresh.

◆ Bread with lots of sugar and starch browns the best.

Master Plan
Asian-Style Toast

1. Take a monstrous 2-inch (5 cm) thick slice of fresh bread with a crispy crust and a light center.
2. Slash an X across the surface to absorb toppings, then toast it.
3. Go for straight butter or range out into garlic butter, Nutella or preserves.

OUTSIDE THE BOX

Scrape burnt toast more efficiently. Rub two burnt slices together rather than scraping them with a knife.

◆ To keep a large quantity of toast warm, place a rack on a baking sheet, stand the toast upright between the slats and hold it in a 200°F (100°C) oven. (If the rack isn't sized right, you can lay the toast flat.)

Bread Crumbs

Dry VS. Fresh?
Some recipes call for dry bread crumbs, the gritty, powdery kind, generally store-bought. Some specify fresh bread crumbs; these are fluffier, generally homemade. The two types are not interchangeable.

◆ Make fresh crumbs by pulsing day-old bread in a food processor.

◇ Always let toasted bread and crackers cool before crushing them into crumbs.

◇ Measure bread crumbs in dry measures, not cups. They settle.

◇ For all-purpose bread crumbs, go with French or Italian bread.

5 Ways to Make Dry Bread Crumbs

1. Spread fresh bread crumbs on a baking sheet. Bake them in a 300°F (150°C) oven for 10 to 15 minutes or until they start to turn golden and are crisp but not browned. Let them cool.
2. Microwave bread on a piece of paper towel until it is crisp, about 1 minute per slice. Let it cool. Break it into chunks and crush it.
3. Toast slices of bread in a 300°F (150°C) oven until very crisp, then cool and crumble them.
4. Crisp Melba toast or bland crackers in a 200°F (100°C) oven, but do not let them brown. Crush them.
5. For speed, crumble sliced bread into chunks and crisp them in a 200°F (100°C) oven. Then cool and finely crumble them.

Ways to Crush and Crumble

- Place parchment over top and crumble with a rolling pin.
- Pulse in the food processor.
- Grind in a rotary grater.
- Put through a meat grinder with a bag tied over the mouth to catch the crumbs.
- Push through a sieve for the finest, most uniform crumbs.

◇ You can freeze fresh and dry bread crumbs.

Croutons

3 Ways to Make Croutons

1. Dice day-old bread (or even fresh bread) into ½-inch (1 cm) cubes. Sauté the cubes in oil or a 1:1 mixture of oil and butter over low heat. The bread should sizzle when it goes in. Stir gently with a spoon for about 10 minutes or until the croutons are browned and crisp.
2. Drizzle cubes with oil and/or melted butter and seasonings. Toss them to coat. Bake them in a single layer at 250°F (120°C) for 15 minutes. Stir. Bake for 10 minutes or until the croutons are golden and crisp.
3. Preheat oven to 200°F (100°C), then turn it off. Butter slices of stale bread. Season them with garlic powder or herb blends. Set slices directly on the rack in the oven. Leave them overnight or until they're completely dry. Cut the bread into cubes. This is the laziest method, but not the best.

- To season croutons, you can toss them, while they're hot, in a paper bag along with a spice blend or grated dry Parmesan. Or toss them with chopped herbs while they're warm.

- Use cookie or candy cutters to make crouton hearts or other shapes.

 **Healthier Eater**

- For fat-free croutons, toss cubes of bread with whisked egg whites instead of oil, then with seasonings, and bake.
- Beware: Plain toasted croutons get soggy fast without a protective coating of butter or oil — especially in soup.

Cookies

 Healthier Eater

Many cookie recipes have high amounts of sugar and fat. You can replace up to a quarter of the granulated sugar in a cookie recipe with skim milk powder. A test batch was puffed, cakier and spread less than a fudgy, chewy batch made with all the sugar.

Ways to Make Cookies Chewier

- Do not overbake them. Remove them from the oven while they are still soft, or even 5 minutes before they are due to be done. Let them finish baking in the residual heat from the pan.
- Bake at 25°F (10°C) lower than the recipe calls for, but for the same amount of time.
- Refrigerate the dough for 1 hour beforehand. It will spread less in the oven, and be denser and possibly chewier.
- Use more butter.
- Substitute brown sugar for the white sugar.
- Add an (extra) egg yolk to the dough.
- Beat in eggs one at a time.
- Store cookies in an airtight container to keep them moist.

◆ For moister cookies, substitute liquid honey for half the granulated sugar.

◆ The temperature of the butter and eggs determines how much cookies spread. If they are cool, cookies will spread more slowly, and thus be denser and lighter. If they are warm, cookies will spread more quickly, and thus be thinner and crispier.

12 Ways to Make Cookies Crispier

1. Use a bit more liquid.
2. Reduce the flour.
3. Replace some of the egg with milk.
4. Start with softened or melted butter.
5. Use more sugar. Or, if the recipe calls for brown sugar, switch to granulated sugar.
6. Substitute baking soda for baking powder, say $\frac{1}{2}$ tsp (2 mL) per 2 cups (500 mL) flour. Also, replace some or all of the water with lemon juice.
7. Start with warmer dough. It will spread more quickly and thinly.
8. Grease the baking sheet to help cookies spread.
9. Drop dough onto warm baking sheets so it will spread faster.
10. Arrange cookies farther apart on the baking sheet to crisp the edges.
11. Bake them longer.
12. Store cookies on a platter, loosely covered, rather than an airtight tin or tub.

Ways to Make Cookies Browner

- Replace some of the granulated sugar with corn syrup. Substitute no more than 2 tbsp (25 mL) corn syrup per 1 cup (250 mL) granulated sugar.
- Replace some of the all-purpose flour with whole wheat flour.

Drop Cookies

✧ To make drop cookies more even, chill the dough and quickly roll it into balls.

Ways to Press and Flatten Balls of Cookie Dough

- Push down with your flexed palm.
- Use the bottom of a juice glass.
- Press with a fork.
- Smoosh with a spatula.
- Use the bottom of a ramekin.

✧ You can dust your hands with flour, icing sugar or cocoa powder to prevent sticking when rolling dough balls.

✧ Before pressing balls of cookie dough, moisten or grease your implement. Then dip it in flour, granulated sugar, cocoa powder or even cornmeal.

✧ Use a thimble or a cork to indent thumbprint cookies.

✧ To use a rolled cookie dough recipe for drop cookies, add more liquid to the batter.

Chocolate Chip Cookies

✧ Make a batch of cookies with the more delectable milk chocolate chips, instead of the standard semisweet chips.

✧ Give chocolate chip cookies that perfect magazine look. Don't fold all your chips into the batter. Arrange 5 to 10 upright on top of each cookie once the dough is sitting on the baking sheet.

Oatmeal Cookies

✧ For chewier, nuttier, browner oatmeal cookies, toast the oatmeal in the oven before mixing the dough. Measure the oatmeal before toasting. Toast it on a baking sheet at 325°F (160°C) for 10 minutes or until barely golden. Shake the sheet after removing it from the oven. Let the oatmeal cool before using it.

Cut Cookies

4 Steps to Fast, Efficient Cookie Cutouts

1. Roll out the dough on a sheet of parchment.
2. Punch out your shapes 1 inch (2.5 cm) apart.
3. Peel off the excess dough in one piece.
4. Slide the parchment with the cutouts right into the fridge or onto a baking sheet.

Chewy Milk Chocolate Chip Cookies

Chocolate chip cookies are irresistible when they are chewy. **Makes about 32 cookies**

- **2 baking sheets, greased and floured**

Tip

When forming the cookie dough balls, be quick rather than obsessively precise. Don't let the dough warm up too much.

Variation

You can use semisweet chocolate chips.

2 cups	all-purpose flour	500 mL
1¼ tsp	baking soda	6 mL
1 tsp	salt	5 mL
1 cup	unsalted butter, at room temperature	250 mL
1½ cups	packed brown sugar	375 mL
¼ cup	granulated sugar	50 mL
2	large eggs	2
1 tsp	vanilla extract	5 mL
2 cups	milk chocolate chips, divided	500 mL

1. In a medium bowl, whisk together flour, baking soda and salt. Set aside.

2. In a large bowl, using an electric mixer, cream butter on medium speed for 1 minute. Beat in brown and granulated sugars until fluffy, about 3 minutes. Scrape the bowl. Beat in eggs and vanilla. Scrape the bowl. Add the flour mixture. On low speed or with a wooden spoon, blend until dough is moistened and clumpy. Stir in about three-quarters of the chocolate chips, reserving the remainder. Refrigerate the dough for at least 1 hour.

3. Meanwhile, preheat oven to 325°F (160°C).

4. Using a 2-inch (5 cm) disher or large spoon, scoop the dough and quickly form it into balls about 1½ inches (4 cm) in diameter. Place them 3 inches (7.5 cm) apart on the baking sheets. Pressing with your palm, flatten each ball to a ½-inch (1 cm) thick disc. Press some of the reserved chocolate chips on top of each cookie. Refrigerate the remaining dough.

5. Bake on the two racks closest to the center of the oven for about 14 minutes, switching pans between racks halfway through the baking time, until the edges are golden and the tops look dry. Let cool on baking sheets on wire racks for 2 minutes. Using a thin spatula, carefully transfer cookies to racks to cool completely. Repeat with the remaining dough.

Ways to Help Shapes Hold Their Shape

- Chill cookie dough for at least 1 hour before rolling it out.
- Chill the dough after rolling it, too. When you cut out shapes, the edges will be firmer and look more defined. Roll out the dough between two pieces of parchment and place it in the fridge with this protective covering. Don't leave it for longer than half an hour or it will dry out.

❖ Before baking sandwich cookies, punch a small hole in the top circle to show off more filling.

Master Plan
Gingerbread House

1. Mix a very firm dough.
2. Make paper templates of the front, back and side walls, and the roof pieces.
3. Roll out the dough, then lay the templates on top. With a pizza cutter, cut around the templates. Cut out the windows and door with a sharp knife.
4. Transfer the cutouts to baking sheets lined with parchment. Refrigerate until firm.
5. Bake at 350°F (180°C) until the edges are golden.
6. Let the gingerbread sections cool completely on racks before trying to assemble the house.
7. Cut out a large piece of thick cardboard for a base, or use a large cake board or tray.
8. Coat the top of the base with a thick layer of royal icing. Embed one of the side walls in the icing. Place the back wall perpendicular to it. Get a helper to hold the side wall while you cement the adjoining edges with the icing. Use sharp, tapered toothpicks as nails, if necessary. Hold for 5 minutes or until set. Repeat to join the other walls.
9. With the icing, glue the roof pieces on top. Hold for 5 minutes or until set. (You need a helper!)
10. Decorate with icing "snow." While the icing is wet, press in gumdrops, licorice, jelly beans and other candies as doorknobs and decorations.

Ideas for Decorating a Gingerbread House

- Use pretzel sticks to create a log-cabin effect.
- Stack a log pile of cinnamon sticks in the yard.
- Breakfast cereals of various shapes make fine roof tiles.
- Shredded coconut mimics icy snow.

❖ It's tricky, but you can make a basket out of cookie dough.

Master Plan
Cookie Dough Basket

1. Mix a batch of extra-firm dough (such as gingerbread). On a lightly floured surface, roll it out to $1/8$- to $1/4$-inch (0.25 to 0.5 cm) thickness. With a cookie cutter, punch out $1\frac{1}{2}$-inch (4 cm) circles.
2. Use an upturned loaf pan or heatproof bowl as the mold. Press foil over it. Lightly spray the foil with oil.
3. Cover the mold with overlapping dough circles, starting at the bottom centre and working toward the rim. Overlap each adjoining cutout by about 50%, then press the joints together with your hands to secure them. Otherwise, the cookies will fall off as they bake. (In fact, they may fall off no matter what you do. I did say it was tricky.)
4. If desired, place the mold on a baking sheet. Bake it at 350°F (180°C) until the basket is firm.
5. Transfer the mold to a wire rack and let cool completely.
6. Carefully lift the cookie basket off the mold.

Sliced Cookies

Shaping Cookie-Dough Logs

- After rolling the dough into a cylinder, moisten your hands to massage away cracks on the surface.
- With one palm against each end, push in the dough cylinder to compact and flatten the ends.
- To smooth out the log, run your hands over the dough after you wrap it in plastic, not before.
- Roll the log on the counter to make it rounder, before and after refrigerating it.

Ways to Prevent Flat Bottoms

- Turn and reroll refrigerated logs frequently.
- Slide the wrapped log into a fresh cardboard tube from toilet paper, paper towels, waxed paper, foil or parchment.
- Cut cardboard tubes into troughs to hold logs of dough.
- Place the logs in a baguette pan.

Slicing Cookie-Dough Logs

- Refrigerate a log for 1 to 2 hours before cutting it. If you're impatient, stash the log in the freezer.
- Before slicing, evenly flatten the ends by tapping them against the counter.
- You can mark the log at evenly spaced intervals with the tines of a fork or gripper (used to hold food for carving). Follow the markings and you'll wind up with even slices. For thicker cookies, cut at every second or third dot.
- To avoid squashing the circles of dough, cut with a serrated knife and give the log a quarter turn each time you cut.

Gussy It Up

- To make a decorative border for a cookie-dough log, roll it in chopped nuts or shredded coconut before slicing and baking.
- Make two-tone pinwheels. Stack two sheets of different-colored dough, then roll them into a cylinder, chill and slice.
- If the dough is firm, you can roll the log in granulated sugar. For shiny cookies, mist the sliced dough with water from a spray bottle, then sprinkle it with granulated sugar before baking.

Shortbread

- ✧ Don't overmix shortbread (or dough for other rich cookies, such as sugar cookies). Handle it as gently and as little as possible.

- ✧ Blend shortbread batter with a wooden spoon. Wet ingredients clump on the spoon and attract the dry ones. The ingredients slide off metal or plastic spoons.

Master Plan
Shortbread Dough

1. In a large bowl, beat butter and sugar until it is fluffy, about 2 minutes.
2. Use a wooden spoon to stir in the flour just until it is moistened.
3. Scrape the dough onto your work surface. Finish mixing with your hands. Pat the dough into a disc. Or roll it into a log.
4. Wrap the dough in plastic and refrigerate it for at least 12 hours. The more butter or fat in the dough, the longer it should be refrigerated.
5. Slice the dough. Or press it into a baking pan. Or roll it out to $\frac{1}{4}$-inch (0.5 cm) thickness between two sheets of plastic wrap or waxed paper, then use a cookie cutter.
6. Bake it.

Baking Cookies

✧ Give thin cookie dough something to grip. Flour a cookie sheet as well as greasing it. The dough will spread less. This also helps if the dough is at room temperature.

Making Do

A heavy, flat baking sheet is best for cookies. The rims on jelly roll pans deflect heat and the cookies bake unevenly. If you don't have a flat sheet, turn a jelly roll pan upside down.

✧ Avoid using an insulated jelly roll pan. The cookies won't brown enough.

✧ Always put cookie dough on cold baking sheets. When baking in batches, cool a hot sheet briefly in the sink, then spray tepid water over it to hasten the task. (Be careful not to shock a hot sheet with cold water, or it may buckle.)

✧ Space cookies that hold their shape, such as shortbreads, 1 inch (2.5 cm) apart. Space cookies that spread, such as chewy chocolate chippers, at least 2 inches (5 cm) apart.

✧ Try to fill an entire sheet for even baking. If you have only a few cookies left to bake, put them on the bottom of a pie plate or small baking dish.

✧ It's best to bake one sheet at a time in the center of the oven. Rotate it halfway through the baking time.

✧ If you want to do two baking sheets at once, place them on the racks just above and below the center, then switch and rotate them halfway through the baking time.

✗ No-No

Don't bake more than two sheets at once. The heat in the oven won't circulate properly.

Is It Done?

- One sign that firm cookies, such as sugar cookies, are done: They lift cleanly and lightly off the baking sheet.
- To test chewy cookies, press halfway between the edge and center of the cookie. Your finger should leave an indent, but encounter some resistance. If the indent is large and easily made, the cookie is apt to be cakey or firm, rather than chewy.

✧ Do not overbake cookies. They continue to cook on the baking sheet and firm up as they cool.

✧ Let cookies cool on the baking sheet on a rack for up to 5 minutes. Cookies will crack and crumble if they are removed too soon. The moment they are set enough to transfer directly to a rack without incident, do so.

✧ If you get distracted and the cookies harden and stick to the baking sheet, return them briefly to the oven, then pry them off with a spatula.

Cookie Doctor

The cookies are too flat.
- The butter was too cold and hard.

The bottoms are burnt.
- Switch to a lighter-colored baking sheet.
- Line the baking sheet with parchment.

The cookies are firm, dry and tough.
- Use less flour. Measure accurately.

The cookies spread too much.
- Use more flour.

The shortbread or sugar cookie is too crumbly.
- Add an egg white.

Decorating Cookies

 Waste Not

Decorate cookies on a rack. Slide a piece of waxed paper underneath the rack to capture the excess. Then you can reuse it.

No-No

Don't decorate cookie dough directly on the baking sheet unless it is too fragile to be transferred. The debris that falls off will burn.

❖ Toppings stick better to warm dough than to cold dough.

❖ Sugary toppings, such as crushed pralines, stick best because they start to melt. Dry toppings, such as shredded coconut, don't stick as well.

❖ Crushed hard candies are good for stained-glass cookies or shortbreads about to go into the oven.

❖ If you're baking with crushed hard candies, it's easier and tidier to use individually wrapped ones. Smash the tiny packets with a rolling pin until the contents are powdery. Snip open the tops and pour the candy over the dough.

Master Plan
Simple Stained-Glass Cookies

1. Roll out the dough.
2. Use two different-size cookie cutters to make rings of dough that are at least ¾ inch (2 cm) wide. For example, use a serrated 2½-inch (6 cm) round cookie cutter, then pop out the centers using a smooth 1¾-inch (4 cm) round cutter.
3. Place the rings on a baking sheet lined with parchment.
4. Fill the centers with pulverized hard candies in bright flavors and colors, such as Life Savers or Campinos. Avoid coarse chunks; they don't melt properly.
5. Bake at 350°F (180°C) for about 8 minutes or until the cookies are golden and the candy has melted. Let the cookies cool in the pan until the candy has set.
6. Use the leftover dough circles for other cookies.

✗ No-No

Don't brush egg paint on cookies before they bake or after they cool. For even color and coverage, brush the paint on cookies hot out of the oven. If this is done before baking, the white looks uneven and the yolk becomes cracked. If done after cooling, the color is mottled and the white remains sticky.

Gussy It Up

- To garnish a plain cookie, dip a halved nut into syrup or lightly beaten egg white and press it onto the dough before baking.
- Make small, soft cookies cuter by pressing chocolate "kiss" and "hug" candies on top. Do this on cookies straight out of the oven. Swirled dark-and-white chocolate candies melt into a pretty pattern, while chocolate ones hold their peaks. Use the ones with nuts if you enjoy a bit of crunch.
- Decorate with brightly colored sanding sugar. It keeps its shape on cookies baked for a short time.
- Create designs. Cover parts of cookies with waxed paper or a spatula before sprinkling on toppings. Or use a stencil.
- Brush cookies with egg paint. Stir a few drops of food coloring into an egg yolk or lightly beaten egg white. Dyed whites have truer color. Dyed yolks are more neon.

Storing Cookies

✦ Let cookies cool completely before storing them.

✦ Store similar cookies together, opposites apart. Separate dry and moist cookies, and those with clashing flavors. No biscotti with oatmeal cookies, or peppermint with gingerbread.

✦ Keep most cookies in an airtight tub or tin at room temperature. Hard, crisp cookies can be stored between layers of waxed paper in a loosely covered cookie jar.

✦ Arrange cookies in single layers in the tin, separated by parchment or waxed paper.

✦ Revive stale cookies by heating them on a baking sheet in a 275°F (140°C) oven for 10 minutes. This even softens biscotti enough that they won't break your teeth. The bad news: The cookies tend to revert when they are cold again.

Ways to Keep Cookies Fresher or Soften Cookies

- Put a slice of bread or an apple wedge in the tin. Replace it every few days.
- Dampen a paper towel, wrap it in foil, then pierce with a fork. Place it in the cookie tin.
- Crumple white tissue paper and put it in the bottom of the cookie jar.

 No-No

Don't store cookies in the fridge. This dries them out.

✦ Cookie dough can be frozen. Wrap it in plastic, then put it in a freezer bag. Freeze it in logs that you can slice and bake from frozen. Or freeze it in a disc, then thaw just to the point where you can roll out the dough.

✦ Baked cookies can be frozen, then thawed and decorated.

Ways to Thaw Frozen Baked Cookies

- Heat them directly on a rack in a 300°F (150°C) oven until crisp.
- Let them thaw at room temperature on a wire rack lined with paper towels to absorb any moisture.

Cakes

3 Steps to a Typical Cake Mix

1. Creaming butter with sugar.
2. Mixing in eggs.
3. Adding flour and milk.

♛ Two Golden Rules

• Use low-gluten cake flour for the lightest, most delicate cakes.
• Be slow and vigorous when creaming butter with sugar, swift and gentle when adding flour. (The former fluffs; the latter toughens.)

✧ After the eggs are added, the batter should run in a ribbon from a spoon. There should be no grittiness evident from the sugar. Rub a bit of the mixture between your fingers to check.

Tips for Adding Flour

• Sift the flour with the rest of the dry ingredients. This reduces the time it will take to blend the batter.
• For the lightest cake, add the flour mixture alternately with the milk. Add the flour mixture in three stages and the milk in two. Begin and end with the flour mixture.
• Beat until there are no lumps. This should take no longer than 2 minutes.
• When mixing by hand, start stirring in the center and widen the circle as you go, to moisten and blend.
• When adding just a flour mixture (not alternating with milk) to a creamed base, some pastry chefs switch off the mixer and fold it in. That way, the batter stays airy.

✧ Ways to lighten a cake, homemade or from a mix:
• Separate the eggs. Beat the yolks into the batter. Beat the whites to soft peaks, then fold them in at the end of the mixing time.
• Add club soda instead of water. The cake will rise higher.
• Add 1 tsp (5 mL) white vinegar or lemon juice per 1 tsp (5 mL) baking soda called for in the recipe.

✧ Instead of trying to smooth the top, level batter in a cake pan by tilting it.

✧ For a flatter top on a cake made with firm batter, push a hollow into the center of the batter.

✧ The center of the oven is the best position to bake a cake, except for angel food cake.

✧ A wet kitchen towel does miraculous things for a cake. Wrap and tie one around the sides of the pan, then bake.

Advantages of a Wet Towel

• The edges of the cake pull away nicely from the sides of the pan, instead of sticking.
• The sides of the cake turn out soft and white, not crusty and browned.
• The cake rises higher.
• The top doesn't crack.
• The cake remains level. The center doesn't heave up.

✧ Some shops sell cake pan strips that work the same way as a wet towel. They are about 1½ inches (4 cm) wide. When saturated with water, they help equalize the heat in the pan.

Is It Done?

- The temperature in the center is 195°F (91°C).
- The cake doesn't jiggle.
- The batter no longer looks shiny or wet.
- The edges are pulling away from the sides of the pan.
- The top is golden brown (for a white cake).
- The top is evenly domed.
- The cake springs back when it's pressed gently near the center. If an indent remains, give the cake another 5 minutes in the oven, no more, before testing again. (Note that this test doesn't always apply. Some rich cakes or chocolate cakes may hold a dent when they're done.)
- A tester comes out almost clean, with a few moist crumbs clinging to it. Exception: thick, dense specimens such as mud cake.

How to Make Pudding Cake

You can transform a standard cake into an English-style "pudding," such as sticky toffee cake, by adding sauce.

1. Instead of baking the cake dry, steam the pan in a bain-marie.
2. Heat the sauce. It can be anything from caramel to hot chocolate pudding.
3. While the cake is still warm, poke the top all over with a skewer, then pour the sauce over the top. Gently lift the edges of the cake with a spatula to allow the sauce to seep underneath. Keep adding sauce as the cake sucks it up. Eat it warm.

OUTSIDE THE BOX

- For moist chocolate cake, add 1 tbsp (15 mL) mayonnaise (not the "lite" kind) to the batter. It does make a difference.
- You can bake a cake in a metal bowl. It turns out as a dome. For a girlie-girl birthday party, stick a Barbie torso in the center and let the decorated cake be her skirt.
- Bake batter in flat-bottom ice cream cones for kid-pleasing cupcakes. Careful — ice cream cone cupcakes want to tip as the batter rises. For support, stand the filled cones in a muffin tin or hang them between the grates of an oven rack. For the latter, arrange the filled cones in a row, then bolster the row at each end, using ovenproof dishes like bookends.

✧ Here's another seasonal treat: You can make a Christmas tree out of cupcakes.

Master Plan
Cupcake Tree

1. Start with 14 cupcakes and a rectangular cake board or platter.
2. Pipe spikes of green icing onto 12 cupcakes. Make sure the tops are covered right past the edges.
3. As you work, dab the bottom of each cupcake with icing to secure it to the platter.
4. Arrange 10 green cupcakes in a tight triangle on the board. Center another 2 at the bottom of the triangle.
5. Scatter red sprinkles over the green icing. Decorate the tree with tiny Christmas ball ornaments (or use round candies). Put a small star-shaped cookie at the peak.
6. Center another 2 cupcakes at the bottom to form the trunk. Pipe chocolate icing back and forth over both, in continuous ridges to resemble bark.

✧ You can make Christmas logs with ginger or chocolate cookies and whipped cream.

Master Plan
Easy Cookie Log

1. Whip heavy or whipping (35%) cream with icing sugar and vanilla extract.

2. On a small platter, stand ginger or chocolate cookies on their edges and stack them sideways by spreading each one generously with cream and gluing it to its neighbor.

3. Slather the remaining cream evenly over the log.

4. Cover the platter with plastic and refrigerate for at least 6 hours or until the cookies are as soft as cake.

5. Unwrap and decorate. Chopped, candied ginger is seasonal. Try sliced toasted almonds or candies.

6. You can vary the flavors of the cream. Mint cream tastes good with chocolate cookies. Make mocha cream by dissolving instant espresso powder in the vanilla extract or some of the cream. You can add a dash of almond or lime extract to the cream.

✧ Use a muffin tin to make individual gingerbread cakes or fruitcakes.

Gussy It Up
Embellish packaged cake mixes to make them your own.

• Add cold brewed coffee, instead of water, to chocolate cake.

• Add cold brewed tea, instead of water, to spice cake.

• Add chocolate chips to vanilla cake.

• Add orange extract to chocolate cake.

• Add poppy seeds to lemon cake and bake it in a loaf pan.

Cake Doctor
The cake is tough or dense.

• Don't use cold ingredients.

• Batter that isn't aerated properly makes a heavy cake. Cream the butter and sugar longer, but don't mix too long after adding the flour.

• If the cake is too flat or dense to turn into a layer cake, cut circles out of it with a large, serrated cookie cutter. Serve them as cute tea cakes. A 13- by 9-inch (33 by 23 cm) sheet cake yields 12 circles if you use a 2¾-inch (7 cm) cookie cutter.

The texture is coarse, with tunnels or holes.

• The batter has too much air. Don't beat the eggs for so long. Run a thin spatula through the batter in the pan to get rid of air pockets. Rap the bottom of the pan a couple of times before putting it into the oven. (Exception: Don't rap the pan or disturb the batter when making a cake lightened with whipped egg whites. Handle it with kid gloves.)

The cake fell.

• It was underbaked.

• Don't introduce cold air into the oven.

• Don't slam the oven door. It can jolt the cake and deflate air bubbles in the batter.

• A cake will sink a bit as it comes out of the oven. Some cooks believe in dropping the pan from a height of about 4 inches (10 cm) to make the cake more even. Others say slamming the cake straight out of the oven will deflate it too much.

• If the cake is badly sunken in the middle, cut a circle out of the center and fill the ring with whipped cream and fruit.

The cake is lopsided.

• The flour mixture wasn't blended thoroughly with the wet ingredients.

• Oven temperatures are uneven. Next time, rotate the cake halfway through the baking time.

• The floor under the oven is tilted. Test it with a carpenter's level. Prop up the oven with a shim (a thin wooden wedge).

The cake is too peaked.

- Flatten it. Put a plate on top right after removing it from the oven. Don't push aggressively. You can add a weight, such as a can.

The top is cracked and/or dry.

- The batter was overmixed.
- The surface of the cake was too close to the top element in the oven.
- Next time, bake the cake for a longer time at a lower temperature.
- Cover the hot cake with a damp kitchen towel when it comes out of the oven. This will reduce cracks, but it won't heal them.
- Cover the hot cake with a large bowl and leave it for 5 minutes.
- As a preventive measure, add an envelope of unflavored gelatin powder to the dry ingredients before mixing the batter.

The cake is dry.

- Brush flavored sugar, liqueur, reduced fruit juice or strained preserves over each layer. (This helps when freezing a cake, too.)
- Dip pieces of cake in sweetened cold milk and heat them in a 350°F (180°C) oven. Eat them at room temperature.

The cake has a rough rim, but is not destined to be iced.

- Trim it with a small serrated knife and hide your handiwork with a sprinkling of icing sugar.

The cake is burnt.

- Freeze it. Slice off the burnt bottom with a large serrated knife. Thaw the cake. Apply icing.

Angel Food Cake

✧ Like meringue, angel food cake batter should not come in contact with fat.

✧ To help you release the cake, line the bottom of the pan with a ring of parchment.

✧ Use a tube pan — something for the batter to grip as it climbs. Rinse it well with hot water and dry it. Or wipe it with a paper towel dipped in vinegar. Never grease the pan.

✧ Angel food cake is better when it's made with cream of tartar. The grain is finer and it shrinks less than angel food cake made with a bit of vinegar or lemon juice. But some recipes call for both cream of tartar and vinegar or lemon juice. In that case, reduce the cream of tartar to, say, 1 tsp (5 mL) instead of $1\frac{1}{2}$ tsp (7 mL).

✧ If the egg whites are overbeaten, angel food cake may collapse.

✧ For extra stability, beat part of the sugar from the recipe into the whites once they reach soft peaks.

✧ Use cake flour for lightness. Sift it two or three times with the sugar. Fewer lumps mean less mixing, meaning less chance of deflating the foamy egg whites.

✧ Do not use an oven temperature higher than 350°F (180°C). The cake must be able to rise uninhibited by a crust that has formed too quickly. For the same reason, bake angel food cake in the lower third of the oven, away from the top element.

✧ For a thick, brown crust, bake at 350°F (180°C). For a thinner, golden crust, bake at 300°F (150°C) or 325°F (160°C).

✧ Invert angel food cake in the pan to allow air circulation after baking. The cake will collapse if the pan stays too hot or if it is removed from the pan while still warm.

✦ A serrated knife is the best tool for cutting angel food cake. Some folks prefer using two forks, back to back. They also sell a special comb for cutting angel food cake.

Cheesecake

9 Ways to Prevent Cracked Cheesecake

1. Grease the pan well.
2. Don't overbeat it.
3. Don't bake it too fast.
4. Don't let the oven get too hot.
5. Bake it in a bain-marie.
6. Don't submit the cheesecake to sudden temperature changes.
7. Don't bake it for too long.
8. Loosen the edges when the cheesecake is done.
9. Chill it before removing it from the pan.

✦ Two reasons for clumps or dents on the surface of finished cheesecake:
- The filling wasn't blended well.
- The cream cheese was too cold when beaten.

✦ Beat the cream cheese with the sugar until it's fluffy, but don't overbeat when adding the remaining ingredients. Too much air, and the cheesecake puffs too high in the oven, then collapses and cracks.

✦ Cold cream cheese makes the batter lumpy. Use cheese at room temperature and you won't be tempted to overbeat it.

✦ Use the mixer on medium speed, not high. Beating too much air into the batter will create bubbles on the surface of the cheesecake.

Gussy It Up

Pour a layer of chocolate between the base and filling, for a bit of snap. Let it set before adding the filling.

✦ Always use a springform pan. Grease the sides to reduce sticking. Line the bottom with a parchment round to make removal and serving easier. The parchment stays put when you cut the slices. For a prettier presentation, you can buy a springform pan with a glass bottom.

✦ For slow, even baking, put the cheesecake pan in a bain-marie (a hot-water bath). Wrap foil around the bottom of the springform pan, in case of leaks.

OUTSIDE THE BOX

Some cooks swear that super-creamy, super-quick cheesecake can be made in a springform pan in a pressure cooker. I haven't tried it.

Virgin Cheesecake

I call this Virgin Cheesecake because it's pure and simple. Plus, it is a good basic cheesecake that is full of possibilities. The last time I made it, I used a chocolate crumb crust, flavored the filling with lime extract and decorated the top with strawberries sliced crosswise for a topographical effect. **Makes 12 servings**

- **Preheat oven to 325°F (160°C)**

- **9-inch (23 cm) springform pan, bottom lined with parchment, sides liberally greased**

- **Large, shallow baking pan**

Variations

I used block cream cheese to get the right heft. Deli cream cheese will make a silkier, softer version.

This is just slightly sweet. You can add another 2 tbsp (25 mL) granulated sugar. Or, depending on the topping you use, you could reduce the sugar to as little as ¾ cup (175 mL).

Cinnamon Graham Crust

1 cup	graham cracker crumbs	250 mL
2 tbsp	packed light brown sugar	25 mL
1 tsp	ground cinnamon	5 mL
3 to 4 tbsp	melted unsalted butter	45 to 60 mL

Filling

4	packages (each 8 oz/250 g) block cream cheese, at room temperature	4
1 cup	granulated sugar	250 mL
4	large eggs	4
2 tbsp	freshly squeezed lemon juice	25 mL
1 tsp	vanilla extract	5 mL

1. *Crust:* In a bowl, using a fork, stir together crumbs, brown sugar and cinnamon. Stir in 3 tbsp (45 mL) butter just until moistened. If necessary, add the remaining butter. Press into the bottom of the prepared pan. Tamp it down evenly with the bottom of a glass. Refrigerate while making the filling.

2. *Filling:* In a large bowl, using an electric mixer, beat cream cheese and sugar on medium-low speed for 1 to 2 minutes or until well blended. Increase to medium speed and beat until fluffy. Beat in eggs, lemon juice and vanilla until blended. Do not overbeat. Pour filling over crust.

3. Overlap two squares of foil at an angle. Place the pan on the foil. Fold the foil up to cover the bottom. Place the springform pan in the baking pan. Pour very hot tap water into the baking pan until it reaches about a third of the way up the sides of the springform pan.

4. Bake in preheated oven for 45 to 60 minutes or until the top looks dry and is beginning to puff and the edges start to turn golden. The center will still be slightly jiggly. Turn off the oven. Prop the door open with a folded dishcloth. Let the cheesecake rest in the oven for 1 hour.

5. Run a small offset spatula around the edges to gently loosen them. Refrigerate the cheesecake for at least 2 hours or until cold. Carefully remove the sides of the pan. Decorate the top as desired.

♦ Keep hot cheesecake away from drafts. Once the baking time is up, leave it in the oven with the door propped open slightly. You can use a rolled kitchen towel as a wedge.

♦ Cheesecake tends to crack as it cools and shrinks. Run a thin spatula around the edges to release them.

♦ Refrigerate the cheesecake until it's cold, about 2 hours, before releasing it from the springform pan.

♦ Moisture may condense on the surface of the cheesecake. To prevent this, let the cake cool, then cover the pan with a paper towel and an inverted plate before refrigerating it.

♦ You can hide imperfections, such as cracks, by covering the top of the cheesecake with a mixture of sour cream and sugar.

Is It Done?

• Cheesecake should have golden brown sides but a jiggly center. Take it out of the oven when it reaches 150°F (65°C).

---

4 Steps to Tidier Cuts

1. Run taut floss or fishing line all the way through the creamy part.
2. Let go of one end and pull it out sideways, not upward.
3. Wipe it off and repeat until the entire cheesecake is scored down to the crust.
4. Finish the job by cutting down through the crust with a knife as you serve or plate each piece.

♦ You can also slice a cheesecake with a knife dipped in hot water, then wiped dry before each cut.

Fruitcake

Factoid Fruitcake is almost indestructible. There are urban legends of fruitcakes that have seen the quarter-century mark.

≡Fast Fix

Reincarnate old, dry fruitcake (and no, not as a doorstop). Turn it into steamed pudding.

1. Cut the fruitcake into chunks. Toss the chunks into a bowl.
2. Add about ¼ cup (50 mL) melted butter and 2 tbsp (25 mL) brandy per 1 lb (500 g) fruitcake. Coarsely mash the mixture with a fork.
3. Press it firmly into a heatproof bowl or pudding bowl. Tie a piece of parchment around the top to seal it.
4. Steam the bowl in a pot of water for an hour.
5. Serve the pudding with custard sauce.

OUTSIDE THE BOX

• For deeper color and flavor, substitute brewed coffee or tea for the liquid in the batter.
• Add crunchy peanut butter to the batter.
• A weird addition is ½ tsp (2 mL) mustard powder per 1 lb (450 g) flour. It's supposed to enhance the fruitiness and the color.
• For extra-long storage, bury the boozy cake in superfine sugar.

- To impregnate fruitcake with liquor, poke it all over with a skewer first.

- Wrap fruitcake in a piece of cheesecloth soaked in brandy or wine, then in foil. Or stash it in a tin.

- To keep cut fruitcake moister, slip a wedge of apple into the tin.

Jelly Rolls

How to Help a Jelly Roll Hold Its Shape without Cracking

1. Bake a thin layer of batter on a rimmed baking sheet lined with well-greased parchment that hangs over the edges.
2. Dust a clean kitchen towel with icing sugar. As soon as you remove the cake from the oven, loosen the edges and invert it onto the towel.
3. Peel off the paper. Trim any crusty edges.
4. While it's still warm, roll up the cake in the towel. Place it seam side down and let it cool.
5. Unroll, fill and reroll. Serve it seam side down.

Lava Cakes

- Don't overcook lava cakes; the molten core will solidify. Bake lava cakes just until they puff up and the tops start to crack. The cakes should still be wobbly.

- The batter for little lava cakes can be frozen in ramekins. Bake them without thawing.

Red Velvet Cake

- Red velvet cake is not bright red. To get the right velvety color, use both red food coloring and sifted cocoa powder in the batter.

Upside-Down Cakes

Ideas for Fruity Upside-Down Cakes

- They'll stick less and look prettier if you line the pan with buttered parchment.
- Instead of sugar, pour golden syrup over the parchment to create a caramel for the fruit.
- Add a bit of corn syrup to the brown sugar and butter glaze. It will be smoother and less likely to separate or get grainy.
- Arrange the fruit in a pretty design. Pour the batter slowly over the rows of fruit so they don't dislodge.

- You can make pineapple upside-down cupcakes instead of a whole cake. Put one pineapple ring in the bottom of each muffin tin. Use canned pineapple; the rings are smaller.

Preparing Cake Pans

- Cakes stick to pans that haven't been properly prepped. You don't want a cake to break after all your work. Grease and flour the pan, then line the bottom with parchment for extra insurance, especially for large cakes. Parchment also makes the flat bottom — often destined to be the top — smoother.

- Even if you're using cake flour in your recipe, flour the baking dish with all-purpose. Cake flour is too fine and clumpy.

✦ If you don't like white streaks on chocolate cake, you can dust the pan with cocoa powder instead of flour. Sift it first, right into the pan.

Parchment Tips

- To get the right size, place the pan on top of the parchment. Trace around the bottom with a pencil. Cut slightly inside the pencil marks. Lay it in the pan, penciled side down.
- Greasing and flouring the pan first helps the parchment stick and lie flat.
- Don't let the parchment wrinkle. If you are lining the bottom and sides, cut out a shape for the base and a separate strip for the sides. Don't try to stuff a crinkly piece of parchment into the corners of a square cake.

Greasing and Flouring a Bundt or Tube Pan

- It can be tricky getting into all the nooks and crannies. Paint the grease on with a pastry brush.
- Use oil or melted butter. Softened butter coats unevenly.
- To flour the funnel section of a tube pan with a removable base, grease it and dip it into a container of flour. The container can be a deep, narrow bowl, a tall, wide tumbler or even a vase. If you use up flour fast and frequently, you can dip the funnel right into the flour bin.

Gussy It Up

Create a shiny, sticky, chewy crust on a Bundt cake. Thickly coat a 10-inch (25 cm) Bundt pan with 1 tbsp (15 mL) softened butter, then ½ cup (125 mL) turbinado sugar. (It's easiest to coat the tube with the sugar first.) Carefully pour in the batter and bake.

 No-No

Don't use foil instead of parchment to line a pan. It sticks and pulls away chunks of cake.

✦ No springform pan? Crisscross two folded, greased strips of heavy-duty foil over the bottom of a cake pan. They should be long enough to hang over the sides so you can use the ends as handles. Pour in the batter. After baking, make sure the cake is cool enough to survive without breaking when you pull it out by the handles.

Releasing Cake from the Pan

✦ Remove a cake when you are just able to handle it and the pan without calling the burn unit. Let it cool for about 10 minutes on a rack, first.

✦ Removed too soon, hot cake becomes a structural disaster and breaks apart when inverted. Left too long, the cake becomes soggy and cements itself to the pan, and the edges overcook.

✦ To prevent grooves on a cake, cover the cooling rack with a kitchen towel.

✦ Ways to coax a stubborn cake or loaf˙ from its pan:
- Set the hot pan on a damp kitchen towel for 5 minutes. Press another damp towel against the sides.
- Rub an ice cube over the bottom of the pan. (Be careful with a glass pan. You don't want it to crack.)
- Rewarm the cake in the oven.
- If the cake is stuck to the removable bottom of a tube or springform pan, insinuate a small offset spatula between the metal and the cake.

7 Steps for Releasing Cake from the Pan

1. Rub the cooling rack with oil to prevent sticking.

2. Slide a small offset spatula around the edge of the pan to loosen the sides. (This works for cupcakes, too.) Press against the metal to avoid wounding the cake.

3. To loosen a cake clinging to the funnel of a tube pan, run a metal skewer around the edges of the funnel.

4. Place the rack over the cake and flip the pan. Pull the pan up and away.

5. If the cake has risen too high to flip that way without damaging the top, hold the pan over the rack, shield your hand with an oven mitt and invert the cake onto your palm, then gently release it.

6. Peel off any parchment. If you leave parchment on until the cake has cooled, it sticks and pulls off chunks.

7. Flip the cake upright on the rack.

❖ To loosen a Bundt cake, let it cool on a rack for 15 minutes, then gently tap the bottom of the pan on a work surface while rotating it.

❖ To remove a soon-to-be layer cake from a springform pan, unclasp the sides of the pan, cool the cake, then cut off the first two layers before removing the base.

♻ Waste Not

If a cake refuses to exit the pan, breaks or collapses, or if you have trimmings left after cutting and decorating, recycle.

- Fire up a fondue. Dip pieces of cake in molten chocolate or caramel. Offer sides such as sanding sugar, sprinkles, nuts and shredded coconut.

- Whip up a sundae featuring chunks of cake. This is especially good with bar cakes such as brownies.
- Use the chunks as a shortcake base.
- If the cake is a sponge, try it as a tiramisu layer.
- Sprinkle trimmings with liqueur and make a trifle.
- Turn the bits into cake crumbs for baking.

❖ To cool a cake quickly, set it on a rack for 10 minutes, then refrigerate it for up to an hour. Don't put a hot cake in the freezer.

Making Layer Cake

Arranging Separately Baked Cakes into Layers

- Don't slice the dome off the bottom cake to level it (unless it is very high). Instead, place the cake upside down. This gives you the flat surface you want, but fewer crumbs to contend with. Plus, you end up with more cake.

- For a double-layer cake, set the second cake on top, right side up. With both of the rougher, flatter bottoms facing the center, fillings and frostings will adhere better.

- If you're making a triple-layer cake, set the first and second cakes rounded side down, and the third cake rounded side up.

Cutting a Single Cake Evenly into Layers

- Use toothpicks as markers, both for slicing and realigning the layers after icing. Measure from the bottom and insert the toothpicks into the sides of the cake halfway up.

- Cut a small slit with a serrated knife. Insert floss, fishing line or sewing thread into the slit. Holding it taut in both hands, saw through the cake.

- If you do a lot of cake cutting, pick up a cake leveler. It's a metal bow strung with wire. You can adjust the height of the wire.
- If you wish to cut all the way through with a serrated knife, bolster the cake by laying your forearm gently across the top while you slice parallel to the work surface with your other hand.

Transferring Cut Layers So They Don't Crack

- After slicing a layer, slide a thin, firm support underneath before lifting it off. The disc from a two-part tart pan is ideal. Other ideas: cardboard, a baking sheet, the base of a springform pan.
- After frosting, tilt the next layer back onto the cake using the same disc. Position it where you want it, push on the cake and pull away the disc.

✖ No-No

Never slice or ice a cake until it is completely cooled. The icing will become slick and slippery. If in doubt, refrigerate the layers briefly.

Frosting and Filling Cake

- ✧ When frosting or serving a cake, anchor the bottom to the platter or cake board with a dab of icing.

How to Frost a Cake

1. Center a big blob of frosting on top of the cake. Sweep it out from the center.
2. Slap frosting generously on the sides. Spread it from bottom to top.
3. Tidy up the sides by smearing frosting with an offset spatula held almost upright while you turn the cake.
4. Tidy up the top, working from the edges to the center.

- ✧ The best tool for frosting is an offset spatula. This is sometimes called a baker's spatula or a frosting knife. The blade is long and narrow, and bent near the hilt. The second-best tool is a piping bag. The third is your hand (for dipping).

Making Do

The best way to frost a cake is to put it on a lazy Susan. If you don't have one, place the cake on a large plate or board. Set that on a large bowl turned upside down on the counter. You can turn the plate or the board as you ice. Keep a firm grip; this is a disaster in the making.

- ✧ How to keep the serving plate or cake board free of frosting:
- Put four strips of waxed paper on the plate in a square pattern underneath the cake. Or use two sheets that overlap in the middle. When you're done frosting the cake, pull out the paper and, voila, clean plate.
- Put sturdy strips of folded parchment under a cake directly on a lazy Susan. When you're done frosting, use the strips to transfer the cake to a platter or board, then pull them out.

Ⓒis for Crumb Coating

The crumb coating is a baker's secret. It is a thin layer of frosting that seals in crumbs, caulks gaps and creates a smooth canvas for the cake decorator.

- ✧ You should also sweep crumbs off a cake before dusting or glazing.

OUTSIDE THE BOX

For a crumb coating, you can cover the cake with melted jelly instead of frosting. Brush a thin layer onto the cake and let it set in the fridge. Then finish frosting.

5 Steps to a Crumb Coating

1. Brush the crumbs off the top of the first cake layer. Apply the usual quantity of frosting or filling. If there's a middle cake layer, do it again. Put on the top cake layer

2. Trim the layers flush, if necessary. Stand on a stool and look down at the cake from above. Slice around the sides, sawing in an up-and-down motion with a small serrated knife or sharp paring knife.

3. Brush the crumbs off the top and sides. On the sides, use frosting to caulk any gaps between the layers. Cover the entire cake with a thin, see-through coat of frosting.

4. Refrigerate the cake until the crumb coating is cold and firm, about an hour.

5. Finish frosting and decorating the cake.

Alternatives to Frosting in the Middle of a Layer Cake

- Lemon curd
- Nut spread
- Jam
- Whipped cream and berries
- Dulce de leche
- Mousse
- Cream cheese blends

✧ How to prevent frosted or filled layers from shifting and slipping:
- Push thin skewers down through the cake, after applying the crumb coating. Once the cake is cold, remove the skewers. The final frosting will hide the holes.
- Pack the cake into a springform pan after applying the crumb coating.

How to Fill a Tube Cake

1. Cut off about 1 inch (2.5 cm) from the top and set it aside as a lid.

2. Following the perimeter of the cake, cut a ring 1 inch (2.5 cm) in from the outside wall. Cut another ring 1 inch (2.5 cm) in from the center wall. Do not cut all the way to the base of the cake; stop within 1 inch (2.5 cm) of the bottom.

3. Make diagonal cuts between the incisions, alternating the direction of the cuts until you have a ring of triangles. Again, cut to within 1 inch (2.5 cm) of the bottom, no deeper. This will allow you to tidily pull out the cake in chunks. Do so.

4. You should end up with a ring-shaped tunnel. Even out the bottom of the tunnel using the curved tip of a grapefruit knife.

5. Fill the tunnel. (Mousse is good.)

6. Replace the lid. Spread icing over the entire cake.

Ways to Fill Cupcakes

- Put 2 to 3 tbsp (25 to 45 mL) batter into each muffin cup or paper liner. Top with a dollop of filling. Spoon in the remaining batter.

- Let cooked cupcakes cool. Carefully cut out a conical plug from the bottom of each one. Scoop out a tiny bit of cake. Add filling and replace the plug.

✧ Build a dam to prevent a soft filling from oozing. Pipe thick, stiff frosting around the perimeter of the bottom cake layer. Spoon the filling into the center. Spread it carefully and evenly up to the dam. If the filling is very soft, chill it before setting the next cake layer on top.

Ways to Create Frosting Effects

- Swirl it with the back of a spoon to make whorls or waves.
- Press the back of a spoon into the icing and pull up peaks.
- Draw a spatula or butter knife across the cake in S shapes.
- Run a (new) comb, the tines of a fork or the edge of a serrated knife over the icing. You can buy an official decorating comb, if you wish. Run the lines straight, or in zigzags or waves.

Ways to Create a Smooth Finish

- Use an offset spatula dipped in cold milk.
- Before spreading firm, dense frosting, such as chocolate ganache, dip the spatula in boiling water.
- Chill the frosted cake. Press, dab and rub a small square of waxed paper over it to smooth out dents and creases. This works for firm icings that set, not buttercream.
- Run the straight edge of a scraper across the top of the cold, frosted cake. (An offset spatula or ruler can do the job, too.) Then do the sides; hold the scraper perpendicular to the sides as you rotate the cake. This is also great for sharpening the edges on a square cake.

✧ An easy way to give a cake a professional-looking finish is to shake crazy drizzles of melted chocolate over smooth white frosting. Or use white chocolate on dark frosting. Let it set before serving.

OUTSIDE THE BOX

- Make psychedelic frosting by dabbing three different colors on a cupcake. Swirl a toothpick through the frostings. Or do an entire cake that way.
- You can use a fresh, fine-tip watercolor brush dipped in gel food dye to write a message or draw designs on firm frosting.

Quantity Guides
Fluffy or buttercream icing

- 9-inch (23 cm) round cake (top and sides): 1 to $1\frac{1}{2}$ cups (250 to 375 mL) for a single layer, 2 to $2\frac{1}{2}$ cups (500 to 625 mL) for a double layer, 3 cups (750 mL) for a triple layer
- Loaf (top and sides): 1 to $1\frac{1}{2}$ cups (250 to 375 mL) for a single layer
- 9- or 10-inch (23 or 25 cm) tube pan: 3 cups (750 mL) for a single layer
- 12 small cupcakes: 1 to $1\frac{1}{2}$ cups (250 to 375 mL)

Glaze

- 9- or 10-inch (23 or 25 cm) cake: 1 cup (250 mL)

Rolled fondant

- 8-inch (20 cm) square cake about 4 inches (10 cm) tall, with 4 layers: 1 lb (500 g)

Frosting and Icing

Frosting VS. Icing?

- Frosting is fluffy and thick. Examples: buttercream, chocolate ganache, cream cheese frosting, the stiff piping cream used for cake decorations.
- Icing is thinner and drier. Royal icing is made with confectioner's (icing) sugar and egg whites; it hardens when it dries.
- Fondant is a thick sugar paste that can be kneaded and rolled.

- Glaze is syrupy and shiny. It is often poured over Bundt cake and allowed to drip artfully down the sides. Glaze isn't meant to coat an entire cake. It is more flavorful than icing. Citrus, caramel and mocha are common glazes.
- Dusting is a sprinkling of confectioner's (icing) sugar or perhaps cocoa powder.
- Filling is looser and not as sweet as frosting. It can be chocolaty, fruity or nutty. It may be a mousse, custard or whipped cream. It can be made crunchy, with chopped candy.

Making Do

Quickie mock buttercream, mixed from butter and confectioner's (icing) sugar, is a modern shortcut to real buttercream whipped with hot syrup.

Ways to Improve Mock Buttercream

- For a satiny texture, beat buttercream frosting made with confectioner's (icing) sugar for 10 to 15 minutes. Scrape the bowl occasionally. You can use the paddle attachment of a stand mixer on medium to medium-high speed.
- Get rid of the raw cornstarch flavor by warming the mixture in the top of a double boiler over barely simmering water for 10 minutes. Do not let the butter melt.

Fast Fix

You can flavor mock buttercream with store-bought butterscotch, caramel or chocolate sauce.

Colorful Tips

- Use a toothpick to scoop and shake drops of gel dye into frosting. Stir to evenly distribute the dye. Repeat until you get the desired color.
- If the dye is in a tube, don't squeeze — accidental blobs can ruin your plans.

- A frosting's color darkens and deepens as it sits. You can make it a day ahead for a richer hue. Use a light hand at first. If the tint is crucial to your cake design, wait an hour.
- Set aside some undyed frosting, in case you need to lighten the color.
- Use white food dye to lighten a tint.
- For the blackest frosting, mix black dye into chocolate frosting.
- Dye frosting blue for a seaside cake design. Use coarse brown sugar for the sandy beach.

Frosting Doctor

It's too thick.
- Add milk 1 tsp (5 mL) at a time. The consistency changes fast.

It's too thin.
- Divide it in half. Add more confectioner's (icing) sugar to just one half. Otherwise, you'll use massive amounts. (Save the other half for another project.)

It's dry, grainy or cracked.
- Add a pinch of baking powder.

It's too wet or slippery.
- If this is due to a hot day, place the frosting in the fridge to thicken before continuing.

It's too dense after refrigeration.
- Revive frosting by fluffing it with a whisk or even beating it with a mixer.

✦ Stretch store-bought icing in a tub by whipping it with a mixer. This aerates and fluffs it, making it less dense.

B is for Boiled Icing

Fluffy boiled icing is sometimes called 7-minute icing because it is beaten for 7 minutes in the top of a double boiler over simmering water. Then, off the heat, it is beaten until cooled, about 10 minutes. It is usually made like an Italian meringue, by pouring hot syrup into egg whites, or sometimes by boiling ingredients in a saucepan, then beating them.

◆ For boiled icing made like a meringue, add a bit of lemon juice, vinegar, cream of tartar or light corn syrup near the end of the whipping time. This prevents it from becoming gritty and hardening too much.

◆ Boiled icing is ready to spread when it begins to harden at the edges of the bowl.

◆ If boiled icing hardens too soon, soften it with 1 tsp (5 mL) boiling water or lemon juice.

Royal Icing Mixtures

• For piping, use 1 to 2 tbsp (15 to 25 mL) water per 4 oz (125 g) confectioner's (icing) sugar.
• If you want royal icing thick enough to knead and roll like fondant, reduce the amount of water.
• For glaze, add water or another liquid to reach the consistency you want.

◆ Use hot water for royal icing. It will dissolve the sugar for a better blend.

G is for Glycerin
Glycerin is a colorless, odorless, syrupy liquid. It helps food stay moist. Look for it in cake-decorating shops and drugstores.

◆ Make thick royal icing for piping more pliable by adding 1 tsp (5 mL) glycerin per 1 lb (500 g) confectioner's (icing) sugar.

Gussy It Up
You can add vanilla extract, cocoa powder or orange extract to royal icing, or substitute lemon juice or rum for the water.

Fondant

F is for Fondant
Fondant is a sweet, chewy paste made with confectioner's (icing) sugar, shortening, glycerin and cornstarch. It's easier to buy than to make. Once rolled out, fondant is draped over cake for a smooth but not hard coating. It can be cut into shapes, or into strips for ribbons. Commercial fondant keeps for 1 year at room temperature. Seal it in plastic. Poured fondant is a looser type. It is poured over petits fours, then allowed to set.

◆ Do not freeze or refrigerate fondant. Moisture plus sugar equals gummy.

◆ Before kneading fondant, lightly grease your hands with oil. Do not use wet hands. That would encourage the sugar to melt.

◆ When rolling out fondant, dust the work surface or parchment sheet with cornstarch or confectioner's (icing) sugar. Roll the fondant as thin as possible, $1/16$ to $1/8$ inch (2 to 3 mm).

◆ Keep extra fondant from drying out while you work. Cover it with plastic or return it to its storage tub.

◆ Frost cake with buttercream before applying fondant. It glues on the fondant and adds a welcome creaminess. Make the frosting layer thin but not transparent.

◆ When applying fondant, place the rolled side, with its wee creases and lines, on the inside.

◆ Lightly press the fondant onto the cake, to help it stick. Trim it to fit around the bottom. A pizza wheel or box cutter leaves the cleanest edges.

Ways to Transfer Fondant

- Roll it out on parchment. Flip it onto the cake using the parchment.
- Wind it around a rolling pin, then unroll it onto the cake.
- Sprinkle it with confectioner's (icing) sugar to prevent sticking, fold it into quarters, then unfold it over the cake.

❖ If the fondant tears on the cake, moisten your fingers with shortening or oil and roll them over the tear. Don't use water; it will dissolve the sugar in the fondant.

❖ After the fondant is trimmed to fit, press it in at the bottom of the cake with a metal spatula or scraper. This makes it look cleaner and more professional.

❖ Press a scraper over the fondant on the cake to flatten it.

❖ Smooth creases by lightly running your buttered fingers or a strip of waxed paper over the fondant.

❖ If you didn't trim the sides of the cake properly and all the layers have left obvious ridges, hide your mistake in plain sight. Run your fingers over the fondant along the layers to indent and emphasize the ridges, as if you wanted them there.

Gussy It Up

Once a cake is covered with fondant, create a 3-D effect by sticking fondant cutouts, such as stars or flowers, all over the cake. Secure them with dabs of icing.

❖ Pipe frosting around the bottom edge of the fondant to hide the seam where it meets the plate or cake board.

❖ For marbled or psychedelic fondant, stop kneading in the dye when it is still streaky.

Ways to Dye Fondant

- Put it into a clear, heavy-duty plastic bag. Add dye and massage the fondant to spread the color.
- Place fondant on a sheet of waxed paper or parchment on the counter. Massage dye into the fondant. Wear thin gloves.

Glaze

❖ Confectioner's (icing) sugar glaze should be opaque. Stir in barely enough liquid to make it drippable. For the most opaque glaze, use cream or milk instead of lemon juice or water.

How to Apply Glaze

1. With a wide pastry brush, sweep crumbs and crusty bits off the sides of the cake.
2. If desired, sprinkle flour over the cake to slow the glaze down.
3. Place the cake on a rack set over waxed paper for easy cleanup.
4. The glaze should be warm enough to pour. However, if it drips too quickly and pools at the bottom, thicken it by whisking in confectioner's (icing) sugar.

Glaze Effects

- Drizzle glaze from a fork, spoon or whisk.
- Pour glaze into a measuring cup with a spout. Pour it over a round cake in a swirling motion, or over a square cake in a back-and-forth motion.

✦ Let excess glaze drip off and set before moving the cake.

✦ When pouring glaze or soft icing over a cupcake or tea cake, hold the cake on a large spatula over the glaze or icing bowl. The excess will drip back into the bowl. Use a blunt knife to push the cake off the spatula and onto a rack.

✦ After decorating the top of a cake with fresh fruit, brush the fruit with glaze. The easiest glaze: melted jelly.

✦ Brush glaze over fruit on a cake from the outside in, in a spoke pattern. That way, there is less chance of dislodging the fruit.

OUTSIDE THE BOX

Make a crispy glaze.
1. In a small saucepan, stir together about 1 cup (250 mL) granulated sugar, 2 tbsp (25 mL) water and a pinch of cream of tartar.
2. Boil it over medium-high heat, without stirring, until it is honey-colored.
3. Pour it onto parchment and swirl it into a circle about 12 inches (30 cm) in diameter. Let it cool briefly. While it's still pliable, invert it over a cake, peel off the parchment and gently press the glaze to mold it onto the cake.

Master Plan
Cake with Shiny Gelled Glaze

1. Make sure the top of the cake is completely flat. Trim it, if necessary. Frost the sides with a crumb coating. Refrigerate it until firm.
2. Stir together 2 tsp (10 mL) unflavored gelatin powder and 2 tbsp (25 mL) water. Let it soften for 10 minutes.
3. In a small saucepan, warm 1 cup (250 mL) preserves over medium heat until hot but not boiling. Strain. You should have about $\frac{2}{3}$ cup (150 mL). Return it to the pan.
4. Add enough juice to make 1 cup (250 mL). Heat until it is almost boiling. Stir in the gelatin mixture until it dissolves.
5. Refrigerate, stirring occasionally, until it is slightly gelatinous but still spreadable.
6. Meanwhile, create a collar with a thick strip of folded foil. Wrap it snugly around the cake, raised slightly above the top. You can use an elastic band or kitchen string to secure the collar around the circumference, then paper-clip the ends at the top edge.
7. Apply the gelled glaze to the top of the cake. Refrigerate until it is set.
8. Remove the collar. Carefully finish frosting the sides. Decorate the top with frosting rosettes and bits of fruit.

Ⓖ is for Ganache

Ganache is simply made with melted chocolate and cream. It can be poured over cake as a thick glaze. Or you can add some softened butter and whip it into a fluffy frosting.

✦ When applying ganache, puddle it onto the top of the cake at the center, then let gravity do its work. You can help gravity along by swirling the ganache outward with the back of a spoon.

✦ Once ganache is set, you can drizzle melted chocolate over it in sharp lines, to create a sculptural, chocolate-on-chocolate effect.

Dusting Cake

❖ Two ways to dust a cake evenly:
- Put confectioner's (icing) sugar or cocoa powder in a small sieve. Instead of shaking it, stir it slowly with a small spoon as you move the sieve over the cake.
- Put confectioner's (icing) sugar or cocoa powder in a mesh tea ball and shake it over the cake.

❖ Let a refrigerated cake come to room temperature before dusting it.

❖ You can brush edible gold dust over chocolate cake.

❖ Create patterns by dusting over a stencil.

❖ When using a stencil, be liberal with the confectioner's (icing) sugar.

Making Do
- Use a paper doily as a stencil. It must have a large, clear pattern.
- Make a homemade stencil. Use clip art. Print out or photocopy it to the size you need. For a sturdier stencil, use cardboard. Carve out the design with a box cutter.
- Use tiny cookie cutters as stencils. To make a design on a frosted cake, press a cookie cutter into the frosting. Fill it in with sanding sugar or candy sprinkles. Lift the cutter straight up and off. Use large, clear, simple shapes only.

Make It Easier to Lift Off Stencils
- Make handles for the stencil. Attach two pieces of masking tape (each folded over itself) at opposite edges, such as 3 and 9 p.m. for a round cake. When finished, lift the stencil straight up without disturbing the design.
- Coat the underside of the stencil with shortening or oil.

❖ Burn a design into the top of a cake. Sprinkle the top with confectioner's (icing) sugar. With a kitchen torch or over a gas flame, heat a metal skewer until it is red hot. Press the skewer into the sugar to make a pattern, such as crisscrosses.

❖ Lightly rub the top of the cake with oil to help dusting stick better. If dusting with coarse sugar, brush the cake with honey. The sugar needs something to stick to.

❖ To apply edible shimmer dust more evenly to cake, mix it with a flavoring extract such as lemon or coconut. (Not vanilla, it's too dark.) Paint it on the cake. This only works on a flat, cold frosting that's not too sticky.

Decorating Cake

9 Simple Decorating Options

1. Chocolate, butterscotch or mint chips, for a polka-dot effect.
2. Candies or jelly beans, to spell out names, create flowers or patterns.
3. Themed candies and chocolates, such as Valentine's Day hearts.
4. Chocolate curls or shavings.
5. Sanding sugar in neon colors. (Beware: The color bleeds when wet.)
6. Crumbled meringue. (You can use store-bought meringue nests.)
7. Flowers (fresh, organic and preferably edible) or candied violets.
8. Whole small fruit, with leaves and stems intact, arranged into a still life.
9. Toasted shredded coconut.

✧ To pat nuts or shredded coconut onto the sides of a cake, hold the cake over waxed paper, fill one hand with the nuts or coconut and pat gently. Turn the cake and repeat.

Fun Inedible Cake Toppers

- Toy dinosaur
- Barbie doll
- Barbie furniture
- Dump truck
- Cocktail umbrella
- Sunglasses
- A keepsake (for example, mark an anniversary by digging out the original topper from a couple's wedding cake)

Master Plan
Chocolate Border

1. Cut a strip of parchment ½ inch (1 cm) longer than the circumference and ½ to 1 inch (1 to 2.5 cm) taller than the cake. (The height depends on how you plan to decorate the top. For instance, you may want to pile whipped cream and/or fruit on the cake. In that case, you would create a higher border.)
2. Lay the parchment flat. Melt semisweet chocolate. Use a spatula to smear it evenly over the parchment. Two oz (60 g) of chocolate is more than enough for a 9-inch (23 cm) round cake.
3. For even edges, lift the coated strip and move it to a clean location. Let it stand for 20 to 30 minutes or until most of the chocolate is no longer shiny. Wrap the strip around the cake.
4. Refrigerate it for 15 minutes or until firm. Peel off the parchment.
5. If the border is too high, you can trim it with scissors.
6. As for the top of the cake, pipe frosting inside the border. (Or frost the top before the border is applied.)

✧ Decorate the sides of a cake with ladyfingers. Trim one end of each ladyfinger so it stands level, then surround the cake. Royal icing makes good glue.

≣Fast Fixes

- Melt ¼ cup (50 mL) whipping cream and ¾ cup (175 mL) butterscotch chips in the microwave on High for 30 to 60 seconds. Whisk until smooth. Let cool briefly. This makes enough to ice 12 cupcakes.
- One to 2 minutes before they come out of the oven, top cupcakes evenly with mini marshmallows. They'll melt and spread. Or try marshmallow fluff from a jar to frost a cooled cake.
- Melt milk chocolate in the microwave on Medium, then pour it over cake.
- Go rocky road, with marshmallows, chocolate chips and chopped nuts. Sprinkle these over a cake a couple of minutes before removing it from oven.
- Sprinkle confectioner's (icing) sugar on cake batter just before baking. This creates a crusty effect, though it's uneven.
- Place small chunks of chopped or shaved chocolate on top of cupcakes hot from the oven. Or press a chocolate "kiss" on top of each one and return the pan to the oven for a minute. The kiss will hold its shape. You can spread it with a spatula.
- Glaze tea cakes or cupcakes by dabbing 1 tsp (5 mL) of store-bought frosting in the center of each one, then returning them to the turned-off oven. The results may be uneven, though.

OUTSIDE THE BOX

Dollop meringue on top of cupcakes instead of frosting. Brown the meringue with a kitchen torch or under the broiler.

Fun with Cupcakes

- Make a sunflower cupcake. Pipe a couple of overlapping layers of yellow frosting petals around the perimeter on top. Fill in the center with chocolate sprinkles.
- Make a wreath cupcake. Pipe a couple of overlapping layers of green frosting leaves around the perimeter on top. Leave the center bare. Scatter a few red sprinkles or tiny balls over the frosting to mimic holly berries.
- Spell out a message or a name on cupcakes. Pipe a letter on top of each cupcake.
- Make a cupcake clock. Arrange 12 cupcakes in a circle on a platter or cake board. Pipe a number on top of each cupcake. In the center, set the hands of the clock with strings of licorice.
- Cut the tip off an ice cream cone and perch it on a cupcake as a witch or wizard hat. Create a face on the cupcake with piped icing or candies.
- Ice cupcakes with wavy blue frosting. Make shark fin shapes out of construction paper or cardboard. Push the fins into the frosting.
- Decorate a cupcake like a baseball. Spread white icing on top. Cover it with white sprinkles. Pipe curved stitches on either side of the top with red frosting.

Using a Piping Bag

- ✧ Buy metal tips for piping bags. They're more precise than plastic, and easier to clean. Use cotton swabs to clean the tips. Remove grease by swishing the tips in a vinegar-and-water solution.

- ✧ To secure a tip, cut only a tiny hole in the bag and screw the collar tightly over the plastic.

How to Fill a Piping Bag

1. Stand it in a tall glass. Soda fountain glasses are the perfect shape.
2. Put a folded, damp paper towel in the bottom of the glass to prevent the tip from drying out.
3. To prevent leaking, twist the bag above the tip and push it in. (Untwist it after filling, when you are ready to pipe.)
4. If the bag is very tall, fold the top down over the rim of the glass.
5. Dollop frosting into the bag.

- ✧ Hold piping bags filled with different colored frostings, doughs or cream mixtures in separate glasses. Use clear glasses so you can tell them apart at a glance.

- ✧ Until you are ready to pipe, seal the top of a piping bag with a chip-bag clip or elastic band. You can also buy piping bag clips.

- ✧ Test each bag of frosting on another surface before you go ahead on your cake or cookies. There's always a blob.

- ✧ Twist the top of a piping bag as you work, to create even pressure and flow.

✪ Waste Not

To squeeze the last bit of frosting out of a piping bag, push your pinkie into the tip.

F is for Flower Nail

A flower nail has a stem and a flat head to hold piped flowers and rosettes. To work faster, cut a pile of tiny waxed paper squares. Place one on the head of the flower nail. Pipe a flower. Remove the paper and set it aside to allow the flower to dry. Repeat.

❖ Don't just attack a cake with colored frosting. Stop and think. Four ways to plan a design:
- Use a bamboo skewer or toothpick to sketch a design on the cake. Firm up the frosting in the fridge first. If you make a mistake, smooth out the frosting with your finger and repeat.
- Use a cutout for a template. Poke holes around it, remove it, then connect the dots.
- Make a paper sketch with colored pencils.
- Cut out a piece of waxed paper to scale. Do a test run of the entire design using colored frosting.

Tactics for Nervous Cake Decorators
- Pipe some frosting onto waxed paper to see how it will turn out.
- Pipe rosettes and other designs onto waxed paper. Refrigerate or freeze them until they are firm. Pick and choose the best ones. Peel them off the paper and arrange them on the cake. Recycle mangled or misshapen ones back into the frosting.
- Pipe messages or designs in chocolate or royal icing onto waxed paper. Once they've set, transfer them to the cake.

Tactics for Writing a Message on a Cake
- First, lay thread or floss across the cake as a guide for lining up the letters.
- Score the message with a toothpick or skewer, then go over it in icing.

- You can use a needle to prick a hole in a small plastic bag. Add icing, then write.
- Stand on a stool to lean directly over the cake to write your message.

Storing and Serving

❖ Refrigerate with caution: Cakes made with oil, such as carrot cake, can be kept cold without hardening. Cakes made with butter, such as pound cake, harden in the cold.

❖ Leave cold cake at room temperature for 30 minutes before serving.

❖ Company's coming, but you don't know when? Freeze cake batter in its baking dish, then loosen and transfer it to a plastic freezer bag. Pop it back into the pan and bake it without thawing. It will take a bit longer to bake, but not much. Use lower oven temperatures; you don't want the outside to overcook.

Common Serving Sizes
- A 9-inch (23 cm) two-layer round cake serves 12.
- A 10-inch (25 cm) two-layer square cake serves 16.
- A 13- by 9-inch (33 by 23 cm) single-layer rectangular cake serves 18.

❖ Set aside leftover frostings and decorations for touch-ups before serving the cake.

❖ If you don't want a cake to stick, dust the plate with confectioner's (icing) sugar.

❖ You can buy round, square or rectangular cake boards in various sizes at bulk food stores and cake-decorating shops. Buy a board 2 inches (5 cm) larger than the circumference or length of your cake.

Making Do

- Press a plastic cutting board into service as a board for a rectangular cake.
- Make a homemade, custom cake board. Cover thick cardboard with wrapping paper or themed paper, such as sheet music or a map. Seal it tightly with new cellophane.

OUTSIDE THE BOX

- Turn a large, round plastic storage tub into an instant cake box (or pie transporter). Set the cake on the lid and invert the tub over the top. Press to snap the tub shut. This protects decorated cakes, yet they remain easy to remove.
- Do the same with a cake tin. Use it upside down.
- Cover a cake on a platter with the bowl of a salad spinner, a large sieve or colander, or a mixing bowl.
- Keep a loaf cake fresher longer. Cut slices from the center, then push the cut edges together.

✧ Transfer a small, frosted round or square cake using two metal, short-handled spatulas held underneath opposite ends.

✧ Put a slice of apple in a tin with leftover cake to keep it moist.

✧ Put a foil or parchment sling under a cake in a tin or box to make it easier to lift out.

✧ Serving that first slice of cake can be tricky. Cut two slices. The first slice will slide out more easily.

✧ For uniform pieces, cut a cake into quadrants, then slice each quadrant.

✧ Even the thinnest slices are overkill in some round cakes, especially the tall or dense ones. Use this portion-control approach: Cut a ring around the center of the cake. Cut slices from the outside ring. Use a knife with a rounded end, not a sharp end, or an offset spatula. When that's done, cut wedges from the small, inner circle.

✧ When transporting a cake in a car, stop it from slipping from side to side and smushing. Place the cake board or platter on a kitchen towel inside a cardboard box or a large baking dish. Bolster the box on all sides with heavy objects. To remove the cake easily, you can cut away the sides of the box with a box cutter.

✧ Hold and transport iced cupcakes in a muffin tin.

5 Tactics for Cutting Cake

1. Use a large serrated knife.
2. Heat the blade in a container of hot water or hold it under hot tap water for a few seconds. Or heat it with a kitchen torch or over a gas flame — but not a good knife.
3. Use the knife dry for fresh, crumbly cake.
4. Use the knife wet for cakes that are creamy, iced or dense, such as flourless chocolate cake or cheesecake.
5. Keep a glass or container of water next to you. Wipe the knife after each pass, if necessary. Use an opaque glass. A clear glass reveals the unappetizing, murky, crummy, greasy water.

Pie and Tart Crusts

Crumb Crust

✦ For the simplest crumb or shortbread base for bars or pie, blend flour or crumbs with sugar, then bind them with melted butter.

✦ Is the mixture sticky enough? Squeeze some between your fingers. It should clump. If it doesn't, add more butter.

⫶Fast Fixes
- Grind cookies in a food processor or pour crumbs into the bowl. Then add cold butter and pulse. You skip melting butter this way, and cold crumbs are easier to press into a pan.
- Mix a crumb crust right in the pie plate or baking dish. Mash it with a fork.

✪ Waste Not
Graham and chocolate Oreo crumbs are sold in supermarkets. But you can grab any type of dry cookie from your cupboard and pulverize it in the food processor. You can also use dry, leftover cake crumbs.

OUTSIDE THE BOX
You can use all kinds of goodies to make a crumb crust. How about crushed pretzels or pulverized granola? Crushed oatmeal cookies are good, too.

✦ A crumb crust can be used as is, but it's better to heat it. This encourages the sugar to melt and bind. If you're not baking it, chill the crust to firm up the butter. Otherwise, the filling may make it soggy.

✦ How to tamp a crumb or shortbread crust evenly into the pan:
- If you're using a pie plate, press another pie plate the same size firmly on top of the crumbs.
- Use the pusher from a food processor.
- Press with a short-handled metal spatula. This creates tidy edges in a square baking dish.
- Use the bottom of a juice glass.
- Use a dry measure with a curved base.
- Use a meat pounder, the stamping kind.
- Cover the crumb with plastic wrap. Spread it with your fingers and press down on it.
- Smooth shortbread with moistened fingers.

Pie Crust

⚛ A Bit of Science
Pie pastry has a simple character. Flour is mixed with cold fat, a bit of liquid is added, and the dough is rolled out. In the oven, the fat melts, leaving layers and air pockets. Thus is born a tender, flaky crust. So why do we fear it?

♛ Two Golden Rules
- Handle with care. Work the pastry as little as possible. That way, you don't develop the gluten that makes it tough and you don't force all the air out.
- Keep it cold. Say after me, "Hot oven, cold pastry." Keep all your ingredients cold and your hands cold. Chilling the dough makes it easier to roll out, keeps the fat firm, gives the flour time to evenly absorb the water and helps the pastry hold its shape. It relaxes the gluten, increasing tenderness and preventing shrinkage.

❖ Fat equals flakiness, but there can be too much of a good thing. A pie pastry that has overdosed on fat is greasy and crumbly. While you're at it, avoid too much water (heavy and shrunken pastry) or too much flour (tough and dry pastry).

Flour Tips

• Using cake/pastry flour for pie crust makes a noticeable difference. The crust resists shrinking and is more tender. That's because this flour has less gluten.

• If you want to use it, add at least 1 part cake/pastry flour to 3 parts all-purpose flour.

• Gluten sucks up more liquid. So add more water to dough made with all-purpose flour, less to dough made with cake/pastry flour.

❖ Always combine the flour and fat before adding water, juice or any other liquid.

❖ Choose ice water rather than cold tap water.

❖ Be a miser with the water. Stir it in gradually with the tines of a fork, just until a clumpy dough forms. Or here's an idea: Spritz it into the flour mixture with a spray bottle, for even coverage. Barely moisten the flour.

❖ Is there enough water? Gently squeeze a bit of dough. It should just hold together. If it still crumbles, add water. If it comes together without squeezing, it's too wet. Add flour.

❖ You'll need less liquid for a sweetened crust. Sugar hinders flour from absorbing it. Reduce the liquid by about 1 tbsp (15 mL) per crust recipe.

4 Ways to Alter the Liquid

1. For lighter pastry, add an acid to relax the gluten. In place of all or some of the cold water, use lemon juice, cider vinegar, wine, or even orange or apple juice.
2. For more tender pastry, use cream or an egg yolk in place of the water. Or add a yolk.
3. Sour cream, buttermilk and yogurt do both jobs.
4. Try club soda instead of water.

❖ Some tart pastries and rich doughs benefit from the light touch of baking powder. About $\frac{1}{2}$ tsp (2 mL) baking powder per $2\frac{1}{2}$ cups (625 mL) flour is recommended. Or try adding the same amount of baking soda with an acidic liquid.

Mythstakes

• Please don't mix the flour with the fat until it resembles coarse crumbs or bread crumbs, though many recipes say so. If it does, you've gone too far. The mixture should look like coarse meal with pea-size lumps or flakes in it.

• When using a food processor, ignore recipes that tell you to pulse until the mixture forms a ball. Just pulse until it clumps, then finish patting it together with your hands.

❖ A couple of kneading motions should bring the dough together. The disc should be pliable, with no cracks or crumbles.

✧ Unless the dough is ridiculously dry, don't resort to adding water until it is formed into a disc. Then, simply moistening your hands and running them over the disc may do the trick.

Master Plan
Pie Dough Like a Pro

1. Scoop flour onto the counter. Sprinkle salt evenly over top.
2. Toss chunks of cold butter over top. With a scraper, chop in the butter until the mixture looks gravelly.
3. Make a well in the middle. Pour water or beaten egg into the well.
4. Use your hands to gradually blend in the flour mixture from the edges of the well. Use a scraper to return stray clumps to the fold.
5. Pull the dough together and pat it into a disc.

✧ Many cooks attack the tender job of making pie pastry with a muscular food processor. There's nothing wrong with that, if you know when to stop.

Master Plan
Processor Pie Dough

1. Put flour and salt in the bowl of a food processor fitted with a metal blade. Pulse three times to mix.
2. Add butter chunks and pulse until they are about the size of peas. (Some pieces will be bigger, some smaller.)
3. Add liquid. Pulse just until the flour is moistened and starts to clump.
4. Dump the dough onto the counter. Gather it gently into ball. Pat it into a disc.

Alternative Ways to Cut In Fat

- My favorite: Don't cut it in. Shred cold butter against the large holes of a box grater. Toss it with the flour, using your hands or a fork. You can freeze the butter beforehand. If you want to substitute shortening, freeze it. If it's a hot day, chill the mixture before adding the water.
- Squeeze it in with your fingers. Freeze $\frac{1}{2}$-inch (1 cm) butter cubes for 15 minutes. Toss them in the flour. Pinch and rub to blend the mixture to the right texture.
- Some bakers use a rolling pin to add butter or shortening to pie pastry. Toss bits of cold butter with the flour mixture onto the work surface. Flatten it all with a rolling pin. Push it together with a scraper and roll it, twice more. Stick the mixture in the freezer for 5 minutes before adding in the liquid.
- Use a stand mixer. Put the flour and chunks of butter into the bowl. Set the mixer on low speed, or on a stir setting as some pro bakers do, then quickly turn the butter into flakes and lumps. You can carry on with the mixer and add the water. Mix until a ragged dough forms, then dump it onto the counter and finish the job.
- Use a hand-held electric mixer on low speed. Use stabbing motions to cut the butter into the flour.
- Use a whisk. This is the low-tech version of the hand-held mixer technique.

F is for Fraisage

The French use this technique. It cuts fat more evenly into pie and tart pastry, and is supposed to prevent tearing or cracking. Dump the dough onto the counter while it's still crumbly. It must be cold. Using the heel of your hand, smear the dough. Do this in quick, short pushes away from you. Smear small amounts at a time, say about a tenth of the dough. Collect the dough with a scraper and form it into a disc. It should be streaky, not well blended.

- If there are cracks at the edges, massage the dough lightly, but don't overwork it.

- Big bits of butter make pastry flakier; smaller bits make it more crumbly.

- Keys to flaky pastry (the traditional fruit pie type):
  - Choose lard or (second best) shortening over butter.
  - Keep the fat cold.
  - Flatten the fat or use large pieces.

- Keys to a tender crust (with fewer layers):
  - Use a blend of butter and shortening — butter for flavor and a deeper brown color, shortening for lightness.
  - Keep the fat in lumps or bits.

- Keys to tart pastry (firmer and richer):
  - Choose butter.
  - The fat can be at room temperature.
  - Add an egg yolk.

♡ Healthier Eater

If you want to use shortening to make pie crust, buy the trans fat–free type.

Crucial Times to Chill the Dough
- After mixing
- After rolling
- After filling

Quantity Guides
- **9-inch pie:** 12 oz (375 g) dough per bottom crust, 8 oz (250 g) dough per top crust (unless we're talking mile-high pie)
- **12 tart shells:** 1 lb (500 g) dough

- When making dough for a double-crust pie, cut it into two pieces, but make one slightly larger for the bottom. Mark it with an X.

8 Tips for Chilling Out

1. Chill the bowl, tools and ingredients for an hour in the fridge.
2. Each time the pastry is handled, cover it with plastic and let it rest for 30 minutes in the fridge.
3. Don't chill the dough for any longer than that, or you'll have to manhandle it when you roll it out. Plus, it cracks.
4. The pastry should be firm but not hard, and pliable but still cold. Press it with your finger. A slight indent should remain.
5. If pastry has been chilled overnight or frozen, let it sit on the counter for at least 15 minutes before rolling it out.
6. Instead of your naturally warm hands, use a ball of dough scraps twisted in plastic to press pastry into a pie plate.
7. Save time by chilling the top and bottom crusts at the same time. Lay the bottom one in its pie plate. Roll out the top one on plastic wrap, waxed paper or parchment, then refrigerate it.
8. You can speed up the process in the freezer. Some cooks like to briefly freeze a filled pie until the dough is firm, then pop it in the oven. This increases the baking time, so adjust accordingly.

- Cut the dough disc in half with a knife. To form each piece into a disc, press it cut side down on the counter.

- Pie dough doesn't have to be an exact circle, but it should be somewhat round. I've rolled out some strange shapes in my day.

Rolling a Circle of Dough

- Before you pick up that rolling pin, pat the top of the disc flat on both sides. Straighten the edges by cupping the sides with both hands and rotating it.
- Don't roll the pin back and forth. Roll the dough from the center to the top edge, then from the center to the bottom edge. Give the dough a quarter turn. Repeat until the diameter is right.
- Stop frequently to cup your hands around the perimeter to try to maintain the circle.
- You might need to flip the dough. Do so only if it starts to stick to the work surface and resists stretching.
- If your circle ends up shaped like an amoeba, trim it into a rough circle. Use the scraps to patch the edges. Roll the pin over the seams.
- To cut a perfect circle, put the bottom of a springform or tart pan, a cake board, a plate or a bowl over the dough as a template. Roll around the edges with a pizza cutter.

OUTSIDE THE BOX

Dough hard to roll? "Iron" it using the bottom of a heavy skillet or a sturdy flat metal spatula. Press in a swirling motion from the center to the edges. Don't press down at the edges.

✧ Patch tears rather than rerolling the dough.

✧ Use a pastry brush to sweep excess flour off the pie dough.

✧ Some bakers trim the surplus off the edges right after putting the dough in the pan. It's better to do so after chilling it. You can cut it more neatly. Scissors work well.

Sizing Guides

- Roll out a bottom crust to a diameter that's 3 inches (7.5 cm) wider than the rim of the pie plate — or 4 inches (10 cm) wider if the pastry edges are very uneven.
- Roll out a top pastry to a diameter that's 2 inches (5 cm) wider than the rim of the pie plate.
- If your filling is mile-high, roll out the top pastry to the same diameter as the bottom one.
- Aim for a $\frac{1}{2}$-inch (1 cm) overhang for a single pie crust. Fold it under and flute it. It should not be too high above the rim or it will sag as it heats, particularly if baked blind.
- For tart shells, cut circles 4 to 5 inches (10 to 13 cm) in diameter.

Fast Fix

For a free-form pie, roll out the dough between two sheets of parchment. Remove the top sheet. Transfer the parchment with the dough onto a baking sheet. Add a filling. Lift the parchment at the sides to help you fold the dough over the filling without touching it.

Gussy It Up

Save the scraps of dough. Form letters and write a short message on top of your sweet or savory pie. Cut pretty shapes, such as hearts or stars, or put an apple on top of an apple pie.

Ways to Transfer Dough to a Pie Plate

- Roll it out on plastic wrap, waxed paper or parchment. Flip it onto the pie plate. Peel off the wrap or paper.
- Roll the dough around a rolling pin. Unroll it over the pie plate.
- Sprinkle the dough with flour, fold it into quarters, place it in the pie plate, then unfold it.

OUTSIDE THE BOX

You can roll out the dough on parchment, transfer it directly into the pie plate (paper and all), then bake it that way. It's unwieldy, but the pie will be easy to remove if you want to take it somewhere without its baking dish.

✧ Did your dough fall apart when you tried to transfer it into the pie plate? Refrigerate it for 15 minutes. Shape it into a disc and reroll.

✧ Give frozen packaged pie pastry a rustic, homemade look. Use a sharp knife to cut off the crimped edges flush with the metal container. Bake. Let it cool for 5 minutes. Pull off the foil plate.

✧ Cement the top and bottom crusts firmly or they will shrink and separate.

Ways to Crimp and Flute

• Push on the outside edge of the dough with the thumb and index finger of one hand held about 1/2 inch (1 cm) apart. At the same time, push into the gap with the knuckle of your other index finger. Continue all around to scallop the edges.

• Position the knuckle of your index finger on the inside edge of the dough at the rim. Place the thumb and index finger of your other hand on the opposite side of the dough and pinch it against the knuckle.

• Press the tines of a floured fork around the edges.

How to Seal a Double-Crust Pie

1. Size the bottom crust so it has a 1-inch (2.5 cm) overhang.
2. Add the filling.
3. Brush milk or egg wash around the perimeter of the bottom crust and the filling side of the top crust.
4. Place the top crust over the filling.
5. Press the edges of the two crusts together.
6. Make the edges of the pie thicker and thus less likely to burn. Fold the dough under to quadruple the thickness. Or you can make a triple thickness by tucking the top pie crust under the bottom one, then pinching them together to seal.
7. Smooth the top of the pastry and even out any lumps from the filling with your hands.
8. Crimp the edges.

Ways to Make Tarts

• Bake small tarts, such as butter tarts, in lightly greased muffin tins. Roll out the pastry 1/8 inch (3 mm) thick. Punch out 4-inch (10 cm) circles using a cookie cutter or a cup. Drop the circles into the muffin cups and gently ruffle the edges.

• Lay out molds or ramekins in tidy rows, about 1 inch (2.5 cm) apart. Roll out a rectangle of pastry dough. Lay it over the molds. Use an empty mold of the same size to push the pastry down into the molds. Cut between the rows, leaving at least a 1/2-inch (1 cm) overhang. Trim excess dough with a small, sharp knife.

- ◆ Instead of fussing with a lattice top right on the pie, where the strips get moist and flaccid, weave it on parchment paper. Cut out a circle of parchment that's about 1 inch (2.5 cm) wider than the top of the pie. After weaving the lattice, refrigerate or freeze it until it's cold but still pliable. Invert it over the pie. Peel off the parchment.

OUTSIDE THE BOX

Practice weaving a lattice crust using strips of cold bacon.

- ◆ For even lattice edges, chill the dough before cutting it into strips.

- ◆ You can vary the width and number of the strips. Use shorter strips at the edges.

- ◆ Refrigerate the lattice strips until they are firm enough to weave without stretching.

- ◆ Attach a lattice loosely, as the strips can shrink.

- ◆ Use egg wash or milk on the perimeter of the bottom crust and the ends of the lattice strips to help them stick together.

Ways to Seal a Lattice Crust

- Tuck the lattice strips under at the edges.
- Cut the edges of the lattice flush with the overhanging bottom crust. Seal and crimp them together.
- For a neater look, add a tidy strip of pastry around the rim to cover the ends of the strips. Then crimp.

✘ No-No

Don't try to make a lattice with whole-grain or nutty pastries. They're too crumbly.

17 Steps to Weaving a Lattice

Weaving a lattice crust is so simple, you will slap your head. It's far simpler than the instructions. The key is to alternate.

1. Imagine a grid with 5 strips running north to south, numbered 1 to 5, and 5 strips running east to west, named A to E. Five is a good number for a 9-inch (23 cm) pie. Make each strip about ¾ inch (2 cm) wide and 7 to 10 inches (18 to 25 cm) long. Leave ¾ to 1 inch (2 to 2.5 cm) between each strip.
2. Place 1 to 5 on a square of parchment.
3. Fold down 2 and 4 a bit more than halfway, from top to bottom.
4. Place C across the midpoint of the odd-numbered strips.
5. Unfold 2 and 4 over C.
6. Fold down 1, 3 and 5 over C, from top to bottom.
7. Place B above C.
8. Unfold 1, 3 and 5 over B.
9. Fold down 2 and 4 over B, from top to bottom.
10. Place A above B.
11. Unfold 2 and 4 over A.
12. Fold up 1, 3 and 5 over C, from bottom to top.
13. Place D below C.
14. Unfold 1, 3 and 5 over D.
15. Fold up 2 and 4 over D, from bottom to top.
16. Place E below D.
17. Unfold 2 and 4 over E.

- ◆ Sprinkle granulated or coarse sugar over the lattice.

Ways to Prevent a Lattice Crust from Sinking

- Overfill the pie or else the lattice will go concave as the fruit shrinks.
- Cook the filling before putting it in the pie crust. Then lay the lattice flat across the top.

✧ You can reduce shrinkage in a pie crust, but you can't eliminate it. The gluten strands that were stretched during rolling spring back in the heat.

Ways to Reduce Shrinkage

- Use the minimum amount of water. Wet dough shrinks as moisture evaporates in the oven.
- If the pastry keeps shrinking back as you try to roll it out, let it rest for at least half an hour in the fridge, then try again.
- Don't stretch the dough. Transfer it gently into the pie plate. Fit it in by lifting and shifting. Do not press it firmly into the corners.
- Fill the shell with pie weights when blind-baking.

✧ Ceramic pie weights conduct heat evenly. Pie weights may also be in the form of metal balls or chains.

Making Do

- Dried beans are traditionally used as pie weights. Some ceramic pie weights are actually shaped like beans.
- Finally, a use for those useless pennies — they can double as pie weights.
- Raw rice is sometimes pressed into service. Be careful: It will stick to any exposed surface on the dough.

B is for Blind-Baking

This is the term for baking a pie shell, completely or partially, without filling. The shell wants to shrink and sag, puff and blister, so we must take steps to prevent that.

Master Plan
Blind-Baked Pie Shell

1. Fit a round of cold dough into the pie plate.
2. Prick the bottom and sides with a fork.
3. Place an aluminum pie plate over the pastry. (It'll be easy to lift out.) Or put foil or a parchment circle over the pastry.
4. Pour in about 4 cups (1 L) pie weights.
5. Refrigerate or freeze it until the pastry is very cold.
6. Bake it on the bottom rack of a 425°F (220°C) oven for 15 minutes. Baking it hot and fast sets the crust quickly, and thus prevents the sides from flopping over or caving in.
7. The pastry should look matte rather than shiny. If you are partially baking it, remove it from the oven now and let it cool on a rack. Remove the weights.
8. If you are baking the shell completely, remove the pie weights. Prick the bottom with a fork to prevent bubbling. Reduce the oven temperature to 350°F (180°C) and bake until the edges start to turn golden brown.

✧ You can blind-bake flat rounds of pastry as tops for tarts or pies.

Master Plan
Blind-Baked Pastry Rounds

1. Roll out the pastry 1/8 inch (3 mm) thick and to a diameter that's 1 inch (2.5 cm) wider than you need.
2. Prick it all over with a fork and place it on a baking sheet. Bake it at 400°F (200°C) for about 12 minutes.
3. Top and flatten the pastry with a second baking sheet.
4. Bake it until golden, 10 to 12 minutes.

Pâte Brisée

Here's a tasty, slightly sweet pastry crust. **Makes pastry for one 9-inch (23 cm) double-crust pie or two 9-inch (23 cm) single-crust pies**

Tip
You can use half and freeze the rest for a future pie.

1½ cups	all-purpose flour	375 mL
½ cup	cake/pastry flour	125 mL
2 tbsp	granulated sugar	25 mL
¼ tsp	salt	1 mL
¾ cup	cold unsalted butter, cut into pieces	175 mL
¼ cup	cold shortening, cut into pieces	50 mL
4 to 6 tbsp	ice water	60 to 90 mL

1. In a food processor, pulse all-purpose flour, cake/pastry flour, sugar and salt to combine. Add butter and shortening. Pulse until the mixture is crumbly, with pea-sized bits of fat.

2. While pulsing, pour in 4 tbsp (60 mL) ice water through the feed tube. Pulse until the dough looks ragged. Add some or all of the remaining ice water if the mixture is too dry to clump.

3. Turn the dough out onto a work surface. Gently gather it into a ball. Cut it in two. (If planning to bake a double-crust pie, make one piece slightly larger.) Press each piece into a disc. Wrap in plastic and refrigerate for 30 to 60 minutes or until firm but not hard.

◇ Lower the fuss factor with blind-baked tart shells. Put squares of foil in the muffin tins or tart molds you will be using. Fill them with pie weights. Twist the tops closed. When the time comes, plop the packets into the tart shells.

Gussy It Up

- Add a couple of tablespoons (25 mL) unsweetened cocoa powder to a single, sweet crust made with sugar and egg.
- Work 3 oz (90 g) of shredded sharp Cheddar into pie dough. Apple pie, anyone?
- Substitute peanut butter for half the fat in a pie crust to create an interesting base for custard or chocolate pie. This makes soft dough, so refrigerate it until cold and roll it out quickly.
- Make piebald pastry. Blend the flour and fat. Evenly divide the mixture into two bowls. Mix unsweetened cocoa powder into the mixture in one bowl. Add half the wet ingredients to each bowl. Press the dough into discs. After refrigerating, press the disc of plain pastry onto the chocolate disc. Roll them out together.
- You can bake handles from strips of dough inserted into muffin tins or ramekins. Then gently push the handles into filled tarts to make them look like baskets. This works best with firmer dough, such as butter pastry.

Pie Pastry Doctor

The dough ripped during rolling.

- Rub water along either side of the fissure. Pinch the edges together.

The pastry split in the pie plate.

- Don't stretch it. Cut a small slit across the tear. Dab it with water. Rub in a circular motion until the scar disappears.

The baked shell split.

- Press a thin scrap of fresh pastry over the crack.
- Brush beaten egg over the fissure. Bake the shell at 300°F (150°C) for about 2 minutes to set the egg.

Better Leftovers

- Use scraps of pie dough to make cookies fast. Roll them out to 1/4 inch (0.5 cm) thick. Sprinkle them with cinnamon sugar or smear them with jam. Bake at 375°F (190°C) until golden.
- Make sandwich cookies. Roll out the scraps of dough. Punch out circles with a cookie cutter. Bake them. Put dollops of leftover cooked pie filling in the sandwiches.

 KID STUFF

Give dough scraps to the kids to use as play-dough. (No eating, please.)

Pies

◇ Never put hot filling in a raw crust. The fat in the pastry will melt. To cool a fruit filling quickly, spread it over a large baking sheet. Once it nears room temperature, refrigerate or freeze it briefly.

Quantity Guides for a 9-Inch (23 cm) Pie

- You'll need about 4 cups (1 L) of fresh fruit.
- You'll need 2 to 3 lbs (1 to 1.5 kg) of apples, depending on how high-rise you want the pie.

◇ Toss fruit for pie filling with a large rubber spatula, lifting from the bottom. The fruit won't bruise as much.

◇ When cutting apples (or any other fruit that browns), toss the fruit in a bowl with 1 to 2 tbsp (15 to 25 mL) lemon juice from the pie recipe, instead of adding the juice later.

Reasons to Toss Fruit with Lemon Juice

- It retards browning.
- It brightens the flavor and cuts sweetness.
- It tenderizes fruit and prompts the release of juices.

◇ If the fruit isn't juicy enough, macerate it by tossing it with granulated sugar. Drier fruit, such as rhubarb, can macerate for 30 minutes. If the fruit is still not juicy enough, add 1 to 2 tbsp (15 to 25 mL) orange or apple juice.

OUTSIDE THE BOX

You can freeze filling in a pie plate. When you're ready to bake, toss the frozen disc into a pie shell.

◇ For a pretty yet simple fruit filling, halve the fruit, then thinly slice it crosswise. Place the fruit in the pie crust around the perimeter, then fill in the center. As you go, fan out the fruit by pressing it lightly with your palm. This works nicely with apples, freestone peaches, apricots and plums.

◇ For fresh-tasting, not too sweet or glutinous blueberry pie, cook half the berries for the filling, then fold in the remaining fresh berries.

◇ Apple pies are not "as easy as pie," because of all the variables. Apples differ in sweetness, juiciness and spiciness. Some hold their shape; some dissolve. The way they are cut affects the cooking time. For the best of two worlds, combine soft, sweet apples and firm, tart apples — such as Macs and Grannies — in one pie. The soft ones dissolve into a saucy base for the firm ones.

◇ Thin wedges work best for apple pie. Use a corer/wedger to cut an apple into 12 wedges, then halve each wedge lengthwise.

⌁Fast Fix

For a makeshift pie or turnover filling, combine shredded apple with applesauce.

✧ You can caramelize apples before filling a pie. Mix the apples with butter, brown sugar and spices such as cinnamon. Cook them in a skillet in a single layer, without crowding, until they are golden brown. Let them cool before filling a partially baked pie shell.

Gussy It Up

• Customize pecan pie and butter tarts by switching syrups in the filling. Switch from cane to maple syrup, for example. For deep flavor, throw a bit of molasses into the mix.

• In place of some of the sugar, drizzle maple syrup over sliced fruit before baking it in a pie.

• Add crystallized ginger to pear, peach or apple pie.

• Perk up fruit pie by adding dried cranberries, blueberries or cherries to the filling. Or add chopped nuts.

• A tasty surprise: Cut about 10 caramels into quarters and sprinkle them into the pie shell before adding the fruit filling and baking. This is especially good with apples or even peaches. Alternatively, you can melt the caramels and pour them over an open pie.

• Add mini marshmallows to pumpkin pie filling after you pour it into the shell. Make sure they are evenly distributed. Use enough to eventually cover the top in a single layer. As the pie bakes, the marshmallows rise and melt to form a topping.

• Top a pumpkin or custard pie with nut crunch. Stir together chopped nuts, brown sugar, flour and butter. Broil the mixture on a baking sheet until it's golden. Let cool. Crumble over the baked pie while it's still warm.

• Dust confectioner's (icing) sugar over the top crust of a pie while it's hot from the oven. The part closest to the pie will melt and be sticky, while the top remains powdery.

• Sprinkle the top crust with neon-bright sanding sugar. This is pretty.

• Redeem a dull fruit pie by serving custard sauce alongside.

✧ For cream pies that are firm enough to slice neatly, add about 1 tbsp (15 mL) softened unflavored gelatin powder to the recipe.

✧ You'll need 1 egg to set each ⅔ cup (150 mL) pumpkin pie purée.

♻ Waste Not

If a custardy pie filling doesn't all fit in the shell, bake the pie halfway, then drizzle leftover filling over the top in a thin layer. This only works for small extra amounts of up to ½ cup (125 mL).

✧ Reduce the liquid in fruit destined to sit atop pastry cream. Cut the fruit into wedges and bake it in a covered dish at 375°F (190°C) until much of the liquid is released. Drain, saving the juices. Arrange the cooked fruit on the pastry cream. Boil the juices to reduce them to 1 tbsp (15 mL), then drizzle them over the fruit.

✧ A hollow space develops underneath the crust as the fruit cooks and shrinks while the pastry gets firmer. You can minimize the effect:

• Avoid high-rise pies.

• Mound fruit more evenly, so there's not so much of a peak in the center.

• Simmer the filling, such as apples, over low heat for 15 minutes first.

• Gently press down on the filling as you apply the top crust. Smooth the top down with both hands.

• Use lots of fat in the crust. It will help the crust sink.

• After you take the pie out of the oven, lightly press down on the crust if you see the filling shrinking. Try this only when the crust is hot and pliable. Careful: It can break.

24 Remedies for Soggy Pies

For pie-makers, a soggy bottom is almost as bad as a saggy bottom.

1. Use thickeners, such as flour, cornstarch and tapioca, to suck up juices.
2. Sprinkle 1 tbsp (15 mL) instant tapioca granules into the bottom of the pie shell to absorb fruit juices. Pulverize the tapioca first in a spice grinder. Or use tapioca flour.
3. Stir ground nuts into the fruit filling.
4. Increase the fat in the pastry. Or use lard.
5. It can be tricky to cook the bottom crust before the top crust gets too brown. Keep the lower layer of dough thin. The upper crust can be a bit thicker.
6. Do not prick the bottom of an unbaked pie shell before adding the filling.
7. Chill the shell for at least 20 minutes before filling it.
8. Brush the shell with lightly beaten egg white, then chill it for 15 minutes before filling.
9. Brush the shell with egg wash. Bake it at 350°F (180°C) for 5 to 10 minutes or until the egg has solidified. Then add the filling. In some cases, you may need to cool the shell before adding the filling.
10. Brush the shell with melted butter, then refrigerate it until it's firm.
11. Sprinkle toasted ground nuts, cake crumbs or bread crumbs over the bottom of the shell. Press them into the dough with the back of a spoon.
12. Another anti-sog technique is lining the bottom with frangipane, which cooks with the fruit but absorbs the liquid. Frangipane is a paste made with almonds, sugar, butter and eggs.
13. For custard and cream pies, turn to graham crumbs for crisping and browning. Sprinkle your work surface with 2 tbsp (25 mL) graham crumbs, then roll out the dough on top. Sprinkle more crumbs over the dough as it is rolled out.
14. Partially bake the bottom crust before adding the filling. This works with fillings that cook quickly or are semi-cooked.
15. Before filling a custard pie, you can prebake the crust, brush on 1 oz (30 g) melted chocolate, then let it cool and harden.
16. Don't let fruit sit for a long time in sugar at room temperature. Too much juice seeps out.
17. To create a pie with more intense flavor and less liquid, sprinkle chunks of fruit with sugar to encourage them to release their juices. Drain, saving the juices. Boil the juices to reduce them before returning them to the fruit.
18. In the same vein, cook berries with a bit of water or juice until they release their liquid. Strain, reserving the liquid. Boil the liquid until reduced, then thicken it with cornstarch (or tapioca flour). Stir it back into the berries. Berries have a lot of liquid and, usually, too much cornstarch is added to compensate. That makes a pie gluey.
19. Apples can be roasted or grilled first. Cut each apple into no more than 8 wedges. Sprinkle with granulated sugar and toss. Spread the apples on a rimmed baking sheet. Broil, turning them once, for 5 minutes or until they are golden brown. Or cut them in half, grill them, then slice them. In a bowl, toss together the roasted or grilled apples, brown sugar, lemon juice, spices and flour. This works with other fruit, too.
20. Put raw fruit in a baked crust lined with lemon curd or pastry cream, then serve it.

21. Cut steam vents in the top crust or use the ultimate steam vent, a lattice top.
22. Bake the pie in a glass dish. It lets you check on the bottom crust.
23. Bake on a rack in the bottom third of the oven. This helps cook the bottom crust and prevents the top from getting too brown before the filling is done.
24. Cool the pie on a rack.

V is for Vent

Pies need to vent. Once steam from the hot filling is offered an escape route, the liquid in the filling is reduced, the crust is saved from sogginess and the heat is distributed more evenly.

Making Do

A pie bird, a little funnel that sits in the center of the pie, is made specifically for venting. If you don't have one, press a piece of rigatoni or penne into service.

✧ Along with a vent in the center, cut a vent or two near the edges. It's easier to check bubbling juices there.

✧ Cutting slashes in the top crust is such a rudimentary way to vent. Think ahead, and you can decorate the top crust before it goes over the pie.

Fun Ways to Vent

• Use a thimble or spice jar lid to punch holes in the pastry. Replace the cutouts in the holes for a polka-dot effect.
• Cut out a large star from the center of the pie crust and tiny stars across the top. Use the cutouts to decorate the top.

✧ Start baking at a higher temperature, such as 400°F (200°C), for 10 to 15 minutes, then reduce the heat to 350°F (180°C). The intense heat at the beginning creates steam that pushes up pockets of fat and makes the crust flaky. Exception: Cook custard pies at 300°F (150°C). If the heat is too high, the eggs seize and the pie becomes watery.

OUTSIDE THE BOX

A pizza stone is great for pies. It distributes heat in the oven and crisps the bottom crust. If you don't have a pizza stone, put the pie on a preheated baking sheet.

Pie Doctor

The bottom is not cooked.
• Drape the pie with foil and put it back in the oven.

The bottom is not cooked, but the top and filling are threatening to burn.
• Carefully cut off the top crust. Scoop the filling into small bowls. Dollop with whipped cream. Decorate with shards of top crust.

The filling is runny.
• It may be underbaked. Give it 5 to 10 more minutes.

The pie crust is done, but the filling isn't.
• Wrap the pie loosely but completely in foil and return it to the oven.

✧ Pie fillings thickened with flour will be too thick if overcooked. Pie fillings thickened with cornstarch will be watery if overcooked.

✧ To distribute tapioca flour or cornstarch more evenly in a bowl of fruit and juices, first combine it with the sugar.

High Apple Pie

Plenty of spiced and creamy filling is what I like. Purists will have none of it. **Makes 8 to 10 servings**

- **9-inch (23 cm) deep-dish pie plate**

- **Small round or star-shaped cookie cutter**

- **Baking sheet, lined with a silicone mat or parchment paper**

Tips

I've tried this with Northern Spies (perfect), Cortlands (fine), a mixture of Grannies and Macs (firm yet creamy) and Spartans (so-so). The Spartans take longer to cook.

The pie shell will be very full. Don't worry: You can make it all fit, and the fruit will settle.

	Pastry for a double-crust pie	
	Finely grated zest of 1 lemon	
1 tbsp	freshly squeezed lemon juice	15 mL
2¾ to 3 lbs	apples (about 8)	1.25 to 1.5 kg
6 tbsp	granulated sugar	90 mL
6 tbsp	packed brown sugar	90 mL
¼ cup	all-purpose flour	50 mL
½ tsp	ground cinnamon	2 mL
¼ tsp	salt	1 mL
⅛ tsp	ground nutmeg	0.5 mL
2 tbsp	unsalted butter, cut into pieces	25 mL
3 tbsp	half-and-half (10%) cream	45 mL
1	large egg	1
1 tbsp	cold water	15 mL
	Turbinado sugar	

1. Roll out slightly more than half of the pastry dough into a 12- or 13-inch (30 or 33 cm) circle. Transfer it to the pie plate. Refrigerate for 30 minutes.

2. In a large bowl, combine lemon zest and lemon juice. Working with one apple at a time, peel, core and cut the apple into 24 wedges. Add to the lemon mixture and toss gently.

3. In another bowl, using a fork, combine granulated sugar, brown sugar, flour, cinnamon, salt and nutmeg. Sprinkle over the apples. Toss gently with a rubber spatula, lifting the apples from the bottom to coat thoroughly.

4. Trim the edges of the pie shell, leaving a 1-inch (2.5 cm) overhang. Mound the apple mixture in the shell, pressing down as much as possible. Dot the filling with butter. Drizzle cream over top.

5. In a small bowl, whisk together egg and cold water.

6. Roll out the remaining pastry into an 11-inch (28 cm) circle. Cut a vent in the center with the cookie cutter.

Tips

Turbinado sugar is coarse and yellowish.

Cover the edges with a pie-crust protector or foil if they start to brown too much.

7. Brush the edges of the bottom crust with egg wash. Place the top crust over the filling. Smooth and press down gently with your palms. Press the edges of the crusts together. Slash a few vents on top, radiating from the center like spokes on a wheel. Fold the edges of the pastry underneath. Crimp the edges. Refrigerate for 30 minutes.

8. Meanwhile, preheat oven to 450°F (230°C).

9. Place pie on prepared baking sheet. Brush the top with egg wash. Sprinkle with turbinado sugar.

10. Bake on the bottom rack for 15 minutes. Reduce the oven temperature to 350°F (180°C). Bake for 45 to 60 minutes or until apples are tender and juices are bubbling. Let cool on a wire rack. If the filling starts to sink as it cools, press down gently to remold the top crust.

✧ Instead of using a lot of a thickener, which can make a pie stodgy or gummy, incorporate more natural pectin.

Ways to Work with Pectin

- Add shredded apple, a high-pectin fruit, to blueberry and other berry pies, along with a bit of thickener.
- Thicken an apple pie with pectin syrup. While the pie is baking, put the peels and cores in a saucepan. Add about 1 cup (250 mL) water and 1 tbsp (15 mL) granulated sugar per 1 lb (500 g) of original apples. Simmer the mixture over low heat, uncovered, for half an hour. Strain, discarding solids. Pour 2 to 4 tbsp (25 to 50 mL) of the syrup (depending on the juiciness of your apples) into the vent in the pie once it's out of the oven. Lightly tap the pie plate to distribute the syrup. Let the pie cool. (Save the rest of the syrup and use it for other pies.)
- Use a masher to crush fruit to release pectin. Heat the mashed fruit just until it breaks down. Combine it with fresh fruit.

✧ As a thickener, choose flour for high-pectin fruit, such as apples. Choose tapioca flour for berries.

✧ For clear juices, choose tapioca flour.

✧ Avoid tapioca granules as a thickener in a lattice-topped or open pie. Hard granules may be left behind. They need to be covered to soften.

Is It Done?

- The pastry looks dry and golden but not brown, except for tinged edges.
- The juices are thick. They bubble rather than spit.
- A skewer pushed through the vent encounters a hint of resistance. This applies to pies made with apples and other firm fruit. If it's mushy, it's overcooked.
- In a custard pie, the center should jiggle slightly. It will firm up as it cools. If you are unsure, turn off the heat and leave the pie in the oven until it's cooled.

- If the edges of your pie begin to turn too brown, cover the perimeter with a pie-crust protector, a ring of metal or, better, silicone.

Making Do

If you don't have a pie-crust protector, forget those suggestions to use strips of foil. That's too awkward.

- Cut the center out of an aluminum pie plate. Leave a 2-inch (5 cm) rim. Turn it upside down over the pie.
- Cut a square of foil that's 1 inch (2.5 cm) wider than the pie plate. Fold it in half. Cut out the center. Leave a 3-inch (7.5 cm) border. Spray one side with oil to prevent sticking. Lay the ring, oil side down, over the pie.

Ways to Make Cleanup Easier

Pies spit. The juices stick and burn. Don't put a pie in the oven without something underneath it to catch the drips.

- Put parchment on the baking sheet or stone.
- Set a pie on a baking sheet. (A small sheet is preferable, to encourage air and heat circulation.) Line the sheet with parchment, foil or a silicone mat.
- Put a pie plate directly on the oven rack. Lay foil, parchment or a silicone liner on the oven floor or on a rack underneath.
- If any juices drip onto the oven floor, quickly sprinkle salt on them to cut smoke and odors.

- If juices leak over the edges of the pie plate, loosen those spots when you take the pie out of the oven. Otherwise, once cooled, they will glue the pie to the plate.

- To extract a tart from a pan with a removable bottom, set it on a coffee can or an upturned narrow bowl. Ease the rim off the sides and pull it down. Slide a long, thin spatula under the tart to remove the base while sliding the pastry onto a serving platter.

- If wee tarts are stuck in their pan, put them in the freezer for 15 to 30 minutes, then remove them.

- Let a pie cool to room temperature before cutting it. The juices have to gel. If you want warm pie, gently heat a slice in the microwave or oven.

✗ No-Nos

- Don't serve cold pie. Fatty pastry becomes hard and unpleasant in the fridge.
- Don't let a fruit pie sit at room temperature overnight. The filling starts to ferment.

- Use a buttered knife to cut through a soft, sticky pie.

Pastries

Choux Pastry

✦ Beaten in a saucepan on the stove, then baked, airy choux has more in common with the popover than its fellow pastries. Choux pastry is split and filled, most famously for éclairs. It can also be fried.

✦ Choux pastry relies on steam to rise. Heat the water quickly. You don't want too much evaporation.

⫶Fast Fix

Traditionally, eggs are beaten into the warm batter with a wooden spoon. Why bother? Use a hand-held electric mixer on low speed.

✦ Beat in the eggs one at a time until fully incorporated, 10 to 20 seconds each.

✦ How to avoid cooking the eggs before they're blended:
  - Before adding the eggs, let the batter sit for 1 minute once it's off the burner.
  - Break the eggs, one at a time, into a small bowl. Slip each one into the batter while the mixer is running.

✦ For the puffiest pastries, bake the dough right away. Alternatively, cover the surface of the dough with butter and plastic wrap, and stick it in the fridge.

✦ Choux pastry needs a hot oven to rise properly. Start baking it at 425°F (220°C), then reduce the heat to 350°F (180°C) at halftime.

✦ Lightly brush the tops with egg wash. Don't let it run down the sides.

Is It Done?

- The cooked flour mixture pulls away from the sides of the pan and starts to film the bottom of the pan. It looks like mashed potatoes and feels like an earlobe.
- After the eggs are added, the dough is smooth, shiny and very thick.
- The baked pastry is golden brown and light. It should slide around the baking sheet.

✗ No-No

Some recipes recommend cutting the finished pastry and pulling out soggy bits. There should be no need for that.

6 Ways to Avoid Sogginess

1. Don't undercook the pastry. Bake it until a skewer inserted in the center comes out clean.
2. Release steam. When the puffs are finished baking, make a 1-inch (2.5 cm) slit in the side of each one with a small, sharp knife.
3. Turn off the oven, but put the pastry back in for 15 minutes. The drier, the puffier.
4. Let the baked puffs cool on a rack.
5. Don't fill them until serving time. Creamy fillings make them soggy.
6. If the puffs sit around and soften, crisp them in a hot oven for 5 minutes.

✦ Choux pastry puffs can be frozen. Wrap them well.

Choux Pastry

This foolproof choux recipe was inspired by the late, great Julia Child. **Makes 12 pastries, 3 to 3$\frac{1}{2}$ inches (7.5 to 9 cm) in diameter**

- **Preheat oven to 425°F (220°C)**

- **Piping bag, fitted with a large, round tip (optional)**

- **2 baking sheets, lined with parchment paper**

Tips

Choux pastry recipes generally stick to equal proportions of flour and water. This one follows the lead of Julia Child, who called for slightly less flour and more eggs.

For firmer pastries, you can increase the flour to 1 cup (250 mL).

Don't worry if you don't pipe out even amounts; you can go back and add dough to each mound.

You can make cylinders if desired.

If you don't have a piping bag, use spoons to dollop the paste onto the baking sheets.

Pastry

1 cup	water	250 mL
6 tbsp	unsalted butter	90 mL
1 tsp	granulated sugar	5 mL
$\frac{1}{8}$ tsp	salt	0.5 mL
$\frac{3}{4}$ cup	all-purpose flour	175 mL
4	large eggs	4

Egg Wash

1	large egg	1
1 tsp	water	5 mL
Pinch	salt	Pinch

1. *Pastry:* In a medium saucepan, bring water, butter, sugar and salt to a boil over medium-high heat. Remove from heat. Immediately dump in flour and, using a wooden spoon, beat vigorously to blend thoroughly. Return to heat. Beat until the mixture forms a mass that looks like mashed potatoes, pulls away from the sides of the pan and begins to film the bottom of the pan, about 1 minute. Remove from heat. Let stand for 1 minute.

2. While beating with a hand-held electric mixer on low speed, add eggs, one at a time, beating for 10 to 20 seconds or just until each egg is absorbed. Beat for about 2 minutes or until the paste is thick and shiny.

3. Spoon the paste into the piping bag. Pipe 6 mounds onto each prepared baking sheet, spacing them out evenly.

4. *Egg wash:* In a small bowl, using a fork, lightly beat egg, water and salt. Using a pastry brush, coat the top of each mound smoothly and lightly with egg wash.

5. Place one baking sheet in the lower middle of the preheated oven and the other in the upper middle. Bake for about 15 minutes or until the mounds have doubled in size and are lightly browned.

6. Switch the baking sheets' positions on the racks and rotate them. Reduce the heat to 350°F (180°C). Bake for about 15 minutes or until the puffs are golden brown, firm and crusty. Turn off the oven.

7. Using a small, sharp knife, cut a 1-inch (2.5 cm) slit in the side of each puff. Return the baking sheets to the oven for 15 minutes. Transfer puffs to wire racks to cool completely.

- If you don't want to frost the tops like éclairs, sprinkle them with confectioner's (icing) sugar.

Gussy It Up

- Turn choux pastry into savory gougères by adding cheese and herbs.
- Cut the puffs in half and use them to serve salad.
- Add fillings, such as smoked salmon or shrimp salad, and serve the puffs as hors d'oeuvres.

Phyllo Pastry

Phyllo VS. Strudel Dough?

Phyllo is made with flour, hot water, oil and vinegar. Strudel is similar, but richer, with egg and butter added. Both are rolled paper-thin — ideally sheer enough to read a newspaper through. Both are baked in multiple layers. Strudel has the better reputation, praised as more tender and delicate enough to blow away in a puff of wind. You can roll most anything, savory or sweet, in phyllo or strudel dough.

- Handle phyllo and strudel dough the same way. If you don't have one, use the other.

- Defrost phyllo overnight in the fridge. Let it come to room temperature for 20 to 30 minutes before unfolding it.

- To avoid cracking and tearing, brush sheets with melted butter from the edges inward.

- When covering strudel dough or phyllo with a fruity filling, first brush it with melted butter and sprinkle it with bread crumbs or powdery chopped nuts to absorb the juices.

- Patch tears or breaks with pieces of dough. Use broken pieces inside your pastry.

- While you're working, cover unused dough with a sheet of plastic wrap, then a damp kitchen towel. That way, it won't dry out, but the sheets won't get damp and stick together either.

✪ Waste Not

- You can refreeze leftover phyllo, but it will become very brittle.
- You can wrap thawed phyllo in plastic and return it to the fridge for 2 to 3 days.

- You can place strudel dough or phyllo on a large kitchen towel. After adding the filling, use the towel to help you to roll the dough.

Puff Pastry

Ways to Cut Puff Pastry

- Slice it with a hot, sharp, thin knife.
- Press down on it with a hot scraper.

- As a template for a large circle of puff pastry, use the bottom of a springform pan or the removable base of a tart pan. Cut around it.

ⲷ Fast Fix

A free-form fruit tart prepared with puff pastry is quicker to make than a pie. Cook and cool the fruit filling first, so the pastry stays crisp. Leave a 2-inch (5 cm) border between the filling and the edges of the pastry. Casually fold the edges over part of the fruit to create a rustic dessert.

◆ Move puff pastry in and out of fridge to keep it firm as you work with each portion.

◆ If the dough seems tough, sprinkle it with ice water.

Better Leftovers

Freeze the trimmings from puff pastry.
- Roll them out as a topping for pot pie.
- Bake them into little cheese sticks. You can roll them in or around grated cheese.
- Prepare vegetable- or mushroom-filled triangles.

Doughnuts

◆ Chill the dough slightly before cutting. You won't need as much flour on the cutting board.

◆ Cut rings of dough with round biscuit cutters, one large and one small.

◆ Help doughnuts keep their shape. Dip a short-handled spatula in the hot oil. Use it to transfer the dough from the cutting board to the pan or deep-fryer.

◆ To keep the heat even, do assembly-line frying. Add the first batch at intervals. Add a new ring of dough each time you remove a completed doughnut. Go with the rhythm.

✿ Waste Not

Fry the leftover doughnut holes, too.

Gussy It Up

- Instead of dusting the hot doughnuts with plain sugar, go upscale with maple sugar.
- Dip the hot doughnuts in vanilla sugar.

Turnovers

◆ When making date turnovers, it's easier and tidier to fold the soft dough over the filling if you use plastic wrap. Place the dough cutouts on a small sheet of plastic wrap, apply the filling, then fold.

◆ To seal the dough for turnovers, wet the edges and press them together with the tines of a fork.

Meringues

Types of Meringue

French, common or cold

- Egg whites are beaten to soft peaks, the sugar is gradually added, then the meringue is beaten until shiny and stiff, about 10 minutes. The oven is preheated to 250°F (120°C). Immediately after adding the meringue, the oven temperature is reduced to 200°F (100°C). The meringue is baked until the top and bottom are dry.
- This type has the weakest structure, less gloss and a grainier texture. It is used to make Pavlovas and meringue kisses.

Hard

- This is the same as the common meringue, but with double the sugar, say ¼ cup (50 mL) per egg white.
- Use it for meringue shells and dacquoise cakes.

Swiss

- Egg whites, sugar and cream of tartar are whisked in the top of a double boiler or heatproof bowl over simmering water. The mixture is heated until it reaches 120°F (49°C) and feels warm and smooth. (Rub some between your fingers to check for gritty sugar.) The mixture is removed from the heat, beaten on high speed for 5 minutes, then on low speed for 5 minutes, until it's very stiff.
- This type is stronger, smoother and glossier. The technique tempers meringues to withstand humid weather. It is used for decorations and icing.

Italian

- Sugar and water are heated to 250°F (120°C) in a saucepan. Meanwhile, the egg whites are beaten to firm peaks. The syrup is poured into the egg whites in a thin stream while beating on medium-low speed. Don't let the syrup touch the beaters or the sides of the bowl or it will turn into hard sugar threads and blobs. The meringue is beaten, interminably it seems, until it is cool.
- This type is strong, glossy and super-smooth. It is good for fluffy buttercream frosting, pie filling and pudding.

✘ No-Nos

- Please don't beat the hell out of egg whites at top speed until they are super-stiff. Overbeating a meringue maximizes the volume, but the cells actually need a bit of stretch and give during baking. Overbeating also makes the air bubbles smaller and expels water.
- Don't wait until firm peaks are forming before you add the sugar. By the time the sugar dissolves properly, the meringue may be overbeaten.

How to Whip Meringue

1. Using an electric mixer, beat egg whites on low speed until they are frothy.
2. Add cream of tartar or another stabilizer. Beat on medium speed until the whites are billowy, with large bubbles forming at the edges. This will take about 5 minutes if you're using a stand mixer.
3. With the mixer running, add the sugar, 1 tbsp (15 mL) at a time, until it is incorporated.
4. Rub some meringue between your fingers to make sure the sugar is dissolved. If it feels gritty, keep going.

Signs of Overbeating

- The egg whites are dull. (They should be shiny.)
- If you turn the bowl upside down, the whites cling firmly. (Use a tipped bowl test instead. The meringue should move a bit.)
- Liquid separates out and puddles beneath the foam.

Signs That the Meringue Is Stiff Enough

- It supports the weight of an egg.
- It hangs from the beater in a stable tuft.

✧ If you are beating egg whites to be folded into batter, the peaks should be perky but not stiff. They should flow slightly when the bowl is tilted. Otherwise, it will be too difficult to fold in the flour without deflating the whites.

✧ To disperse flour more evenly through a meringue, sift it with a quarter of the sugar from the recipe first, instead of beating the sugar into the meringue all at once.

✧ For the finest meringue, use superfine sugar.

✧ Meringues work with brown sugar. It makes them ivory-colored and caramel-flavored.

✧ For a soft meringue, add about 2 tbsp (25 mL) sugar per egg white. For a firm meringue, add about ¼ cup (50 mL) sugar per egg white.

✧ For a firm crust and soft interior, bake the meringue at contrasting temperatures. Start at 250°F (120°C) for a few minutes (time depends on size), then reduce the heat to 200°F (100°C). For a more evenly cooked meringue, bake at a steady 225°F (110°C).

✧ Do not open the oven door while a meringue bakes. A rush of colder air may deflate the bubbles.

✧ Once a meringue is done, turn off the oven and open the door slightly, then let it cool slowly inside. For crispier meringue shells and cookies, let the meringues sit in the oven overnight.

OUTSIDE THE BOX

Brown meringue on a pie with a cook's torch.

⚛ A Bit of Science

Meringue insulates. That's the secret of baked Alaska. The ice cream doesn't melt because the meringue protects it from the heat.

Master Plan
Baked Alaska

1. Line a bowl with plastic wrap. Press softened ice cream into the bowl.
2. Drizzle a single-layer cake with liqueur. Press it on top of the ice cream.
3. Cover the bowl with plastic wrap. Freeze it until the ice cream is firm.
4. Unmold the cake and ice cream dome onto a heatproof platter. Discard the plastic wrap. Cover the dome with meringue. Make sure it is completely sealed. You could also pipe the meringue over the dome and decoratively around the base.
5. Bake at 500°F (260°C) until the meringue's peaks are golden, about 5 minutes.

✧ To make meringue discs for a torte, or dacquoise, cut out 8- or 9-inch (20 or 23 cm) circles of parchment paper. Lay the circles on a baking sheet. Spoon the meringue onto the circles, leaving a ½-inch (1 cm) border. For Pavlova, pile on the meringue and form a well in the center.

◈ When building a torte with meringue layers, set the first layer top up and the other layers bottom up (the smooth sides).

Meringue Doctor

The whites won't whip.

- Fats stop proteins in egg whites from coagulating. Rub the bowl with a wedge of lemon before mixing. This cleans it and the acid stabilizes the meringue.
- Use a stainless-steel bowl, instead of plastic, which retains grease.
- When using a rubber spatula, make sure it is grease-free.

The whites won't whip properly.

- Use cream of tartar to increase the acidity of the egg-white foam, which stabilizes it. Add $1/8$ tsp (0.5 mL) cream of tartar for every 2 egg whites.
- Use another stabilizer: lemon juice, white vinegar, salt or cornstarch. (Beware: Too much acid can prevent the proteins from coagulating during baking. Follow the recipe.)
- Let the egg whites come to room temperature before beating. They fluff better that way.
- Add sugar to the meringue gradually, only after soft peaks are starting to form.

The whites are overbeaten.

- Add another egg white and beat it in slowly, just until the meringue is glossy.
- Next time, turn off the mixer just before the egg whites hit the right texture. Pull off the whisk attachment and use it to do the final bit of whipping by hand.

The whites are floating on a thin, watery puddle at the bottom of the bowl.

- Don't let them sit so long before mixing or baking.
- Stabilize them with cream of tartar.
- Add a bit of sugar and whisk to soft peaks.

The meringue is grainy.

- Sugar particles did not dissolve, because the egg whites were either too cold or not beaten slowly enough.
- Add sugar 1 tbsp (15 mL) at a time.
- Set the mixing bowl over a bowl partially filled with hot water. Make sure the bottom is not touching the water. Whisk until the meringue feels smooth when you rub it between your fingers. Remove it from the warmth and beat for 30 to 60 seconds on high speed.

The meringue pie topping is weeping.

- Cook it longer. Undercooked egg whites leak moisture as they stand. This leaves a watery layer between the meringue and the pie filling.
- Don't cook it for so long. The proteins have coagulated, which squeezes out moisture.
- Time the meringue so it's ready to spread over a hot, hot filling.
- Sprinkle fine cake crumbs over the filling first, to absorb moisture from the meringue.
- Don't make a meringue in humid weather. Meringues will weep (or even fail to whip). The sugar in them absorbs moisture from the air.

The meringue is beading.

- The beading may be from sugar or moisture.
- There's too much sugar in the meringue.
- The meringue was put in the fridge while it was still warm.
- The pie was cooked for too long or at too high a heat. The egg proteins are leaking moisture.
- Bake at a higher heat for a shorter time, rather than at a low heat for a longer time.

The meringue shrinks and cracks.

- Spread it all the way to the edges to seal in the filling. Otherwise, it will pull away as it bakes.
- The meringue was cooled too quickly or exposed to cold air. After turning the oven off, let the meringue cool in it with the door ajar.

- Use more meringue next time.
- Stabilize the egg whites with cornstarch paste. Dissolve ½ tsp (2 mL) cornstarch in 1 tbsp (15 mL) water. Heat it in the microwave on High for 15 seconds or until a clear paste forms. Beat it into a meringue mixture of 4 egg whites, ½ tsp (2 mL) cream of tartar and ½ cup (125 mL) superfine sugar. Add the paste, 1 tsp (5 mL) at a time, once firm peaks have formed.

No-No

Adding cornstarch paste is supposed to make a meringue tender, easy to cut, and less prone to shrinking or overcooking. However, don't add cornstarch directly; it sucks up moisture. Don't use confectioner's (icing) sugar in meringues, either. It has cornstarch in it.

Fast Fix

Make a meringue-like topping instantly. Arrange marshmallows on top of baked puddings, custards or pie fillings about 15 minutes before the end of the cooking time.

✧ Meringue turns out better when baked at a higher temperature for a shorter time, but the opposite is recommended for food-safety reasons.

Baking Conundrums

- For food safety, a meringue made with 3 egg whites on a hot pie filling in a 350°F (180°C) oven should be cooked until it reaches 160°F (71°C), about 15 minutes. If there are more egg whites, the meringue should be baked at 325°F (160°C) for 25 to 30 minutes. These meringues end up overcooked and prone to weeping, beading and shrinking.
- A meringue cooked at 425°F to 450°F (220°C to 230°C) for 5 minutes has fewer problems, but the interior doesn't reach a temperature high enough to kill salmonella.

Custards and Puddings

❖ Custards can be simmered, like crème anglaise, or baked, like crème caramel. Custards are also used as bases for ice cream, pudding, mousse, cream and pumpkin pies, and lemon curd.

♛ A Golden Rule

Turn the heat down. On the stove, do not boil custard; just bring it to a boil. In the oven, bake it at a low temperature, say 300°F (150°C). High heat curdles the eggs and squeezes out moisture.

❖ For the lushest, silkiest custards, whip the yolks with the sugar until thick and fluffy, about 3 minutes, before whisking in the scalded milk.

❖ How long should you leave custard on the stove to thicken? Until it starts to bubble and the foam dissipates from the top.

Is It Done?

- It coats the back of a spoon.
- A line traced through the custard coating the spoon is distinct. If it's not cooked enough, the custard will flow together after you trace a line. If it's overcooked, you'll notice small chunks.

❖ Ways to deal with custard that is threatening to curdle:

- Transfer it to a cool bowl and whisk it quickly.
- Whisk in a spoonful of cold cream.
- Beat it with a hand-held mixer.
- Pour it into a blender and whirl it until it is cooler. The custard will be thinner but usable.

❖ Reasons to continue whisking for 30 to 60 seconds after removing custard from the heat:

- It stops curdling in the layer of custard in contact with the hot base of the pan.
- It helps steam escape. Otherwise, your custard will "sweat" and become diluted.

⚡ Lightning Won't Strike If ...

You decide not to strain finished custard through a sieve. Just don't handle custard roughly or overheat it to begin with. Straining does, however, create the smoothest, softest custard.

☰ Fast Fix

For a quick chocolate custard, start with scalded chocolate milk instead of plain milk. To turn this into a pudding, add a cornstarch or tapioca slurry and heat the mixture to the boiling point.

❖ When preparing a baked custard, beat the eggs lightly. Otherwise, the custard will be foamy and insubstantial.

Is It Done?

- A tester inserted near the edge comes out clean.
- The center remains wobbly. It will firm up as it cools.
- The tip of a knife tip inserted ½ inch (1 cm) deep in the center comes out clean. Any deeper and it comes out coated. (Try this only if the custard will be inverted or covered, or you don't care about the mark.)
- If a tester comes out clean in the center, the custard is overcooked. Immediately set the baking dish in ice water.

- Adding butter to custard, say for a lemon tart filling? Let the custard cool a bit first. It should not be so hot that the butter melts instantly.

- Making mousse with custard? Cool the custard before folding in whipped cream and/or egg whites. Otherwise, the foam will deflate.

- Make sure crème brûlée is super-cold before you apply the torch to the sugar. Otherwise, the delicate custard may break down and overheat.

3 Keys to Curd

1. One is the secret number for lemon curd. For every egg yolk, you'll need 1 tbsp (15 mL) each granulated sugar, lemon juice and butter, as well as the zest of 1 lemon.
2. No curdled curd, please. Do not let it boil.
3. Adding butter makes curd thick and shiny when it's cool. Whisk in butter 1 tbsp (15 mL) at a time, and only off the heat.

Lemon Curd

This is a very tangy specimen. **Makes about 1 cup (250 mL)**

Variation
You can substitute other fruit juices for the lemon juice. Choose strong, tangy juice when you experiment. You may have to reduce the amount of sugar.

4	large egg yolks	4
¼ cup	granulated sugar	50 mL
	Grated zest of 1 lemon	
¼ cup	freshly squeezed lemon juice	50 mL
¼ cup	unsalted butter, cut into 4 pieces	50 mL

1. In a heatproof bowl, using an electric mixer, beat eggs and sugar for 2 to 3 minutes or until pale, smooth and fluffy. Whisk in lemon zest and juice.
2. Set the bowl over a pan of simmering water over medium-low heat. The bottom of the bowl should not touch the water. Heat, whisking constantly, for about 2 minutes or until the mixture is as thick as pudding. Do not let it boil. Remove the bowl from the heat. Let it stand for 30 seconds. Whisk in butter, one piece at a time, until melted.
3. Transfer the curd to a storage container. Smooth plastic wrap directly over the surface. Let cool. Snap on the lid. Store the curd in the fridge up to 1 week.

☰ Fast Fix

Cool custard, pastry cream and pudding more quickly. Spread it on a rimmed baking sheet lined with plastic wrap. Cover the surface with plastic wrap. With a razor blade, cut a few slits through the plastic to let steam escape. Once it has cooled, peel the wrap off the top. Scrape the custard into a tub. Squeeze the plastic to extract the remaining custard.

How to Lighten Dense Bread Pudding

1. Separate the eggs.
2. Put the yolks in the pudding mixture.
3. Whip the whites. Fold them in.
4. Bake the pudding right away.

✧ For a custardy bread pudding, bake it in a bain-marie, or water bath. For a firm, structured texture, bake it on the oven rack.

♻ Waste Not

During the Christmas season, some people receive too much fruitcake. Others, meanwhile, especially Italians, become loaded down with gifts of panettone. You can transform stale panettone into bread pudding.

✧ Preferably cook pudding or custard in a nonstick pan.

OUTSIDE THE BOX

You can make pudding in a blender.

Blender Pudding

Pudding lovers in a hurry have turned the blender into their secret weapon. Here's one take on the technique. **Makes 6 servings**

Variations

Use other types of chocolate.

Add flavorings such as instant espresso powder to the cream before heating it.

6 oz	semisweet chocolate, coarsely chopped	175 g
½ cup	granulated sugar	125 mL
1	large egg	1
1 tsp	vanilla extract	5 mL
Pinch	salt	Pinch
1 cup	heavy or whipping (35%) cream	250 mL
½ cup	whole milk	125 mL

1. In a blender, finely grind chocolate with sugar. Add egg, vanilla and salt. Blend it briefly into a paste. Scrape the sides.

2. In a microwave-safe glass measuring cup, combine cream and milk. Microwave on High for about 3 minutes, or until scalded and steaming. Do not boil.

3. With the blender running, immediately drizzle hot cream through the feed tube into the chocolate mixture. Blend for about 1 minute or until smooth and thickened.

4. Transfer to a food storage tub. Smooth plastic wrap directly over the surface. Snap on lid. Refrigerate overnight or until cold and thick.

✧ Create a crusty, caramelized top on rice pudding as you would for crème brûlée. Sprinkle the top with granulated sugar and blast it with a kitchen torch.

✧ Increase the eye appeal of a trifle or mousse. Arrange it in a clear dish lined with spiral slices of jelly roll. Pretty.

Steamed Pudding Tips

• Scatter bread crumbs, cake crumbs, granulated sugar or chopped nuts on the sides and bottom of a greased mold for steamed pudding. This will help the pudding release.

• Protect steamed pudding from moisture by covering it with a large piece of buttered parchment or foil. Tie it in place with kitchen string.

• Steamed pudding can be made in advance. Let it cool, then refrigerate it. To reheat, wrap the pudding in foil and bake it at 300°F (150°C) until warm, about 20 minutes.

Frozen Treats

✧ When preparing frozen desserts, whip cream only to soft peaks. Otherwise, they tend to leave a greasy or buttery residue on the tongue.

✧ Add whipped cream to the base for a frozen dessert after the base is partially frozen. Otherwise, it may separate.

✧ Let a creamy frozen dessert sit in its mold at room temperature for 15 to 30 minutes before serving.

✧ To unmold a stubborn frozen dessert, run cool water over the bottom of the mold. Don't use anything hot.

✧ How to keep homemade ice cream and ices creamy rather than icy and granular.
  ○ Use plenty of sugar. Sugar prevents an iced treat from freezing rock-hard. That's why Popsicles are so sweet. One estimate: Use 1 part sugar to 4 parts liquid.
  ○ Add alcohol, but not too much. It inhibits freezing and keeps ices softer. Wait until an ice has begun to freeze before stirring in spirits.
  ○ Use emulsifiers and stabilizers, such as egg yolks, egg whites, whipped cream, butterfat, gelatin or carrageenan (jelly made from Irish moss seaweed).
  ○ Churn them. Churning in an ice cream machine prevents large ice crystals from forming. If a frozen dessert is not churned, it must be beaten several times while it's freezing to break up the crystals.

Types of Ices

  ○ **Ice cream:** Made with cream, with or without eggs. The expensive stuff has lots of fat and less air.
  ○ **Gelato:** Italian ice cream. Denser but served softer. Sometimes lower in fat, with more milk.
  ○ **Soft-serve ice cream:** Served without fully hardening. More air, less fat and less sugar. If you freeze soft-serve, it will become hard-serve.
  ○ **Ice milk:** Lower in fat.
  ○ **Kulfi:** Indian ice cream. Often made with condensed milk.
  ○ **Parfait:** Dessert made with whipped, frozen cream, or a layered ice cream dessert.
  ○ **Frozen yogurt:** Just that.
  ○ **Sherbet:** A fruit and dairy ice.
  ○ **Sorbet:** A smooth ice made with fruit juice, sugar and water. No dairy.
  ○ **Granita:** A coarse Italian ice.

Ice Cream

✧ Store ice cream between 0°F and –5°F (–18°C and –21°C). Keep it as cold as possible in the main part of the freezer, not in the door. Protect it from temperature fluctuations that can make it icy.

✧ Serve ice cream that's between 6°F and 10°F (–14°C and –12°C). It should be easy to scoop but firm enough to hold its shape. Let it get there in the fridge, not on the counter. Depending on the size of the container, it could take 20 minutes to reach the right texture for serving.

Remedies for Icing

- Melted ice cream and frozen yogurt become icy and granular when refrozen. Scoop out the melted bits at the edges before returning these treats to the freezer.
- To quickly refreeze ice cream that has gotten very soft, say at the dinner table, cut it or scoop it into balls, place the pieces on a tray, freeze them, then transfer them to the tub.
- Soften crystallized ice cream or frozen yogurt by swirling it in a food processer until it's smooth. Return it to the freezer immediately.

✧ To quickly remove all of the ice cream from a tub, cut with scissors from top to bottom in the corners or slash with a box cutter.

✧ If you need ice cream for baked Alaska, a frozen cake creation or a mold, you can soften it slightly in the microwave. Twenty seconds at Medium-Low (30%) is perfect for 2 cups (500 mL).

Gussy It Up

If the ice cream you bought or made is boring, let it soften a bit, stir in tidbits and treats, then refreeze it. Some tasty ideas:

- Toasted nuts
- Toasted shredded coconut
- Yogurt- or chocolate-covered nuts
- Crushed brittle or praline
- M&Ms or Smarties
- Dried fruit (soak it in rum or brandy first)
- Chopped candied ginger
- Cookie shards
- Chopped caramels

✧ For the smoothest homemade ice cream, start with a custard base. Ice cream can also be made with a juice, syrup or puréed fruit base. These are more likely to ice up. Compensate by adding lots of cream.

Master Plan
Homemade Ice Cream

1. In a medium saucepan, combine heavy or whipping (35%) cream and milk over medium heat. Bring it to the verge of boiling, but don't let it boil.
2. Add flavorings, such as a vanilla bean, cinnamon stick or chai tea. Remove from heat, cover and steep for 1 hour. Strain.
3. In a large heatproof bowl, whisk together eggs, sugar and salt. Heat the cream mixture in a medium saucepan over medium heat just until it's warm. Slowly whisk it into the egg mixture until it is smooth.
4. Return the mixture to the pan. Cook over medium heat, whisking, until the mixture is thickened. Do not allow it to boil.
5. Remove it from the heat. Whisk for 30 to 60 seconds to lessen the chance of curdling from extended contact with the base of the hot pan. Strain it into a storage tub with a tight lid. This is your custard base.
6. Stir in flavorings such as vanilla extract, lemon zest, espresso powder paste or chopped chocolate. (If using chocolate, stir it in the warm custard until it melts.)
7. Cover and refrigerate until very cold, preferably overnight.
8. Process the mixture in an ice cream maker according to the manufacturer's instructions.
9. Add toasted nuts, chocolate chunks or other tidbits, or liqueur, 2 minutes before the end of the churning time.
10. Scrape the ice cream back into the tub. Cover and freeze until firm.

OUTSIDE THE BOX

Add tang to ice cream by replacing some of the milk with buttermilk. Or make crème fraîche ice cream.

Cold Facts

- Pricier ice cream machines have their own refrigeration units. Standard models employ insulated canisters with coolant. Cover the canister in plastic and store it in the freezer. Otherwise, it will take a couple of days to be ready. The coolant must be completely frozen — no sloshing sounds.

- Always chill an ice cream base, whether it is a custard or a fruity purée, until it is super-cold before putting it in an ice cream maker. It's best to refrigerate it overnight. Ice cream must be frozen as quickly as possible to prevent large ice crystals.

- Chill additions, such as chocolate chips or nuts, in the fridge before using them.

- Ice cream is not ready once it's churned. Most home machines don't make it firm enough. Return the mixture to the freezer and your patience will be rewarded.

- The point of churning is not to freeze the mixture solid but to fluff it with air bubbles and distribute ice crystals.

ⓞ is for Overrun

That's the commercial term for the air in ice cream. Cheaper ice creams have more overrun — that is, more volume but less ice cream.

- Lightness is not necessarily bad. If you want more overrun at home, fill the canister halfway to give the ice cream more room to expand.

- For denser ice cream, fill the canister almost to the top.

- Filling it three-quarters creates a happy medium — rich but not dense.

- ✧ The texture of homemade ice cream is right if the scoop forms a natural ball as it is rolled about $\frac{1}{2}$ inch (1 cm) deep across the surface. Shards are a bad sign.

- ✧ Homemade ice creams don't hold their shape as long in the serving bowl because they don't contain all those industrial emulsifiers.

Ways to Mimic Commercial Ice Cream

- Use gelatin. Add softened unflavored gelatin to the chilled custard base of your ice cream. Put the mixture straight into the bowl of the ice cream machine. Churn and freeze. Per 1 cup (250 mL) custard base, use 1 tsp (5 mL) gelatin, softened in 1 tbsp (15 mL) water, then heated until liquid. The resulting ice cream is smoother and takes a dramatically longer time to melt. It is a bit chewy when very cold. You could reduce the amount of gelatin. Note: Don't be tempted to stir the gelatin into the ice cream base while it's hot; the mixture will set overnight.

- Use jelly extracted from Irish moss seaweed. Irish moss is the source of the additive carrageenan, an emulsifier and thickener. (See extraction instructions in the Produce Department chapter.) Add about 1 tbsp (15 mL) Irish moss jelly per 1 cup (250 mL) warm custard base. Refrigerate the base overnight. Churn as usual. The ice cream will be thicker, though not smoother, and it will sit longer without melting.

⚛ A Bit of Science

A sudden ice cream headache is caused when the cold treat comes in contact with a nerve bundle in the roof of the mouth. The nerves send a message to the brain telling it to dilate blood vessels in the head. You can get an ice cream headache from cold drinks too, such as iced coffees and smoothies.

ⓈÂ is for Still-Freezing

Ice cream can be made without a machine using a technique called still-freezing.

1. Freeze the ice cream mixture in a shallow metal bowl, covered, for 1 to 2 hours or until the edges are firm but the center is still slushy.
2. Beat it with an electric mixer until it is smooth but not melted. Freeze it.
3. Beat three or four more times, every 30 minutes.
4. Cover and freeze it until it is solid.

Ices

✧ Use gelatin to make homemade ice pops more like the Popsicles you buy at the corner store (slushy rather than hard and glassy). Add 1 tsp (5 mL) softened unflavored gelatin per $1\frac{1}{2}$ cups (375 mL) fruit purée base.

✧ Granita should have large ice crystals, so don't churn it in an ice cream machine. It's a step down (or up) from a sorbet.

How to Make Granita

1. Pour your granita mixture into a shallow metal pan. Put it in the freezer.
2. When ice forms on the sides, scrape it down with a fork and stir it into the mixture. Don't use a spoon to scrape or stir.
3. Do this repeatedly until the mixture is solid.
4. To serve granita, scrape off layers of ice crystals with a fork. It should be fluffy and slushy.

How to Make Sorbet Without an Ice Cream Machine

1. Freeze your sorbet mixture until it turns to slush.
2. Scrape it into a food processor with 2 pasteurized egg whites. Blend the mixture and return it to the freezer.
3. Once it has frozen solid, toss chunks into the food processor. Blend again.
4. Return it to the freezer until it's firm.

Chocolate

Cacao **VS.** Cocoa?

Cacao refers to the tree, pod and beans. Cocoa refers to the processed products produced from the beans.

- **Pod:** Fruit of the cacao tree. Size and shape of a large papaya. Interior is oily, gray and fleshy, with embedded beans, or seeds.
- **Beans:** Fermented, dried in the sun, hulled and roasted.
- **Nibs:** Broken particles of roasted beans.
- **Liquor/mass:** Cocoa liquor, or cocoa mass, produced from ground nibs. Thick, bitter, dark brown paste. Consists of cocoa butter and cocoa powder, the building blocks of chocolate.
- **Cocoa butter:** Fat extracted from the cocoa liquor. Solid at room temperature, yet melts in the mouth. Gives chocolate a long shelf life.
- **Cocoa powder:** Made by extracting some of the fat from cocoa liquor.

Anatomy of a Chocolate Bar

- Thick cocoa liquor, or mass, is transformed into dry crumb, then into a paste.
- The paste is squeezed through giant rollers to create chocolate flakes.
- The flakes are mixed and kneaded in a heated tub, called a conche, until smooth and molten.
- Along the way, lecithin is added for a smooth texture. It is an emulsifier that keeps the cocoa butter from separating out. Other potential additives: whole or skim milk, powdered milk, sweetened condensed milk, cream, butter, sugar, corn syrup, cocoa butter, spices, flavorings.
- The chocolate is poured into plastic molds and refrigerated. Once firm, the bars are wrapped.

✧ The chocolate type depends on the amount of cocoa butter and solids. The more cocoa mass, the stronger the chocolate. The content may be noted as a percentage on the package. The rest is mainly sugar and dairy products.

Categories of Chocolate

- **Dark chocolate:** At least 35%; better quality 50% to 100%. May be unsweetened, bittersweet or semisweet.
- **Milk chocolate:** At least 10%, all the way up to 50%, but 30% considered high.
- **White chocolate:** Not technically chocolate. Contains no chocolate liquor, just cocoa butter, sugar, dairy products, lecithin, often vanilla. Mild, sweet and creamy. Amount of cocoa butter varies.

Buyer Beware

- White chocolate is not actually white. It's ivory. If it's white, you may be looking at a cheap imitation made with shortening, or maybe with palm oil or cottonseed oil.

✧ Check labels. The best lineup is chocolate, sugar, cocoa butter, vanilla and lecithin. It's dire if sugar is the first ingredient, or there are other fats or oils.

Options for Quality Cooking

- Choose dark chocolate with at least 60% cocoa solids. Otherwise, it will be too sweet. Dark chocolate may be too strong once you get past 85%. If you are using an intense dark chocolate, add sugar and reduce the baking time.
- Choose milk chocolate with at least 30% cocoa solids.

OUTSIDE THE BOX

You can eat nibs. They're intense, bitter, crunchy and not at all sweet. Use them as a garnish or toss them into Mexican dishes or salads.

C is for Couverture

You can bake with a chocolate bar or supermarket squares, but pastry chefs prefer couverture. It has more cocoa butter, so it flows better when melted. It is conched longer, so it is smoother. It is particularly good for coating and molding, but it also makes dough and batter silky and moist.

D is for Dutched

Natural cocoa powder is acidic. Dutched, or Dutch-process, cocoa powder is treated with an alkaline to counteract that, and thus make it less bitter. It is reddish brown, darker than natural cocoa powder, as well as smoother and more soluble. Some swear that sweets made with it taste more chocolatey. Dutched is standardized, so there's more consistency among different brands. Natural varies more.

- If you're not sure whether a cocoa powder is Dutched, check the label for mention of alkalines.
- If a recipe doesn't specify, use either type. Choose Dutched for drinks or recipes with few ingredients or a small amount of sugar. Use natural in recipes with many ingredients or lots of sugar.
- Natural cocoa powder, with its higher acidity, works well with baking soda, which needs acid for leavening. Dutched cocoa powder, being alkaline, works well with baking powder, which is acidic.
- To substitute for Dutched cocoa, add a pinch of baking soda to regular cocoa powder when sifting.

 Lightning Won't Strike If ...

You switch natural cocoa powder for Dutched, or vice versa. Most recipes will turn out acceptable.

✧ Cocoa powder is lumpy. You have to smooth it out before cooking or baking. Four ways to smooth out lumps:
- Shake the tub.
- Sift it.
- Press it through a sieve.
- Dissolve it into a paste in some of the liquid from the recipe, instead of sifting.

✧ For eating, the best temperature for dark chocolate is between 66°F and 77°F (19°C and 25°C).

Ways to Assess Dark Chocolate

Tasting dark chocolate is like wine tasting. You use your senses.
- **Sight:** Glossy is good. Waxy is bad.
- **Smell:** A strong chocolate aroma should be evident. Search for accents of vanilla, nuts or fruit.
- **Touch:** The chocolate should snap decisively, leaving crisp edges. It should not be grainy. It should melt smoothly.
- **Taste:** You want a rich chocolate taste and aftertaste. Chew a piece 5 to 10 times. (Don't suck it like milk chocolate.) Breathe in through your mouth and out through your nose to let the flavor fill your head.

✧ Don't serve fresh fruit with dark chocolate. It pairs better with dried fruit. It is also good with mint leaves.

- When making hot chocolate from scratch, first dissolve the cocoa powder into a smooth paste in the mug with some milk and sugar, then pour in scalded milk. Stir well.

- Do not substitute instant cocoa drink for cocoa powder in cooking. It has sugar and emulsifiers.

☰Fast Fix

Turn hot chocolate into hot mocha. Add instant coffee. About ½ tsp (2 mL) instant coffee granules per 1 cup (250 mL) hot chocolate should do it.

Chopping Chocolate

Ways to Make Decorative Chocolate Shavings and Sprinkles

- Scrape a room-temperature block of chocolate with a vegetable peeler or cheese slicer.
- For firmer, larger shavings, zap the chocolate in the microwave on Medium (50%) until just before the surface starts to melt. (Example time: 45 seconds for 4 oz/125 g.) You could also run a blow-dryer over it — very briefly.
- For sprinkles, chill the chocolate, then use the teardrop holes of a box grater (for tiny sprinkles) or a rasp grater (for powder).
- Use a scraper to transfer curls or sprinkles, so the heat from your hands doesn't mar them.

- Chop white and milk chocolate finely for faster melting. They scorch more easily. Dark chocolate can be chopped coarsely, then exposed to heat longer.

Chopping Tips

- It's easier to chop chocolate with a serrated bread knife. Chunks don't go flying.
- If you want just chunks and chips, sift the broken chocolate through a colander to catch the larger pieces and leave the powder behind.
- Cold chocolate is harder to chop by hand. It splinters and jumps around.
- Break a chocolate bar in its wrapper. First, put it in the fridge to firm up. Whack it with the side of a mallet or smack it down onto the cutting board.

- Don't melt big or uneven pieces. One piece may threaten to scorch before another piece melts. Break chocolate into pieces that are about 1 inch (2.5 cm) square or smaller.

- You can shred chocolate against the large holes of box grater for even and fast melting.

- To grate chocolate more easily, refrigerate it overnight.

Melting Chocolate

- Use chocolate chips, rather than chopped chocolate, for cookies, and use chunks or bars for melting. The chips are meant to hold their shape.

⑤ is for Seizing

When chocolate melts, it becomes smooth, velvety and shiny. But if it separates into a dry, clumpy, grainy or gummy mess, we say it has seized. There are various degrees of seizure: The chocolate may be matte and refuse to soften, or it may separate into lumps in a watery liquid. Once seized, chocolate may be repaired, but it will never be the same.

◆ The higher the cocoa butter and sugar content, the more easily chocolate melts — and the more sensitive it is to heat. White chocolate and milk chocolate are more prone to scorching and seizing than dark chocolate.

Causes of Seizing

- Adding water (a few drops will do it)
- Overheating (the cocoa butter separates out)

 **A Bit of Science**

Fine, dry cocoa particles and sugar are suspended in fat. The cocoa particles love water. Even a few drops of moisture prompt them to stick together. (This could be a drop of peppermint extract or errant steam from the bottom of a double boiler.) But if you add enough liquid, they don't clump. Fancy that.

◆ Never place chocolate over direct heat. Use low heat only.

7 Ways to Melt Chocolate

1. **The safest way:** With the cream and/or butter from your recipe — if there's plenty. Melt them together. They should be at similar temperatures from the start.

2. **In the microwave:** This is best for amounts less than 1 lb (500 g). Microwave dark chocolate on Medium (50%), milk and white chocolate on Low (10%). Chocolate may be melted yet hold its shape, so beware of burning. Microwave in short bursts, no more than 30 seconds each, stirring each time. Stop while the chocolate is warm but not molten. Stir to finish the job. You can use the Defrost setting to go really slowly.

3. **Over barely simmering water:** Put larger quantities and larger pieces (chunks of up to 2 oz/60 g) in the top of a double boiler or in a heatproof bowl. Make sure the bottom of the pan or bowl doesn't touch the water. Stir until the chocolate is melted. If it gets too hot, remove it briefly from the heat. To melt a small amount, bring the water to a boil, remove it from the heat, then place the chocolate over it and stir.

4. **In the oven:** Put chopped chocolate in a heatproof bowl. Heat it in a 200°F (100°C) oven until it starts to melt. Not too long — you don't want the chocolate to reach that temperature.

5. **In a skillet:** Pour 1 inch (2.5 cm) of water into the skillet. Bring it to a boil. Remove it from the heat. Set a heatproof bowl of chocolate in it. Let it stand for 5 minutes. Stir.

6. **With butter in a pan:** Put softened butter in the bottom of a wide saucepan. You need at least 1 cup (250 mL). Add chocolate chopped into ½- to ¾-inch (1 to 2 cm) pieces. Put the pan over very low heat. The butter will melt first and cushion the chocolate from the heat. Stir occasionally.

7. **In hot water:** Put chopped chocolate in a sturdy zip-lock bag and immerse the bottom in hot tap water for 5 minutes. Use a fresh bag — a leak would be terrible. If necessary, use a can or plate to submerge the chocolate. Dry the bag. Knead it for a minute. You can carry on by snipping a hole in a bottom corner. Drizzle the chocolate decoratively or squeeze it into your batter.

✧ To prevent seizing, you must have at least 1½ tsp (7 mL) liquid for every 2 oz (60 g) chocolate. Some sources even say 1 tbsp (15 mL) liquid per 1 oz (30 g) chocolate. This may be a problem for truffles.

OUTSIDE THE BOX

Chocolate can be melted on a heating pad (set in a metal bowl), hot tray or electric skillet. Put a heatproof bowl of chopped chocolate on top. Careful, the lowest setting may be too hot. Put a towel between the chocolate bowl and the heat source.

✧ You don't need to melt chocolate completely before removing it from the heat. Once you see the edges go from sharp to soft, stir every 15 to 20 seconds until it's smooth. If necessary, briefly return the chocolate to the heat.

Factoid Chocolate's melting point happens to be just below body temperature, so it melts in the mouth.

Temperature Guidelines

- Heat dark chocolate no higher than 120°F (49°C).
- Heat milk chocolate no higher than 115°F (46°C).
- Heat white chocolate no higher than 110°F (43°C).
- Cocoa butter separates out at 120°F (49°C).
- Cocoa solids blacken at below 130°F (54°C).

✧ There is no remedy for burnt chocolate. Throw it out. It tastes bad.

Ways to Avoid Moisture That Causes Seizing

- Melt chocolate over barely simmering water, no more than 1 inch (2.5 cm) deep.
- Use a bowl with a lip to discourage any steam from entering.
- Make sure the top of the double boiler fits snugly.
- Don't cover the pan or bowl. Steam condenses on the lid and water falls into the chocolate.
- When removing the pan or bowl from a double boiler, wipe the bottom to prevent stray drops from falling into the chocolate when you pour it out.
- Use dry tools. Some cooks even avoid introducing a wooden spoon into melted chocolate because it can retain moisture. (It's also porous and may impart old flavors to the chocolate.)
- Flavor extracts count as liquids. Don't put drops of peppermint, orange or other wet extracts in melted chocolate. But you can add oil of peppermint or citrus oil.
- Don't melt chocolate with a small amount of butter. Butter is one-fifth water.

Seized Chocolate Doctor

Seized chocolate can be treated but never restored to its former glory.

- Add 1 tsp (5 mL) or more of shortening or oil per 1 oz (30 g) chocolate. Do not add butter or margarine (they contain water).
- Add enough liquid to wet all of the particles, then whisk vigorously. The chocolate will be thinner and grainy.
- Whisk in cream or corn syrup.
- Turn seized chocolate into a glaze. Bring heavy or whipping (35%) cream to a simmer. Pour it into the chocolate. Whisk until the mixture is smoother. Small, gritty bits will linger. Use about 2 tbsp (25 mL) cream per 1 oz (30 g) chocolate.

- Whisking cold chocolate into a hot liquid can cause seizing. Whisking hot chocolate into a cold liquid makes the cocoa butter congeal. That frosting or milkshake will end up with tiny flecks.

Tempering Chocolate

🅣 is for Tempering

Tempering involves slow heating and cooling to stabilize the cocoa butter in chocolate. It makes chocolate stronger and glossier, and gives it a nice snap. Temper chocolate for coating, dipping and molding. Berries dipped in untempered chocolate will be dull, matte and crumbly. Chocolate cups won't harden and shape properly.

⚛ A Bit of Science

Cocoa butter contains different types of fat crystals that crystallize, or hold their shape, at temperatures ranging from 63°F to 97°F (17°C to 36°C). If chocolate is melted and simply cooled, its structure changes. The chocolate becomes dull, soft, greasy and more meltable. We say it is "out of temper." If chocolate is melted, cooled, then reheated to about 90°F (32°C), this encourages the crystallization of the most desirable type of fat. When the chocolate cools again, it is hard and shiny. It snaps instead of crumbling. It is stable enough at room temperature for molding, shaping into cups or flowers, or spreading into sheets. It is also less likely to bloom. We say it is "in temper."

Tempering Basics
- **Melt:** Dark chocolate up to 120°F (49°C), milk chocolate up to 115°F (46°C), white chocolate up to 110°F (43°C).
- **Cool:** To 80°F (27°C).
- **Reheat:** Dark chocolate to 88°F to 90°F (31°C to 32°C), milk chocolate to 85°F to 87°F (29°C to 31°C), white chocolate to 82°F to 84°F (28°C to 29°C).

- The chocolatier's traditional tempering method is messy and frustrating: Melt the chocolate. Pour three-quarters onto a marble slab. Keep smearing and folding the chocolate over itself until it cools. Work quickly. Return this chocolate to the remaining melted chocolate. Use residual heat or reheat to raise it to the required temperature.

🅢 is for Seed Crystals

The cocoa butter crystals in tempered chocolate are called seed crystals. Why do you care? Since most chocolate sold is already tempered, you can use it to "seed" melted chocolate, or encourage it to form the right crystal structure. Use the good stuff.

Master Plan
Simplest Tempered Chocolate
1. Melt 1 lb (500 g) of chocolate chunks.
2. Stir in 4 oz (125 g) of large chunks. Stir until the chocolate feels almost cool. (Test: Touch the stirring spoon just above your upper lip.) If the added chunks melt completely, stir in another 2 oz (60 g).
3. With a fork, lift out unmelted chunks and set them aside for other uses.
4. Scrape the chocolate onto a cold surface. Spread it evenly.
5. Refrigerate the chocolate until it is set, say 15 to 20 minutes.
6. Break it unto chunks. Reheat and melt to no higher than 90°F (32°C). Use it at this temperature for dipping and molding.

Making Do
If you don't have a marble slab, use a baking sheet. Rap the sheet on the counter to even out the layer of chocolate.

Master Plan
Precise Tempered Chocolate

1. Start with at least 12 oz (375 g) of chocolate. Chop it into chunks no bigger than ½ inch (1 cm).

2. Melt it over barely simmering water, stirring with a rubber spatula, until it reaches at least 110°F (43°C). This dissolves the fat crystals.

3. Remove it from the heat. Pour it into a dry, room-temperature bowl.

4. Immediately add chunks of unmelted chocolate. Use about a third of the amount you started with — 4 oz (125 g) in this case. (Don't be tempted to use grated chocolate.)

5. Stir until the chocolate cools to 80°F (27°C). Or spread it out on a cool surface. Remove any chunks of unmelted chocolate.

6. Reheat to no higher than 88°F to 90°F (31°C to 32°C) for dark chocolate, 85°F to 87°F (29°C to 31°C) for milk chocolate, 82°F to 84°F (28°C to 29°C) for white chocolate.

7. Place the chocolate over simmering water for 3 to 5 seconds at a time, rather than just leaving it there. If you reheat it above the proper temperature range, the gong sounds and you have to start over.

8. Use the chocolate immediately at the holding temperatures listed in Step 6. Maintaining the temperature is difficult. Some people use a heating pad with adjustable settings. Some dip the bowl of chocolate in and out of a bowl of hot water.

Is It Done?

- Smear the chocolate on a piece of foil and refrigerate it for 2 minutes to firm it up.
- The top should look smooth and even.
- Peel off the chocolate. The bottom should be shiny and firm. It should not be sticky or streaky.
- If it didn't work, you can scrape the whole mess back into the pan or bowl and start over.

C is for Compound Chocolate

The chocolate may be in temper, but you will lose your temper trying to get it that way at home. That's why they make compound chocolate. It contains cocoa powder, but most or all of the cocoa butter that causes the trouble is replaced by vegetable oil. Chocolate sans cocoa butter tastes similar to real chocolate, but doesn't act like it. It may not shine or melt in your mouth. It doesn't have to be tempered after it's melted.

There are different types of compound chocolate. Read the label. One is compatible with real chocolate. It includes some cocoa butter, and is meant for coating but not molding. Another replaces the cocoa butter with palm kernel oil. These two fats tend to bloom, or streak, when they come in contact. So if you want to pipe this kind on real chocolate, cool it down to at least 90°F (32°C), so it will set fast.

- If you don't want to temper chocolate, add 1 tbsp (15 mL) shortening to melted chocolate. However, it will be glossier and softer, with less snap than it had before.

Chocolate Creations

- Cool melted chocolate before adding it to batters or custards.

Ways to Ramp Up Chocolate Flavor

- Use cocoa powder in addition to real chocolate. To incorporate it, pour boiling water on the cocoa powder. Let it cool before using. Reduce the amount of liquid in the recipe to compensate.
- Substitute bottled chocolate syrup for corn syrup in a recipe. Chocolate syrup is basically corn (or another) syrup with cocoa powder.

Making Do

For 1 oz (30 g) unsweetened chocolate, substitute:

- 3 tbsp (45 mL) cocoa powder and 1 tbsp (15 mL) unsalted butter.
- One oz (30 g) semisweet chocolate. Plus remove 1 tbsp (15 mL) sugar and $\frac{1}{3}$ tsp (1.5 mL) butter from the recipe.

For 1 oz (30 g) semisweet chocolate, substitute:

- 1 tbsp (15 mL) plus $1\frac{3}{4}$ tsp (9 mL) cocoa powder, 1 tbsp (15 mL) plus $\frac{1}{2}$ tsp (2 mL) sugar and $1\frac{1}{2}$ tbsp (22 mL) unsalted butter.
- $\frac{3}{5}$ oz (18 g) unsweetened chocolate and $2\frac{1}{3}$ tsp (12 mL) sugar.

For 1 oz (30 g) couverture, substitute:

- One oz (30 g) semisweet chocolate and $\frac{1}{2}$ tsp (2 mL) cocoa butter.

❖ Milk chocolate lovers can use it in place of bittersweet and semisweet chocolate in mousses, puddings, pots de crème and the like. However, milk chocolate will make these not only sweeter but runnier.

❖ Alterations when switching milk chocolate for bittersweet:
- Increase the amount of chocolate in the recipe by 20%. Use 12 oz (375 g), say, instead of 10 oz (300 g).
- Reduce the sugar by a third. Use 4 tbsp (60 mL), say, instead of 6 tbsp (90 mL).

Chocolate Drizzling Tips

- When drizzling molten chocolate over cake or a dessert, jerk your spoon or fork back and forth quickly so the chocolate hits the plate, too. This looks nice.
- You can use a honey drizzler to drizzle melted chocolate.
- To make melted chocolate glossier, whisk in about $\frac{1}{2}$ tsp (2 mL) each corn syrup and butter per 1 oz (30 g) chocolate.

Dipping Tips

- When dipping fruit in chocolate, the fruit should be cool but not cold, and completely dry.
- To dip strawberries in chocolate, press a thin skewer into the top of each through the hull. Or use a toothpick. If you hold them by the tender green leaves, you are liable to pull out the leaves.
- When you are getting low on chocolate in the dipping bowl, bring it close with a wide rubber spatula. Scrape and hold, then roll fruit or whatever you are dipping against it.
- Place dipped berries or candies on a rack to allow the excess to drip off. Set waxed paper under the rack. You can reuse the drippings.

❖ If chunks are left after whisking chocolate and cream for a ganache, microwave the mixture on High for a few seconds. Be brief, very brief. Whisk until smooth.

❖ For baking, toss chocolate chunks or chips with some of the flour from the recipe. The flour helps them cling to the batter instead of sinking. Toss 2 cups (500 mL) chips or chunks with about 1 tbsp (15 mL) flour. This isn't necessary for brownies or dense muffins.

Ways to Flavor Homemade Truffles

- Add coffee-shop syrups. Raspberry is a lovely accent.
- Scald and flavor the cream. Steeping chai tea in the cream is one favorite.

⊗ Waste Not

- To get that last bit of melted chocolate out of a bowl, sprinkle in some flour from the recipe and scrape.
- Frugal chocolate lovers can buy bunnies at half-price after Easter, then freeze them. Chop them up for cookies, icings and desserts.

✧ Refrigerate a chocolate mixture for truffles until it is firm enough to roll. Or stash it briefly in the freezer.

✧ You can set dipped truffles on a drum sieve.

OUTSIDE THE BOX

Here's a trick to use when coating truffles with cocoa powder: Put the cocoa on a baking sheet. Create an incline by putting a rolled towel under one end. Roll truffles down the hill through the cocoa.

✧ Keep homemade truffles firm in the fridge. Let them stand at room temperature for 5 minutes before serving, to bring out the flavors.

How to Make Chocolate Leaves

1. Start with real leaves with prominent veins. Pick firm small or medium ones. Clean them with vegetable wash or vinegar. Dry them thoroughly.
2. With a pastry brush, paint melted chocolate onto the underside of the leaves.
3. Let the chocolate cool until it is firm. Carefully peel off the leaves. If you refrigerate the chocolate, don't let it get too cold or it will splinter.

How to Pipe Chocolate Shapes and Designs

1. Pour melted chocolate into a piping bag.
2. Refrigerate the chocolate until it is firm enough to pipe, about 15 minutes for 4 oz (125 g).
3. Work quickly. It should be runny enough not to clog the tip, but firm enough not to leak out.
4. Pipe shapes and designs, from rosettes to initials, onto waxed paper. Let them cool until hardened.
5. Use them as cake decorations or garnishes.

How to Mold a Chocolate Bowl

1. Blow up a balloon. Dip the bottom in melted chocolate.
2. Even the edges with your fingertip.
3. Set the balloon upside down in a small bowl to allow the chocolate to firm up.
4. Repeat the dipping and cooling once or twice to make a thick bowl.
5. Prick the balloon and discard it.

How to Rim Hot Chocolate or Latte

About 1 oz (30 g) of chocolate is enough to rim two to four mugs, depending on how narrow they are.

1. Dip the rim of a clear coffee mug in melted white chocolate. (Or use dark chocolate.)
2. Dip the chocolate in bright, crushed candies or sprinkles.

Storing Chocolate

✧ The secret of chocolate's success in the pantry: Unlike other fats, cocoa butter keeps for years without going rancid.

✧ Dark chocolate lasts longer than white or milk chocolate because it has fewer milk solids.

---

6 Storage Tips

1. Store chocolate in a cool, dry cupboard, away from fluctuations in temperature or humidity. The humidity should be low. Don't store chocolate next to the fridge or stove.

2. Store chocolate at temperatures from 60°F to 75°F (16°C to 24°C). The optimal temperature is 63°F (17°C).

3. Keep chocolate away from spices or strongly scented food, or items that contain chemicals or perfumes. It is easily tainted by foreign aromas and flavors.

4. Wrap chocolate in foil or, if unopened, leave it in its original packaging. Plastic wrap holds moisture and prevents air circulation.

5. Do not refrigerate or freeze chocolate unless the temperature at home goes above 75°F (24°C). It will sweat when it warms up and exhibit a greater tendency to bloom. Fridge temperatures also fluctuate.

6. Exception: You can freeze nibs if you want to keep them for more than a few weeks. Refresh nibs by warming them for 5 minutes in a 250°F (120°C) oven.

Ⓑ is for Bloom

Chocolate with bloom looks like it has gone bad, but it is fine to eat. Bloom is not mold. The cure for bloom: Melt the chocolate or use it in baking. Bloom is caused by temperature changes, exposure to direct sunlight or damp, or old age. There are two types.

- **Fat bloom:** Warmth causes cocoa butter to separate out and drift to the surface. When the fat resolidifies, the chocolate is left with gray or white patches or bumps. They may feel oily.
- **Sugar bloom:** Moisture or humidity leaches out sugar and it rises to the surface. When the sugar dries again, the chocolate is left with dots, streaks or hazy sections. They may feel gritty.

✧ Milk chocolate is less likely to bloom, as it contains less cocoa liquor, or mass. Out-of-temper chocolate, filled chocolates and chocolates with rough surfaces are more likely to bloom.

✧ Chocolate doesn't have to be old to bloom. Old chocolate that has bloomed will be crumbly, as slow-forming, big, coarse crystals of fat develop.

Carob

✧ Also known as Saint John's bread, this chocolate substitute and thickener is made from the pods of the carob tree. The pulp is roasted and ground into powder. This powder may be made into syrup, or into chips or bars with the help of added fat.

✧ Carob is sweeter than chocolate but doesn't taste as good. Use less sugar when cooking with carob powder and turn down the heat.

Candy

✧ When rolling no-bake balls, such as rum balls or sugarplums, coat your palms lightly with butter.

✧ Use mini marshmallows when making crispy rice squares and other desserts. They melt faster and more evenly than the big ones.

✧ It's less messy to melt marshmallows in the microwave. Butter the bowl to reduce sticking. Eight oz (250 g) takes 2 to 3 minutes on Medium. Stop and stir a couple of times.

 No-No

Don't attempt hard candy, fondant, nougat, divinity or fudge on a hot, humid day.

Hard Candy

✧ When making candy, choose a pan that accommodates about four times the volume of your mixture, to avoid boil-overs.

✧ Roll round candy until it has cooled; otherwise, one side will be flattened.

✧ To crush hard candy, put it in a heavy-duty plastic bag, seal well and whack it with a mallet.

Uses for Broken Candy

- Sprinkle it on ice cream.
- Garnish creamy desserts.
- Add it to chocolate bark.
- Decorate a cake.
- Add it to cookies.

8 Steps to Better Brittle

1. Don't put nuts straight from the freezer into the hot syrup. It will set too quickly.

2. Pour the hot syrup and nut mixture onto a large sheet of lightly oiled parchment paper laid on a heatproof surface. (A ceramic stovetop is perfect.) Cover it with a second sheet of lightly oiled parchment.

3. Immediately roll out the mixture to ¼-inch (0.5 cm) thickness, pressing firmly with a rolling pin from the center outwards.

4. It shouldn't harden faster than you can finish, but if it does, transfer it to a large baking sheet and warm it in a 350°F (180°C) oven for 5 minutes, then continue rolling.

5. Let cool until the mixture is firm but still pliable, 2 to 5 minutes.

6. Remove the top sheet of parchment. Use a lightly oiled pizza cutter to score the brittle into squares. About 1½ inches (4 cm) is a good size. If it's too firm to score, go back to the oven trick.

7. Let it cool until it is firm. Peel off the parchment. Break it into pieces.

8. Store brittle in an airtight container at room temperature. Keep the pieces in layers separated by parchment paper.

Fudge

✦ Wrap the fudge in foil and store it in a cool, dry place. Do not refrigerate it. Fudge will become more sugary and granular in 2 to 3 days.

Fudge Doctor

It's too stiff to beat.

- Perhaps it cooled too much. Stir in a few drops of warm cream and try again.

It's grainy.

- The fudge was disturbed before it was cool enough to beat, or not beaten long enough.

It's too soft.

- The syrup wasn't cooked to the right temperature.
- The fudge was beaten while it was too warm.
- The fudge was not beaten long enough.
- If your fudge doesn't set properly, add heavy or whipping (35%) cream, beat it with an electric mixer until it is fluffy, then use it to ice a cake. You can scrape unset fudge into a tub and freeze it until you need it.

It's crumbly or too hard.

- You overbeat it. Fudge may lighten suddenly, turn crumbly and weep fat.
- Chop it and use it like broken candy.
- Crumble it to use as part of a parfait or layered mousse or pudding.

Tips for Cheaters

- Classic fudge made with sugar syrup and an eye on the thermometer is temperamental. It requires lots of tedious stirring and can go from gooey to crumbly in the blink of an eye. Cheat with recipes that replace the syrup with marshmallows or sweetened condensed milk.
- Add baking soda to cheater's fudge to make it firmer, lighter and drier, rather than chewy and dense. Half a teaspoon (2 mL) baking soda is enough for fudge made with $1\frac{1}{4}$ cups (300 mL) sweetened condensed milk and 14 oz (400 g) chocolate.
- Mock fudge tends to be softer. For cleaner cuts, chill it in the fridge beforehand.

8 Steps to Successful Fudge

1. Grease the sides of the pan. Add $\frac{1}{8}$ tsp (0.5 mL) baking soda to the fudge mixture. If it doesn't foam up high when it comes to a boil, add another pinch of baking soda. Boil, without stirring, to the soft-ball stage, 234°F to 240°F (112°C to 116°C).

2. Immediately pour the mixture into a clean, large, wide-bottom bowl. Never scrape the pan clean. That causes "sugaring," or grittiness.

3. This is crucial: Let the mixture cool on a rack until it reaches 110°F (43°C), which can take 1 to 2 hours. You should be able to comfortably stick your finger into the mixture right to the bottom of the bowl.

4. For quicker cooling, set the bowl in ice water or pour the mixture onto a marble slab or buttered baking sheet.

5. Beat it until it is very thick, lighter in color and glossy-turning-to-matte. If you're not Arnold Schwarzenegger, give your biceps a break by using a stand mixer fitted with the paddle attachment. Beat on medium-low speed for perhaps 15 minutes.

6. Quickly stir in nuts or other tidbits.

7. Scrape the mixture into a glass baking dish lined with a sling of greased foil or parchment. Let it cool completely on a rack.

8. Wait at for least 12 hours before consuming. It will get creamier.

Syrup and Caramel

A Bit of Science

Molten sugar is a chemistry lesson. Sugar breaks down as it is heated, getting hotter, thicker, darker, more bitter and less sweet in stages.

Stages of Molten Sugar

- **Thread:** 215°F to 234°F (102°C to 112°C). Forms threads, from fine to coarse, depending on how hot it is. At the high end, it should form a 2-inch (5 cm) long coarse thread.
- **Soft-ball:** 234°F to 240°F (112°C to 116°C). Forms a squishy ball that flattens out on its own when picked up. Has a chewing-gum texture. Best for fudge, fondant and pralines.
- **Firm-ball:** 244°F to 248°F (118°C to 120°C). Forms a ball that holds its shape but flattens if pressed. Used for caramel candies.
- **Hard-ball:** 248°F to 265°F (118°C to 129°C). Forms a rigid but pliable ball. Used for divinity and nougat.
- **Soft-crack:** 270°F to 290°F (132°C to 143°C). Forms firm but bendable threads. Brittle but sticks to the teeth. Used for some caramels and taffy.
- **Hard-crack:** 290°F to 310°F (143°F to 154°C). Forms hard threads that snap when bent. Brittle and does not stick to the teeth.
- **Caramel:** 320°F to 375°F (160°C to 190°C). Rapidly colors from golden to deep brown, and changes from sweet to bitter.
- **Browning:** 375°F to 380°F (190°C to 193°C). In its latter stages, caramel loses its sweetness. It can be turned into a coloring agent called browning or caramel coloring.

- **Black Jack:** 410°F (210°C). Burnt black, decomposed and inedible.

Lightning Won't Strike If ...

You don't test sugar syrup the traditional way, by dripping it into water. This is awkward and inconvenient, involving fishing around, peering closely and squeezing. Just use a reliable thermometer.

5 Tips if You Do Want to Go the Water Route

1. Test about ½ tsp (2 mL) syrup.
2. Pour the syrup off the side of the spoon.
3. Use cold, not icy, water.
4. Use fresh water for each test.
5. Remove the syrup from the burner each time you test, to prevent overcooking.

Syrup Doctor

You passed the right stage.

- Say you've hit firm-ball when you want soft-ball. Pull the syrup off the heat and add an ice cube to try to reverse the process.

The caramel is too light after being removed from the stove.

- Bring it back to a boil without stirring. Boil until it is darker.

The caramel darkens suddenly.

- Dip the base of the pan in cold water to stop the cooking.
- If you are making sauce, add liquid to the caramel.

Two Safety Tips

- Molten sugar is excruciatingly hot and causes nasty burns. It hardens on your skin. Get it off fast. Run to the sink and spray it immediately with cold water to stop the heat and melt off the sugar.
- Pour hot syrup with the edge of the pan away from you, and from only a few inches up, so you don't get spattered.

A Bit of Science

Sugar is a crystal. Crystals like to gang up. In hot sugar syrup, one lone crystal attracts another, then another. Suddenly you have crusty clumps on the side of your pan. Stirring them back into the syrup just speeds up the reaction.

- ✧ The easy way out: Change the chemical structure of the syrup so the crystals are no longer attracted to each other.
- Add another form of sugar, such as corn syrup or honey — say 1 tbsp (15 mL).
- Add an acid, such as lemon juice, vinegar or cream of tartar.

Other Ways to Deal with Crystallization

- Never stir sugar syrup once it has melted.
- Do not let dry crystals fall back into the pan.
- Use a wet pastry brush to wipe down the sides of the pan.
- Cover the pan for a couple of minutes. Steam condenses on the lid and the water rinses the sides.
- Make sure the thermometer or testing spoon is clean each time. You don't want to introduce sugar crystals.
- Oil the sides of the pan beforehand to prevent crystals from sticking. (This also prevents boil-overs).
- Remove the pan from the heat, let it cool slightly, then stir in a bit of water until the crystals dissolve.
- Don't scrape the pan when you are done.

Light VS. Dark Caramel?

Caramel goes from straw to amber. The darker the caramel, the deeper the flavor, and the more bitter and the weaker when hardened.

8 Tips for Stovetop Caramel Syrup

1. Use a wide saucepan, not a deep one. Otherwise, the sugar closest to the metal may brown before the rest even melts.
2. For even melting, sprinkle sugar in a bit at a time.
3. Sugar caramelizes unevenly. A cast-iron skillet offers steady, uniform heat. The bad news: It's hard to assess the color in a black pan.
4. Caramel turns and burns as it goes from straw to golden to brown. Reduce the heat when it starts to color.
5. Golden amber is okay. Dark amber is bitter.
6. For even coloring, swirl the pan occasionally.
7. To judge color, put a few drops on a white plate, as it may look darker in the pan. Or dip a strip of white cardboard in the syrup.
8. Caramel syrup continues to darken off the heat. Take it off the burner just before it has reached the shade you want.

Wet VS. Dry?

Caramel can be prepared dry, by melting sugar, or wet, by boiling sugar and water. The former gives you a darker caramel. The latter gives you more control over the color.

- ✧ If caramel sets too quickly, warm it over low heat until it melts.

Microwave Caramel Syrup

The easiest way to make caramel: in the microwave. Caramel syrup may be turned into sauce or candy garnishes, or used in cakes, pies, puddings, frostings, ice cream bases and coffee creations. **Makes about ¹/₂ cup (125 mL)**

Tip

This is a fast, simple method, but you must remain vigilant or the syrup will burn.

¹/₂ cup	granulated sugar	125 mL
¹/₄ cup	corn syrup	50 mL
1 tbsp	water	15 mL

1. Put sugar in a 4-cup (1 L) microwave-safe glass measuring cup. Stir in corn syrup and water until sugar is moistened.

2. Microwave on High. You will see cascading bubbles. Watch carefully. As soon as the color changes from straw to gold, remove the cup. This takes less than 3 minutes. (If you take it out when it's honey-colored, you've gone too far; it turns dark and bitter as it sits.)

3. Let it stand for at least 1 minute. Check the color. If you want it darker, microwave it for 10 seconds longer. Wait 30 seconds, then check the color. Repeat this until you are satisfied.

❖ To keep caramel liquid, set it in the top of a double boiler over simmering water.

❖ To make crisp caramel, pour it onto oiled parchment. Spread quickly into a thin sheet. Once it has cooled, you can break it into slivers to decorate desserts. Or create decorative swirls. Let them cool, then peel them off when they're solid.

Keep It Clean

Caramel syrup coats a pan when it hardens. Don't scrape the pan. Don't try to clean it off with cold water; the coating will stick more firmly. Fill the pan with hot water, or add water and bring it to a boil. The caramel will melt off.

❖ Caramel doesn't store well. It softens as it absorbs humidity in the air.

❖ Caramel syrup bubbles up when you add a liquid such as cream. Adding it quickly can be explosive.

Ways to Deal with Foaming and Spitting

- Use a large saucepan so the syrup doesn't bubble over.
- Warm cream or another liquid to the boiling point before adding it.
- Remove the syrup from the heat before adding the cream or liquid.
- Slowly whisk in the cream or liquid as you pour it in a thin, steady stream.
- Stand as far away as possible from the pan. Certainly do not lean over it.
- Move the pan into the sink and whisk it there, if you're worried.

Easy Caramel Sauce

This is a very sweet, rich sauce for sundaes. It thickens as it sits, but is not a firm caramel.
Makes about 1¾ cups (425 mL)

Variation

Whisk in finely chopped bittersweet chocolate along with the butter. Try 2 to 4 oz (60 to 125 g) chocolate.

2 cups	granulated sugar	500 mL
1 cup	water	250 mL
2 tbsp	corn syrup	25 mL
1 cup	heavy or whipping (35%) cream	250 mL
1 tsp	vanilla extract	5 mL
⅛ tsp	salt	0.5 mL
2 tbsp	unsalted butter	25 mL

1. In a large saucepan, stir together sugar, water and corn syrup over medium heat. Bring to a boil. Cook, without stirring, until the mixture is honey-colored.

2. Meanwhile, place cream in a microwave-safe bowl. Microwave on High for 30 to 60 seconds or until hot but not boiling.

3. Remove the syrup from the heat. Gradually whisk in half the cream. The mixture will bubble up. Whisk to blend it. Whisk in the remaining cream, vanilla and salt. Whisk in butter until it melts.

4. Serve the sauce hot, warm, at room temperature or cool. Store it in an airtight container in the refrigerator for up to 1 week.

≣ Fast Fix

For the easiest caramel sauce, buy individually wrapped caramel candies. Melt them with a bit of cream in the microwave. Stir frequently.

Ⓓ is for Dulce de Leche

Dulce de leche is a Latin American caramel made with sweetened condensed milk. When prepared with goat's milk, it is called *cajeta*. D is also for delectable and delicious.

✦ The longer you heat the sweetened condensed milk, the darker and thicker the dulce de leche. It also firms and darkens a bit as it cools.

Master Plan
Oven Dulce de Leche

1. Pour two 14-oz or 300-mL cans of sweetened condensed milk into a 9-inch (23 cm) deep-dish pie plate. Stir in a pinch of salt.

2. Cover the dish with foil. Crimp the edges to seal it firmly and securely.

3. Put the dish in a roasting pan. Add enough boiling water to come halfway up the sides of the dish.

4. Bake it in a 425°F (220°C) oven for 45 minutes.

5. Top up the boiling water. Bake for 45 minutes or until smooth, set and caramel-colored.

Healthier Eater

You can use low-fat sweetened condensed milk for dulce de leche.

Master Plan
Traditional, Dangerous Dulce de Leche

1. Place an unopened 14-oz or 300-mL can of sweetened condensed milk in a small, deep saucepan and cover generously with water. Simmer it over low or medium-low heat for 2 hours.
2. Turn the can upside down. Simmer it for 1 hour.
3. Let it cool completely before opening.

Beware: Never let the water boil down far enough to expose the can. It may explode and injure you. Make sure the can is covered by at least 2 inches (5 cm) of water at all times. Makers of sweetened condensed milk advise consumers to avoid this method because of safety issues.

Master Plan
The Best and Easiest Dulce de Leche

1. Scrape a 14-oz or 300-mL can of sweetened condensed milk into the top section of a double boiler over simmering water.
2. Cover and simmer it over low heat, stirring very occasionally, for about 3 hours or until it is thick and caramel-colored.
3. Whisk until it is smooth.

Master Plan
Fastest Dulce de Leche

1. Scrape a 14-oz or 300-mL can of sweetened condensed milk into an 8-cup (2 L) microwave-safe glass measuring cup. (The milk will bubble right to the top.)
2. Microwave it on Medium (50%) for 5 minutes. Stir it well.
3. Microwave it on Medium-Low (30%) for 7 to 10 minutes or until it is thick and caramel-colored. Stir briskly after the first 3 minutes, then check and stir every minute.

Note: The microwave method is fast, but the resulting dulce de leche is coarser and the color is not as pleasing.

Gelatin

Leaf VS. Powder?

Chefs favor leaf gelatin, though you may never encounter it. It comes in brittle sheets, which should be soaked in cold water for 10 minutes, then squeezed dry. For our purposes, powdered gelatin works fine. When translating recipes, 4 leaves equal 1 tbsp (15 mL) gelatin powder.

Gelatin Measurements

- If a recipe calls for 1 tbsp (15 mL), just use one envelope — although an envelope actually contains about $2\frac{1}{2}$ tsp (12 mL).
- One $\frac{1}{4}$-oz (7 g) envelope of unflavored gelatin sets 2 cups (500 mL) of liquid, broth or juice.
- Reduce the liquid to $1\frac{3}{4}$ cups (425 mL) for a solid set.

How to Mix Unflavored Gelatin

1. Sprinkle 1 tbsp (15 mL) gelatin powder into $\frac{1}{4}$ cup (50 mL) cold liquid from the recipe.
2. Let it soften and swell for about 5 minutes.
3. Add it to the rest of the liquid — $1\frac{3}{4}$ to 2 cups (425 to 500 mL) water, stock, milk, juice, wine or the like. The liquid should be hot.
4. Stir until the gelatin dissolves or you'll end up with rubbery lumps. To check, splash some of the mixture against the side of the bowl. There should be no particles visible.
5. Refrigerate the mixture until it sets. Allow 2 hours to firm up 2 cups (500 mL) liquid.

♦ One manufacturer notes that you don't have to soften gelatin if you mix it with sugar, which also separates the granules.

X No-Nos

- Do not try to cool gelatin quickly in the freezer. It's apt to crack and crumble.
- If you add softened gelatin to a cold mixture, it will be lumpy.

♦ How to dissolve gelatin without adding it to a hot liquid:

- Soften it as usual with liquid in a small, heatproof bowl. Pour boiling water into a slightly larger bowl. Set the gelatin dish in the water. Stir constantly to dissolve the gelatin. It should be fluid. It's okay if it looks foggy. If necessary, change the boiling water.
- Soften the gelatin as usual with liquid in a small, microwave-safe bowl. Microwave it on High for about 20 seconds or until it is close to boiling. Do not boil. Stir it rapidly.

♦ Test a gelatin mixture beforehand if you are unsure how firm the end result will be. Put a large spoonful in a shot glass and place it in the freezer for 20 to 30 minutes. Then poke your finger in the middle. Or pour a spoonful onto a small, flat plate and refrigerate it for at least 30 minutes.

♦ If you are adding acidic ingredients, such as fruit, to a gelatin dessert, you may need to:

- Double the time for gelling.
- Add extra gelatin.
- Reduce the amount of water.

- How to speed up setting a package of flavored gelatin:
- Dissolve the gelatin powder in half the boiling water. Substitute ice cubes for the rest. Use 2 cups (500 mL) ice cubes to replace 1 cup (250 mL) water. Stir for 3 to 5 minutes or until it thickens. Discard ice cubes that haven't melted. Refrigerate.
- Set the bowl or mold of gelatin in ice water. Stir constantly until it is almost set. It should thicken in 5 minutes. Refrigerate.

Gelatin Doctor

There's a rubbery layer at the bottom of the fruit-flavored gelatin.

- The gelatin didn't dissolve properly.
- Stir the gelatin with boiling water for at least 2 minutes to dissolve it completely. Be patient. Look closely at a spoonful. If there are no particles, it's good to go.

There's foam on top of the set gelatin.

- Stir slowly to minimize bubbles while mixing gelatin with boiling water.
- Get rid of stubborn bubbles by pressing them against the side of the bowl with the back of a spoon.

The gelatin refuses to set.

- Certain fruits contain enzymes that destroy protein bonds in gelatin. The troublemakers include pineapple, kiwifruit and figs, along with gingerroot. This affects not only gelatin molds, but desserts that are stabilized by gelatin, such as mousses and cream pies. It can't be helped. Next time, disable the enzymes. Purée and boil the fruit first. Or use canned fruit.

Gelatin Mold Techniques

- Stirring the gelatin with the liquid for 2 minutes prevents it from pulling away from the solid ingredients once it sets.

- Wipe the mold lightly with oil before adding the gelatin mixture. The gelatin will be easier to remove and will hold its shape.
- For firmer molds, or shapes such as squares, reduce the water by 25%. For small cutouts, such as letters of the alphabet, reduce the water by half. Measure in favor of the boiling water, not the cold.
- Serve a mold on a platter set in a glass bowl of crushed ice. This will help maintain its shape.
- You can use paper cups or candy cups as individual molds. This is an efficient way to make Jell-O shots.
- If you don't want your molded gelatin to stick, sprinkle the serving platter with cold water. You will be able to slide the mold or arrange gelatin shapes on the platter.

Suspending Fruit

- Wait until the gelatin is partially set, with the consistency of unbeaten egg whites, before adding solids. (Chill it for about an hour.) That way, the solids will remain suspended.
- Use room-temperature fruit. Cold fruit is more likely to sink.
- Patiently set the gelatin, layer by layer, with fruit or other additions in each section.

The Easiest Way to Make a Gelatin Mold

- Set gelatin until it is the consistency of raw egg whites.
- Mix in fruit or other items with different densities and let them find their own space.
- Banana slices, apple, grapefruit or pear wedges, strawberry halves and marshmallows are floaters.
- Orange slices, fresh grapes and canned fruit, such as peaches, are sinkers.

The Hardest Way to Make a Gelatin Mold

- Tip and roll the mold to create a thin layer of gelatin coating. Refrigerate until it is set.
- Form a design by picking up bits of food with a skewer or toothpick, dipping each in the gelatin and placing it on the set layer of gelatin. Fill in the spaces in between with more gelatin. Refrigerate until set.
- Repeat until the mold is filled — if you don't have a life.

Ways to Unmold

- Loosen the edges with the tip of a knife to introduce air between the mold and the gelatin. Or use a thin rubber spatula if you are worried about damaging the shape.
- Invert the mold onto a serving plate sprinkled with cold water. Run hot water over a kitchen towel, wring it and place it over the mold. Wait a minute, remove the towel and gently shake the mold. The gelatin should slip out.
- Dip the mold up to its edge in warm water for about 5 seconds. If the gelatin doesn't fall onto the plate when you invert the mold, dip it again.
- Warm the mold with a blow-dryer.

OUTSIDE THE BOX

Use a square or rectangular baking dish to set gelatin. Unmold it. Cut it into squares to serve.

- You can mix fresh blueberries into partially gelled gelatin for a polka-dot effect. Lime gelatin with blueberries is pretty.

A is for Agar

This seaweed product is the vegetarian's equivalent of gelatin. It suffers from a whiff of seaweed and the tendency to break into brittle shards, but it sets quickly and stays set at room temperature. It comes in powder and flakes.

Agar Measurements

- One tsp (5 mL) agar powder equals 1 tbsp (15 mL) agar flakes.
- Recipes seem to call for too much. One tsp (5 mL) agar sets 2 cups (500 mL) water handily.

How to Use Agar

1. Soak agar powder in a cold liquid for 10 minutes.
2. Bring the mixture to a simmer over medium heat. Reduce the heat to low and stir until the agar is dissolved, about 5 minutes.
3. Let it stand at room temperature for about an hour. If you want to add fruit or other tidbits, do so as soon as possible after removing it from the heat.
4. Refrigerate.

- Unlike gelatin, agar does set with pineapple. But if you are using acidic fruit and berries, add a bit more agar.

Entertaining

Recipes

From Ordinary to Extraordinary

Taking Shortcuts

◆ Make takeout barbecued whole chicken your friend. Strip and go crazy. Five ideas for a stripped rotisserie chicken:

- Prepare chicken pizza, using barbecue sauce instead of tomato sauce.
- Top corn chowder with strips of chicken and chopped herbs.
- Place chicken on mixed baby greens for a big dinner salad.
- Roll chicken in tortillas, bake with shredded cheese on top and garnish with spicy sautéed, chopped tomatillos.
- Create a quick jambalaya with rice, tomato sauce, vegetables and chicken.

◆ Go to Chinatown and buy a roast duck. For instant intrigue, substitute it for stripped rotisserie chicken. Two ideas for stripped Chinese duck:

- Arrange a bed of sticky rice, then top with mixed greens. Drizzle with Asian dressing. Top with duck.
- Smear wheat tortillas with hoisin sauce. Add duck, bean sprouts, julienned carrots and shredded green onions. Roll.

Mythstake

Although people refer to them as Peking ducks, the birds commonly sold ready-to-go in Chinese butcher shops are actually a simpler type of barbecued, or roast, duck. The preparation of Peking duck is long and involved, and includes pumping air under the skin to separate it from the flesh.

◆ Extend a basic three-course meal by adding hors d'oeuvres at the beginning, a palate-cleansing sorbet in the middle and, at the end, crackers and cheese with port, and/or truffles and liqueur.

◆ You can put anything on pizza dough. Read up on pizza cookery, then either go crazy or take it easy with toppings.

Simple Pizza Ideas

- Bake a round of dough in a 500°F (260°C) oven until it is crispy, about 12 minutes. Smear it with pesto. Serve with tomato salad.
- Brush dough with herbed oil and sprinkle on minced garlic. The garlic becomes tender yet crunchy as the crust cooks. You can arrange very thinly sliced, drained plum tomatoes on top, if you wish.
- Buy a prepared crust, then go all out with the toppings. How about crème fraîche, smoked salmon and dill sprigs?

Fun, Easy Retro Ideas

- Haul out the fondue — preferably the disco-era one in avocado green.
- Serve breakfast for dinner. People love it in diners. Use diner-style decorations and serving ware.
- Bake in hobo packs. Arrange three food groups in each individual parchment packet. Drizzle with dressing or sauce. Sprinkle with herbs. Stick the packs in the oven.

- Go with the big supper salad. It's fast, healthful and a good way to use up leftovers. Two super supper salad ideas:
  - Sear salmon or fresh tuna and place it atop a mound of baby greens.
  - Cut firm, leftover veggies — such as asparagus, cauliflower or broccoli — into chunks, toss with assertive salad dressing and top with strips of leftover grilled steak.

OUTSIDE THE BOX

You can turn homemade or bottled salsa into passable gazpacho. Simmer it with stock, then zap it in a blender. Serve it drizzled with sour cream and topped with croutons or tortilla chips. You can add some texture with finely diced cucumber.

- For fast dips, start with sour cream, yogurt or deli cream cheese. Stir in salsa, pesto, chutney, curry paste or a spice blend. Don't stir in onion soup mix, please, unless you are a university student.

- Open a can of consommé. Add mini ravioli or tortellini. Sprinkle with chopped herbs.

- Bake store-bought tartlet shells. Make hors d'oeuvres by filling them with antipasto, chopped fresh tomato and basil, sautéed wild mushrooms or anything tasty but easy that you can think of.

- Buy a baked, unfrosted cake. Cut it into a shape such as a heart or an initial. Frost it in a wild color. Add pretty decorations.

- Improve a scoop of ice cream. Squeeze it between two oversized cookies.

Going from Plain to Fancy

- Turn dinner into an '80s party. Serve whatever you happen to have in crêpes. Either the batter or the crêpes can be made in advance and refrigerated or frozen.

- Make sandwiches dinner-worthy. Carefully choose the bread, filling and presentation.

Simple Ways to Improve a Sandwich

- Roll a pesto wrap or stuff a ciabatta. Don't settle for boring bread.
- Pad the filling with roasted red peppers or baby arugula.
- Use quality condiments, such as mayonnaise mixed with roasted garlic or wasabi.
- Substitute fresh tuna or salmon for the canned kind.
- Experiment with unusual fillings, such as roasted artichokes and cheese.
- Grill the sandwich or press it.

- Use an attractive fruit or vegetable as a pincushion for plain hors d'oeuvres. Cut a slice off the bottom for stability. Insert cocktail toothpicks holding cubes of cheese or single shrimp.

- In place of simple croutons, toast thin ovals from a baguette. Smear the bread with anything from liverwurst to goat cheese. Float it on top of soup.

- Stuff things with cheese. Example: Fill pitted Medjool dates or halved cherry tomato shells with cream cheese.

9 Cheese Ball Techniques

Turn a soft, bland cheese into a cheese ball.

1. Use block cream cheese for firmness, instead of the fluffy deli kind.
2. Mix in herbs (preferably fresh), seasonings and/or nuts, chopped but not too finely.
3. If you have trouble rolling it, refrigerate the cheese to firm it up.
4. Wet your hands to form the mixture into a ball.
5. You can cover the cheese with plastic wrap as you roll.
6. Wrap the ball in plastic. Refrigerate it for at least an hour to firm up, or overnight to meld flavors.
7. Roll it into a nicer sphere before removing the wrap.
8. Decorate the ball. Roll it in finely chopped herbs, nuts or bell peppers, or cracked peppercorns.
9. If you are in a hurry, you can instead line a bowl with plastic wrap and push the cheese into it. Firm the cheese in the fridge, then unmold it and serve it as a mound. Press whole nuts or halves decoratively around the base.

✧ Turn boring cubes of cheese into kebabs. Thread them onto skewers with grape tomatoes, grapes, pitted olives, mini cucumber or pickle slices, or chic star fruit.

✧ Serve an exotic fruit paste or jam with a slab of cheese. Examples: fig jam, quince paste, guava jam, mango chutney.

✧ Defend yourself from boring food by keeping an arsenal of spice blends. From Cajun to za'atar (tart, includes sumac), spice blends are great in sauces, dips, rubs, marinades and more.

Ideas for a Spice Blend

- Mix it into ground meat for burger patties or meatloaf.
- Stir it into a paste with olive oil. Spread it on flatbread, or smear it on dough and bake.
- Stir it into softened butter.
- Stir it into thick yogurt to make a zingy dip for fresh fruit or vegetables.
- Mix it with spreadable cheese for sandwiches.
- Sprinkle it on roasted vegetables. Dukka (an Egyptian nut-and-spice mixture) is fabulous on roasted sweet potatoes.

✧ Make a meal beautiful with a handful of edible flowers. You can buy bags of mixed petals or whole flowers.

Ideas for Edible Flowers

- Add them to salads.
- Sprinkle them over an omelet.
- Decorate a cake with them.
- Use them singly as garnishes.
- Brew fragrant tea.

✧ Embellish with gourmet salts, particularly smoked salt. Three foods uplifted by smoked salt:
- French fries
- Popcorn
- Steamed vegetables (toss them with olive oil and smoked salt; edamame is fabulous this way)

✧ Pipe things — right down to the soft cheese in a celery stalk and the creamy yolk in a deviled egg. They will look more appetizing.

3 Ways to Make Butter Cute

1. Press butter through a piping bag into swirls and let them set, instead of serving plain hunks or pats.
2. Press softened butter into candy molds.
3. Roll balls of butter in paprika or black pepper.

❖ Add ethnic flavors to old standards.

Cross-Cultural Matches

- Creamed spinach tastes great with Indian spices.
- Jerk sauce and mango salsa make meatloaf interesting.
- Freeze a batch of Spanish romesco sauce (intense, with smoky peppers, tomatoes and nuts). Serve it with seafood, pasta or vegetables, or add a dollop to plain soup.
- Always have pesto on hand to use with hot and cold dishes. You can make chicken salad with pesto mayonnaise.

❖ Add spirits. A bit of beer, wine, hard liquor or liqueur immediately transports a dish from suburbia to uptown.

OUTSIDE THE BOX

You can add beer or wine to soup.
- Beer is good in hearty soup with beans or cabbage. Use about 1 cup (250 mL) beer per 3 cups (750 mL) soup.
- Add red or white wine to tomato soup or seafood chowder. Use about ½ cup (125 mL) wine per 4 cups (1 L) soup.

❖ Turn fruit into a tropical treat. Just add heat and booze.

Tips for Grilling or Sautéing Fruit

- First, dip fruit in crunchy dark brown or turbinado sugar.
- Use high heat to brown fruit quickly without softening it too much.
- Cook it in a buttered panini press, grill it or sauté it in butter.
- Flambé it with rum, for a kick.
- A squeeze of lime juice at the end combats sweetness.
- Serve it with tropical ice cream. Coconut ice cream, for example, is lovely with caramelized banana or pineapple slices.

❖ Hide a coin in the steamed pudding. This is an old Christmas tradition. Whoever gets the coin will have financial luck in the coming year. Just warn diners beforehand so they don't break their teeth.

❖ Serve a hot drink with a chocolate spoon alongside. To make one, dip the bowl of a teaspoon in melted chocolate. Stand the spoon upright in a glass or cup until the chocolate hardens. Repeat until the coating is thick enough. You can also dip a plastic or metal spoon in chocolate to give away with a gift of coffee.

Sweet Ways to Make Sugar Festive

- Put granulated sugar in a zip-lock bag, add a drop of food coloring and massage it in.
- Use a fork to mix in a drop of extract, such as peppermint, citrus, coconut or maple.
- Mix homemade maple sugar. Using a fork, stir 3 to 4 tbsp (45 to 60 mL) maple syrup into 1 cup (250 mL) granulated sugar. Yum.

Taking a Step up the Ingredient Ladder

Upscale an Ingredient in a Home-Style Dish or Comfort Food

- Use ground lamb and Guinness in shepherd's pie.
- Replace the chicken in pot pie with lobster chunks.
- Make burgers with bison meat.

Put Unusual Ingredients in the Usual Dishes

- Prepare brisket, chili, marinade, gravy, barbecue sauce or salad dressing with brewed coffee.
- Replace the liquid in honey cake with strong tea.
- Poach delicate scallops or mussels in green tea.
- Reduce fine, dry wine and use it in place of vinegar in salad dressing.
- Put smoked and flavored salts in ground meat for better burgers.
- Use sweet potatoes or cabbage, instead of potatoes, in latkes.
- Sprinkle cocoa powder into chili or stew and give a nod to Mexican mole.

❖ Crank up the quality. Example: Switch to fresh tuna in a dish to which you'd normally add canned tuna.

Find a New Use for Old Ingredients

- Put roasted asparagus in a sandwich with cheese.
- Add coconut rum or Baileys to gelatin. Surprise guests with upscale Jell-O shots.

Faking It

❖ At your next get-together, make it look like you've worked harder than you have.

Items That Can Help You Fake It

Flavored butter

- This is called compound butter in chefdom. Put a pat on plain grilled meat or fish, or steamed vegetables, or serve it alongside dinner in individual little pots.
- Make flavored butter intense (like chipotle), savory (like classic herb and garlic) or sweet (like cinnamon or vanilla, for French toast).

Flavored mayonnaise

- Start with homemade or bottled mayonnaise. Add flavorings, from truffles to horseradish, from salsa to pesto. Include garlic and call it aioli. Burgers, sandwiches and grilled vegetables all benefit.

Roasted nut oils

- Gourmet oils, such as hazelnut and pistachio, are precious and delicious. You won't be able to stop sniffing once you start.
- Use nut oils to transform mashed potatoes, drizzle them into soup or create a special vinaigrette (try walnut oil with cider vinegar). You can even pour nut oil over ice cream.

Mixed organic baby greens

- These are not just for salad, and there's no need for dressing. Put anything hot or cold on a bed of these greens and it will look elegant and colorful.

Alternative "dishes" or containers

- Parmesan bowls
- Tortilla bowls
- Bread bowls
- Lettuce cups and wraps

Puff pastry or phyllo

- Wrap your food. These are store-bought, simple to work with and versatile.

- Think beyond dessert. Make roasted vegetable strudel. Roll asparagus spears, herbs and butter in puff pastry; leave the decorative asparagus tips sticking out. For phyllo, combinations with soft goat cheese or crumbled feta are bound to please.

Edible gold foil and flakes

- Turn even rice pudding into a glittering dessert with these melt-in-your-mouth embellishments.
- Head to Little India to pick some up. You can buy edible silver, too.

Coulis

- A coulis is an easy, fresh fruit sauce. Purée berries or other soft, sweet fruit, strain and stir in superfine sugar. Coulis is vivid and gorgeous, but simple.

- Drizzle coulis over plain pudding, custard, pound cake or cheesecake. Use it to decorate a plate.

Flavored whipped cream

- Pile it atop plain coffee or dollop it on an ordinary pie.
- Potential additions to whipped cream: Baileys, raspberry liqueur, ground cinnamon or cardamom, instant espresso powder, chopped crystallized ginger, maple syrup.

Chocolate cups

- These come in various sizes and are so versatile. Fill the $\frac{1}{4}$-cup (50 mL) size with mousse or pudding (store-bought is okay). Fill the 1-tbsp (15 mL) size with a shot of liqueur.

Bread Bowl

Fill a bread bowl with chili, stew or chowder. Bread bowls are also great serving vessels for dips, especially warm spinach or crab dip. **Makes 1**

- **Preheat oven to 350°F (180°C)**

Tips

Waste not. Bake the top too and use it as a lid. While you're at it, brush the pulled-out bread with oil and make croutons.

You can make this with any size loaf as long as you leave the shell 1 inch (2.5 cm) thick.

Variation

Make mini bread bowls out of dinner rolls.

| 1 | round pumpernickel or sourdough loaf (about 8 inches/20 cm in diameter) Olive oil | 1 |

1. Cut about $\frac{1}{2}$ inch (1 cm) off the top of the loaf. Pull out the bread in tufts, leaving a shell about 1 inch (2.5 cm) thick. Brush the interior with olive oil to help seal the bowl and prevent leaking.

2. Bake directly on the middle rack of the preheated oven for 20 minutes or until browned and crusty outside.

Meringue nests

- Create a unique Pavlova. Fill one large nest or individual nests with whipped cream, custard, lemon curd or ice cream. Top with mouthwatering ripe fruit. Drizzle with fudge or caramel sauce. Sprinkle with toasted shredded coconut, grated chocolate or chopped toasted nuts. It can all be store-bought. Talk about something being more than the sum of its parts!

Master Plan
Fine Herb Butter

1. Using a fork, blend 1/2 cup (125 mL) each finely chopped herbs and butter at room temperature.
2. Put the butter on a square of waxed paper and form a log. Twist the ends closed. Place it in a sealed zip-lock bag or wrap it in foil.
3. Refrigerate or freeze it. Once the butter is firm, you can slice it off in coins as you need it.

Parmesan Bowls

Add oomph to your salad course. Pile delicate greens into these savory, edible little bowls.
Makes 6 bowls

- **Preheat oven to 350°F (180°C)**

Tips

These are tricky to make. I used Grano Padano Parmesan with 32% moisture. Only moist, fresh Parmesan will work. Avoid store-bought, dry, gritty, pre-grated Parmesan. Grate fresh Parmesan using a Microplane (rasp) grater. It must be fluffy.

For thicker cups, divide the Parmesan among 4 circles.

Variation

Make lacy Parmesan crisps to garnish or accompany salad. Use about 1/4 oz (7 g) cheese per circle. Let the crisps cool without molding.

3 oz	Parmesan cheese, freshly grated	90 g

1. Draw two 6-inch (15 cm) circles on a sheet of parchment paper. Lay it marked side down on a baking sheet. Sprinkle 1/2 oz (15 g) Parmesan evenly on each circle.
2. Bake in preheated oven for 2 to 3 minutes or until the cheese bubbles and starts to become dry and golden at the edges. Let cool for a few seconds.
3. Here's a tricky bit: When the circles are firm enough to pick up with a spatula, yet still pliable, drape each one over the bottom of a juice glass or tiny bowl. Gently flute with fingers. Let cool until set.
4. Repeat twice more with the remaining Parmesan.

Restaurant Tricks

Thinking Big, Thinking Small

✧ Serve a pretty, perfect tidbit on a really large, elegantly sculpted plate.

✧ Create height when you're plating a dish. Don't ladle food into separate piles. It looks boring.

• At the very least, ladle onto a bed of mashed potatoes or rice. Example: Lean lamb chops against a mound of mashed sweet potato. Top the arrangement with a sprig of mint, planted like a flag.

• Use tongs to twist spaghetti, linguine or other string pasta into a nest and mound it high.

✧ A large wedge of iceberg lettuce fills the plate but doesn't overwhelm the stomach. Drizzle creamy dressing over top. (Try Roquefort.) Scatter cherry tomatoes around the base. Crisscross a couple of crisp slices of bacon and lean them against the lettuce.

✧ Make a giant sandwich or a tiny sandwich. Fill an entire baguette or sourdough round, then cut it on the diagonal or in pie wedges when serving. Alternatively, serve finger sandwiches or pinwheels with smooth soup.

✧ Circulate with soup — hot or cold — in shot glasses, teacups or glass espresso cups. Garnish with tiny pea sprouts, corn sprouts or onion sprouts, or baby herb sprigs.

Ideas for Shooters

• Gazpacho in cucumber "cups."
• Steamed oysters in sake cups. Put a shucked oyster and its liquor into each cup. Top it up with vodka, sake or mignonette sauce (a tangy spiced liquid that usually includes wine or vinegar). A Caesar blend of vegetable cocktail and vodka is good, too. Drink it straight like a shot or warm it first (only slightly, please) in a steamer basket.

Ways to Follow the Small-Plate and Tapas Trends

• Serve an array of appetizers only.
• Prepare lots of courses in small sizes instead of a few big ones.

✧ During a large meal, diners will feel less full if you follow the French tradition of serving a simple green salad after the main course.

✧ Slice meat and vegetables very thinly and fan them out rather than serving hunks and chunks.

✧ Buy baby vegetables. They are so cute.

✧ Serve food on cocktail toothpicks or in spoons. Examples: a single coconut shrimp on a decorative toothpick; one wonton with sweet chili sauce on a spoon. You don't need to prepare these; you can buy them at the supermarket.

Personal Pot Pies

I like to make mini pot pies with leftover turkey. That way, everyone gets a tidy portion of filling and crust. Don't be intimidated by the number of ingredients. Everything comes together fairly easily. **Makes 10 mini pot pies**

- **Ten ¾-cup (175 mL) ramekins**

- **Baking sheet**

Tips

Use the pastry recipe for other dishes.

If you want to take a shortcut, buy pie or tart shells and adapt them.

Pastry

2 cups	all-purpose flour	500 mL
½ tsp	kosher salt	2 mL
½ cup	cold unsalted butter, cut into pieces	125 mL
6 tbsp	cold shortening, cut into pieces	90 mL
⅓ cup	cold water	75 mL
1 tbsp	cider vinegar	15 mL

Filling

20	red pearl onions (about 6 oz/175 g)	20
3 cups	chicken stock	750 mL
1 to 2	inner stalks celery, with leaves, cut into ¼-inch (0.5 cm) dice	1 to 2
1	large carrot (about 6 oz/175 g), cut into ¼-inch (0.5 cm) dice	1
1	parsnip (about 6 oz/175 g), cut into ¼-inch (0.5 cm) dice	1
¼ cup	unsalted butter	50 mL
½ cup	all-purpose flour	125 mL
1 cup	whole milk	250 mL
2 tbsp	chopped fresh parsley	25 mL
1½ tsp	poultry seasoning	7 mL
½ tsp	kosher salt	2 mL
	Freshly ground pepper	
½ cup	frozen peas, thawed and drained	125 mL
10	cremini mushrooms (about 4 oz/125 g), quartered	10
1½ to 2 cups	diced roast turkey (¼-inch/0.5 cm dice)	375 to 500 mL
1 cup	diced smoked ham (¼-inch/0.5 cm dice)	250 mL

Egg Wash

1	large egg	1
1 tbsp	cold water	15 mL
Pinch	salt	Pinch

Variation

You can use roast chicken.
Or try seafood.

1. *Pastry:* In a large bowl, stir together flour and salt. Using a pastry blender, two forks or your hands, blend in butter and shortening until the mixture resembles coarse crumbs, with some pea-sized lumps or flakes.

2. In a small bowl, combine cold water and vinegar. Add to flour mixture. Blend with a fork just until mixture almost comes together in a ball. Press into a disc. Cover with plastic wrap and refrigerate for 30 minutes. Meanwhile, preheat oven to 350°F (180°C).

3. *Filling:* Bring a large saucepan of water to a boil over high heat. Add pearl onions. Blanch for 30 seconds. Drain. Rinse with cold water. Drain. Peel.

4. Pour stock into the same pan. Bring it to a boil over high heat. Add celery, carrot and parsnip. Boil for 1 minute. Using a skimmer, transfer vegetables to a colander to drain, reserving the stock in a separate bowl.

5. In same pan, melt butter over medium heat. Stir in flour. Cook, stirring, for 1 minute. Gradually whisk in the reserved stock until smooth. Cook, whisking frequently, until the mixture returns to a boil. Whisk in milk. Stir in parsley, poultry seasoning, salt and pepper to taste. Stir in pearl onions, celery, carrot, parsnip, peas, mushrooms, turkey and ham. The mixture will be very thick; it will thin as it bakes.

6. Divide the filling among the ramekins. Place ramekins on the baking sheet. Bake for 15 minutes.

7. Meanwhile, on a lightly floured surface, roll out pastry to $\frac{1}{8}$ to $\frac{1}{4}$ inch (0.25 to 0.5 cm) thick. Cut out 10 circles about $\frac{1}{2}$-inch (1 cm) diameter wider than the mouths of the ramekins (about $4\frac{1}{2}$ inches/12 cm). Prick the circles with a fork. Roll the scraps into thin ropes.

8. *Egg wash:* In a small bowl, beat the egg, cold water and salt with a fork.

9. Remove the ramekins from the oven. Line the circumference around the top of each ramekin with a rope of dough. Moisten the ropes with egg wash. Cover them with dough circles. Press to seal.

10. Brush egg wash over the pastry. Return the ramekins to the oven. Bake for 45 minutes or until the pastry is golden, the filling is bubbly and the vegetables are tender.

- Buy a set of tiny, lovely dipping bowls to serve condiments. Buy individual gravy boats for sauces.

- Miniaturize old favorites into single servings or bites. Even chicken pot pie, meatloaf and cobbler are chic and alluring in size small. Example: Mini burgers are crowd pleasers. Make about 6 per 1 lb (500 g) of ground meat. Grill them, put them in mini buns (up to 3 inches/7.5 cm in diameter) and slather them with flavored mayo.

Deconstructing

- Like an haute chef, gather the ingredients for a familiar dish, but don't meld them.

Creative Ways to Deconstruct a Salad

- Skewer it. Two examples: Make *insalata caprese* by alternating cocktail bocconcini balls, grape tomatoes and basil leaves. Serve the dressing as a dip. As an alternative to sloshy fruit salad, skewer chunks of watermelon, banana rounds and large berries. Serve the kebabs with yogurt dip.
- Create a salad bouquet.

Master Plan
Entertaining Salad Bouquet

1. Hollow out segments of baguette to make "vases" open at both ends. Each should be 3 to 4 inches (7.5 to 10 cm) tall. Rub them inside and out with olive oil. Place them on a baking sheet with the holes facing sideways. Bake for 15 minutes at 350°F (180°C).
2. Place vases on serving plates. Stuff whole lettuce leaves upright in each vase. You can add anything else that's tall. Tuck in a

couple of crispy cooked bacon slices or a few stalks of steamed asparagus.
3. Drizzle dressing around the perimeter of the plate for dipping.
4. Pluck from the bouquet and eat with your hands.

- Stew looks neater and even chic when it is deconstructed.

Master Plan
Deconstructed Stew

1. Once the stew is cooked, strain it. Set the meat aside.
2. Discard the limp vegetables, such as onions and carrots.
3. Degrease the sauce. Thicken it, if necessary.
4. Sauté diced smoked bacon with a fresh set of vegetables, such as pearl onions, blanched baby carrots and thickly sliced mushrooms, until the vegetables are tender but still firm.
5. Arrange the meat in the center of a wide serving bowl. Pour some sauce over it. Spoon sautéed bacon and vegetables on top. Garnish with chopped fresh herbs.

Putting on a Show

- Prepare food at the table. The simplest example is the archetypal Caesar salad tossed at the table in a big wooden bowl on a stand.

Master Plan
Caesar at the Table

1. Rub the bowl with a cut garlic clove.
2. Use a fork to whisk dressing in the bottom of the bowl. Include a coddled egg for authenticity.
3. Add torn romaine to the bowl and toss.
4. Sprinkle on grated Parmesan cheese, bacon bits and croutons. Freshly grind black pepper over top.

❖ People always clap when something is set on fire. Do it with appetizers, main courses and desserts. Go overboard and do it all in one meal.

F is for Flambé

Flambé is the French term for sprinkling your food with liquor and setting it on fire. Do this safely as well as flamboyantly.

11 Tips for Playing with Fire

1. For best results, the pan, food and liquor should be warm.
2. For flambéed meat, allow 1 oz (30 mL) liquor per serving.
3. Do not pour straight from the bottle into the pan.
4. Warm the liquor. Pour it into a heatproof glass measuring cup, then set the cup in a bowl of very hot water or zap it for a few seconds in the microwave on High. Do not boil the liquor.
5. Make sure the food in the pan is at least 75°F (24°C).
6. If you're using a gas stove, turn off the burner before flambéing.
7. To flambé fruit, warm it and sprinkle it with sugar beforehand.
8. Use a barbecue lighter instead of matches. It'll keep you farther away from the flames.
9. Tilt the pan away from you when lighting the alcohol.
10. Prolong the flames by jiggling and tilting the pan.
11. Admire it while it's burning. Wait until the flame expires before serving.

✗ No-No

Don't flambé in a nonstick pan. The surface is not meant to cope with flames. Cast iron is best for flambéing.

Mixing and Matching

❖ Surprise the palate by playing with temperature, texture and taste combinations. Match hot with cold, soft with firm, sweet with sour.

Hot-and-Cold Ideas

• Hot fudge sauce over ice cream, sprinkled with toasted nuts, is so elemental. Play with the idea. How about hot mango coulis over coconut ice cream with toasted macadamia nuts? Hot caramel sauce over chocolate ice cream with broken peanut brittle?
• Turn cold vichyssoise into a hot cream soup, or vice versa.
• Do a role reversal. Serve tomato soup cold with an herb garnish, alongside gourmet grilled cheese.

❖ Aim for balance when planning a menu. Pair the rich and the simple. Examples: simple steamed vegetables with a rich, saucy meat dish, or an elaborate vegetable casserole with plain grilled meat or fish.

Providing Service with More Than a Smile

❖ Hand out steamed towels after dinner. Dunk small white facecloths in a bowl of water pleasantly scented with lemon juice or rosewater. Microwave on High for 20 to 30 seconds per cloth. Wring the cloths and roll them up. (Be careful: Don't burn yourself.)

✧ Serve another round — of food, that is.

3 Ways to Get a Second Wind

1. Take a cue from the traditional seafood buffet that arrives at a Portuguese wedding at midnight to fuel more dancing and drinking.
2. Wheel around a dessert cart.
3. Carry a New Year's Eve party deeper into the new year by serving breakfast at 12:30 a.m.

✧ Serve from the left and remove empty dishes from the right.

✧ Send home doggie bags. In particular, there's always too much of a good thing at potlucks. Hand takeout containers to guests before they leave. The leftovers the next day will double the pleasure of the memory of your party. Save restaurant delivery containers, plastic supermarket bakery boxes, and sour cream, margarine or yogurt tubs to treat guests to takeout *chez vous*.

✧ Set the timer on the coffee maker so it is brewed just as you start dessert.

✧ Leave a bowl of public transit tokens or tickets by the door for guests who are too cheerful to drive. They take tickets and drop their car keys into the bowl. Or you can stand by the door and phone for taxis.

Presentation Plus

♛ A Golden Rule

Presentation is half the battle. We feast with our eyes first. If it looks good, it tastes better. Size matters. So do garnishes and a table dressed to impress.

✧ Food styling starts with sketches. Decide how you want your dish to look.

Uses for Squeeze Bottles

- Squeeze pancake batter into shapes on the griddle.
- Decorate plates with drizzles and swirls of reduced balsamico, fruit coulis, or chocolate or caramel sauce. You can use store-bought sauce or make your own.

✧ Decorate a plate using a stencil. Anything goes; you don't need an official stencil. At a chefs' seafood competition, one charming plate featured the outline of a fork at one edge. It was created by dusting paprika over a fork.

Ways to Add Colors and Patterns

- Halve round vegetables, such as Brussels sprouts or juicy cherry tomatoes. Arrange them as a border around the plate.
- Small touches are appreciated: chopped green herbs on mashed potatoes, rice cooked in tomato sauce, diced red pepper among the corn kernels, toasted whole pecans on salad greens.

✧ Make neat, tidy, even cuts. Grease, wet or heat the knife, if necessary. Example: Let a quiche or tart cool until you can slice a wedge without sloppy edges. Put the slice on a serving plate. Warm it for a few seconds in the microwave, if necessary.

✧ Garnishes should be edible — and call to the eater to do so. No one feels compelled to consume a sprig of parsley.

Green Garnish Ideas

- Ultra-thin fried or baked vegetable chips
- Fried fresh herb leaves
- Fried baby spinach leaves
- Carved vegetables
- Browned garlic slices
- Long slivers of green onion

Savory Garnish Ideas

- Shaved Parmesan or other hard cheese
- Preserved lemon wedges or fried lemon slices

Sweet Garnish Ideas

- Wonton crisps (brush wonton dough with a mixture of butter, maple syrup and cinnamon, then bake at 375°F/190°C until golden, 5 to 10 minutes)
- Peanut brittle shards
- Cookies (try star-shaped ones or wafers)

✧ Serving on ice is wise as well as impressive. Put the ice on a rack in the serving bowl, so food doesn't end up in a puddle of water.

✧ Keep tablecloths simple. Form and color should come from the food, dishes and table decorations.

Creamy Chocolate Drizzle

You can use this to decorate a dessert plate or as a dip for fresh strawberries. **Makes 1 cup (250 mL)**

Tip

Chocolate drizzle can be refrigerated for up to 2 weeks. If it thickens too much in the fridge, warm it in a bowl of very hot water.

½ cup	heavy or whipping (35%) cream	125 mL
2 tbsp	corn syrup	25 mL
3 oz	bittersweet chocolate, chopped	90 g

1. In a microwave-safe bowl, combine cream, corn syrup and chocolate. Microwave on Medium-High (70%) for about 1½ minutes or until just starting to steam. (Or heat in a small saucepan over medium heat.) Whisk or stir until smooth and shiny.

2. Pour into a squeeze bottle. Let cool on the counter until just thick enough to control. Or speed things up by refrigerating it for 5 to 10 minutes.

 KID STUFF

Set the table with a paper tablecloth and give young guests crayons to draw pictures.

Centerpiece Tips

- Keep floral arrangements and candles low. It's annoying to have to peep around them or crane your neck to talk to someone.
- Avoid strongly scented flowers. They may clash with the aroma of the food.
- Instead of flowers, you can use a gingerbread house. Then demolish it for dessert.
- For a fast centerpiece, drop flowers or sprigs of pine and other decorations onto a cake pedestal.
- Create a centerpiece from colorful, shapely fruit. Pile pomegranates, pears, mandarin oranges and even fresh cranberries into a large, clear glass vase. Add sprigs of foliage, or holly at Christmastime.

Alternatives to Place Cards

- Use a decorated cookie; add initials or a symbol with icing. Take a shortcut by buying the cookies and icing.
- Tag wineglasses with nail-polish symbols or names. (Nail-polish remover will erase it all.)
- Write names or initials on ribbons. Tie each ribbon around the stem of a flower or an evergreen sprig.
- For Easter, used dyed, decorated eggs marked with names or initials.
- For a Christmas feast, use a gold gilt pen, gel pen or permanent marker to inscribe ornaments.

- ❖ A dinner party is not all about the food. Set a theme. Examples:
- Decorate your dining room like a '50s diner. Serve burgers or omelets with fries. Play jukebox hits.
- At a buffet for a sporting event, set the mood by covering the table with Astroturf. Set a small portable TV, tuned to the game, right on the table.

✧ Gift catalogues and barbecue shops sell steak-branding irons. You can go with a house monogram or the letters R and M (for rare and medium).

✧ Save labor and make your cocktail party more memorable at the same time. Designate a house cocktail or a theme drink de jour. Mix the drink, or at least the base, before the party.

✧ Don't forget the olfactory senses. You can fill the kitchen with heavenly scents by simmering cinnamon sticks, bay leaves, dried citrus peel, vanilla extract or nutmeg in a small pan of water.

Using Creative Vessels

♛ A Golden Rule

A colored plate looks best when it is empty. Stick to a white plate. It's a blank canvas and your food is the art. If you want to get fancier, look for a white plate that's oversized, embossed or a captivating shape.

Coffee and Tea Themes

- Bake lava cakes in heatproof coffee mugs. Dollop coffee-flavored whipped cream on top.
- Serve mocha pudding in see-through glass espresso cups.
- Pour Earl Grey or chai custard onto fruit from a teapot.
- Serve coffee gravy for brisket or steak in a coffee pot.

✧ For a garden party or barbecue, line a wheelbarrow with a plastic tablecloth and fill it with ice and drinks. Wheel it to shady spots as the sun moves.

Food Bowl Ideas

- Serve flavored mayonnaise in a scooped-out bell pepper or tomato shell.
- Serve stuffing in a pumpkin shell. Note: This works only if you're grilling your turkey, deep-frying it or have two ovens going at once.

Master Plan
Stuffing in a Pumpkin Shell

1. Cut off the top of a pumpkin to use as a lid. Leave on the stem, to use as a handle. Hollow out the pumpkin.
2. Fill it with stuffing. Put fatty trimmings and maybe the wing tips from your bird on top.
3. With the cap sitting next to it, roast it in a 350°F (180°C) oven until the stuffing is hot (at least 165°F/74°C).
4. Discard the wing tips and fat. Cover with the cap to serve.

✧ You can serve tuna or egg salad in ice cream cones.

☺ KID STUFF

For a kid's birthday party, serve the food on toys. Some playful ideas:

- Pile hot dogs in a dump truck (new or well washed, and lined with waxed paper).
- Set up little bowls of treats on different floors of a dollhouse.
- Pile a Barbiemobile with cheesies and let the kids wheel the snacks instead of passing them. Expect a mess.
- Fill a cash register with M&Ms or Smarties and jelly beans; the kids will have fun ringing in sales to pop open the drawer. They can even buy the treats with funny money.
- Stick cocktail toothpicks into melon or cheese cubes and place them on a new, clean game board. Kids can play checkers, for example. The opponent's pieces are eaten once captured.

- Serve do-it-yourself soup. Fill a gravy boat with cream soup and invite diners to pour it over spicy grilled shrimp.

- If you are serving an Asian feast, consider putting each dinner in a bento box.

Playing with Shapes

- Change the shape of things to come to the dinner table. Example: Pizza suddenly becomes a conversation piece if it's heart-shaped for your sweetheart.

- Use a cookie cutter to punch cute shapes from pumpernickel cocktail squares or party rye. Nudge the bread out of the cutter with the base of a knife. Make canapés.

- Freeze ice cream in a heart-shaped mold or small Bundt pan for a pretty side dish to serve with cobblers, brownies or pound cake. Line the mold with plastic wrap to make the ice cream easy to extract.

Better Buffets

- Put cutlery and napkins at the end of the buffet line, not the beginning. People won't have to fumble as much.

- Put food on pedestals for drama. Use cake stands, boxes or overturned bowls.

- Serve assorted cheeses, hors d'oeuvres or mini desserts on a large lazy Susan to make them more accessible.

- Set up a pasta bar. Prepare a variety of pastas and sauces. Set out grated cheeses, sautéed mushrooms and onions, steamed broccoli florets, chopped herbs and a shaker of hot pepper flakes. Let guests mix and match.

- At a housewarming, serve different courses in different rooms or areas, such as the deck or sunroom. Nothing in the bathroom, please.

- Host a crêpe party. Invite guests to help themselves to a choice of crêpes (such as plain and tomato-flavored) and fillings (such as ham and cheese sauce). Or make it a dessert buffet and offer chocolate crêpes with a variety of fillings (such as Nutella, whipped cream and berries).

Wine and Cheese Parties

- For a wine and cheese party, allow $\frac{1}{2}$ lb (250 g) of cheese and 3 glasses of wine per person.

- For a party platter, buy 2 to 4 oz (60 to 125 g) of cheese per person.

Ways to Identify Cheeses

- Serve them on a slate board. You can write the names of the cheeses in chalk. Slate cutting boards are sold in kitchen shops, and slate tiles in home renovation stores. Stick felt squares to the bottom of tiles.
- Make toothpick flags with the names written on them. Stick them in the cheeses.
- Put a place card beside each cheese.

- Serve milder cheeses with light wines or beers, aggressive cheeses with full-bodied wine or liquor.

Options for a Cheese Tasting
- Serve three tiers of cheeses, arranged according to mildness.
- Group cheeses in soft, semisoft and firm categories.

Display cheeses on top of large, clean, dry, colorful autumn leaves. (Note: Some leaves are toxic if eaten, including oak, red maple, yew, laburnum, black walnut and choke cherry. If you don't want to use real leaves, you can buy remarkable parchment facsimiles of autumn and spring leaves.)

Options for an After-Dinner Cheese Plate

- Serve one superb cheese.
- Serve three wedges or chunks on a flavor scale from mild to sharp or a texture scale from soft to firm.

9 Accompaniments to Cheese Platters

1. Firm, neutral crackers.
2. Bread that complements the texture and intensity of the cheese, such as walnut bread with blue cheese.
3. Figs or dried fruit.
4. Nuts in the shell, with a nutcracker alongside.
5. Pickles and pickled vegetables such as asparagus.
6. Salsa.
7. Jam, jelly or chutney.
8. Tapenade.
9. Grapes (tiny, sweet champagne grapes are never mundane).

 No-No

Don't serve citrus fruit (too acidic) or tropical fruit (too sweet) with cheese platters.

Halloween Tricks and Treats

✦ To make floating ice "hands" for punch, fill plastic gloves with water, tie them tightly at the cuffs and freeze. To make "diseased hands," add cranberries or blueberries to the water. Pull or cut off the gloves.

Master Plan
Monster Eyes

1. Cook jumbo pasta shells until barely tender.
2. Fill the shells with spiced ricotta mixture.
3. Press a miniature, store-bought, cooked meatball into the center of the cheese in each shell.
4. Bake the shells on top of tomato sauce at 350°F (180°C) until the fillings are warm and the sauce is bubbling.
5. Glue a green olive slice to the middle of each meatball eye using a bit of the sauce.

✦ Snack on bocconcini eyeballs. Wrap each eye in prosciutto and use an olive slice as the iris.

✦ Cut plain sandwiches into coffin shapes.

✦ Fill a pumpkin shell with soup, stew or chili.

✦ Use a jack-o'-lantern with a candle inside as a chafing dish for a bowl of warm dip.

Master Plan
Moldy Bones

1. Buy breadstick dough at the supermarket.
2. Tie a knot at both ends of each length of dough.
3. Brush the dough with lightly beaten egg white.
4. Sprinkle on dry grated Parmesan and crumbled dried basil.
5. Bake as directed on the package.
6. Serve "gore" (a.k.a. tomato sauce) as a dip.

◇ Serve a cake cut in the shape of a gravestone. Pipe a sad message in icing.

Master Plan
Dirt Pudding

1. Stir crushed chocolate sandwich cookies with chocolate pudding.
2. Stir in gummy worms.
3. Serve the mixture in a new flowerpot. You can shove a fake flower in the pot.
4. Ladle it with a new trowel.

◇ For creepy fudge, press gummy bugs into the surface of fudge before it sets. Use foolproof fudge, not the sensitive kind.

◇ Make alien cookies. Give circles of sugar cookie dough two big round eyes, a straight slash of a mouth and two toothpick holes for nostrils.

◇ Decorate cupcakes with a spiderweb design on the frosting.

Master Plan
Kitty Litter Pudding

1. Stir crumbled spice cake with vanilla pudding. The mixture should be fairly dry.
2. Crush white sandwich cookies. Dye about a quarter of them green with a few drops of food coloring.
3. Stir half the crumbled cookies, white and green, into the cake mixture.
4. Put the mixture in a shallow, rectangular, new, food-safe plastic box.
5. Heat Tootsie Rolls until they are pliable. Twist each one slightly. Bury the rolls in the litter.
6. Toss the remaining crushed cookies over top.
7. Serve this disgusting dessert with a new scooper.

Party Planning

♔ A Golden Rule

When throwing a dinner party, don't prepare a dish you've never tried before. That's a recipe for nasty surprises and last-minute panic. Murphy's Law says the cooking time will be way off, or the dish will look ugly. It may even be inedible. Stick to a recipe you trust and know.

✧ Try to give each diner elbow room — at least 30 inches (75 cm) from the center of one plate to the next.

✧ The night before a large family dinner, such as the Christmas feast, put out serving dishes with utensils in them and a sticky note stating what to put in each.

✧ For a theme party, cover all the bases: food, tableware, decor, dress code, games and activities.

✧ At Christmastime, make charity the theme of your party. Ask guests to bring food bank donations instead of wine or hostess gifts. Serve an afternoon feast, then visit a nursing home or head to a local church or soup kitchen to serve dinner to the homeless.

✧ Instead of the usual barbecue cookout, invite guests to a backyard picnic. Spread colorful blankets on the lawn. Bring out the food in picnic baskets.

✧ Try a medieval feast. Serve hunks of roasted meat and other foods to be eaten by hand at a long table.

✧ You don't have to stick to lunch or dinner. Breakfast can be an entertaining event. If you have workout buddies, run to your house afterward.

Breakfast Party Ingredients

- Strata or French toast that can be prepared the night before.
- Bagels and flavored cream cheeses.
- Premium coffees and teas.
- Smoothies in liqueur glasses, instead of dessert.

✧ For cocktail parties and tapas parties, plan on 10 hors d'oeuvres or small bites per person. For dinner parties, plan on 5 per person.

✧ Calculations for a cocktail party lasting for 2 or 3 hours:
- Plan on 3 drinks per person.
- One 750-mL bottle of wine makes 6 drinks.
- One quart (1 L) of liquor makes 20 mild drinks.
- Plan on 1 lb (500 g) of ice per person.

✧ Use a cooler to keep large amounts of food chilled if there's no more room in the fridge.

Transporting Food

◆ Secure food being transported in a cardboard box in the trunk of car. Wedge books or bricks against the side of the dish so it doesn't overturn or slide around.

◆ Hot foods that travel well: easily reheated dishes such as casseroles, mac and cheese, soups, stews.

◆ When bringing a warm dish to a party, wrap the container in newspaper, then a towel. If you have an insulated shopping bag, use it.

◆ Transport breakable bottles and bowls cushioned inside oven mitts and tea cosies.

◆ Save plastic clamshells from supermarket produce, aluminum pie plates and baking pans, and takeout boxes (the sturdy ones with the black bases and clear covers) for transporting baked goods to the office or potlucks.

Making Do

You can transport cookies, small sandwiches and hors d'oeuvres in plastic supermarket bags. Put a generous piece of foil on a paper plate. Fill the plate with food, but don't mound it high. Wrap the foil up and over the food completely, then crimp the edges. Top it with an inverted paper plate. Staple the plates together around the edges. You can stack several of these packages in a plastic bag.

◆ When transporting an item covered in foil, such as a cake, don't place the foil over top and crimp it under the plate. Put a large piece of foil under the plate like a sling. Bring the top edges together and crimp the foil shut. That way, the edges won't keep coming loose.

Safety and Hygiene

Food Safety

♔ Five Golden Rules

- Wash your hands before and after handling food. Wash work surfaces frequently.
- Keep raw and cooked foods separate.
- Cool or cook. Refrigerate promptly. Cook or heat to proper temperatures.
- Keep cold foods cold and hot foods hot. Don't leave food in the danger zone for more than 2 hours.
- When in doubt, throw it out.

Supermarket Food Safety Tips

- Go to the dairy case and the meat case at the end of your shopping trip. At home, put these items away first.
- In the store, slip meat packages into produce bags to prevent dripping.
- Haul meat in separate grocery bags, away from produce, bread and packaged foods.
- Obtain one or more reusable totes with an insulation lining, for your ice cream, meat and milk.
- For the trip home, pack dairy products, eggs and separately wrapped meat with frozen products.
- Keep a cooler in the trunk of the car to transport frozen and easily spoiled foods.
- Sanitize reusable shopping bags by washing them frequently.

Safe Temperatures

- ✧ Marinate in the fridge, never at room temperature.

- ✧ Refrigerate cooked food as soon as possible. Try to cool it to room temperature first. Otherwise, it will warm up the food next to it and hasten spoilage. It can also create icy buildups in the fridge.

Ⓓ is for Danger Zone

The danger zone is 40°F to 140°F (4°C to 60°C). Between these temperatures, bacteria begin to multiply out of control. After 2 hours, they reach dangerous levels.

- Until they are served, keep hot foods at least 140°F (60°C) and cold foods cooler than 40°F (4°C).
- Set the fridge at 40°F (4°C) or colder.
- Check temperatures of raw and cooked foods with a thermometer, instead of guessing.

The Most Hazardous Temperature Ranges

- Bacteria reproduce the fastest and most vigorously between 70°F and 120°F (21°C and 49°C). Cool food fast to at least 70°F (21°C) — think room temperature — before refrigerating it, or heat it fast to 120°F (49°C) — think warm to hot tap water.
- The most dangerous zone is 90°F to 110°F (32°C to 43°C). At temperatures above 90°F (32°C), the time limit is just 1 hour before bacteria reach critical levels.

⚛ A Bit of Science

Why are we worried about the 2-hour limit? After all, the bacteria will be killed once a dish is cooked. Yes, but they produce toxins that they can leave behind. These toxins can make you sick, too. Within 2 hours in the danger zone, bacteria can invade food in overwhelming numbers.

- ✧ Freeze juice boxes to keep the contents of lunch bags cool and safe.

✦ If food doesn't cool down enough in 1 to 2 hours to refrigerate it, you'll have to help it along.

7 Ways to Cool Food Faster

1. Remove it from the hot pan, if possible.
2. Chill it in a large bowl or sinkful of ice water.
3. Toss ice packs or sealed bags filled with ice into it.
4. Divide it and put it into smaller, shallow containers.
5. Stir it often.
6. Don't cover it. Food cools faster without a lid.
7. In winter, you can set a pan or container in the snow, cover it and pack snow around it.

Safe Buffet and Party Food Tips

- Use smaller dishes. Keep the rest of the food in the fridge or in a low-temperature oven. Replenish as needed. It's more work, but safer.
- Nestle cold foods into ice.
- If you're using chafing dishes, check with a thermometer to make sure the food is above 140°F (60°C). Chafing dishes with candles won't necessarily keep food at a safe temperature.
- An electric slow cooker will keep cooked food hot enough to be safe. But you must heat the food before putting it in.
- Throw out any leftovers held at room temperature for more than 2 hours.

☼ A Bit of Science

Freezing doesn't kill bacteria. It just puts them in suspension. As food thaws, bacteria awaken from their frozen slumber and begin to go forth

and multiply. At 40°F (4°C), it's party time. That's why food should be thawed in the fridge or, second best, in cold running water. Don't thaw food on the kitchen counter, outdoors or in the dishwasher. At room temperature or in warm water, the center of the food may still be frozen while the thawed surface crawls with bacteria. Exceptions: frozen pastries (no cream), bread, fruit and vegetables can be thawed on the counter.

✦ Thaw only as much food as you need at one time.

Thawing Food in the Fridge

- Loosen the wrappings.
- Put meat in a pan or tray on the bottom shelf.
- Drippings can contaminate other food in the fridge. Make sure they don't fall on or touch other food.
- Speed things up by putting food that's defrosting in the warmest part of the fridge, closer to the door rather than the back or walls.
- Be patient. Even a small amount of food can take an entire day to defrost.

Thawing Food in Cold Water

- Keep the water below 70°F (21°C).
- Use slowly running water, if possible.
- If food is thawing in a bowl or sink, replace the water every half-hour. This flushes any bacteria down the drain.
- Put food in a leak-proof bag. Careless handling can spread bacteria from food thawed directly in water. Also, food can get soggy.
- When thawing meat, massage it once in a while.
- Don't thaw food until it is completely softened, just until it is pliable.
- If food isn't thawed within 2 hours, cook it or continue thawing in the fridge.

- The ultimate solution: Don't thaw. Cook food from the frozen state whenever possible. (In particular, frozen turkey and other large roasts do fine.)

Cooking from Frozen

- Allow 50% more cooking time.
- Rinse off frost and icy chunks with warm water beforehand.

 ## No-No

Do not defrost meat or fish in the microwave, no matter how encouraging the instruction booklet is. The fussing, turning and shielding is a pain and, despite all your efforts, parts of the food will start to cook. One section may be in the danger zone while another is still icy. Use the microwave as a last resort — if you plan to cook food immediately or if you are thawing and reheating prepared foods.

Power Failures

- How long food stays safe in the fridge and freezer after a power failure or breakdown is affected by outside factors such as the room temperature and how many times the appliance door is opened. The 2-hour rule is the hard line for the fridge, but food may still be safe after up to 4 hours.

- If a storm is coming and you fear a blackout, turn the fridge and freezer to their coldest settings.

- Worried about a power failure while you're on vacation? Put a bag of ice cubes in the freezer. Check it when you get back.

- When the power comes back on, if food still feels cold and has been above 40°F (4°C) for less than 2 hours, you can keep it. Cook it as soon as possible.

7 Steps to Take During a Power Failure or Breakdown

1. Keep the appliance doors closed. The fridge should stay cool for 4 to 6 hours if the door is kept closed. Food will stay frozen for a couple of days in a loaded freezer, but for only 1 day in a half-full freezer.
2. If your freezer is half full, quickly stack packages close together to hold the cold.
3. Cover the top and sides of the freezer with a blanket to insulate it, but don't cover the compressor.
4. Pack the fridge and freezer with ice or dry ice.
5. Don't try to lug a freezer outside into the snow. It can heat up in the sun, even though it's cold outside. Frozen food, however, can be kept outside, in a shady spot, on a bone-chilling day.
6. Use coolers filled with ice as backups. If freezer food is cooling below fridge temperatures, transfer it to the fridge or to the coolers.
7. Leave a bedroom light on when you go to sleep. When the power snaps on, you'll wake up and know how long the blackout lasted and thus how long the food was in danger.

- Boil thawed veggies at room temperature for 10 minutes before eating them. Or throw them out.

- Discard thawed vacuum-packed meat that has reached room temperature.

- Discard any food exposed to drippy meat juices.

✧ If food has thawed and dripped in the fridge or freezer, particularly meat, clean the area with a bleach solution or a commercial disinfectant.

Mythstake

Cooking thawed food is the safest option. However, many foods can be refrozen if they were kept at a safe temperature in the refrigerator and still feel very cold. Do you want to refreeze? That's another question, and the answer is often no. The quality and texture may be terrible. If, for example, you thaw a fish fillet safely in the fridge, then refreeze it, the delicate flesh will turn into a soggy mess.

Bottom Lines

- If it still has ice crystals and the temperature is not above 40°F (4°C), especially if has been in the fridge for less than 1 day, you can refreeze it.
- If it has thawed to room temperature, you can't refreeze it. In fact, you should cook it right away. Refreezing won't lower the bacteria count. So, when it's defrosted, the food would start out at a disadvantage.

Foods That Can Be Refrozen

- Cooked food
- Previously frozen meat, poultry or fish from the supermarket, butcher or fishmonger, as long as it was properly stored
- Meat that thawed to room temperature, but was immediately cooked
- Flour
- Nuts
- Bread and pizza dough
- Packaged fruit and fruit juice, unless it smells yeasty or fermented, or seems slimy

Foods That Shouldn't Be Refrozen

- Ice cream and frozen yogurt
- Fruit pies, juices and high-acid fruit held at room temperature for more than 2 hours

✧ Most food sitting above 40°F (4°C) for 2 hours must be discarded. But some types can be kept, then refrigerated as soon as possible. Beware: This is not a license to store food on the counter.

Foods You Should Discard

- Dairy products, including soft and semisoft cheeses (such as cream cheese and bocconcini)
- Fresh and cooked meat and seafood
- Deli meats, bacon, sausages and hot dogs
- Tuna, chicken and egg salad
- Casseroles with meat or cheese
- Soups and stews
- Cooked pasta and rice dishes
- Pizza
- Gravies and sauces
- Mayonnaise, tartar sauce, creamy dressings and dips
- Prepared horseradish
- Cut produce
- Custards and puddings
- Creamy cakes, pastries and pies
- Cheesecake, cheese-filled pastries and desserts
- Raw pie and cookie dough

Foods You May Keep

- Butter, margarine, shortening and lard
- Hard, dry, grated cheese, such as Parmesan
- Eggs (in the shell)
- Mushrooms, raw vegetables and fruit
- Herbs
- Commercial, non-creamy salad dressing
- Ketchup, mustard and barbecue sauce
- Relish
- Olives and pickles

- Breads and rolls
- Plain cakes, muffins and quick breads
- Fruit pies
- Jams and jellies

Borderline

- Discard cooked fruit, vegetables, vegetable juices and fruit juices if they have been above 40°F (4°C) for more than 6 hours.

Germs (and Dirt)

Germs VS. Dirt?

Worry more about what you can't see than what you can see. Germs are worse than dirt. The two, however, often go together.

F is for the Five-Second Rule

The rule says you have 5 seconds to scoop something off the floor before it gets too dirty and germy. Scientists say timing does play a part, but location is more important. The kitchen floor may be the worst place to drop food. Even the bathroom floor might be cleaner. So forget about the 5 seconds. Just wash the food or throw it out, if the dog doesn't grab it first.

H is for Hamburger Disease

Hamburger disease is food poisoning caused by *E. coli* bacteria. It is linked to eating undercooked hamburgers, but these bacteria can be found in any food. On raw meat, they seethe on the surface. Grinding meat into hamburger or sausage blends the *E. coli* throughout and gives it more room to flourish. Ground meat should always be cooked to well-done. Long gone are the days when James Beard put an ice cube inside the burger patty to make sure the center stayed medium-rare.

✧ Don't spoon, lick and double-dip to test food you are cooking unless it is hot enough to kill germs.

C is for Cross-Contamination

Raw is raw, cooked is cooked, and never the twain should meet. Neither should meat juices and produce.

- Don't cut up raw meat or fish, then use the same board for raw ingredients for salad, say, or cooked food.
- Every barbecuer should know this one: Use two separate platters, two separate sets of tongs, even two separate brushes for the raw and the cooked.
- Don't use an instant-read thermometer on raw meat or fish, then on the cooked versions. Disinfect it in between.
- Wash utensils and cutting boards immediately after they come in contact with meat.
- Protect raw meat with plastic before putting it in the fridge.
- Store meat on the bottom shelf of the fridge so it doesn't accidentally drip on food below.
- Keep raw meat separate from the other items in your grocery cart.
- Use a plastic bag as a glove when inspecting drippy packages of meat in the supermarket.

☺ KID STUFF

Don't let your children sneak food directly from a serving bowl or storage tub. Germs on their hands and in their saliva contaminate the food, and it will go bad faster. It's unappetizing, too.

✧ Wipe the tops of cans before opening them. Dust, germs and chemical residues can get into the food.

✧ Some herbs and spices, especially those with more antioxidants, inhibit bacteria. A few identified as bacteria fighters: cayenne pepper, cloves, cinnamon, rosemary, thyme, nutmeg, bay leaves. Onions and garlic also have antibacterial qualities. Don't get too excited: These will not sterilize bacteria-laden food and make it safe to eat.

7 Things That Fight Bacteria

1. Drying (dry-curing, brining, salting, packing in sugar or sugar syrup all draw the water out of bacteria).
2. Pickling (bacteria can't tolerate acids such as vinegar).
3. Smoking (chemicals in the smoke kill bacteria).
4. Bleach.
5. Alcohol.
6. Irradiation.
7. Vacuum (vacuum-packed meat keeps longer).

Sanitizing and Sterilizing

Using a Bleach Solution

- Keep a bleach solution sink-side for sanitizing. You can make it as strong as 1 part bleach per 4 parts water. However, some experts say as little as 1 tsp (5 mL) bleach per 3 cups (750 mL) water will suffice, especially for soaking.
- Spray bleach solution on sponges, dishcloths, cutting boards, utensils and counters that have been in contact with raw meat, fish or eggs. Leave it for a few seconds. Wash with soapy water, if desired. Rinse with lots of plain hot water. Air-dry or use a clean towel. Don't smear germs back on with a used towel.
- Wash or spray anything that has been contaminated secondhand after you touched it. Don't forget the faucet handle.
- Once you're done, wash your hands for at least 20 seconds. Scrape under your fingernails, too.

Mythstakes

- Using latex, disposable or plastic gloves is no guarantee of sanitation. Gloves are harder to clean than your hands. Also, they tend to be washed less, and so accumulate more bacteria.
- You think you are wiping something clean, but you are just smearing germs around with that stinky wet sponge or dishcloth. Don't let sponges and dishcloths fester sink-side for more than a day without sterilizing them.

✧ How to sterilize dishcloths, sponges and non-metal scrubbing pads:
- In the laundry. Wash them in water that is at least 140°F (60°C).
- In the dishwasher. Put dishcloths on the top shelf. Put sponges and scrubbing pads in the utensil holder or toss them on the bottom shelf while you wash dishes.
- In the microwave. It takes 2 minutes on High to kill 99% of the bacteria on a sponge, 4 minutes to get them all, scientists have found. Note: The sponges must be wet. They should be cellulose and contain no metal. This also works with loofahs and, probably, dishcloths. Beware of burns when removing steamy sponges from the microwave.
- On the stove. At least once a week, boil them for 3 to 5 minutes.
- In bleach or vinegar. Sterilize slimy sponges and cloths in a solution of 1 part bleach and 9 parts water for 3 to 5 minutes. Or soak them overnight in a pan of water with $\frac{1}{2}$ cup (125 mL) vinegar.

✧ Wash out lunch bags and boxes every night.

- A wet sponge can be the most dangerous item in your home. It may harbor millions of virulent bacteria. You can make a sponge inhospitable to microbes and spores by allowing it to dry out completely between uses. For convenience, alternate between two dry sponges.

- Assign different-colored sponges for different jobs, such as washing dishes and wiping grime off the stove. Or you can cut off a corner of the dish sponge to differentiate it.

Safe Produce

Mythstake

Some people don't realize you can get food poisoning from fresh fruit and vegetables. As we have seen in a number of food scares, it's not just meat that's perilous. Produce may be tainted with bacteria.

- Bag the fresh fruit and vegetables at the supermarket to avoid contamination from packages of meat, or even from the grocery cart.

- Germs grow more quickly on precut produce.

- Washing produce before refrigerating or storing it promotes the proliferation of mold and bacteria.

- Refrigerate, eat or use produce within 2 hours of peeling or cutting it.

- Pull off the outer leaves of leafy vegetables such as lettuce or cabbage. Besides being wilted or browned, they have been handled a lot and are most likely to be contaminated or harbor more bacteria.

- Handle fruit and vegetables gently, to avoid bruising and crushing. Bacteria thrive on bruised patches, so cut them off and discard. There are also more germs in crevices and in the scar at the stem end.

- Some experts recommend peeling all fruit before eating, unless it's organic. The peels, however, contain nutrients.

♛ A Golden Rule

Wash all fruit and vegetables to get rid of dirt, pesticides and chemical traces, and to slough bacteria off the surface.

- Rub the produce with your hands while washing. Scrub firm produce with a soft brush.
- First soak leafy greens, broccoli and cauliflower in cool water to loosen dirt, then rinse them under running water.
- Wash produce even if you're not eating the peel. Germs can be transferred to the flesh when you cut, say, a cantaloupe. Germs can be transferred to your hands and then your mouth from the peel of, say, a banana.
- Greens and other produce sold in bags labeled "washed" should be rinsed anyway.
- After washing produce, clean your hands with soap and water.

- When it comes to banishing microbes, studies have found that a vigorous wash with water is as effective as commercial fruit and vegetable washes. The latter, however, appear to be better at removing pesticide residues.

Commercial VS. Homemade?

You can use a commercial produce wash or make your own. Store-bought washes have a viscous, slippery quality. Ingredients may include citric acid, baking soda, grapefruit oil, oleic acid, glycerol and ethyl alcohol. Homemade ones are simple. They may be rubbed on, sprayed on or used as a soaking solution.

8 Simple Homemade Washes

1. Baking soda paste.
2. Salt paste or salt-and-vinegar paste.
3. 1 part vinegar and 1 to 2 parts water.
4.. ¼ cup (50 mL) grapefruit juice and 1 tsp (5 mL) baking soda.
5. Grapefruit seed extract, marketed as a killer of germs and fungi. You can use 10 to 12 drops per 1 cup (250 mL) water.
6. ⅓ cup (75 mL) water, 1 tsp (5 mL) lemon juice and 2 tsp (10 mL) baking soda.
7. 1 cup (250 mL) distilled water and ½ to 1 cup (125 to 250 mL) vinegar in a spray bottle.
8. 12 cups (3 L) cold water, ¼ cup (50 mL) vinegar and 2 tbsp (25 mL) salt in a soaking tub. Note: Vinegar can kill germs, but not in such a small ratio.

Soaking VS. Spraying?

Soaking fruit for 5 to 15 minutes in a large bowl of water mixed with vegetable wash is awkward, but it's more effective than spraying. It even helps to strip some of the wax that seems welded on. The spray, scrub and go method is more convenient for a single fruit. If you spray, try to leave the solution on the produce for 5 minutes before rinsing it off.

✧ Ozone is another cleaning option. Machines sold for home use employ super-oxygenated water, or water infused with ozone, to sanitize anything from a dishcloth to a chicken leg to a stalk of broccoli to a pacifier to a garbage bin. The machines are pricey.

Old and Spoiled Food

✧ Is it spoiled? Let your senses be the guide, but leave your sense of taste out of it. If you're suspicious, never dip a finger in to try a morsel. Throw out food that looks or smells bad. The catch? Food can go bad without smelling bad.

Mythstake

You can't just scrape mold off the top of jam or jelly and carry on consuming it. The mold is not as harmless as was once thought. Mycotoxins, or fungal poisons, can be invasive and insidious. If you see mold or get a whiff of ferment or yeastiness, discard the entire contents of the jar — just in case.

Signs of Spoilage

- A mixture in the fridge thickens or slimes mysteriously.
- The lid of a plastic storage tub holding food in the fridge bubbles up. The contents may be fermented or contaminated. Bacteria and yeast produce gas.
- You see air bubbles in the food.
- There are streaks of dried food near the top of a jar.
- The color is unnatural.

⑤ is for Salmonella

Salmonella are bacteria that cause food poisoning. They are mainly found on the surfaces and cavities of poultry and eggshells, but can contaminate other foods as well. There are no signs to detect. Cooking food to 165°F (74°C) will kill salmonella. The risk of contracting salmonella is low. The very old, the very young, pregnant women and people with chronic illnesses or suppressed immune systems are particularly warned to avoid consuming raw eggs.

B is for Botulism

Botulism is food poisoning caused by a toxin so powerful it can even lead to paralysis. The bacteria that cause it are at home in moist, airless environments. The toxin is found most often in home-canned foods with a low acid content. It is not common in commercially canned food. Chopped garlic in oil is another potential source of contamination. Don't make your own for extended storage. If you do make some, stick to a small batch, refrigerate it and keep it no longer than a day or two.

How to Discard Spoiled Food

Here's how to get rid of food that may contain botulism toxin or other contaminants:

1. If the suspect jars or cans are sealed, cushion them with newspaper and toss them in the garbage.
2. If they are open or leaking, boil them, covered in water, for 30 minutes. Then toss them in the garbage.
3. Wash your hands well.
4. Scrub the counters, containers, any utensils or can opener that came in contact with the food. Wipe with a bleach solution, then rinse.
5. Put the sponge or dishcloth that you used to wipe up in a plastic bag, tie the bag and throw it in the garbage.
6. Wash your hands again.

Pests

15 Ways to Prevent Insect Infestations

1. Beware of bulk food bins.
2. Birdseed and dried flower arrangements are an overlooked source of pantry pests.
3. Carryout cardboard boxes from supermarkets and warehouse shopping chains can be hiding places for eggs or adult insects.
4. Never leave partly opened packages in the cupboard. Store dried food in airtight glass or plastic containers. Don't think unopened packages are safe, either. Beetles can chew through foil and cardboard. Larvae are small enough to enter sealed zip-lock bags.
5. Store dried food in the freezer. Or put new packages of grain products in the freezer for 4 days to kill any eggs, then transfer them to the pantry.
6. Clean up spilled food promptly. Check in cracks, under appliances and behind cupboards.
7. Caulk crevices.
8. Lay shelf paper flat. Avoid self-adhesive shelf paper. Bugs may find the glue tasty.
9. Don't buy a lot of food that's infrequently used.
10. Maintain door and window screens.
11. Don't leave dirty dishes lying in the sink or on counters.
12. Remove garbage promptly. Don't overfill the kitchen garbage can.
13. Put cedar wood in the cupboards.
14. Get rid of cupboard clutter and give bugs fewer places to hide.
15. Spices, no matter how pungent, are not safe from infestation. Spices in bottles are more resistant than those in metal boxes with flip tops. Flimsy plastic packages are the worst, especially once they have been opened; don't store spices in them.

Mythstake

Putting dried chiles in with the dry goods will not repel pests. Having no bugs to test this on, and wanting none, I have not verified this for myself. But pantry moths are known to even eat dried chiles, and bugs have been found in cayenne pepper.

⨯ Fast Fix

Use a hand-vac to quickly suck up any roaches, beetles or moths you happen to see. Go outside to empty the bag.

OUTSIDE THE BOX

Extreme cold can be a pest-control tool. It will kill roaches and pantry bugs, and their eggs. I am reminded of the frustrated guy who shut off his water pipes in the depths of winter, turned off the heating and moved his family to a hotel for a week. When they got home, all the roaches were dead.

Flies and Wasps

✦ Basil is supposed to repel fruit flies and all kinds of bugs, inside and out.
  • Put a basil plant in the windowsill.
  • Scatter fresh basil leaves over the fruit.
  • Put dried basil in the bottom of the fruit bowl.

✦ Plagued by flies and wasps attracted to your food? They are easy to swat if you blast them with hairspray to make their wings stiff and sticky. Who needs pesticides?

✦ If you are dive-bombed by wasps while trying to enjoy dinner in your backyard, distract them with something pungent a few feet away. Three suggestions:
  • An open bottle of beer
  • A can of tuna
  • Overripe fruit

Ways to Trap Fruit Flies

They say you can catch more flies with honey than vinegar, but that's not so in the case of fruit flies. Here's how to trap those pesky flies.

• Top choice: Fill a small jar with cider vinegar and poke a tiny hole in the lid to allow the flies to enter. Put it beside the fruit or right in the middle of the bowl.
• Fill the jar with red wine.
• Put overripe banana chunks in the jar.
• Add water to a leftover jam jar, shake, then poke a hole in the lid.
• Lure fruit flies with leftover beer or pop. You can mix the beer with vegetable juice.
• You can set a small funnel in the jar instead of punching a hole in the lid.

Pantry Pests

P is for Pantry Pest

A number of beetles and moths are known as pantry pests. Though destructive, they are not poisonous or harmful, relatively speaking. They stick close to their food sources in the pantry, so it's easier to get rid of them without resorting to chemical means.

8 Ways to Deal with Pantry Pests

1. Freeze the food for 4 days to kill the eggs.
2. The eggs are also killed by heat, but less conveniently. Spread the contents of a package or container on a baking sheet and heat the food above 140°F (60°C) for 30 to 60 minutes.
3. Throw everything out. Some experts say you can use the food once you get rid of the pests, or just sift the pests out, but I shudder at the idea.
4. Vacuum the cupboard.
5. Throw away the shelf paper.
6. Scrub the cupboard, especially in the joints and cracks. Larvae like to crawl into crevices.
7. Spray with a bleach solution. Then wash with hot, soapy water.
8. Scrub the storage containers or clean them all in the dishwasher before refilling.

W is for Weevil

The weevil is a type of beetle that may infest your pantry. The name is incorrectly applied to any number of its cousins with colorful names such as the sawtoothed grain beetle, cigarette beetle, drugstore beetle, confused flour beetle and spider beetle. Even carpet beetles, in the larval stage, prefer the kitchen.

- Kitchen moths can turn into a pantry plague. Known as Indian meal moths or cereal moths, these pests start out as small worms, cocoon themselves in webbing, then emerge as tiny moths that restart the cycle.

- Mother Hubbard's cupboard, the one that was bare save for the single moth that flew out, may have been empty because of pantry pests. They are not finicky. Some of the beetles prefer whole grains, but pretty well any type of food comes under attack: cereal, rice, flour, pasta, beans, nuts, seeds, pet food, sugar, dried fruit, even chocolate.

Signs of Pantry Pests

- No signs at first. Eggs hatch in infested food after you bring it home. Then the bugs appear, seemingly out of nowhere.
- Tiny holes in packages, grains or other food. Some weevils will hatch and eat a bean or whole grain from the inside out.
- Gray webbing.
- Clumped grains with sticky secretions.
- Insects may be spied in several stages, from larvae to adults. A tiny moth flitting near the cupboard door is a bad sign.

- Consider bug sprays or other pesticides as a last resort. Avoid using them in food cupboards.

Roaches, Ants and Silverfish

- You may, however, have to get serious with poisons and pesticides to rid yourself of roaches, ants and silverfish. In contrast to pantry pests, these bugs roam more widely, under appliances, behind baseboards, under sinks, near water pipes, and into parts of the house other than the kitchen. They may nest within the walls or floors.

- Pheromone traps are sold to lure various pests, but the traps are better at detecting their presence than controlling the population. In the case of cockroaches, pheromone traps and sticky paper can be used to get an indication of where they are hanging out.

- The roach is the world's most disgusting bug. It spreads germs and dirt, and causes allergic reactions.

- Cockroaches like dark spots near moisture and food. If you see them brazenly running around in the light, the population has reached crisis level. Subtler signs include roach specks (droppings), carcasses and skins.

Mythstake

Slovenly housekeepers are not the only ones plagued by cockroaches. Roaches will infest clean and dirty kitchens alike. Clutter, however, gives them more places to hide.

- Look for signs of silverfish outside the kitchen, too. They feed on any type of carbohydrate, including wallpaper paste, book bindings and even cellulose in shampoo.

- Ants come in from the outside or through the foundation. Some are attracted to sweets, some to fatty foods.

Ant Remedies

- If you know where ants are entering the house, draw a line on the floor with petroleum jelly, chalk or baking soda. Apparently, ants don't like to walk across these.
- Scatter the contents of minty tea bags or coffee grounds where ants seem to congregate.
- Try to lure and kill ants with a mixture of 1 cup (250 mL) borax and 2 tbsp (25 mL) icing sugar.

Ways to Control Roaches, Ants and Silverfish

- Clean up food debris on the counters, in the depths of the cupboards, behind appliances and under sinks.
- Lay traps along the routes they like to follow.
- Treat baseboards, cracks, dark hiding places and damp spots with pesticides.

Physical Hazards

Fire

Ways to Prevent Kitchen Fires

- Be patient. Don't leave oil or other fats unattended on the stove.
- Keep the stovetop clean of grease and food particles, which can spread a fire.
- Don't leave anything flammable near the stove, such as hanging cotton or paper towels.
- When roasting high-fat meat, such as duck or lamb, drain it often.
- Don't store cooking wine, alcohol or messy bottles of oil near the stove.
- Prevent spattering when deep-frying. Fill the pot no more than half-full. Dry food well before dropping it in.
- Don't reuse frying oil too often. Old oil has a lower smoke point and is more likely to catch on fire. The same goes for high-quality, unrefined olive and nut oils.

✧ Call 911 for anything more than a small flare-up. If a small fire spreads from the stove, call 911 before doing anything else. Otherwise, contain it.

✧ Keep a multipurpose dry fire extinguisher handy, but make sure you know how to use it. An extinguisher can do more harm than good if the force of the blast spreads burning grease, knocks down a pan or appliance, or blows a burning towel onto other flammable objects. If you aim it at the base of the fire, flames can shoot up and hit the cupboards.

✧ If an appliance starts to spark or flame, don't toss water on it. You may throw baking soda on it, but first turn off the breakers.

♛ A Golden Rule
Never, ever, throw water on a grease fire.

 A Bit of Science
Water is heavier than oil. If you throw it on a grease fire in a pan, it sinks to the bottom, where the intense heat zaps it into steam. The result can be volcanic, with a fireball exploding toward the ceilings and walls.

6 Ways to Deal with a Grease Fire

1. Turn off the burner and/or power.
2. Smother it. Put a lid on the pot and tamp it down with a thickly wadded, damp (not sodden) towel.
3. Toss baking soda on it. Keep a large open box next to the stove. You will need a lot to put out a fire. Do it carefully. Tossing baking soda into a deep pan of oil can cause spattering and spreading of the flames.
4. Do not move the pot away from the stove. Trying to move the pot to the sink is almost instinctive, but you may drop it and cause the fire to spread.
5. Move anything flammable and loose away from the fire.
6. If the grease fire is in the oven, don't open the door. Turn off the heat.

✘ No-Nos

- Do not throw flour or sugar on a fire. They are combustible.
- Beware of throwing salt or even baking soda in a large clump. Firefighters worry that tossing these can cause splashing and spreading of flames.

❖ Water, baking soda or salt can be used to quell a dry fire involving paper, cloth or wood.

❖ Keep smoke detectors in good working condition. Change the batteries once a year at the same time. Designate a date that's easy to remember. Examples: New Year's Day or the first day of spring.

❖ Don't store propane tanks in the sun or under your deck. Keep them away from the house.

Burns

❖ What temperature should your water heater be set at? That's a controversial question. To prevent scalding (particularly in children, seniors and the disabled), some safety advocates recommend setting the thermostat so the temperature of tap water does not exceed 120°F (49°C). Others counter that the temperature must reach 140°F (60°C) to kill bacteria. There is a compromise. The water can be stored at the higher temperature. Valves can be installed to reduce the temperature of the water coming out of the tap, or anti-scald devices can be installed in individual taps to slow the water to a trickle if it gets too hot.

❖ Test the temperature: Run your tap until the water is at its hottest. Direct the flow into a pan with a candy thermometer affixed to the side.

Ways to Prevent Burns

- Turn pot handles inward, so kids don't overturn them and you don't catch on them.
- Put boiling liquid at the back of the stove.
- Lift the lid of a pot on an angle, facing away from you, so you don't get blasted by steam.
- Tilt your head away when approaching a hot pot or skillet filled with crackling oil.
- Drape a potholder or kitchen towel over the hot handle of a pan as a reminder not to pick it up absentmindedly. You could also mark it with a sprinkling of flour.
- Don't pick up a hot pot or baking dish with a damp towel or potholder. The cloth immediately gets steamy and burns.
- Steam can rise up and burn you as you pour boiling water from pan to sink to drain potatoes or pasta. Minimize the potential danger by partly filling the sink with cold water.
- Hot liquids, syrup and foods such as spaghetti sauce or stew are less likely to splash and splatter you if you direct the flow over the back of a large spoon or ladle.

Treating Burns

- Burned skin is hot, so cool it under running water. Do this at intervals for up to an hour.
- Apply a dry, sterile gauze dressing.
- Do not cut or remove burned skin or any material sticking to it.
- See your doctor, if necessary.

Mythstake

Butter is not a good remedy for burns. Neither is mustard. They will seal in the heat and make the burn worse, plus increase the chance of infection if the skin is broken.

Cuts

Ways to Prevent Cuts from Glass

- A drinking glass is less likely to crack when hot liquid is added if you put a metal spoon in it. Metal absorbs heat.
- Wash delicate glassware, crystal or ornaments in a plastic bowl to avoid chipping.
- Get all the shrapnel. After sweeping up broken glass, give the area a careful swipe with a wet paper towel to catch the splinters that are almost too small to see. You can also dab up tiny shards with a damp cotton-wool pad.
- Wrap broken glass in newspaper before throwing it into the garbage or recycling bin.

Ways to Prevent Cuts from Knives

- Never grab for a falling knife.
- Don't toss a sharp knife into a sink of soapy water. You might grope around and get a nasty surprise. Bouncing around in the sink also dulls the knife.
- Don't leave sharp tools, such as skewers or fondue forks, loose in the kitchen drawer. Put them in bags, secure them with elastic bands or shove corks on the ends so you don't stick yourself.

✧ If you have a splinter or tiny shrapnel of glass in your skin, and tweezers don't work, try putting clean adhesive tape or duct tape over the top and pulling.

✧ Cover any cuts to prevent germs from entering your skin during food preparation.

Making Do

You can paint clear nail polish over a small cut if you don't have a "liquid bandage." Drugstores sell small vials or spray bottles of liquid bandage. Regular bandages get ragged, dirty and contaminated during a bout of cooking. A liquid bandage neatly keeps food and germs out of the wound.

OUTSIDE THE BOX

Black pepper is supposed to stop bleeding. Restaurant cooks may use it, and some people carry those little takeout packets of pepper in their purse for first-aid. If you want to try pepper, use it only on superficial cuts and rinse well first. Take the top off the shaker and sprinkle a generous amount on the cut. Cayenne pepper is also supposed to stop bleeding. Pepper and cayenne may sting. I haven't tried either.

Accidents

Ways to Prevent Accidents

- Never leave a little kid alone in the kitchen.
- If you drop slick or greasy food on the floor, like the proverbial banana peel, clean it up right away. You don't want to go flying.
- Buy childproof latches for the fridge, freezer, oven door, drawers and cupboards.
- Dress appropriately for the kitchen. Tie your hair back. Wear sensible, protective shoes. Avoid voluminous caftans and fairy sleeves that can catch on fire.

Keep It Clean

Green Clean

✧ Humble kitchen ingredients can tackle a lot of chores. You can clean and deodorize without harsh chemicals. You won't necessarily get astounding results. Be realistic. Home remedies don't work as quickly, efficiently or thoroughly as commercial products, but they are kinder to the environment.

Useful Items

- **For cleaning:** Vinegar, lemon juice, cream of tartar, ketchup, Worcestershire sauce, rhubarb leaves, apple peels, citric acid, pickle juice, waxed paper, onion, chopped potato, barley, bread, meat tenderizer, club soda, milk, ice cubes, boiling and cold water, borax.
- **For blotting:** Cornstarch, salt, flour, cornmeal, talcum powder.
- **For scrubbing:** Baking soda, salt, toothpaste, raw rice, pumice stone, emery board, cork, citrus rinds, foil, eggshells.
- **For deodorizing:** Baking soda, lemon juice, vinegar, newspaper, mustard powder, coffee beans, essential oils, activated charcoal.

Mythstake

No, baking soda is not a powerful odor eater. It is a mild one. One lonely box tucked into a small area with just the top layer exposed is a random remedy for the fridge. A box with "flo-thru" vents is more efficient. However, baking soda is a good cleanser. Keep a shaker box of baking soda sink-side.

Ⓐ is for Activated Charcoal

Baking soda works best on odors from acidic foods. Activated charcoal is better at absorbing odors in general. You may find activated charcoal at a pet shop, hardware store or drugstore. It may come in a small sheet. Activated charcoal takes a couple of days to banish odors.

Ⓑ is for Borax

Borax is a naturally occurring mineral that contains boron, sodium, oxygen and water. It has had many uses, from cleaning to preserving mummies, for thousands of years. It removes stains, brightens laundry and kills bugs. It can be naturally mined or a refined compound.

♻ Waste Not

When you're done with squeezing lemons, run the halves over your hands or the cutting board, sink and faucets. Or save them in the freezer for future cleaning jobs. Citrus rinds make good scrubbers when dipped in baking soda or salt.

✧ As an all-purpose cleanser, mix 12 cups (3 L) hot water, $\frac{1}{2}$ cup (125 mL) vinegar and $\frac{1}{4}$ cup (50 mL) baking soda.

Ways to Make a Clean Getaway

- Tackling a messy job? Line the counter with waxed paper. When you're done, lift, fold and toss.
- If you're bold, you can follow the lead of Chinese restaurants. Line the counter or table with a thick plastic sheet, lift everything up and off, and cart it away.

✧ If you splat egg on the counter or floor, sprinkle it with salt to turn it into a manageable sludge.

Ways to Clean Off Egg Stuck to Dishes and Cutlery

- Wash with cold water. Don't let it dry on. Hot water will cook the egg onto the plate.
- Rub dried egg off with salt, using a paper towel dipped in oil if desired.

OUTSIDE THE BOX

When making pastry or bread, sweep up the flour on the work surface with a stale but still soft bread crust.

Ways to Unstick Gum

- Apply ice to harden the gum. Lift it off with a scraper.
- Put the item in a plastic bag, then into the freezer. Break off the gum.
- Loosen it by soaking it in vinegar.
- Rub it with peanut butter. This works on gum stuck in hair.

✧ How to peel off a stubborn adhesive sticker, label or price tag:
- Rub it with vinegar. This works well on the paper, but leaves remnants of glue.
- Spray it with WD-40 and rub with a paper towel. This is good at removing the glue.
- Run a blow-dryer over it for a minute. Immediately pull it off or rub it under warm running water. If there's glue residue, rub some soap over it and rinse.
- Rub it with oil and leave it overnight.

Ways to Remove Wax

- Rub it with an ice cube. Lift it with a scraper.
- Freeze the candleholder or tablecloth it's stuck on, then break off pieces of wax.
- Iron it with a paper bag over top.

⊟ Fast Fix

Sweep, then rub the floor with a mop that has waxed paper attached to the head. It will give the floor some shine and pick up leftover dust. Depending on the mop, you may be able to clamp the paper onto the head.

Odd Ways to Clean Shoes

- Wipe off dirt with a paper towel dampened with vinegar.
- Rub scuffs with a chunk of potato before applying polish.

Removing Stains

♛ Three Golden Rules

- Don't give up on a stain until you have worked on it twice or thrice in a row. The washer, dryer and even the dishwasher can set a stain, then it's too late.
- Don't wash a protein stain, such as blood, in hot water. Otherwise, it will cook and set.
- Completely remove a greasy stain caused by oil, gravy or mayonnaise before putting the item in the dryer. The heat will set the stain.

✧ If food dye has caused a stain, soak the item immediately in lukewarm water and bleach. It may be impossible to remove.

Chocolate Stains

- Rinse the item in lukewarm water with detergent. Dry it.
- If the stain is stubborn, launder it in hot water with bleach (for whites).

Stains on Fabric from Coffee, Tea or Fruit Juice

- Stretch the fabric over a bowl. Pour boiling water onto the stain from a height of 1 to 2 feet (30 to 60 cm). Beware of splashing. Do this right away, before the stain dries.
- Rinse the item in the hottest tap water possible. Then soak it with bleach (if it's white) or a laundry presoak (if it's colored) before washing.
- As an alkaline, baking soda may counter mild acidic stains. Make a paste with baking soda and water. Rub it on the stain. Leave it for 30 minutes. Sponge it off.

Bright Red Fruit or Beet Stains

- Blot the stain with bread.
- Soak the stained item in milk. Rinse it with cold water. Launder it.
- Rub it with a cut lemon before tossing it in the washing machine.
- Try the fruit juice stain remedies.

Red Wine Stains

- Pour club soda over the stain. Cover it with a paste of 1 part borax and 1 part water. Leave it for 5 minutes. This lifts most of the stain like magic. Keep working on the residue, which is purplish gray, with more paste or other remedies.
- Smear a mixture of 1 part dish soap and 1 part vinegar over the stain. Leave it for 5 minutes. Rub it with cold water.
- Blot the stain with salt. Vacuum up the salt. Soak the stain in cold water.
- If you can't remove the stain, try the fruit juice stain remedies.

Curry Stains

- The culprit is bright yellow turmeric. Soak the item in a mixture of water and baking soda for several hours.
- Cover the stain with a paste of hydrogen peroxide and cream of tartar for several hours.

- You may be able to lighten, but not remove, the stain.

Stains from Blood or Meat Juices

- Rub the stain under cold running water.
- Soak the item in strongly salted cold water. Keep changing the water until it runs clear.
- A paste of cornstarch and water works well on bloodstains (and beet stains). Smear it over the stain, leave it for 10 to 15 minutes and rinse it off.
- Soak the item in lukewarm water for 30 minutes. Rub detergent into the remaining stain. If it's stubborn, apply a few drops of ammonia.
- Rub the stain with salt paste.
- Sprinkle meat tenderizer over the stain, particularly if it isn't fresh. Then rinse it in cold water.

Stains on Your Hands

- Sprinkle a used lemon rind with salt or baking soda, and scrub.
- Clean off fruit stains by rubbing your fingers with vinegar.

Stains on Cloth or Carpet from Grease, Gravy or Mayonnaise

- Generously sprinkle on cornstarch to blot the stain. Leave it for an hour. Vacuum or brush it off. This will minimize the grease. It may leave a white residue.
- Dab the stain with solvent or cleaning fluid. Wash it in hot water.
- Soak the stain in a mixture of 1/4 cup (50 mL) laundry detergent and 2 cups (500 mL) water. Wash the item in hot water with bleach and extra detergent. Do this several times, if necessary.

Getting Rid of Grease and Oil

✦ If you've spilled oil on the floor, counter or stovetop, clean it up efficiently. Sprinkle a load of flour over it to prevent spreading. Lift it with a scraper. Wipe the surface clean with hot, soapy water.

✦ If a spray bottle or nozzle is clogged or encrusted with oil, soak it in a container of vinegar for 5 minutes. Transfer it to hot, soapy water. If you can, pump the hot water through it.

Greasy Plastic Containers
- Scrub them with a paste of baking soda and water.
- Wipe them with vinegar. Then wash them in hot, soapy water.

Greasy Dishes
- Sprinkle salt on them and rub.
- Add a spoonful of baking soda to the wash water.
- Pour $\frac{1}{4}$ cup (50 mL) vinegar into a sinkful of hot, soapy water.

✦ If your floor is greasy, add vinegar to the wash bucket. This will make the floor shinier, too.

✦ To clean off a grease stain on the filter over the fan in the range hood:
- Cover it with a paste of vinegar and cream of tartar. Leave it for 30 minutes. Scrub it clean using a toothbrush, then rinse. This removes brown grease stains very well. You won't need to scrub hard.
- You can run the filter through the dishwasher, but that's not as effective.

✦ If your hands are coated with grease, dissolve it under hot running water before trying to soap it off.

Cleaning the Sink and Drain

✦ If there are rust stains on the sink or faucet, pour a few drops of hydrogen peroxide on the rust, then sprinkle on cream of tartar. Leave it for 30 minutes. Wipe.

✦ If porcelain and tiles are dull, shine them up with vinegar and water.

✦ Scrub off soap scum with a solution of 3 parts water and 1 part citric acid.

Unclogging the Drain
- Stop pouring grease down the sink. Saturated fat is the worst; it solidifies.
- Try to dissolve grease by running the hottest water from the tap until the drain flows freely.
- Pour $\frac{1}{4}$ cup (50 mL) baking soda, then hot vinegar, into the drain hole. Let these do their work by putting in the plug and waiting — anywhere from 5 minutes to 5 hours. Fill the sink with the hottest tap water. Pull the plug to flush the drain.
- Pour a strong sludge of salt dissolved in hot water down the sink regularly to cut odors and grease buildup. Don't run the water for half an hour afterward.

Cleaning the Oven

Cleaning a Film of Yellow Grease off the Window
- Clean it while it's warm. Heat the oven to 200°F (100°C) if necessary.
- Make a paste of baking soda and water. Dip a damp cloth in the paste. Rub in circles.

Cleaning Up Spills
- Sprinkle salt liberally over a spill while it's warm. Let the oven cool. Scrape up the crud.

- Wet any remaining stain with a sponge. Spread a thin layer of baking soda over it. Rub with steel wool. Wipe with a paper towel or sponge.

Degreasing the Interior
- Rub it with a sponge dipped in a solution of 1 part vinegar and 1 part hot water.
- Prevent a greasy buildup by wiping with this mixture after each use.

Getting Rid of Food Baked onto the Rack
- Soak the rack in a solution of 1 cup (250 mL) vinegar, ¼ cup (50 mL) baking soda and 12 cups (3 L) hot water.
- Rub the rack with a ball of foil. (This helps on a barbecue grate, too.)
- Run a scraper over the rack.

Dealing with Dirty Cookware

Scrubbing off Cooked-On Fat
- Scrub it with baking soda and a damp cloth.
- If the situation is serious, fill the pan with hot water, add a spoonful of baking soda and boil it for 5 minutes. Drain, then rub the hot pan with baking soda.

- ✧ If a pot is coated with starch from potatoes, flour or dough, or rice is stuck to the bottom of the pan, rinse the pan right away in cold water, or soak it. Hot water just plasters it to the pan.

Removing Burnt Food
- Don't scrape or you'll scratch the pan. Don't let the burnt pan sit around. Loosen the crud right away. Fill the pan with soapy water and soak it overnight.
- Make a paste with meat tenderizer and water. Smear it on the pan. Leave it for half an hour. Scrub it off.

- Sprinkle the bottom with baking soda. Add ½ cup (125 mL) each water and vinegar. Bring it to a boil. Remove the pan from the heat. Leave it overnight.
- Scrub the pan while it's warm with lots of baking soda.
- Generously sprinkle baking soda over the pan. Cover the baking soda with water. Boil for 5 minutes.
- Add about 1 inch (2.5 cm) water and a squirt of dish soap. Bring it to a boil. Reduce the heat and simmer for 15 minutes. Loosen the crust with a spatula.
- Boil it with water.
- Sprinkle salt on the burnt area. Heat it on the stove. The burnt surface may flake off.

- ✧ If burnt milk is stuck to the pan, add baking soda and a bit of water. Bring it to a boil. This should lift up the burnt milk in a layer.

Cleaning Stains or a Dirty Coating Off Enamel Cookware
- Cover the bottom of the pan with water and ¼ cup (50 mL) salt. Soak it overnight. Bring it to a boil.
- Put a spoonful of baking soda in a pan full of water. Bring it to a boil.
- Soak the pan in hot water and dish detergent. Rub with baking soda.
- For old stains, fill the pan with cold water and a spoonful of bleach. Leave it overnight. Rinse it well.
- Soak it for an hour or two with a solution of hot water, baking soda and detergent.

- ✧ If a nonstick pan is stained, sprinkle the surface with baking soda. Cover that with a thin layer of lemon slices and water. Heat to the boiling point. Turn off the heat and leave the pan for several hours.

❖ If heatproof glass has baked-on food, fill the pan or dish with water. Cover it. Heat it in the microwave until the water boils. Leave it for 5 minutes. Drain and wash.

Removing Stains or Discolorations from Aluminum Pots

- Simmer water with a spoonful of cream of tartar added.
- Simmer a solution of 3 parts vinegar to 1 part water for 15 minutes.
- Fill it with 1 to 2 inches (2.5 to 5 cm) water. Add an apple peel and boil for 5 minutes.

❖ If a pie plate has burn marks on the edges, wet the plate. Scrub the spots with salt.

Cleaning Stubborn Stains from Cookware

- Boil a 3:1 solution of vinegar and water. Wash the cookware in soapy water.
- Cover the bottom with a single layer of pearl barley. Add just enough water to cover the barley. Bring it to a boil, then immediately remove it from the burner and leave it overnight.
- Boil rhubarb leaves in water for a few minutes. This should make a dull pot shine.
- Add water with half an onion. Bring it to a boil.

Cleaning Coffee and Tea Vessels

Purging Scale from a Kettle

- Pour in 2 cups (500 mL) vinegar, top it up with water and boil. If there is lots of scale, leave it overnight. Rinse well.
- Pour a can of cola in the kettle. Boil. Rinse well.

Removing Tannin and Mineral Deposits from a Teapot

- Fill it with boiling water. Add 1 tbsp (15 mL) vinegar and 2 tbsp (25 mL) baking soda. It will fizz. Leave it for 15 minutes. Rinse and repeat, if necessary. Wipe the pot with a paper towel.
- Scrub with a paste of water or vinegar and baking soda.

Eliminating Dirt or Scale from a Coffee Maker

- Run a 1:1 solution of vinegar and water through the brewing cycle. Brew plain water to rinse it out.
- Clean a stained, burnt carafe with 1 cup (250 mL) boiling water and 1 tsp (5 mL) baking soda. Heat until the stain dissolves. Let it cool.
- While it's still warm, rub the carafe with baking soda paste.

Cleaning a Vacuum Flask or Insulated Mug

- Add warm water and 3 tbsp (45 mL) baking soda. Cover and shake. Leave it for 15 minutes. Rinse.
- Add a spoonful of raw rice and shake for 30 seconds. Rinse.
- Add a crushed eggshell. Shake it with warm water. Rinse.

Caring for Metal

❖ If a stainless-steel appliance has fingerprints and water spots, rub it with a cloth dampened with warm water. Or use a glass cleaner. Then rub it dry.

❖ Wash grease and dirt from a stainless-steel appliance with hot soapy water and a soft sponge. Wipe it dry. Apply commercial stainless-steel polish. Buff with a towel.

- Polish dull stainless steel with crumpled newspapers.

Polishing Copper
- A vinegar-and-salt slurry scrub works like magic. You could also use lemon juice.
- Smear it with ketchup. Leave it for a few minutes. This shines it up fine.
- Rub it with pickle juice.
- Scrub it with WD-40.

- How to remove water spots from steel knives, bowls or pans:
- Rub them with a lemon slice.
- Wipe them with a paper towel dipped in vinegar.

Polishing Silver and Pewter
- Clean without rubbing. Line a bowl with foil. Add boiling water, then about 2 tbsp (25 mL) baking soda per 4 cups (1 L) water. Add the silver. Leave it until it is cool enough to handle. Rinse well and wipe dry.
- Soak silver in cooled potato cooking water for several hours.
- Polish with Worcestershire sauce.

Brightening Up Aluminum
- Scrub it with a 1:1 paste of salt and vinegar.
- Smear it with a paste of cream of tartar and water. Leave it for a few minutes. Scrub and rinse.
- Rub it with foil.

Cleaning Rust Spots from Chrome or Other Metal
- Rub off rust with a piece of crumpled foil.
- Use a hunk of raw potato dipped in powdered dishwashing detergent.
- Use a cork dipped in oil.
- Fight rust on knives by running them through an onion.
- Shine metal up by soaking it in cola.

- Rub it with a 2:1 solution of cream of tartar and hydrogen peroxide. Leave it for 10 minutes.
- Rub with citric acid crystals and a damp paper towel.

- To prevent steel wool from rusting, store it in a zip-lock bag in the freezer. If it starts to rust:
- Prevent a mess by wrapping it in foil.
- Keep it completely covered in soapy water.

Beautifying Glass and China

Shining Glassware
- For sparkly glasses, add $\frac{1}{4}$ cup (50 mL) each of salt and baking soda to the dishwasher along with the detergent.
- Rub glassware with a paste of baking soda and water. Rinse it in cold water. Dry it. Polish it with a soft cloth.
- Rinse it with a 3:1 solution of water and vinegar.

- To remove wine stains from a decanter, fill the bottom with raw rice or chopped raw potato. Add water. Shake. Rinse.

Removing Mineral and Hard-Water Deposits from Glass
- Scrub it with steel wool dampened with vinegar.
- Soak it in a solution of 1 part vinegar and 2 parts hot water. (This works for plastic, too. Use boiling water.)

- If china is stained by tea and coffee, rub it with a paste of lemon juice or vinegar and baking soda.

- How to remove dirt lodged in hard-to-reach crevices in a vase, pitcher or bottle:
- Add a bit of water. Drop in an Alka-Seltzer tablet. Shake.

- Add baking soda and vinegar. Shake.
- Add soapy water and two spoonfuls of raw rice. Shake.
- Add a crushed eggshell and warm water. Shake.

Caring for Wood

✧ To polish furniture, combine 2 parts olive oil with 1 part lemon juice. Keep this in a spray bottle. Shake before using.

✧ How to remove water stains from the dining table or a wooden tray:
- Rub with a spoonful of lemon oil.
- Rub real mayonnaise over the spot.
- Rub the spot with Vaseline.
- Rub with an oil-and-salt paste.

Restoring Wood

✧ If a wooden bowl or another wooden item is scarred and faded:
- Restore the deep brown color and hide scratches by rubbing it with a paste of instant coffee granules and water.
- Stain the wood lightly with double-strength brewed tea or coffee.

✧ To clean a wicker basket, scrub it with a damp brush dipped in salt. Let it dry, then brush off the salt.

✧ To remove grime from a cork coaster or board, spray it with cold water. Rub it with a pumice stone or emery board.

Eliminating Odors

Deodorizing Your Hands

- Rub them on stainless steel to get rid of persistent onion and garlic odors. They even sell bars of stainless steel "soap" for this purpose. But a spoon, faucet or the side of a pan will do.
- Rub a lemon wedge over them.

- Scrub with salt, then wash your hands in soapy water.
- Rub coffee beans or ground coffee in your hands.
- Scrub them with white toothpaste.
- Rub them with mustard powder.

✧ A quick breath check: Lick the back of your hand and sniff.

Freshening Your Breath

- Chew parsley, citrus peel, fennel seeds or coffee beans.
- Eat an apple.

✧ How to remove a bad smell from a vacuum flask, bottle, jar or plastic container:
- Stuff it with crumpled newspaper and put on the lid. Leave it overnight.
- Add equal amounts of vinegar and baking soda. Shake.
- Add 1 tsp (5 mL) mustard powder per 4 cups (1 L) warm water. Leave it overnight.
- Add 20 whole cloves per 4 cups (1 L) warm water. Leave it overnight.
- Store an empty covered container with a spoonful of salt inside.

✧ If a lunch bag smells stale, dip a day-old hunk of bread in vinegar. Pop it in the bag. Close the top. Leave it for an hour or two. Rinse and dry well.

✧ What to do if cutting boards or other kitchen tools smell fishy or oniony:
- Rinse them in cold water. Rub leftover citrus rind or prepared mustard over them. Wash them in soapy water.
- Rub baking soda paste over them, then rinse.
- Rub them with coarse salt, then rinse with cold water.

Removing a Fishy Smell from a Pot or Pan

- Bring a mixture of vinegar and hot water to boil in it.
- Scrub it with a baking soda paste. Wash it in hot, soapy water. Dry. Wipe with vinegar. Rinse.

Clearing the Air of Frying Odors

- Fry some celery in the oil afterward.
- Fry a piece of gingerroot in the oil afterward.

Freshening the Air in the Kitchen

- Simmer 2 tbsp (25 mL) ground cinnamon in 2 cups (500 mL) water.
- Sprinkle coffee grounds onto a warm element if you have a flat, ceramic stovetop. Or just brew a pot of coffee.
- Put a drop or two of essential oil on the warm light bulb in your range hood.
- Get rid of smoke lingering in the air by whirling a damp towel.

- ◈ To get rid of a foul smell in a cupboard, lay a piece of stale bread in a dish of vinegar. Set it in the cupboard.

Deodorizing the Microwave

- Stuff crumpled newspaper in the compartment. Leave it overnight.
- Fill half a citrus rind with salt. Heat until it is steamy. Leave it for several hours.

- ◈ If the dishwasher smells rancid, sprinkle baking soda over the dishes while they sit waiting to be washed.

- ◈ How to improve the aroma from the garbage can or compost pail:
- Line the bottom with a newspaper section.
- Sprinkle a few spoonfuls of borax on the bottom.

- ◈ To freshen up the garbage disposal, toss in citrus rinds.

Deodorizing the Fireplace

- Throw coffee grounds in the fire.
- Toss in used citrus rinds.

Chemical Solutions

✗ No-No

Never mix commercial cleansers. You don't know what hazardous concoction may result. In particular, never combine bleach or ammonia with other cleaning agents — or with each other. Also, never mix bleach with an acid. You'll create toxic gases and carcinogens.

is for Ammonia

Ammonia is a gas in its natural form, but a liquid in the guise of household ammonia. This foul chemical will work when nothing else does. It will cut through anything greasy and cruddy. It will also strip the skin from your nostrils and throat. Use it with caution.

Ammonia Safety Tips

- Dilute ammonia with water. Use 9 parts water per 1 part ammonia.
- Use ammonia in a well-ventilated room.
- Wear a mask and gloves.
- Wash your skin with cold water if it comes in contact with ammonia.

Cleaning Fabric Stains with Ammonia

- Nothing cuts grease — even the worst kind — like ammonia. On cloth, it cleans fresh oil stains very efficiently.
- It works on stubborn stains such as mustard and chocolate. Dab with ammonia, then wash.

Dealing with Grease-Encrusted Kitchen Cabinets

- The top surfaces of kitchen cabinets become coated with thick, stubborn, yellow grease. Strip it off with an application of ammonia and elbow grease.
- Save yourself the trouble next time and line the surfaces with brown paper or wallpaper. When cleaning time arrives, strip it off and throw it out.
- To slow down the greasy buildup, buff the tops of the cabinets with paste wax. This works for the top of the fridge and the wall behind the stove, too. These areas will be easier to wipe clean.

How to Clean Soot and Grease off a Barbecue Grate

1. Put the grate in a sturdy green garbage bag. Pour in 2 cups (500 mL) household ammonia. Close it tightly. Be careful not to poke holes in the bag.
2. Leave the bag in a sunny, airy spot outside for 4 to 8 hours.
3. Open the bag quickly and run away. Don't put your face near it. Let the fumes evaporate for a few minutes.
4. Rinse the bag and grate with a garden hose.
5. Toss out the bag. Wash the grate immediately in hot, soapy water.

❖ The barbecue grate technique works for oven racks and stainless-steel cookware, too, although one might wonder how it all got into a condition bad enough to require such drastic cleaning.

❖ You can also stick barbecue grates in your self-cleaning oven. Be forewarned that this may strip any shiny coating.

How to Clean a Greasy Oven

1. Heat the oven to 200°F (100°C).
2. Put a heatproof glass bowl with $1/2$ cup (125 mL) ammonia on the top rack. Put a large bowl of boiling water on the bottom rack. Close the door. (It stinks!) Leave it for an hour.
3. Turn off the oven. Leave it overnight. (Do not open the door.) The fumes from the ammonia soften baked-on crud.
4. Open the oven door to air it out. Turn on the fan. Open a kitchen window, too.
5. Wipe the oven clean with hot, soapy water.

❖ Use oven cleaner to remove burnt-on stains on the bottom of a pan. You can heat the pan before applying the cleaner. Rinse well. It stinks.

❖ Oven cleaner is corrosive. Handle it only with rubber gloves. Rinse with plenty of cold water. Avoid inhaling the fumes. Keep the room well ventilated.

How to Turn a Stained, Yellowed Sink Sparkly White

1. Line it with paper towels.
2. Pour bleach evenly over the towels.
3. Wait half an hour. At halftime, press down on the yellow patches where the paper has bubbled up, so that it makes contact with the enamel again.
4. Wipe and marvel.

❖ To dry the kitchen floor quickly after washing, turn on a fan or open the doors and windows.

Advice to Ignore
A collection of silly, useless tips that are passed around

- An **apple** is easy enough to peel. There's no need to pour boiling water over it and let it sit for a minute first.

- Tossing the trimmed ends of **asparagus** into a freezer bag sounds frugal and wise. But the payoff is miserly. It takes a lot of work just to get a thin asparagus gruel. You have to simmer the ends in stock until they are very soft, purée them in a food processor and press them through a food mill. There's not much left once all the stringy bits are discarded. If you wish, save the trimmings, but skip the puréeing. Pour the asparagus liquid into soup.

- We are advised to add some of the **asparagus**-cooking water to vinaigrette. So who wants water in vinaigrette?

- Wavy **bacon** sounds attractive. But don't bother weaving cooked bacon through a rack and letting it cool. It tears when you try to pull it out and it's uneven. Too bad.

- Use the inside of a **banana** peel to polish silver. Then grab some other fruit to remove the banana gunk from the silver.

- You can polish dark shoes with a **banana** peel if you don't mind slime on them.

- Your hopes will be dashed if you think spraying **barbecue** grates with Windex while they are still warm will strip the crud.

- A **barbecue lighter** won't brûlée or brown a topping. The flame is too lazy.

- **Basil** blackens more — not less — if you roll the leaf from stem to tip and cut slivers parallel to the vein. Mint leaves can be rolled either way.

- **Batter** for fish is supposed to cook extra crispy when you add 1 tbsp (15 mL) vinegar per 1 cup (250 mL) batter. Too bad it makes no difference.

- Adding $\frac{1}{2}$ tsp (2 mL) sugar to 1 cup (250 mL) **batter** does not help it stick to food better, as advertised.

- Adding oil to the soaking water for **beans** does not reduce foaming.

- Do not put **berries** frozen solid through a meat grinder to purée them more smoothly. The grinder strains and shakes. In fact, don't put anything frozen solid through the grinder.

- **Blanching** in the microwave does not save time or energy and is not as effective when you need to deactivate those enzymes that cause browning.

- Don't **bleach** stained plastic dishes and cups in a solution of $\frac{3}{4}$ cup (175 mL) bleach, $\frac{1}{4}$ cup (50 mL) baking soda and 1 cup (250mL) vinegar. Mixing bleach with acids releases chlorine gas.

- You can fill a baking sheet with $\frac{1}{2}$ inch (1 cm) of water and put it on the lower rack while baking **bread**. Sure, it creates steam, and steam is good. It also blocks air circulation and draws heat away from the dough. The bread won't turn out well.

- **Bread** can be warmed or thawed in a dampened paper bag in a 350°F (180°C) oven, but the microwave does it better and faster. Plus, the bag imparts a strange taste.

- Popping bread in the toaster is not a good shortcut if you are making dry **bread crumbs**.

- When **brining**, some chefs add a spoonful of saltpeter per 12 cups (3 L) liquid to prevent beef and pork from turning gray. Yuck!

- You can put on cotton gloves and stretch hot **brittle** with your hands. It's easier and more accurate to use a rolling pin.

- **Brussels sprouts** are supposed to transform from bitter to sweet if you freeze them outdoors overnight in winter. They actually transform into ghastly mush.

❖ Putting a dab of **butter** under the spout of a teapot is supposed to stop drips. But it just melts on the hot pot. It may be okay for cold jugs.

❖ Using a melon baller to make **butter** balls sounds like a great idea, but it doesn't work. You have to finish the balls by hand-rolling. Dipping the baller in hot water doesn't help. The best you'll get are little footballs.

❖ Don't press **butter** with a warm whisk to soften it. The butter gets stuck in the whisk.

❖ Sorry, you cannot make **buttermilk** cheese the way you make yogurt cheese, by straining it through cheesecloth.

❖ You have better things to do with your time than trying to scrub out a stain on the carpet with a **cabbage** leaf.

❖ Please don't put a pan of hot water on the rack right underneath your **cake** as it bakes. This is supposed to make it moist, but the cake ends up with a weird sunken center.

❖ Dusting a **cake** with cornstarch is supposed to prevent glaze from running off and icing from slipping. It is more apt to prevent the glaze or icing from sticking.

❖ Don't try to cool a hot **cake** quickly by sticking layers in the freezer. First of all, you shouldn't cut a hot cake. Second of all, it's no good for the freezer.

❖ It's not that clever to dust a pan with some of the **cake mix** you are using — the mix is too fine and clumpy.

❖ You can line a **cake pan** with large paper coffee filters. But why?

❖ You don't need to dust an angel food **cake pan** with flour. In fact, the pan should be bare.

❖ Never mind pouring a thin layer of oil over the surface of foods in open **cans** in the fridge, to prevent mold. And never mind the lids they sell for cans. Get rid of those open cans. Scoop food into safe and secure airtight tubs.

❖ Soaking **candles** overnight in salt water is supposed to make them drip-proof, but they burn down faster.

❖ Making a **caramel** lattice is difficult. It's worse when you attempt to trail caramel syrup over an oiled ladle, leave it to cool and detach it in one piece. Good luck!

❖ Do not try to make browning or **caramel** coloring by boiling brown sugar with water. At first, it's syrupy enough, but too sweet. Afterwards, it's too thick. As it cools, it hardens.

❖ You will die of old age waiting for hard, set **caramel** to melt in the top of a double boiler. It will happen eventually ...

❖ Boiling **carrots** for 5 minutes is a silly way to make the skins slip off. It doesn't work, though the surface gets mushy. Just use a vegetable peeler.

❖ Don't add an extra cup of shredded carrots to the **carrot cake** to make it moister. It will be denser and heavier.

❖ Don't wrap **cheese** in vinegar-soaked cheesecloth. It's supposed to kill germs, but it makes the cheese taste and smell bad.

❖ Worried about hardening **cheese**? Wrapping it in a cabbage leaf is an awkward preventive measure.

❖ Whirling cold water in the food processor bowl does not rid it of sticky **cheese** residue. Hot water helps, though.

❖ This one is incomprehensible: When transporting **cheesecake**, cut a circle from a disposable pie plate to fit over the bottom of the springform pan. If the cake is released from the springform, but still sitting on the base of the pan, it could be carried in an intact pie plate. However, reattaching the side of the springform pan seems the simplest remedy.

❖ Do not broil **chestnuts** in pursuit of smoky, roasted flavor. The shells will burn before the nuts are done.

❖ Some people prick **chestnuts** with a fork instead of slitting them. This does release steam, but the shells aren't as easy to open.

❖ You can transform **chicken wings** into "mock legs." Cut off the tips and straighten the two sections to look like a small double leg. The trouble is, they retract when cooked.

❖ Afraid your eyes will sting if you accidentally rub them after cutting hot **chiles**? Rinsing your hands with milk beforehand is not good insurance.

❖ Rubbing your hands with baking soda doesn't get rid of burning **chile** juices.

- Brushing **china** with toothpaste to get rid of gray scratch marks is a good attempt, but futile.

- Yes, one must be cautious when melting **chocolate**. But melting it in a gas oven with just the heat of the pilot light seems excessive.

- Here's a dubious household **cleanser**: Combine 12 cups (3 L) hot water, 1 cup (250 mL) ammonia, $\frac{1}{2}$ cup (125 mL) vinegar and $\frac{1}{4}$ cup (50 mL) baking soda. This formula is supposed to cut grease and mildew. However, chemists say ammonia and vinegar neutralize each other.

- Instant **coffee** is supposed to foam less if you add the granules to boiling water, not vice versa. It makes not a whit of difference. Maybe this was the case with the original coffee powders?

- Don't strain soup, sauce, used oil or most anything else besides coffee through a paper **coffee filter** unless you are a paragon of patience.

- Unfortunately, if gum is stuck in your child's hair, rubbing it with **cola** will not remove it.

- Don't brush **cookie dough** with egg white to help colorful sanding sugar stick. You don't need it and the dye will run.

- Shoving a couple of lumps of sugar in the tin in the hopes of keeping **cookies** crisp doesn't do anything.

- Stuffing paper towels between layers of baked **cookies** in the freezer is supposed to absorb fat. Actually, this makes no difference in taste and texture. In the same vein, putting a paper towel in with baked goods is supposed to prevent freezer burn by sucking up moisture. If that much moisture is released, it's too late.

- It takes more skill than I can hope for to detect freshness in **corn** simply by holding the ear. This is how it's supposed to work: If it's cool, it's fresh. If it's warm, the sugars are turning to starch.

- Adding **corn flour** to the salt shaker keeps it dry. It also makes it yellow and gritty, and falls out the holes.

- Making clotted **cream** at home is tricky. You are supposed to heat milk and heavy or whipping (35%) cream for several hours, or just heat heavy or whipping (35%) cream in the top of a double boiler over simmering water, until skin and clots form. It takes all day and the butter separates out. The result is granular and chunky.

- You may be able to make homemade **crème fraîche** by heating 1 cup (250 mL) heavy or whipping (35%) cream with 2 to 4 tbsp (25 to 50 mL) buttermilk, sour cream or yogurt to 110°F (43°C), then leaving it overnight at room temperature. You may be able to get food poisoning, too. Besides, if the cream is more than barely warm, it won't work.

- Trying to make rectangular **crêpes** by using a rectangular pan and doubling the amount of batter doesn't work. Keep them round.

- Using a vegetable peeler to cut spirals out of a **cucumber** makes a mess, not an attractive garnish.

- It's not easy to clean old stains from a **cutting board**, wood or plastic. Pouring on vinegar and wiping won't do the job. Neither will covering the board with bleach and salt, then scrubbing.

- Microwaving dates and other **dried fruit** does not make them easier to chop — quite the opposite.

- It's fine to know that **dough** will stick to the grout if you try to knead it on a tile counter. But who has a tile counter?

- Apparently, **dulce de leche** can be made with whole milk, sugar and baking soda. Put it out of your mind and just open a can of sweetened condensed milk.

- Avoid vague salt-water tests to check the freshness of an **egg**. All eggs will float if there's enough salt in the water.

- When you are trying to dye an **egg** with a natural agent such as beet skins, it seems to make sense to contain everything in pantyhose, instead of simmering them loose. Actually, it makes no difference to the intensity of color. Meanwhile, the color ends up uneven because of the puffy air pocket in the hose.

- One physicist argued that the best way to cook a perfect "3-minute" **egg** is to heat it for 1 hour at 140°F (60°C). The method is called LTLT (low temperature, long time).

- Holding raw **eggs**, whole or just whites, at 140°F (60°C) in the top of a double boiler over simmering water for 5 minutes before beating them is supposed to cut the risk of salmonella. This seems impossible. Even when you whip them the whole time, there are cooked bits.

- Avoid shiny **eggs** — for no apparent reason.

- Using a baster or medicine dropper to suck up bits of stray yolk from **egg whites** is a fool's game.

- If you are so inclined, and have no glue, you can use raw **egg white** to sort of seal an envelope that has lost its sticking power.

- Here's an icky mess worse than the pesky kitchen **flies** it is supposed to lure and suffocate: Simmer 1 cup (250 mL) milk, ¼ cup (50 mL) sugar and 2 tbsp (25 mL) black pepper for a few minutes, then leave it out in a shallow dish.

- Don't try to smooth out **frosting** by dipping the spatula in hot water. You'll make a mess.

- Making your own **garlic juice** is a foolish endeavor. The garlic is puréed, then pushed through a strainer. But you need a lot. You can buy this product.

- Don't bother rinsing a mold with cold water before adding **gelatin**. It's supposed to be easier to remove once it firms up. But this makes no difference and no sense. The gelatin is wet when you pour it in.

- There are several ways to test how solidly **gelatin** will set. Pouring a spoonful onto a small plate and shoving it in the freezer for up to half an hour is not a good way. The gelatin becomes brittle and opaque.

- Please don't soak your stinky feet in fruity flavored **gelatin** mixed with warm water in the hopes of making them smell sweet. The powder will dye your feet.

- Don't try to frost a **glass** by wetting it and sticking it in the fridge. That's underkill. Churning crushed ice in it before sticking it in the freezer is overkill.

- If two **glasses** or **bowls** are stuck together, don't put the bottom one in hot water. Scientists say the material will swell evenly, not expand outwards.

- Refrigerating wilted **green beans** in a plastic bag will not firm them up.

- Do not cover the skillet when making **grilled cheese**. You'd think this would hasten the cheese melting, but it just hastens the bread burning. The sandwich gets soggy, too.

- Puréeing **herbs** with oil? Pouring boiling water over them in a colander beforehand is supposed to give them a better color, but doesn't.

- Chopping **herbs** such as basil, oregano and mint with a drizzle of oil is supposed to prevent them from darkening, but actually promotes it.

- You can blanch **herbs** before making flavored oil. That's supposed to soften them and encourage the flavors to blend better. It just purges the essential oils and makes the herbs wetter. Botulism bacteria love that.

- If you don't have **honey**, mixing 1¼ cups (300 mL) granulated sugar with 1 cup (250 mL) water is a sad substitute. Use another viscous syrup.

- Tossing a bunch of **ice** into warm stock or stew is supposed to be a quick way to defat. It's just a quick way to melt ice cubes.

- Tossing **ice cubes** in a paper bag versus a plastic one doesn't make them less likely to stick. Neither does spraying them with soda water before transferring them to a bag. That just makes them look cloudy.

- Spraying an **ice cube tray** with oil is supposed to prevent sticking. But it leaves a film on the ice. Get a flexible tray you can twist; the ice pops out easily.

- Never mind the gimmick about rolling around a coffee canister to make **ice cream**. It takes so long, even the kids get tired of kicking the thing around.

- Starch harvested from raw potato soaking water can be added to **latke** batter. It does help them hold together. It also makes them gummy and stodgy.

- You can stir lemon curd into béchamel to make a **lemon sauce**. The sauce, however, is too sweet for savories and too pasty for sweets.

- Got a big batch of **lettuce** to dry? Tie it in a clean pillowcase and spin it in the dryer on the Air Only setting — if you don't mind bruised, limp lettuce.

- The worst torture devised for a live **lobster** is sticking a skewer into the opening at the end of the tail to drain urine before cracking and chopping the creature to pieces. Would a lobster even hold still for that?

- Here's another fruitless way to torture the creature: Tie a spoon or table knife to the **lobster**'s tail to keep it straight while it boils. The cutlery won't stay put and the bondage stresses out the crustacean.

- Trying to add color to a stock or seafood dish by simmering crushed **lobster** and **shrimp** shells is a waste of time. The shells change color, not the water.

- **Mayonnaise** is an unusual adhesive for the coating on fried chicken. Use the word "adhesive" lightly. Oily equals slippery.

- You cannot stiffen homemade **mayonnaise** with a hard-cooked egg yolk. You will end up with a grainy mess.

- For crispier chicken skin, we are advised to rub **mayonnaise** over it before roasting. But it's slimy. Just rub the bird with oil. Don't add mayonnaise to the marinade for fried chicken, either.

- Apparently, **meat** should be defrosted fat side down in the microwave. I say don't struggle with defrosting meat more than partially in the microwave. The edges are bound to cook.

- Placing plastic wrap over **meat** before you whack it with a tenderizing mallet just tears the plastic — or even drives it into the meat. The same goes for waxed paper.

- Marinating **meat** in vinegar overnight will indeed kill bacteria, but it also "cooks" the proteins into a gray, fibrous mess. Don't use any strong vinegary marinades, unless you intend to prepare sauerbraten.

- Brushing cold water or an ice cube over the top of **meatloaf** is supposed to prevent cracking. You won't notice any difference.

- **Meringue** beaten in a glass bowl is supposed to be dry or grainy, but I noticed no particular difference.

- Here are two dubious ways to prevent **milk** from leaving a sticky coating on the bottom of a pan: Rinse the pan in cold water before pouring in the milk. Sprinkle sugar on the bottom of the pan.

- Adding cream of tartar is suggested as a way to sour **milk**. Never mind. It just clumps at the bottom.

- Adding a spoonful of water to boiled **milk** does not prevent a skin from forming.

- **Milk** won't boil over if you put a wooden spoon in the pan — you wish.

- You can grease only the bottom and ½ inch (1 cm) up the sides of **muffin** cups. This is supposed to create evenly rounded muffin tops and give the batter something to cling to as it rises. More like it gives the batter something to stick to. And it doesn't do a thing for the tops.

- **Mussels** that won't close tight after sitting in the freezer for a minute or two are not lost causes.

- **Mussels** that float are suspect, but this is not a cut-and-dried test.

- Rubbing a **mustard** stain with glycerin just creates an oil stain.

- Toasted **nori** cannot be rehydrated and used in salad. Soaking it in boiling water for 15 minutes is one silly suggestion. The result looks like pond scum. Reducing the soaking time and/or using cold water makes no difference.

- Rubbing scratched wood with a broken **nut**, such as a pecan or walnut, just gives you a shinier scratch mark.

- The scent from a pierced lemon or orange that's baked at 300°F (150°C) for 15 minutes is not powerful or widespread enough to clear a kitchen of fishy or frying **odors**, even if the oven door is left ajar. Leaving out a bowl of vinegar is ineffectual, too. Putting a glass of bleach nearby on the counter, out of the way, while you fry helps a bit, but the scent is disgusting.

- Don't use olive or any other cooking **oil** to soften or polish leather. Cooking oils eventually go rancid and stink.

- Don't rub **oil** on stainless-steel appliances to get rid of fingerprints. That's overkill. Don't use oil to clean dirt or grease buildup, either. That's underkill.

- Extra virgin **olive oil** turns bitter when beaten into mayonnaise. Blending it with a wooden spoon is supposed to prevent that. It doesn't.

- It's too difficult to roll an **omelet** by jerking the pan toward you to make the farthest edge roll over.

- Instead of weeping when you chop an **onion**, you can look like a fool. Put a votive candle next to your chopping board (and pray it works) or lodge a small hunk of bread between your lip and gums or between your teeth (and hope no one sees you).

✧ Another stupid **onion** remedy: Keep cold water running in the sink while you cut an onion on the board.

✧ Here's a convoluted way to cut an **onion**: Cut it in half from top to bottom. Cut off the root end at a 45-degree angle. Cut each piece in half lengthwise. Slice about halfway through. Take the leftover hunk, turn it around and continue to slice.

✧ You could grow old trying to extract the juice of an **onion** with a citrus reamer or by scraping it with a spoon.

✧ Were **oranges** with larger navels overripe when picked? It's hard to tell the difference when you eat them.

✧ It is indeed easier to shuck **oysters** that have been stashed in the freezer for half an hour, but, alas, the flesh freezes.

✧ Don't use a baster to squeeze round **pancakes** or create shapes. The opening is too small.

✧ Rubbing a griddle or cast-iron pan with salt to prevent **pancakes** from sticking just makes them salty.

✧ In my college days, we used to throw **pasta** against the wall to see if it was done. It sticks once there is enough starch on the surface. This is fun, but pasta will stick whether it's ready or not. It depends on how long you have it in your hand (the longer, the stickier) and how close you are to the wall.

✧ Don't run a rolling pin over the top of a pie plate to cut off the **pastry**. The edges will be mangled and too short to crimp.

✧ Why does everyone mention using two knives to cut butter into flour for pie **pastry** or shortbread? It's awkward and inefficient.

✧ **Pears** do not ripen faster or better if you cover the bowl with a damp cloth.

✧ Rubbing a vegetable **peeler** with steel wool is supposed to sharpen it, but doesn't do much.

✧ The stem and most of the seeds should — but don't — pull away when you cut a **pepper** from the base almost to the tip, then pull the halves apart. This doesn't work in the other direction, either.

✧ **Peppers** are supposed to be easier to peel if you fry them before roasting them. Sounds like another case of overkill.

✧ They say blanching basil beforehand makes smoother **pesto**. I say it makes blander pesto.

✧ Sticking a grape leaf in with homemade **pickles** is an old-fashioned way to prevent them from going soft.

✧ Alum is an old-fashioned additive to avoid in your **pickles**. It will make them bitter and upset your stomach.

✧ When blind-baking a **pie shell**, greasing the dish is supposed to help the pastry grip so it doesn't sag down the sides. Wouldn't that make it even more slippery? The dough is greasy enough.

✧ Making a **piping bag** out of a square of waxed paper is for the nimble or desperate. Curl the paper into a cone. Tape down the edge near the tip. Evenly cut off the top. Fill the cone halfway. Cut a small hole in the point. Now you are free to make a mess. Piping from a makeshift foil bag is no picnic, either.

✧ You can prepare a **pizza** ahead if you want to save a minuscule amount of time. Cook the dough for 3 minutes on a hot stone in a 500°F (260°C) oven, to prevent sogginess. Add the toppings. Freeze or refrigerate. Cook it when you are ready. Beware: The edges will blacken.

✧ Don't try to brush oil on the bottom of the stretched dough for grilled **pizza**. You'll end up wrestling with the dough.

✧ You can stretch **pizza dough** and freeze it flat. But why?

✧ **Plastic wrap** will stick less to itself if stored in the freezer. It will also stick less to a bowl.

✧ In search of crispier kettle **popcorn**? Don't use a splatter screen instead of a lid on the pot. Moisture and oil spit through the screen. The pot is hard to handle and you can burn yourself. The popcorn turns out tough and chewy.

✧ You can use a melon baller to carve **potato** balls from a large, waxy spud. Most of them turn out dome-shaped and there's a lot of waste. Just buy potato balls.

- Peeled **potato** chunks are supposed to help suck up salt faster while salt cod is soaking. One Portuguese chef calls that a joke — with good reason. The potato can't absorb enough to make a discernible difference.

- Testing a boiled **potato** by poking it with a knife doesn't tell you enough. A sharp knife always slides out easily. In the same vein, if the potato refuses to cling to a skewer or knife when pierced, it is not only done, it is overdone.

- A hunk of **potato** dipped in salt is not an effective scrubber for beet stains and the like. The salt slips off due to the starch. It doesn't scrub stains from the fingers well, either.

- Storing an apple with a **potato** to prevent sprouting will lead to sprouting frustration. The potato actually sprouts more and gets wrinkled.

- If you are of a scientific bent or unsure how starchy your **potatoes** are, you can make brine of 12 cups (3 L) water and 1 cup (250 mL) salt. Spuds that float in the brine are less dense, which supposedly means they contain less starch. But the shape and weight are variables. In the end, this doesn't tell you much more than simply looking at the potato.

- A paste of vinegar and cream of tartar will not remove burnt black stains from **pots and pans**, not even if you let it sit for half an hour. It will remove greasy brown stains, though.

- You may be advised to fill **preserve** jars, invert them to blast heat on the seal, then cool them upright. Careful — this can loosen the seal. Process jars in a hot-water canner instead of relying on this dubious technique.

- Once upon a time, some people would put Aspirin in **preserves** and skip the hot-water processing. Please don't.

- Don't put Epsom salts in **preserves**. Yes, people did that, too. The salts would help jams and jellies gel. Drugstore Epsom salts cause nausea, vomiting, cramps and diarrhea if ingested.

- It's not true that **puff pastry** rises higher on a dampened baking sheet. A test showed the opposite, in fact.

- Baking **puff pastry** in muffin cups is supposed to make it rise higher. But the circles shrink and get tiny as they bake. They may be fine for hors d'oeuvres.

- Don't bother cutting strips to form a tidy little border on a rectangle of **puff pastry**. It rises, separates and shifts in the oven.

- Adding a bit of vinegar to **rice** cooking water does not, alas, make the pot easier to clean.

- Overnight **rice pudding** is a great idea. You put raw rice and sugar into a wide Thermos, add boiling milk, cover and shake. Too bad it doesn't work.

- There are better ways to prevent sticking than by trying to wrap a **rolling pin** in waxed paper.

- Some say **roux** must be hot when it's added to cold liquids or cold when it's added to hot liquids. No difference is noticeable.

- **Salt** prevents browning in cut fruit. It also prevents you from eating the fruit.

- Don't attempt to revive a dying fire by tossing a handful of **salt** on it. The salt is inorganic. It is more likely to smother the fire. Sugar might work; it is combustible.

- When filling **sausage** casings, you may be advised to secure the links by twisting in alternate directions each time. It doesn't make any difference.

- Don't apply **shortening** to stop bleeding. In fact, don't put anything unsanitary in a cut.

- Don't scrub your **silver** with baking soda. This can scratch it.

- To extend the life of **sour cream**, you can add 1 tsp (5 mL) vinegar per 1 cup (250 mL) sour cream. Bad news: It will smell unpleasant.

- Holding a piece of plastic wrap over the bowl keeps **spices** from falling overboard when you're grinding with a mortar and pestle. You have to be nimble, though.

- Extracting liquid chlorophyll from **spinach** to use as a food dye is not worth the effort. The color is too light. The spinach has to be blended with water, puréed and strained. The liquid is heated to coagulate, strained at length, left undisturbed, then covered with a thin layer of oil.

- **Split peas** are not supposed to stick to the pot if a slice of bread is added to the pan with the peas and liquid. But they do.

- It's expensive to add ½ cup (125 mL) dishwashing detergent to the washing machine to clean **stains** from kitchen towels. Other cleaners work just as well. Try bleach or borax.

- Unfortunately, a twisted wire hanger doesn't work as a makeshift branding iron for grilled **steak**.

- Faux **steak sauce** made from soy sauce, hot sauce, lemon juice and brown sugar tastes horrid —and nothing like steak sauce. Adding tomato paste doesn't help.

- You can make mini prebaked **tart shells** by hanging 5-inch (12.5 cm) dough rounds over the cups of an inverted muffin tin. They will be messy and large.

- If a **tomato** has no stem, you are advised to tape over the scar. Too much TLC!

- A **tomato** sliced vertically is supposed to leak less. A test showed no difference. And horizontal slices are prettier.

- Another way to skin a **tomato**: Stroke the skin with the dull edge of a knife until it wrinkles and can be lifted off. This is rough and damaging.

- A juicy hunk of ripe **tomato** is supposed to erase ink stains on furniture. It will lift very light stains, but so will soap and water. Save the juicy tomato for eating.

- Spraying a white plastic tub or bowl with oil before adding **tomato sauce** should prevent staining. It doesn't. Putting the container in the sun all day is another way to rid plastic of tomato stains. You wish!

- Using old kitchen **towels** as shelf liners makes no sense. They crumple and shift.

- Funny thing: You can tie cotton **twine** tighter if you wet it. But when it dries, it winds up looser than twine that was not moistened. You can't win, unless you need to use it wet.

- A **turkey** will supposedly thaw more evenly at room temperature if you insulate it in 10 layers of newspaper. The trouble is, you shouldn't thaw a turkey at room temperature.

- You can turn a roast **turkey** using wadded paper towels, but there are better ways.

- A cotton ball soaked in **vanilla** is a feeble fridge deodorizer.

- Boiling ½ cup (125 mL) water with 1 tsp (5 mL) **vanilla** in a bowl doesn't get rid of the burnt-popcorn smell in the microwave, either.

- Don't try to deodorize plastic tubs with **vanilla** and water. It's a waste of expensive vanilla. So is rubbing your hands with vanilla to get rid of odors.

- Don't bother rubbing your hands with **vinegar** to get rid of unpleasant fish or onion odors. You will stink of vinegar instead.

- Got a plastic tub or bowl that smells garlicky or oniony? Soaking a sponge in a 1:1 **vinegar** and water solution, then sealing it overnight in the container isn't great. All you get is a smelly sponge.

- Pouring **vinegar** on frozen meat or other food is supposed to make it defrost faster. It just stinks. And you need a lot.

- Dish soap is not the best fruit and vegetable **wash**. Sure, it will clean produce, but ingesting soap can cause diarrhea. Its proponents recommend using no more than 1 tsp (5 mL) dish soap per 12 cups (3 L) water.

- Using hydrogen peroxide as a produce **wash** is another unappetizing idea. Recommended concentrations include ¼ cup (50 mL) drugstore (3%) hydrogen peroxide per sinkful of cold water or up to 4 drops of food-grade (35%) hydrogen peroxide per cup (250 mL) of water. Drugstore peroxide (normally used for cuts and the like) is meant for disinfection, not ingestion. If not adequately diluted, food-grade peroxide is also dangerous to ingest.

- Putting a dish of cloves or lemon juice in water on your outdoor table is supposed to repel **wasps**, but the scent covers such a limited area.

- To make **waxed paper, plastic wrap** and **foil** easier to tear, insert a length of metal pipe inside the paper tube to make it heavier. Or don't.

- Never line baking pans with **waxed paper**. It melts and smokes.

- Want to fight **wine** with wine? Pour white wine on a red wine stain. But there are other methods that don't involve wasting good wine.

✧ Stirring **yogurt** gently in one direction until it comes to a low simmer is supposed to prevent curdling. Stir in any direction you want — it will curdle in the heat.

✧ Alas, there are false hopes of making **yogurt** simply by putting a spoonful of commercial yogurt in a pot of warm milk and heating it slowly for many hours. This does not work, even with live cultures.

✧ Sounds plausible: Stick a piece of parchment or plastic wrap on the back of the grater so **zest** that gets stuck will peel off with it. Too bad the parchment or plastic simply falls off. When you are finished zesting, however, you can brush zest off the back of the grater more efficiently with a square of parchment than with your fingers. Waxed paper is not a good alternative; it's too sticky.

Library and Archives Canada Cataloguing in Publication

Sampson, Susan
    12,167 kitchen and cooking secrets : everyday tips, hints, techniques and more / Susan Sampson.

Includes index.
ISBN 978-0-7788-0222-8

1. Cookery—Miscellanea. 2. Home economics—Miscellanea.
I. Title. II. Title: Twelve thousand one hundred sixty-seven kitchen and cooking secrets.

TX651.S24 2009   641.5   C2009-902209-5

Index

Entries in bold indicate recipe and Master Plan (MP) titles